AF819958

All in One

A Guide cum Practice Book for All Subjects

Maths, English, Hindi & EVS

Class 4

Authors

Maths Astha Singhal

English Vaishali Jaiswal

Hindi Richa Shukla

EVS Parneet Kaur

arihant

SUCCESS AND NOTHING LESS

Published by

ARIHANT PRAKASHAN

(School Division Series)

卐 ADMINISTRATIVE & PRODUCTION OFFICES

Regd. Office

'Ramchhaya' 4577/15, Agarwal Road, Darya Ganj, New Delhi -110002
Tele: 011- 47630600, 43518550; Fax: 011- 23280316

卐 Head Office

Kalindi, TP Nagar, Meerut (UP) - 250002, Tel: 0121-7156203, 7156204

卐 SALES & SUPPORT OFFICES

Agra, Ahmedabad, Bengaluru, Bareilly, Chennai, Delhi, Guwahati, Hyderabad, Jaipur, Jhansi, Kolkata, Lucknow, Nagpur & Pune.

PO No : TXT-XX-XXXXXXX-X-XX

Published By Arihant Publications (India) Ltd.

For further information about the books published by Arihant, log on to www.arihantbooks.com or e-mail at info@arihantbooks.com

Follow us on

卐 PRICE ₹395.00

PRODUCTION TEAM

Publishing Managers	Project Head	Cover Designer	Inner Designer	Page Layouting
Mahendra Singh Rawat & Keshav Mohan	Ashwani, Manju, Mohit, Shivam	Bilal Hashmi	Ankit Prajapati	Amit Agarwal

EXCLUSIVE FEATURES

1. Quick Summary at the start of each Chapter

2. Solutions/Answers of All NCERT Questions

3. Additional Practice Questions in each Chapter

Content List

Maths Magic (Maths)

Marigold (English)

रिमझिम (हिंदी)

Looking Around (EVS)

Allinone

MATH-MAGIC
(Maths)

CHAPTER 1

BUILDING WITH BRICKS

Brick Wall

Brick wall is a structure made by bricks, assembling them in different patterns. Some of Brick Wall are shown in the figures.

For stronger brick wall, a masons put the bricks on the top of the joint of two bricks.

Brick Pattern

A brick pattern refers to a layout where bricks are arranged in such a manner that it enhance the strength and beauty of wall or floor. Some of Brick Pattern are shown in the figures.

Jaali

It refers a decorative lattice used in buildings to allow light and air to pass through. Some Jaalis are shown in the figures.

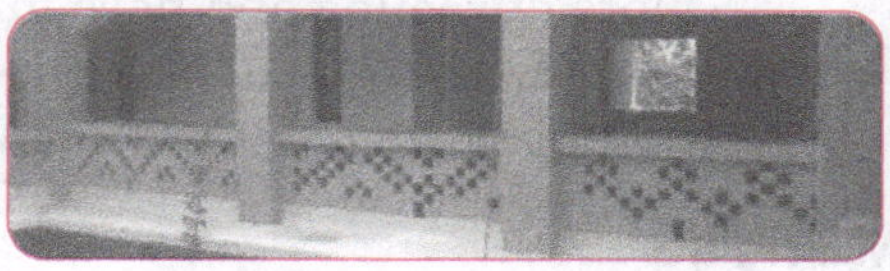

Jharokha

'Jharokha' is a term referring to a type of overhanging balcony or window. Some Jharokhas are shown in the figures.

Arch

An arch is a curved structure made of bricks with a curved shape.

NCERT FOLDER

Brick Patterns for Jagriti School (NCERT Pg 1-2)

Q.1

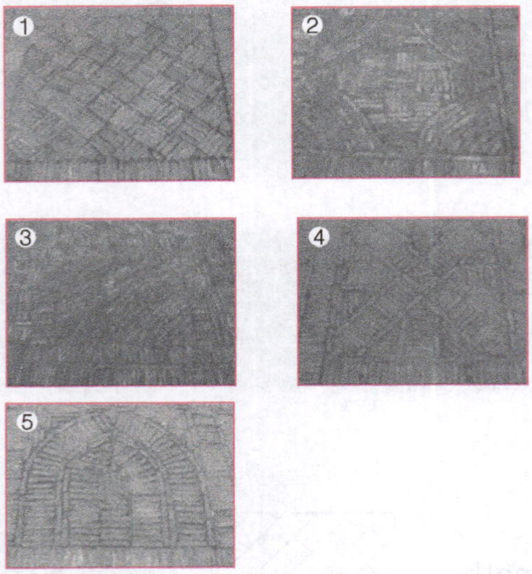

(i) Which floor pattern do you like the most?

(ii) Have you seen such patterns anywhere?

Ans. *(i) I like floor pattern- 4 because it seems more attracting and have mirror half also.

*(ii) Yes, I have seen such patterns in old houses, forts and monuments.

NCERT Pg 3

Q.2

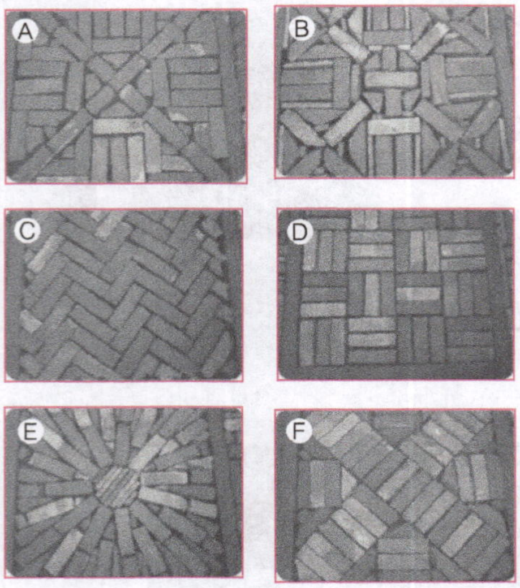

(i) Which pattern is made in a circle?

(ii) In which pattern can you show mirror halves? Draw a line.

(iii) Now you draw some new floor patterns.

Ans. (i) Pattern - J is made in a circle.

(ii) Patterns - A, B, H and J have mirror halves.

*(iii)

How to Draw a Brick? (NCERT Pg 4)

Q.3

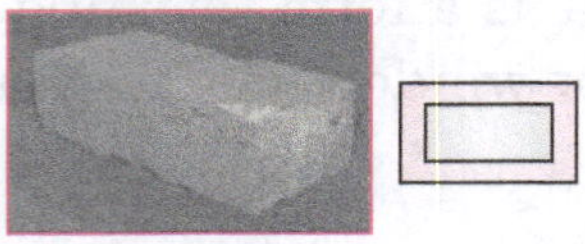

(i) How many faces in all does a brick have?

(ii) Is any face a square?

(iii) Draw the smallest face of the brick.

Ans. (i) A brick has 6 faces in all.

(ii) No, all the faces of a brick are rectangle.

(iii) Smallest face of the brick.

** Students can write alternate answer as per their choice.*

Q.4 Which of these are the faces of a brick? Mark a (✓).

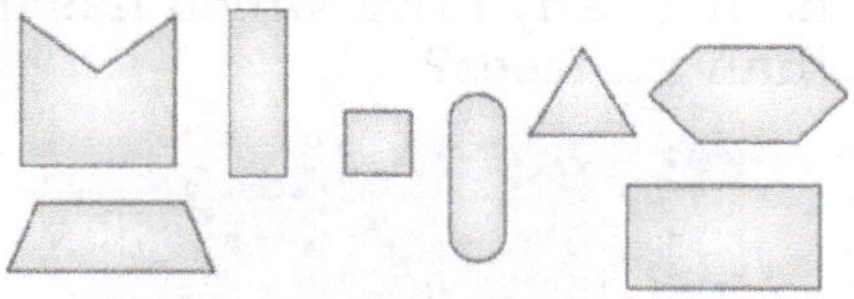

Ans.

(✓) (✓)

Q.5 Which of these are the drawing of a brick? Mark a (✓).

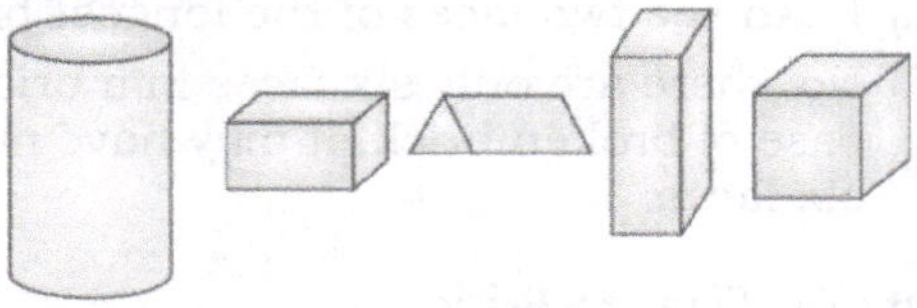

Ans.

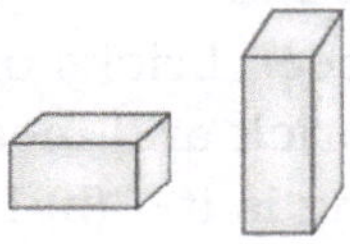

(✓) (✓)

Q.6 Make a drawing of this box to show 3 of its faces.

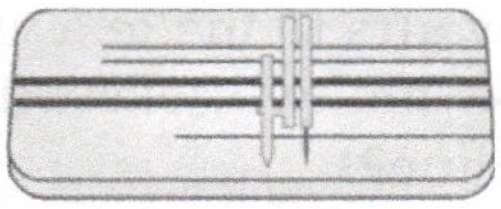

Ans.

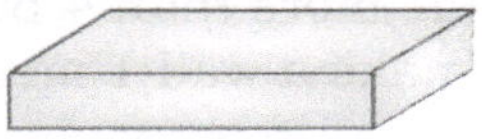

Q.7 Can you make a drawing of a brick which shows 4 of its faces?

Ans. No, such drawing can not be possible which shows 4 of its faces.

A Wall that will not Fall (NCERT Pg 5)

Q.8 One day Muniya and Zainab are playing with bricks and making their walls. Each makes a different wall.

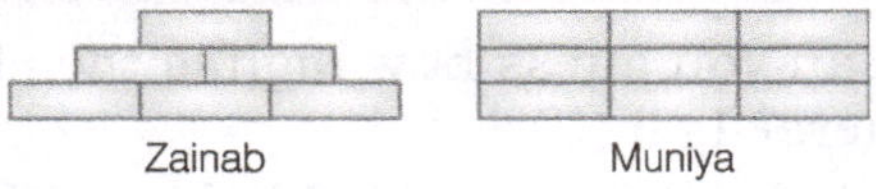

What do you think? which wall will be stronger?

Ans. The wall made by Zainab is stronger than the wall made by Muniya because in Zainab wall's masons put the bricks on the top of the joint of two bricks.

Q.9 Here are photos of three kinds of brick walls. Can you see the difference in the way the bricks are placed?

Ans. Yes, I can see the difference in the way the bricks are placed.

Q.10 Now, match the photo of each wall with the correct drawing below:

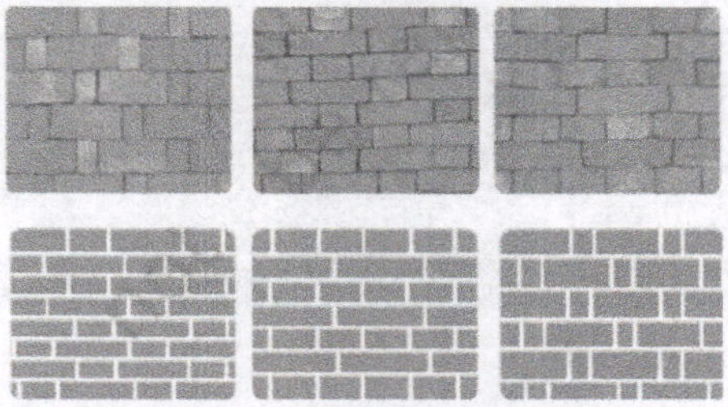

Ans.

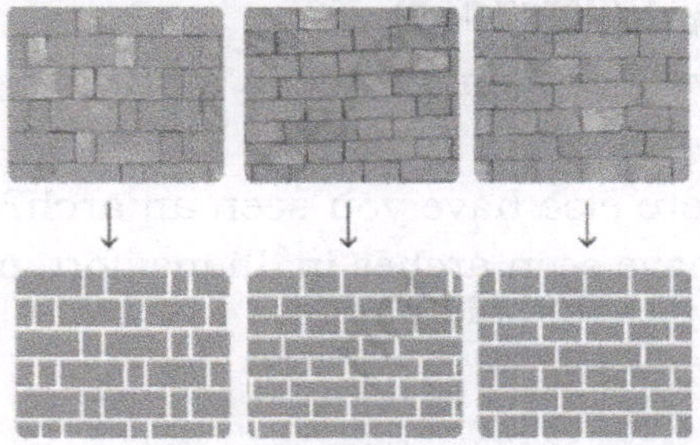

Looking Through a Brick 'Jaali' (NCERT Pg 6)

Q.11

How many different 'Jaali' patterns can you see in these two photos?

Ans. In these two photos, there are 5 different 'Jaali' patterns.

NCERT Pg 7

Q.12 Now colour some bricks red and make your own 'Jaali' patterns in the wall drawn below.

Ans. Do Yourself.

Q.13 Now draw some 'Jharokha' patterns on the wall here. You can shade it black.

Ans. Do Yourself.

A Special Arch (NCERT Pg 9)

Q.14 Have you seen arches in a bridge?

Ans. Yes.

Q.15 Where else have you seen an arch?

Ans. * I have seen arches in Jhansi fort, old temples and old bridges.

Q.16

Isn't the 'Jaali' of this window beautiful? It is made of thin bricks. Have you ever seen thin bricks? Look around.

Ans. *Yes, the 'Jaali' of this window is very beautiful. I have seen thin bricks used in old temples and buildings.

NCERT Pg 10

Q.17 (i) Which of these bricks have curved edges?

(ii) How many faces do you see of the longest brick?

(iii) Is there any brick which has more than six faces?

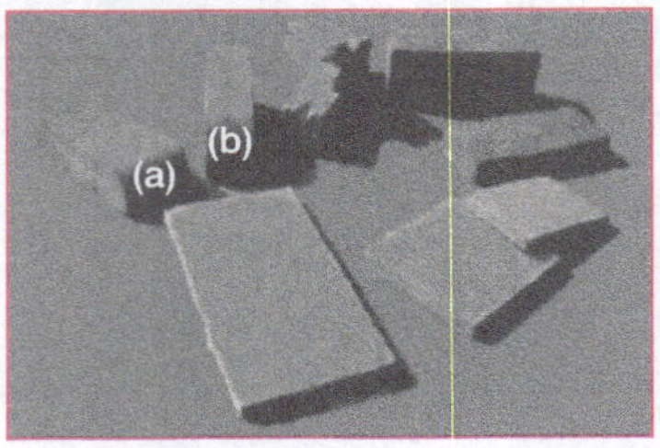

Ans. (i) Bricks (a) and (b), given in figure have curved edges.

(ii) I can see two faces of the longest brick.

(iii) No, there are only six faces in a brick but in case of broken brick, it may have more than six faces.

Find Out : The Size of a Brick

Q.18 (i) Have you seen bricks of different sizes.

(ii) Take one brick and measure it.

(a) How long is it? (b) How wide is it?

(c) How high is it?

Ans. (i) Yes, I have seen bricks of different sizes.

(ii) (a) 9 inches (b) 4 inches (c) 3 inches

Q.19 Muniya wants to make a wall 1 metre long. How many bricks will she need to put in a line?

Ans. Muniya needs more than 4 but less than 5 bricks to make a wall 1 metre long.

Bricks and Bricks – Hot and Fresh! (NCERT Pg 10-12)

Q.20

Can you guess how high is the chimney here? Is it.

(a) about 5 metres? (b) about 15 metres?

(c) about 50 metres?

Ans. (c) The height of chimney about 50 metres.

Q.21 Here are four pictures from the brick kiln. These pictures are jumbled up. Look at them carefully.
Write the correct order. ....

(A) 

(B) 

(C) 

(D) 

Ans. The correct order of the given figures is C, D, B and A.

Q.22 Have you seen a brick kiln? Did you try to guess the number of bricks kept there?

Ans. Yes, I have seen a brick kiln. I think, there are 10 to 15 Lakhs bricks kept there.

Q.23 Can you try to write it? (1 Lakh).

Ans. 1 Lakh = 100000

Find Out (NCERT Pg 12)

Q.24 Look at these photos and guess how many bricks are carried by this truck.

Ans. Around 6000 bricks are carried by this truck.

Mental Math : Bhajan Buys Bricks (NCERT Pg 12)

Q.25 Bhajan went to buy bricks. The price was given for one thousand bricks. The prices were also different for different types of bricks.

Old bricks - ₹ 1200 for one thousand bricks.

New bricks from Intapur - ₹ 1800 for one thousand bricks.

New bricks from Brickabad - ₹ 2000 for one thousand bricks.

(i) Bhajan decided to buy the new bricks from Brickabad. He bought three thousand bricks. How much did he pay?

(ii) Guess what he will pay if he buys 500 old bricks.

Ans. (i) Price of one thousand bricks = ₹ 2000
Thus, price of three thousand bricks
= ₹ 2000×3
Therefore, he paid ₹ 6000.

(ii) Price of 1000 old bricks = ₹ 1200
Price of one old brick = ₹ $\frac{1200}{1000}$
Thus, price of 500 old bricks
= ₹ $\frac{1200}{1000} \times 500$ = ₹ 600
Hence, he will pay ₹ 600.

PRACTICE QUESTIONS

1. Fill in the blanks.
 (i) A rectangular block has .... number of faces. [4/6]
 (ii) A Mathematics book has .... number of edges. [8/12]
 (iii) A geometry box has .... shape faces. [rectangular/square]
 (iv) A dice has .... shape faces. [rectangular/square]

1. Multiple choice questions.
 (i) This closed shoes box has

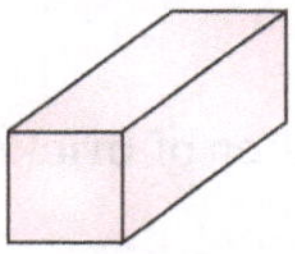

(a) 1 square face and 2 rectangular faces.

(b) 2 square faces and 4 rectangular faces.

(c) 2 square faces and 4 faces which are neither square nor rectangular.

(d) 4 square faces and 2 rectangular faces.

(ii) A cube has 6 faces. Two cubes are joined face to face to form a solid shape like the one shown. How many faces will this solid have?

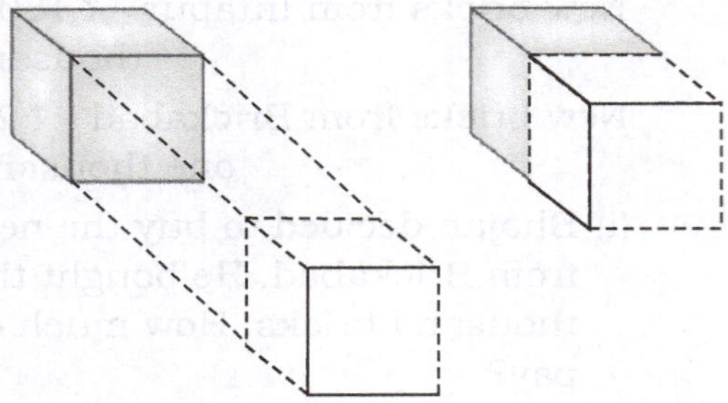

(a) 6 (b) 10

(c) 8 (d) 5

(iii) Which of the following wall pattern will not fall easily?

(a) 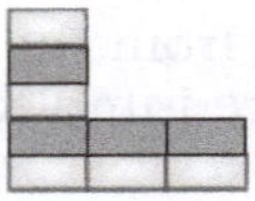 (b) 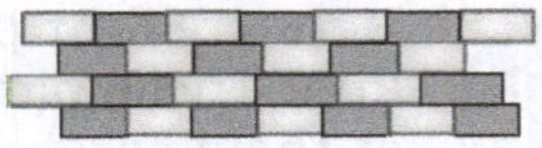

(c) 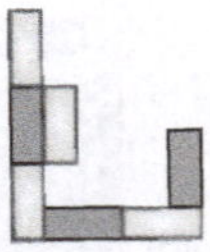 (d) 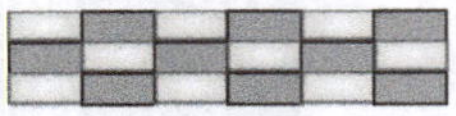

3. Mohan went to brick market to buy bricks for his house. The price of one thousand bricks for different kiln fields are given below.

Kiln field	Price of one thousand bricks
STAR	₹ 4000
OM	₹ 3800
JK	₹ 4100

(i) Mohan buys 1200 bricks of STAR. How much he paid for bricks?

(ii) Mohan have ₹ 5320. How many bricks of OM kiln can he buy?

(iii) If Mohan buys 700 bricks of OM kiln and 1200 bricks of JK kiln, then how much he pay for all bricks?

ANSWERS & SOLUTIONS

1. (i) 6 (ii) 12

(iii) rectangular (iv) square

2. (i) (b) (ii) (a)

(iii) (b)

3. (i) Price of 1000 bricks of STAR kiln = ₹ 4000

Price of 1 brick of STAR kiln $= ₹\,\frac{4000}{1000} = ₹\,4$

Therefore, price of 1200 bricks of STAR kiln = ₹ 4 × 1200 = ₹ 4800

Hence, he paid ₹ 4800.

(ii) Number of bricks purchased in ₹ 3800 = 1000

Number of bricks purchased in ₹ 1 $= \frac{1000}{3800}$

∴ Number of bricks purchased in ₹ 5320

$= \frac{1000}{3800} \times 5320$

= 1400 bricks

(iii) Price of 1000 bricks of OM kiln = ₹ 3800

Price of 1 brick of OM kiln $= ₹\,\frac{3800}{1000}$

∴ Price of 700 bricks of OM kiln

$= ₹\,\frac{3800}{1000} \times 700$

= ₹ 2660

Price of 1000 bricks of JK kiln = ₹ 4100

Price of 1 brick of JK kiln $= ₹\,\frac{4100}{1000}$

∴ Price of 1200 bricks of JK kiln

$= ₹\,\frac{4100}{1000} \times 1200$

= ₹ 4920

Hence, he will pay = ₹ 2660 + ₹ 4920

= ₹ 7580

CHAPTER 2 LONG AND SHORT

Long

It refers to a larger value whenever something is measured which is big.

Short

It refers to a smaller value whenever something is measured which is small.

Distance

Distance refers to the amount of space between two places or things. It can be measured in various units such as metres, kilometres, miles, etc. e.g. Distance between Kanpur and Lucknow, distance between two points *A* and *B*, etc.

Height

The distance from bottom to top of something standing up right. e.g. Height of building, height of man, etc.

Length

Length is defined as the measurement of something from end to end. e.g. Length of rope, length of field, etc.

Conversion of units into another units

The conversion between different units and measurements of the same quantity done by the process of multiplication or division.

1 kilometre = 1000 metres

1 metre = 100 centimetres

1 centimetre = 10 millimetres

1 metre = 1000 millimetres

1 millimetre = $\frac{1}{1000}$ metre

1 millimetre = $\frac{1}{10}$ centimetre

1 centimetre = $\frac{1}{100}$ metre

1 metre = $\frac{1}{1000}$ kilometre

NCERT FOLDER

How Far Apart are the Dots? (NCERT Pg 13)

Q.1

(i) Guess the distance between any two dots.

How many centimetres is it? Now measure it with the help of a scale. Did you guess right?

(ii) Which two dots do you think are farthest from each other? Check your answer.

(iii) Which two dots are nearest to each other? Check your answer.

Ans. *(i) The guessed distance between dot-A and dot-E is 3.7 centimetres. The actual distance between dot-A and dot-E is 3.5 centimetres.

No, I did not guess right but my guess is nearly correct the right answer.

(ii) I think dot-O and dot-M are farthest from each other.

Yes, I am right. The distance between them is 10.2 centimetres.

(iii) The dot-D and dot-O are nearest to each other. The distance between them is 1.2 centimetres.

** Students can write alternate answer as per their choice.*

The Shorter Line (NCERT Pg 14)

Q.2 How Birbal made Akbar's line shorter?

Ans. Birbal drew a another line which is longer than the line drawn by Akbar.

Try This (NCERT Pg 14)

Q.3 Make her right arm 1 centimetre longer than the left arm.

Ans. Length of left arm is 1.3 centimetres.

Therefore, length of right arm is,

$1.3 + 1 = 2.3$ centimetres.

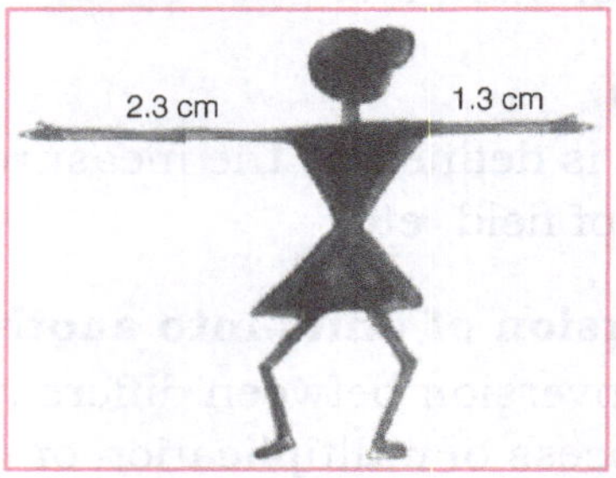

Q.4 Draw a cup 1 centimetre shorter than this cup.

Ans. *Height of given cup

$= 2.4$ centimetres.

So, height of shorter cup

$= 2.4 - 1 = 1.4$ centimetres.

Q.5 Draw a broom half as long as this broom.

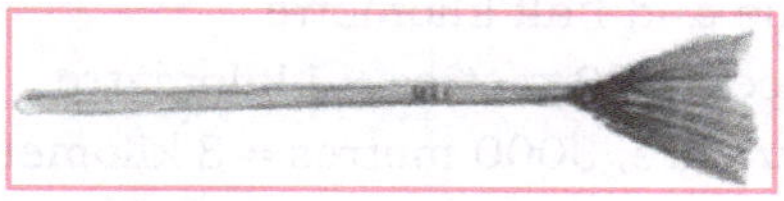

Ans.

Q.6 Draw another hair of double the length.

Ans.

How Tall Have You Grown? (NCERT Pg 15)

Q.7 Do you remember that in class 3 you measured your height?

Ans. * Yes, I remember that. At that time, my height is 107 centimetres.

Q.8 Do you think you have grown taller?

Ans. * Yes, I have grown taller. Now, my height is 112 centimetres.

Q.9 How much? (in centimetre)

Ans. * About 5 centimetres.

Q.10 Have your friends also grown taller?

Ans. * Yes, most of them grown taller.

Q.11 Find out and fill the table below.

Friend's Name	Last Year's height (in centimetre)	This Year's height (in centimetre)	How many centimetre have they grown?

Ans. *

Friend's Name	Last Year's height (in centimetre)	This Year's height (in centimetre)	How many centimetre have they grown?
Gaurav	120	124	4
Abhishek	122	127	5
Ankit	121	125	4
Rahul	123	127.5	4.5
Rohan	121.5	126	4.5

Q.12 Jhumpa once read a list of the tallest people in the world. One of them was 272 centimetres tall! That is just double of Jhumpa's height. How tall is Jhumpa? (in centimetre)

Ans. Height of tallest people = 272 centimetres.

Since, height of tallest people

$= 2 \times$ height of Jhumpa

Therefore, height of Jhumpa $= \frac{272}{2}$

$= 136$ centimetres.

So, Jhumpa is 136 centimetres tall.

Imagine (NCERT Pg 15)

Q.13 Could that person pass through the door of your classroom without bending?

Ans. * No, because the height of the door is 220 centimetres.

Therefore, he cannot pass through the door.

Q.14 Will his head touch the roof of your house if he stands straight?

Ans. No, his head will not touch the roof of my house if he stands straight because the height of the roof is 350 centimetres from the floor.

The Long and Short of Your Family! (NCERT Pg 15)

Q.15 Who is the tallest in your family?

Ans. * My father is the tallest in my family.

Q.16 Who is the shortest in your family?

Ans. * I am the shortest in my family.

Q.17 What is the difference between their heights?

Ans. * The difference between my height and my father's height is 48 centimetres.

Inter-School Sports Meet (NCERT Pg 16-17)

Q.18 **Race**

This is a 100 metres race for girls. Arundhati is nearest the finishing line. She is about 6 metres from it. Behind her is Rehana. Konkana and Uma are running behind Rehana. Look at the picture. To answer the questions below choose from these distances:

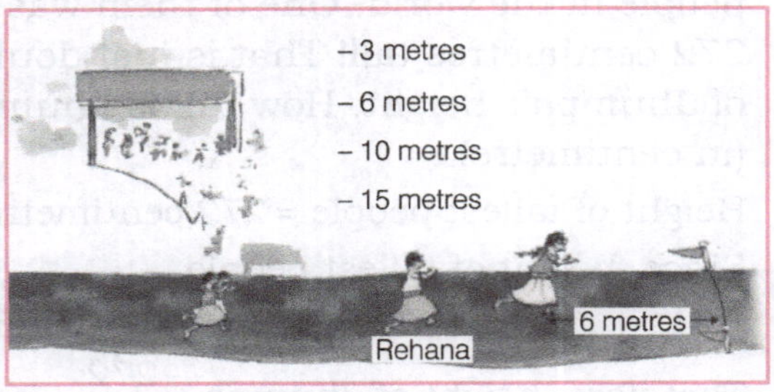

(i) How far is Rehana from Arundhati?

(ii) How far ahead is Rehana from Konkana and Uma?

(iii) How far are Konkana and Uma from the finishing line?

Ans. (i) Rehana is 3 metres far from Arundhati.

(ii) Rehana is 6 metres far ahead from Konkana and Uma.

(iii) Konkana and Uma are $6 + 3 + 6 = 15$ metres far from the finishing line.

Q.19 Have you heard about a 1500 metres or 3000 metres race? (you remember that 1000 metres make 1 kilometre and 500 metres make half a kilometre.)

So, you can say—

(i) In a 1500 metres race people run .... kilometres.

(ii) In a 3000 metres race people run .... kilometres

Ans. Yes, I heard about those races.

(i) Since, 1000 metres = 1 kilometre and 500 metres = half a kilometre.

Therefore, 1500 metres

= 1000 metres +500 metres

= 1 kilometre + half a kilometre

= one and half kilometre

(ii) Since, 1000 metres = 1 kilometre.

Therefore, 3000 metres = 3 kilometres.

Q.20 Have you heard about marathon races in which people have to run about 40 kilometres? People run marathons on roads because the track of a stadium is only 400 metres.

(i) 10 rounds of a stadium track = ... kilometres.

(ii) So, if you run a marathon on a stadium track, you will have to complete .... rounds!

Ans. Yes, I heard about marathon races.

(i) Since, one round = 400 metres.

Therefore, 10 rounds

$= 400 \times 10 = 4000$ metres

Now, 1000 m = 1 kilometre

So, 4000 m = 4 kilometres

$\therefore$ 10 rounds of a stadium track

= 4 kilometres

(ii) Length of marathon = 40 kilometres

$\because$ 1 kilometre = 1000 metres

$\therefore$ 40 kilometres = (40×1000) metres

= 40000 metres

Length of track = 400 metres

Number of rounds to complete the marathon

$= \frac{40000}{400} = 100$ rounds

Long Jump (NCERT Pg 17-18)

Q.21 This is the long jump for boys.

Dhanu has the longest jump of 3 metres 40 centimetres. Gurjeet is second. His jump is 20 centimetres less than Dhanu's. Gopi comes third. His jump is only 5 centimetres less than Gurjeet's jump.

How long are Gurjeet's and Gopi's jumps?

Ans. Since, Gurjeet's jump is 20 centimetres less than Dhanu's jump.

Therefore, Gurjeet's jump
= 3 metres 40 centimetres
– 20 centimetres
= 3 metres 20 centimetres

Now, Gopi's jump is 5 centimetres less than Gurjeet jump.

Therefore, Gopi's jump
= 3 metres 20 centimetres – 5 centimetres
= 3 metres 15 centimetres

Q.22 Try and see how far you can jump.

Ans. * I can jump 1 metre 73 centimetres long.

Q.23 How far can you throw a ball?

Ans. * I can throw a ball to a distance of 16 metres.

Q.24 Look for a big ball, like a football or volleyball. How far can you kick it?

Ans. * I can kick a big ball, like a football to a distance of 10 metres.

Q.25 Here are the Indian Records and World Records for some jumps.

Sports	World Record	Indian Record
High Jump (Men)	Javier S. (2 metres 45 centimetres)	Chandra Pal (2 metres 17 centimetres)
Long Jump (Men)	Mike P. (8 metres 95 centimetres)	Amrit Pal (8 metres 8 centimetres)
High Jump (Women)	Stefka K. (2 metres 9 centimetres)	Bobby A. (1 metre 91 centimetres)
Long Jump (Women)	Galina C. (7 metres 52 centimetres)	Anju G. (6 metres 83 Centimeters)

Find out from the table

(i) How many centimetres more should Chandra Pal jump to equal the Men's World Record for high jump?

(ii) How many centimetres higher should Bobby A. jump to reach 2 metres?

(iii) Remember that 1 metre
= 100 centimetres

Half metre = ?

(iv) Galina's long jump is nearly

(a) 7 metres (b) 7 and a half metres

(c) 8 metres

(v) Look at the Women's World Records. What is the difference between the longest jump and the highest jump?

(vi) If Mike P. could jump .... centimetres longer, his jump would be full 9 metres.

(vii) Whose high jump is very close to two and half metres?

(a) Stefka K. (b) Chandra Pal

(c) Javier S. (d) Bobby A.

Ans. (i) Men's world record for high jump
= 2 metres 45 centimetres

Chandra Pal's high jump
= 2 metres 17 centimetres.

Difference between both high jumps
= 2 metres 45 centimetres – 2 metres 17 centimetres
= 28 centimetres

Therefore, Chandra Pal requires to 28 centimetres more high jump to equal the men's world record for high jump.

(ii) High jump of Bobby A
= 1 metre 91 centimetres

$\because$ 1 metre = 100 centimetres

$\therefore$ 1 metre 91 centimetres = 191 centimetres

and 2 metres = 200 centimetres

Required height to reach 2 metres
= 200 centimetres – 191 centimetres
= 9 centimetres

Therefore, Bobby A requires to 9 centimetres more higher jump to reach 2 metres.

(iii) ∵ 1 metre = 100 centimetres

∴ Half metre = $\frac{100 \text{ centimetres}}{2}$

= 50 centimetres

(iv) (b) Galina's long jump is 7 metres 52 centimetres.

Therefore, Galina's long jump is nearly 7 and a half metres.

(v) Women's world record for long jump

= 7 metres 52 centimetres

and Women's world record for high jump

= 2 metres 9 centimetres

Difference between the women's longest jump and the women's highest jump = 7 metres 52 centimetres − 2 metres 9 centimetres = 5 metres 43 centimetres

(vi) Long jump of Mike P. = 8 metres 95 centimetres = 895 centimetres

and 9 metres = 900 centimetres.

Required length to jump to full 9 metres

= 900 centimetres − 895 centimetres

= 5 centimetres.

(vii) (c) High jump of Stefka K.

= 2 metres 9 centimetres,

high jump of Chandra Pal

= 2 metres 17 centimetres,

high jump of Javier S

= 2 metres 45 centimetres

and high jump of Bobby A

= 1 metre 91 centimetres

Therefore, high jump of Javier S. is very close to two and half metres.

Running Exercise (NCERT Pg 19)

Q.26 The doctor has told Devi Prasad to run 2 kilometres every day to stay fit.He took one round of this field. How far did he run?

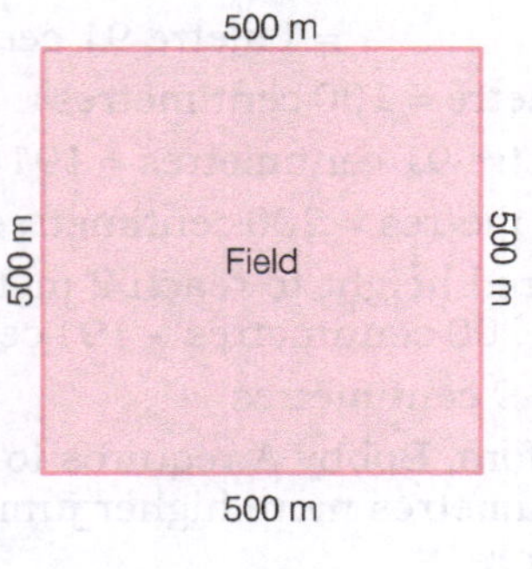

Ans. Length of one round

= 500 metres + 500 metres + 500 metres + 500 metres

= 2000 metres

∵ 1000 metres = 1 kilometre

∴ Length of one round = 2 kilometres

Since, Devi Prasad took one round of this field.

Therefore, he ran 2 kilometres.

Q.27 The field was very far from his home. So he chose a park nearby. The boundary of the park was about 400 metres long.

(i) How many rounds of the park must Devi Prasad run to complete 2 kilometres?

(ii) One day the weather was very good and a cool breeze was blowing. He felt so good that he kept jogging till he got tired after 8 rounds. That day he ran ………… kilometre and ……… metres!

Ans. (i) Boundary of the park = 400 metres

∵ 1 kilometre = 1000 metres

∴ 2 kilometres = 2000 metres

Number of rounds of the park to complete 2 kilometres = $\frac{2000}{400}$ = 5

Therefore, Devi Prasad must run to 5 rounds of the park to complete 2 kilometres.

(ii) Boundary of the park = 400 metres

Distance covered in 1 round of the park

= 400 metres

So, distance covered in 8 rounds of the park = 400 × 8 = 3200 metres

∵ 1000 metres = 1 kilometres

∴ 3200 metres = 3 kilometres and 200 metres

Therefore, that day he ran 3 kilometres and 200 metres.

How Many Rooms High? (NCERT Pg 19)

Q.28 The Qutab Minar is 72 metres high. About how many metres high is your classroom?

Ans. * My classroom is about 4 metres high.

Q.29 (i) Guess how many rooms, one on top of the other, will be equal to the Qutab Minar.

(ii) Explain how you made a guess.

Ans. *(i) Since, the height of Qutab Minar = 72 metres

and height of room = 4 metres

Number of rooms, one on top of the other

$$= \frac{72}{4} = 18$$

Therefore, 18 rooms, one on top of the other, will be equal to the Qutab Minar.

(ii) On the basis of the height of the classroom. I made my guess.

From Kozhikode of Thalassery (NCERT Pg 20)

Q.30 Subodh is going to Kozhikode which is 24 kilometres (km) away.

Manjani is going to Thalassery which is 46 kilometres away in the opposite direction.

How far is Kozhikode from Thalassery?

Ans. As shown in figure, distance of Kozhikode = 24 kilometres

and distance of Thalassery = 46 kilometres

Since, both Kozhikode and Thalassery in opposite direction.

So, distance between Kozhikode and Thalassery = 24 + 46 = 70 kilometres

Therefore, Kozhikode is 70 kilometres far away from Thalassery.

How Far is your Home from School? (NCERT Pg 20-21)

Q.31 Momun comes to school from very far. He first walks about 400 metres to the pond. With slippers in his hands, he then walks 150 metres through the pond.

Next he runs across the 350 metres wide green field. Then, he carefully crosses the 40 metres wide road to reach his school.

(i) How much does Momun walk every day to reach school?

(ii) Is it more than 1 kilometre?

Ans. (i) Distance between school and home

= Distance of pond from his home
+ Distance covered to cross the pond
+ Distance covered to cross the green field
+ Width of road

= 400 + 150 + 350 + 40

= 940 metres

Hence, Momun walks 940 metres everyday to reach school.

(ii) Since, 1 kilometre = 1000 metres

and distance covered by Momun to reach school = 940 metres

As 940 metres is less than 1000 metres.

Therefore, It is not more than 1 kilometre.

Q.32 Find out how far your friends live from school and fill the table.

Write in metres or kilometres.

S.No.	Friend's name	Distance of home from school	
		Metres	Kilometres
1	Diwakar	6000m	6km
2	Abhijeet	2500m	2km 500m
3	Umesh	1700m	1km 700m
4	Neelesh	500m	0km 500m
5	Rohit	3250m	3km 250m

(i) Who among them lives nearest to the school?

(ii) Who lives farthest from the school?

(iii) How many children live less than 1 kilometre away from your school?

(iv) Is there anyone who lives more than 5 kilometres away from the school? How do they come to school?

Ans. *(i) Neelesh lives nearest to the school.

(ii) Diwakar lives farthest from the school.

(iii) Only one child (Neelesh) lives less than 1 kilometre away from school.

(iv) Yes, Diwakar lives more than 5 kilometres away from the school. He comes to school by bus.

Guess and Find Out (NCERT Pg 21)

Q.33 How long is the thread in a reel?

Ans. * Length of thread in a reel depends on the size of reel. On the basis of size of a reel, thread may 100 metres to 500 metres long.

Q.34 How long is the string of a kite reel? Can it be more than a kilometre long?

Ans. * The length of the string of a kite reel may be 250 metres to 2000 metres. Yes, it can be more than a kilometre long.

Q.35 If a handkerchief is made out of a single thread, then how long would that thread be?

Ans. * If a handkerchief is made out of a single thread, then thread would be 10000 metres or 10 kilometres long.

I Wish I Were! (NCERT Pg 22)

Q.36 Which is the highest building that you have seen? About how many rooms high was it?

Ans. * The highest building which I have seen is Qutab Minar. It is about 18 rooms high.

Q.37 How high can a kite go? Can it go higher than the Qutab Minar?

Ans. A kite can go up to 200 metres to 300 metres. Yes, it can go higher than the Qutab Minar.

Q.38 How high can a plane fly? Can it fly higher than Mount Everest which is about 9 kilometres high?

Ans. A plane can fly upto 11600 metres. Yes, it can fly higher than Mount Everest.

Q.39 Have you ever seen clouds below you?

Ans. * Yes, When I visited to ' Vaishno Devi ' temple, I have seen clouds below me.

PRACTICE QUESTIONS

1. Multiple choice questions.

(i) Shown below is a map showing 4 towns *P*, *Q*, *R* and *S* and the roads connecting them of the four, the shortest road is the one connecting

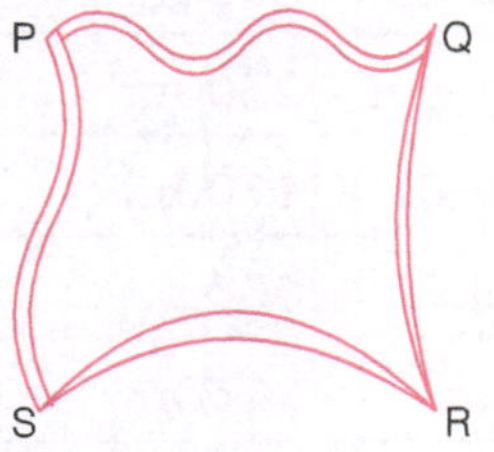

(a) Town *P* to Town *Q* (b) Town *Q* to Town *R*
(c) Town *R* to Town *S* (d) Town *S* to Town *P*

(ii) The distance jumped by Faisal in a Long Jump Competition is shown below. How many centimetres did Faisal jump?

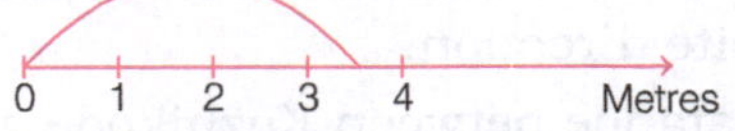

(a) 30 (b) 35 (c) 350 (d) 450

(iii) An ant comes out of its hole and travels along the dotted lines to the piece of sugar. How much distance does it cover?

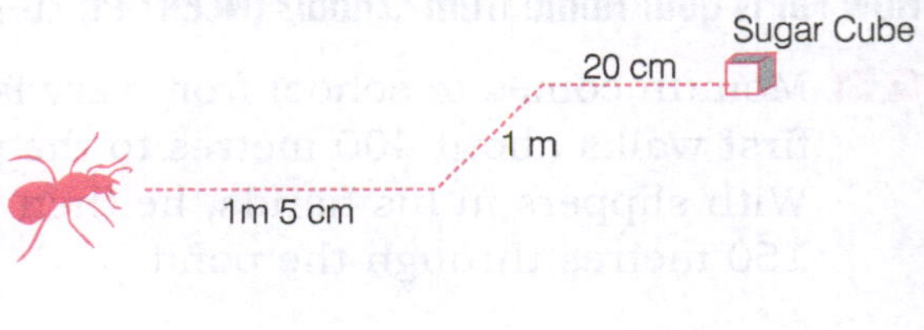

(a) 1m 26m (b) 2m 25m
(c) 2m 70cm (d) 22m 5cm

2. Rahul's longest jump is 4 metres 95 centimetres and he is second. Arjun's longest jump is 15 centimetres more than Rahul. Find the longest jump of Arjun.

3. Add the followings.
(i) 10 metres 15 centimetres and 8 metres 88 centimetres. (in centimetres)
(ii) 10 kilometres 45 metres, 17 kilometres 580 metres and 5 kilometres 475 metres. (in kilometres)

4. Subtract the followings
(i) 85 metres 95 centimetres from 90 metres 9 centimetres. (in metres)
(ii) 10 kilometres 870 metres from 17 kilometres 815 metres. (in kilometres)

ANSWERS & SOLUTIONS

1. (i) (b) (ii) (c)
(iii) (b) Distance covered by ant
= 1 metre 5 centimetres
+ 1 metre + 20 centimetres
= 2 metres 25 centimetres

2. Rahul's longest jump
= 4 metres 95 centimetres
∴ Arjun's Jump
= 4 metres 95 centimetres
+ 15 centimetres
= 5 metres 10 centimetres

Hence, longest jump of Arjun is 5 metres 10 centimetres.

3. (i) We know that 1 metre
= 100 centimetres
∴ (10 meters 15 centimetres)
+ (8 metres 88 centimetres)
= (10 × 100 centimetres
+ 15 centimetres)
+ (8 × 100 centimetres
+ 88 centimetres)
= (1000 centimetres
+ 15 centimetres)
+ (800 centimetres
+ 88 centimetres)
= 1015 centimetres
+ 888 centimetres
= 1903 centimetres

(ii) We know that 1 kilometer
= 1000 kilometres
∴ 10 kilometres 45 metres
+ 17 kilometres 580 metres
+ 5 kilometres + 475 kilometres
= 10.045 kilometres
+ 17.58 kilometres
+ 5.475 kilometres
= 33.1 kilometres

4. (i) We have,
(90 metres 9 centimetres)
− (85 metres 95 centimetres)
= (90 metres + 0.09 metre)
− (85 metres + 0.95 metre)
$\left[\because 1 \text{ cm} = \frac{1}{100} \text{ m}\right]$
= 90.09 metres − 85.95 metres
= 4.14 metres

(ii) We have,
(17 kilometres 815 metres)
− (10 kilometres 870 metres)
= (17 kilometres + 0.815 kilometre)
− (10 kilometre + 0.870 kilometre)
$\left[\because 1 \text{ m} = \frac{1}{1000} \text{ km}\right]$
= 17.815 kilometres
− 10.870 kilometres
= 6.945 kilometres

CHAPTER 3

A TRIP TO BHOPAL

Distance

Distance is a quantity that tells how much path to be covered between two points. The distance can be measured in terms of metres, centimetres or kilometres.

e.g. (i)

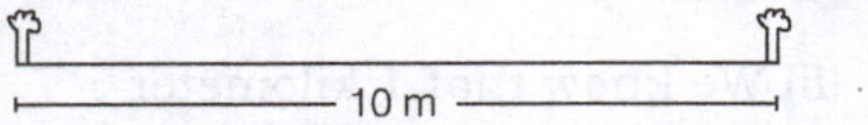

(ii) Distance between kanpur and Lucknow is 100 kilometres.

Units of distance

S.No.	Units	Uses
1.	Centimetre (cm)	used to measure length of objects and shorter distances usually by a scale. Example : Size of book, Size of pen, etc.
2.	Metre (m) (1 m = 100 cm)	used to measure cloths, distance between two objects like tree, building etc.
3.	Kilometre (km) (1 km = 1000 m)	used to measure long distance like distance between two cities, length of road, etc.

Length

Length is the longest measure of an object on a planar surface. It indicates how long the given object is. e.g. Length of bridge is 500 metres, length of bus is 5 metres etc.

Width

Width is the smallest measure of an object on a planar surface. It indicates how wide the given object is. e.g. Width of road is 10 metres, width of table is 150 centimetres etc.

Price

Price is the amount of money required to purchase a product or services. e.g. Price of 1 ticket is ₹ 50, price of 1 kg sugar is ₹ 40 etc.

NCERT FOLDER

NCERT Pg 23

Q.1 Today Sugandha is very excited. All the children of her school are going on a trip to Bhopal with their teachers.

Ms. Meenakshi and Mr. Rakesh are talking about the number of buses needed.

Ms. Meenakshi — We will need 4 buses.

Mr. Rakesh — I think we need at least 5.

Ms. Meenakshi — Each bus has 50 seats.

Mr. Rakesh — Let us see how many children are going.

Class	Number of children
I	33
II	32
III	42
IV	50
V	53
Total	______

(i) So, there are a total of .... children going.

(ii) If they get 4 buses, how many children will get seats?

(iii) Will there be any children left without seats?

Ans. (i) Total children

$= 33 + 32 + 42 + 50 + 53 = 210$

(ii) Since, each bus has 50 seats.
So, total number of seats in 4 buses
$= 4 \times 50 = 200$ seats

Therefore, 200 children will get seats.

(iii) Total number of children = 210

Total number of seats = 200

Number of children without seats
$= 210 - 200 = 10$

Therefore, 10 children will be left without seats.

Waiting for the Buses (NCERT Pg 24)

Q.2 Each mini bus can take 35 students. How many mini buses are needed?

Ans. Total number of students = 210

Seats in each mini bus = 35

Number of mini buses needed

$$= \frac{\text{Total number of children}}{\text{Seats in each mini bus}}$$

$$= \frac{210}{35} = 6$$

Therefore, 6 mini buses are needed for all students.

The Journey Begins (NCERT Pg 25-27)

Q.3 As the buses start moving from Hoshangabad, children sing at the top of their voices. Some look outside to enjoy the view of the green fields and the hills.

(i) Indra — When will we reach Bhopal?

** Students can write alternate answer as per their choice.*

If we do not stop anywhere, we should reach there in 2 hours, that is around .... o'clock.

(ii) If they go to Bhimbetka, they will reach there

(a) Before 10 o'clock

(b) Between 10 o'clock and 11 o'clock

(c) After 11 o'clock

Ans. (i) The buses started the journey at 9 o' clock.

Time taken to reach Bhopal is 2 hours.

Therefore, the bus will reach Bhopal at = 11 o'clock

(ii) (b) Between 10 o'clock and 11 o'clock.

Q.4 Victoria - It must be more than half a kilometre.

Ms. Asha - Look, it is written - 'This bridge is 756.82 metres long'. So we can guess that the Narmada must be about 500 metres wide at this place.

(i) Was Victoria right?

(ii) Ms. Asha - See, our bus is about 5 metres long. Imagine how many buses can stand in a line on this bridge.

Ans. (i) Yes, Victoria was right.

(ii) Length of bridge = 756.82 metres

Length of one bus = 5 metres

Number of buses that can stand in a line on this bridge

$$= \frac{756.82}{5}$$

$$= 151.364$$

Therefore, 151 buses can stand in a line on this bridge.

Q.5 Have you ever crossed a long bridge? About how many metres long was it?

Ans. * Yes, I have crossed a long bridge. It was about 900 metres long.

Q.6 What is the difference between the water level of the Narmada in the rainy season and Now? .... metres

Ans. Now a days, the water level of the Narmada = 40 metres

In the rainy season, the water level of the Narmada = 15 metres

The difference between the water level of the Narmada in rainy season and now

= 40 metres – 15 metres

= 25 metres

Q.7 Each bus takes about 15 minutes to refill and there are two buses to be refilled. So, they stop there for about .... minutes, which means they are late by about .... minutes.

Ans. Time taken by one bus to refill = 15 minutes

Therefore, time taken by two buses to refill $= 2 \times 15 = 30$ minutes

which means they are late by about 30 minutes.

Q.8

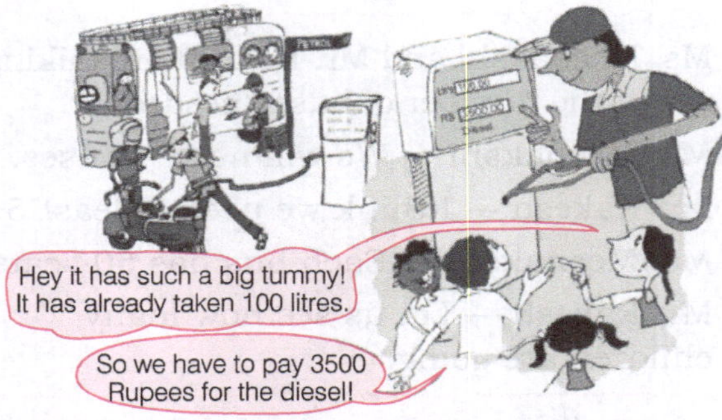

Look in the picture and find the price of 1 litre of diesel.

Ans. Price of 1 litre of diesel

$$= \frac{\text{Total rupees paid}}{\text{Total litres of diesels}}$$

$$= \frac{3500}{100} = ₹\,35$$

Q.9 How much time did Aman take to come out of the toilet? ....

Ans. Time taken by Aman to come out

= Time taken by one bus to refill

= 15 minutes [from Q.7]

Hence, Aman takes 15 minutes to come out of the toilet.

To Bhimbetka (NCERT Pg 28-29)

Q.10

(i) How many more deer are there than bisons?

(ii) But Bonomala is the happiest because the number of people is even more than the number of deer and bisons together. Her count is less than 200. How many people must Bonomala have counted?

214 / 154 / 134 / 177

Ans. (i) Number of deer = 117

Number of bisons = 37

Number of more deer than bisons

= Number of deer- Number of bisons

= 117 − 37 = 80

Hence, there are 80 more deer than bisons.

(ii) Total number of animals (Deer + Bisons)

= 117 + 37 = 154

Since, total number of people is more than the number of deer and bisons together.

∴ Total number of people is more than 154.

Also, total number of people is less than 200.

Therefore, Bonomala has counted 177 people.

Q.11 They have spent 1 hour there. What time is it?

Ans. They reached there at 11 o'clock and spent 1 hour here.

Therefore, it is 12 o'clock.

Q.12 They are now moving towards Bhopal. They should reach there in less than 1 hour, at about __________ o'clock.

Ans. They started at 12 o'clock from Bhimbetka.

The distance to Bhopal from Bhimbetka

= 70 − 50 = 20 kilometres

So, they reached Bhopal at 12 : 45 o'clock.

That is around 1 o'clock.

Lunch Time (NCERT Pg 30-31)

Q.13

Each child is to be given 1 orange, 1 banana and 5 biscuits.

All the children take oranges and biscuits but 38 children do not take bananas. How many oranges, biscuits and bananas are distributed?

Ans. Total number of students = 210

Number of oranges distributed

$= 210 \times 1 = 210$

Number of biscuits distributed

$= 210 \times 5 = 1050$

Number of students who took bananas

= 210 − 38 = 172

Number of bananas distributed

$= 172 \times 1 = 172$

Q.14 I gave four toffees each to four of my friends and three toffees are left with me. How many toffees did I have?

Ans. Number of toffees given to a friend = 4,

number of friends = 4,

number of toffees given to 4 friends $= 4 \times 4 = 16$

and number of toffees left = 3

Total number of toffees = 16 + 3 = 19

Hence, he had 19 toffees.

Q.15 What numbers can you make using 3, 5 and 7? You can make 357 and 537. What others?

Ans. Numbers can made using the digits 3, 5 and 7 are 357, 375, 537, 573, 735 and 753.

Numbers made using the digits 3, 5 and 7 other than 357 and 537 are 375, 573, 735 and 753.

Q.16 A number becomes double if it is increased by 8. What is the number?

Ans. The number will be 8.

Because 8 + 8 = 16 and 16 is double of 8.

Q.17 Think of a number which can be divided by 2, 3 and 5 and comes between 25 and 50.

Ans. A number which can be divided by 2, 3 and 5 = Number should be multiple of each 2, 3 and 5.

So, required number $= 2 \times 3 \times 5 = 30$

The number 30 also comes between 25 and 50.

$\therefore$ Required number is 30.

Q.18 A small ant climbs 3 centimetres in 1 minute but slips down 2 centimetres. How much time will it take to climb to 2 centimetres?

Ans. Distance covered by ant in 1 minute

= 3 centimetres − 2 centimetres

= 1 centimetre

$\therefore$ Distance covered by ant in 2 minutes

$= 2 \times 1 = 2$ centimetres

Hence, it will take 2 minutes to climb 2 cm.

Which Boat do we Take? (NCERT Pg 31-33)

Q.19 There are different kinds of boats. Each has a different ticket price and also different trip times.

S. No.	Name of the Boat	Ticket-price	Trip-time
1.	Double-decker	₹ 30	45 minutes
2.	Paddle-boat	₹ 15	30 minutes
3.	Motor-boat	₹ 25	20 minutes
4.	Boat with oars	₹ 15	45 minutes

(i) Indra and Bhanu first went in the motor-boat and then took the oar-boat.

(a) How much did they pay for both the boats?

(b) How much time did they get for both rides?

(ii) One group of children went for the double-decker trip. They paid ₹ 450 in total. How many children went for the double-decker trip?

(iii) Which boat makes two trips in 1 hour?

(iv) Which boat takes less than half an hour to complete a trip?

(v) Which boat gives them the most time taking the least money?

(vi) Javed went twice for boating. He paid a total of ₹ 40 and boated for 50 minutes. Which two boats did he take?

Ans. (i) (a) Ticket price of motor-boat = ₹ 25 and ticket price of oar-boat = ₹ 15

Total price paid by Indra and Bhanu

$= 2 \times 25 + 2 \times 15$

= 50 + 30 = ₹ 80

Hence, they paid ₹ 80 for both the boats.

(b) Trip time for motor-boat = 20 minutes

Trip time for oar-boat = 45 minutes

Total time they get for both rides

= 20 + 45 = 65 minutes

(ii) Ticket price of double-decker boat = ₹ 30

Total amount paid by the group = ₹ 450

Number of children went for double-decker trip

$$= \frac{\text{Total amount paid by group}}{\text{Ticket price of double-decker boat}}$$

$$= \frac{450}{30} = 15$$

(iii) $\because$ Time for two trips = 1 hour = 60 minutes

[$\because$ 1 hour = 60 minutes]

$\therefore$ Time for one trip $= \frac{60}{2}$

= 30 minutes

Since, Paddle-boat completes 1 trip in 30 minutes.

Therefore, Paddle-boat makes two trips in 1 hour.

(iv) Motor boat takes less than half an hour to complete a trip.

(v) Double-decker and oar-boat give most time but oar-boat takes less money than double-decker.

Therefore, oar-boat gives them the most time and taking the least money.

(vi) Javed boated 50 minutes, it means he took paddle-boat and motor-boat.
So, he paid ₹ 40.

Time to Return (NCERT Pg 33)

Q.20 Children enjoy different boat rides till 4 o'clock. It is time to return. Now they will not stop anywhere and reach back in two hours.

So, they should reach Hoshangabad by .... o'clock.

Ans. Travelling time to reach Hoshangabad
= 2 hours

Time to reach Hoshangabad
= Starting time to return + travelling time
= 4 o'clock + 2 hours
= 6 o'clock

Find Out (NCERT Pg 34)

Q.21 Have you ever been on a school trip? How many children were there in all? How did you go and how far? How much time did it take? Try to find out the cost of travel for each child.

Ans. * Yes, I had been on a school trip on children day.
There were 75 children in all. We went by bus and the place was about 40 kilometres far from my school.
It took 1 hour. Cost of travel for each child was ₹ 60.

Practice Time (NCERT Pg 34)

Q.22 There are four very old cave-paintings. Mark the oldest

(a) 4200 years old (b) 1000 years old
(c) 8500 years old (d) 1300 years old

Ans. (c) 8500 years old.

Q.23 One bus can carry 48 children. How many children can three buses carry? About-

(a) 100 (b) 200 (c) 150

Ans. (c) Number of children carried by one bus
= 48

Total number of children carried by three buses = $3 \times 48 = 144$

Therefore, option (c) is correct answer that is about 150.

Q.24 Which pair of numbers add to make more than 500?

(a) 152 and 241
(b) 99 and 299
(c) 321 and 192
(d) 401 and 91

Ans. (c) From option (a), on adding 152 and 241, we get $152 + 241 = 393$

From option (b), on adding 99 and 299, we get $99 + 299 = 398$

From option (c), on adding 321 and 192, we get $321 + 192 = 513$

From option (d), on adding 401 and 91, we get $401 + 91 = 492$

So, option (c) is correct.

Q.25 What happened at what time? Draw lines to match.

(i)	Crossed the Narmada bridge	(a)	3:00 pm
(ii)	Looked at Bhimbetka paintings	(b)	6:00 pm
(iii)	At the petrol pump	(c)	9:10 am
(iv)	Boating in the lake	(d)	12:30 pm
(v)	Had lunch	(e)	11:30 am
(vi)	Returned to Hoshangabad	(f)	9:30 am

Ans. (i) → (c), (ii) → (e), (iii) → (f),
(iv) → (a), (v) → (d), (vi) → (b)

PRACTICE QUESTIONS

1. Multiple choice questions.

   (i) Shivam goes to a birthday party at 8 o'clock and come back after 2 and half hour. At what time he come back?

   (a) 10 o'clock
   (b) 11 o'clock
   (c) Between 10 o'clock and 11 o'clock
   (d) Between 11 o'clock and 12 o' clock

   (ii) The height of a plant is 2 metres. After 2 years, it grows to 15 metres. Find out how much height the plant grew in 2 years?

   (a) 15 metres (b) 13 metres
   (c) 17 metres (d) 12 metres

   (iii) If 175 pens, 70 pencils and 140 books are equally distributed to 35 students, then find how many of items will each child get?

   (a) 5 pens, 2 pencils, 3 books
   (b) 2 pencils, 4 books, 5 pens
   (c) 5 pens, 2 books, 5 pencils
   (d) 2 pencils, 5 books, 4 pens

   (iv) If the cost of 65 litres of milk is ₹ 3445, then the cost of one litre of milk is

   (a) 47 (b) 49 (c) 55 (d) 53

   (v) Counting backwards, Jaya wants to write down all numbers from 600 to 1 (600, 599, 598, ... and so on upto 1). Among the following numbers, which one will come first in her list?

   (a) 445 (b) 544 (c) 545 (d) 454

2. Make all three-digit numbers using digits 0, 9 and 7. And find the difference between smallest and greatest number.

3. A book self has 17 sections and each of the section has same height of 16.8 centimetres. Find out how many books the book shelf can hold, if each book has 2.1 centimetres of thickness.

ANSWERS & SOLUTIONS

1. (i) (c) Time of going to birthday party = 8 o'clock

   Spent time = 2 and half hour

   Time of come back

   = Time of going to birthday party + Spent time

   = 8 o'clock + 2 and half hour

   = 10 : 30 o' clock

   Hence, time of come back in between 10 o'clock and 11 o'clock.

   (ii) (b) Height of plant = 2 m

   Height of plant after 2 years = 15 m

   ∴ Height of plant grew in 2 years

   = 15 m − 2 m = 13 m

   (iii) (b) Number of pens = 175, number of pencils = 70, number of books = 140 and number of students = 35

   ∴ Number of pens distributed to each student $= \frac{175}{35} = 5$ pens,

   number of pencils distributed to each student $= \frac{70}{35} = 2$ pencils

   and number of books distributed to each student $= \frac{140}{35} = 4$ books

   (iv) (d) Cost of 65 litres of milk = ₹ 3445

   Cost of 1 litres of milk $= \frac{3445}{65} =$ ₹ 53

   (v) (c) As 545 > 544 > 454 > 445

2. All three-digit numbers using digits 0, 9 and 7 are 709, 790, 907 and 970.

   Here, smallest three-digit number is 709 and greatest three-digit number is 970.

   ∴ Difference between smallest and greatest number = 970 − 709 = 261

3. Sections in a book shelf = 17

   Height of each section = 16.8 cm

   Height of book shelf = 17 × 16.8 = 285.6 cm

   Thickness of each book = 2.1 cm

   ∴ Number of books, the book shelf can hold $= \frac{\text{Height of book shelf}}{\text{Thickness of each book}}$

   $= \frac{285.6}{2.1} = 136$ books

CHAPTER 4

TICK-TICK-TICK

Hands of a clock

There are three types of hands in a clock.

(i) **Hour hand** The shortest hand in the clock is hour hand. It completes one revolution in 12 hours.

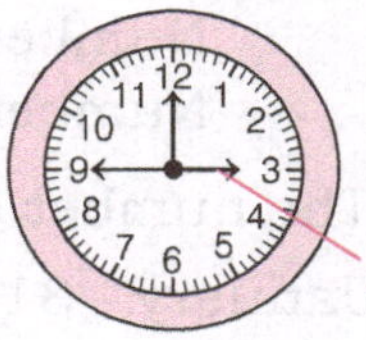

(ii) **Minute hand** The longest hand in the clock is minute hand. It completes one revolution in 60 minutes or 1 hour.

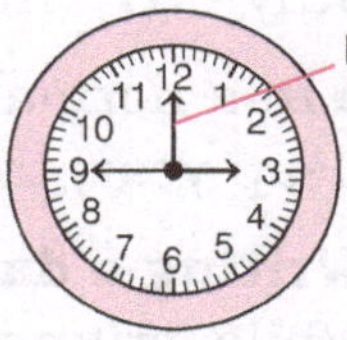

(iii) **Second hand** A thin long hand in the clock is second hand. It completes one revolution in 60 seconds or 1 minute.

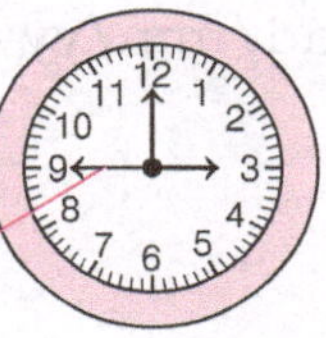

Division in a clock

There are 2 types of division in a clock.

(i) **Big division** A clock is divided in 12 big divisions which is shown by numbers 1 to 12. If a hour hand moves from one number to the next number, it counts as 1 hour and a minute hand moves from one number to the next number, it counts as 5 minutes.

(ii) **Small division** Every big division divided into 5 small divisions. Therefore, a clock is divided into ($12 \times 5 = 60$) small divisions. It is shown by thin lines between the numbers. If a minute hand moves from one thin line to the next thin line. It counts as 1 minute.

12-hour clock

There are 24 hours in a day and we use such a clock which shows the time maximum 12 hours. Therefore, in a day, hour hand of this clock makes two revolutions.
We use 'am' to represent the time from midnight to 11 : 59 before noon and 'pm' to represent the time from 12 : 00 noon to 11 : 59 midnight.

e.g. (i) 6: 45 am means it is 6 hours 45 minutes in the morning.

(ii) 5 : 15 pm means it is 5 hours 15 minutes in evening.

24-hour clock

We seen such clocks at railway stations. In a 24 hour format, we do not use 'am' and 'pm' while telling the time. We use 1 to 24 hours to tell the time. The table shows the time representation in 12-hour clock and 24-hour clock.

Time in 12-hour clock	Time in 24-hour clock
11:30 AM	11:30 hours
3:30 PM	15:30 hours

Calendar

- Number of days in a year are 365 or 366.
- Number of months in a year are 12.

The number of days in each month is given below.

January - 31, February - 28 or 29, March - 31, April - 30, May - 31, June - 30, July - 31, August - 31, September - 30, October - 31, November - 30, December -31.

Note In a normal year, there are 365 days in the year and February has 28 days. In a leap year, there are 366 days in the year and February has 29 days.

Writing a date

While writing a date, we represent the date, month and the year in format of dd/mm/yyyy. e.g. 29 March 2024 is written as 29/03/2024.

NCERT FOLDER

Practice Time (NCERT Pg 36-37)

Q.1 Three friends read time from a clock. Who is right?

	Cheecku	Bittu	Pinki
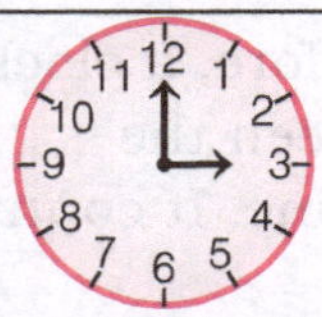	12 : 03	12 : 15	3 : 00
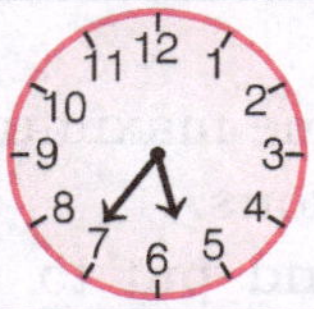	7 : 25	5 : 07	5 : 35
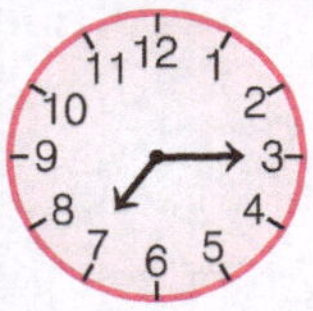	3 : 35	7 : 03	7 : 15

Ans. In first clock, minute hand is pointing to 12 and hour hand pointing to 3. Hence, the time is 3 o'clock. Therefore, Pinki is right.
In second clock, the clock is showing the time 5 : 35. So, Pinki is right.
In third clock, the clock is showing the time 7 : 15. So, again Pinki is right.

Q.2 Show the following times in the clock:

3 : 10

6 : 40

4 : 45

2 : 20

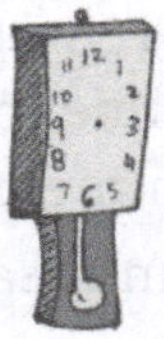

3 : 15

7 : 35

* *Students can write alternate answer as per their choice.*

Ans.

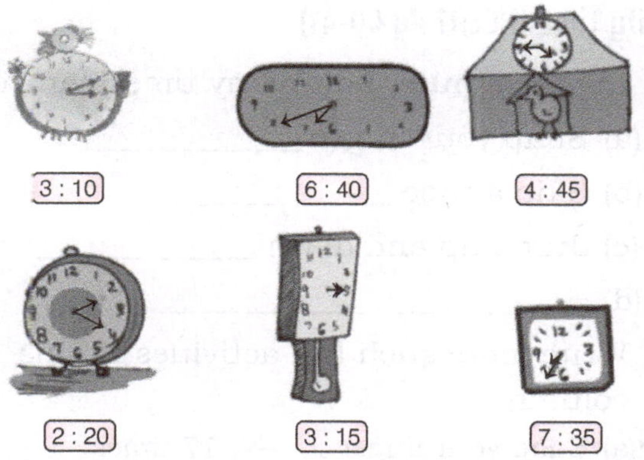

Q.3 Do you like sky watching? If yes, then this one should interest you.

(i) At what time does the sun rise at your place?

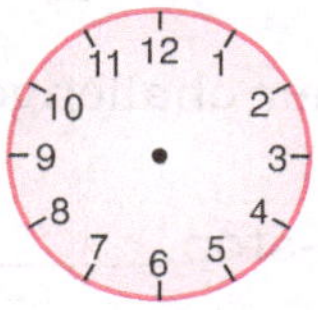

(ii) When does the sun set ?

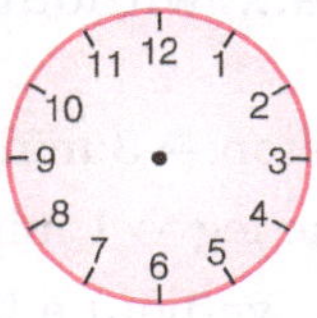

Ans. *(i) At my place, the sum rises at 5 : 30 am in summers.

(ii) In summers, the sun sets at 7:15 pm at my place.

Q.4 Does the sun rise and set at the same times every day?

Ans. No, the sun does not rise and set at the same times every day.

Q.5 Look at a newspaper and see the time of sunrise and sunset in different months.

Ans. * The sunrise and sunset time in different months in my town is given below.

Date - Month	Sunrise time	Sunset time
15 January	6 : 54 am	5 : 19 pm
15 February	6 : 35 am	5 : 45 pm
15 March	6 : 15 am	5 : 59 pm
15 April	5 : 48 am	6 : 28 pm
15 May	5 : 29 am	6 : 47 pm
15 June	5 : 13 am	7 : 15 pm
15 July	5 : 16 am	7 : 22 pm
15 August	5 : 29 am	7 : 09 pm
15 September	5 : 46 am	6 : 59 pm
15 October	6 : 08 am	6 : 27 pm
15 November	6 : 21 am	6 : 02 pm
15 December	6 : 43 am	5 : 49 pm

Find Out (NCERT Pg 38-40)

Q.6 How long will it take the minute hand to move from

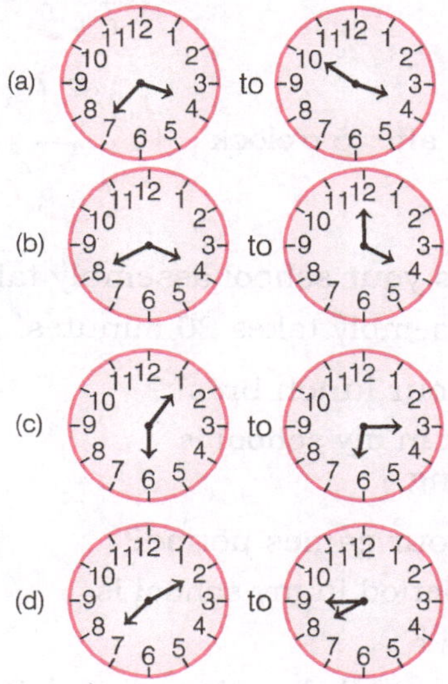

Ans. (a) 15 minutes (b) 20 minutes
(c) 10 minutes (d) 35 minutes

Q.7 Draw where the hands will be:

(a) 20 minutes after 6 o'clock

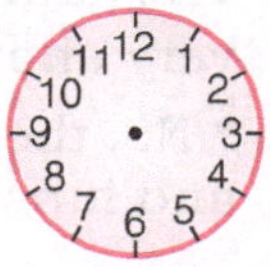

(b) 30 minutes after 8 o'clock

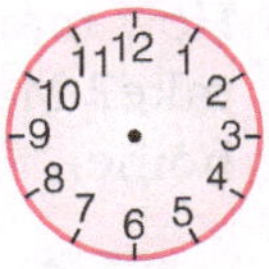

(c) 10 minutes after 7 o'clock

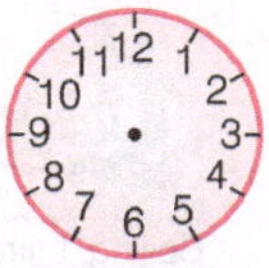

(d) 15 minutes after 5 o'clock

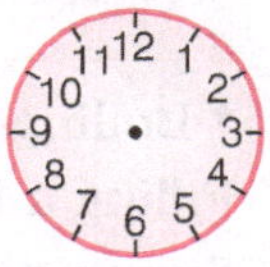

Ans.

(a) 20 minutes after 6 o'clock

(b) 30 minutes after 8 o'clock

(c) 10 minutes after 7 o'clock

(d) 15 minutes after 5 o'clock

Q.8 How long does your school assembly take?

Ans. *My school assembly takes 20 minutes.

Q.9 How long is your lunch break?

Ans. * Lunch break in my school is 30 minutes long.

Q.10 How long is your games period?

Ans. * The games period in my school is 45 minutes long.

Q.11 Is it the same as all the other periods?

Ans. * Yes, all the other periods have the same time as games period.

Q.12 The games period and lunch break seem very short! Are not they?

Ans. * No, the time is enough for games period and lunch break.

Q.13 How many minutes can these activities take? Make a guess and then check at home.

Boiling 1 litre milk ________

Filling a bucket ________

Sweeping your room ________

Ans. * Boiling 1 litre milk → 7 minutes
Filling a bucket → 3 minutes
Sweeping your room → 5 minutes

Activity Time (NCERT Pg 40-41)

Q.14 In one minute, how many times can you

(a) Snap your finger ____________

(b) Skip a rope ____________

(c) Jump up and down ____________

(d) ____________ ____________

Write more such fun activities in this column.

Ans. *(a) Snap your finger → 17 times

(b) Skip a rope → 35 times

(c) Jump up and down → 38 times

(d) Blink my eyelids → 70 times

(e) Squats → 30 times

Q.15 Here is another challenge for you. How long can you

(a) Speak non-stop ____________

(b) Stand on one leg ____________

(c) Sing 'Aaaa...' without a break ____________

Ans. *(a) Speak non-stop → 3 minutes

(b) Stand on one leg → 1 minute

(c) Sing 'Aaaa...' without a break → 1 minute.

Q.16 How long do you take to

(a) Run a 50 metre race ____________

(b) Collect 50 pebbles from the ground ____________

(c) Count 1 to 100 ____________

Ans. *(a) Run a 50 metre race → 1 minute

(b) Collect 50 pebbles from the ground → 5 minutes

(c) Count 1 to 100 → 2 minutes

Q.17 Let's look at a clock again! Solve this one

(a) The minute hand started from 2. How many minutes will it take to come back to 2 again? ____________

(b) What happens to the hour hand ? Does it also move ? How long will it take to move from one number to the next?

(c) Look around you and list the activities that take about one hour to complete.

(i) ____________ (ii) ____________

(iii) ____________ (iv) ____________

(v) ____________

Ans. (a) After 1 rotation minute hand came back to 2 again. Therefore, it take 1 hour or 60 minutes.

(b) Yes, the hour hand also moves. The hour hand takes 1 hour to move from one number to the next number.

*(c) (i) Cleaning of house.

(ii) Cooking food

(iii) Playing hockey

(iv) Completing the home work.

(v) Going to temple and worship there.

Q.18 How long does it take to cook dinner at home? More than an hour/less than an hour.

Ans. It takes more than an hour to cook dinner at home.

Q.19 Ask your father if he can cook as fast as your mother does. Yes / No

Ans. * No.

Q.20 Which games take less than an hour to finish?

Ans. Games like kabaddi, kho-kho, wrestling, boxing, swimming, judo, etc. takes less than one hour to finish.

Q.21 How long does a football match take?

Ans. The duration of a football match is 90 minutes, which is divided into two halves of 45-45 minutes.

Rani's Diary (NCERT Pg 42-44)

Q.22

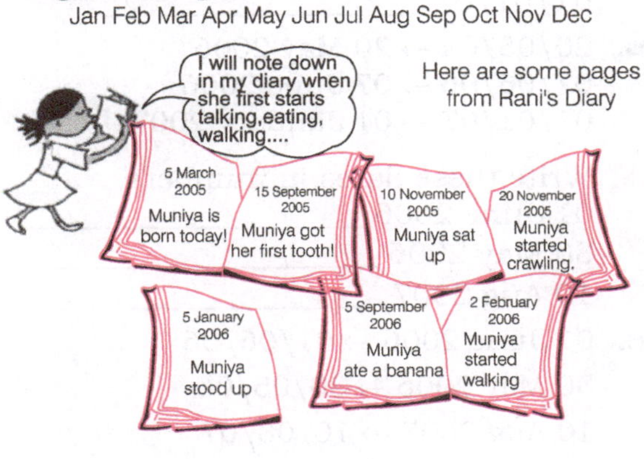

Mark these in the correct order on Muniya's time line.

Ans.

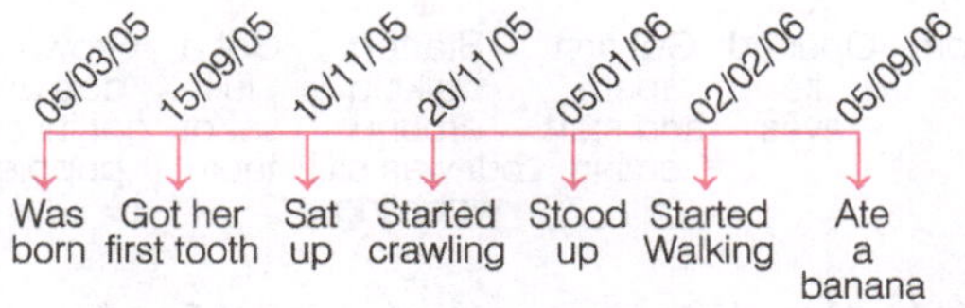

Q.23 Muniya got her first tooth in September. How many months old was she then?

Ans. When Muniya got her first tooth in September, she was 6 months old.

Q.24 How old was Muniya when

(a) She first sat up?

(b) She got her first tooth?

Ans. (a) She was 8 months old when she sat up first.

(b) Muniya was about six months old when she got her first tooth.

Q.25 What did she do first

(a) Walking / eating a banana?

(b) Crawling / standing?

Ans. (a) Walking (b) Crawling

Q.26 Rani had a pet puppy. After 2 weeks it opened its eyes. She watched it grow like this:

After 3 weeks, it got its first teeth and started eating.

After 4 weeks, it started walking around but was still wobbling.

It had a full set of teeth by the time it was 7 months old.

After 1 year, it was a grown-up dog and got its own puppies.

Now, make a time-line of this dog life in your notebook.

Ans.

	After 2 weeks	After 3 weeks	After 4 weeks	In 7 months	After 1 year
Born	Opened its eyes	Got first teeth and start eating	Started walking around but was still wobbling	Got a full set of teeth	Grown up dog and got its own puppies

Q.27 Note the differences between Muniya and Rani's puppy.

Ans.

Positions	Muniya (age)	Puppy (age)
Started walking	About 11 months old	4 weeks old
Ate food for the first time	18 months old	3 weeks old
Got the first tooth	About 6 months old	3 weeks old

Find Out (NCERT Pg 45)

Q.28 Do all animals grow at the same speed?

Ans. No, all animals do not grow at the same speed.

Q.29 Discuss about the growth of
(a) a hen (b) a cow (c) a bird

Ans. The animals mentioned above grow in the following order-a bird, a hen, a cow.

Q.30 Draw pictures of the baby animal and the big animal.

Ans. *

Q.31 Here are the pictures of grandfathers posing for a photograph. Who looks the oldest to you?

Elephant Appu's grandfather (95 years old)

Chachoo rat's grandfather (2 years old)

Rani's grandfather (70 years old)

Ans. Elephant Appu's grandfather is oldest. He is 95 years old.

Q.32 How much older is Appu's grandfather than Rani's grandfather?

Ans. The age of Appu's grandfather = 95 years
and age of Rani's grandfather = 70 years
Difference between their age = 95 − 70
= 25 years

So, Appu's grandfather is 25 years older than Rani's grandfather.

Q.33 Will Chuchoo's grandfather ever grow as old as Appu's grandfather?

Ans. Chuchoo's grandfather will never grow as old as Appu's grandfather.

Q.34 How much younger is Chuchoo rat's grandfather than Rani's grandfather?

Ans. Age of Chuchoo rat's grandfather = 2 years
Age of Rani's grandfather = 70 years
Difference between their age = 70 − 2
= 68 years.

Hence, Chuchoo rat's grandfather is 68 years younger than Rani's grandfather.

Holidays are Fun! (NCERT Pg 46-48)

Q.35 Atif wrote his letter on 01/05/06. You remember how we write a date in numbers?

Ans. Yes, I remember that a date is written in number in the format of day/month/year.

Q.36 1/05/06 is 1 May 2006

Now, write which dates these stand for

05/05/06 ____05 May 2006____
20/05/06 ________________
07/06/06 ________________
01/01/07 ________________

Ans. 20/05/06 → 20 May 2006
07/06/06 → 07 June 2006
01/01/07 → 01 January 2007

Q.37 Write these dates in numbers.

01 June 2006 ________________
30 May 2006 ________________
10 Aug 2007 ________________

Ans. 01 June 2006 → 01/06/06
30 May 2006 → 30/05/06
10 Aug 2007 → 10/08/07

Q.38 How long did it take the letter to reach from Ajmer to Nagpur?

Ans. Atif wrote this letter on 01/05/06 and Shabana got it on 06/05/06. So, it took 5 days to reach from Ajmer to Nagpur.

Q.39 How many days will Atif spend at his Nani's place?

Ans. Atif is going to his Nani's place on 05/05/06 and returned on 20/05/06. So, he spent (20 – 5) = 15 days at his Nani's place.

Q.40 Fill the table :

	Dates		Number of days
	From	To	
Shabana's holiday			
Atif's holiday			

Ans.

	Dates		Number of days
	From	To	
Shabana's holiday	1 June 2006	9 August 2006	70 days
Atif's holiday	1 May 2006	29 June 2006	60 days

Q.41 Who has got longer holidays - Shabana or Atif ?

Ans. Shabana has got longer holidays.

Q.42 Which long holidays do you get in school? Fill the table.

Occassion	Dates		Number of days
	From	To	
Summer holidays			
Autumn Break			
Winter Break			
Holidays after the exam			

Ans. *

Occassion	Dates		Number of days
	From	To	
Summer holidays	25th May	2nd July	39 days
Autumn Break	12th October	19th October	8 days
Winter Break	25th December	5th January	12 days
Holidays after the exam	15th March	1st April	18 days

I got long summer holidays in the school.

Q.43 On 15 May 2006 Chandran went to a shop to buy butter. He checked the packet to see if this butter was safe to eat.

It was written on the packet - Best before 180 days from the date of packing.

Then, he checked the date of packing. It was 15/01/06.

Help him find out if he should buy this butter or not.

(i) In which month was the butter packed?

(ii) Which month will it be 180 days after 15/01/06?

(iii) Can Chandran eat it on 15th May 2006?

Ans. (i) The butter was packed in the month of January.

(ii) Calculation of 180 days after 15/01/06

16/01/06 — 31/01/06 = 16 days
01/02/06 — 28/02/06 = 28 days
01/03/06 — 31/03/06 = 31 days
01/04/06 — 30/04/06 = 30 days
01/05/06 — 31/05/06 = 31 days
01/06/06 — 30/06/06 = 30 days

Now, 180 – 166 = 14 days

So, 180 days after 15/01/06 is 14 July 2006.

Therefore, it will be July month, 180 days after 15/01/06.

(iii) Yes, Chandran can eat it on 15th May 2006.

Q.44 Do you ever check the date of packing of things you buy?

Ans. * Yes, I am always check the date of packing of things when I bought.

Q.45 Have you seen medicines which have the expiry date written on them?

Ans. Yes, every medicine has expiry date.

Find Out (NCERT Pg 48)

Q.46 (i) Which are the other things that come with an expiry date?

(ii) On a cough syrup, it was written :

Mfg. date **7/03**

This shows, it was made in July 2003.

Exp. date **7/05**

This shows the month and year till when it is safe to take.

What month and year is written as 07/05?

(iii) Would it be safe to take the cough syrup in September 2005?

Ans. (i) Other things which come with an expiry date are medicines, packaged food, etc.

(ii) 07/05 shows July month of year 2005.

(iii) No, It would not be safe to take the cough syrup in September 2005, because expiry date of this cough syrup is July 2005.

Tutun Missed the Train (NCERT Pg 49-51)

Q.47 Can you guess why they missed the train?

Ans. Railways uses 24-hours clock. And their ticket shows 5 : 30. It means 5 : 30 at morning but they reached 5 : 15 at evening. Therefore, they missed the train.

Q.48 Look at this chart. It tells the difference between your watch and a 24-hour clock. Try to complete it.

Time by your watch (12-hour clock)	Time by a 24-hour clock
1 o'clock in the afternoon	13 : 00 hours
2 o'clock in the afternoon	14 : 00 hours
3 o'clock in the afternoon	
3 : 30 in the afternoon	15 : 30 hours
6 o'clock in the evening	
9 o'clock in the evening	
12 o'clock at midnight	

Ans.

Time by your watch (12-hour clock)	Time by a 24-hour clock
1 o'clock in the afternoon	13 : 00 hours
2 o'clock in the afternoon	14 : 00 hours
3 o'clock in the afternoon	15 : 00 hours
3 : 30 in the afternoon	15 : 30 hours
6 o'clock in the evening	18 : 00 hours
9 o'clock in the evening	21 : 00 hours
12 o'clock at midnight	00 : 00 hours

Q.49 Can you tell why a 24 hours clock is called so?

Ans. A 24-hour clock shows the time for whole day which is 24 hours. Therefore, it is called 24-hour clock.

Q.50 Suppose a train leaves at 8 : 30 at night. The time written on the railway ticket would be ________ .

Ans. Railway uses 24 hours clock. So, in that clock 8 : 30 at night shows as 20 : 30 hours.

Q.51 You must have noted the time of sunrise and sunset. Write, here using am and pm.

Time of sunrise

Time of sunset

Ans. * Time of sunrise - 5 : 45 am

Time of sunset - 6 : 38 pm

Q.52 Where have you seen a 24 - hour clock being used?

(i) ________________

(ii) ________________

(iii) ________________

Ans. (i) Railway stations

(ii) Airports

(iii) Bus stands

PRACTICE QUESTIONS

1. Multiple choice questions.

(i) The clock 

shows in time

(a) 2 : 3 (b) 2 : 15
(c) 3 : 10 (d) 3 : 2

(ii) The short hand of this clock at quarter to 8 in/on

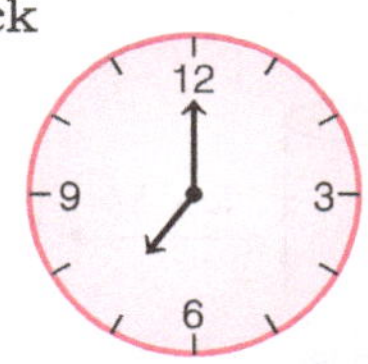

(a) between 8 and 9
(b) exactly at 9
(c) between 7 and 8
(d) exactly at 8

(iii) Which of these hand moves fastest in a clock?

(a) Minute hand (b) Second hand
(c) Hour hand (d) None of these

(iv) If the time is 11 : 00 am. Now, after how many hours will the time be 1 : 00 pm?

(a) 1 (b) 2 (c) 10 (d) 14

(v) Sanjeev is celebrating Diwali with his friends. He knows the fire-crackers can be burst only till 10 pm. The time being shown by the wall clock now is 9:20 pm. For how much more time can Sanjeev and his friends enjoy bursting crackers?

(a) 20 minutes (b) 40 minutes
(c) 45 minutes (d) 56 minutes

(vi) In 24 hours clock, 6 : 15 am shows as

(a) 6 : 15 hours
(b) 16 : 15 hours
(c) 18 : 15 hours
(d) 20 : 15 hours

2. Find odd one out.

(i) (a) 6 : 15 am (b) 18 : 30 hours
(c) 12 : 30 pm (d) 9 : 30 am

(ii) (a) 19 : 30 hours (b) 21 : 15 hours
(c) 13 : 45 hours (d) 11 : 55 am

3. Ramesh is 15 month younger than his sister Radha. If Radha born in october 2012, then find the birth of Ramesh.

4. Ramesh checked his grandfather's medicine. He found that the expiry date is 18 months after the manufacturing date. If expiry date is 03/20, then found the manufacturing date of medicine.

ANSWERS & SOLUTIONS

1. (i) (b) (ii) (c) (iii) (b)

(iv) (b) Difference between 1: 00 pm and 11: 00 is 2 hours.

(v) (b) Time shown by given clocks

= 9 : 20 pm

∴ Time for which Sanjeev and his friends enjoy bursting crackers

= Minute hand moves from 4 to 12

$= (12 - 4) \times 5 = 8 \times 5 = 40$ minutes

(vi) (a)

2. (i) (b) (ii) (d)

3. Given, birth of Radha is October 2012 and Ramesh is 15 months younger than Radha.

∴ Birth of Ramesh

= Birth of Radha + 15 months

= October 2012 + 1 year 3 month

[∵ 12 months = 1 year

∴ 15 months = 1 year 3 months]

= January 2014

4. Given, expiry date of medicine

= 3/20 or March 2020

∵ Expiry date is 18 months after the manufacturing date.

∴ Manufacturing date of medicine

= Expiry date of medicine − 18 months

= March 2020 − 1 year 6 months

[∵ 1 year = 12 months

∴ 18 months = 1 year 6 months]

= September 2018 = 09/18

CHAPTER 5

THE WAY THE WORLD LOOKS

Top view

This view shows the object as seen from above. It provides the information about the object's length and width.

e.g. 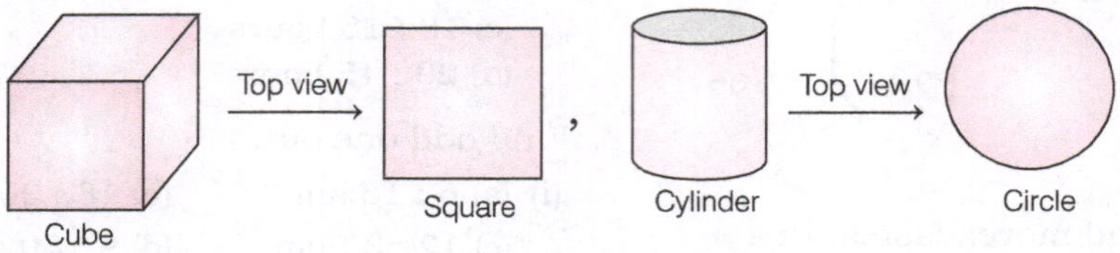

Front view

This view shows the object as seen from the front. It provides information about the object's height and width.

e.g. 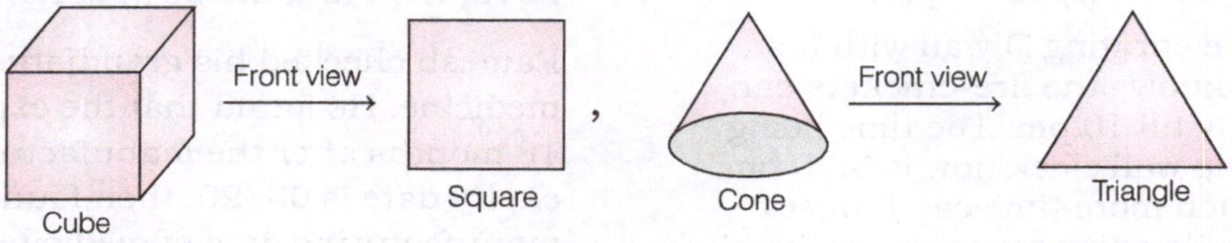

Side view

This view shows the object as seen from the sides. It provides information about the object's height and length.

e.g. 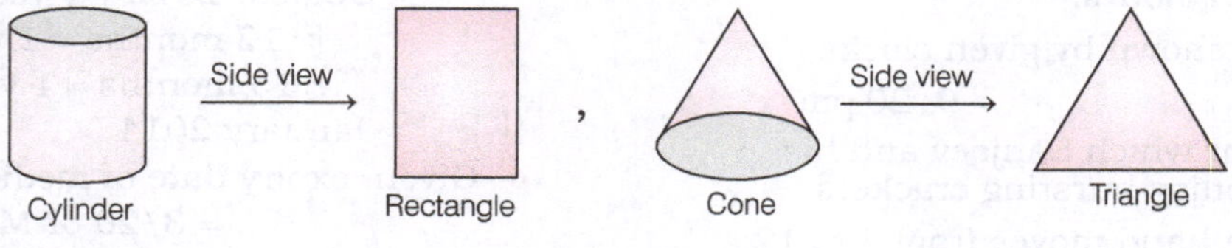

NCERT FOLDER

Gappu's Air Journey (NCERT Pg 52-55)

Q.1 Draw how the fan looks from below.

Ans. When we see the ceiling fan from below, it looks like the given figure.

Q.2 Can you think why Gappu could see the cheese on the jug but Chinky could not?

Ans. Gappu saw the cheese on the jug because he saw from above while Chinky was on floor, so she could not see.

Q.3 When I ran around in my house, it looked so big! But from here, it looks small. How is that?

Ans. Objects appear smaller as distance increases. Since, Gappu was looking things from higher in the air. Therefore, the house looks smaller.

Q.4 Imagine how your classroom looks from above. Try to draw it and mark the benches, black board, doors, windows etc.

Ans. *

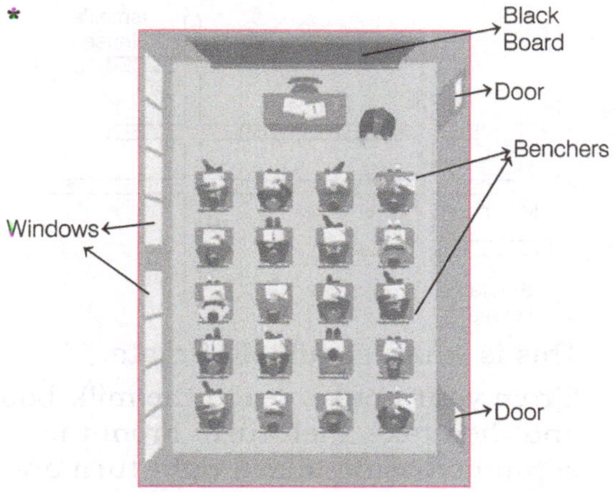

** Students can write alternate answer as per their choice.*

Q.5 Look at these pictures and discuss why things look wide and big at this end but narrow and small at the other end.

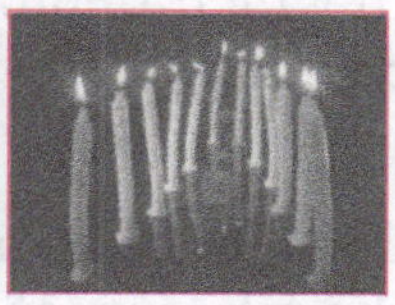

Ans. Objects appear smaller and narrow as the distance increases. Therefore, things look wide and big at this end but narrow and small at the other end in these pictures.

Match Two Views of the Same Pose (NCERT Pg 55-56)

Q.6 This is a top view of a girl in a yoga pose.

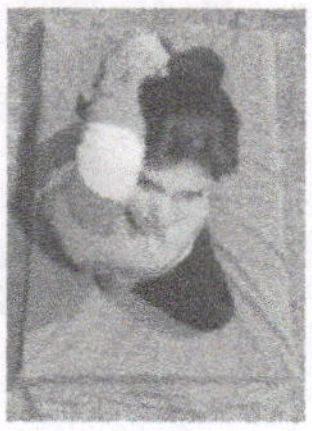

Only one of the photos below is the correct match of the same yoga pose. Mark it.

Ans.

Q.7 These are two different views of the same bowls.

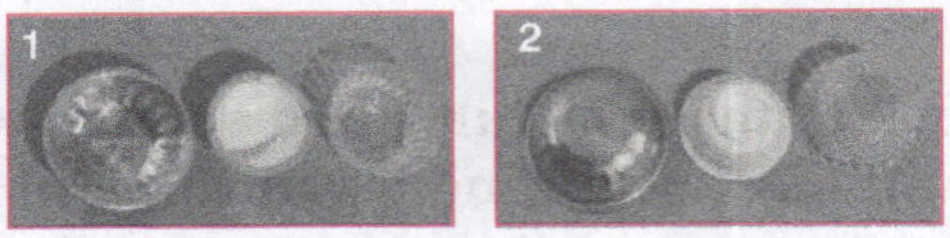

In which photo are the bowls upside down? ....

Ans. In photo-2, the bowls are upside down.

Q.8 Draw lines to match the side view with the top view of

- A pipe - A funnel

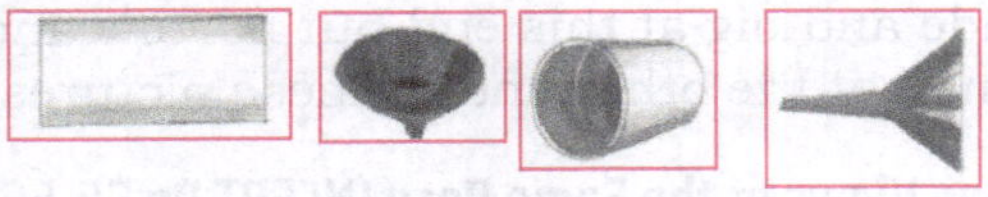

Ans.

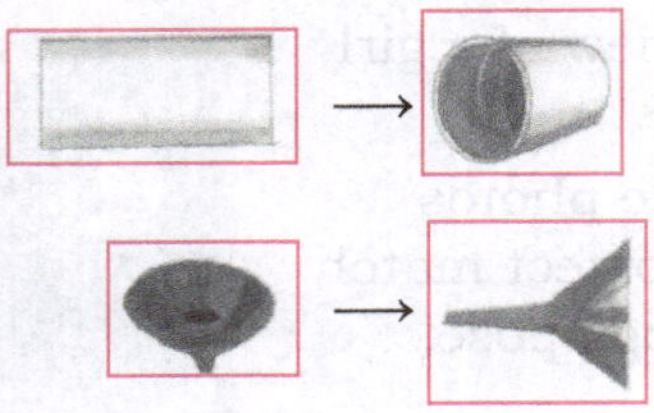

Q.9 Try to draw pictures of a shoe from the side, top, front etc.

Ans.

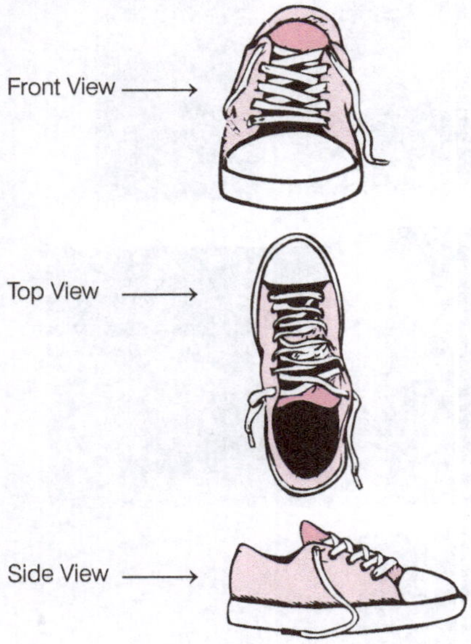

The Park Behind Gappu's House (NCERT Pg 57)

Q.10 Here is a bigger picture of that park. Look at it carefully and answer the questions.

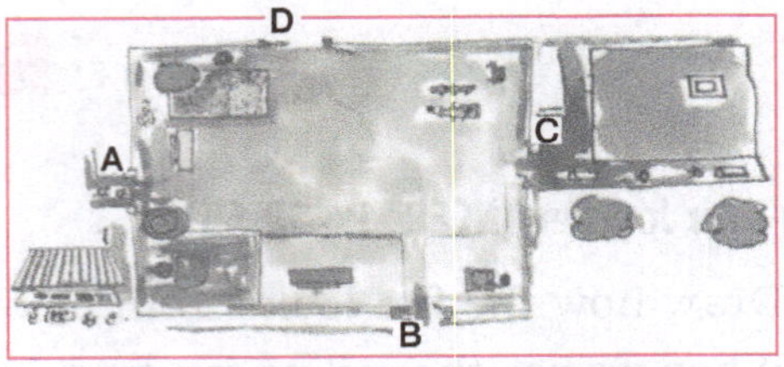

(i) Mark the gate nearest to the sweet shop. *A* / *B* / *C* / *D*

(ii) Which gate is nearest to Gappu's house?

(iii) If you enter from gate-*B*, the bench will be to your-Left/Right/Front

(iv) When Suhasini entered the park, the flower bed was to her right. Which gate did she enter from?

(v) Which of these is nearest to you if you enter from gate-*C* ?

(a) Basketball court (b) Flower bed

(c) Green bench (d) See-saw

Ans. (i) Gate-*A* is the nearest to the sweet shop.

(ii) Gate-*C* is nearest to Gappu's house.

(iii) If I enter from gate-*B*, the bench will be to my left.

(iv) When Suhasini entered the park through gate-*D*, then the flower bed was to her right.

(v) (d) See-saw is nearest to me if I enter from gate-*C*.

Ismail's Home (NCERT Pg 58)

Q.11 On the phone Ismail told Srijata the route to his house from her house. The route map is shown here.

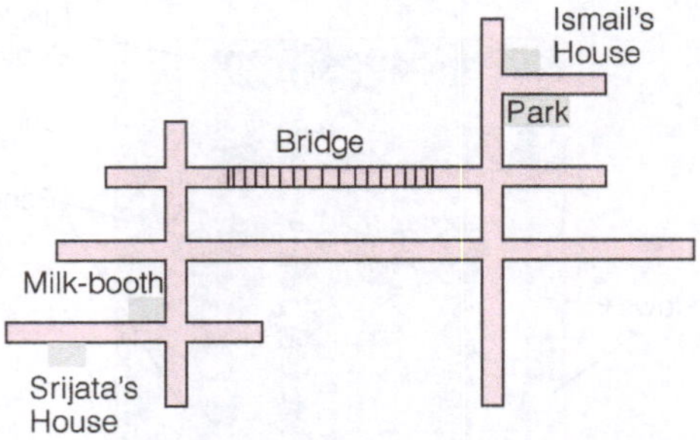

This is what Ismail told Srijata.

'From your house, reach the milk-booth and then take a left turn. From the second crossing take a right turn and go over the bridge.

Go straight and then take the first right turn. After about 100 metres you will see a big park. When you cross the park you will come to a side lane. My house is the first house in that lane'.

(i) Did Ismail go wrong somewhere? Can you correct him?

(ii) Show where Srijata will reach if she takes the route he told her.

(iii) Write the directions for going from Ismail's house to Srijata's house.

Ans. (i) Yes, Ismail was wrong. He should have told Srijata to go straight and then take the left turn instead of the first right turn.

(ii) Srijata will reach opposite to Ismail's house, if she takes the route he told her.

*(iii) Start from Ismail's house. Take second right turn and go straight and then take left turn you reach the milk booth. Then, take right turn and go straight. Now, Srijata's house is left to you.

Gibli and the Big Box (NCERT Pg 59)

Q.12 Well, one day Gibli saw a big box on her way.

It looked like this.

Gibli moved across and turned left. Now, she could see the other face of the big box.

Gibli was confused. What was this box? She climbed on a cup and tried to see from there. The box looked like this.

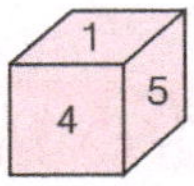

(i) Can you guess what that box-like thing was?

(ii) The numbers on the opposite faces of this box add up to 7.

Which number was on the opposite side of 5?

(iii) In the picture, which number will be at the bottom?

(iv) Which number will Gibli see if she again turns left from 5?

(v) What will this box look like if you opened it up? Mark the correct picture.

(a)
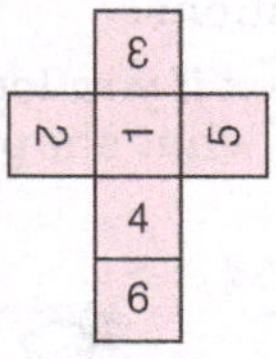

(b)
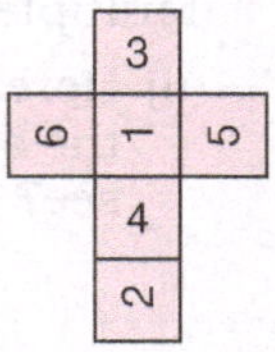

(c)
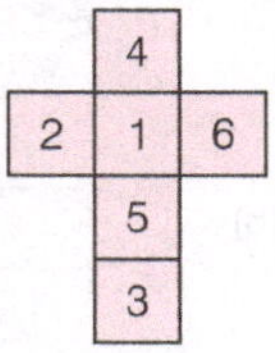

(d)
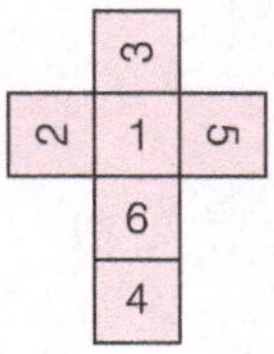

Ans. (i) That box was a die.

(ii) Since, the numbers on the opposite faces of this box add up to 7.

Therefore, opposite side of $5 = 7 - 5 = 2$

Hence, 2 was on the opposite side of 5.

(iii) The number, which is top of a die = 1

So, opposite number of $1 = 7 - 1 = 6$

Hence, 6 will be at the bottom of the die.

(iv) If Gibli again turns left from 5, she will see the opposite side of number 4.

And opposite side of number $4 = 7 - 4 = 3$

Hence, if Gibli again turns left from 5, she will see the number 3.

(v) (a)

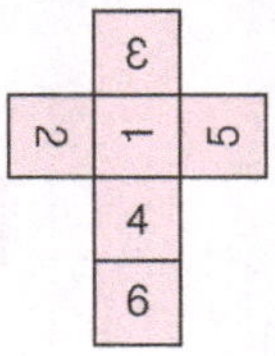

Try it Out (NCERT Pg 59)

Q.13 (i) Draw a shape like this on a thick paper. Cut it out and colour the different faces in different colours.

(ii) Can you use this box to play a game?

Ans. (i) Do yourself.

*(ii) No, I cannot use this box to play a game.

PRACTICE QUESTIONS

1. Multiple choice questions.

(i) Here is a shoes box if you look at it from the side as show, what shape would you see?

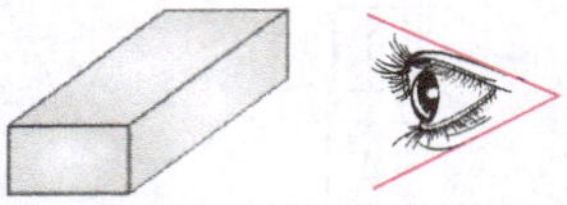

(a) 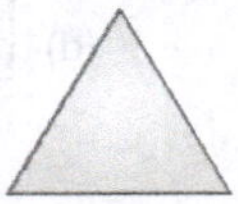

(b) 

(c) 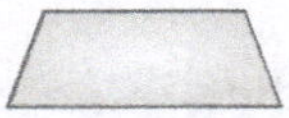

(d) 

(ii) Look at the map below, how many times does Meera have to turn to her left if she walks to school along the path shown?

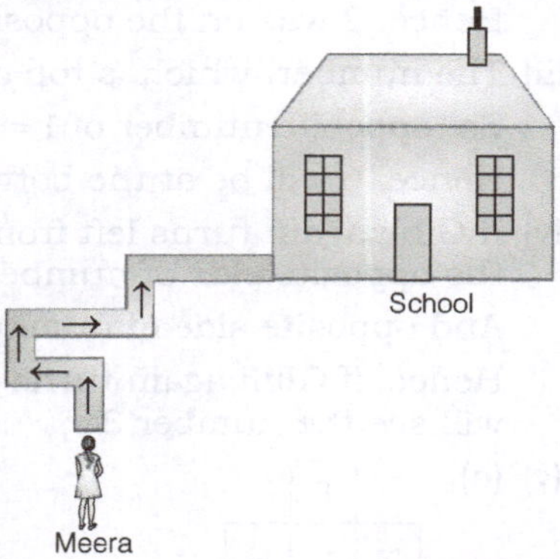

(a) 2 (b) 3 (c) 5 (d) 6

(iii) Find the opposite number of 2 in given figure

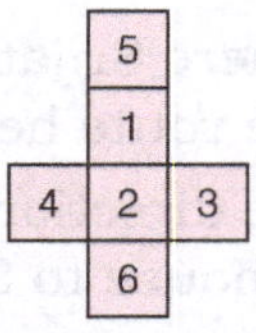

(a) 3 (b) 1 (c) 5 (d) 4

2. A close die is shown below.

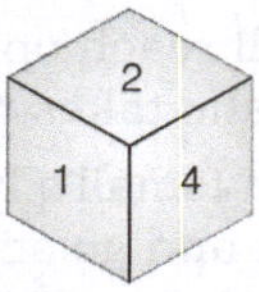

On the basis of given dice, fill these open dice.

(i) 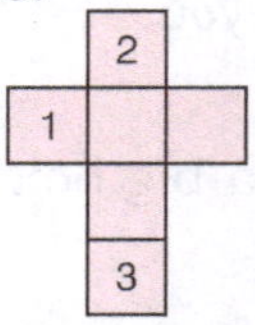

→

(ii) 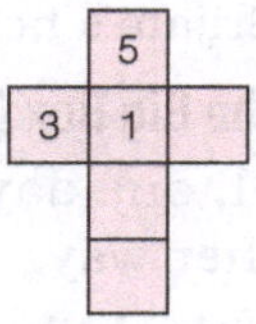

→

(iii) 

→

ANSWERS & SOLUTIONS

1. (i) (d) (ii) (a)

(iii) (c) Since, the numbers on the opposite faces of a die add up to 7.

∴ Opposite number of 2 = 7 − 2 = 5

2. (i) Since, the numbers on the opposite faces of a die add up to 7.

∴ Opposite side of 2 is 7 − 2 = 5,
opposite side of 3 is 7 − 3 = 4
and opposite side of 1 is 7 − 1 = 6

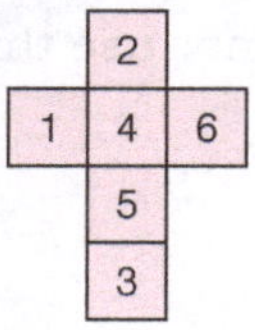

(ii) Since, the numbers on the opposite faces of a die add upto 7.

∴ Opposite side of 3 is
7 − 3 = 4,
opposite side of 5 is 7 − 5 = 2
and opposite side of 1 is 7 − 1 = 6

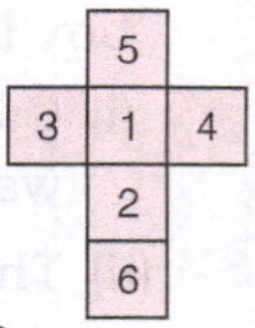

(iii) Since, the numbers on the opposite faces of a die add upto 7.

∴ Opposite side of 6 is
7 − 6 = 1,
opposite side of 2 is 7 − 2 = 5
and opposite side of 4 is 7 − 4 = 3

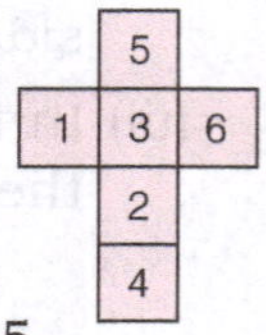

CHAPTER 6

THE JUNK SELLER

Loan or Credit

Loan is a sum of money that one or more individuals or companies borrow from banks, which he has to pay back with interest within a given period of time.

Buying and Selling

- To obtain something in return for money or the equivalent is called 'Buying'. The price at which something is purchased is called **cost price**.
- To offer something to someone who pays for it and then owns it, is called 'Selling'. The price at which something is sold is called **selling price**.

Earning

Earning is the amount of money that you make from doing a business or a job.

Profit and Loss

The money that you gain when you sell something for more than its price is called **profit**. The amount, the seller lose after selling the product less than its cost price is called **loss**.

Profit = Selling price – Cost price

Loss = Cost price – Selling price

NCERT FOLDER

NCERT Pg 60

Q.1 What about you? Do you also find Maths difficult?

Ans. * No, Maths is not difficult. It becomes easy if we practice it regularly.

Q.2 What is the most difficult thing in your Maths book?

Ans. * Nothing, all the topics that I have read are easy to understand.

** Students can write alternate answer as per their choice.*

Q.3 What do you think is the easiest lesson?

Ans. * All the lessons are of equal level. It depends on practice.

Find Out : How Much for a Cup of Tea? (NCERT Pg 61)

Q.4 Ask people and find out the cost of a cup of tea

(i) at a tea stall (ii) at a hotel

Ans.*(i) The cost of a cup of tea at a tea stall is ₹ 10.

(ii) The cost of a cup of tea at a hotel is ₹ 30.

Q.5 If a person who runs a tea stall earns ₹ 30 in a day, how much will be earn in 10 days?

Ans. Since, earning in 1 day = ₹ 30

So, earning in 10 days = 30×10 = ₹ 300

Q.6 And in a month?

Ans. Number of days in a month = 30 days

Since, earning in 1 day = ₹ 30

Therefore, earning in 30 days = 30×30

= ₹ 900

Q.7 How did you get the answer? Discuss.

Ans. If you know the price of 1 item, then you can find the price of any number of item by multiplying the price and quantity of the items.

Find Out : What is a Loan? (NCERT Pg 61-63)

Q.8 Have you ever heard of someone taking a loan? For what?

Ans. * Yes, I have heard of someone taking a loan for farming.

Q.9 How much loan was taken?

Ans. * He took a loan of ₹ 20000.

Q.10 How much money was paid back?

Ans. * He paid back ₹ 21000 after 5 months.

Q.11 Hariya and Babu want to buy a handcart for ₹ 300.

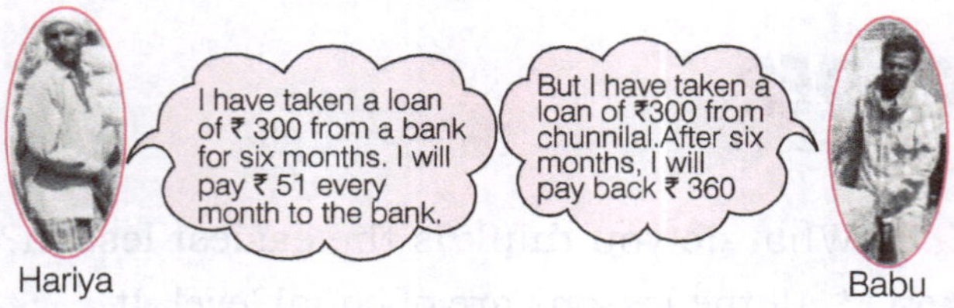

Who has to pay back more Hariya or Babu?

Ans. Amount paid by Hariya every month = ₹ 51

Total money that he pay in 6 months

= 6×51 = ₹ 306

Amount paid by Babu after six months

= ₹ 360

Hence, Babu has to pay back more money than Hariya.

Q.12 I have 9 rickshaws of my own. I give the rickshaws on rent, each for ₹ 20 a day. On Sundays I do not take any money for them. How much does Kiran earn from 9 rickshaws in a day?

Ans. Since, Kiran earns from one rickshaw in a day = ₹ 20

Therefore, she earns from 9 rickshaws in a day = 9×20 = ₹ 180

Hence, Kiran earns ₹ 180 from 9 rickshaws in a day.

Q.13 For 1 rickshaw, she gets ₹ 20 per day. So, for 9 rickshaws, she will earn ₹_____ . How did you do it?

Ans. ∵ For 1 rickshaw, she gets ₹ 20 per day.

∴ For 10 rickshaws, she will get

₹ 20 × 10 = ₹ 200

So, for 9 rickshaws, she will get

₹ 200 – ₹ 20 = ₹ 180.

Q.14 In a week, how much does Kiran earn from one rickshaw?

Ans. Number of days in a week = 7

Since, Kiran gives each rickshaw for ₹ 20 a day.

On Sunday, she does not charges any money for them. Therefore, she took money for 6 days in a week.

Amount of money earned by Kiran in a week from one rickshaw = ₹ 20 × 6 = ₹ 120

Q.15 Do it mentally and write the answers.

2×6 = ...	4×80 = ...
20×6 = ...	4×81 = ...
2×60 = ...	9×25 = ...
3×42 = ...	31×9 = ...

Ans.

$2 \times 6 = 12$	$4 \times 80 = 320$
$20 \times 6 = 120$	$4 \times 81 = 324$
$2 \times 60 = 120$	$9 \times 25 = 225$
$3 \times 42 = 126$	$31 \times 9 = 279$

Q.16 4×81 is 4 more than 4×80. Am I right?

Ans. Yes, she is right because $4 \times 81 = 324$

and $4 \times 80 = 320$

So, 324 is 4 more than 320.

How Much to Pay for this Junk? (NCERT Pg 63-64)

Q.17 Kiran has bought some junk from junk collectors. How much will kiran pay for 31 kg of newspaper?

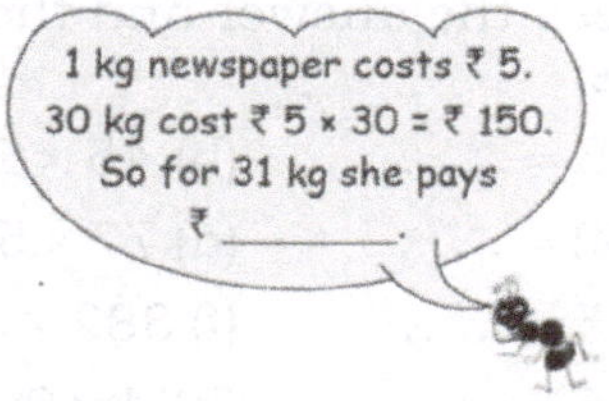

Ans. Cost of 1 kg newspaper = ₹ 5

∴ The cost of 31 kg newspaper = ₹ 5×31

= ₹ 155

Hence, Kiran will pay ₹ 155 for 31 kg of newspaper.

Q.18

Rate–List

Kind of Junk	Price of 1 Kg
1. Waste Paper	₹ 4/-
2. Newspaper	₹ 5/-
3. Iron	₹ 12/-
4. Brass	₹ 170/-
5. Plastic	₹ 10/-

(i) How much will Kiran pay for 42 kg of newspaper?

(ii) Also find the cost of

(a) 22 kg of plastic

(b) 23 kg of waste paper

(c) 12 kg of iron

Ans. (i) ∵ Price of 1 kg newspaper = ₹ 5

∴ Price of 42 kg newspaper = ₹ 5×42 = ₹ 210

Hence, Kiran will pay ₹ 210 for 42 kg newspaper.

(ii) (a) ∵ Cost of 1 kg of plastic = ₹ 10

∴ Cost of 22 kg of plastic = ₹ 10×22

= ₹ 220

(b) ∵ Cost of 1 kg of waste paper = ₹ 4

∴ Cost of 23 kg of waste paper = ₹ 4×23

= ₹ 92

(c) ∵ Cost of 1 kg of iron = ₹ 12

∴ Cost of 12 kg of iron = ₹ 12×12

= ₹ 144

Q.19 Can you do this without writing?

Ans. Yes, I can do this without writing.

Q.20 Guess the total money Kiran will pay to the junk collectors. Will it be

- more than 600?
- less than 600?

Ans. It will be more than 600 because

$210 + 220 + 92 + 144$ is ₹ 666.

Smart Kiran Sells the Junk (NCERT Pg 64-66)

A. How much will Dinu pay for 63 kg plastic?

Q.21

Dinu's Rate-List

Kind of Junk	Price of 1 Kg
1. Newspaper	₹ 6/-
2. Iron	₹ 14/-
3. Brass	₹ 180/-
4. Plastic	₹ 12/-
5. Waste paper	₹ 4.50/-

(i) Kiran bought 1 kg plastic for ₹ 10, but sold 1 kg plastic for ₹ 12. How much money does she earn on selling 1 kg plastic?

(ii) How much money does she earn for 63 kg?

Ans. (i) Kiran bought 1 kg plastic for ₹ 10, but sold it for ₹ 12.

So, she earns = $12 - 10$

= ₹ 2

Hence, Kiran earns ₹ 2 on selling 1 kg of plastic.

(ii) ∵ Earning of Kiran on selling 1 kg of plastic = ₹ 2

∴ Earning on selling 63 kg of plastic

= ₹ 2×63 = ₹ 126

Hence, she earns ₹ 126 for selling 63 kg plastic.

It can be calculated as

	60	3
2	60×2	3×2
	120	6

On adding the numbers, we get

$120 + 6 = 126$

B. Kiran sells 32 kg iron.

Q.22 (i) How much money will Dinu pay for 32 kg iron?

(ii) Kiran buys 1 kg iron for ₹ 12, but sells it for ₹ 14.

How much does she earn when she sells 32 kg iron?

Ans. (i) ∵ Price of 1 kg of iron = ₹ 14

∴ Price of 32 kg of iron = ₹ 14 × 32 = ₹ 448

It can be calculated as

	30	2
10	30×10	2×10
	300	20
4	30×4	2×4
	120	8

Then add the numbers in the boxes:

$300 + 20 + 120 + 8 = 448$

Hence, Dinu paid ₹ 448 for 32 kg iron.

(ii) Kiran buys 1 kg of iron for ₹ 12 and sells it for ₹ 14.

Therefore, Kiran earns by selling 1 kg of iron

= ₹ 14 − ₹ 12 = ₹ 2

Earning of Kiran when she sells 32 kg iron

= ₹ 2 × 32 = ₹ 64

Hence, Kiran earns ₹ 64 by selling 32 kg iron.

C. What will Dinu pay for 152 kg newspaper?

Q.23 Kiran bought 1 kg newspaper for ₹ 5, but sold it for ₹ 6. How much money did Kiran earn by selling 152 kg of newspaper?

Ans. Kiran bought 1 kg newspaper for ₹ 5, but sold it for ₹ 6.

So, she earns by selling 1 kg newspaper

= ₹ 6 − ₹ 5 = ₹ 1

Earning by selling 152 kg of newspaper

= ₹ 1 × 152 = ₹ 152

D. What does Dinu pay for brass?

Q.24 How much money will Dinu pay for 4 kg brass?

Ans. ∵ Money paid by Dinu for 1 kg brass

= ₹ 180

∴ Money paid by Dinu for 4 kg brass

= ₹ 180 × 4 = ₹ 720

Hence, Dinu will pay ₹ 720 for 4 kg brass.

NCERT Pg 67

Q.25 First guess the answer and then calculate:

(a) 37 × 18 = ...   (b) 45 × 24 = ...

(c) 69 × 52 = ...   (d) 77 × 55 = ...

(e) 142 × 5 = ...   (f) 382 × 3 = ...

(g) 2 × 175 = ...   (h) 4 × 206 = ...

Ans. (a) My guess is 37 × 18 is nearly equal to 40 × 15 = 600

Calculation

	10	8
30	30×10	30×8
	300	240
7	7×10	7×8
	70	56

On adding the numbers, we get

$300 + 240 + 70 + 56 = 666$

(b) 45 × 24 is nearly equal to 50 × 20 = 1000

Calculation

	20	4
40	40×20	40×4
	800	160
5	5×20	5×4
	100	20

On adding the numbers, we get

$800 + 160 + 100 + 20 = 1080$

(c) The value of 69 × 52 is near about 70 × 50 = 3500

Calculation

	50	2
60	60×50	60×2
	3000	120
9	9×50	9×2
	450	18

On adding the numbers, we get

$$3000 + 120 + 450 + 18 = 3588$$

(d) The value of 77×55 is near about

$80 \times 50 = 4000$.

Calculation

	50	5
70	70×50	70×5
	3500	350
7	7×50	7×5
	350	35

On adding the numbers, we get

$$3500 + 350 + 350 + 35 = 4235$$

(e) The value of 142×5 is near about the value of $150 \times 5 = 750$.

Calculation

	5
100	100×5
	500
40	40×5
	200
2	2×5
	10

On adding the numbers, we get

$$500 + 200 + 10 = 710$$

(f) My guess that the value of 382×3 is about 1100.

Calculation

	3
300	300×3
	900
80	80×3
	240
2	2×3
	6

On adding the numbers, we get

$$900 + 240 + 6 = 1146$$

(g) My guess that the value of 2×175 is about 350.

Calculation

	100	70	5
2	200	140	10

On adding the numbers, we get

$$200 + 140 + 10 = 350$$

(h) My guess that the value of 4×206 is about 810.

Calculation

	100	100	6
4	4×100	4×100	4×6
	400	400	24

On adding the numbers, we get

$$400 + 400 + 24 = 824$$

Fill my Diary (NCERT Pg 68)

Q.26 Kiran paid ₹ 919 to the junk collectors. When she sold the junk. She got these notes and coins from Dinu.

28 coins of 

18 notes of 

5 notes of 

1 note of 

9 notes of 

Now, you make a record in her diary. Find out how much she earned this time.

Ans.

18 March 2007

Money she paid – ₹ 919

Money she got from Dinu

5 × 100 – ₹ 500

1 × 50 – ₹ 50

9 × 20 – ₹ 180

18 × 10 – ₹ 180

28 × 5 – ₹ 140

Total – ₹ 1050

Total money she got : ₹ 1050

Money she paid : – ₹ 919

Money she earned : ₹ 131

PRACTICE QUESTIONS

1. Fill in the blanks.

(i) $5 \times 45 =$ ......

(ii) $30 \times 12 = 30 \times 10 + 30 \times$ ......

(iii) $40 \times 9 = 40 \times 10 -$ ......

(iv) $124 \times 67 =$

	60	7
100	6000	700
20		140
4	240	28

2. Multiple choice questions.

(i) The price of two pens is ₹ 6, then the price of 16 pens is

(a) ₹ 96 (b) ₹ 45
(c) ₹ 48 (d) ₹ 50

(ii) Ramesh earned ₹ 5 for selling 1 kg of sugar. How much he earns if he sells 14 kg of sugar?

(a) ₹ 14
(b) ₹ 70
(c) ₹ 5
(d) ₹ 75

(iii) ₹ 5000 = ... × ₹ 200

(a) 25
(b) 30
(c) 50
(d) 10

3. A coffee mug costs ₹ 32 each. A company manager wants 60 mugs for a celebration in their company. So, how much do 60 coffee mug cost?

4. Each student in grade four was given 16 raffle tickets to sell to raise funds for their school. The price of each ticket is ₹ 20. If Simran sold all her tickets, how much money did she raised for her school?

5. Aman earns ₹ 80 per day by working on fields. How much will he earn in 25 days?

ANSWERS & SOLUTIONS

1. (i) 225 (ii) 2
(iii) 40 (iv) 1200

2. (i) (c) (ii) (b)
(iii) (a)

3. Cost of one mug = ₹ 32
Cost of 60 mugs = 32×60
= ₹ 1920

4. Number of tickets Simran has = 16
Price of each ticket = ₹ 20
Price of 16 tickets = 16×20 = ₹ 320
Hence, Simran raised ₹ 320 for her school.

5. Earning of Aman per day = ₹ 80
Earning of Aman in 25 days = ₹ 80 × 25
= ₹ 2000

CHAPTER 7 JUGS AND MUGS

Measurement

Measurement is a method by which the properties of an object can be determined by only comparing them to a standard quantity.

Volume

The amount of space that something contains or fills is called volume. It can be measured in litres, millilitres, cubic metres, etc. e.g. 10 litres, 500 millilitres, etc.

Conversion of Units of Volume

- 1 litre = 1000 millilitres (mL)
- 1 litre = $\frac{1}{1000}$ kilolitre
- 1 kilolitre = 1000 litres
- 1 millilitre = $\frac{1}{1000}$ litre

NCERT FOLDER

Bunny and Banno Celebrate their Wedding Anniversary (NCERT Pg 69-72)

Q.1 The donkey looked confused and asked – Ten glasses of 100 mL each. How much is that? The fox got another chance to show off ! He said - Ah. That is simple! 10 times hundred millilitres is .... millilitre = ... litre.

Ans. ∵ Quantity of kheer in each glass = 100 mL

∴ Quantity of kheer in ten glasses

$= 100 \text{ mL} \times 10 = 1000 \text{ mL}$

$= 1$ litre [∵ 1000 mL = 1 litre]

Q.2 Now, you write it 10×100 mL = ...

Ans. $10 \times 100 \text{ mL} = 1000 \text{ mL}$

$= 1$ litre [∵ 1000 mL = 1 litre]

Q.3 So, 1000 ants drink:

1000×1 mL = ...mL

Ans. $1000 \times 1 \text{ mL} = 1000 \text{ mL}$

* *Students can write alternate answer as per their choice.*

Who can have 1 Litre Kheer? (NCERT Pg 73)

Q.4 (i) Do you like kheer? What do you call it at home?

(ii) How much kheer can you have?

Ans. *(i) Yes, I like kheer. We also call it 'kheer' at home.

*(ii) 1 litre

Q.5 Can you drink 1 litre water at one time?

Ans. *No, I cannot drink 1 litre water at one time.

Q.6 The donkey is trying to look for different ways to add upto 1 litre. Help him complete the chart.

Ans. *

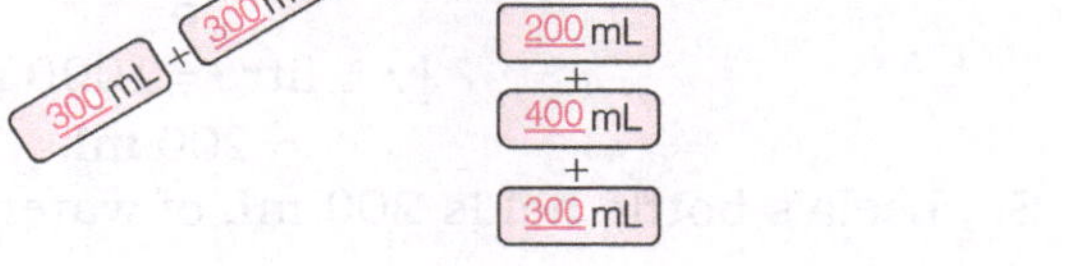

Look Around (NCERT Pg 74)

Q.7 Look at these pictures. Now, look for some other things, we get in packets or bottles like these. Make your own list.

Ans. *

Paket	How many mL or L?	Paket	How many mL or L?
	500 mL		50 mL
	1L		600 mL
	10 mL		100 mL
	200 mL		

Q.8 Have you seen a one-litre water bottle?

Ans. *Yes, I have seen a one-litre water bottle.

My Litre Bottle (NCERT Pg 75)

Q.9 Look what Adithyan is saying. I poured two small bottles of water to fill this 1 litre bottle. How much water does his small bottle hold?

Ans. ∵ Capacity of 2 small bottles of water

$= 1$ litre

∴ Capacity of 1 small bottle of water

$$= \frac{1 \text{ litre}}{2} = \frac{1000}{2} \text{ mL}$$

[∵ 1 litre = 1000 mL]

= 500 mL

So, his small bottle holds 500 mL of water.

Q.10 To fill the 1-litre bottle I need to pour water 5 times from my small bottle. Then, how much water does Leela's bottle hold?

Ans. ∵ 5 times of capacity of small bottle = 1 litre

∴ Capacity of 1 small bottle $= \frac{1 \text{ litre}}{5}$

$$= \frac{1000}{5} \text{ mL}$$

[∵ 1 litre = 1000 mL]

= 200 mL

So, Leela's bottle holds 200 mL of water.

Ramu's Measuring Bottle (NCERT Pg 75)

Q.11 Ramu got an empty 250 mL coconut oil bottle. Look at the picture and discuss what he did to make his big measuring bottle.

Ans. **Step I** He took 250 mL coconut oil bottle and fill it with water.

Step II Then, he poured one bottle of water in big bottle and marked the water level as 250 mL.

Step III Again he poured 250 mL of water in big bottle and marked the water level as 500 mL.

Step IV By pouring third time 250 mL of water in big bottle, he marked the water level as 750 mL.

Step V After pouring fourth time 250 mL of water in big bottle, he marked the water level as 1000 mL or 1 litre.

My Measuring Bottle (NCERT Pg 76)

Q.12 Find your own way to make a bottle which can measure 200 mL, 400 mL, 600 mL, 800 mL and litre. Discuss with your friends and teacher how you made this.

Ans. Take a 200 mL bottle and a large bottle.

(i) I filled water in 200 mL bottle and poured it in the big bottle and marked the water level as 200 mL.

(ii) Again, I poured 200 mL of water in big bottle and then marked the water level as 400 mL.

(iii) By pouring third time 200 mL of water in big bottle, I marked the water level as 600 mL.

(iv) Again, poured fourth time 200 mL of water in big bottle and I marked the water level as 800 mL.

(v) After pouring fifth time 200 mL of water in big bottle, I marked the water level as 1000 mL or 1 litre.

Guess and Check (NCERT Pg 76)

Q.13 Look at the buckets, mugs, glasses and other things in your house. Guess how much water each can hold. Check if your guess is right by using your measuring bottle.

Ans. *

Objects	My Guess	My Measure
	250 mL	300 mL
	200 mL	220 mL
	12 L	10 L
	2 L	2 L
	10 L	10 L
	1 L	1 L
	8 L	10 L

Neetu in Hospital (NCERT Pg 77)

Q.14 Neetu has to take 3 injections in a day for 5 days. One injection gives 5 mL of the medicine to her body.

(i) How much medicine will she need for one day?

(ii) How much medicine in all for 5 days?

Ans. (i) $\because$ Quantity of medicine given by one injection = 5 mL

$\therefore$ Quantity of medicine given by 3 injections $= 5 \times 3 = 15$ mL

So, Neetu needs 15 mL of medicine for one day.

(ii) $\because$ Medicine taken by Neetu in a day = 15 mL

$\therefore$ Medicine taken by Neetu in 5 days $= 5 \times 15$

$= 75$ mL

So, 75 mL medicine in all for 5 days.

Q.15 How much do we use at a time?

Ans. *(i) Eye drops — We use less than 1 mL at a time.

(ii) Cough syrup — We take 10 mL at a time.

(iii) Milk — We take 250 mL at a time.

(iv) Coffee — We take about 60 mL at a time.

(v) Juice — We take about 200 mL at a time.

(vi) Shampoo — We use less than 5 mL at a time.

Q.16 List things we use more than one litre at a time.

(i) Water for taking bath.

(ii) ....

(iii) ....

(iv) ....

(v) ....

Ans. *(ii) Water for washing clothes.

(iii) Petrol or diesel to fill the tank of bike or car.

(iv) Paint for painting the house.

(v) Watering the plants.

Practice Time (NCERT Pg 78)

Q.17 Amina's water bottle holds one litre of water. She drank 250 mL of water and her friend Govind drank 150 mL. How much water is left in her bottle?

Ans. Water holds by bottle = 1litre

= 1000 mL

Water drunk by Amina = 250 mL

and water drunk by Govind = 150 mL

Total water drunk by Amina and Govind

$= 250 + 150$

$= 400$ mL

So, water left in the bottle $= 1000 - 400$

$= 600$ mL

Q.18 Yusuf runs a tea shop. For making a glass of tea, he uses 20 mL of milk. Yesterday he made 100 glasses of tea. How much milk did he use?

Ans. ∵ Quantity of milk used for making a glass of tea = 20 mL

∴ Quantity of milk required for making 100 glasses of tea = 20 mL × 100

= 2000 mL

= 2 litres [∵ 1000 mL = 1 L]

Q.19 Radha's grandma was ill. The doctor gave her a bottle with 200 mL of medicine. She has to take the medicine every morning for 10 days. How many millilitres of medicine does she have to take every morning?

Ans. ∵ Quantity of medicine Radha's grandma has to take for 10 days = 200 mL

∴ Quantity of medicine taken by Radha's grandma in 1 day = $\frac{200}{10}$ mL

= 20 mL

Hence, Radha's grandma has to take 20 mL of medicine every morning.

Water-Water (NCERT Pg 79)

Q.20 The table shows the water used in one day by a family of 5 people. They live in Goodallur village.

Activity	Water (in litres)
Cooking and drinking	30 litres
Washing clothes	40 litres
Cleaning pots, pans	20 litres
Bathing	75 litres

Total water used by them ....

Ans. Total water used by them

= 30 + 40 + 20 + 75

= 165 litres

Q.21 How many litres of water does your family use in a day? Guess and fill in this table.

Activity	Water used (in buckets)	Water used (in litres)
Cooking and drinking	2	20
Washing clothes	6	60
Cleaning pots, pans	3	30
Cleaning of house	2	20
Watering plants	4	40
Bathing	8	80

Ans. * Total water used in my family

= 20 + 60 + 30 + 20 + 40 + 80

= 250 litres

Drops and Drops Make an Ocean (NCERT Pg 79-80)

Q.22 (i) Is there any tap in your school or your home which is leaking?

(ii) How much water do you think we waste through a leaking tap?

(iii) Place your litre jar below the leaking tap so as to catch all the drops in the bottle. Note the time. After one hour check how much water is in the bottle.

Ans. *(i) Yes, there is one tap in my school which is leaking.

*(ii) I think about 30 litres to 35 litres of water is wasted through a leaking tap in a day.

*(iii) In one hour, about 1 litre and 500 mL of water is collected in the bottle.

Q.23 Find out how much water is wasted

(i) In a day ? (ii) In a week?

(iii) In a month? (iv) In a year?

Ans. *(i) ∵ Water wasted in 1 hour

= 1 litre and 500 mL

= 1500 mL

∴ Water wasted in a day = 1500 mL × 24

[∵ 1 day = 24 hours]

= 36000 mL

= 36 litres

[∵ 1000 mL = 1 litre]

*(ii) $\because$ Water wasted in a day = 36 litres

$\therefore$ Water wasted in a week = 36 litres × 7

[$\because$ week = 7 days]

= 252 litres

*(iii) $\because$ Water wasted in a day = 36 litres

$\therefore$ Water wasted in a month = 36 litres × 30

[$\because$ 1 month = 30 days]

= 1080 litres

(iv) $\because$ Water wasted in a day = 36 litres

$\therefore$ Water wasted in a year = 36 litres × 365

[$\because$ 1 year = 365 days]

= 13140 litres

Puzzle (NCERT Pg 80)

Q.24 Chelannur village has a milk society. Geetha and Ammini went there to buy 4 litres of milk. But the man could not find the one litre measure. He had only a 3 litres and a 5 litres bottle with him. But he gave them exactly 4 litres of milk. Explain how he did this.

Ans. At first, the milkman will fill 5 litres bottle with milk, then he pours it down into 3 litres bottle. Now, 2 litres of milk is remaining in 5 litres bottle. He pours down this 2 litres milk in Geetha's bottle. Again repeat the process.

Now, Geetha has 4 litres milk in her bottle.

PRACTICE QUESTIONS

1. Fill in the blanks.
   (i) A glass can hold 200 ...... of water. [mL/litre]
   (ii) Capacity of a water tank is 500 ...... [mL/litre]
   (iii) 4 litre 75 mL = ... mL. [4750/4075]
   (iv) 2000 mL = 8 × ...... mL. [200/250]
2. Multiple choice questions
   (i) The unit to measure the capacity of hair oil in a travelling pack is
   (a) grams (b) millilitres
   (c) litres (d) metres
   (ii) Which of the following can hold the maximum liquid?
   (a) A juice glass (b) A cup of tea
   (c) A water tank (d) A pond
   (iii) Capacity of a tablespoon is
   (a) 300 mL (b) 3 mL
   (c) 30 mL (d) 35 mL
   (iv) 10 litres are equal to
   (a) 1000 mL (b) 100 mL
   (c) 10000 mL (d) 100000 mL
3. If you are trying to pour coffee in 50 mL cups from a 500 mL kettle but you spilled 70 mL while doing it. What is the amount of coffee in last cup?
4. The weekly consumption of the milk in a family is 14 litre. Find the total consumption of milk in 3 months.

ANSWERS & SOLUTIONS

1. (i) mL (ii) litre (iii) 4075 (iv) 250
2. (i) (b) (ii) (d) (iii) (b) (iv) (c)
3. Amount of coffee in kettle = 500 mL
   Amount of coffee spilled = 70 mL
   Amount of coffee left in the kettle = 500 − 70
   = 430 mL
   Number of 50 mL cups that can be filled
   $= \frac{430}{50} = \frac{43}{5} = 8\frac{3}{5}$
   So, 8 cups will be completely filled and the last cup will have 30 mL of coffee.
4. Consumption of milk in a family in one week (7 days) = 14 litres
   Consumption of milk in a family in one day
   $= \frac{14}{7} = 2$ litres
   Number of days in 1 month = 30
   Number of days in 3 months = 3 × 30
   = 90
   Consumption of milk in a family in 3 months
   = 90 × 2 = 180 litres

CHAPTER 8 CARTS & WHEELS

Circle

A circle is the collection of points which are at an equal distance from a fixed point in the plane. e.g. wheels, rings, bangles, coins, etc.

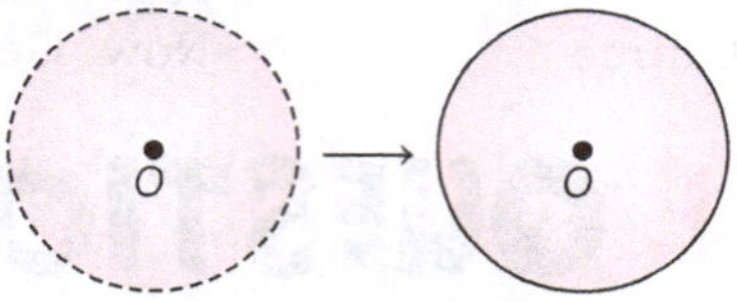

Parts of circle

- **Circumference of the circle** Circumference of the circle is the measurement of the boundary of the circle. If we open a circle and make a line out of it, then length of line is equal to the circumference of the circle.
- **Centre** The centre of a circle is the point inside the circle which is at the same distance from all the points on the circle's circumference. It is also known as the origin of the circle.
  It is the point where the compass tip is placed when drawing a circle.
  In the figure given below, point *O* is the centre of the circle.

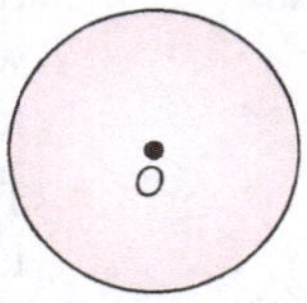

- **Radius of the circle** The line joining the centre of circle and any point on the circumference of the circle is called the radius of circle. It is denoted by *r*.
  In the figure given below, *OA* is the radius of circle.

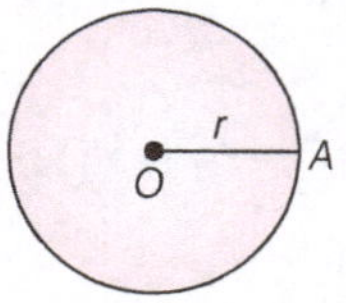

NCERT FOLDER

NCERT Pg 81

Q.1 You must have seen many such round things around you.

List some more in your notebook.

Ans. (i) Plate (ii) Bread (Roti)
(iii) Ball (iv) Bangles
(v) Ring (vi) Wheels
(vii) Coins (viii) Bindi
(ix) Orange
(x) Top and bottom of a bowl and glass

Round Bangle (NCERT Pg 82)

Q.2 Have you ever gone to a bangle shop?

Ans. Yes, I have gone to the bangle shop with my mother.

Q.3

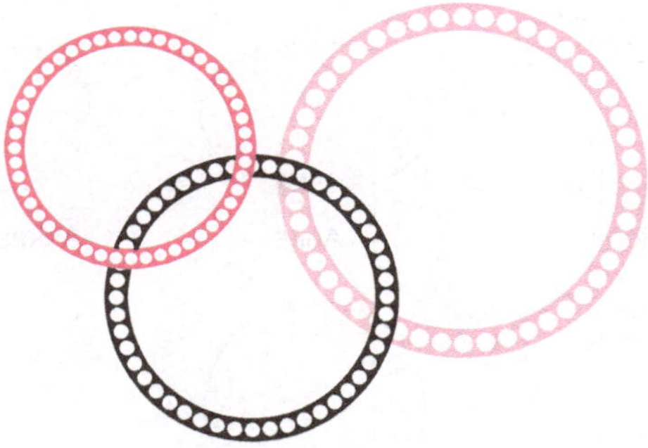

Guess which of these bangles is of your size.

Ans. * The smallest bangle is of my size.

Q.4 Take a wire and make a bangle for yourself. Can your madam or mother wear this bangle?

Ans. * I made a bangle by wrapping the wire around a pipe. No, my madam or mother cannot wear this bangle.

Q.5 A bangle can be used to trace a circle. What are the other things around you that you can use to trace a circle?

Ans. The other things that can be used to trace a circle are coins, glass, bowl, ring, caps of bottle, plates, etc.

* *Students can write alternate answer as per their choice.*

Q.6 Trace a circle with the help of some of these things in your notebook or on the ground.

(i) Which thing makes the smallest circle?
(ii) Which thing makes the biggest circle?

Ans. (i) A ring makes the smallest circle.

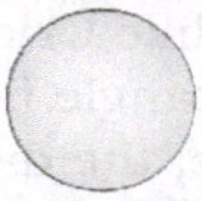

(ii) The biggest circle could be made in my notebook by the wheel.

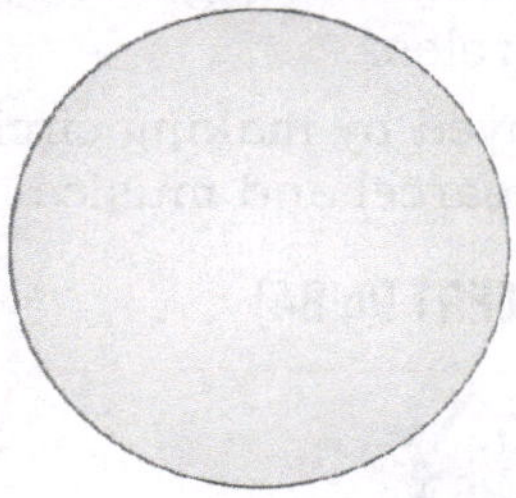

Games with Circles (NCERT Pg 83)

Q.7 Children are playing some games.

(i) Do you play these games?
(ii) Which song do you sing when you play these?

Ans. (i) Yes, I play these games.
*(ii) We sing 'RAIN-RAIN GO AWAY, COME AGAIN ANOTHER DAY' while playing these games.

Q.8 Why do we make a circle in each of these games?

Ans. We make a circle in each of these games because circle has no corner and each child standing on the circle is at the same distance from the centre. So, we get equal importance and opportunity.

Q.9 What if a rectangle was made ? Discuss.

Ans. There are some games played by making rectangles like Kabaddi, Hockey, Football, etc. But games like Cricket needs a circle because if a rectangle field is constructed to play the game, the distance of boundary from the pitch will be unequal.

Q.10 Think of some other games you play by making circles.

Ans. Games played by making circles are passing a parcel and musical chair.

Making a Circle (NCERT Pg 84)

Q.11

Is any of these a good drawing of a circle? Discuss.

Ans. No, none of these is a good drawing of a circle.

Q.12 Can you draw a circle on the floor with a chalk? Try.

Ans. Yes. Do yourself.

Q.13 Also draw a circle in your notebook using a pencil.

Ans.

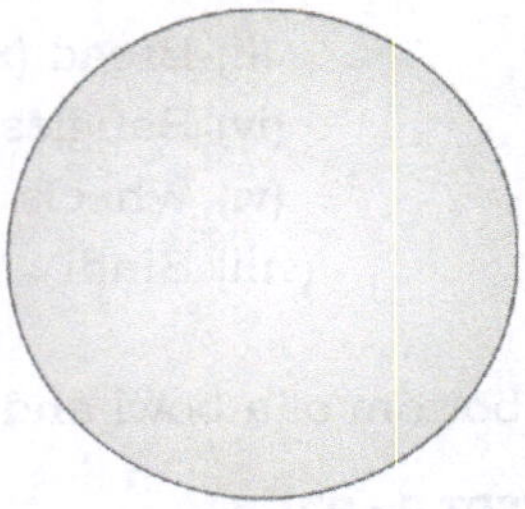

Q.14 Look at the circles drawn by your friends. Who has drawn the best circle?

Ans. *Circle drawn by some of my friends are given below.

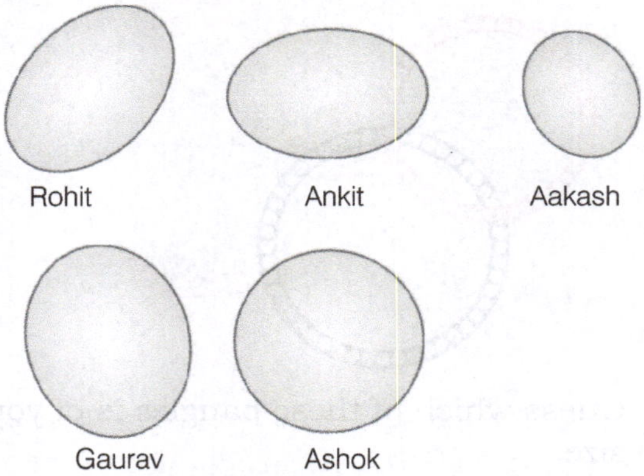

A circle drawn by Ashok is the best.

Making a Circle with a Rope (NCERT Pg 85)

Q.15

Can you also make a circle with a rope and nails like Ariba?

Ans. Yes, I can make a circle with a rope and nails like Ariba.

Q.16 Do the activity in small groups. Each group should take a rope of a different length.See the circles made by different groups.

(i) Which group made the smallest circle?

(ii) How long was their rope?

(iii) Does a longer rope make a bigger circle? Why is it so?

(iv) What was the radius of the smallest circle?

Ans. *(i)

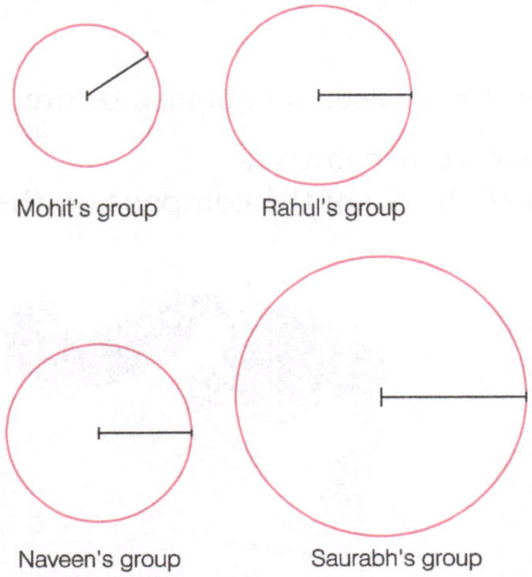

Mohit's group made the smallest circle.

*(ii)

Group	Length of their rope
Mohit's group	1 metre
Rahul's group	1.5 metres
Naveen's group	2 metres
Saurabh's group	3 metres

(iii) Yes, a longer rope makes a bigger circle because longer rope acts as a bigger radius.

*(iv) Smallest rope was 1 metre long. So, radius of the smallest circle was 1 metre.

Q.17 Draw the radius of this bangle using a ruler. Measure the length of the radius.

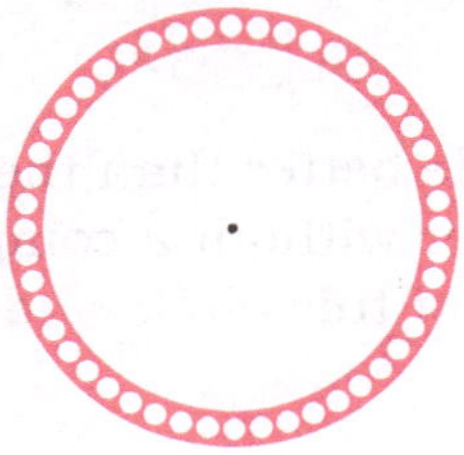

Ans. * Take any point *A* on the boundary of circle and mark the centre as point *O*. Join the point *A* and point *O* using scale.

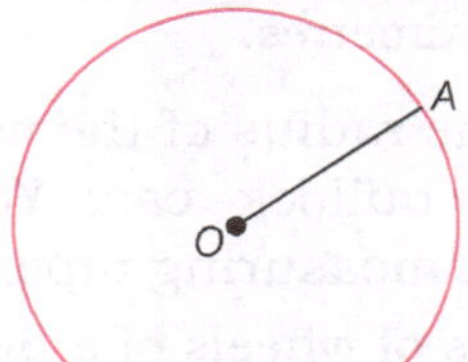

Now, measure the *OA*. Hence, radius of this circle is the length of *OA*.

Q.18 See what your friends have drawn. Discuss the length of the radius they measured. Is it the same as yours?

Ans. Do yourself.

Q.19

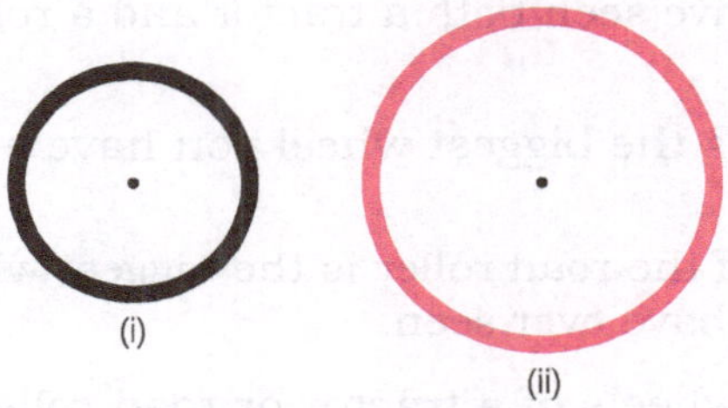

(i) Draw the radius of these circles.

(ii) Guess which circle has the longer radius.

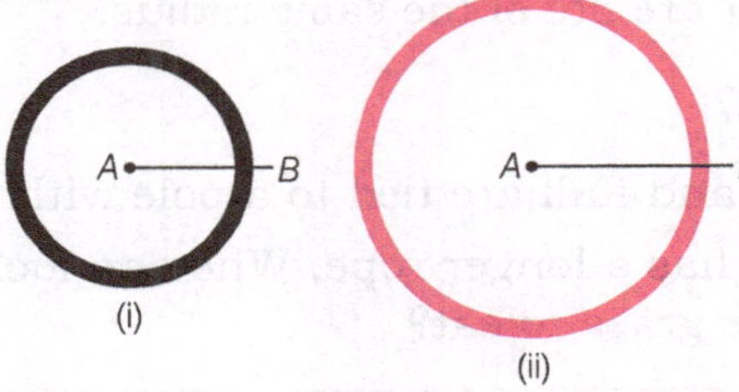

(iii) Measure the radius of both the circles using a ruler. Write the length of their radius.

(a) Radius of the circle (i) ________.

(b) Radius of the circle (ii) ________.

Ans. (i)

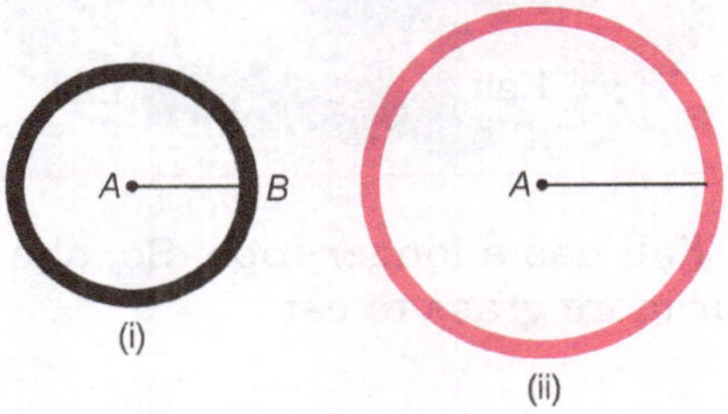

(ii) Circle (ii) has longer radius.
(iii) (a) Radius of the circle (i), AB is 1 Centimetre.
(b) Radius of the circle (ii), CD is 1.5 Centimetres.

Q.20 Measure the radius of the wheels of a bicycle or a bullock- cart. You can use a thread or a measuring tape.

Ans. * The radius of wheels of a bicycle is 40 Centimetres and the radius of the wheels of a bullock-cart is 50 centimetres.

Q.21 Are all the wheels of a bicycle or a bullock-cart of the same radius?

Ans. Yes, all the wheels of a bicycle or a bullock-cart are of the same radius.

Q.22 Have you seen a tractor or a road roller?

Ans. Yes, I have seen both a tractor and a road roller.

Q.23 Which is the biggest wheel you have ever seen?

Ans. Wheel of the road roller is the biggest wheel which I have ever seen.

Q.24 Are all wheels of a tractor or road roller of the same radius?

Ans. No, All the wheels of a tractor or a road roller are not of the same radius.

NCERT Pg 87

Q.25 Lali and Kali are tied to a pole with ropes. Kali has a longer rope. Who can look for more grass to eat?

Ans. Since, Kali has a longer rope. So, she can look for more grass to eat.

Using a Compass (NCERT Pg 88)

Q.26 Have you seen a compass before?

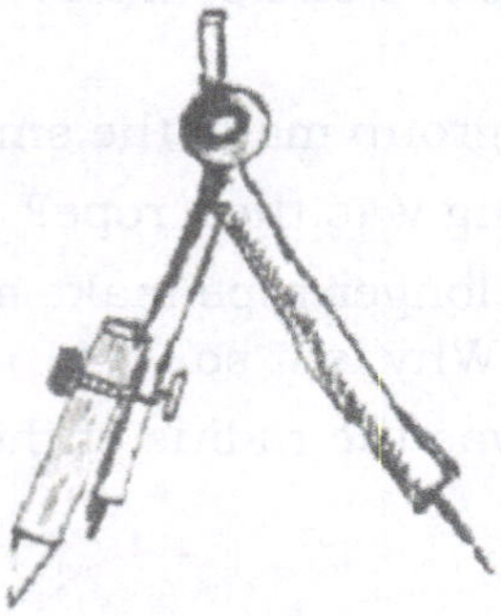

Ans. Yes, I have seen a compass before.

Q.27 Open your compass.
Press the tip of the compass on the paper.

Hold the compass from the top.
Without moving the tip, try to move the pencil around.
Do you get a circle?

Ans. Yes, If we follows these steps, we get a circle.

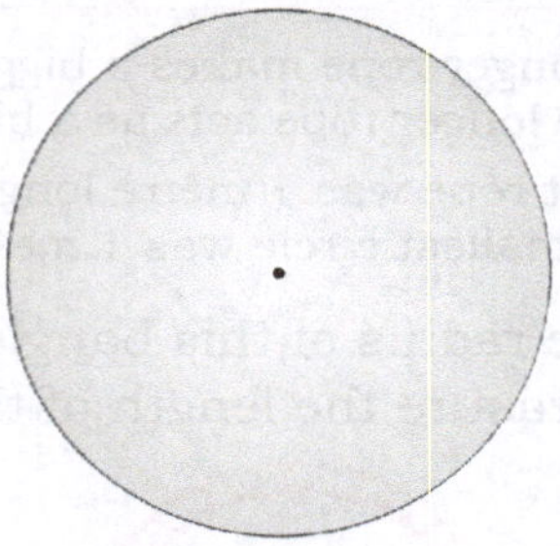

Q.28 Is this circle better than the one you made earlier without a compass? Draw the radius of this circle and measure it.

Ans. Yes, this circle is better than the one I made earlier without a compass.

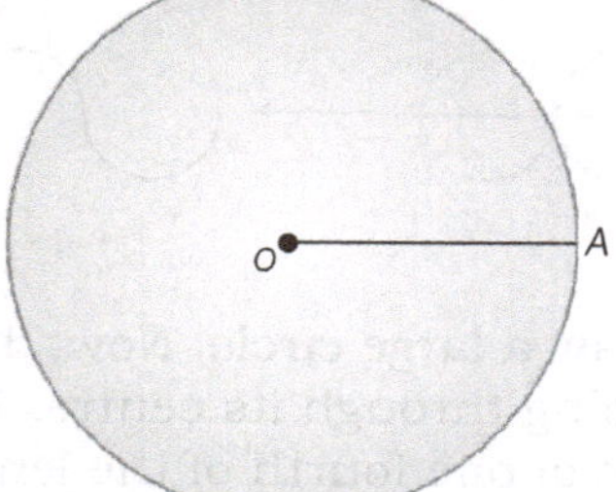

OA is the radius of this circle and radius of this circle is 1.4 centimetres.

Q.29 Now you can make your own designs like Daljeet had made. How many did you make?

Ans. Do yourself.

Q.30 Guess how this design has been made. Use a compass to make a similar one in the box.

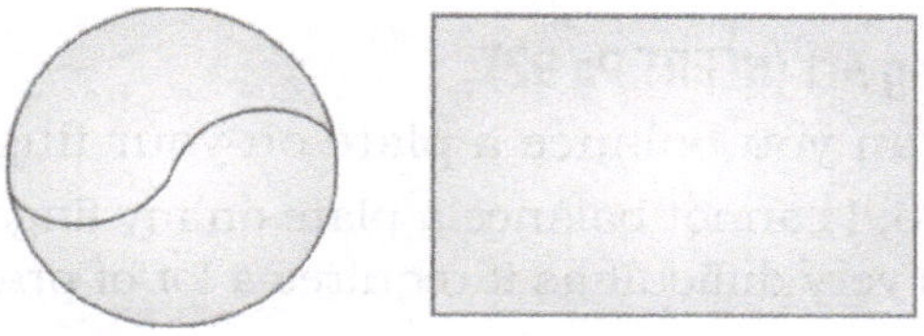

Ans.

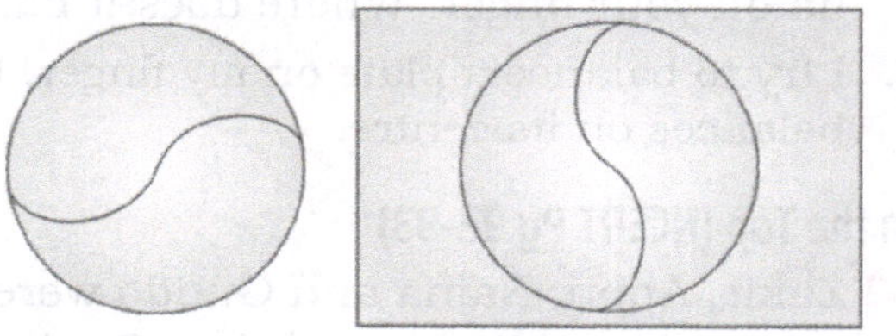

NCERT Pg 89

Q.31 **Is it a circle?**

Naina was making a circle?

Ravi asked her for an eraser. She kept her compass and gave him the eraser.

Then, she started again to complete her circle. But she got this.

Guess

Why did Naina get such a drawing? Discuss.

Ans. Naina did not put the tip of her compass again on the same place where she had put before going to find an eraser. So, she get such a drawing.

Q.32 Can a circle have more than one centre?

Ans. No, a circle has not more than one centre.

Q.33 Did any one of you ever get a shape like Naina's?

Ans. Yes, so many times, I get a shape like Naina's. When I draw a circle using compass with loose screw or using more than one centres.

Find the Centre (NCERT Pg 90-91)

Q.34 Sadiq and Sameena want to make circles for themselves.

Then, they cut their circle.

She folded her circle into half. 

Then, she folded it again like this. 

She opened the folded circle.

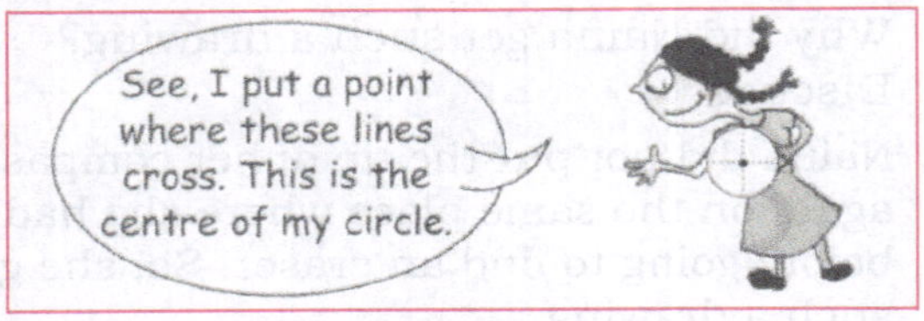

Now you trace a circle on a paper using a bangle. Cut it. Then, find its centre like Sameena did.

Ans. First we draw a circle using a bangle on notebook, then we cut the circle from its outline.

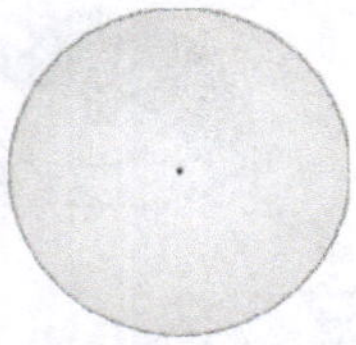

Now, fold the circle into half.

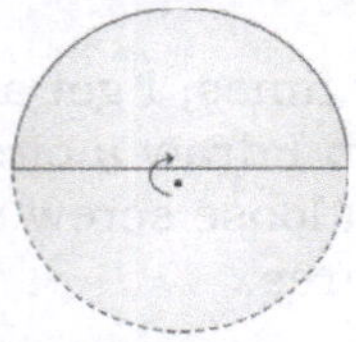

Again fold it into half

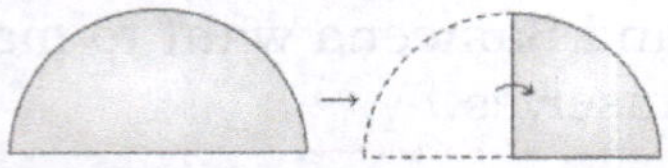

Now, we open the folded circle. We found the crossing point of two creased lines. This crossing point is the centre of circle.

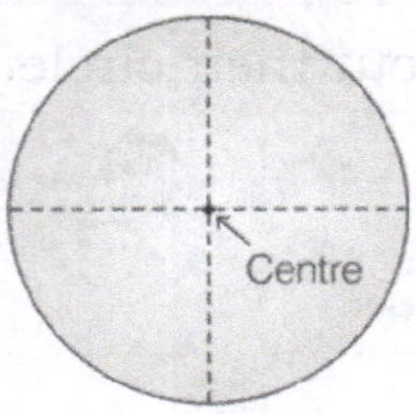

Q.35 We can also make the design on NCERT page 88 like this. How did you do it?

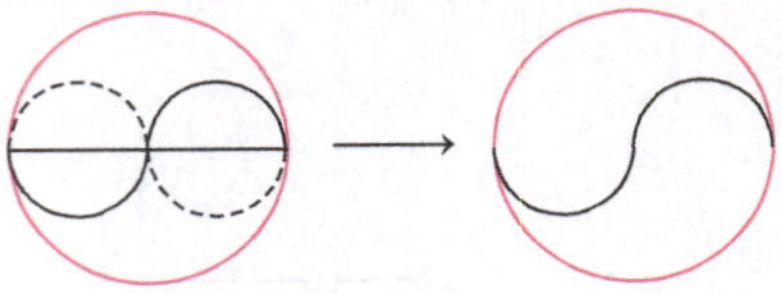

Ans. First draw a large circle. Now, draw a line *AB* passing through its centre. Take a distance of one fourth of the length of *AB* in compass and put the tip on *A* mark a point *C* on *AB* as centre and draw a semicircle with centre *C*. Similarly, find centre *D* and draw another semicircle with centre *D* as shown in the figure given below.

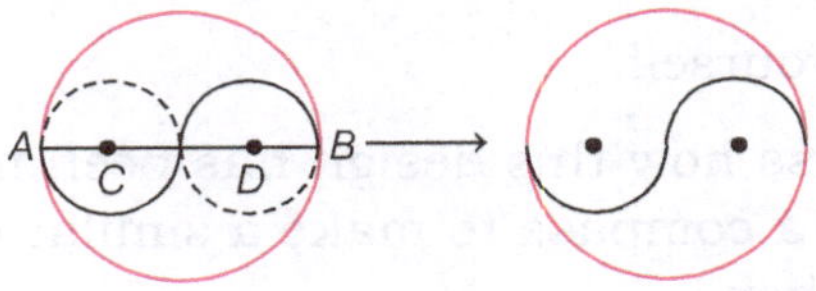

Balancing Act (NCERT Pg 92)

Q.36 Can you balance a plate on your finger?

Ans. No, I cannot balance a plate on my finger. It is very difficult as it requires a lot of practice.

Q.37 You also try to balance a plate or a round lid on your finger. Where does it balance?

Ans. I try to balance a plate on my finger. It balances on its centre.

Spin the Top (NCERT Pg 92-93)

Q.38 Zakir, Appu, Naina and Guddo were getting bored. It was raining. So they could not go out to play. Suddenly Appu said – Let's each make a top.

They took a piece of cardboard traced a circle on it. Then, they made a hole and put a matchstick in it.

Now, everybody was excited to spin their tops which looked like this.

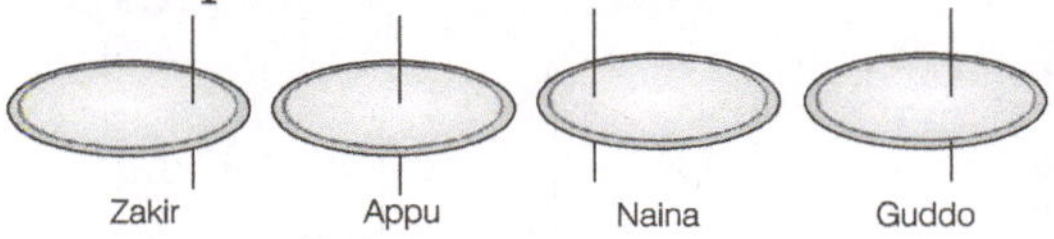

Guess

(i) Whose top will not spin at all?

(ii) Whose top will spin a little?

(iii) Whose top will spin the best?

(iv) In whose top is the stick nearest to the centre?

Ans. (i) Zakir and Naina's top will not spin at all.

(ii) Top made by Guddo will spin a little.

(iii) Appu's top will spin the best.

(iv) The stick is nearest to the centre in Appu's top.

Make Your Own Top (NCERT Pg 93)

Q.39 To make the top spin well, where you make the hole?

Ans. I will make the hole at the centre of the circular piece of cardboard to make the top spin well.

PRACTICE QUESTIONS

1. Name the following in the given figure.

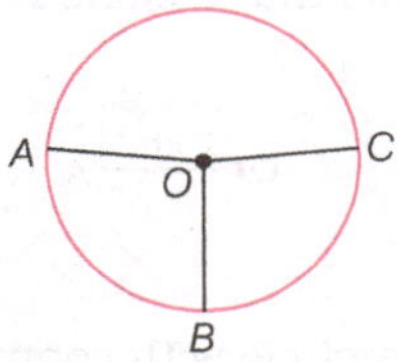

(i) Centre (ii) Radius

2. In the figure below, O is the centre of the circle.

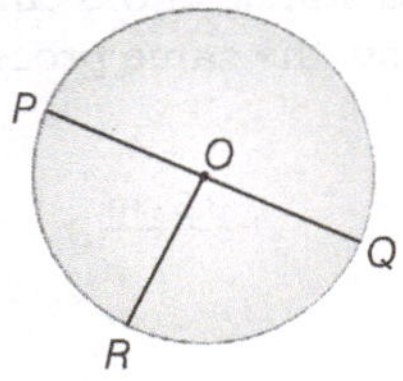

(i) What is OQ?

(ii) If $OP = 5$ centimetres, then find the length of OR.

(iii) Find the length of PQ.

3. Draw a circle of radius 6 cm using a compass and pencil. Also, write the steps which are followed by you to drawing it.

4. A cow and a buffalo are tied to a pole with two ropes of 10 metres and 12 metres long respectively in a field. Who look for more grass to eat?

5. Make a design like number 8 in a circle having radius of 4 centimetres.

6. Draw the circles of following radius using a compass.

(i) 2 centimetres

(ii) 3.5 centimetres

(iii) 5 centimetres

7. Using different sizes of circular things, make circles of different sizes and measure the radius of these circles.

8. Raj, Rahul and Adil are three friends. They have different ropes of different lengths. They made different circles using the ropes which are given below.

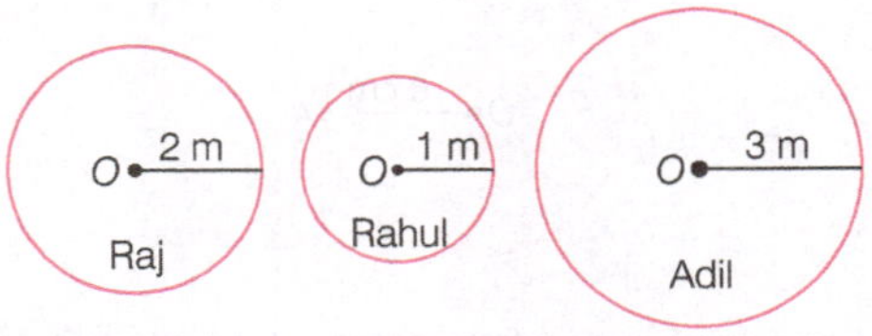

On the basis of above information, answer the following questions.

(i) Which is the smallest circle?

(ii) Which is the largest circle?

(iii) If Raj and Rahul have ropes of length 2 m and 1 m respectively, then find the sum of radius of Raj and Rahul's circles.

ANSWERS & SOLUTIONS

1. (i) In the given figure, O is the centre of given circle.

(ii) In the given figure, OA, OB and OC are the radii of the circle.

2. (i) Given, O is the centre of the circle.

We know that the line joining the centre of circle and any point on the circumference of the circle is said to the radius of circle.

Hence, in given figure OQ is the radius of the circle.

(ii) Given that $OP = 5$ centimetres

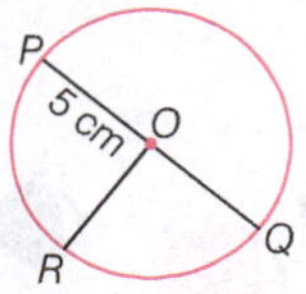

Here, OP, OQ and OR are the radius of the circle. Also, we know that all the radii of a circle are equal in length.

Therefore, $OP = OQ = OR = 5$ cm [given]

Thus, $OR = 5$ cm

(iii) We have, $OP = OQ = 5$ cm

Now, $PQ = OP + OQ = 5 + 5 = 10$ cm

Hence, the length of PQ is also 10 cm.

3. To drawing a circle of radius 6 cm, I followed the following steps.

Step I Set the compass needle at 0 on the scale and open the compass equal to 6 cm.

Step II Set the compass needle in the centre of a paper sheet.

Step III Move the pencil around the fixed needle to draw the required circle.

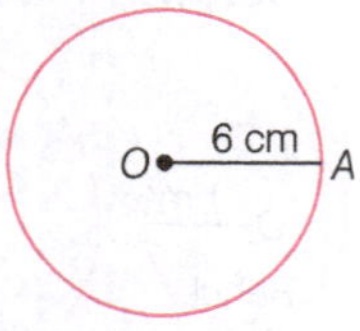

4. Length of rope of the cow = 10 metres

Length of rope of the buffalo = 12 metres

Here, we can think of the ropes as the radius of the circular grazing ground because they are tied at the centre of the ground. As we can see that the buffalo is tied with a longer rope than that of the cow. So, it has access to more grass to eat.

5. First draw a vertical line of length of 16 cm. Now, taking a radius of 4 centimetres in a compass, mark point O from point A and point O' from point B and draw two circle with centre O and O', respectively.

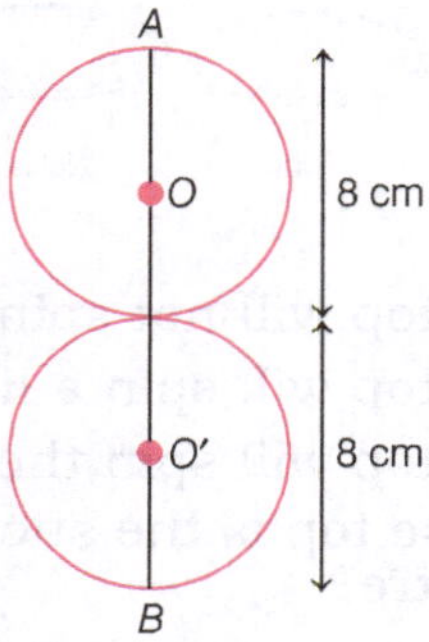

6. (i) Radius = 2 cm

To draw a circle with radius 2 cm follow the steps given below.

Step I Take a point O in the paper.

Step II Take a distance of 2 cm in the compass. Place the compass pointer at O and rotate the pencil leg of compass all around so that a circle is drawn.

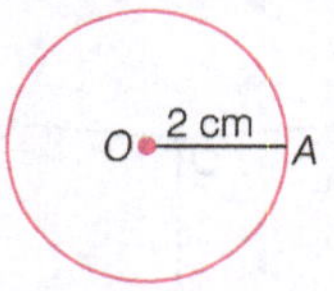

Hence, a circle with centre O and radius $OA = 2$ cm is drawn as shown in above figure.

(ii) Take a distance of 3.5 cm in the compass and follow the same process as part (i).

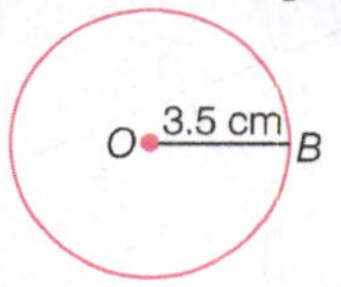

(iii) Take a distance of 5 cm in the compass and follow the same process as part (i).

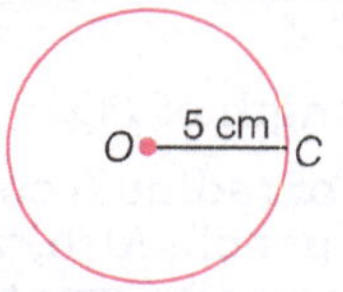

7. Do yourself.

8. (i) Since, Rahul has smallest rope.
So, Rahul's circle is the smallest circle.

(ii) In the given figures of circles, we can see that Adil has largest rope i.e. length of 3 m.
So, Adil's circle is the largest circle.

(iii) We have, length of rope Raj has = 2 m
length of rope Rahul has = 1 m

Therefore, sum of radius of Raj's circle and Rahul's circle = 2 m + 1 m = 3 m

CHAPTER 9

HALVES AND QUARTERS

Half

Half means dividing a whole thing or object into two equal parts. Each part is known as half. Some figures are given below.

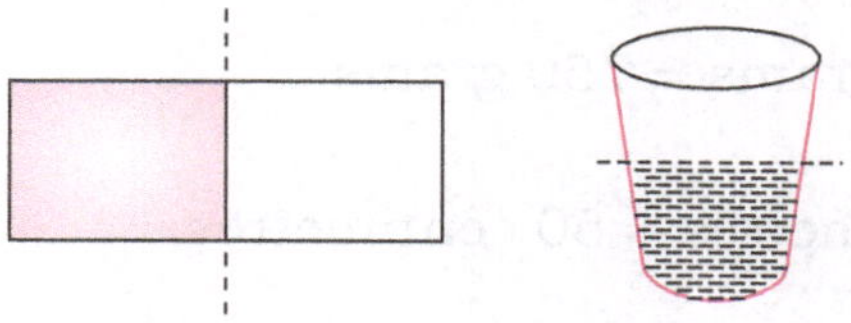

Half means 1 part out of 2 parts. So, half is written as $\frac{1}{2}$ in fraction form.

Different ways to cut into half

We can cut an object into two equal halves in different ways.

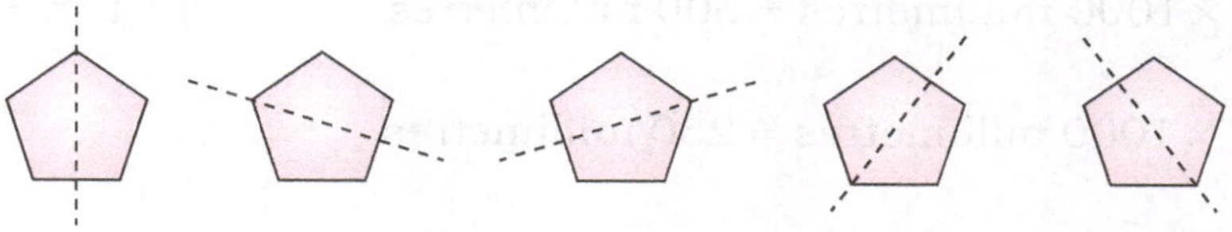

Quarter

Quarter means dividing a object into four equal parts where each part is known as quarter. Some figures of quarter are given below.

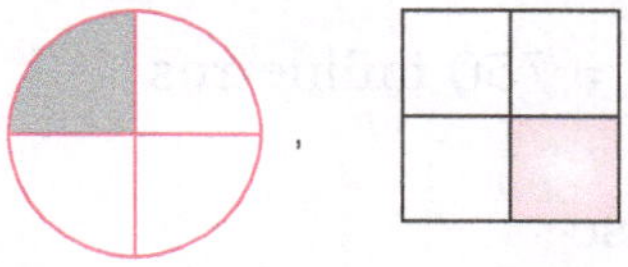

We can also get the quarter by dividing the half of one whole object into two more equal parts.

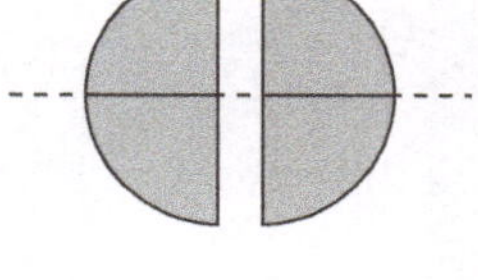

Quarter means 1 part out of 4 parts. So, quarter is written as $\frac{1}{4}$ in fraction form.

Different ways to cut into quarters

We can cut an object into 4 equal quarters in different ways.

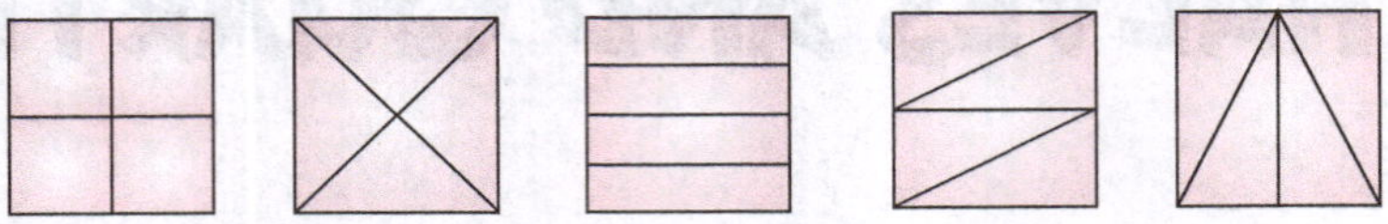

Half and Quarters of different units

- $\frac{1}{2}$ kilogram = $\frac{1}{2} \times 1000$ grams = 500 grams [∵ 1 kilogram = 1000 grams]
- $\frac{1}{4}$ kilogram = $\frac{1}{4} \times 1000$ grams = 250 grams
- $\frac{3}{4}$ kilogram = $\frac{3}{4} \times 1000$ grams = 750 grams
- $\frac{1}{2}$ metre = $\frac{1}{2} \times 100$ centimetres = 50 centimetres [∵ 1 metre = 100 centimetres]
- $\frac{1}{4}$ metre = $\frac{1}{4} \times 100$ centimetres = 25 centimetres
- $\frac{3}{4}$ metre = $\frac{3}{4} \times 100$ centimetres = 75 centimetres
- $\frac{1}{2}$ metre = $\frac{1}{2} \times 1000$ millimetres = 500 millimetres [∵ 1 m = 1000 millimetres]
- $\frac{1}{4}$ metre = $\frac{1}{4} \times 1000$ millimetres = 250 millimetres
- $\frac{1}{2}$ litre = $\frac{1}{2} \times 1000$ millilitres = 500 millilitres [∵ 1 litre = 1000 millilitres]
- $\frac{1}{4}$ litre = $\frac{1}{4} \times 1000$ millilitres = 250 millilitres
- $\frac{3}{4}$ litre = $\frac{3}{4} \times 1000$ millilitres = 750 millilitres
- ₹ $\frac{1}{4}$ = $\frac{1}{4} \times 100$ paise = 25 paise [∵ ₹ 1 = 100 Paise]
- ₹ $\frac{1}{2}$ = $\frac{1}{2} \times 100$ paise = 50 paise
- ₹ $\frac{3}{4}$ = $\frac{3}{4} \times 100$ paise = 75 paise

NCERT FOLDER

Half-Half (NCERT Pg 95)

Q.1 If the cats ask you to divide the chapati equally, how will you divide it?

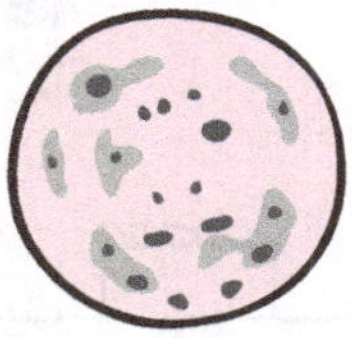

Ans. First, fold the chapati into equal half to get the line and then cut it in two halves along that line.

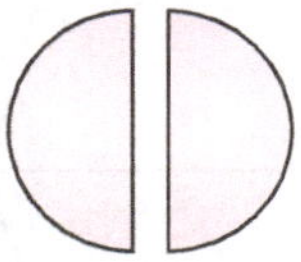

Half of Half (NCERT Pg 95)

Q.2 If two more cats come for food, how will you divide one chapati equally for four cats?

Ans. First, I will fold the chapati into two halves and again I will fold each part into two halves. Then, open the folded chapati and tear it on creased lines.

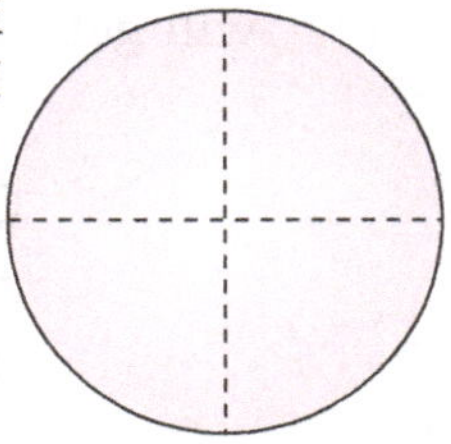

Therefore, I shall get four quarters of chapati.

Half of Many Pieces (NCERT Pg 95-96)

Q.3 Rani got a chocolate. She divided it equally and gave half to her friend Reena.

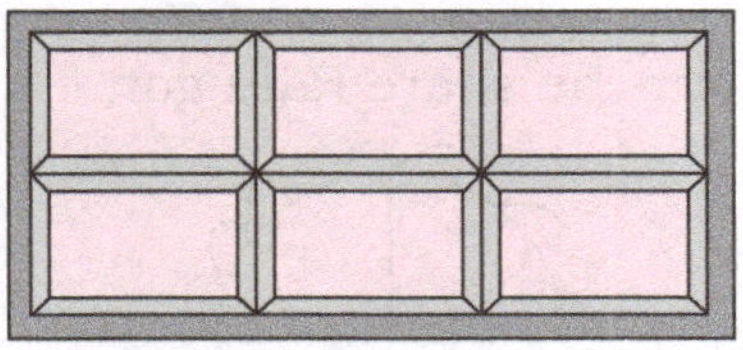

(i) Mark the portion that Reena got.

(ii) How many pieces of chocolate are there?

(iii) How many pieces were left with Rani?

Ans. (i)

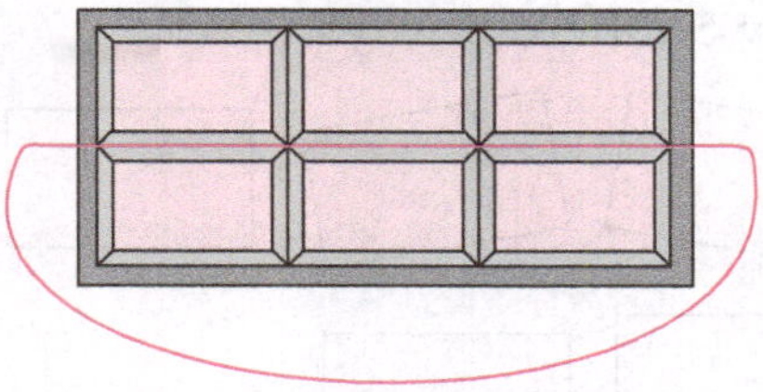

(ii) There are 6 pieces of chocolate.

(iii) Total number of pieces = 6

Number of pieces, Reena got = $\frac{6}{2} = 3$

Total number of pieces left = 6 – 3 = 3

Hence, 3 pieces of chocolate were left with Rani.

Many Shapes from a Half Sheet (NCERT Pg 96)

Q.4 Take a piece of paper. Cut the sheet into two equal triangles so that each triangle is equal to half of the sheet. Shade the two triangles with different colours.

Ans. Do yourself.

Q.5 Draw different shapes using these triangles. One such shape is shown here.

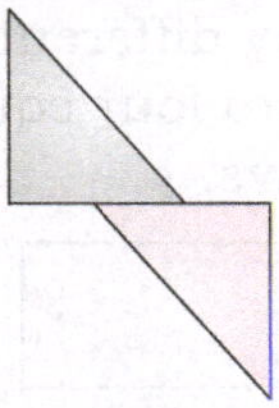

Ans. *

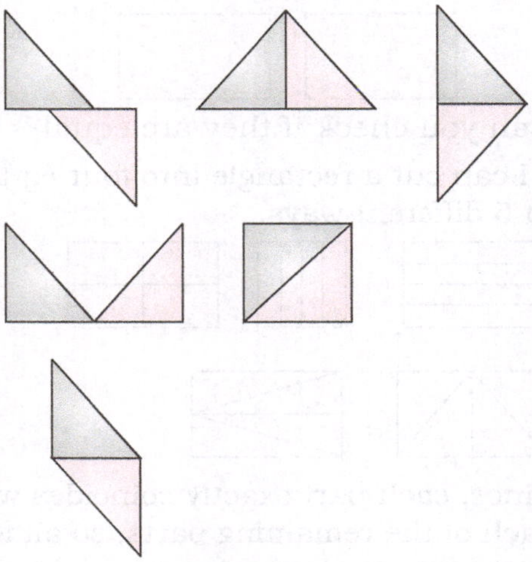

** Students can write alternate answer as per their choice.*

Many Ways to Cut into Half (NCERT Pg 96-97)

Q.6 In how many different ways can you cut a rectangle into half ?

Draw 5 different ways.

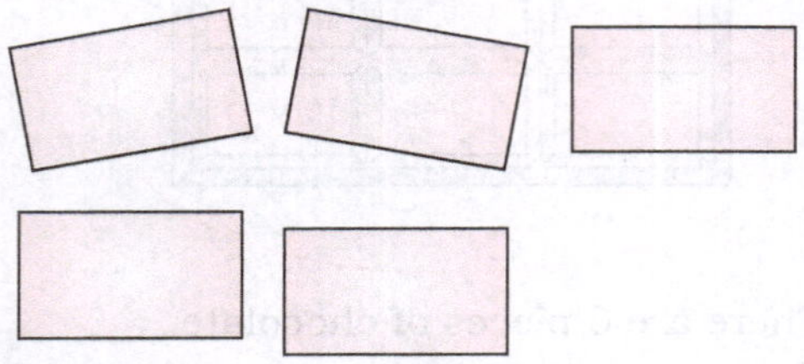

Can you check if they are equal?

Ans. * I can cut a rectangle into half in 5 different ways. There are 5 different ways to cut a rectangle into half as shown below.

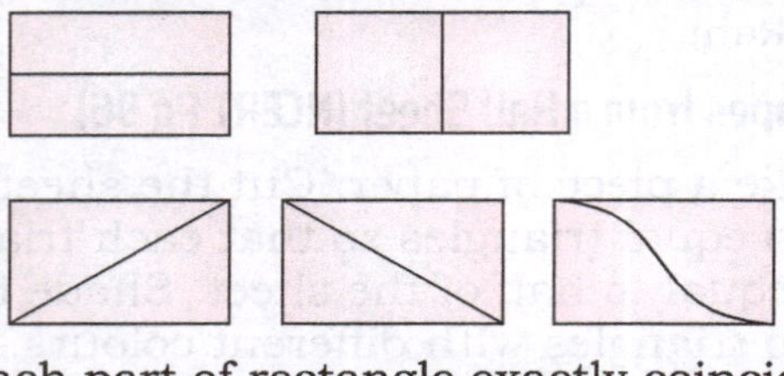

Each part of rectangle exactly coincides with the other part, so two parts are equal.

Many Ways to Make Quarters (NCERT Pg 97)

Q.7 In how many different ways can you cut a rectangle into four equal parts? Draw 5 different ways.

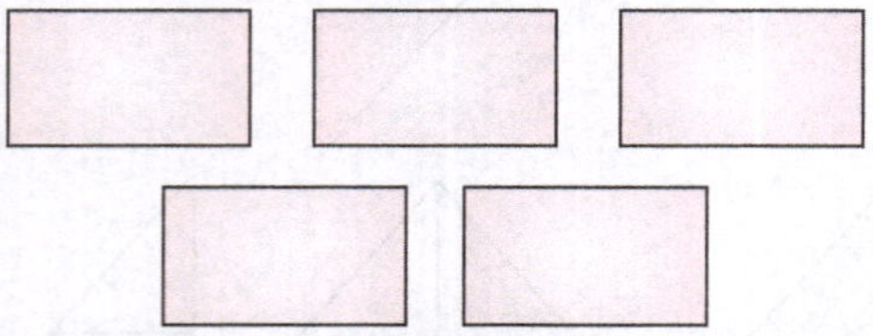

Can you check if they are equal?

Ans. * I can cut a rectangle into four equal parts in 5 different ways.

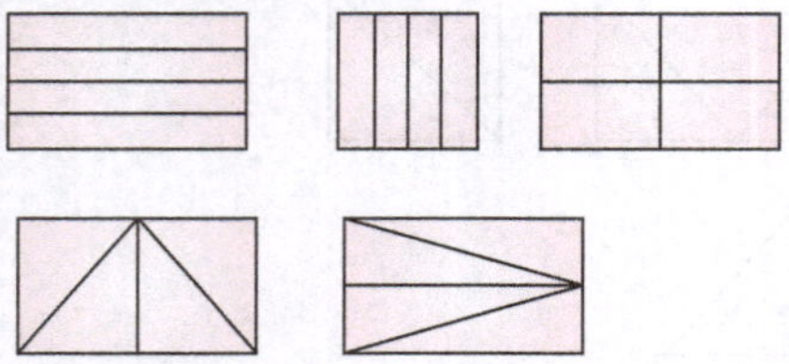

Since, each part exactly coincides with the each of the remaining parts, so all four parts are equal.

Cutting the Cake (NCERT Pg 98)

Q.8 Rajni's father brought a cake. She divided the cake into 4 equal parts, for herself, her brother Raju, her father and her mother.

(i) Colour each share with different colours.

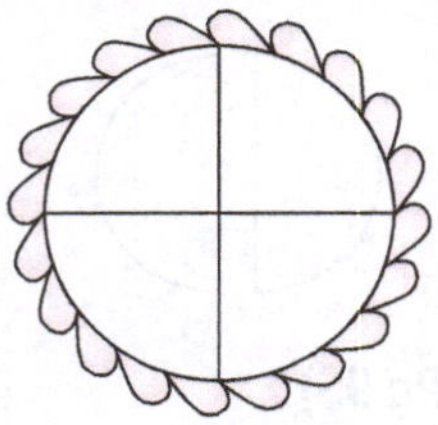

(ii) How much does each get?

(iii) Father gave his share of cake to Rajni.

Now, colour the total part that Rajni will get.

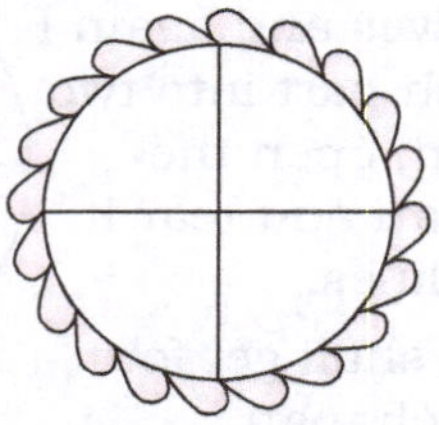

(iv) Out of 4 parts, Rajni will get .... parts which is equal to half of the cake.

So, she can write it as $\frac{}{4}$ or $\frac{1}{2}$.

(v) Colour the share Raju got.

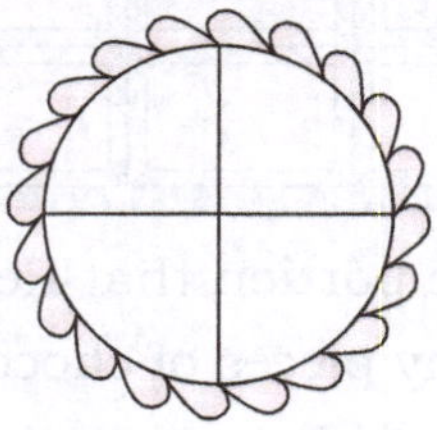

(vi) How much of the cake do Rajni and Raju together get? Colour their total share.

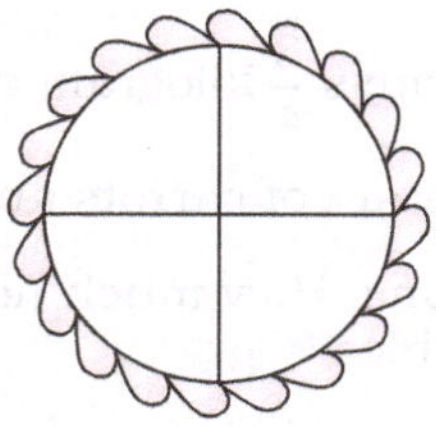

Ans. *(i)

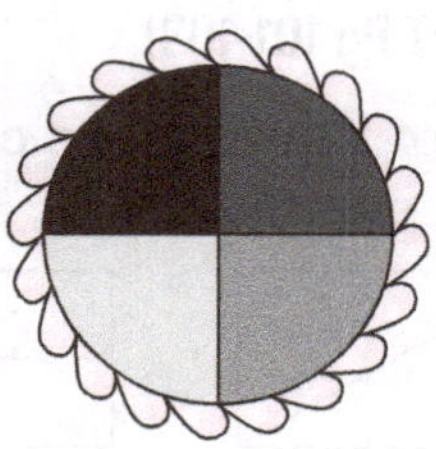

(ii) Each person gets $\frac{1}{4}$ part of cake.

(iii)

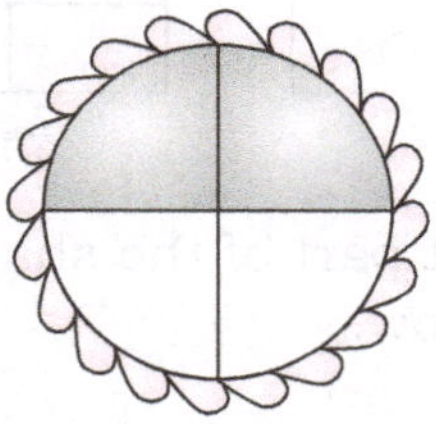

(iv) Out of 4 parts, Rajni will get 2 parts which is equal to half of the cake.

So, she can write it as $\frac{2}{4}$ or $\frac{1}{2}$.

(v)

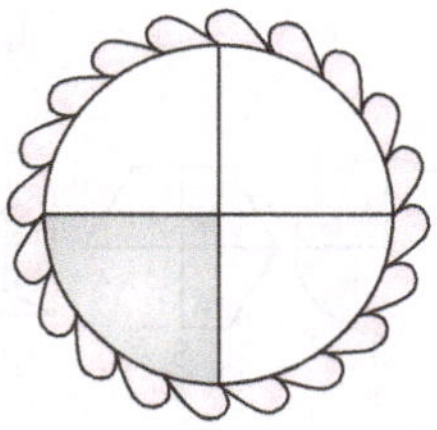

(vi) Altogether they get 3 parts out of 4. So, we can write it as $\frac{3}{4}$.

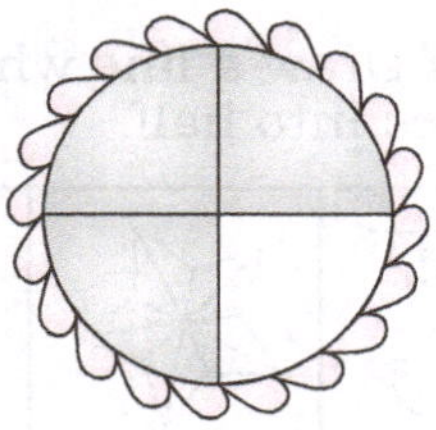

Greedy Kundu (NCERT Pg 99)

Q.9 First pumpkin-seller — $\frac{1}{4}$ of this pumpkin is for ₹ 10.

This full pumpkin will cost ₹ ....

Ans. $\because$ Cost of $\frac{1}{4}$ of pumpkin = ₹ 10

$\therefore$ Cost of 1 pumpkin $= \frac{₹\,10}{\frac{1}{4}} = ₹\,10 \times 4 = ₹\,40$

Hence, this full pumpkin will cost ₹ 40.

Q.10 Kundu — How much of this pumpkin will I get for ₹ 10?

Second pumpkin-seller — Half.

This full pumpkin will cost ₹ ....

Ans. $\because$ Price of half pumpkin = ₹ 10

$\therefore$ Price of full pumpkin $= \frac{₹\,10}{\frac{1}{2}} = ₹\,10 \times 2$

= ₹ 20

Hence, this full pumpkin will cost ₹ 20.

Using a Price List (NCERT Pg 100)

Q.11

Item	Price in ₹ (per kg)
Tomato	8
Potato	12
Onion	10
Carrot	16
Pumpkin	4

(i) How much does $\frac{1}{2}$ kilogram of tomatoes cost?

(ii) Which costs more $\frac{1}{2}$ kilogram of onions or $\frac{1}{4}$ kilogram of carrots?

(iii) What is the price of $\frac{3}{4}$ kilogram of potatoes?

(iv) Keerthi is going for shopping. She has only ₹ 20 with her. Can she buy all the things in her shopping list?

(v) Make two questions yourself from the price list.

(a) ______________________

(b) ______________________

Ans. (i) $\because$ Cost of 1 kilogram of tomatoes = ₹ 8

$\therefore$ Cost of $\frac{1}{2}$ kilogram of tomatoes = ₹ $8 \times \frac{1}{2}$

= ₹ 4

(ii) $\because$ Cost of 1 kilogram of onions = ₹ 10

$\therefore$ Cost of $\frac{1}{2}$ kilogram of onions = ₹ $10 \times \frac{1}{2}$

= ₹ 5

$\because$ Cost of 1 kilogram of carrots = ₹ 16

$\therefore$ Cost of $\frac{1}{4}$ kilogram of carrots = ₹ $16 \times \frac{1}{4}$

= ₹ 4

Therefore, cost of $\frac{1}{2}$ kilogram of onions is more than the cost of $\frac{1}{4}$ kilogram of carrots.

(iii) $\because$ Price of 1 kilogram of potatoes = ₹ 12

$\therefore$ Price of $\frac{3}{4}$ kilogram of potatoes = ₹ $12 \times \frac{3}{4}$

= ₹ 9

(iv) Cost of $\frac{1}{2}$ kilogram of potatoes = ₹ $12 \times \frac{1}{2}$

= ₹ 6

Cost of 2 kilograms of pumpkin = ₹ 4×2

= ₹ 8

and cost of $\frac{1}{4}$ kilogram of carrots = ₹ $16 \times \frac{1}{4}$

= ₹ 4

Total cost of vegetables = ₹ 6 + ₹ 8 + ₹ 4

= ₹ 18

Therefore, Keerthi can buy all the things in her shopping list.

(v) *(a) How much does 2 kilogram of potatoes cost?

(b) Rohit buys $\frac{3}{4}$ kilogram of tomatoes, $\frac{1}{2}$ kilogram of carrots and $\frac{1}{4}$ kilogram of onions. How much he paid for vegetables?

Practice Time (NCERT Pg 101-103)

Q.12 What part of the whole is coloured? Write below each shape.

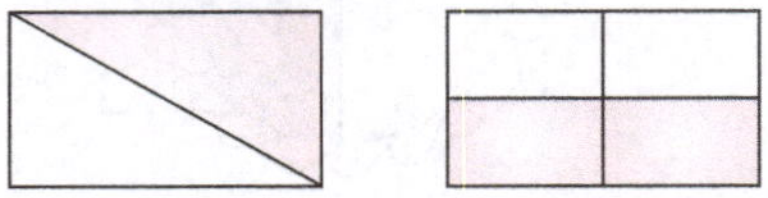

Ans.

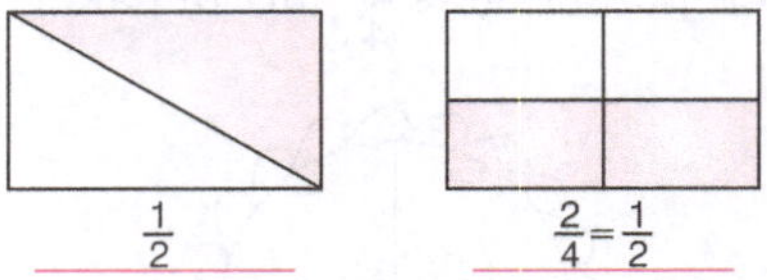

Q.13 Colour that part of the shape which is written below.

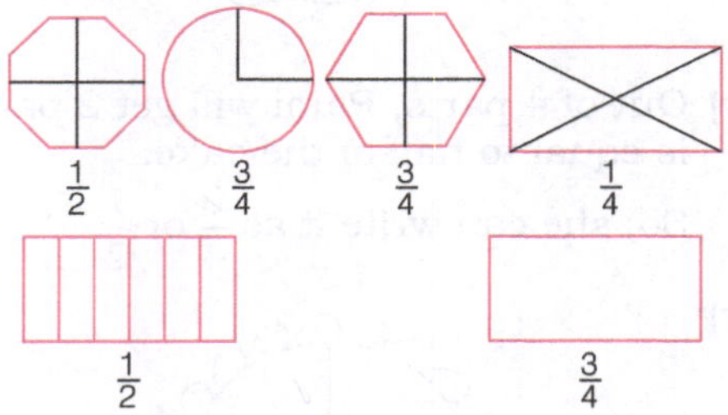

Ans. *

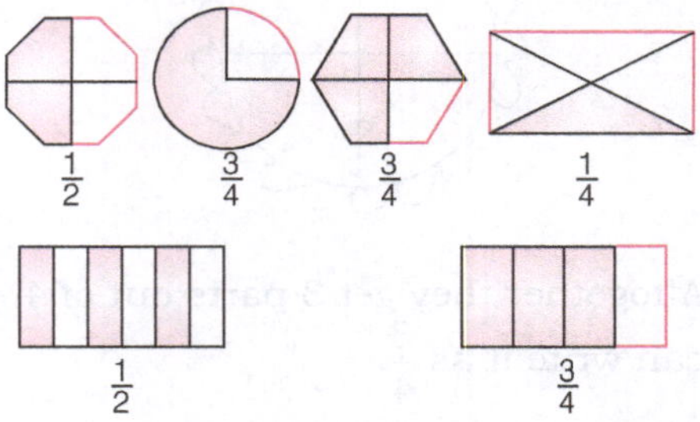

Q.14 **Cut in half** Draw a line which divides these shapes into half.

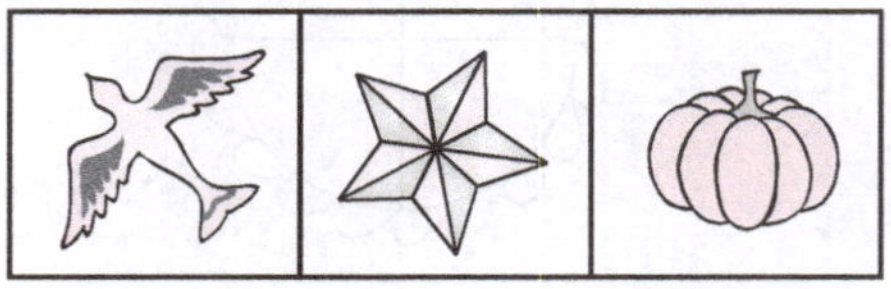

Ans.

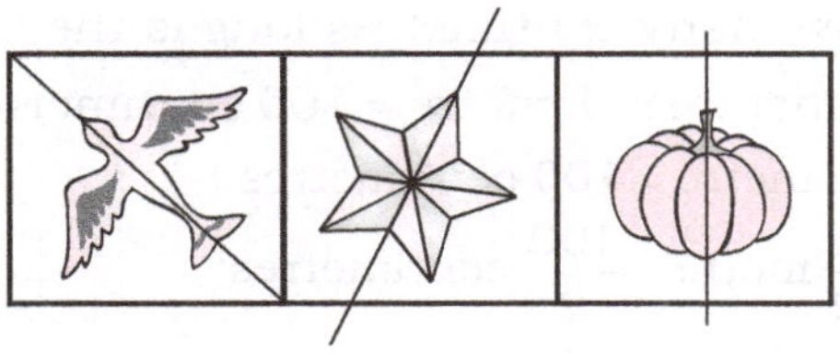

Q.15 Colour half the number of shapes as shown here. One has been done for you.

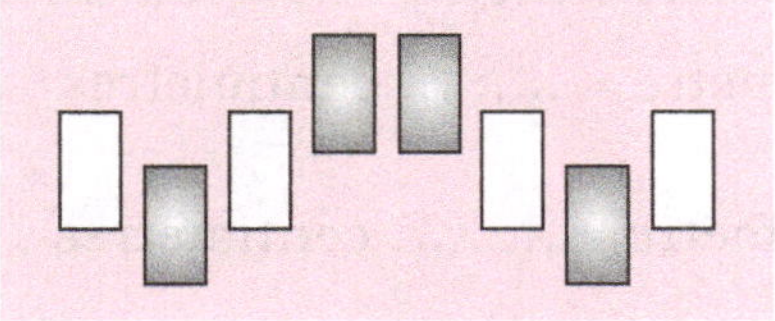

(i)

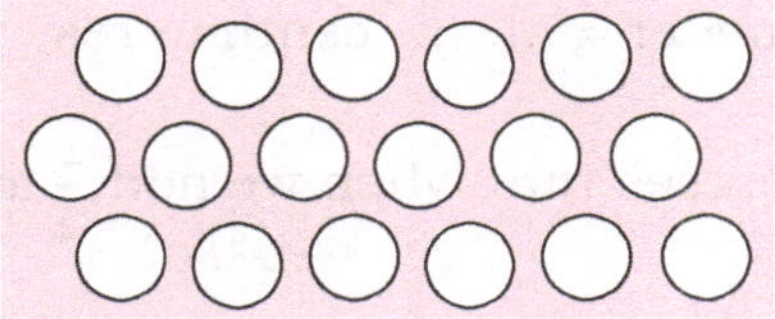

(ii)

Ans. *

(i)

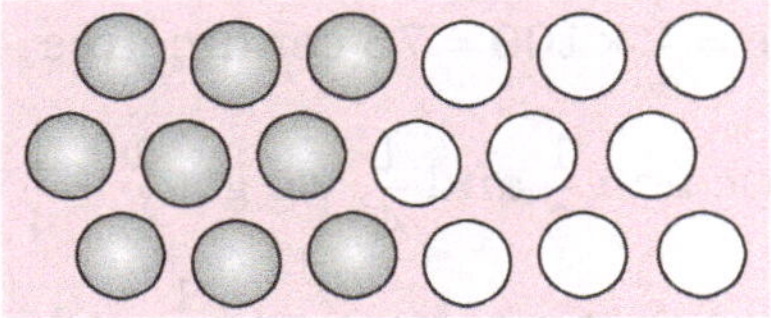

(ii)

Q.16 Colour $\frac{1}{4}$ of these shapes.

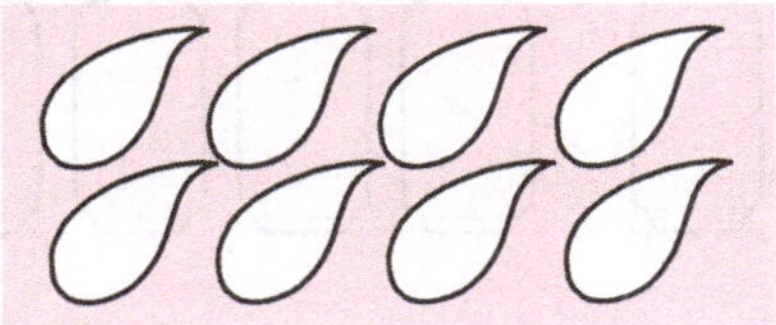

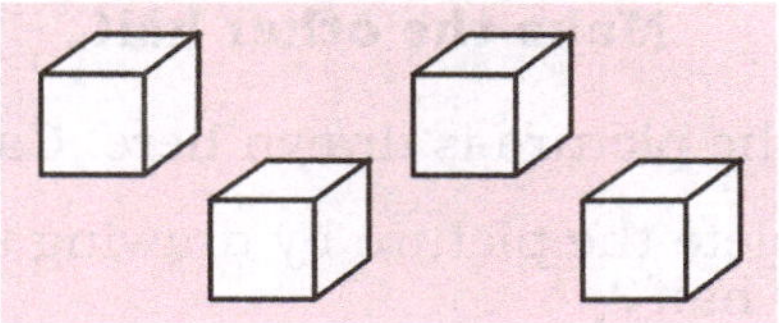

Ans. *

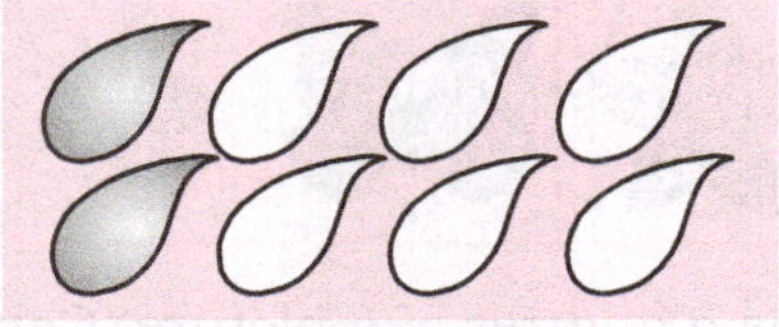

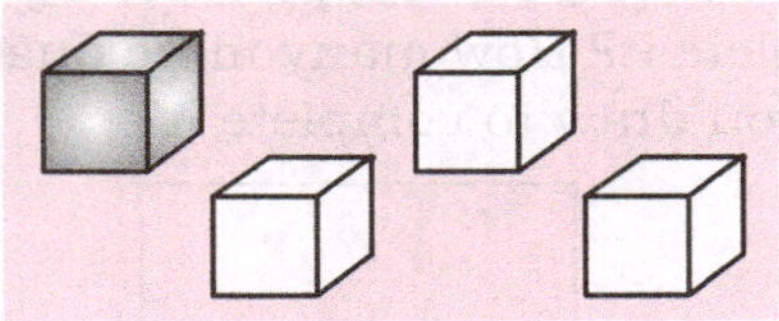

Q.17 Match the coloured part as shown.

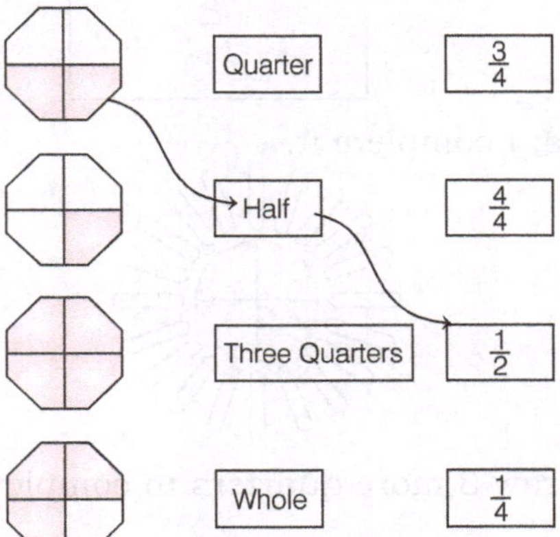

Ans.

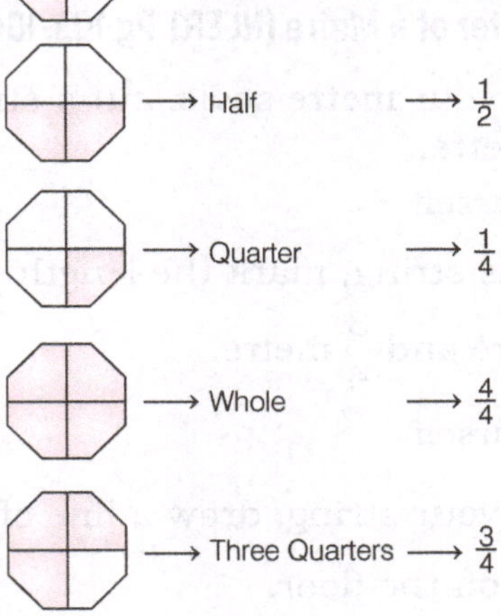

Q.18 **Make the other half**

$\frac{1}{2}$ of the picture is drawn here. Can you complete the picture by drawing the other half?

Ans.

Q.19 This is a quarter of a picture. Can you complete it? How many more quarters will you draw to complete it?

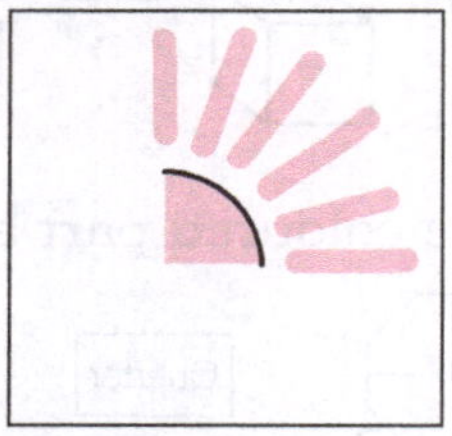

Ans. Yes, I complete it.

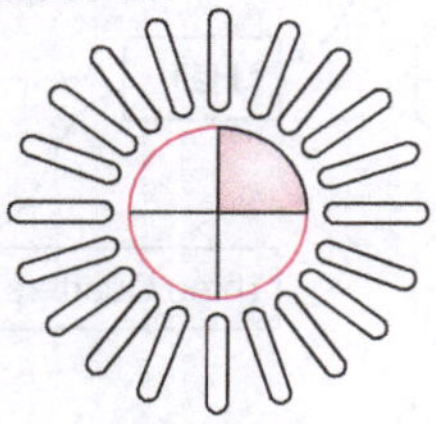

I draw 3 more quarters to complete it.

Half and Quarter of a Metre (NCERT Pg 103-104)

Q.20 Using your metre scale, cut a string of one metre.

Ans. Do yourself.

Q.21 On this string, mark the length $\frac{1}{2}$ metre, $\frac{1}{4}$ metre and $\frac{3}{4}$ metre.

Ans. Do yourself.

Q.22 Using your string, draw a line of length $\frac{1}{2}$ metre on the floor.

How many centimetres long is the line?

Remember, 1 metre = 100 centimetres.

Ans. $\because$ 1 metre = 100 centimetres

$\therefore \frac{1}{2}$ metre $= \frac{100}{2}$ centimetres

= 50 centimetres

Hence, the line is 50 centimetres long.

Q.23 Remember, 1 metre = 100 centimetres.

So, $\frac{1}{2}$ metre = ... centimetres

$\frac{1}{4}$ metre = ... centimetres

$\frac{3}{4}$ meter = ... centimetres

Can you see that when we add $\frac{1}{2}$ and $\frac{1}{4}$, we get $\frac{3}{4}$?

Ans. $\frac{1}{2}$ metre $= \frac{1}{2} \times 100 = 50$ centimetres

$\frac{1}{4}$ metre $= \frac{1}{4} \times 100 = 25$ centimetres

$\frac{3}{4}$ metre $= \frac{3}{4} \times 100 = 75$ centimetres

When we add $\frac{1}{2}$ and $\frac{1}{4}$, we get $\frac{1}{2} + \frac{1}{4} = \frac{3}{4}$.

Yes, I see that when we add $\frac{1}{2}$ and $\frac{1}{4}$, we get $\frac{3}{4}$.

Sharing Milk (NCERT Pg 104)

Q.24 This bottle is full of milk and it holds one litre. The milk is put into 4 other bottles, so that each bottle has $\frac{1}{4}$ litre of milk.

(i) Shade the bottles to show the level of milk in each.

(ii) Remember, 1 litre = 1000 millilitres.

How many millilitres of milk does each bottle have?

Ans. (i)

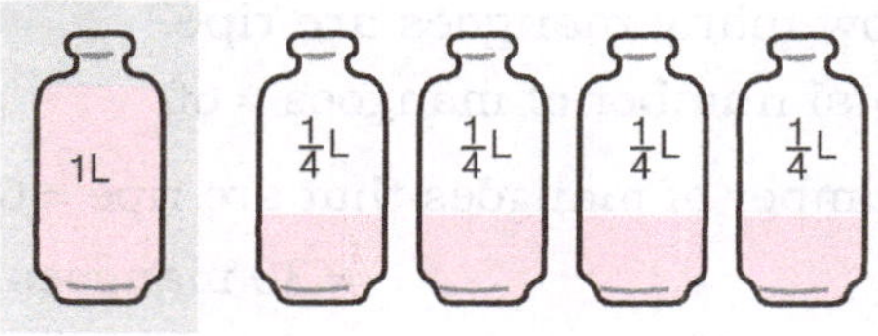

(ii) $\because$ Full bottle holds = 1 litre

= 1000 millilitres

$\therefore \frac{1}{4}$ bottle holds = $\frac{1000}{4}$

= 250 millilitres.

So, each bottle have 250 millilitres of milk.

Q.25 Shan poured 1 litre of milk into two bottle, so that the first bottle holds $\frac{3}{4}$ litre and the other holds $\frac{1}{4}$ litre.

(i) Shade the level of milk in each bottle.

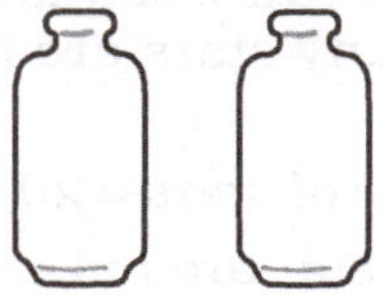

(ii) How many millilitres of milk does each bottle hold?

Ans. (i)

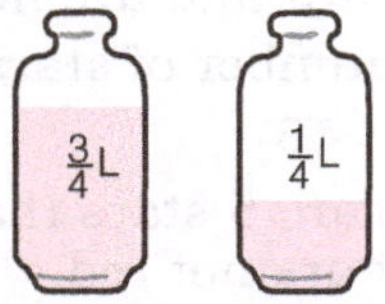

(ii) $\because$ 1 litre = 1000 millilitres

$\therefore \frac{3}{4}$ litre = $\frac{3}{4} \times 1000$ millilitres

= 750 millilitres

$\therefore \frac{1}{4}$ litre = $\frac{1}{4} \times 1000$ millilitres

= 250 millilitres

So, first bottle which holds $\frac{3}{4}$ litre of milk has 750 millilitres of milk and second bottle which holds $\frac{1}{4}$ litre of milk has 250 millilitres of milk.

Balance the Weight (NCERT Pg 105)

Q.26

Choose from the weights above to make the two pans equal. In how many ways can you do it?

Remember, 1 kilogram = 1000 grams

(i) Draw the weights in the empty pan.

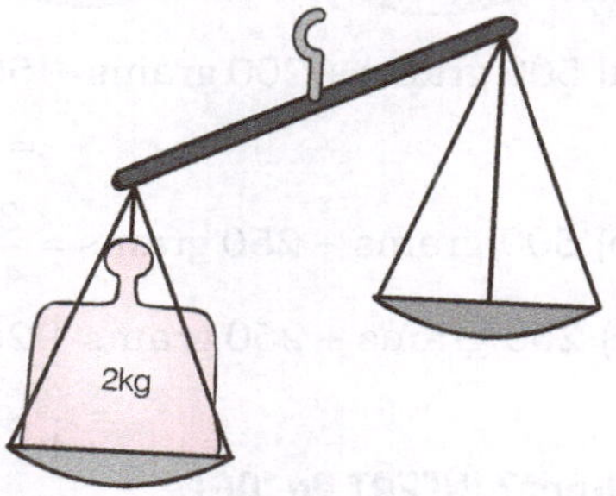

(ii) In how many different ways can you balance this weight of $\frac{3}{4}$ kilogram?

(a) .... (b) .... (c) ....

Ans. *This can be done in many ways.
Some ways to equal the two pans are given below.

(a) 1 kilogram + 500 grams + 500 grams = 2 kilograms

(b) 1 kilogram + 500 grams + 250 grams + 250 grams = 2 kilograms

(c) 1 kilogram + 500 grams + 250 grams + 200 grams + 50 grams = 2 kilograms

(d) 1 kilogram + 500 grams + 200 grams + 200 grams + 100 grams = 2 kilograms

(e) 1 kilogram + 250 grams + 250 grams + 200 grams + 200 grams + 100 grams = 2 kilograms

(f) 1 kilogram + 250 grams + 250 grams + 250 grams + 200 grams + 50 grams = 2 kilograms

(g) 500 grams + 500 grams + 250 grams + 250 grams + 200 grams + 200 grams + 100 grams = 2 kilograms

*(i)

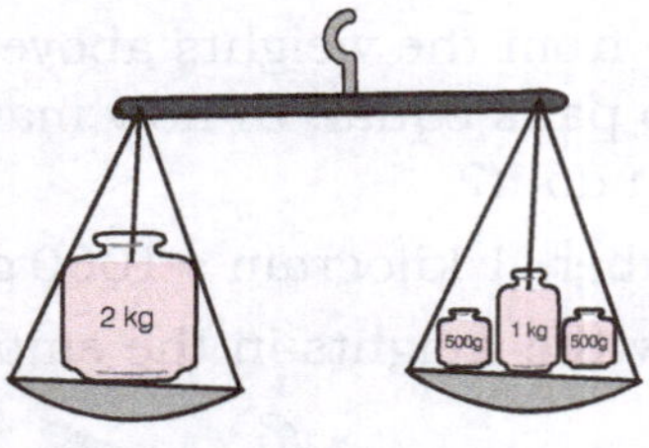

(ii) (a) 500 grams + 200 grams + 50 grams $= \frac{3}{4}$ kilogram

(b) 500 grams + 250 grams $= \frac{3}{4}$ kilogram

(c) 250 grams + 250 grams + 250 grams $= \frac{3}{4}$ kilograms

Why is it Wrong? (NCERT Pg 106)

Q.27 Kannan shaded some parts as shown. But his friend Mini says that it is wrong. Explain why it is wrong.

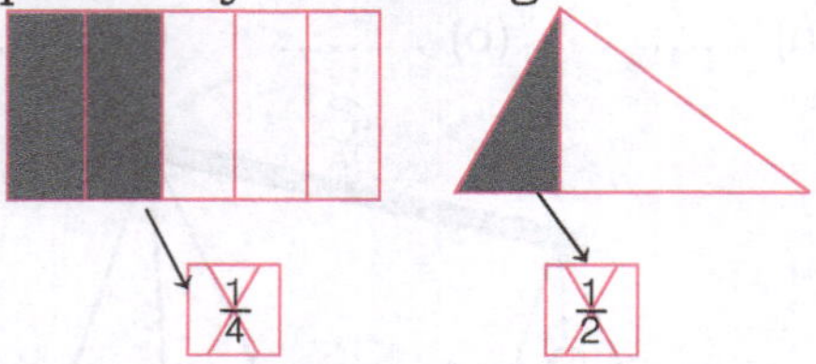

Ans. In rectangle, shaded part is not equal to any other part because shaded part is more than the $\frac{1}{4}$ part of rectangle. So, it can not be said that the shaded part is $\frac{1}{4}$.

In triangle, shaded part is not equal to other part and it looks less than the half of triangle. So, it is not equal to $\frac{1}{2}$.

Practice Time (Pg 106)

Q.28 There are 60 mangoes. $\frac{1}{2}$ of them are ripe. How many mangoes are ripe?

Ans. Total number of mangoes = 60

Number of mangoes that are ripe $= 60 \times \frac{1}{2}$

= 30 mangoes

Hence, 30 mangoes are ripe.

Q.29 There are 32 children. $\frac{1}{2}$ of them are girls. How many children are boys?

Ans. Total number of children = 32

Number of girls $= 32 \times \frac{1}{2} = 16$ girls.

Number of boys = Number of total children − Number of girls

= 32 − 16 = 16

Hence, 16 children are boys.

Q.30 There are 20 stars. A quarter of them are red. How many stars are red? How many are not red?

Ans. Total number of stars = 20

∵ Quarter of star are red.

∴ Number of red stars $= \frac{20}{4} = 5$

Number of stars that are not red

= Total number of stars − red stars

= 20 − 5 = 15

Hence, there are 5 stars that are red and 15 stars that are not red.

Q.31 Ravi wants a pencil. It costs ₹ 2. He gives a one-rupee coin, one half-rupee coin and one quarter-rupee coin. Is it enough?

Ans. Cost of pencil = ₹ 2

Money given by Ravi $= ₹\,1 + ₹\,\frac{1}{2} + ₹\,\frac{1}{4}$

= ₹ 1 + 50 paise + 25 paise

= ₹ 1 + 75 paise = 1 Rupee 75 paise

Since, 1 Rupee 75 paise < ₹ 2

Therefore, money given by Ravi is not enough.

PRACTICE QUESTIONS

1. Fill in the blanks.

(i) $\frac{1}{2}$ kilogram is equal to .... grams.

(ii) $\frac{3}{4}$ metre is equal to .... Centimetres.

(iii) 250 millilitres is equal to .... litre.

2. Multiple choice questions.

(i) Which of these is shaded as $\frac{1}{2}$?

(a) 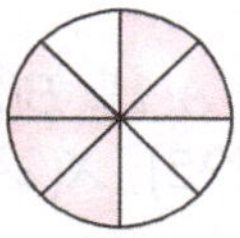

(b) 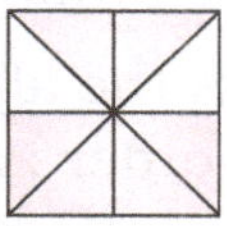

(c) 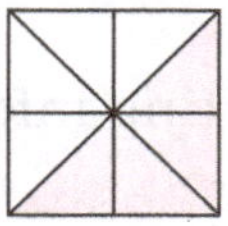

(d) 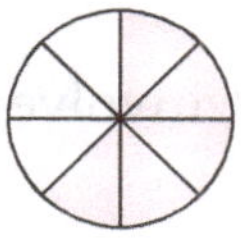

(ii) Which fraction can be used to represent the following figure?

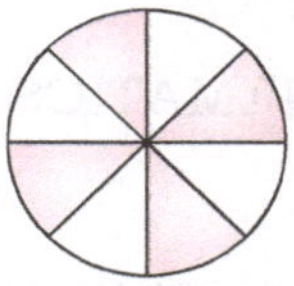

(a) $\frac{4}{5}$ (b) $\frac{1}{2}$ (c) $\frac{5}{11}$ (d) $\frac{7}{10}$

3. Shade the part of following shapes as given below.

(i) 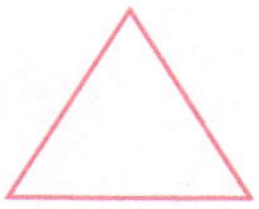

$\frac{1}{2}$

(ii) 

$\frac{3}{4}$

(iii) 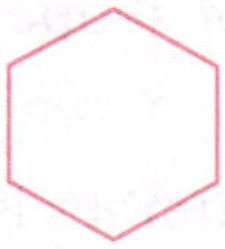

$\frac{1}{3}$

(iv) 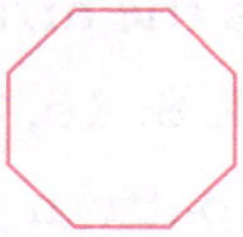

$\frac{5}{8}$

4. Ramesh has a ten rupee note, two ₹ 5 coins, 3 coins of ₹ $\frac{1}{2}$, 2 coins of ₹ $\frac{1}{4}$ and 5 coins of ₹ $\frac{1}{10}$. How much total money Ramesh has?

5. Rohan's father gave him ₹ 120. He spent $\frac{2}{3}$ of it on pizza.

How much money did he spend on pizza?

How much money was left with him?

ANSWERS & SOLUTIONS

1. (i) 500 (ii) 75 (iii) $\frac{1}{4}$

2. (i) (c) (ii) (b)

3. (i) 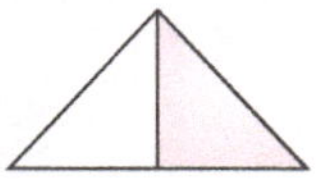

$\frac{1}{2}$

(ii) 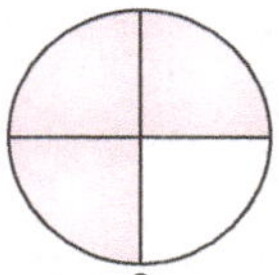

$\frac{3}{4}$

(iii) 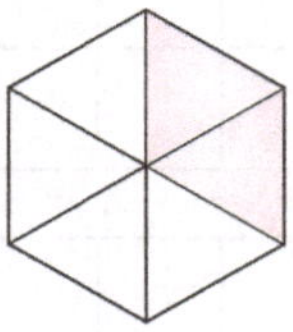

$\frac{1}{3}$

(iv) 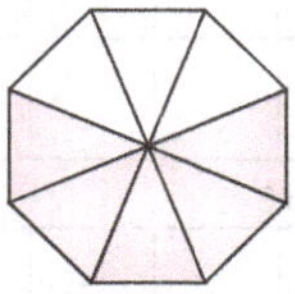

$\frac{5}{8}$

4. Total money that Ramesh has

$= 1 \times ₹\ 10 + 2 \times ₹\ 5 + 3 \times ₹\ \frac{1}{2} + 2 \times ₹\ \frac{1}{4} + 5 \times ₹\ \frac{1}{10}$

$= ₹\ 10 + ₹\ 10 + ₹\ \frac{3}{2} + ₹\ \frac{1}{2} + ₹\ \frac{1}{2}$

= 22 ₹ 50 paise

5. Total money, Rohan get = ₹ 120

Money spent on pizza $= \frac{2}{3} \times ₹\ 120$

= ₹ 80

Money left with Rohan = ₹ 120 – ₹ 80

= ₹ 40

CHAPTER 10 PLAY WITH PATTERNS

Pattern

It refers the arrangement of shapes, numbers and designs.

(i) 2, 4, 8, 16, 32, ... (ii) *AZ, BY, CX, DW, EV, ...*

In first pattern, the next number is double of the previous number.

In second pattern, first letters (*A, B, C*) follow the order of the alphabet : *A*(1), *B*(2), *C*(3) and second letters (*Z, Y, X*) follow in reverse alphabetical order : *Z*(26), *Y*(25), *X*(24).

Coding-Decoding

Coding and decoding are logical reasoning processes that involve converting information into a different form using rules and regulations.

(i) MATHEMATICS → 13 1 20 8 5 13 1 20 9 3 19

In this coding, each letter of the word MATHEMATICS is replaced by its place value.

(ii) 3 12 1 19 19 → CLASS

In this coding, each number represents the place value of the alphabetical letters.

Place value of letters

A	B	C	D	E	F	G	H	I	J	K	L	M	N	O	P	Q	R	S	T	U	V	W	X	Y	Z
1	2	3	4	5	6	7	8	9	10	11	12	13	14	15	16	17	18	19	20	21	22	23	24	25	26

NCERT FOLDER

NCERT Pg 108

Q.1 Can you see how Tinu has made different patterns using the same block? Now, you too make 3 different patterns using  .

Pattern 1

Pattern 2

Pattern 3

** Students can write alternate answer as per their choice.*

Ans. * Pattern 1

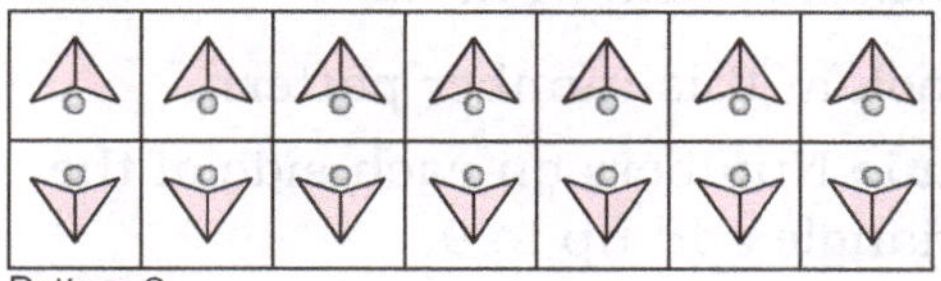

Pattern 2

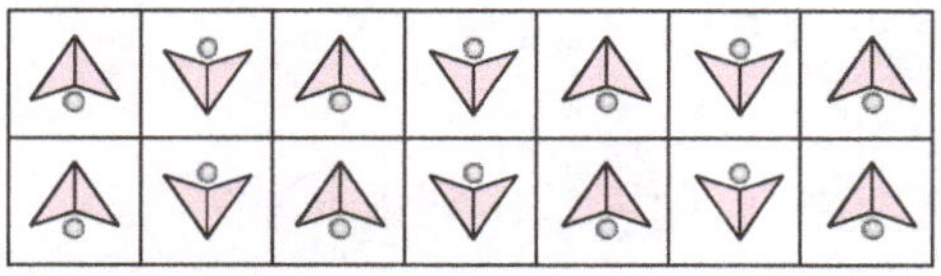

Pattern 3

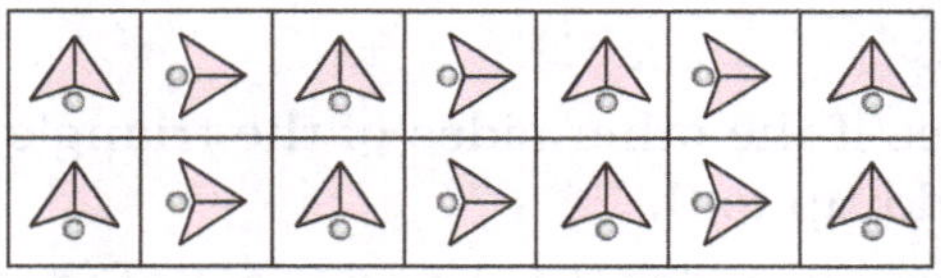

NCERT Pg 109

Q.2 Yamini has used her blocks to make a few patterns. Help her to take these patterns forward.

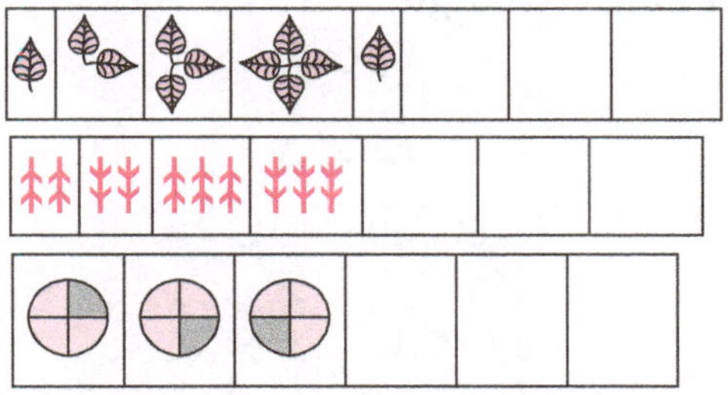

Ans.

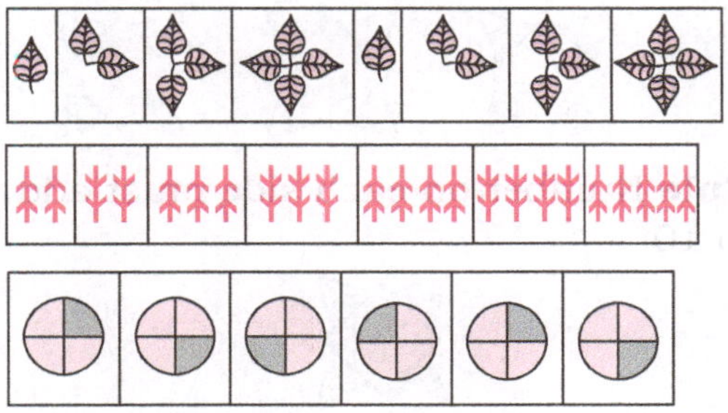

Q.3 We can also make patterns with numbers and letters. Below are a few examples. Can you take them forward?

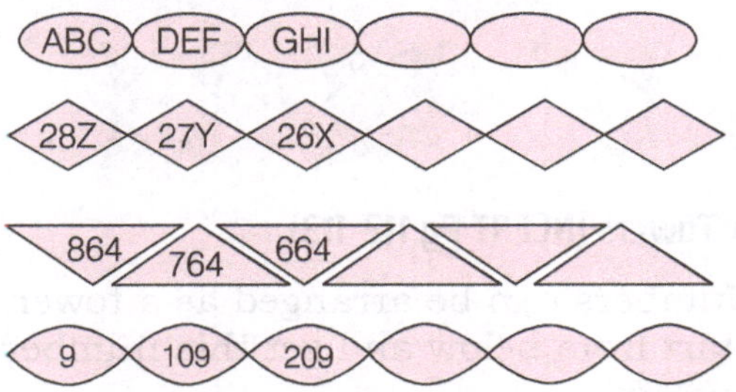

Ans.

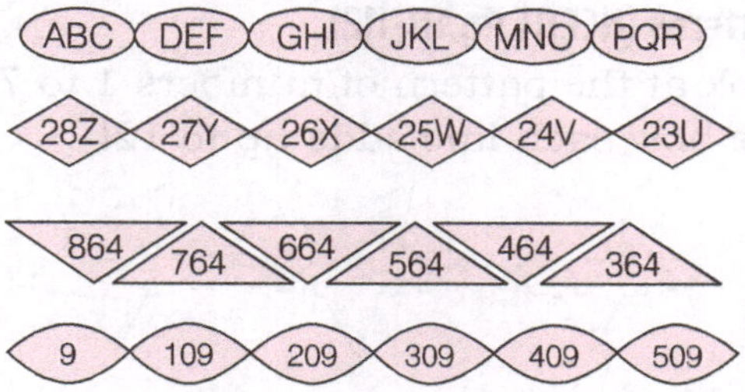

Q.4 Now write your own number patterns.

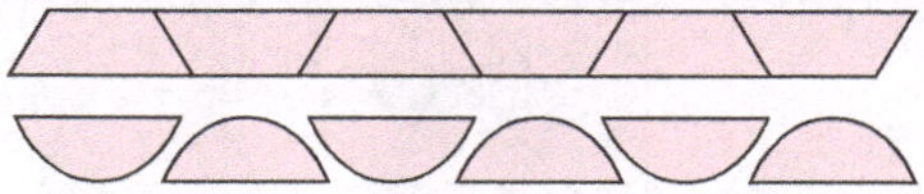

Ans. *

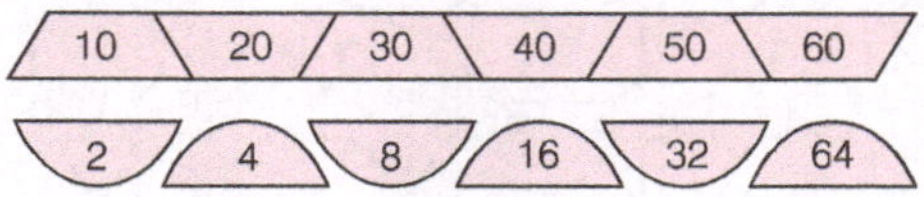

NCERT Pg 110

Q.5 Make a pattern without numbers.

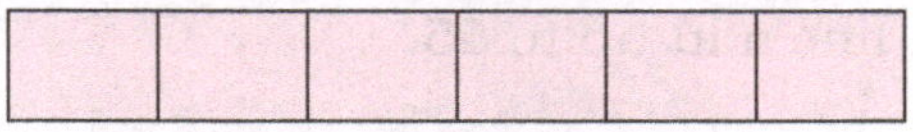

Ans. *

AZ	BY	CX	DW	EV	FU	GT

No Number Comes Twice (NCERT Pg 110)

Q.6 Look at the number box. Can you see a pattern?

Now, you try writing the letters – A, B, C in the box so that no letter comes twice in any line.

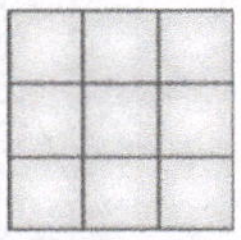

Ans.

A	B	C
C	A	B
B	C	A

Magic Patterns (NCERT Pg 111-112)

Q.7 Look at the pattern of numbers 1 to 7. See how each line adds up to 12!

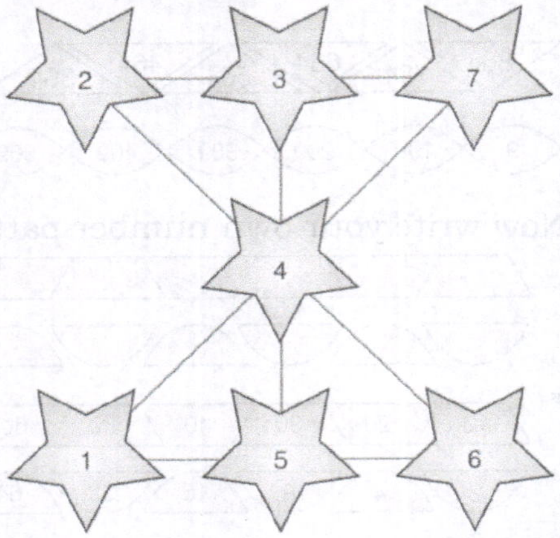

Now, you fill these stars. Use numbers 1 – 9 and the rule that the numbers on each line add up to 15.

Ans. *

Magic Triangles (NCERT Pg 111-112)

Q.8 Look at this number pattern.

Rule Numbers on each side of the triangle add up to 9.

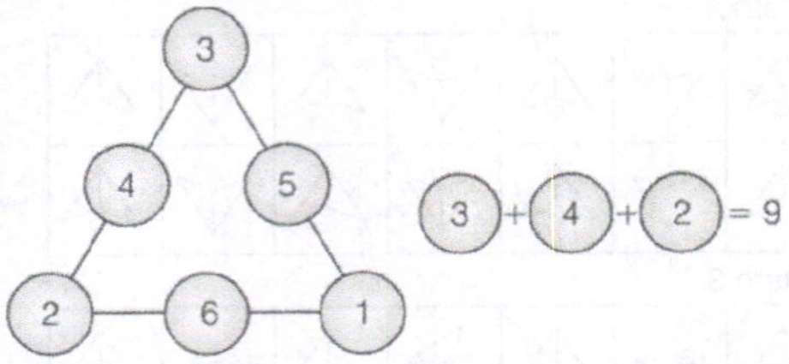

See if the other sides of the triangle also add up to 9.

Ans. Yes, the sides 2-6-1 and 3-5-1 of triangle, also add up to 9.

2 + 6 + 1 = 9 and 3 + 5 + 1 = 9

Q.9 Now, use numbers 1 – 6 to make your own magic triangle.

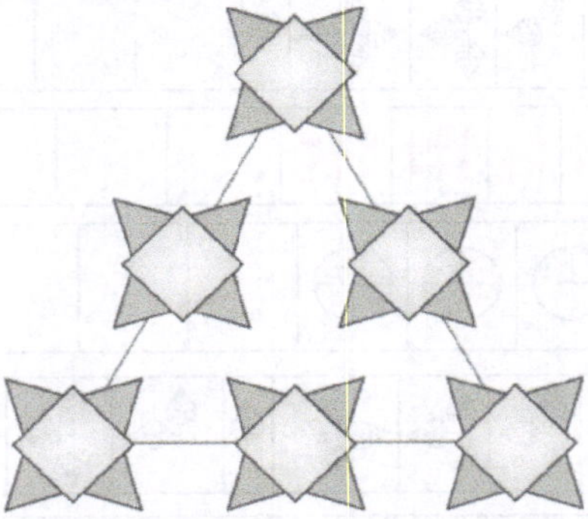

Rule Number on each side must add up to 10.

Ans. *

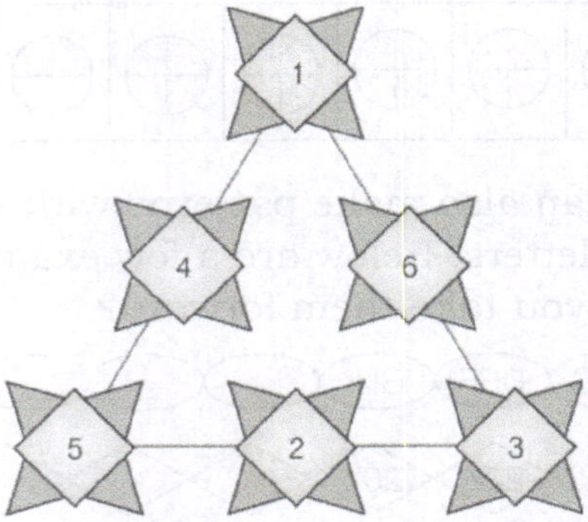

Number Towers (NCERT Pg 112-113)

Q.10 Numbers can be arranged as a tower. We start from below and get this number pattern.

Can you see the rule for this pattern?

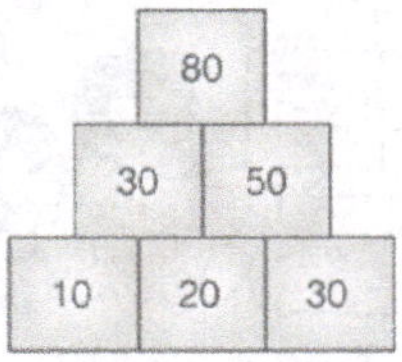

Rule We add 2 numbers below to get the number in the box above them.

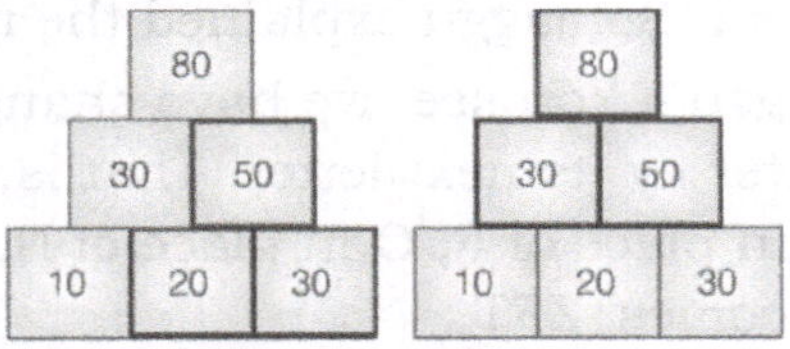

20 + 30 = 50   30 + 50 = 80

Using the same rule, complete these number towers.

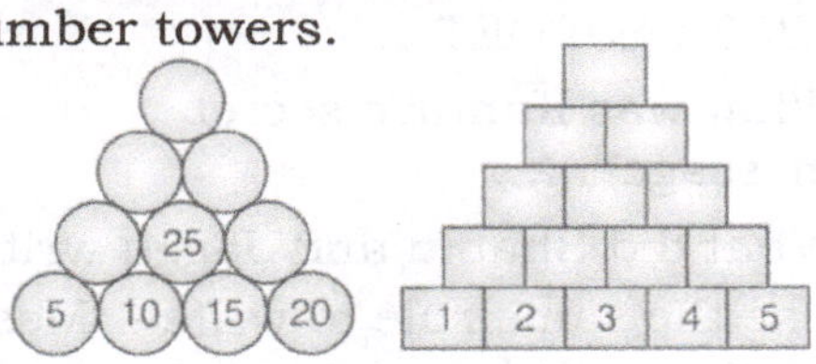

Ans.

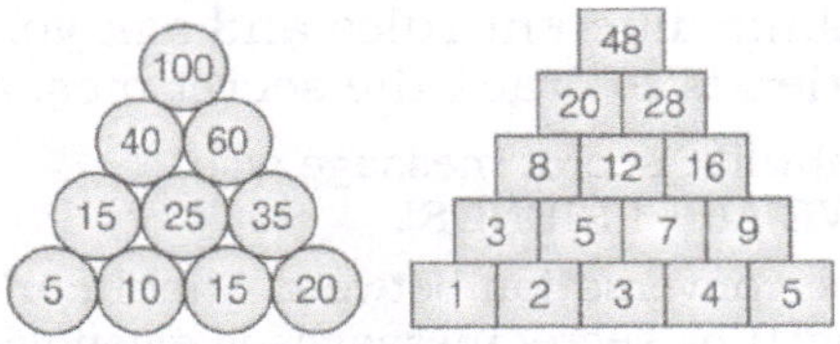

The Same Sum Rule (NCERT Pg 113)

Q.11 Some friends are playing with number cards. See how they add.

Can you see the rule which gives us the same sum each time?

Rule We get, the same sum when we add the two numbers –

11	+	16	=	27
12	+	15	=	27
13	+	14	=	27

First from left and First from right
Second from left and Second from right
Third from left and Third from right

Now, you write any number and the three numbers after that. Make a pattern using the rule.

	+		=	
	+		=	

See if you get the same sum.

Ans. *Number are as given below.

31	32	33	34

31	+	34	=	65
32	+	33	=	65

Patterns with Addition (NCERT Pg 114)

Q.12

Now, you try make such a pattern with 5 numbers in order.

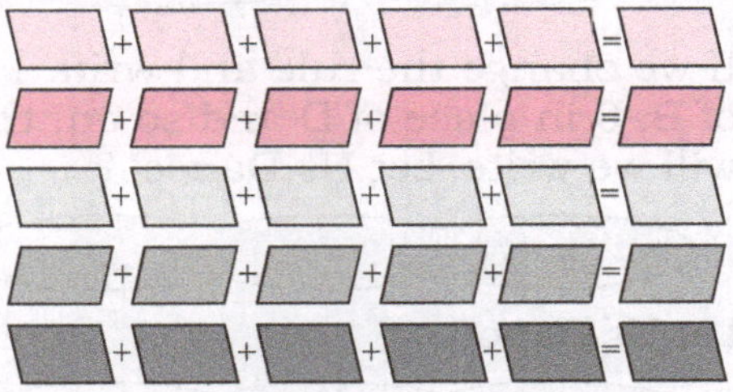

Does the sum grow by 5 each time?

Ans. 1 + 2 + 3 + 4 + 5 = 15
2 + 3 + 4 + 5 + 6 = 20
3 + 4 + 5 + 6 + 7 = 25
4 + 5 + 6 + 7 + 8 = 30
5 + 6 + 7 + 8 + 9 = 35
Yes, the sum grows by 5 each time.

Secret Messages (NCERT Pg 115)

Yamini explained the rule - Numbers have been used for letters.

e.g. J is 10, P is 16.

So, JUMP is 10 21 13 16 .

Q.13 Complete this list of letters and numbers to help you.

A B C D E
1 2 3 4 5

A B C D E
1 2 3 4 5

Ans.

A	B	C	D	E	F	G	H	I	J	K	L	M
1	2	3	4	5	6	7	8	9	10	11	12	13
N	O	P	Q	R	S	T	U	V	W	X	Y	Z
14	15	16	17	18	19	20	21	22	23	24	25	26

Q.14 Teenu wants to write to his friend 'Good Morning'.
What will he write by the same rule?

Ans. Good Morning →

7 15 15 4 13 15 18 14 9 14 7

Q.15 If we change the rule and write 1 in place of B. 3 in place of D and so on, then how will we write 'Let Us Dance' ?

Ans. Let Us Dance →

11 4 19 20 18 3 26 13 2 4

More Secret Message (NCERT Pg 116)

Q.16

Shablu and Jaggu are playing a game. They are writing some secret messages. But Kahuli is not able to understand them. So, jaggu explained the rule –

Jaggu – You see, we have changed each letter by its next letter. That is, we write G in place of F, O in place of N. So, YES becomes ZFT.

Kahuli – Oh! Now, I understand.

Kahuli – See what I have written

XF BSF GSJFOET

(i) What was Kahuli's secret message?......

(ii) What did Shablu and Jaggu write?

(iii) Use the same rule to write – 'Meet me on the moon'.

(iv) Make different rules and ask your friends to crack the secret message.

Ans. (i) Kahuli's, secret message was ' WE ARE FRIENDS'.

(ii) The conversation between Shablu and Jaggu by secret messages is given with their meanings.

Shablu – IFMMP ! IPX BSF ZPV?
– HELLO ! HOW ARE YOU?

Jaggu – GJOF UIBOL ZPV.
– FINE THANK YOU.

Shablu – XJMM ZPV QMBZ XJUI NF?
– WILL YOU PLAY WITH ME?

Jaggu – ZFT !
– YES !

(iii) The secret message for 'meet me on the moon' is 'NFFU NF PO UIF NPPO'.

(iv) **Rule** Replace the letters of words by its opposite letters.

Following this rule the new key will be-

A B C D E F G H I J K L M
Z Y X W V U T S R Q P O N

Secret message - ZIV BLF TLRMT GL HXSLLO?

Upside Down (NCERT Pg 117)

Q.17 Anisha is playing. She is showing her friends that she can stand on her head.

Now, Anisha is playing with this card. Draw what it will look like, when upside down.

Ans. It will look as given below, when it upside down.

Floor Patterns (NCERT Pg 117-119)

Q.18 (i) Have you ever seen a floor with tiles of these shapes?

These designs are made by covering the floor completely with tiles that fit into without any gaps.

(ii) Now, you cover this floor with this tile.

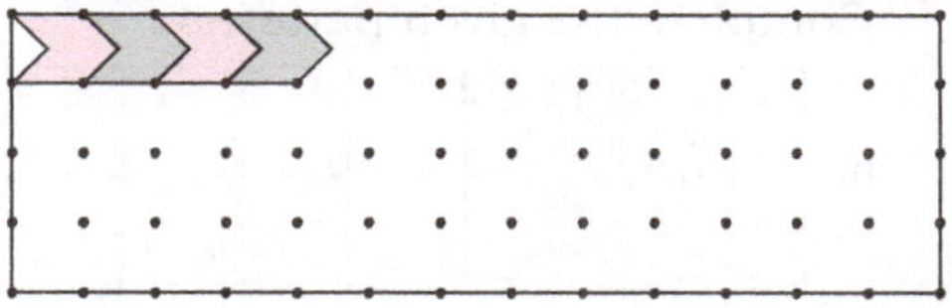

(iii) Can you make such a floor design with a tile like a circle?

(iv) Try with this circle shape tile without leaving a gap. Could you do it? Discuss with your friends.

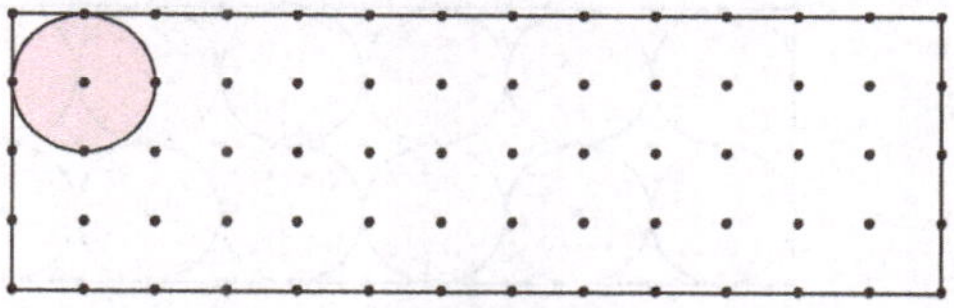

(v) Complete this tiling pattern.

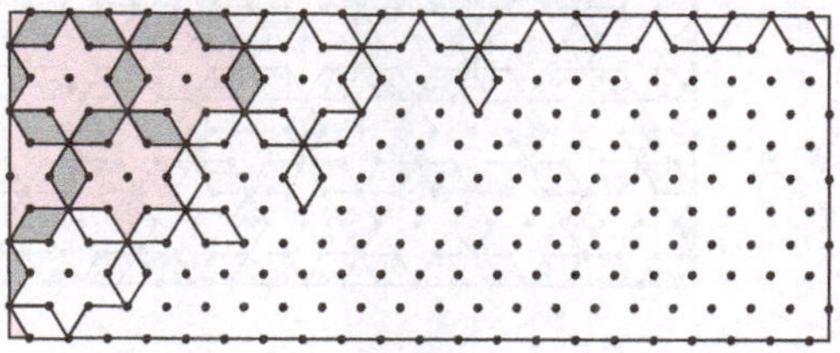

(vi) Ramiya has made a wall with his blocks. Can you complete this for him?

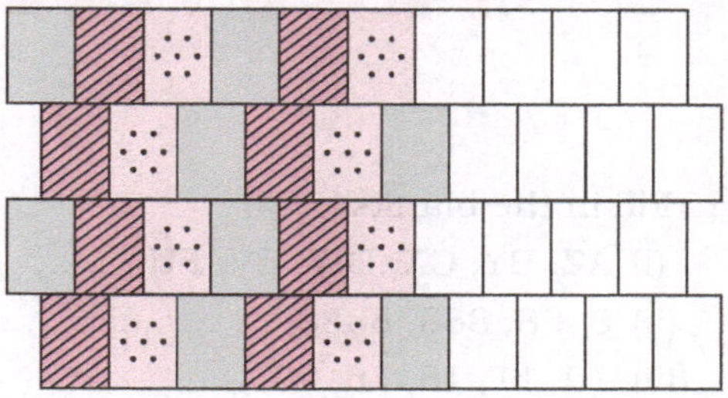

(vii) Renu began to paint this wall. Now, you help her to complete it.

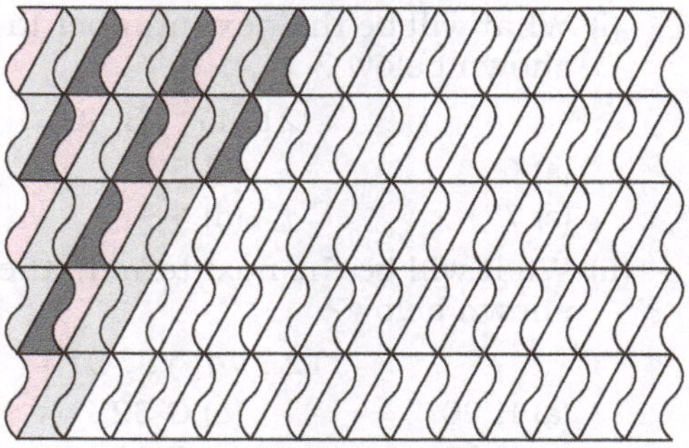

Ans. (i) *No, I have never seen a floor with tiles of these shapes.

(ii)

(iii) No, when we make such a floor design with a tile like a circle, it creates gap between four tiles. So, it is not possible to make such a floor design with a tile like a circle without leaving gaps.

(iv) No, I cannot do it without leaving gap.

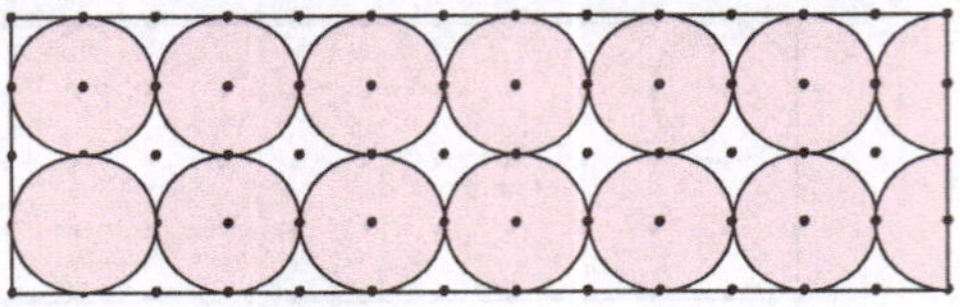

(v)

(vi)

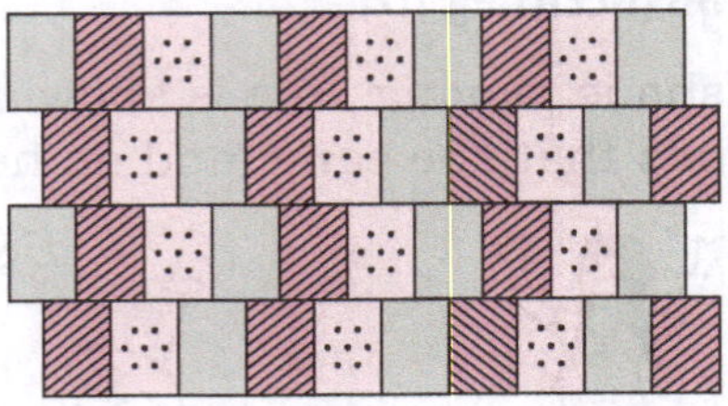

(vii)

PRACTICE QUESTIONS

1. Fill in the blanks.

(i) AZ, BY, CX, DW, EV, FU, ..., ...

(ii) 8, 88, 888, 8888, ..., ...

(iii) 10, 11, 13, 16, 20, ...

(iv) AB, BC, CD, ..., ...FG.

2. Multiple choice questions.

(i) What will be the next number in the pattern shown below ?

21, 17, 13, 9

(a) 6 (b) 5
(c) 7 (d) 4

(ii) What will be the next term in the pattern shown below?

T2 , V4, Y8, C16

(a) H 20 (b) G 32
(c) H 32 (d) G 16

(iii) Given that A corresponds to K, B corresponds to L and D corresponds to N which letter will be there that corresponds to the letter U?

(a) K (b) L
(c) I (d) M

3. Match the following tiling pattern with similar tile?

	Column I		Column II
(i)	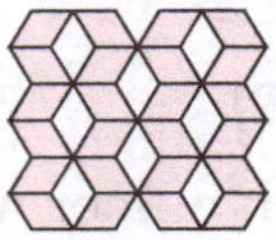	(a)	
(ii)	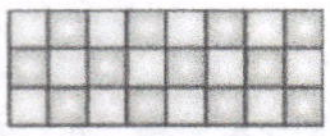	(b)	
(iii)		(c)	
(iv)		(d)	

4. Complete the given patterns.

(i) 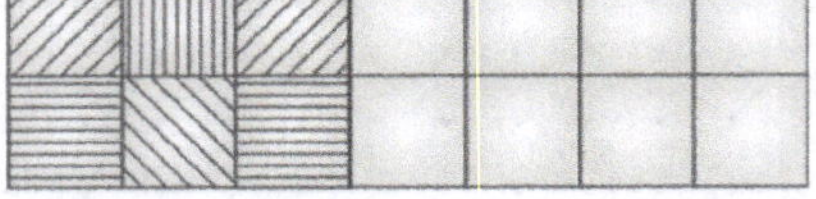

(ii)

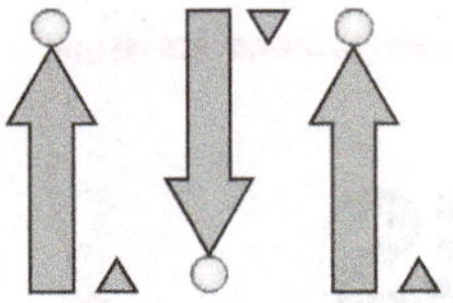

5. Fill these circles, Use numbers 1 - 9 and the rule that the numbers on each line add up to 13.

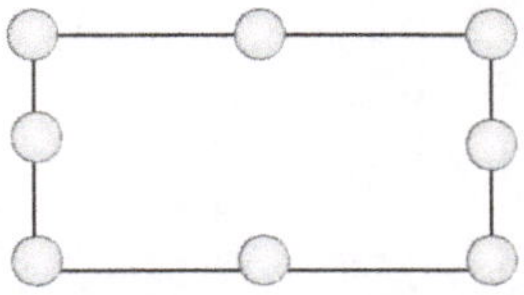

6. If every letter is changed by the previous letter, then find the secret message for 'He is my brother'.

7. Complete the number tower.

(i)

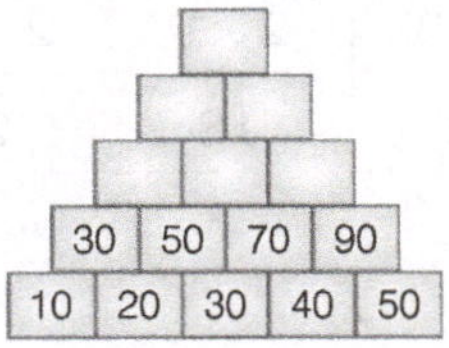

(ii)

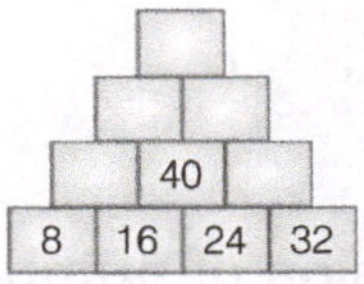

ANSWERS & SOLUTIONS

1. (i) GT, HS (ii) 88888, 888888
(iii) 25 (iv) DE, EF

2. (i) (b) (ii) (c) (iii) (a)

3. (i) → (c) (ii) → (d)
(iii) → (a) (iv) → (b)

4.

(i)

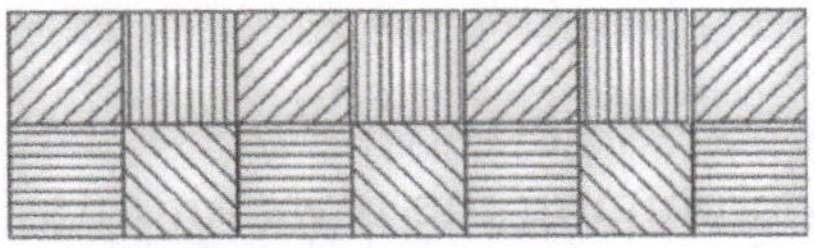

(ii)

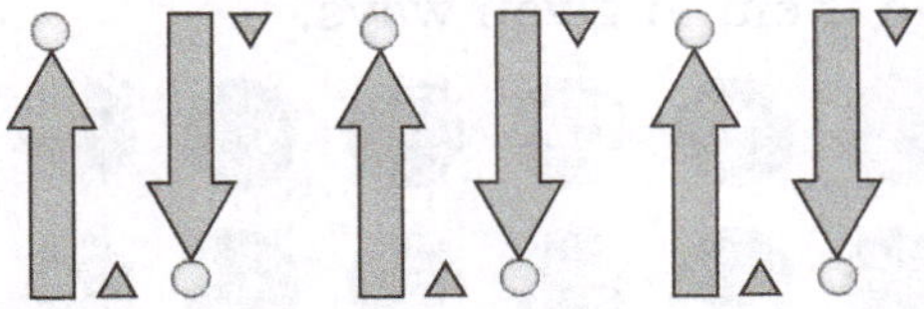

5.

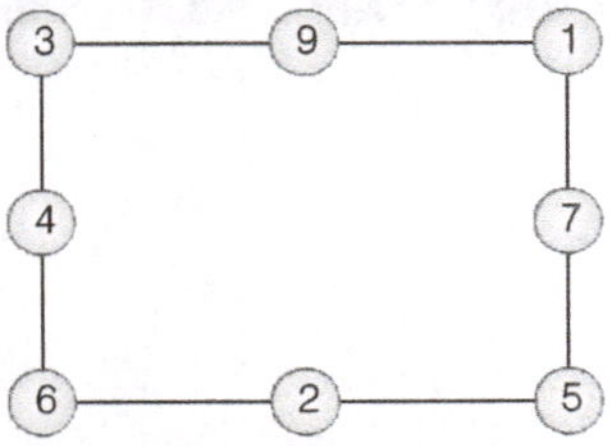

6. 'GD HR LX AQNSGDQ'

7. **Rule** We add 2 numbers below to get the number in the box above them.

(i) $30 + 50 = 80$
$50 + 70 = 120$
$70 + 90 = 160$
$80 + 120 = 200$
$120 + 160 = 280$
$200 + 280 = 480$

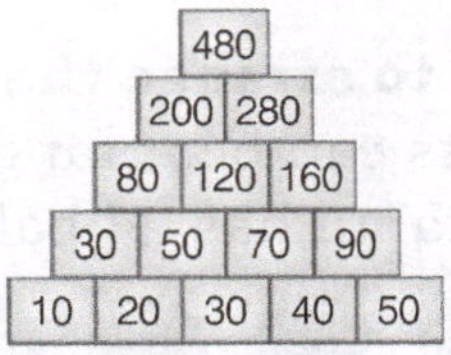

(ii) $8 + 16 = 26$
$24 + 32 = 56$
$24 + 40 = 64$
$40 + 56 = 96$
$64 + 96 = 160$

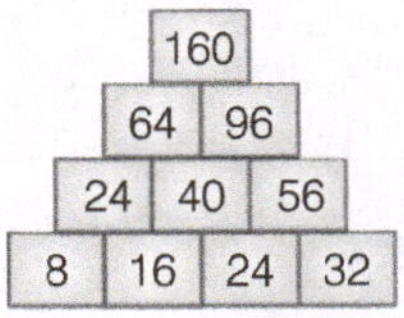

CHAPTER 11 TABLES AND SHARES

Tables

It refers to the multiplication of numbers.

Table of 2

2×1	2×2	2×3	2×4	2×5	2×6	2×7	2×8	2×9	2×10
2	4	6	8	10	12	14	16	18	20

Shares

It refers to the division of numbers.

- Subtracting the small number from the large number until the result is zero.
- Number of times the subtraction occurs, is the 'Quotient' of division.

e.g. $20 \div 4$

First time $\rightarrow 20 - 4 = 16$, Second time $\rightarrow 16 - 4 = 12$,

Third time $\rightarrow 12 - 4 = 8$, Fourth time $\rightarrow 8 - 4 = 4$, Fifth time $\rightarrow 4 - 4 = 0$

The subtraction occurs 5 times to get the result zero.

So, quotient of $20 \div 4$ is 5.

Different ways to arrange the things or objects

Things or objects can be arrange in different ways by changing the rows and its elements. e.g. Rahul has 24 balls. He can arrange them in given ways.

(i) **Row 1**

Row 2

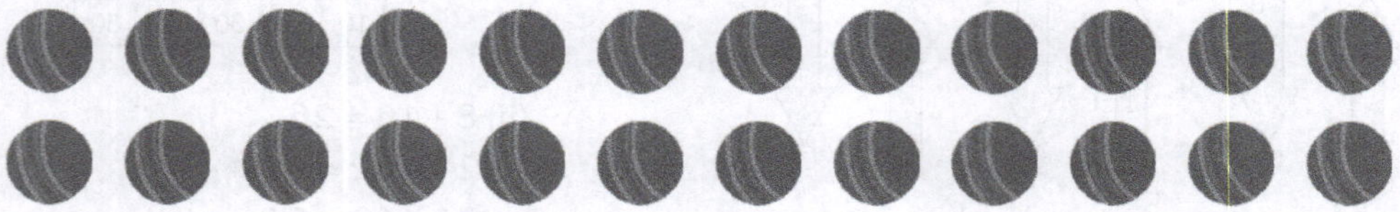

There are 2 rows with 12 balls.

So, total balls $= 2 \times 12 = 24$ balls.

(ii) **Row 1**

Row 2

Row 3

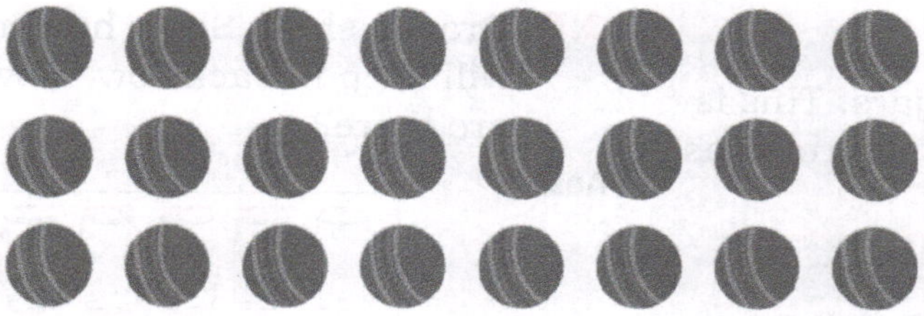

There are 3 rows with 8 balls.

So, total balls = $3 \times 8 = 24$ balls.

Similarly, we can form other different ways.

NCERT FOLDER

Shyama's Garden (NCERT Pg 120)

Shyama has planted sunflower, rose and marigold plants in her garden. She has planted them in three flower-beds. Her garden looks like this.

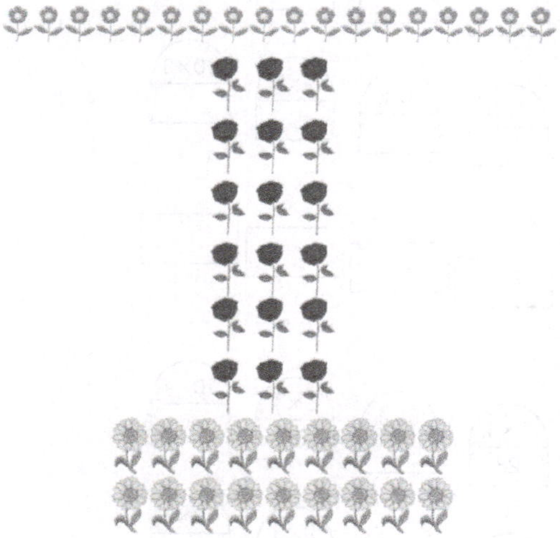

Each flower- bed has a different arrangement.

See how the roses are planted.

$$18 = 6 \times 3$$

So, there are 6 rows with 3 plants each.

Q.1 What are the ways in which the sunflower and marigold are planted?

(i) 18 = ... × ...... So, there is ...... row with ...... plants.

(ii) 18 = ... × ...... So, there are ...... rows with ...... plants each.

Ans. (i) $18 = 1 \times 18$, so there is 1 row with 18 plants.

(ii) $18 = 2 \times 9$, so there are 2 rows with 9 plants each.

Q.2 You too can make your own garden. Draw a garden, showing flower-beds with 48 plants. Each row should have the same number of plants.

Ans. *

I made a garden with 48 flower plants having 4 rows with 12 plants each.

* *Students can write alternate answer as per their choice.*

Jars in the Shelf (NCERT Pg 121)

Q.3 Bheema made a shelf for 30 jars. This is a long shelf with two rows. Each row has the same number of jars.

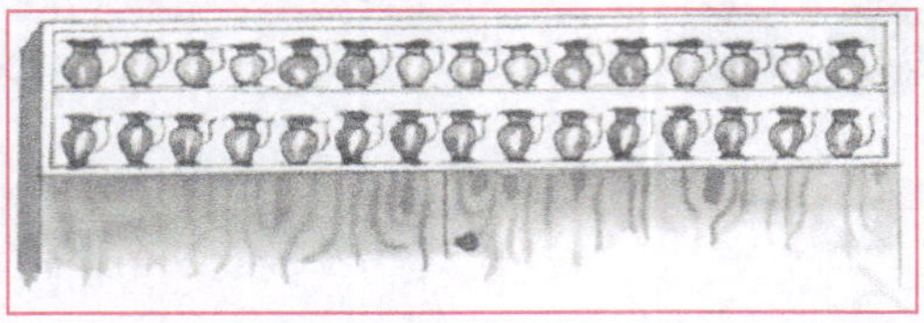

Can you think of other ways to make a shelf to keep 30 jars?

Ans. Yes, I can make a shelf to keep 30 jars in different ways.

(i) 1 row × 30 jars = 30 jars
(ii) 3 rows × 10 jars = 30 jars
(iii) 5 rows × 6 jars = 30 jars
(iv) 6 rows × 5 jars = 30 jars
(v) 10 rows × 3 jars = 30 jars
(vi) 15 rows × 2 jars = 30 jars
(vii) 30 rows × 1 jar = 30 jars

Q.4 Draw a shelf. Show how many jars you will keep in each row. How many rows are there?

Ans. *

The self made for keeping 24 jars. It has 4 rows and each row can keep 6 jars.

Q.5 Have your friends drawn it in different ways?

Ans. Yes, they have drawn it in different ways.

NCERT Pg 122

Q.6 Help Bunty to make the table of 7, using tables of 4 and 3.

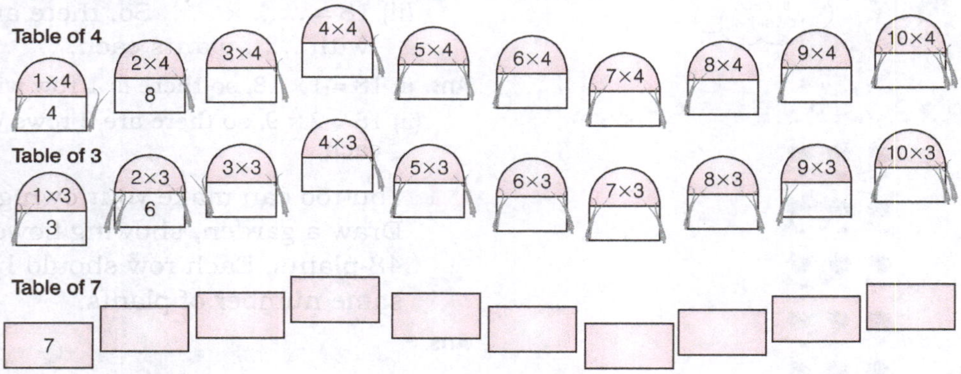

Ans.

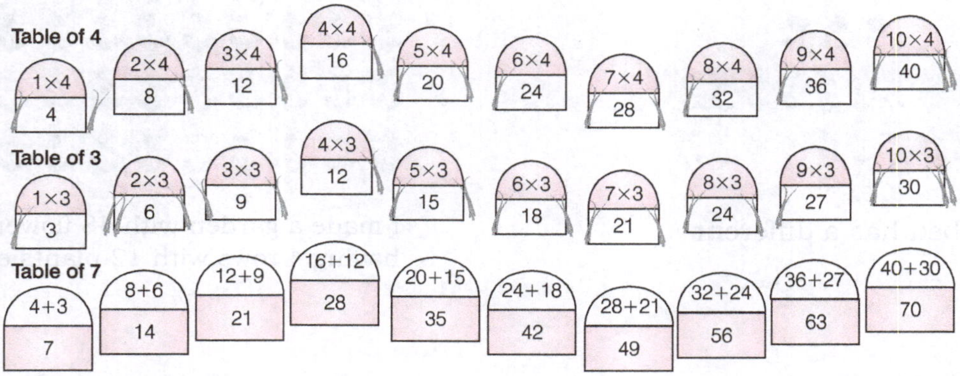

Q.7 Which two tables will you use for writing the table of 12?

Ans. * To write the table of 12, I will use the table of 4 and 8.

The table of 4 is as follows

4 × 1	4 × 2	4 × 3	4 × 4	4 × 5	4 × 6	4 × 7	4 × 8	4 × 9	4 × 10
4	8	12	16	20	24	28	32	36	40

The table of 8 is as follows

8 × 1	8 × 2	8 × 3	8 × 4	8 × 5	8 × 6	8 × 7	8 × 8	8 × 9	8 × 10
8	16	24	32	40	48	56	64	72	80

Now the table of 12 become as given below

4 + 8	8 + 16	12 + 24	16 + 32	20 + 40	24 + 48	28 + 56	32 + 64	36 + 72	40 + 80
12	24	36	48	60	72	84	96	108	120

NCERT Pg 123

Q.8 Some of Gayatri's cats were playing in a box. When she tried to count all, she could see were legs. She counted 28 legs.

(i) How many cats are there in the box?

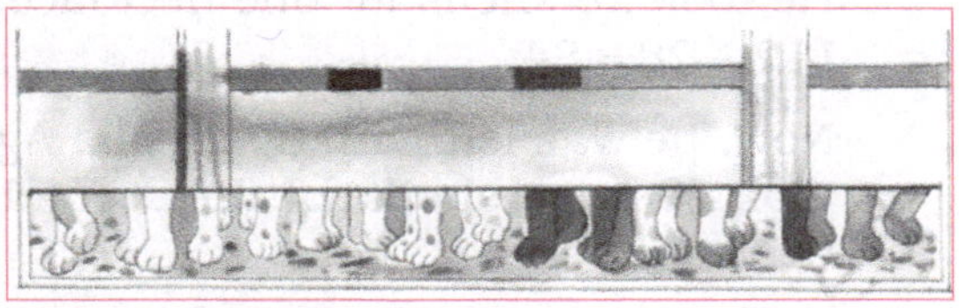

(ii) 8 legs mean 2 cats. 12 legs mean ...... cats.

(iii)

How many legs?	4	8	12				
How many cats?	1	2					

So, 28 legs mean _______ cats.

Ans. (i) Total number of legs is seen by Gayatri in the box = 28

∵ Each cat has 4 legs.

Therefore, number of cats in the box

$$= \frac{\text{Number of legs is seen by Gayatri in the box}}{\text{Number of legs having a cat}}$$

$$= \frac{28}{4} = 7$$

Hence, there are 7 cats in the box.

(ii) 8 legs mean 2 cats. 12 legs mean 3 cats.

(iii)

How many legs?	4	8	12	16	20	24	28
How many cats?	1	2	3	4	5	6	7

So, 28 legs mean 7 cats.

Q.9 Billo has kept his chickens in a box. He counted 28 legs. How many chickens are there?

Ans. A chicken has 2 legs.

∵ Total number of legs = 28.

∴ Number of chickens in the box

$$= \frac{\text{Total number of legs}}{\text{Number of legs having a chicken}}$$

$$= \frac{28}{2} = 14$$

Hence, there are 14 chickens in the box.

Q.10 Leela has not gone to school for 21 days. For how many weeks was she away from school?

Ans. Number of days, Leela has not gone to school = 21 days

∵ Number of days in a week = 7 days.

∴ Number of weeks, she was away from school $= \frac{21}{7} = 3$ weeks

So, Leela has not gone to school for 3 weeks.

Jumping Animals (NCERT Pg 124)

Q.11

(i) A frog jumps 3 steps at a time starting from 0.

(a) Count the jumps he takes to reach 27. So, he has taken 27 ÷ 3 = ... jumps.

(b) He has taken .... jumps, if he is at 36.

(c) If he is at 42, he has taken .... jumps.

(ii) Starting from 0, a rabbit jumps 5 steps at a time.

(a) In how many jumps does he reach 25?

(b) He reaches .... after taking 8 jumps.

(c) He needs .... jumps to reach 55.

Ans. (i) (a) He has taken 27 ÷ 3 = 9 jumps.

(b) He has taken 36 ÷ 3 = 12 jumps.

(c) He has taken 42 ÷ 3 = 14 jumps.

(ii) (a) He has taken 25 ÷ 5 = 5 jumps to reach 25.

(b) ∵ In one jump, rabbit takes 5 steps.

∴ In 8 jumps, he takes = 5 × 8

= 40 steps.

So, he reaches 40 after taking 8 jumps.

(c) In one jump, number of steps taken by rabbit = 5

Number of jumps to reach 55 = $\frac{55}{5}$

= 11

So, rabbit needs 11 jumps to reach 55.

Practice Time (NCERT Pg 124)

Q.12 (i) 28 ÷ 2 = ... (ii) 56 ÷ 7 = ...

(iii) 48 ÷ 4 = ... (iv) 66 ÷ 6 = ...

(v) 96 ÷ 8 = ... (vi) 110 ÷ 10 = ...

Ans. (i) 28 ÷ 2 = 14 (ii) 56 ÷ 7 = 8

(iii) 48 ÷ 4 = 12 (iv) 66 ÷ 6 = 11

(v) 96 ÷ 8 = 12 (vi) 110 ÷ 10 = 11

Sea Shells (NCERT Pg 125)

Q.13 Dhruv lives near the sea. He thought of making necklaces for his three friends. He looked for sea-shells the whole day. He collected 112 sea-shells by evening. Now, he had many different colourful and shiny shells.

He took 28 shells for one necklace.

112 − 28 = 84

Now, he was left with 84 shells. Again, he took 28 more shells for the second necklace.

(i) How many shells are left now?

(ii) Then, he took shells for the third necklace. So, he was left with .... shells.

(iii) How many necklaces can Dhruv make from 112 shells?

(iv) Are the shells enough for making necklaces for all his friends?

Ans. (i) 84 − 28 = 56

There are 56 shells left now.

(ii) 56 − 28 = 28

So, he was left with 28 shells.

(iii) Number of shells needed for one necklace = 28

Number of necklaces made from 112 shells = $\frac{112}{28}$ = 4

So, Dhruv can make 4 necklaces from 112 shells.

(iv) Yes, 112 shells are enough for making necklaces for all his 3 friends.

Try These (NCERT Pg 125-126)

Q.14 Kannu made a necklace of 17 sea-shells. How many such necklaces can be made using 100 sea-shells?

Ans. Total number of sea-shells = 100

Number of sea-shells required for 1 necklace = 17

Number of sea-shells left after making 1 necklace = 100 − 17 = 83

Number of sea-shells left after making 2 necklaces = 83 − 17 = 66

Number of sea-shells left after making 3 necklaces = 66 − 17 = 49

Number of sea-shells left after making 4 necklaces = 49 − 17 = 32

Number of sea-shells left after making 5 necklaces = 32 − 17 = 15

After making 5 necklaces, 15 sea-shells remain.

And it is not possible to make a required necklace with 15 sea-shells.

Hence, Kannu can make 5 necklaces of 17 sea-shells, using 100 sea-shells.

Q.15 One carton can hold 85 soap bars. Shally wants to pack 338 soap bars. How many cartons does she need for packing all of them?

Ans. Total number of soap bars = 338

Number of soap bars can be held by one carton = 85

∴ Number of soap bars left after packing 1 carton = 338 − 85 = 253

Number of soap bars left after packing 2 cartons = 253 − 85 = 168

Number of soap bars left after packing 3 cartons = 168 − 85 = 83

Since, only 83 soap bars are left.

Number of soap bars left after packing 4 cartons = 0

So, Shally needs 4 cartons to pack 338 soap bars.

Q.16 (i) Manpreet wants 1500 sacks of cement for making a house. A truck carries 250 sacks at a time. How many trips will the truck make?

(ii) A driver charges ₹ 500 for a trip. How much will Manpreet pay the driver for all the trips?

Ans. (i) Number of cement-sacks required for making a house = 1500

Number of sacks carried by a truck in one trip = 250

Number of sacks left after first trip
= 1500 − 250 = 1250

Number of sacks left after second trip
= 1250 − 250 = 1000

Number of sacks left after third trip
= 1000 − 250 = 750

Number of sacks left after fourth trip
= 750 − 250 = 500

Number of sacks left after fifth trip
= 500 − 250 = 250

Number of sacks left after sixth trip
= 250 − 250 = 0

So, truck makes 6 trips to carry 1500 sacks of cement.

(ii) Charge for one trip = ₹ 500

∴ Charges for 6 trips = ₹ 500 × 6 = ₹ 3000

So, Manpreet will pay ₹ 3000 to the driver for all the trips.

Gangu's Sweets (NCERT Pg 126-127)

Q.17 Gangu is making sweets for Eid. He has made a tray of 80 laddoos.

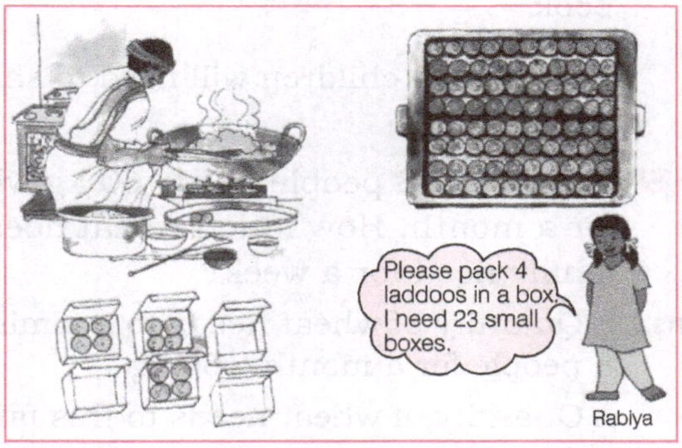

(i) Are the sweets (laddoos) in the tray enough to pack 23 small boxes?

(ii) How many more sweets (laddoos) are needed?

(iii) Gangu also has a bigger box in which he packs 12 laddoos. How many boxes does he need for packing 60 laddoos?

Ans. (i) Total number of laddoos in a tray = 80

Number of laddoos to be pack in a small box = 4 × 23 = 92

∵ 92 > 80

∴ 80 sweets (laddoos) in the tray are not enough to pack 23 small boxes.

(ii) Total number of laddoos in a tray = 80

Total number of laddoos needed for 23 small boxes = 92

Number of more laddoos required = 92 − 80 = 12

So, 12 more laddoos needed to pack 23 small boxes.

(iii) Total number of laddoos to be packed = 60

Number of laddoos to be packed in a bigger box = 12

Number of bigger boxes needed for packing 60 laddoos = $\frac{60}{12} = 5$

So, Gangu needs 5 bigger boxes for packing 60 laddoos.

Practice Time (NCERT Pg 127)

Q.18 Neelu brought 15 storybooks to her class. Today 45 students are present. How many children will need to share one book?

Ans. Number of books are brought by Neelu = 15

Total number of students present in class = 45

Number of children will need to share one book = $\frac{45}{15} = 3$

Therefore, 3 children will need to share one book.

Q.19 A family of 8 people needs 60 kg wheat for a month. How much wheat does this family need for a week?

Ans. ∵ Quantity of wheat needs to a family of 8 people for a month = 60 kg.

∴ Quantity of wheat needs to this family for a day = $\frac{60}{30} = 2$ kg [∵ 1 month = 30 days]

∴ Quantity of wheat needs to this family for a week = 2 kg × 7 = 14 kg

[∵ a week = 7 days]

Therefore, this family needs 14 kg wheat for a week.

Q.20 Razia wants change for ₹ 500.

How many notes will she get if she wants in return

(i) All 100 rupee notes?

(ii) All 50 rupee notes?

(iii) All 20 rupee notes?

(iv) All 5 rupee notes?

Ans. (i) Number of ₹ 100 notes requires to change ₹ 500 = $\frac{500}{100} = 5$

So, 5 notes of ₹ 100 require to change ₹ 500.

(ii) Number of ₹ 50 notes requires to change ₹ 500 = $\frac{500}{50} = 10$

So, 10 notes of ₹ 50 require to change ₹ 500.

(iii) Number of ₹ 20 notes requires to change ₹ 500 = $\frac{500}{20} = 25$

Therefore, 25 notes of ₹ 20 require to change ₹ 500.

(iv) Number of ₹ 5 notes requires to change ₹ 500 = $\frac{500}{5} = 100$

Therefore, 100 notes of ₹ 5 require to change ₹ 500.

Q.21 You have to distribute 72 tomatoes equally in 3 baskets. How many tomatoes will there be in each?

Ans. Total number of tomatoes = 72

and total number of baskets = 3

$\because$ Tomatoes are equally distributed in all 3 baskets.

$\therefore$ Number of tomatoes in a basket $= \frac{72}{3}$

$= 24$

Hence, there will be 24 tomatoes in each basket.

Q.22 There are 350 bricks in a hand-cart. Binod found the weight of a brick to be 2 kg. What will be the weight of all the bricks?

Ans. Total number of bricks in a hand cart = 350

$\because$ Weight of one brick = 2 kg

$\therefore$ Weight of all 350 bricks = 2 kg × 350

= 700 kg

So, weight of all the bricks is 700 kg.

Another Method (NCERT Pg 129)

Q.23 Mridul and Lokesh are trying 70 ÷ 5 in a different way.

Lokesh writes —

	5+6
First, I give ₹ 5 to each. →	5) 70
I have distributed 5 × 5= ₹ 25 →	−25
Next, I give ₹ 6 more to everyone.	45
I have distributed 30 rupees more. →	−30
	?

(i) Now, I am left with .... rupees.

(ii) How will Lokesh distribute the rest of the money? Complete it.

(iii) So, each child gets 5 + 6 + ... = ... rupees.

(iv)

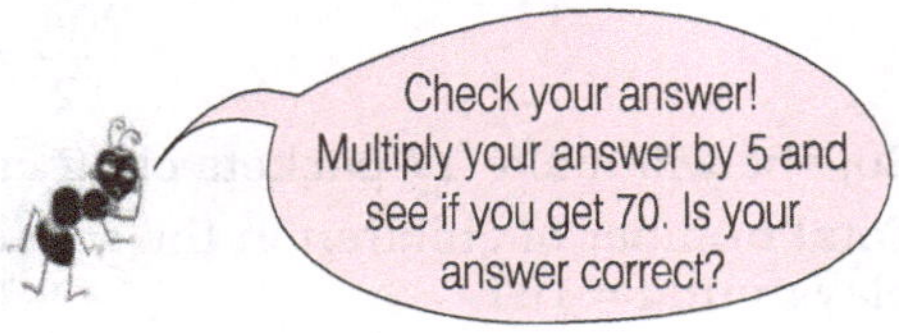

Ans. (i) Now, I am left with 70 – 25 – 30 = 15 rupees.

```
   5+6
5) 70
  −25
   45
  −30
   15
```

(ii) Now, Lokesh is left with ₹ 15.

So, he gives ₹ 3 more to everyone.

```
   5+6+3
5) 70
  −25
   45
  −30
   15
  −15
    0
```

(iii) So, each child gets 5 + 6 + 3 = 14 rupees.

(iv) $\because$ Each child gets ₹ 14.

$\therefore$ Total money to 5 childs = ₹ 14 × 5 = ₹ 70

So, Yes, my answer is correct.

Your Method (NCERT Pg 129)

Q.24 (i) Now use your own method to divide ₹ 70 equally among 5 people. If you want you can start by giving ₹ 2 to each. Or you can even start with ₹ 11 to each.

(ii)

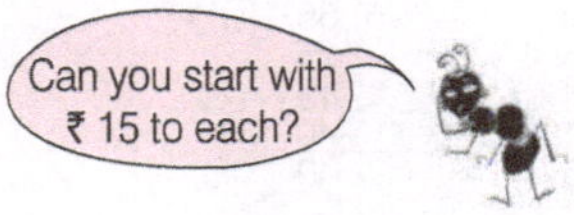

Ans. *(i) Start by giving ₹ 2 to each.

```
   2+5+5+2
5) 70
  −10
   60
  −25
   35
  −25
   10
  −10
    0
```

So, each child gets = 2 + 5 + 5 + 2 = ₹ 14

Now, start by giving ₹ 11 to each.

```
   11+2+1
5) 70
  −55
   15
  −10
    5
   −5
    0
```

So, each child gets = 11 + 2 + 1 = ₹ 14

(ii) Start by giving ₹ 15 to each.

$$\begin{array}{r} 15 \\ 5\overline{)\,70} \\ -75 \\ \hline -5 \end{array}$$

∵ 5 times of 15 is more than 70.

∴ We cannot start with ₹ 15 to each.

Try Doing These (NCERT Pg 129-130)

25. (i) $5\overline{)\,65}$ (ii) $84 \div 2$

(iii) $3\overline{)\,69}$ (iv) $90 \div 6$

(v) $4\overline{)\,72}$ (vi) $9\overline{)\,108}$

(vii) $232 \div 2$ (viii) $2\overline{)\,428}$

(ix) (a) Meera made 204 candles to sell in the market. She makes packets of 6. How many packets will she make?

(b) If she packs them in packets of 12, then how many packets will she make?

(x) On Sports Day, 161 children are in the school playground. They are standing in 7 equal rows.

How many children are there in each row?

Ans. (i)

$$\begin{array}{r} 5+8 \\ 5\overline{)\,65} \\ -25 \\ \hline 40 \\ -40 \\ \hline 0 \end{array}$$

So, $5\overline{)\,65} = (5 + 8) = 13$

(ii)

$$\begin{array}{r} 10+10+20+2 \\ 2\overline{)\,84} \\ -20 \\ \hline 64 \\ -20 \\ \hline 44 \\ -40 \\ \hline 4 \\ -4 \\ \hline 0 \end{array}$$

So, $84 \div 2 = 10 + 10 + 20 + 2 = 42$

(iii)

$$\begin{array}{r} 12+5+6 \\ 3\overline{)\,69} \\ -36 \\ \hline 33 \\ -15 \\ \hline 18 \\ -18 \\ \hline 0 \end{array}$$

So, $3\overline{)\,69} = 12 + 5 + 6 = 23$

(iv)

$$\begin{array}{r} 10+5 \\ 6\overline{)\,90} \\ -60 \\ \hline 30 \\ -30 \\ \hline 0 \end{array}$$

So, $90 \div 6 = 10 + 5 = 15$

(v)

$$\begin{array}{r} 15+3 \\ 4\overline{)\,72} \\ -60 \\ \hline 12 \\ -12 \\ \hline 0 \end{array}$$

So, $4\overline{)\,72} = 15 + 3 = 18$

(vi)

$$\begin{array}{r} 10+2 \\ 9\overline{)\,108} \\ -90 \\ \hline 18 \\ -18 \\ \hline 0 \end{array}$$

So, $9\overline{)\,108} = 10 + 2 = 12$

(vii)

$$\begin{array}{r} 100+10+6 \\ 2\overline{)\,232} \\ -200 \\ \hline 32 \\ -20 \\ \hline 12 \\ -12 \\ \hline 0 \end{array}$$

So, $232 \div 2 = 100 + 10 + 6 = 116$

(viii)

$$\begin{array}{r} 200+10+4 \\ 2\overline{)\,428} \\ -400 \\ \hline 28 \\ -20 \\ \hline 8 \\ -8 \\ \hline 0 \end{array}$$

So, $2\overline{)\,428} = 200 + 10 + 4 = 214$

(ix) (a) Total number of candles = 204

Number of candles in one packet = 6

Number of packets of candles Meera made

$$= \frac{204}{6} = 34$$

So, Meera will make 34 packets of 6 candles.

(b) Total number of candles = 204

Number of candles in one packet = 12

Number of packets made by Meera

$$= \frac{204}{12} = 17$$

So, she will make 17 packets of 12 candles.

(x) Total number of children in the school playground = 161

Number of rows = 7

Given that the number of children in each row is equal.

∴ Number of children in each row = $\frac{161}{7}$

$= 23$

So, there are 23 children in each row.

Story Problems (NCERT Pg 130-132)

26. Look at the pictures and make questions.

(i)

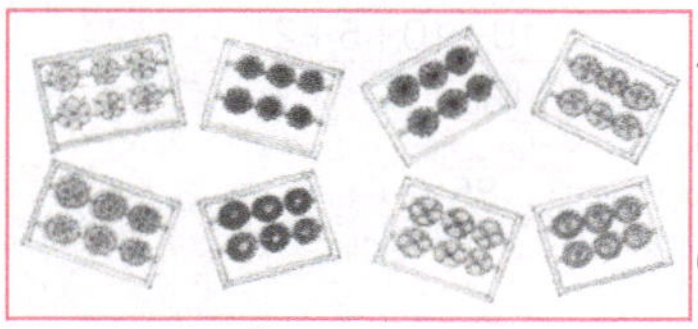

There are 8 packets of rakhis.

Each packet has 6 rakhis in it

Your question ____________________

(ii)

There are 10 packets of sugar. Saurabh paid 110 rupees for all the packets.

Your question ____________________

(iii)

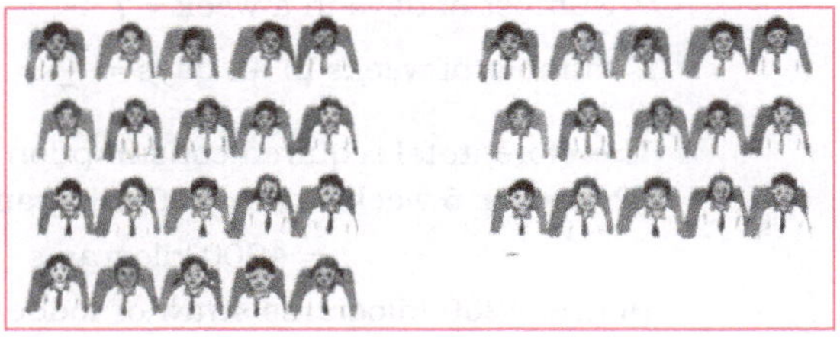

There are 35 students in 7 rows. Each row has the same number of students.

Your question ____________________

(iv) Hari, Seema, Chinku and Lakshmi are going to Guwahati. The cost of one rail ticket is ₹ 62.

Your question ____________________

(v) One metre of cloth costs ₹ 20. Lalbiak bought some cloth and paid ₹ 140.

Your question ____________________

Ans. (i) **My question** How many rakhis are there in all packets?

(ii) **My question** What is the cost of 1 packet of sugar?

(iii) **My question** How many students are there in each row?

(iv) **My question** How many rupees they paid for all 4 tickets?

(v) **My question** How many metres of cloth was bought by Lalbiak for ₹ 140?

PRACTICE QUESTIONS

1. Multiple choice questions.

(i) There are 96 plants in 8 rows and each row has equal number of plants. So, each row has ...... number of plants.

(a) 12 (b) 16 (c) 24 (d) 18

(ii) Ram arranges their books in a self. It has 5 rows and each row has 8 books. Total number of books are

(a) 20 (b) 16
(c) 40 (d) 38

(iii) In a room, Ramesh counted 144 legs of chairs. Number of chairs in the room is

(a) 48 (b) 36
(c) 38 (d) 34

(iv) Radha has 195 pearls. She makes the necklaces using 32 pearls. How many necklaces can she make through 195 pearls?

(a) 8 (b) 7
(c) 9 (d) 6

2. A monkey jumps 6 steps at a time starting from1.

(i) He has taken .... jumps to reach 43.
(ii) If he is at 31, he has taken .... jumps.
(iii) After taking 9 jumps, where did he reach?

3. Complete this division by filling the boxes.

```
    10+10+5+2
5 ) 135
   −□
    85
   −50
    □
   −□
    10
   −□
    0
```

4. Mohan packs 18 pens in a box. How many boxes does he need for packing 144 pens?

5. In a cattle shed, 700 kg straw or fodder consumed in a week. How much fodder does this cattle shed required for 42 days?

6. Frame the questions

(i) There are 45 students in a class. Sohan distributes 4 mangoes to every student.

(ii) In a plant nursery, there are 1800 plants. All the plants are placed in 75 rows.

ANSWERS & SOLUTIONS

1. (i) (a) (ii) (c) (iii) (b) (iv) (d)

2. (i) 7 (ii) 5 (iii) 55

3.

```
    10+10+5+2
5 ) 135
   −[50]
    85
   −50
    [35]
   −[25]
    10
   −[10]
    0
```

4. Total number of pens = 144

Number of pens in one box = 18

∴ Number of boxes need for packing 144 pens

$$= \frac{144}{18} = 8$$

Hence, Mohan needs 8 boxes for packing 144 pens.

5. Given that 700 kilograms straw or fodder consumed in a week.

∵ Number of days in a week = 7

∴ Number of weeks in 42 days $= \frac{42}{7} = 6$

Therefore, total required consumption for 42 days or 6 weeks = (6 × 700) kilograms
= 4200 kilograms

Hence, 4200 kilograms straw or fodder is required for 42 days in the cattle shed.

6. (i) In a class, there are 45 students. Sohan distributes 4 mangoes to each child. Find the number of mangoes distributed by Sohan.

(ii) In a plant nursery, 1800 plants are placed in 75 rows and each row has equal number of plants. How many plants are placed in each row?

CHAPTER 12 HOW HEAVY? HOW LIGHT?

Heavy and Light Objects

The object which has less weight as compared to another object, is called light object and another object is called heavy object. e.g. Cotton and feather are light objects while wood and iron are heavy objects.

Balance

It is an instrument that is used to determine or measure the weight of an object.

Addition or subtraction of the weights

- Weights can be added/subtracted only if they are in same units.

  e.g. (i) 15 kilograms + 45 kilograms = 60 kilograms

  (ii) 1500 grams – 350 grams = 1150 grams

- The weight with different units cannot be added/subtracted directly. First, we convert them in same units, then we add/subtract them.

  e.g. (i) 12 kilograms + 75 grams = 12000 grams + 75 grams

  [∵ 1 kilogram = 1000 grams]

  = 12075 grams

  (ii) 7 kilograms – 500 grams = 7000 grams – 500 grams

  [∵ 1 kilogram = 1000 grams]

  = 6500 grams

NCERT FOLDER

NCERT Pg 133-134

Q.1 Jaiju and Mannu were shifting house. They loaded all their things on a horse-cart. There were many things like-a water tank, five sacks of wheat, three tables, an almirah, four chairs, two mattresses, three sacks of rice, a bamboo ladder, pots and pans.

Father gave them some idea of the weight of each thing.

Thing loaded	Weight
A sack of wheat	100 kg
A sack of rice	35 kg
Water tank	50 kg
Almirah	70 kg
A table	10 kg
A chair	5 kg
A mattress	20 kg
Bamboo ladder	10 kg
Pots and pans	10 kg

(i) Find out the total weight they had loaded on the cart.

(ii) Which things should be removed so that the weight of the load is not more than 700 kg?

Ans. (i)

Things loaded	Weight	Number of items	Their total weights
A sack of wheat	100 kg	5	5×100 $= 500$ kg
A sack of rice	35 kg	3	$3 \times 35 = 105$ kg
Water tank	50 kg	1	$1 \times 50 = 50$ kg
Almirah	70 kg	1	$1 \times 70 = 70$ kg
A table	10 kg	3	$3 \times 10 = 30$ kg
A chair	5 kg	4	$4 \times 5 = 20$ kg
A mattress	20 kg	2	$2 \times 20 = 40$ kg
Bamboo ladder	10 kg	1	$1 \times 10 = 10$ kg
Pots and pans	10 kg		10 kg
			Total = 835 kg

So, they loaded 835 kg of weight on the cart.

(ii) *Total loaded weight on cart = 835 kg

Weight to be removed = 835 kg − 700 kg

= 135 kg

The weight of 3 sacks of rice = 105 kg

The weight of 4 chairs = 20 kg

The weight of a bamboo ladder = 10 kg

Total weight of these three things

$= 105 + 20 + 10 = 135$ kg

Thus, the things that should be removed are 3 sacks of rice, 4 chairs and a bamboo ladder.

NCERT Pg 134

Q.2 Now you also make your own balance. Write down how you made it. Also, draw a picture of your balance in the box below.

Ans. To make a balance, I need a straight and strong stick of suitable length, 2 pans and 6 threads or ropes of equal and suitable length for tying the pans. Pans are tied on the both ends of stick. A hole is made in the middle of stick to hold it. Now, my balance is ready for use.

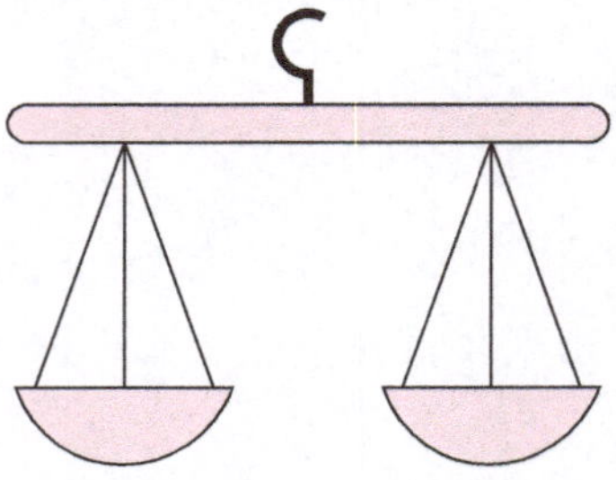

** Students can write alternate answer as per their choice.*

NCERT Pg 135

Q.3 Mannu and Jaiju put a pencil and a geometry box in the two pans of the balance. Which pan will go down? Why? Draw a picture to show it.

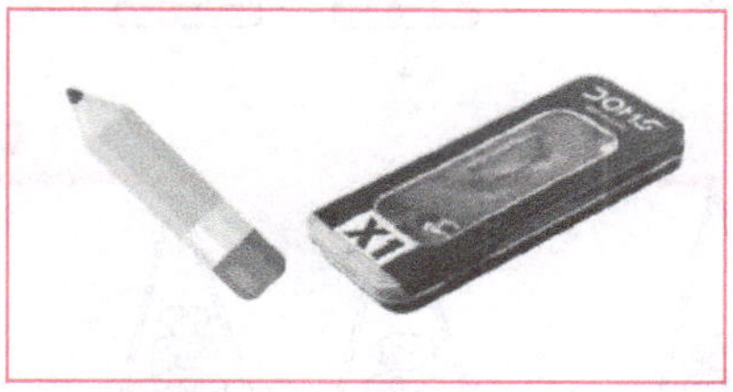

Ans. Since, weight of geometry box is more than the weight of pencil.

So, pan which holds the geometry box will go down.

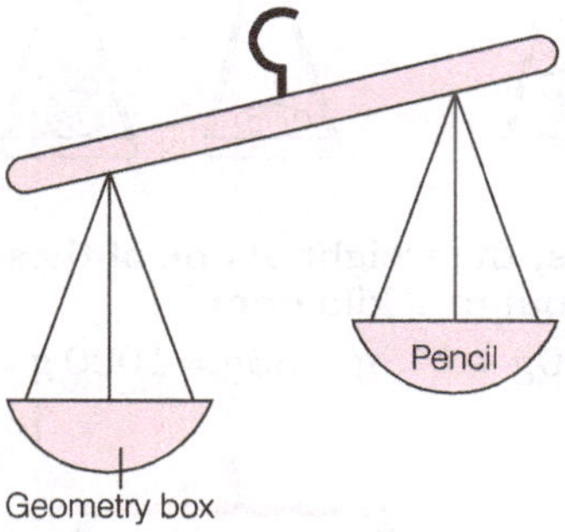

What is Heavier? (NCERT Pg 135)

Q.4 Make pairs of different things and use the balance to decide which is heavier.

First guess which thing will take the pan down and then check with your balance.

Ans. *

S.No.	Pairs	My guess
(i)	Cooker and spoon	Cooker is heavier than spoon.
(ii)	Bat and ball	Bat is heavier than ball.
(iii)	Shoes and shocks	Shoes are heavier than shocks.
(iv)	Bucket and mug	Bucket is heavier than mug.
(v)	Plastic chair and wooden chair	Wooden chair is heavier than plastic chair.

What is the Heaviest? (NCERT Pg 135)

Q.5 Make groups of three things.

For example-eraser, ball and paper. Use the balance to arrange them in order of weight - the lightest, the one with in-between weight, the heaviest.

Complete the table with at least five examples.

Lightest	In-between weight	Heaviest
Paper	Eraser	Ball

Ans. *

Lightest	In-between weight	Heaviest
Paper	Eraser	Ball
Pen	Geometry box	Book
Mug	Bucket	Water tank
Handkerchief	Wrist watch	Mobile
Orange	Papaya	Watermelon

Q.6 Can you find your own weight using this balance?

Ans. No.

Making Weights (NCERT Pg 136)

Q.7 (i) Get a new cake of soap. The packet will have the weight written on it. You can use this soap to make your own different weights.

The soap weighs .... grams (g).

(ii) Take a small plastic packet. Put it in one pan of the balance. Put the soap in the other pan. Slowly add sand to the packet till the pans are balanced. Close the packet with rubber band or string.

Now, stick a strip of paper and write '......... g' on it.

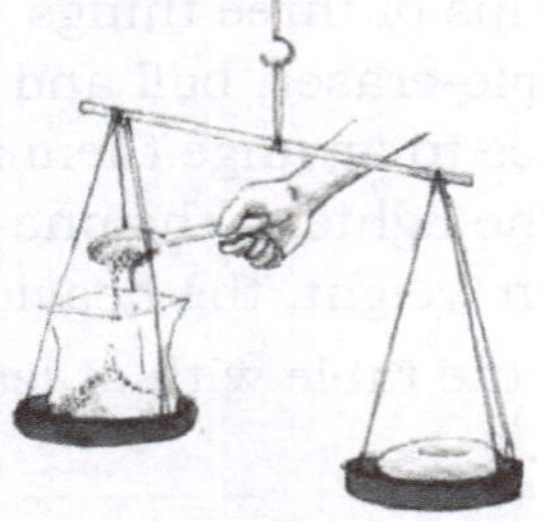

(iii) If you put the soap and the weight you just made together in a pan, how many grams will both these weigh?

Ans. *(i) The soap weighs 50 grams.

*(ii) Now, stick a strip of paper and write 50 g on it.

*(iii) Both of these will weigh 50 g + 50 g = 100 g

Practice Time (NCERT Pg 137)

Q.8 (i) Which pan of the balance will go down? Show by drawing an arrow.

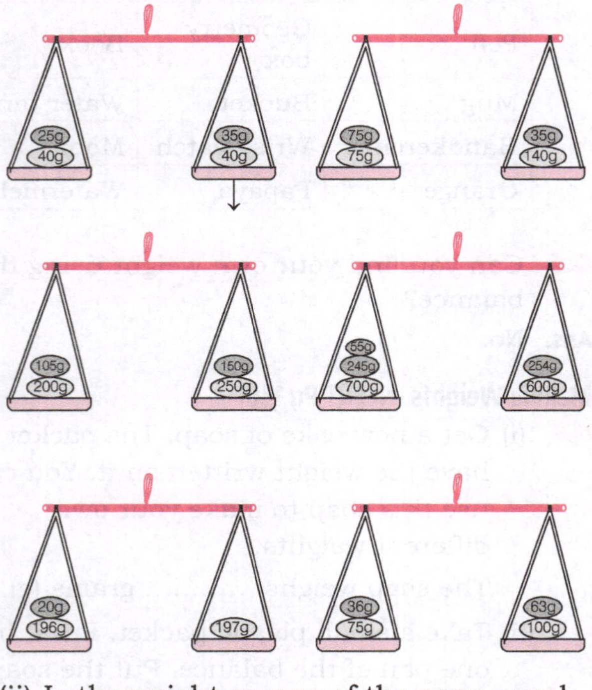

(ii) Is the weight on any of the pans equal to 1 kilogram? Mark it.

Ans. (i)

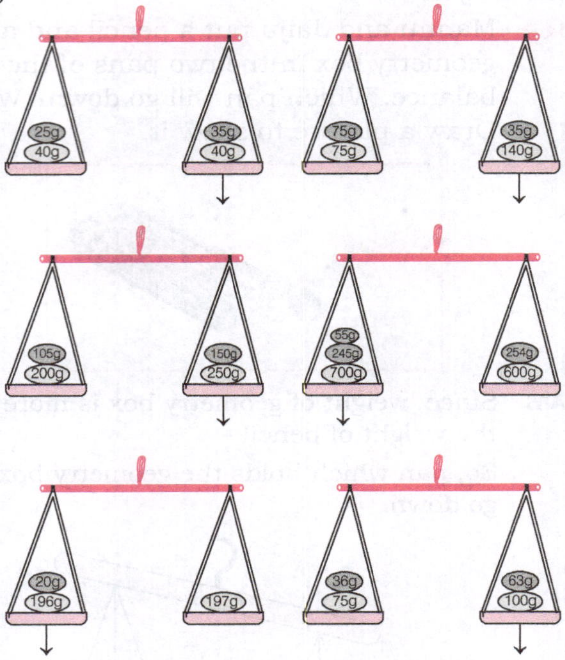

(ii) Yes, the weight of one of these pans is equal to 1 kilogram.

700g + 245g + 55g = 1000 g = 1 kg

[∵ 1000 g = 1 kg]

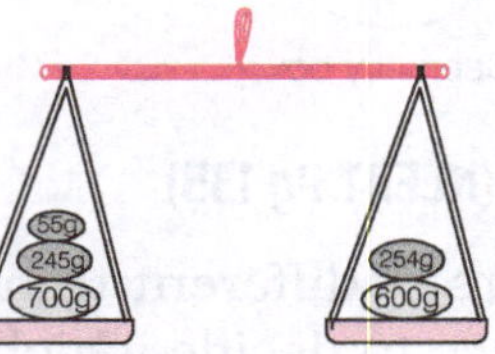

Q.9 How many grams are there in 1 kg?

Ans. There are 1000 grams in 1 kg.

Grams and Kilograms (NCERT Pg 138)

Q.10 Name 5 things that we usually buy –

	In grams		In kilograms
(i)		(i)	
(ii)		(ii)	
(iii)		(iii)	
(iv)		(iv)	
(v)		(v)	

Ans. *

	In grams		In kilograms
(i)	Tea	(i)	Wheat flour
(ii)	Pepper	(ii)	Rice
(iii)	Coriander powder	(iii)	Potato
(iv)	Turmeric powder	(iv)	Sugar
(v)	Alum	(v)	Watermelon

Q.11 Which is heavier - 1 kilogram cotton or 1 kilogram iron?

Ans. Both 1 kilogram cotton and 1 kilogram iron have equal weight. So, both are equal.

Dinesan Went Shopping (NCERT Pg 139)

Q.12 Dinesan went to a shop and bought some things. His younger brother cut the end of the bill where the weights were written.

Guess and write the weight of each thing he bought-in g or kg.

Items	Weight
Rice	5
Sugar	1
Mustard seeds	10
Wheat	3
Dal	500
Tea	250
Pepper	25

Ans.

Items	Weight
Rice	5 kg
Sugar	1 kg
Mustard seeds	10 g
Wheat	3 kg
Dal	500 g
Tea	250 g
Pepper	25 g

Car and Tractor (NCERT Pg 139)

Q.13 Ritu is weighing her toys. She wants to know if her tractor is heavier than her car. How would you help her to find out quickly?

Ans. It can be done by keeping tractor in one pan and car in another pan of the balance and the pan which goes down is heavier than other.

Q.14 Guess which is the heaviest - a real car, a bus or a tractor?

Ans. The bus is the heaviest.

Q.15 Which is the heaviest thing you have seen?

Ans. The heaviest thing, I have ever seen is a train.

Elephant's weight (NCERT Pg 140-142)

Q.16 Now imagine what happened next and complete the story.

Discuss with your friends how Vaidika's daughter found the weight of the elephant.

Ans. After marking the water level on the boat, she requested to remove the elephant from the boat.

Now, she requested to king to put the gold on the boat till the water level touched the raised water level mark when elephant was on the boat.

Now, king was left with no alternatives.

Therefore, he had to give the gold equal to the weight of the elephant to Vaidika.

How Much the Chair Weighs (NCERT Pg 143)

Q.17 Anamika wants to weigh this chair using the weighing machine.

Can you suggest a way for doing this?

Ans. First, put any flat slab on the weighing machine on which chair can be kept easily. Note down the weight of slab. Now, put the chair on the slab and note down the total weight.

Now, subtract the weight of slab from the total weight of slab and chair. The difference is the weight of the chair.

Broken Stones (NCERT Pg 143-144)

Q.18 Now you show how Abdu will use these stone pieces to weigh–

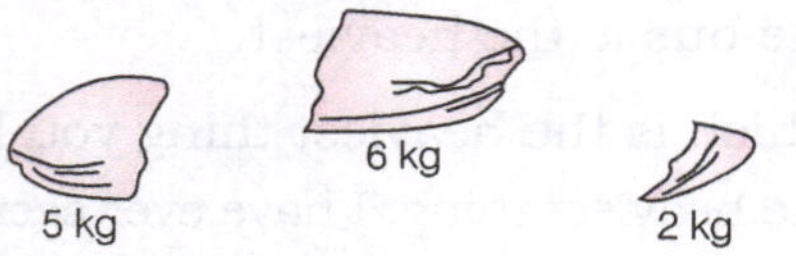

(i) 4 kg of firewood.

(ii) 3 kg of firewood.

(iii) 7 kg of firewood.

Ans. (i)

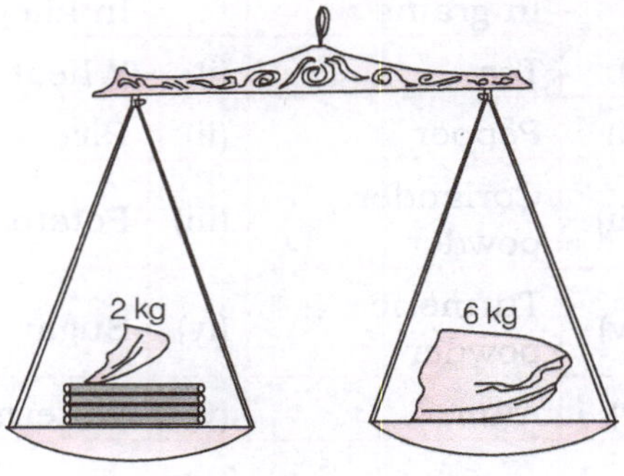

(ii)

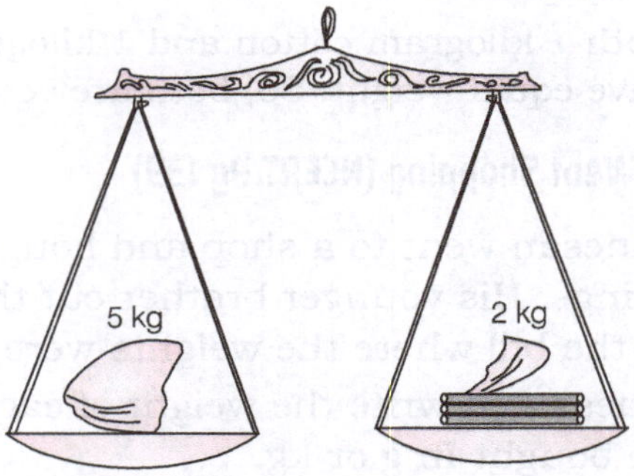

(iii)

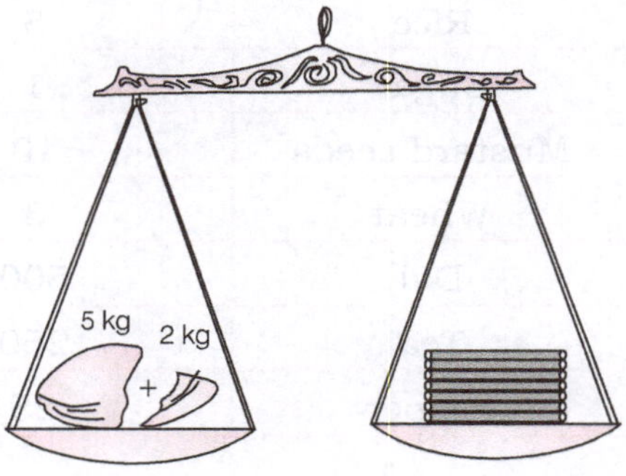

Post Office (NCERT Pg 145-146)

Q.19 (i) Have you ever been to a post office?

(ii) What different things do people go there for?

Ans. (i) Yes, I have been to a post office many times with my grandfather.

(ii) People go to post office to post the letters, parcels, money orders and buy the stamps, envelops.

They also go there for banking reasons.

Q.20 Postal Rates

Postal Items	Postal Rates (in ₹)
Single post card	0.50
Printed post card	6.00
Inland Letter	2.50
Letter weighting-	
(i) 20 grams or less	5.00
(ii) For every additional 20 grams	2.00
Parcel weighing-	
(i) 50 grams or less	5.00
(ii) For every additional 50 grams	3.00

(i) How much does a postcard cost?

(ii) How much does an inland letter cost?

(iii) How much will you have to pay for stamps on a letter weighing 50 grams?

(iv) Akash wants to send a parcel of the Math Magic textbook to his friend Rani in Chennai. The book weighs 200 g. See the chart to find the cost of posting the book.

(v) Read the weight shown in the picture. Find out the cost of sending a parcel of that weight.

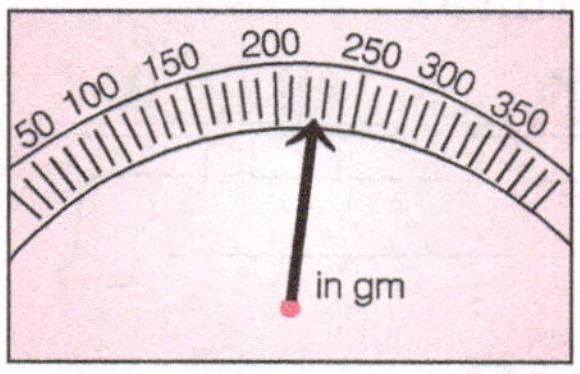

Parcel weight = ________

Cost of stamps = ________

Ans. (i) The cost of single postcard is ₹ 0.50 and cost of printed postcard is ₹ 6.

(ii) The cost of an inland letter is ₹ 2.50.

(iii) For 50 grams letter,

The cost of stamps for first 20 grams = ₹ 5

The cost of stamps for next 20 grams = ₹ 2

and the cost of stamps for last 10 grams = ₹ 2

Total cost of stamps for 50 grams

= ₹ 5 + ₹ 2 + ₹ 2

= ₹ 9

So, I have to pay ₹ 9 for stamps on a letter weighing 50 grams.

(iv) For 200 grams parcel,

The cost of stamps for first 50 grams = ₹ 5

The cost of stamps for second 50 grams = ₹ 3

The cost of stamps for third 50 grams = ₹ 3

and the cost of stamps for last 50 grams = ₹ 3

So, total cost of stamps for 200 grams parcel = ₹ 5 + ₹ 3 + ₹ 3 + ₹ 3 = ₹ 14

Hence, the cost of posting the book is ₹ 14.

(v) The weighing machine showing the weight of parcel = 225 grams

For this 225 grams parcel,

The cost of stamps for first 50 grams = ₹ 5

The cost of stamps for second 50 grams = ₹3

The cost of stamps for third 50 grams = ₹ 3

The cost of stamps for fourth 50 grams = ₹ 3

And the cost of stamps for last 25 grams = ₹ 3

So, total cost of stamps for 225 grams parcel = ₹ 5 + ₹ 3 + ₹ 3 + ₹ 3 + ₹ 3 = ₹ 17

Hence, the cost of sending a parcel of 225 grams weight is ₹ 17.

Parcel weight = 225 grams.

Cost of stamps = ₹ 17

How Many Stamps? (NCERT Pg 146)

Q.21 Rahul needs stamps of Rupees 25 for his parcel. He went to the post office. Only stamps of ₹ 1, ₹ 2, ₹ 5 and ₹ 10 were there at that time. Using those stamps in how many different ways can he make ₹ 25?

(i) Can you show five different ways?

(ii) What is the heaviest parcel he can send using stamps of ₹ 25?

Ans. *(i) Cost of stamps for Rahul's parcel = ₹ 25

Cost of stamps available at that time

= ₹ 1, ₹ 2, ₹ 5 and ₹ 10

He can make ₹ 25 by different ways

(a) ₹ 10 + ₹ 10 + ₹ 5 = ₹ 25

(b) ₹ 10 + ₹ 10 + ₹ 2 + ₹ 2 + ₹ 1 = ₹ 25

(c) ₹ 10 + ₹ 5 + ₹ 5 + ₹ 5 = ₹ 25

(d) ₹ 5 + ₹ 5 + ₹ 5 + ₹ 5 + ₹ 5 = ₹ 25

(e) ₹ 10 + ₹ 5 + ₹ 5 + ₹ 2 + ₹ 1 + ₹ 1 + ₹ 1 = ₹ 25

(ii)

Weight of parcel (in grams)	Cost of stamps (in ₹)	Money left to Rahul (in ₹)
50	5	20
100	5 + 3 = 8	17
150	8 + 3 = 11	14
200	11 + 3 = 14	11
250	14 + 3 = 17	8
300	17 + 3 = 20	5
350	20 + 3 = 23	2

The heaviest parcel that he can send using stamps of ₹ 25 is 350 grams.

Our Weight Together (NCERT Pg 146)

Q.22 A frog was struggling to escape from the mouth of a crow. How can I escape? The frog thought. Suddenly a trick came to his mind.

He asked the crow, Are you good at arithmetic? If yes, then I will ask you a problem. Your weight is 650 g and I am only 145 g. How much do we weigh together? The crow was good at Mathematics, so he happily opened his beak to answer.

What happened after that? So what was the answer the crow wanted to give?

Ans. As crow opened his mouth, frog jumped out from his mouth.

The answer given by crow as - together our weight was 650 g + 145 g = 795 g.

Am I Fit or Fat? (NCERT Pg 147)

Q.23 Now you also fill the table by finding out the age, height and weight of any five friends.

Ans. *

Name	Age	Height	Weight
Rohan	9	4 feet 2 inch	28 kg
Gaurav	7	3 feet 11 inch	26 kg
Abhishek	8	4 feet 1 inch	27 kg
Rohit	9	4 feet	28 kg
Ram	8	3 feet 10 inch	25 kg

How Many Oranges? (NCERT Pg 148)

Q.24 **Puzzle**

All oranges have equal weight. The two papayas have the same weight. The weights in the first and second balances are equal. How many oranges balance the weight in the third?

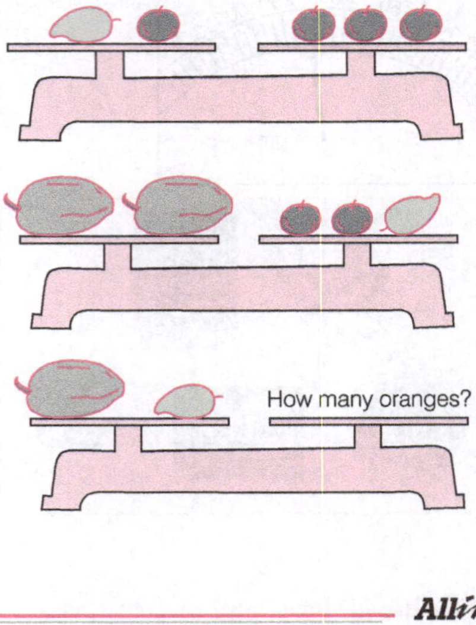

Ans. In first balance,

1 mango + 1 orange = 3 oranges

∴ 1 mango = 2 oranges

In second balance,

2 papayas = 2 oranges + 1 mango

∵ 1 mango = 2 oranges

∴ 2 papayas = 2 oranges + 2 oranges

= 4 oranges

∴ 1 papaya = 2 oranges

In third balance,

1 papaya + 1 mango

= 2 oranges + 2 oranges

= 4 oranges

So, 4 oranges balance the weight in third balance.

Find That Marble (NCERT Pg 148)

Q.25 There are 3 marbles of the same size but one marble is slightly heavier or lighter than the other two. Can you find which is that marble and if it is heavier or lighter? You can use a balance only two times.

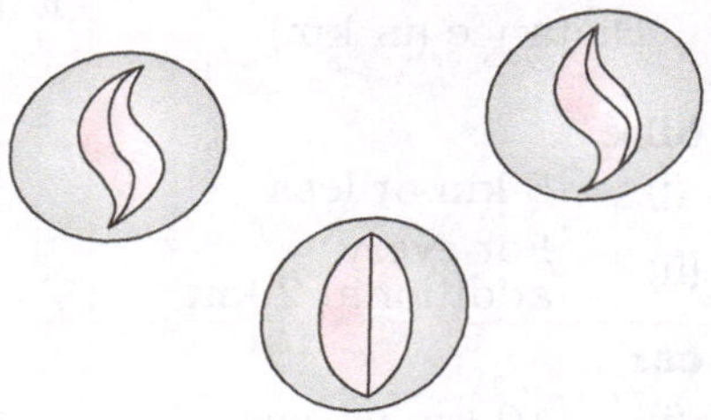

Ans. Let P, Q and R be the three marbles. One of them is heavier or lighter than others.

Case I Put marbles P and Q in different pans. If both will be equal, then R is heavier or lighter than these marbles.

Case II Put P and R in different pans.

(i) If they are equal, then Q is heavier or lighter.

(ii) If $P < R$, then $Q = R$ and P is lighter than Q and R.

PRACTICE QUESTIONS

1. Fill in the boxes.

(i) 6 kg 750g + 8 kg 900 g + 2 kg 350 g = □

(ii) 49 kg + 105 kg + 73 kg 500 g + 15 kg + 350 g = □

(iii) 32 kg – 18 kg 650 g – 3 kg 150 g = □

(iv) 12 kg 75 g – 8 kg 155 g – 2 kg 350 g = □

2. Multiple choice questions.

(i) Which of the following things is heaviest?

(a) Pencil (b) Eraser

(c) Bat (d) Balloon

(ii) A shopkeeper has 15 bags of flour. Each bag is having a weight of 5 kg. What is the total weight of the bags?

(a) 15 kg (b) 5 kg

(c) 50 kg (d) 75 kg

(iii) The weight of a guava can be

(a) 25 g (b) 250 g

(c) 2000 g (d) 3000 g

3. Make different weights of 1 kg, 2 kg and 5 kg using packet of 1 kg detergent powder.

4. Which pan of the balance will go up side? Show by drawing an arrow (↑).

(i)

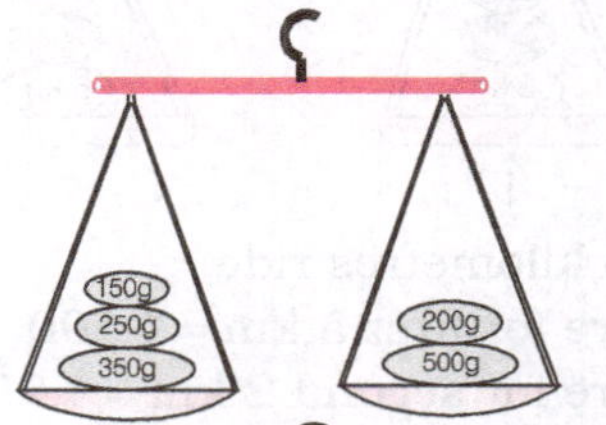

(ii)

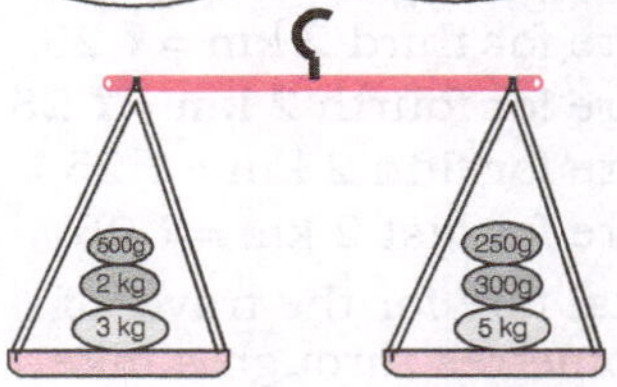

5. In a tourist place, the fare of different vehicles is shown below.

Distance (in km)		Fare Rates (in ₹)
For bike		
(i)	5 km or less	₹ 100
(ii)	For every additional 2 km	₹ 25
For car		
(i)	10 km or less	₹ 350
(ii)	For every additional 5 km	₹ 120

(i) Ranjeet travels 15 kilometres through a bike. How much fare will he pay for this?

(ii) How much money did Mohan pay, if he travelled 38 kilometres by a car?

6. A vegetable vendor uses four weights of 1 kg, 3 kg, 6 kg and 8 kg to weight the vegetables of different weights.

How will he use these weight to weight different things?

(i) 13 kg of potato

(ii) 16 kg of pumpkin

ANSWERS & SOLUTIONS

1. (i) 18 kg (ii) 242 kg 850 g (iii) 10 kg 200 g (iv) 1 kg 570 g

2. (i) (c) (ii) (d) (iii) (b)

3.

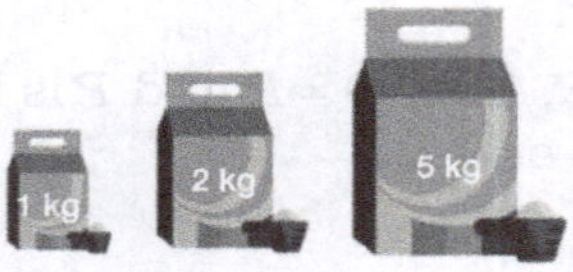

4.

(i)

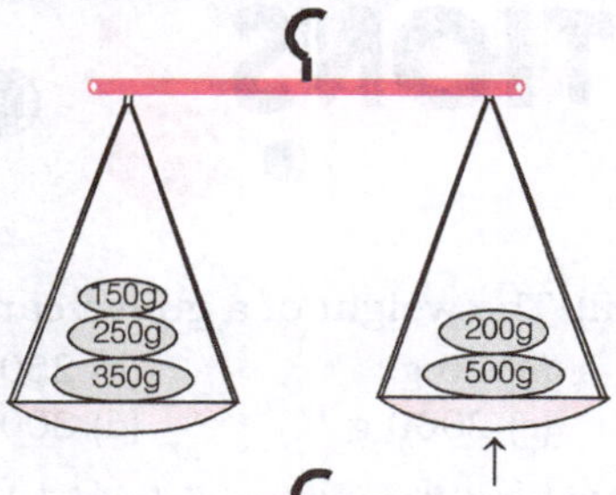

(ii)

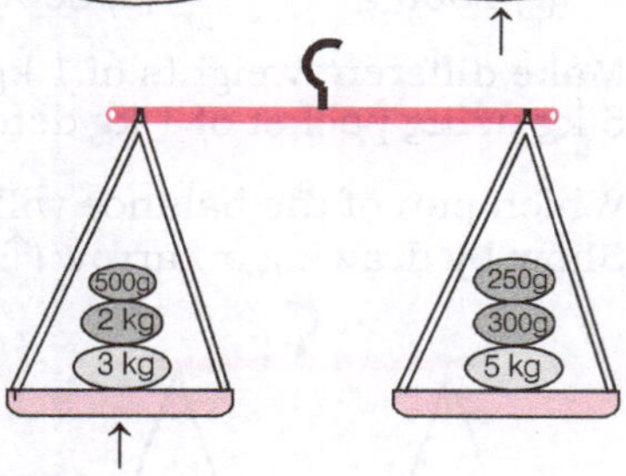

5. (i) For 15 kilometres ride,

The fare for first 5 km = ₹ 100

The fare for second 2 km = ₹ 25

The fare for third 2 km = ₹ 25

The fare for fourth 2 km = ₹ 25

The fare for fifth 2 km = ₹ 25

The fare for last 2 km = ₹ 25

So, total fare for the travel of 15 kilometres through a bike

= ₹100 + ₹25 + ₹25 + ₹25 + ₹25 + ₹25

= ₹ 225

(ii) For 38 kilometres travel,

The fare for first 10 km = ₹350

The fare for second 5 km = ₹120

The fare for third 5 km = ₹120

The fare for fourth 5 km = ₹120

The fare for fifth 5 km = ₹120

The fare for sixth 5 km = ₹120

The fare for last 3 km = ₹120

So, total fare that Mohan has to pay for 38 kilometres travel by car

= ₹350 + ₹120 + ₹120 + ₹120 + ₹120 + ₹120 + ₹120

= ₹1070

6.

(i)

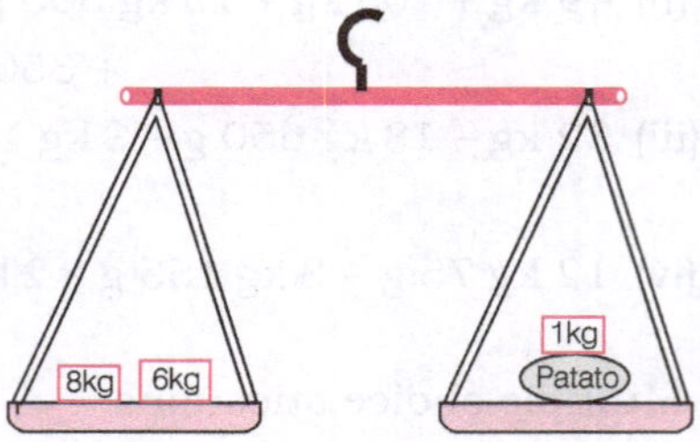

(ii)

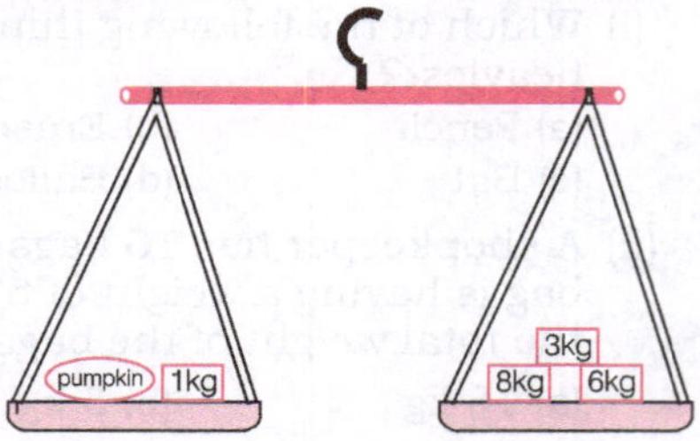

CHAPTER 13 FIELDS AND FENCES

Boundary or Perimeter

The total length around the outside of a shape is called its boundary or perimeter.

e.g. Boundary of this shape = Sum of all sides

= 5 cm + 3 cm + 3 cm + 5 cm + 4 cm = 20 cm

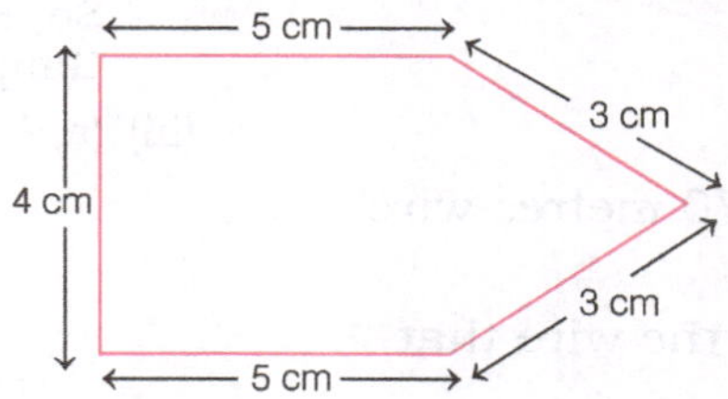

Measurement of Boundary

1. **Boundary of simple shapes**

We can find the boundary of simple shapes like triangle, quadrilateral, pentagon, etc. easily by adding the measurements of sides.

e.g. (i) Boundary = 5 cm + 3 cm + 4 cm = 12 cm

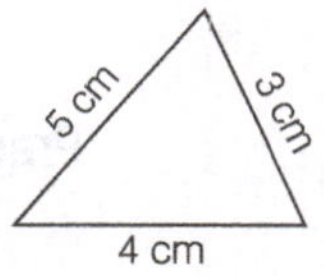

(ii) Boundary = 5 cm + 8 cm + 3 cm + 12 cm = 28 cm

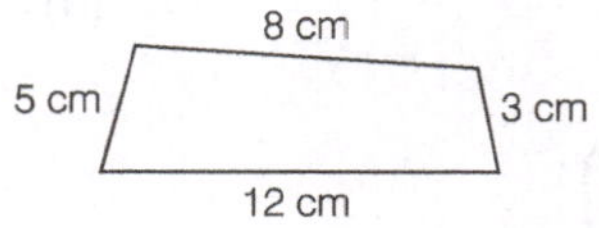

2. **Boundary of complex shapes**

Boundary of complex shapes like fields, etc. are measured by thread or rope. Take a long piece of thread and place it along the boundary of the shape. Then, cut the exact length of thread, needed for covering the shape, starting from one point and coming back to the same point.

Now, measure the length of thread, which is equal to the boundary of the shape.

NCERT FOLDER

NCERT Pg 149-150

Q.1 (i) Rahmat needs to find the length of the boundary of the field. Can you find it from this picture? See the length of each side written near it.

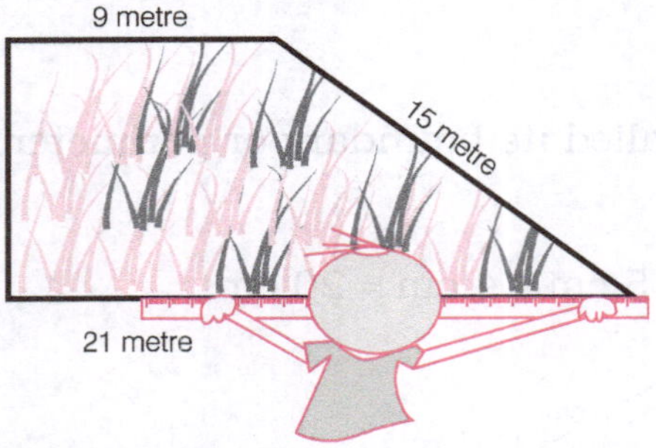

(ii) Rahmat bought a roll of 70 metres wire for the fence.

Ganpat Can you give me the wire that is left with you?

I will use it for my field.

Rahmat Oh sure, why not!

How much wire did Rahmat give to Ganpat?

(iii) Ganpat thanked Rahmat and started fencing his own field. But he needed to get more wire.

(a) How long is the boundary of Ganpat's field?

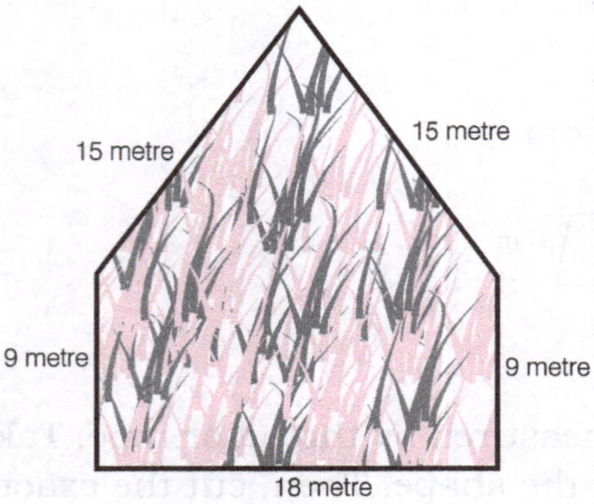

(b) How much more wire will Ganpat need for his field?

Ans. (i) Length of the boundary of the Rahmat's field

= 9 metre + 9 metre + 15 metre + 21 metre

= 54 metre

Hence, the length of the boundary of the Rahmat's field is 54 metre.

(ii) Total length of roll = 70 metre

Length of wire used by Rahmat = 54 metre

Length of wire left to Rahmat = 70 – 54

= 16 metre

So, Rahmat gave 16 metre of wire to Ganpat.

(iii) (a) Length of the boundary of Ganpat's field

= 9 metre + 18 metre + 9 metre + 15 metre + 15 metre

= 66 metre

Hence, the length of the boundary of Ganpat's field is 66 metre long.

(b) Boundary of Ganpat's field = 66 metre

Length of wire received from Rahmat

= 16 metre

Length of required wire = 66 – 16

= 50 metre

So, Ganpat needs 50 metre more wire for his field.

Practice Time (NCERT Pg 151-152)

Q.2 Here are pictures of some more fields. Find out which one has the longest boundary.

(a)

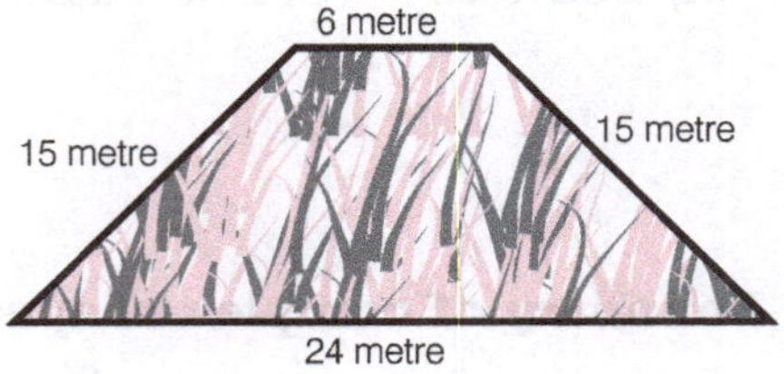

Boundary = ____________ metre

* *Students can write alternate answer as per their choice.*

(b)

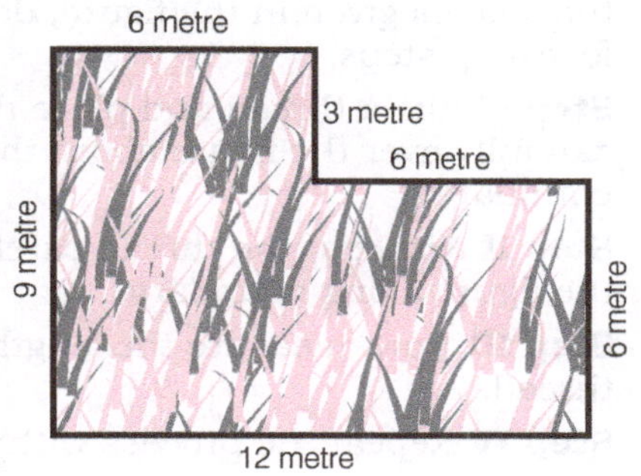

Boundary = ___________ metre

(c)

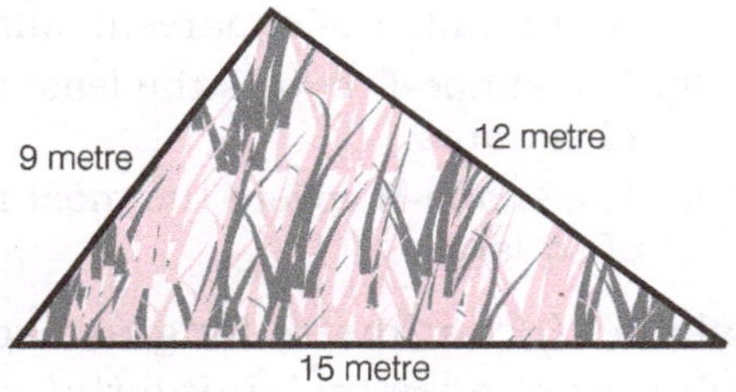

Boundary = ___________ metre

(d)

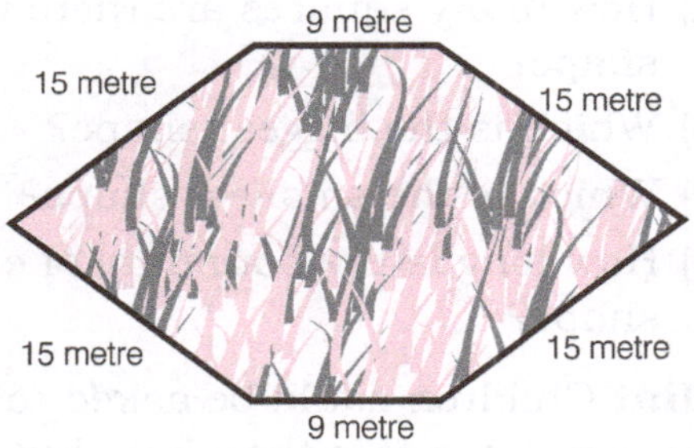

Boundary = ___________ metre

Ans. For field-(a),

Boundary = 6 + 15 + 24 + 15 = 60 metres

For field-(b),

Boundary = 6 + 3 + 6 + 6 + 12 + 9 = 42 metres

For field-(c),

Boundary = 9 + 12 + 15 = 36 metres

For field-(d),

Boundary = 15 + 9 + 15 + 15 + 9 + 15

= 78 metres

Hence, the field-(d) has the longest boundary.

Q.3 Chandu's father is called the 'young old man' in his village.

At 70 years of age, he is fully fit. Do you know his secret?

He goes for a walk around the field every morning. Everyday he takes four rounds of Chandu's field.

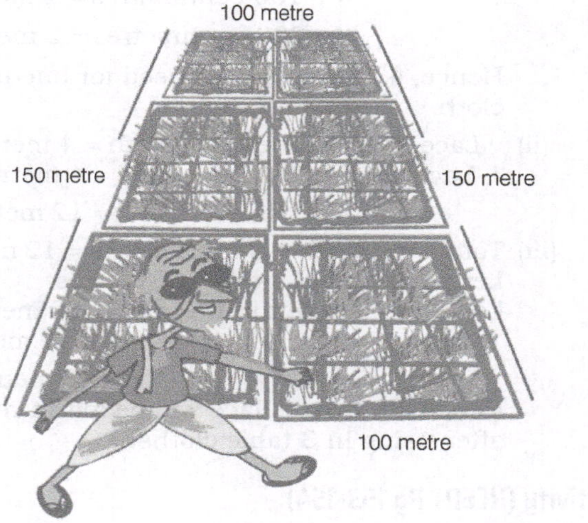

What is the total distance he covers?

4 × ....= .... metre = ...kilometre

Ans. Boundary of the Chandu's field

= 100 + 150 + 100 + 150 = 500 metres

Total distance covered by him

= (4 × 500) metre

= 2000 metres

= 2 kilometres

[∵ 1000 metres = 1 kilometre]

Q.4 Ganpat's wife works in a tailor's shop. She has to fix lace around a table cloth. She bought a 100 metre roll of lace.

(i) Look at the picture of the table cloth and tell how much lace is used for one table cloth.

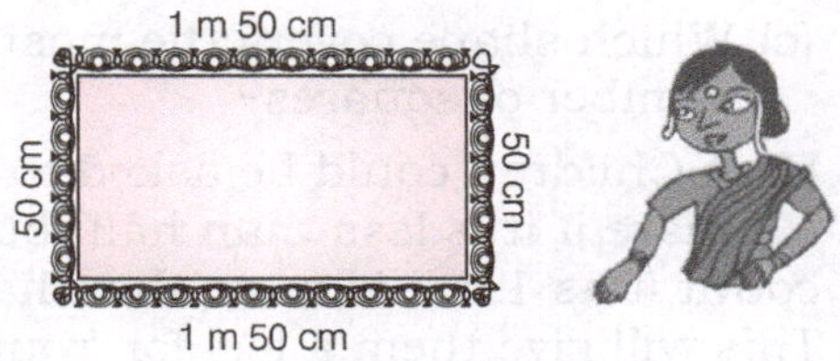

(ii) How much lace will be used in 3 such table cloths?

(iii) How much lace will be left in the roll?

Ans. (i) Length of the boundary of table cloth

= 1 metre 50 centimetres + 50 centimetres + 1 metre 50 centimetres + 50 centimetres

= 2 metres 200 centimetres = 4 metres

$\left[\begin{array}{l} \because 100 \text{ centimetres} = 1 \text{ metre} \\ \therefore 200 \text{ centimetres} = 2 \text{ metres} \end{array}\right]$

Hence, 4 metres lace is used for one table cloth.

(ii) ∵ Lace used in one table cloth = 4 metres

∴ Lace used in 3 table cloths = 4 metres × 3

= 12 metres

(iii) Total lace used in 3 table cloths = 12 metres

Length of roll of lace = 100 metres

Length of lace left in the roll = 100 metres − 12 metres

= 88 metres

Hence, 88 metres lace will be left in roll after using in 3 table cloths.

Activity (NCERT Pg 153-154)

Q.5 (i) Find out the length of the boundary of these shapes. (**Hint** You can use a thread.)

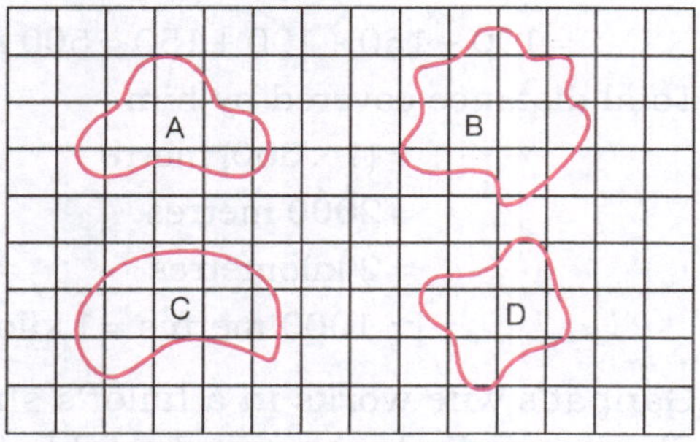

(ii) Count the squares to find out.

(a) How many squares are there in each shape?

(b) Which shape covers the least number of squares?

(c) Which shape covers the most number of squares?

Hint Children could be asked to ignore a square if it is less than half, but count it as 1 if it is more than half. This will give them a feel for 'rounding off'.

Ans. *(i) To find out the length of the boundary of the shapes given in the figure, do the following steps.

Step I Take a thread and place the thread carefully over the figure about the boundary.

Step II Now, cut the thread carefully over the figure along boundary.

Step III Now, measure the length of the thread.

Step IV Repeat the process with all figures.

(ii) (a) The number of squares in shape-A = 5

Number of squares in shape-B = 8

Number of squares in shape-C = 7

And number of squares in shape-D = 4

(b) The shape-D covers the least number of squares.

(c) The shape-B covers the most number of squares.

Q.6 Take a 20 centimetre long thread. Make different shapes by joining the ends. Place on the squared sheet.

Find out.

(a) How many squares are there in each shape?

(b) Which is the biggest shape?

(c) Which is the smallest shape?

(d) How long is the boundary of each shape?

Hint Children could be asked to ignore a square if it is less than half, but count it as 1 if it is more than half. This will give them a feel for 'rounding off'.

Ans. *

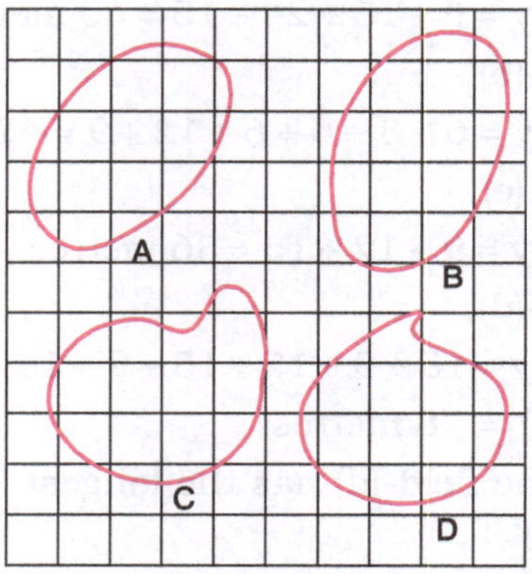

(a) Number of squares in shape-A = 10
Number of squares in shape-B = 13
Number of squares in shape-C = 12
Number of squares in shape-D = 8
(b) The biggest shape is figure B.
(c) The smallest shape is figure D.
(d) We used a 20 cm long thread. So, the boundary of each shape is 20 cm long.

Q.7 (i) How many different shapes can you make by joining two squares? Draw them on the squared sheet given below. How long is the boundary of each shape?

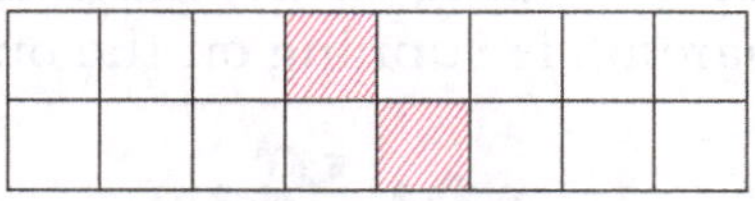

(ii) Try this activity with three squares also.

Ans. (i) I can make four different shapes joining two squares.

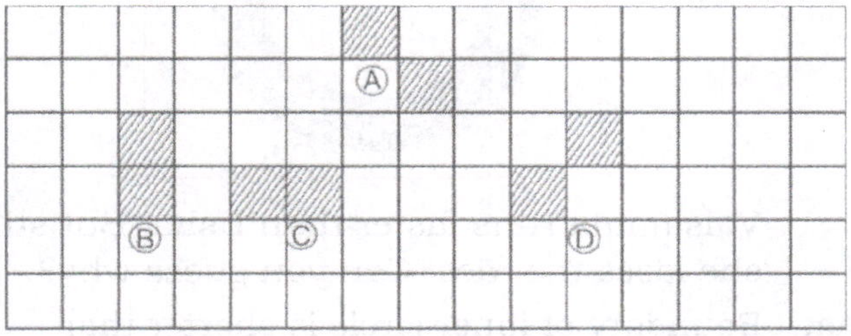

Boundary of shape-A = 8 units
Boundary of shape-B = 6 units
Boundary of shape-C = 6 units
Boundary of shape-D = 8 units

(ii) The shapes formed by joining three squares are given below.

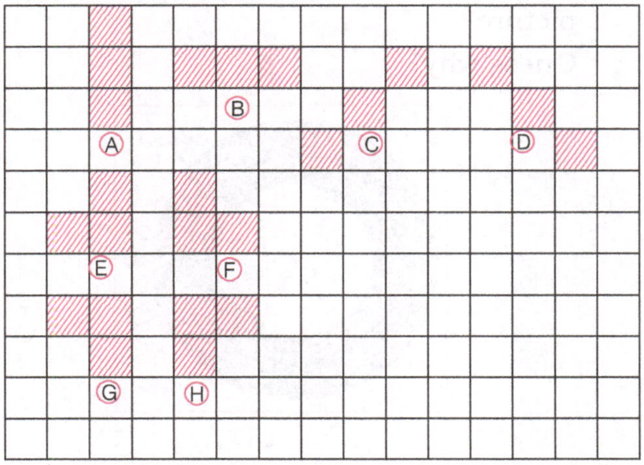

Practice Time (NCERT Pg 155-156)

Q.8 A square has a boundary of 12 centimetres.

(i) From the corner of this square, a small square of side 1 centimetre is cut off. Will the boundary of *B* be less or more? Find its length.

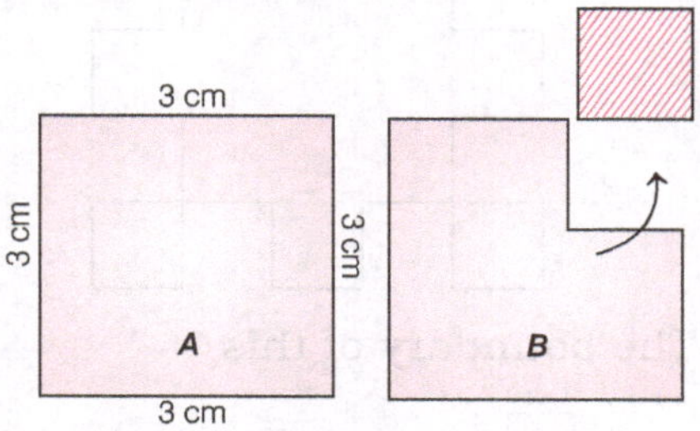

(ii) If you cut a 1 centimetre square to get shape *C*, what will be the length of the boundary of *C*?

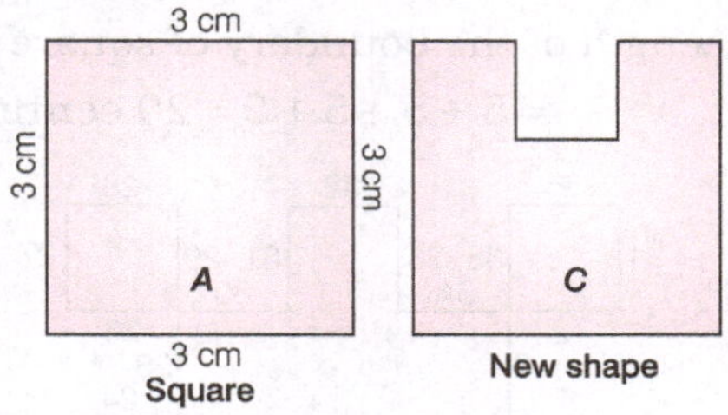

Ans. (i) Length of the boundary of square *A*
= 3 + 3 + 3 + 3 = 12 centimetres
Length of the boundary of shape *B*
= 3 + 3 + 2 + 1 + 1 + 2 = 12 centimetres
There will be no difference in boundary of square *A* and shape *B*
Length of the boundary of shape B is 12 centimetre.

(ii) Boundary of shape *C*
= 3 + 3 + 3 + 1 + 1 + 1 + 1 + 1
= 14 centimetre
Hence, the length of the boundary of shape *C* is 14 centimetre.

Q.9 (i) Find the length of the boundary of square *D*.

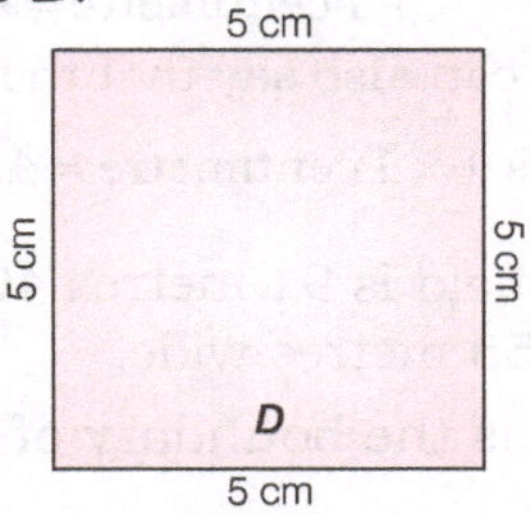

(ii) 8 squares of side 1 centimetre are cut out of the square *D*. Now, it looks like shape *E*. What is the length of the boundary of shape *E*?

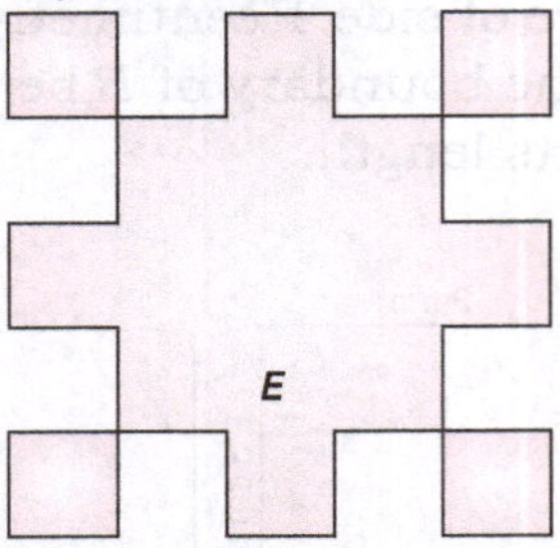

(iii) The boundary of this 

is ____ + ____ + ____ + ____ .

Can we also say that the boundary is 4 × 1 centimetre?

Ans. (i) Length of the boundary of square *D*.

$= 5 + 5 + 5 + 5 = 20$ centimetre

(ii)

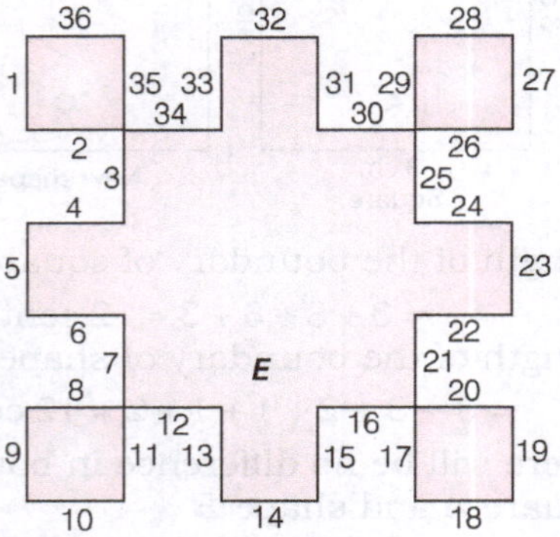

We know that there are 36 edges measuring 1 cm in shape *E*.

∴ Length of boundary of shape,

$E = 1 \times 36 = 36$ centimetres.

(iii) The boundary of this 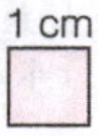

is

1 centimetre + 1 centimetre + 1 centimetre + 1 centimetre = 4 centimetres.

Yes, we can also say that the boundary of 

is 4×1 centimetre = 4 centimetres.

Q.10 A hockey field is 91 metres 40 centimetres long and 55 metres wide.

How long is the boundary of the field?

Ans. Length of hockey field = 91 metres 40 centimetres.

Width of hockey field = 55 metres.

Length of boundary of hockey field

= Length + Width + Length + Width

= 91 metres 40 centimetres + 55 metres + 91 metres 40 centimetres + 55 metres

= 292 metres 80 centimetres

Hence, boundary of hockey field is 292 metres 80 centimetres long.

Q.11 Usha and Valsamma are running a race. Usha is running on the inner circle. Valsamma is running on the outer circle.

Valsamma runs faster than Usha. But still she loses the race. Can you guess why?

Ans. Boundary of inner circle is shorter than boundary of outer circle. So, Valsamma covered more distance as compared to distance covered by Usha. Therefore, Valsamma loses the race.

Q.12 Have you seen any race where runners start from different places - like in this picture?

Guess why?

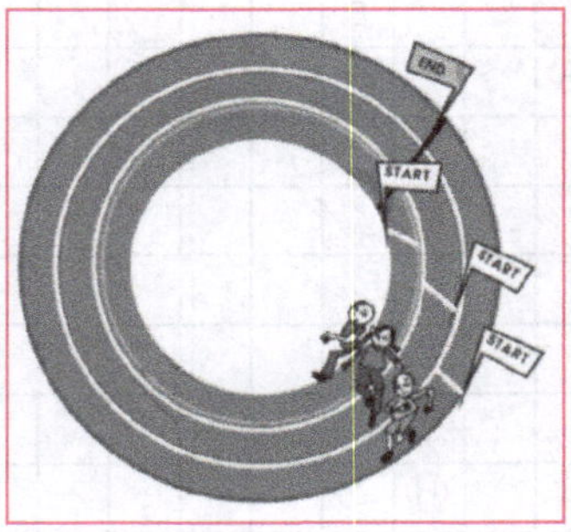

Ans. Yes, I have seen such a race where runners start from different places. Such arrangement is made to equal distances for every participants.

School Garden (NCERT Pg 157)

Q.13 The students of Class III and IV thought of making a vegetable garden. They chose a place which looked like this.

Students of both the classes thought that garden 1 was bigger. So, both wanted to take garden 1. Suddenly Neetu said

How will Neetu find out if the two gardens are equally big?

Ans. Neetu places a long rope along the boundary of garden-1 and measure the length of boundary, with the same length she measures boundary of garden-2.

Finally, she saw that the length of the boundaries of both gardens are equal. Therefore, both the gardens are also equal.

Activity (NCERT Pg 158-160)

Q.14 Look at the table in your classroom. Guess how many Math-Magic books you can place on it.

(Remember, the books should not overlap. Do not leave gaps between the books)

(i) Write your guess here.

(ii) Now, check if your guess was right. How many books could you place?

(iii) What is the difference between your guess and the actual number of books?

Ans. *(i) 8 Math-Magic books can be placed on the table.

*(ii) My guess was right. 8 Math-Magic books can be placed on the table.

*(iii) The difference between my guess and actual number of books is zero.

Q.15 Look for another table.

(i) Is this table bigger than the last table? Yes/No

(ii) Make a guess how many Math-Magic books can be kept on this table.

(iii) Check if your guess was correct. How many Math-Magic books could you keep?

(iv) The difference between the sizes of the two tables is ....books.

Ans. *(i) Yes, this table is bigger than the last table.

*(ii) 14 Math-Magic books can be kept on this table.

*(iii) 12 Math-Magic books could be kept on this table.

*(iv) The difference between the my guess and actual number is 2 books.

Q.16 (i) How many Math-Magic books can be covered with one sheet of newspaper?

(ii) Try covering your Math-Magic book with half a sheet of newspaper.

(iii) Can you cover your book with a smaller sheet?

(iv) Find the smallest sheet which can cover your book. Check if your friend used a smaller sheet than you did.

Ans. *(i) 6 Math-Magic books can be covered with one sheet of newspaper.

*(ii) Should be done by the students.

*(iii) Yes, we can cover the book with a smaller sheet.

*(iv) Should be done by the students.

Q.17 (i) Which is the biggest leaf in this picture?

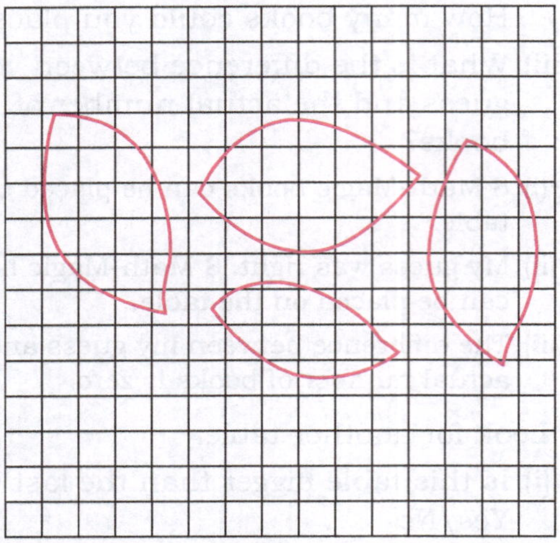

(ii) Collect some leaves from the garden. Place each of them here on this squared sheet. Trace out their edges and check how many squares there are in each leaf.

(iii) Which is the biggest leaf?

(iv) Which is the smallest leaf?

Ans. (i) The leaf in the middle from the top is biggest leaf.

(ii) Do yourself.

(iii) Do yourself.

(iv) Do yourself.

Q.18 (i) How many small squares of size 1 centimetre are there in this big shaded square?

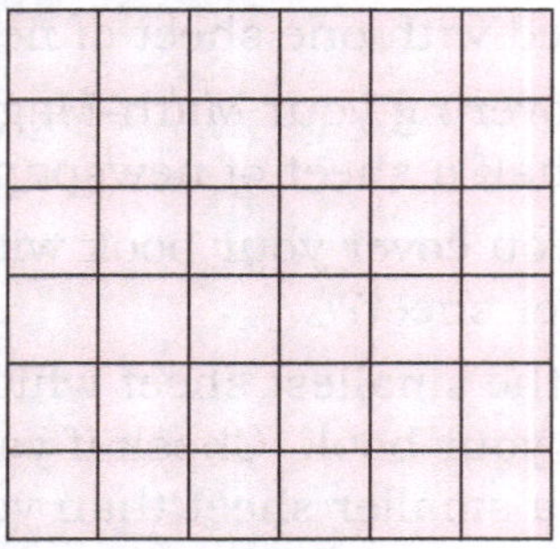

(ii) Can you think of a faster way to know the total number of small squares without counting each?

Ans. (i) There are 36 small squares of size 1 centimetre in this big shaded square.

(ii) Yes, there are 6 rows and 6 columns of size 1 centimetre.

So, number of small squares in this big shaded square = $6 \times 6 = 36$

Q.19 (i) Guess, how many squares of one centimetre can fill this shaded rectangle.

Write your guess here.

(ii) Check your guess by filling it with small squares.

Ans. (i) Number of rows is 4 and number of columns is 8.

So, I think 32 squares of 1 centimetre can fill this blue rectangle.

(ii)

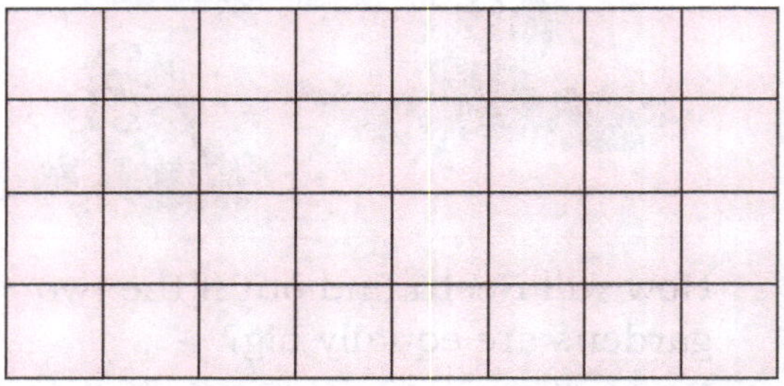

As there are 32 squares in the shaded rectangle. So, my guess is correct.

Q.20 Look at the picture. Can you divide it into 4 equal pieces? Each piece should have the same number of squares.

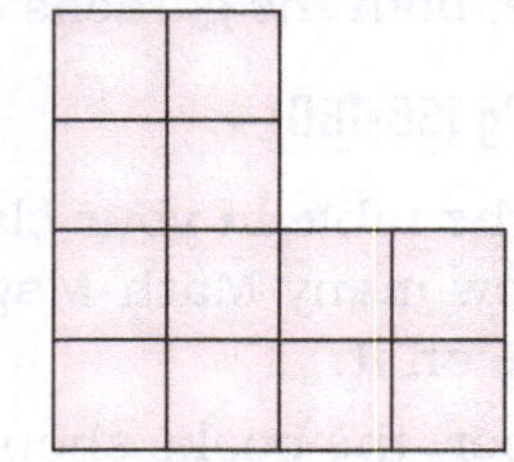

Ans. Yes, I can divide it into 4 equal pieces.

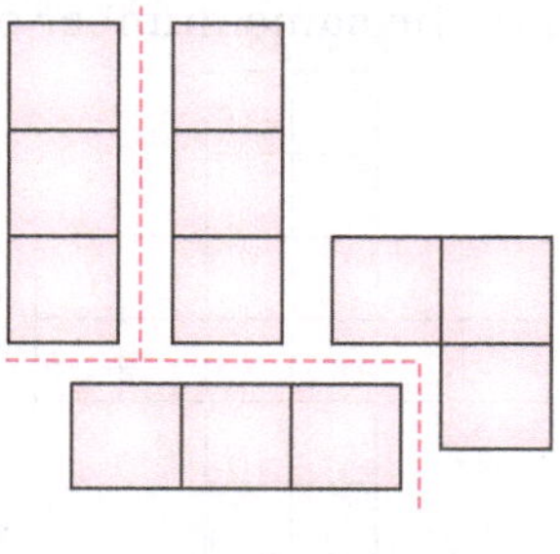

Puzzle: A House and the Well (NCERT Pg 161)

Q.21 Raghavan has a piece of land.

There are 4 houses on his land and in the middle there is a well.

He wants to divide this land equally among his four children.

Each should get one house and be able to use the well without entering the other's land. Can you help him divide the land?

Give different colours to each one's share.

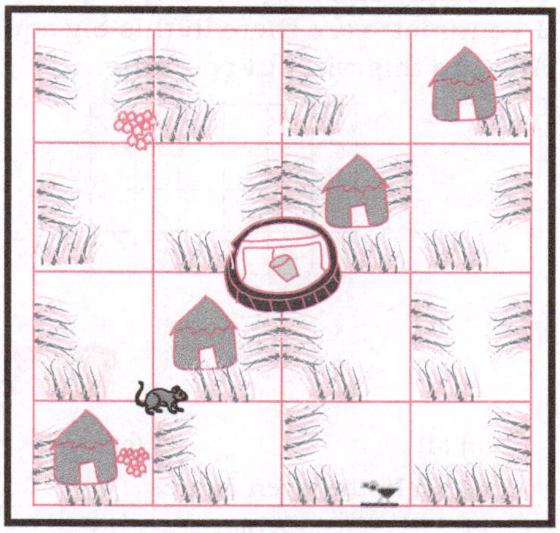

Ans. * The given picture shows how the land can be divided equally among the four children so that each one gets one house and is able to use the well without entering the other's land.

PRACTICE QUESTIONS

1. Multiple choice questions.

(i) Boundary of the given figure is

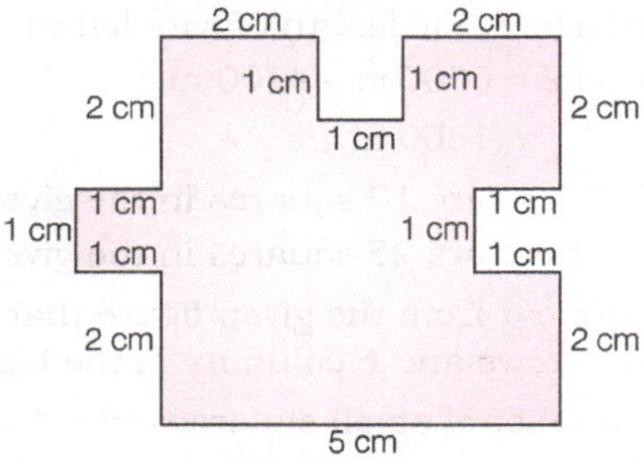

(a) 20 centimetres (b) 29 centimetres
(c) 23 centimetres (d) 26 centimetres

(ii) 12×500 metre is equal to
(a) 12 kilometres (b) 5 kilometres
(c) 6 kilometres (d) 60 kilometres

2. (i) Find the length of the boundary of the following fields.

(a) 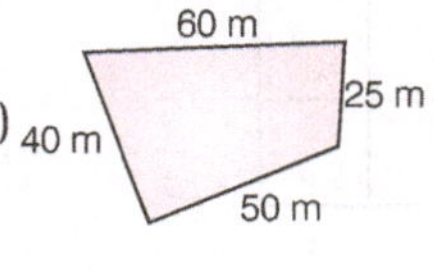

(b) 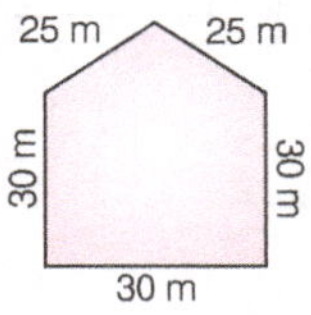

(ii) On the basis of figures in part (i), answer the following questions.

(a) Which figure has the longest boundary?

(b) Ramesh goes for a walk around the field-(b) every morning and he takes 10 rounds of the field. What is the total distance he covers?

3. Amar has a square garden with side 350 metres long. How much wire will be needed for fencing it three times? If Amar bought a bundle of wire and its length is 6000 metres. How much wire will be left in the bundle?

4. Count the square in the given shapes. (you could ignore a square if it is less than half, but count it as 1 if it is more than half)

(i) 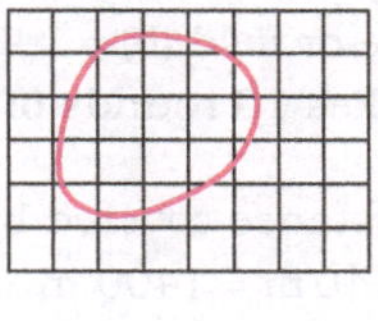 (ii) 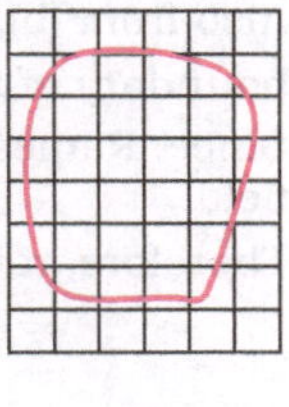

5. Each small square of the given big square is 1 centimetre.

How many small squares of size 1 centimetre are there in this big square? Also, do this without counting.

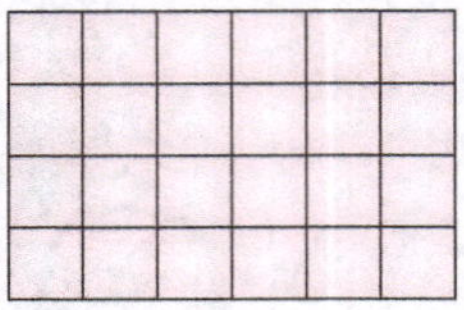

6. Divide it into 4 equal pieces? Each piece should have the same number of squares.

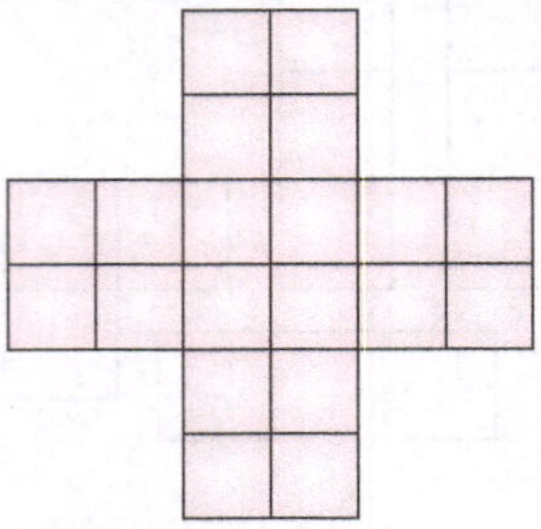

ANSWERS & SOLUTIONS

1. (i) (d) (ii) (c)

2. (i) (a) In the given figure,

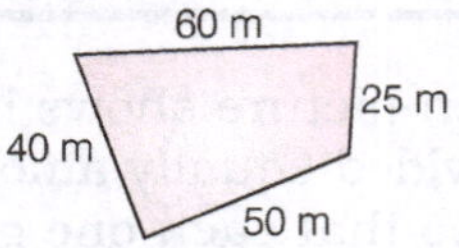

The length of the boundary
= Sum of lengths of all sides
= 60 m + 25 m + 50 m + 40 m
= 175 m

(b) In the given figure,

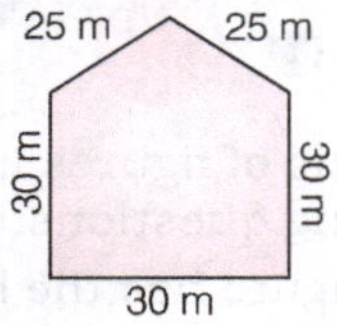

The length of the boundary
= Sum of lengths of all sides
= 25 m + 25 m + 30 m + 30 m + 30 m
= 140 m

(ii) (a) We have,
boundary of figure (a) = 175 m
and boundary of figure (b) = 140 m
$\because$ 175 m > 140 m
Hence, figure (a) has the longest boundary.

(b) Given that
Ramesh goes for a walk around the field (b).
Also from (b), we get
boundary of figure or field (b) = 140 m
Since, Ramesh takes 10 rounds of the field.
Therefore, total distance covered by him
= 10 × 140 m = 1400 m

3. We have,
the length of a side of square garden
= 350 m
$\therefore$ Boundary of square garden = 4 × Side
= 4 × 350
= 1400 m
$\because$ Wire needed for fencing it one time
= 1400 m
$\therefore$ Wire needed for fencing it three times
= 3 × 1400
= 4200 m

Since, Amar bought a bundle of wire of length 6000 m.

Therefore, the length of wire left in the bundle = 6000 m − 4200 m
= 1800 m

4. (i) There are 12 squares in the given figure.
(ii) There are 25 squares in the given figure.

5. It is clear from the given figure that there are 4 rows and 6 columns in the big square.
$\therefore$ Number of small squares = 6 × 4 = 24

6.

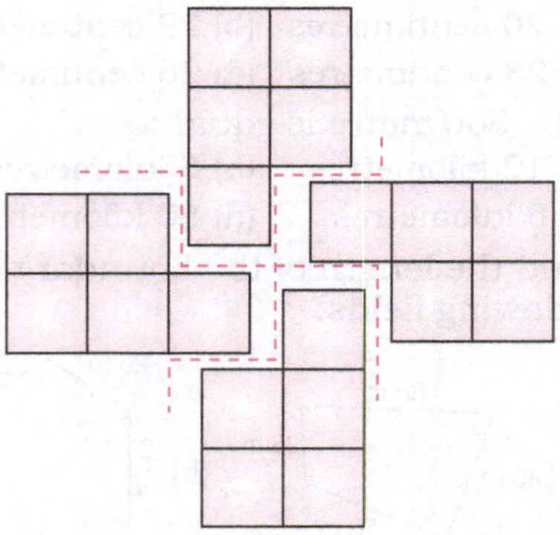

CHAPTER 14 SMART CHARTS

Smart Charts

It is collection of information or data which is collected by observations and measurements. Smart charts are used to make data more presentable, easy and quick to understand. It involves tables, charts etc. e.g. The table shows the number of students of different classes who eat banana and those who eat apple.

Class	Number of students who eat bananas	Number of students who eat apples
I	28	25
II	26	24
III	20	30
IV	25	25

Bar Charts

A bar chart or bar graph is a chart or graph that represents categorical data with rectangular bars with heights or lengths proportional to the values that they represent. e.g. The strength of Class IV in 2021, 2022 and 2023 is shown below.

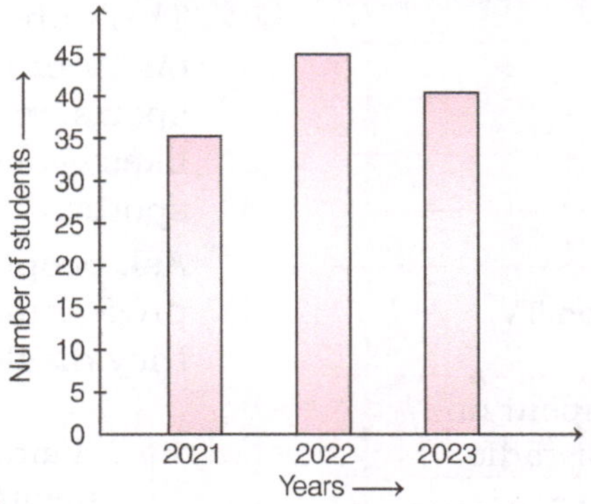

Pie-chart or Chapati chart

It is a circular graph that uses slices to represent the data. e.g. In a class, half of the students like Cricket, one fourth of the students like Football and rest quarter of the students like Kabaddi are shown in given pie-chart.

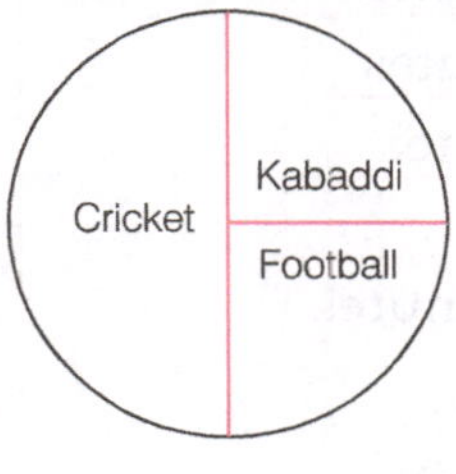

NCERT FOLDER

How many Hours? (NCERT Pg 162-163)

Q.1 (i) All of us enjoy watching television (TV) or listening to the radio. How much time do we spend in this?

(ii) Note the time you spend in front of a TV or radio every day. Do this for one week. The time spent in a week is ...... hours.

(iii) So, in a month, you spend about 30 ×...... = ...hours.

(iv) I can watch TV for 24 hours! Is it good or bad for me?

(v) Find out from your friends the time they spend in a week.

How many hours they watch TV or listen to the radio (in a week)	Number of children
More than 6 hours	
Six hours	
Five hours	
Four hours	
Three hours	
Two hours	
One hour	
Zero hour (do not watch)	

Ans. *(i) I spend about 2 hours daily on TV.

*(ii)

Day	Time spent on TV or radio
Monday	2 hours 15 minutes
Tuesday	2 hours 5 minutes
Wednesday	1 hours 50 minutes
Thursday	1 hours 10 minutes
Friday	1 hours 45 minutes
Saturday	2 hours 5 minutes
Sunday	3 hours
Total time spent = 14 hours 10 minutes	

So, I spent 14 hours 10 minutes in a week.

*(iii) ∵ I spend about 2 hours daily on TV.

∴ In a month, I spend about $30 \times 2 = 60$ hours.

(iv) It is bad for health to watch TV for 24 hours.

(v) Do yourself.

From Your Table (NCERT Pg 163)

Q.2 Watching TV/listening to the radio...

(i) .... children spend more than 6 hours in a week.

(ii) ....children spend no time at all.

(iii) Most children spend .... hours in a week.

(iv) .... children spend more than 3 hours.

Ans. (i) Do yourself. (ii) Do yourself.

(iii) Do yourself. (iv) Do yourself.

Which Programme? (NCERT Pg 163-164)

Q.3 There are different types of programmes on TV or radio such as cartoons, news, sports, music, plays, serials. Juhi's father likes watching serials. Her mother likes sports. Juhi likes news programmes.

Ask people in your family to name one programme they like and one programme they dislike. Make a table.

Family member	Programme they like	Programme they dislike
Mother		
Father		

** Students can write alternate answer as per their choice.*

(i) The kind of programme most family members like ....

(ii) The kind of programme most family members dislike ....

Ans. * In my family, the programmes liked and disliked by them are given below.

Family Members	Programmes they like	Programmes they dislike
Father	News	Serials
Mother	Serials	Movie
Grandfather	News	Serials
Grandmother	Serials	Sports
Brother	Movie	Serials
Sister	Music	News
Me	Sports	Serials

(i) Most of the family members like Serials and News.

(ii) Most of the family members dislike Serials.

Q.4 Find out from 20 friends, the programmes they like and dislike and write in a table.

Kind of programme	Number of children liking it	Number of children disliking it
News		
Serials		
Cartoons		
Comedy shows		
Sports		

(i) Which kind of programme is liked by most children?

(ii) Which kind of programme is disliked by the least number of children?

(iii) How many children like sports programmes?

(iv) Is there any kind of programme not liked by any one? Yes/No. If yes, which one?

Ans. * Liking and disliking of programmes by children.

Kind of programme	Number of children liking it	Number of children disliking it
News	10	10
Serial	2	18
Cartoons	19	1
Music	18	2
Movie	17	3
Sports	20	0

(i) Most of the children like cartoon and sports programmes.

(ii) Cartoon and sports are disliked by the least number of children.

(iii) 20 (All) children like sports programmes.

(iv) No.

Who is my friend? (NCERT Pg 164-165)

Q.5 I've a friend with me always,
In the nights and through the days.
When I run he runs with me,
Sometimes I lead, sometimes he.
When it's dark he can't be seen,
Do you know which friend I mean?

Read the poem carefully and answer these questions :

(i) Which word comes most often in the poem?

(ii) Which letter has been used most?

(iii) Which letter comes the least?

Ans. (i) The word 'I' comes most often in the poem.

To answer the next questions, first of all make a table regarding this.

Letter	Number of letters	Letter	Number of letters
A	9	N	13
B	1	O	6
C	2	P	—
D	7	Q	—
E	21	R	6
F	2	S	10
G	2	T	10
H	14	U	4
I	14	V	1
J	—	W	7
K	2	X	—
L	2	Y	3
M	7	Z	—

(ii) Letter-E has been used most in this poem.

(iii) Letter-B and letter-V come only 1 time and letters- J, P, Q, X and Z never come.

Q.6 Take a paragraph you like from your language textbook. Read carefully and find out :

(i) Which word comes most often? How many times?

(ii) Which word comes least often?

(iii) The letter used most often is ....

(iv) The letter used least often is ....

Ans. (i) Do yourself. (ii) Do yourself.
(iii) Do yourself. (ii) Do yourself.

Food we Eat (NCERT Pg 166)

Q.7 (i) Find out from your classmates and fill the table:

Main food	Number of persons
Rice	
Wheat	

(ii) Look at the table and tell:

(a) Most children eat food made from ....

(b) Compared to children who eat rice, those who eat wheat are more/less/equal.

(c) Compared to those who eat wheat, children eating ragi are more/less.

Ans. *(i)

Main Food	Number of persons
Rice	20
Wheat	25
Maize	5
Ragi	8
Pulses	22
Barley	10

(ii) (a) Most children eat food made from wheat.

(b) Number of children who eat rice are less than the number of children who eat wheat.

(c) Children who eat wheat are more than those who eat ragi.

Preparing for the Class Drama (NCERT Pg 166-167)

Q.8 All children of a class are getting ready for a drama. Some children are acting. Some are busy collecting the dresses. Some are bringing tables and chairs to make the sets.

The Drama Chart

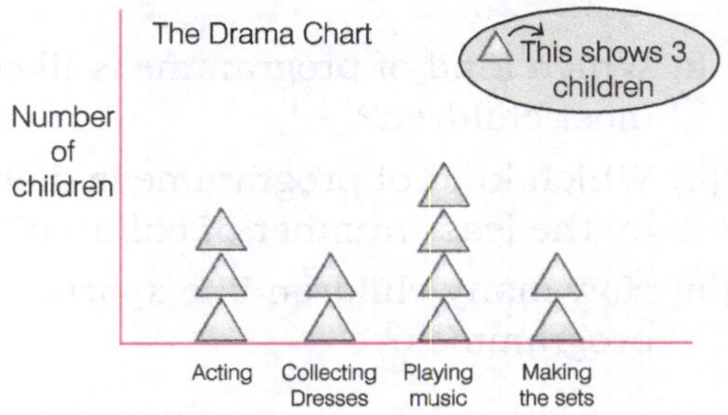

(i) How many children are acting in the drama?

(ii) Which are more-children making the sets or those acting?

(iii) What is being done by most of the children?

(iv) How many children are collecting dresses?

Ans. (i) $\because 1\Delta = 3$ children

$\therefore 3\Delta = 3 \times 3 = 9$ children

Therefore, 9 children are acting in the drama.

(ii) Number of children doing acting $= 3 \times 3 = 9$

Number of children making the sets

$= 3 \times 2 = 6$

Clearly, $9 > 6$

Hence, the children who are acting, are more than those making the sets.

(iii) Most of the children are playing music.

(iv) Number of children collecting dresses

$= 3 \times 2 = 6$

So, 6 children are collecting the dresses.

Whose Head is Bigger? (NCERT Pg 167-168)

Q.9 Cut long paper strips from waste paper. Give one strip to each of your friends.

Now, put the paper strip around your head and tear off the extra strip. On a big sheet, paste these paper strips along a line.

Use a scale and find out from your chart:

(i) The length of the longest strip is .... cm. So, ... has the biggest head.

(ii) The smallest strip is .... cm long. It belongs to ....

Ans. *

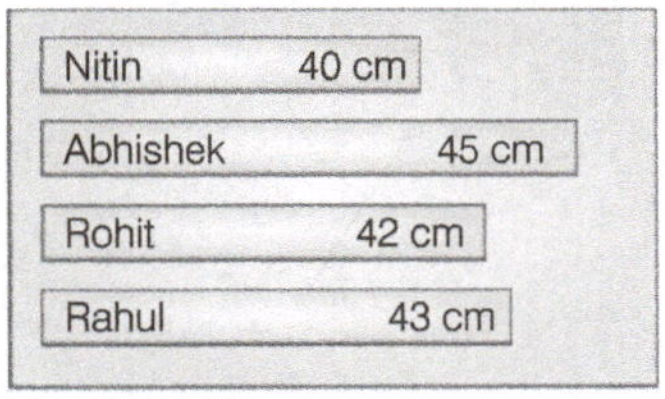

(i) The length of the longest strip is 45 cm. So, Abhishek has the biggest head.

(ii) The smallest strip is 40 cm long. It belongs to Nitin.

Chapati Chart (NCERT Pg 168-169)

Q.10 All children of a school take part in different clubs.

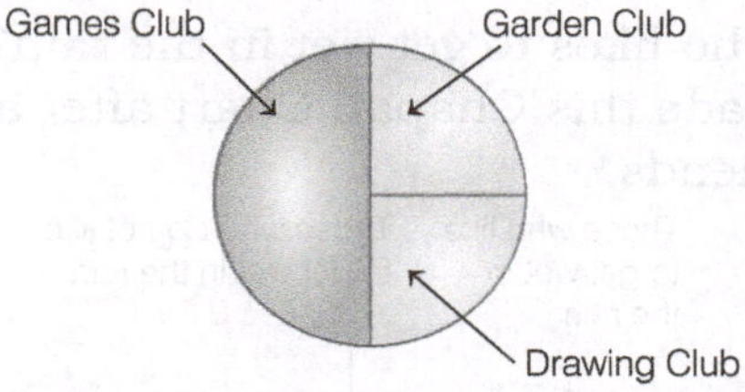

The Chapati Chart shows the number of children in different clubs.

From the picture we can see that :

(a) Half the children in the class take part in the Games Club.

(b) One fourth of the children are members of the Garden Club.

(c) The Drawing Club has one fourth of the children of the class.

If there are 200 students in the school, look at the above Chapati Chart and tell the number of members in each club :

(i) The Games Club has .... members.

(ii) The Garden Club has .... members.

(iii) There are .... members in the Drawing Club.

Ans. (i) Total number of students in the school $= 200$

Number of children who take part in the Games Club = Half of the total children

$= \frac{1}{2} \times 200 = 100$

Hence, the Games Club has 100 members.

(ii) Total number of students in the school $= 200$

Number of children who take part in the Garden Club

= One fourth of the total children

$= \frac{1}{4} \times 200 = 50$

Hence, the Garden Club has 50 members.

(iii) Number of children who take part in the Drawing Club

= One fourth of the total children

$= \frac{1}{4} \times 200 = 50$

Hence, there are 50 members in the Drawing Club.

Getting Wet in the Rain (NCERT Pg 169-170)

Q.11 Who likes to get wet in the rain? A child made this Chapati Chart after asking his friends.

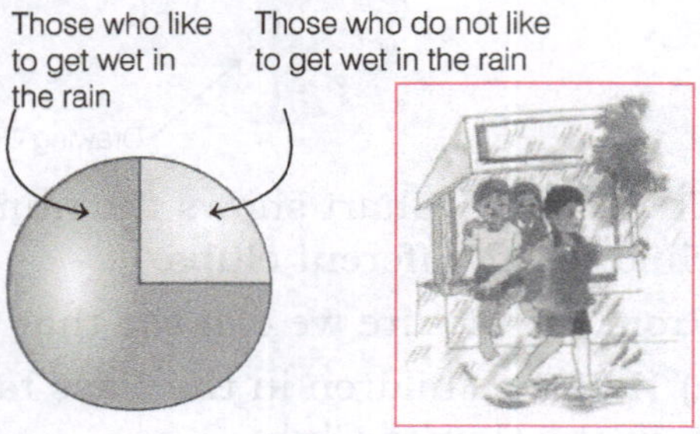

(i) See the chapati Chart and tell :

(A) How many children like to get wet in the rain?

(a) Half
(b) One-fourth
(c) Three-fourth

(B) How many children do not like to get wet in the rain?

(a) Half
(b) One-fourth
(c) Three-fourth

(ii) If the number of children in the class is 28, then tell the number of children

(A) who like to get wet in the rain ....

(B) who do not like to get wet in the rain ....

Ans. (i) (A) (c) Three-fourth (B) (b) One-fourth

(ii) (A) Number of children who like to get wet in the rain $= \frac{3}{4} \times 28 = 21$

(B) Number of children who do not like to get wet in the rain $= \frac{1}{4} \times 28 = 7$

Tea, Coffee or Milk (NCERT Pg 170)

Q.12 Some children were asked which of these they liked most-Tea, Coffee or Milk.

The drink they like	Number of children
Milk	20
Coffee	10
Tea	10

(i) Total number of children .... Find out from the table

(ii) Children who like milk are $\frac{1}{2}$ / $\frac{1}{4}$ of the total children.

(iii) Children who like coffee are $\frac{1}{2}$ / $\frac{1}{4}$ of the total children.

(iv) Show the liking for Tea, Coffee or Milk in a Chapati Chart.

Ans. (i) Total number of children = 20 + 10 + 10 = 40

(ii) Total number of children = 40

Number of children who like milk = 20

Children who like milk $= \frac{20}{40} = \frac{1}{2}$ of the total children.

Hence, children who like milk are $\frac{1}{2}$ of the total children.

(iii) Number of children who like coffee = 10

Children who like coffee $= \frac{10}{40} = \frac{1}{4}$ of the total children.

Hence, children who like coffee are $\frac{1}{4}$ of the total children.

(iv)

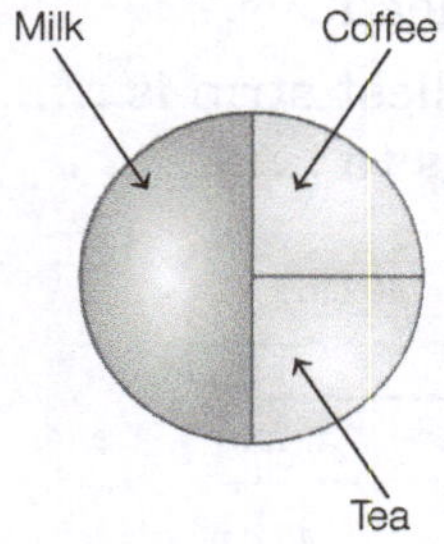

PRACTICE QUESTIONS

1. The following graph is showing the sales of bikes in different months of a year.

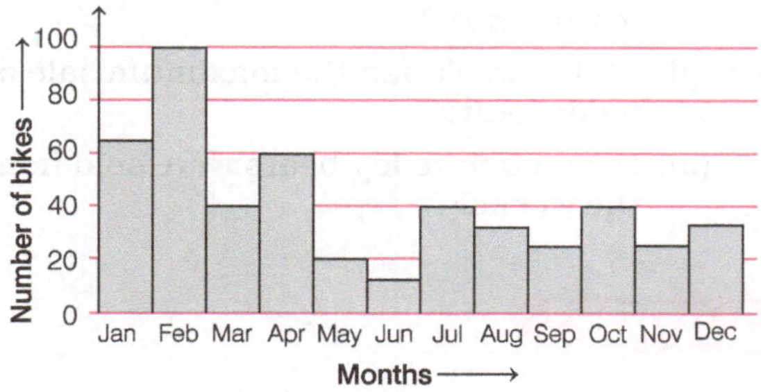

Study the above graph to answer the questions given below.

(i) In which month maximum number of bikes were sold?

(a) January (b) February
(c) June (d) October

(ii) How many bikes were sold in month of April?

(a) 55 (b) 65 (c) 60 (d) 70

(iii) Minimum sales of bikes were in the month of ....

(a) May (b) September
(c) November (d) June

2. Children of Class-IV were asked their favourite food items. The food chart is given below.

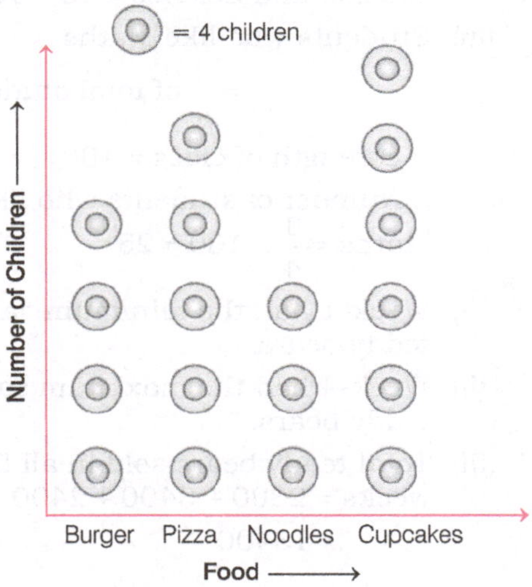

(i) How many children like the Pizza?

(ii) There are .... fewer students who like Noodles than Burger.

(iii) The most popular food item is ....

(iv) How many more children like Cupcakes than Pizza?

3. The following bar graph shows the number of juice bottles sold in the following months. Answer the questions that follow.

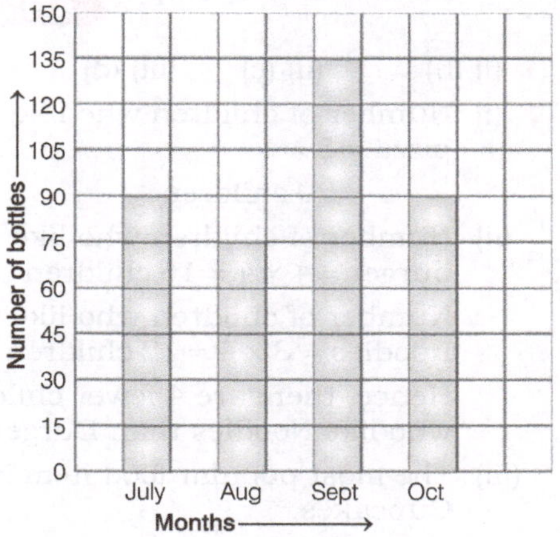

(i) In which month the most number of bottles were sold?

(ii) In which month the least number of bottles were sold?

(iii) How many less bottles were sold in July than September?

(iv) How many more bottles were sold in September than August?

4. Mohan made a Chapati Chart after asking his friends about the subjects they like the most.

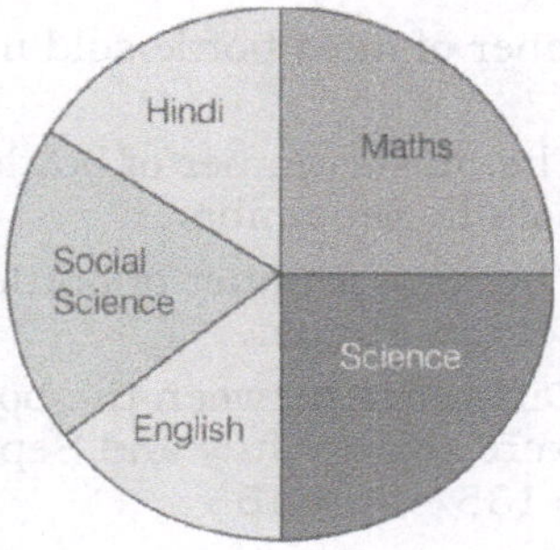

Observe the above Chapati Chart and answer the following questions.

(i) How many students like Hindi?

(ii) If there are 60 students, then how many students like Science and English?

(iii) How many students like Maths? If strength of class is 100.

5. The following table shows the number of teddy bears sold from a factory in 4 weeks.

Weeks	Number of teddy bears
Week-1	2300
Week-2	3400
Week-3	2400
Week-4	5300

Based on the above information, answer the following questions.

(i) Which week had the minimum sale of teddy bears?

(ii) Which week had the maximum sale of teddy bears?

(iii) How much teddy bears were sold in all the weeks?

ANSWERS & SOLUTIONS

1. (i) (b) (ii) (c) (iii) (d)

2. (i) Number of children who like the pizza $= 5 \times 4$
$= 20$ children

(ii) Number of children who like the burger $= 4 \times 4 = 16$ children

Number of children who like the Noodles $= 3 \times 4 = 12$ children

Hence, there are 4 fewer children who like Noodles than Burger.

(iii) The most popular food item is Cupcakes.

(iv) Number of children who like Cupcakes $= 6 \times 4$
$= 24$ children

Number of children who like Pizza
$= 5 \times 4 = 20$ children

Hence, 4 more children like cupcakes than pizza.

3. Number of juice bottle sold in July = 90

Number of juice bottle sold in August = 75

Number of juice bottle sold in September = 135

Number of juice bottle sold in October = 90

(i) The most number of bottles were sold in September.

(ii) The least number of bottles were sold in August.

(iii) Difference between the bottles that were sold in July and September $= 135 - 90 = 45$

Hence, 45 less bottles were sold in July than September.

(iv) Difference between the bottles that were sold in September and August $= 135 - 75 = 60$

Hence, 60 more bottles were sold in September than August.

4. (i) Students who like Hindi
$= \frac{1}{3}$ of $\frac{1}{2}$ students $= \frac{1}{6}$th students

(ii) Total number of students = 60

Number of students, who like Science $= \frac{1}{4} \times 60 = 15$ students

Number of students, who like English $= \frac{1}{6} \times 60 = 10$

Total number of students who like English and Science $= 10 + 15 = 25$

(iii) Students who like Maths
$= \frac{1}{4}$ of total students

$\because$ Strength of class = 100

$\therefore$ Number of students who like Maths $= \frac{1}{4} \times 100 = 25$

5. (i) Week-1 had the minimum sale of teddy bears.

(ii) Week-4 had the maximum sale of teddy bears.

(iii) Total teddy bears sold in all four weeks $= 2300 + 3400 + 2400 + 5300$
$= 13400$

Marigold

(English)

CHAPTER 1 WAKE UP!

Summary of the Poem The poem 'Wake up!' by C. Fletcher is a happy reminder to start the day early. It talks about a lovely morning with birds singing, bees buzzing and animals getting up.

Stanza-wise Explanation

Stanza 1

Wake up! Wake up! Wake up!
It's a lovely day.
Oh! Please get up
And come and play.
The birds are singing in the trees,
And you can hear the buzzing bees.

Word-Meaning *Buzzing* - *Humming sound of bees*

Exp. The poet asks the child to wake up and start their day. He requests the child to get up and play outside. He mentions that the birds are chirping in the trees and the bees are buzzing.

Stanza 2

Wake up! Wake up!
It's a lovely day.
Oh! Please get up
And come and play.
It's much too late to lie in bed,
So hurry up, you sleepy head.

Word-Meaning *Sleepy head* - *Those who sleep a lot.*

Exp. The poet is telling the child to wake up as it's a beautiful day outside.
The poet is requesting the child to get up from the bed and come to play. It's too late to still be sleeping, so they should quickly get up and stop being lazy.

Stanza 3

Wash and dress
And come on out–
Everyone is up and about.
The cow, the horses, the ducks
And the sheep,
The tiniest chicken
Cheep-cheep-cheep
Wake up!

Word-Meaning *Is up and about* - *Woken up and doing their work.*

Exp. The poet asks the child to take a bath, get dressed and go outside because everyone is already awake. Animals like cows, horses, ducks and even tiny chickens are awake and making noises.

NCERT FOLDER

Reading is Fun (NCERT Page 04)

Q.1 What do you think birds say to each other in the morning?

Ans. The birds might be chirping and saying 'good morning' to each other.

Q.2 Who are already awake?

Ans. Everyone including the cow, horses, ducks, sheep and the tiniest chickens are already awake.

Q.3 Which creatures wake up in the morning before the child does?

Ans. The birds, bees, the cows, the horses, the ducks, the sheep and the chickens wake up before the child does.

Let's Listen (NCERT Page 04)

Q.1 Listen to the songs of birds. Say the words boy and bee. Listen to the b sound in - big, bubbles, bin, bag, blue, blow and black.

Ans. Do it yourself.

Q.2 Listen to the baby chicks - cheep cheep cheep

Ans. Do it yourself.

Let's Listen and Talk (NCERT Page 04)

Q.1 Go for a morning walk. Listen to the sounds you hear like the rustling of leaves, the wind blowing, the chirping of birds, the sounds of footsteps.

Ans. Do it yourself.

Q.2 Imagine that a cow, a horse, a duck and a chicken are meeting for a morning meal. What would they say to one another? Talk about it.

Ans. **Cow** Good morning, everyone! The grass is so green today. I'm excited for breakfast. What's everyone planning?

Horse Good morning, Cow! I'm ready for a long trot around the field. Maybe we can race after breakfast?

Duck Quack-quack! That sounds fun, Horse! I'll be swimming in the pond and looking for tasty bugs. Want to join me for a swim later?

Chicken Cheep-cheep! I'm going to peck for worms and seeds. Duck, I'd love your help finding the best spots. And Cow, maybe you can share some grazing tips?

Cow Sure, Chicken! I'll help you find good spots. And Duck, I'd like to swim with you after breakfast. Horse, a race sounds great-let's see who's faster!

Horse Sounds good! I'll save some energy for our race. And Duck, we can splash around together after my trot.

Duck Great! I'll look for tasty bugs and a good swimming path.

Chicken Cheep-Cheep! Let's make the most of this beautiful morning. Here's to a day of fun and friendship!

Cow Agreed! Let's enjoy every moment and have a wonderful day!

Say Aloud (NCERT Page 04)

Betty bought a bit of butter,

But the bit of butter that Betty bought was bitter.

So Betty bought some better butter,

To make the bitter butter better.

Ans. Pronounce the words clearly and fluently.

Let's Write (NCERT Page 05)

Q.1 Connect the pairs of sentences below using and or but.

(a) It is time to get up for school.

(b) I want to sleep for some more time.

Ans. It is time to get up for school **but** I want to sleep for some more time.

(a) Sheila got some chocolates for her birthday.

(b) She got some new clothes too.

Ans. Sheila got some chocolates **and** new clothes for her birthday.

(a) Everyone has gone to sleep.

(b) I want to read my book.

Ans. Everyone has gone to sleep **but** I want to read my book.

(a) Raju plays cricket.

(b) He also plays hockey.

Ans. Raju plays cricket **and** hockey.

Q.2 Fill in the blanks according to the example given below

	tiny	tiner	tiniest
(a)	big	______	biggest
(b)	sleepy	sleepier	______
(c)	______	lovelier	loveliest
(d)	______	later	______
(e)	round	______	______
(f)	small	______	______
(g)	good	______	best

Ans. (a) bigger (b) sleepiest
(c) lovely (d) late, latest
(e) rounder, roundest (f) smaller, smallest
(g) better

PRACTICE QUESTIONS

Multiple Choice Questions

1. What is the main message of the poem?
(a) To go back to sleep.
(b) To ignore nature's sounds.
(c) To wake up and start the day.
(d) To be ignorant of your surroundings.

2. What does the poet suggest about staying in bed?
(a) It is okay to stay in bed.
(b) It is too late to stay in bed.
(c) It is preferable to stay in bed.
(d) It is time to stay and go back to sleep.

3. What should the child do when they hear the birds and bees?
(a) Stay inside
(b) Go to school
(c) Go back to sleep
(d) Wake up and play

4. What does the poem emphasise about the morning?
(a) It is time to start the day with activity.
(b) It is a time to rest.
(c) It is too early to do anything.
(d) It is time to stay in bed and do nothing.

5. Which sound is used to describe the sound of the tiny chicken?
(a) Roaring
(b) Buzzing
(c) Quacking
(d) Cheep Cheep Cheep

Ans. 1. (c), 2. (b), 3. (d), 4. (a), 5. (d)

Fill in the Blanks

1. The poem describes the singing of birds and ________ of bees.
2. The animals mentioned include the cow, horse, duck and ________.
3. In the poem, the poet urges the child to wake up and ______.
4. The poet emphasises that it's ____ to be sleeping and encourages getting up.

Ans. 1. buzzing, 2. sheep, 3. play, 4. too late

Answer the Following Questions

1. How does the poem describe the day?

Ans. The poem describes the day as lovely.

2. What action is the speaker asking the listener to take?

Ans. The speaker is asking the listener to get up from the bed and come out to play.

3. Suppose your brother is having a bad habit of getting up late. How can you help them in improving this habit.

Ans. If my brother had a bad habit of getting up late, I would suggest him to go to bed early.

Then, I would ask him to set an alarm so that he can get up early.

Writing Task

1. Recently you went on a early morning walk with your parents. Describes the sights you saw, the sounds you heard and how you felt.

Ans. Our elders often tell us that a morning walk is a refreshing experience. The fresh air and peaceful surroundings uplifts both the mind and body. The sun had just risen, and the air was slightly cold. It carried the fragrance of fresh flowers and earth. As I walked the path in the park, the usual sights seemed more beautiful. The trees seemed more vibrant, the flowers more coloured and the sky clearer.

The chirping of the birds added another layer of beauty to the scene. As I walked in the park, I saw groups of people exercising. Some were walking, jogging and doing yoga.

CHAPTER 2

NEHA'S ALARM CLOCK

Summary of the Chapter

Neha doesn't like waking up early in the morning. She feels irritated when her alarm rings at 6 a.m. One day, when the alarm clock falls down, she's happy because she thinks it won't ring the next morning. But the birds at her window start waking her up next morning. Neha wishes the birds would leave her alone and they leave. But the bright sun wakes her next morning and she wishes for the sun to let her sleep. Her wish comes true and sun is covered by clouds. Next morning her mother wakes her up. She gets ready.

Next day, nobody wakes Neha up and she gets up on her own. She wonders who woke her up. Her mother explains that she has a clock inside her body that tells her when to wake up, eat and sleep. Neha finally understands and rushes to get ready for school. Her mother relaxes her, reminding her that it is Sunday.

WORD-MEANING

Narrator - The person telling the story; Snuggles - to get comfortable; Mutters - To speak in a low voice; Chirpy - Happy and lively; Unfair - Not right, improper, wrong; Sill - The bottom part of a window; Snores - Makes a loud noise while sleeping.

Reading is Fun (NCERT Page 10)

Tick (✓) the correct answer.

Q.1 What time did Neha's clock ring every morning?

(a) 4 o'clock (b) 9 o'clock
(c) 6 o'clock

Q.2 What did the birds say?

(a) Sleep on (b) Wake up
(c) Go and play

Q.3 What is inside you that makes you get up at the same time everyday?

(a) Our body clock (b) Our eyes
(c) Our feet

Ans. 1. (c) 6 o'clock, 2. (b) Wake up, 3. (a) Our body clock.

Q.4 Put the letters in the right order. One has been done for you.

ilesm — Smile

(a) mrala
(b) ockic
(c) norming
(d) edorns
(e) wodwin

Ans. (a) alarm (b) clock
(c) morning (d) snored
(e) window

Let's Listen and Talk (NCERT Page 11)

Q.1 Listen to the sounds around you when you are on your way to school. Discuss with your friend the sounds that you heard. List them here

Ans.

Sounds you heard		Sounds your friend heard
	Cars honking	Dogs barking
	People talking	Vendors calling out their goods
	Leaves rusting	School bus engine
	Birds chirping	Construction work
	Loudspeak er noise	Airplane flying overhead

Q.2 If there is no clock in the house to wake you in the morning, how will you wake up?
Will you continue to sleep or ...

Ans. If there is no clock to wake me up in the morning, I can wake up by the following ways.

- Stick to a routine.
- Make sure there is a window in my room so that I can wake up due to sunlight.
- Set an alarm on my phone.
- Ask someone to wake me up.

Q.3 What are the different ways of knowing the time during the day?

Ans. There are many ways to check the time during the day.
(a) Wrist watch (b) Wall clock
(c) Mobile phone (d) Sunlight
(e) Certain programmes on television.

Word Building (NCERT Page 12)

Find the hidden words
mother, birds, clock, alarm, happy, morning, holiday, hungry, sunday

Ans.

h	c	d	a	q	r	b	i	r	d	s	e
u	b	f	l	m	a	h	o	s	b	m	n
n	i	e	o	b	t	f	c	a	c	f	o
g	t	m	p	a	b	c	l	i	e	d	p
r	s	u	v	z	a	m	o	t	h	e	r
y	a	w	y	x	k	s	c	b	n	o	k
p	l	o	h	m	t	u	k	c	e	v	r
r	k	p	o	e	i	a	b	o	f	u	s
s	u	a	l	a	r	m	d	o	m	k	f
t	u	o	i	m	k	i	m	n	w	i	g
s	u	n	d	a	y	t	x	z	a	s	c
k	p	i	a	o	l	h	a	p	p	y	o
m	o	n	y	t	m	o	r	n	i	n	g

Say Aloud (NCERT Page 12)

ought	matter	tick – tock	tick – tack
bought	chatter	tell – told	tip – tin
caught	shatter	train – time	take – tall

Let's Write (NCERT Page 13)

Q.1 Who said these words and to whom?

(a) "Wake up, dear! Wake up fast!"

(b) "Ma, who woke me up today?"

(c) "Why do you sleep at nine every night?"

Ans.

Who Said	To Whom
(a) Birds	Neha
(b) Neha	Mother
(c) Mother	Neha

Q.2. Use the help box to fill in the blanks.

was, were

(a) Ram ______ a good football player.

(b) The cows ______ grazing in the field.

(c) My toys ______ broken.

(d) Her frock ______ too long.

(e) The market ______ closed.

(f) The children ______ happy.

(g) The flowers ______ kept in a vase.

Ans. (a) was (b) were (c) were
(d) was (e) was (f) were
(g) were

Q.3. Look at the pictures below and complete the following paragraph. You will need these words

pulled out, inside, called out, behind, under

Yesterday, I lost a book. I looked for it everywhere.

I looked (a)__________ a door.

I looked (b)________ a cupboard.

I looked (c)________ a bed.

I could not find it anywhere. Then, I

(d) ______ Sheroo. 

Sheroo, my dog came running to me.

I asked him to look for my book.

He (e) ________  another book from my bag.

Ans. (a) behind (b) inside
(c) under (d) called out
(e) pulled out

Fun Time (NCERT Page 15)

Q.1. Here is a word, clock. Write down words relating to clock.

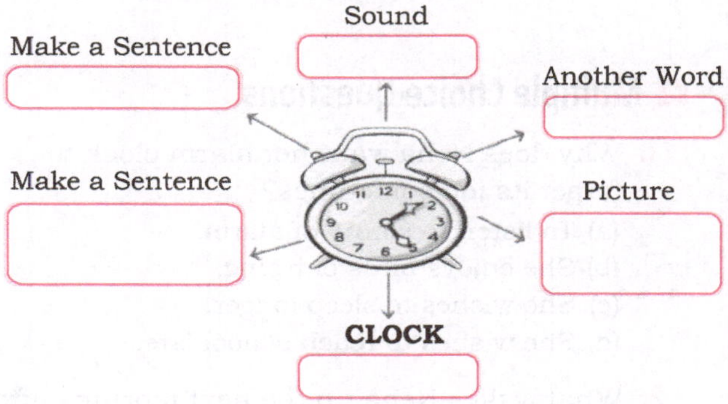

Ans.

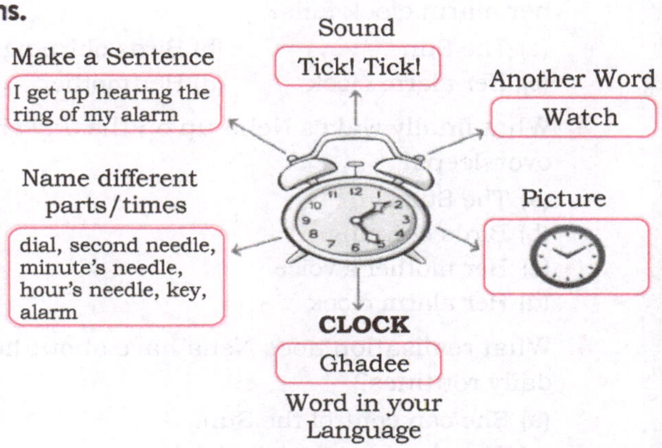

Here is a word, Morning . Now write down words related to it.

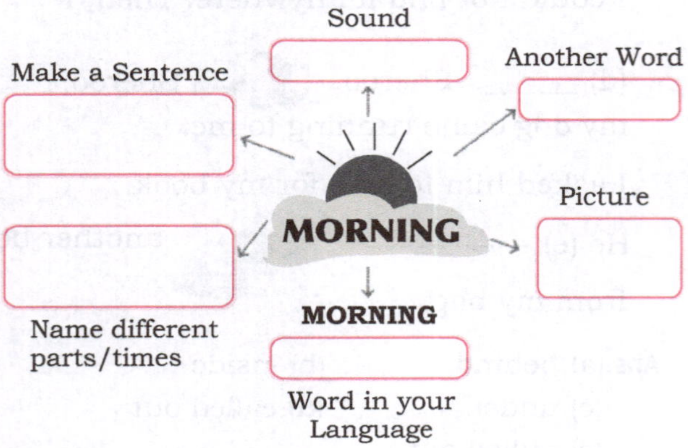

Ans.

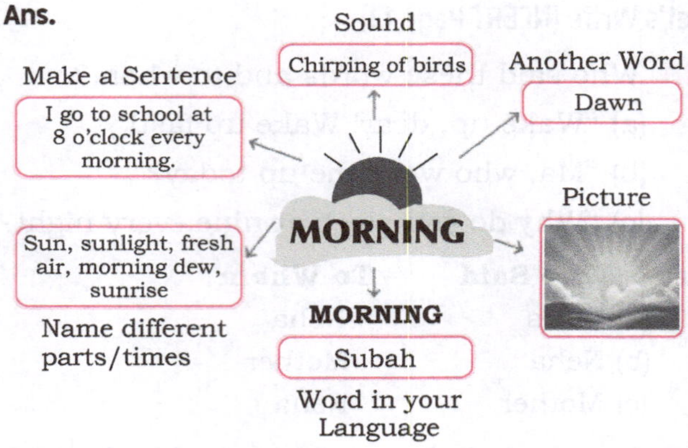

PRACTICE QUESTIONS

Multiple Choice Questions

1. Why does Neha want her alarm clock to forget its job sometimes?
   (a) To listen to sound of alarm.
   (b) She enjoys birds chirping.
   (c) She wishes to sleep longer.
   (d) She wishes to reach school late.

2. What wakes Neha up the next morning after her alarm clock fails?
   (a) The Sun (b) Birds chirping
   (c) Her alarm clock (d) Her mother

3. What finally wakes Neha up on the day she oversleeps?
   (a) The Sun
   (b) Birds chirping
   (c) Her mother's voice
   (d) Her alarm clock

4. What realisation does Neha have about her daily routines?
   (a) She can control the Sun.
   (b) She should wake up early.
   (c) She has a clock inside her.
   (d) She can wake up on her own.

5. Why does Neha sleep late on Sundays?
   (a) She doesn't like to wake up early.
   (b) The Sun wakes her up early.
   (c) Alarm clock doesn't ring on Sunday.
   (d) Its a holiday and she has nothing to do.

Ans. 1. (c), 2. (b), 3. (c), 4. (c), 5. (a)

True or False

1. The birds stop chirping when Neha wishes for quiet.
2. The poem suggests bathing and dressing up after waking up.
3. Neha's mother wakes her up when the Sun is behind the clouds.
4. Neha feels frustrated that the alarm clock rings every morning at six.
5. Neha's mother intentionally hides the alarm clock to teach Neha a lesson.

Ans. 1. False, 2. False, 3. True, 4. True
5. False

Answer the Following Questions

1. What did Neha do when the alarm rings?

Ans. When the alarm rings, Neha wakes up but she is upset. She wants to sleep for some more time and wishes that the alarm does not do its job sometimes.

2. What does Neha wish for the Sun? What happens to the Sun on the next day?

Ans. The Neha wishes for the Sun to leave her alone. On the next day, the Sun is hidden behind the clouds.

3. Why do Neha get up early?

Ans. Neha gets up early because of the clock inside her body which tells her to wake up.

Who said to Whom

1. "Relax! Today is Sunday!"
2. "Wake up dear! Wake up fast!"
3. "But, I was sleeping, how could I ...?"

Ans.

Who said	To whom
1. Mother	Neha
2. Birds	Neha
3. Neha	Mother

Writing Task

1. Write a letter to your younger sister telling her the important of waking up early. Explain the concept of biological clock and how it is beneficial for us.

Ans. XYZ Apartments,

New Delhi

22nd October, 20XX

Dear Riddhi

How are you? I am doing well here and hope that you feel the same. Recently I read about the concept of biological clock of the body. A biological clock is a system that regulates an organism's sense of time. It controls our body's functioning.

It tells us when to go to sleep, when we wake up and when we want food. In fact, remember how we used to wake up early even on a Sunday. It was because of this biological clock.

The purpose of me telling you this is to maintain a schedule, a routine. It will set your biological clock properly and you will remain fit and healthy. Wake up early in the morning and go for a walk. You can even do yoga. Eat healthy meals at proper intervals. And sleep early to get atleast 8 hours of sleep.

Maa and Paa send their love and we all hope to see you soon.

Yours lovingly

Seema

CHAPTER 1 NOSES

Summary of the Poem The girl looks into the mirror and feels that her nose grows in a strange and funny way. She says that if anyone ever wants to laugh but doesn't know why, they should just look in the mirror. The way the nose sticks out is so amusing that it will definitely make anyone smile or laugh.

Stanza-wise Explanation

Stanza 1

I looked in the mirror
and looked at my nose:
it's the funniest thing,
the way it grows
stuck right out where
all of it shows
with two little holes where the
breathing goes.

Word-Meaning *Funniest - Something that makes you laugh; Stuck - Fixed in one place.*

Exp. The girl looks in the mirror and notices her nose. She finds it funny as how her nose stands out on her face, with two small holes for breathing. She notices its shape and where it sits on her face.

Stanza 2

I looked in the mirror
and saw in there
the end of my chin
and the start of my hair
and between there
isn't much space to
spare with my nose,
like a handle, sticking there.

Exp. The girl looks in the mirror again. She notices how her nose sits between the end of her chin and the start of her hair, leaving little space in between. She compares her nose to a handle, that is sticking on her face.

Stanza 3

If ever you want
to giggle and shout
and can't think of what
to do it about,

just look in the mirror
and then, no doubt,
you'll see how funny
your nose sticks out!

Word-Meaning *Giggle - A light and silly laugh; Shout - To make a loud noise or speak loudly; Sticks out - Grows out.*

Exp. The girl suggests that if you ever feel like laughing or shouting but don't know why, all you have to do is look in the mirror. She believes that seeing how funny your own nose looks will definitely make you laugh. She emphasises that your nose sticking out will bring a smile to your face.

NCERT FOLDER

Reading is Fun (NCERT Page 19)

Q.1 Why does the poet feel that the nose is a funny thing?

Ans. The poet feels that the nose is funny because it is stuck on the face like a handle and has two little holes.

Q.2 Why is your nose important for you?

Ans. The nose is important because the two little holes helps us breathe.

Q.3 Does the child in the poem like her nose? Why do you think so?

Ans. The child in the poem likes her nose because she finds it funny and enjoys how it sticks out, making her laugh.

Let's Talk (NCERT Page 19)

Q.1 Describe a few funny things you have seen. Do they make you laugh?

Ans. I have seen some funny things like a dog chasing its tail or a cat jumping but missing its spot. I also laugh when people slip in a harmless way or make funny faces.

Q.2 What does 'features' mean? Look up the dictionary. What are the different kinds of features of people we come across in the world? Discuss.

Ans. 'Features' are the special parts or traits of something. For people, features include facial parts like eyes, nose and mouth, physical traits such as height and build, and personality traits like kindness or humor.

Fun Time (NCERT Page 20)

Q.1 Sit in groups.

Q.2 Look at your friend's face and describe what you see. Use words like long, round, oval, slanted, sharp, flat to help you. You can use other words also.

Ans. My friend Shreya has an oval face with a round chin. Her eyes are almond-shaped and their nose is flat. She has a bit of chubby cheeks and a smooth jawline.

Q.3 What is your favourite fruit? Describe it in five sentences.

Ans. My favourite fruit is mango.

(i) It is sweet and juicy, with a soft yellow flesh.
(ii) The skin is usually green, yellow, or red.
(iii) Mangoes have a large seed in the middle.
(iv) There are many varieties of mangoes. They all taste different.
(v) I love eating them in the summer because they are so refreshing!

(a) How does it smell?

Ans. It smells sweet and fruity.

(b) How does it look?

Ans. It is yellow or orange in colour and sometimes has a red or green skin.

(c) How does it feel?

Ans. It feels smooth and soft.

(d) When you bite it what sound does it make?

Ans. It makes a quiet, soft sound.

(e) How does it taste?

Ans. It tastes very sweet and juicy.

Let's Exercise (NCERT Page 21)

A breathing exercise

- Close your right nostril with your right thumb.
- Inhale slowly through your left nostril till your lungs are filled with air.
- Now close your left nostril with your second and third fingers.
- Remove your finger from the right nostril and exhale through it.
- Repeat this exercise, slowly in the beginning, and with practice, increase your speed.

Let's Write (NCERT Page 22)

Q.1 Do you know a fish breathes from its gills? Write two sentences about other animals which can breathe under water.

Ans. Yes, I know that fish have a special organ called gills to breathe under water.

- Turtles can hold their breathe underwater and breathe when they come up for air.
- Frogs can also breathe through their skin when they're in water, and they use their lungs when they are out of water.

Q.2 Punctuate the following passage Mother father neelam said i have got a fire engine ive got a fire engine whats this whats this called Mother somewhat confused by the noise ive got a fire engine Mother come and see it.

Ans. "Mother, Father," Neelam said, "I have got a fire engine! I've got a fire engine!" "What's this? What's this?" called Mother, somewhat confused by the noise. "I've got a fire engine, Mother. Come and see it."

Q.3 Using a red pencil, choose and circle the things whose smell you like. Now with a blue pencil circle the things whose smell you do not like. Make five sentences like this - I like/do not like the smell of .... because it reminds me of..........

Ans.

(a) I like the smell of chocolate because it makes me think of yummy desserts and happy times.

(b) I do not like the smell of rotten fruit because it makes me think of bad, spoiled food.

(c) I like the smell of roses because it reminds me of lovely gardens and fresh flowers.

(d) I do not like the smell of garbage because it reminds me of trash and dirty places.

(e) I like the smell of coffee because it makes me think of a cozy and comforting start to the day.

Let's Sing (NCERT Page 23)

What is it?

Tall ears,
Twinkly nose,
Tiny tail,
And -hop, he goes!

What is he -
Can you guess?
I feed him carrots
And watercress.

His ears are long,
His tail is small -
And he doesn't make any
noise at all!

What is it
Anns. Babbit

Tall ears,
Twinkly nose,
Tiny tail,
And - hop, he goes!
- Marie Louise Allen

Write three pairs of words that rhyme with each other.

Ans. (a) Nose - Goes
(b) Guess - Watercress
(c) Small - All

PRACTICE QUESTIONS

Multiple Choice Questions

1. What does the poet compare the nose to?
   (a) A box
   (b) A ball
   (c) A lamp
   (d) A handle
2. Where does the poet look to see her nose?
   (a) In the lens
   (b) In a mirror
   (c) In the water
   (d) In the window
3. What does the poet find funny about the nose?
   (a) Its size
   (b) The colour of it
   (c) The way it grows
   (d) The way we breathe through it.
4. How many holes does the nose have, according to the poem?
   (a) One (b) Two
   (c) Three (d) Four
5. What does the poet suggest to do when you want to giggle and shout?
   (a) Play outside
   (b) Dance around
   (c) Look in the mirror
   (d) Stay wherever you are.

Ans. 1. (d), 2. (b), 3. (c), 4. (b), 5. (c)

True or False

1. The poet feels sad when she looks at her nose.
2. The poet finds the nose small and hardly noticeable.
3. The poet describes the nose as having three little holes.
4. Poem suggests that looking at your nose in mirror can make you laugh.
5. The nose is located between the end of the chin and the start of the hair

Ans. 1. False, 2. False, 3. False, 4. True, 5. True

Answer the Following Questions

1. Why is a Nose important for us?

Ans. Nose is important to us as it helps us breathe and stay alive.

2. What other suitable title can you suggest for the poem?

Ans. Another suitable title for the poem could be - 'A Funny Feature on Our Face.'

3. Does the child in the poem like her nose? Why do you think so?

Ans. The child in the poem seems to like her nose as she finds its funny for its size.

Writing Task

1. Imagine that you wake up with the nose of an elephant. How would you look? What would you feel and what are the things that you would do with your new nose?

   You can use the given image to write your answer.

Ans. If I wake up as a nose of an elephant, I think I would look very weird. I like my small nose. So, having a long nose would be strange and funny to watch myself in the mirror. However, I think it would be fun. With the long nose, I could reduce the use of my hands.

I could reach anything that I could not reach with my hands. I can use the nose called trunk to take a bath too. Hence, even though it would be weird to see a trunk every day, I would get used to it and enjoy it.

CHAPTER 2
THE LITTLE FIR TREE

Summary of the Chapter

Shetty was a magician. One day, while he was returning home it started raining. So, he took shelter under a small and beautiful fir tree. Being grateful for its protection, he promised to grant four wishes of the fir tree. First, the fir tree wished for green leaves as it did not like its own needle-like leaves. Its wish was granted but a goat came and ate them.

Next, it wished for golden leaves, but they were stolen by two men. Now; it wished for glass leaves, as no one can steal them. However, a strong wind broke all the leaves. Finally, the fir tree asked for its old needle-like leaves. It happily found its needles restored the next morning.

WORD-MEANING

Shelter - A place giving temporary protection Reward - A kind of award or prize; Grant - To fulfill a wish; Steal/stole - To take something without permission or right, often secretly.

NCERT FOLDER

Reading is Fun (NCERT Page 27)

Tick (✓) the correct answer.

Q.1 The pretty little fir tree was happy with gold leaves but...

(a) a goat came along and ate them.
(b) all the leaves got wet in rain.
(c) a man stole them.

Ans. (c) a man stole them.

Q.2 The fir tree was sad...

(a) because it had yellow leaves.
(b) because it had needle-like leaves.
(c) because it was very short.

Ans. (b) because it had needle-like leaves.

Q.3 The fir tree was not happy with the gold leaves...

(a) because the goats came and ate them up.
(b) a man stole them.
(c) the gold leaves broke.

Ans. (b) a man stole them.

Word Building (NCERT Page 28)

Q.1 By changing the circled word to its opposite, rewrite these sentences. One has been done for you.

(a) I carry a light bag to school every day.

Ans. I carry a heavy bag to school every day.

(b) Rina won the race.

Ans. Rina lost the race.

(c) I love eating vegetables.

Ans. I hate eating vegetables.

(d) This glass of milk is full.

Ans. This glass of milk is empty.

(e) The old man is wise.

Ans. The old man is foolish.

Q.2 Now give the opposite of the words below by adding **un** or **im**.

(a) happy	(b) polite
(c) seen	(d) proper
(e) lucky	(f) possible
(g) important	(h) perfect
(i) healthy	(j) safe
(k) patient	(l) pure

Ans.

(a) unhappy	(b) impolite
(c) unseen	(d) improper
(e) unlucky	(f) impossible
(g) unimportant	(h) imperfect
(i) unhealthy	(j) unsafe
(k) impatient	(l) impure

Q.3 Rita **loved** her dog Sheroo. Everyday, Sheroo would **go out** of the house and **come** back himself. But one day he did not come home. Rita looked **everywhere** for him. Tears rolled **down** her cheeks. Sheroo was **lost**. He was **nowhere** to be found. Rita was **crying** when she reached home. She got into her bed. All of a sudden something jumped on her. Can you guess who it was? Rita was very **happy**.

Give the opposites of the words in bold.

Ans. loved-hated, go out-come in, come-go, everywhere-nowhere, down-up, lost-found, nowhere-somewhere, crying-smiling, happy-sad.

Let's Write (NCERT Page 29)

Q.1 Rewrite the passage below using capital letters where necessary.

(i) one saturday afternoon amarjit and his little sister rani went for a picnic to india gate. there they saw ducks, water and their friend raj

Ans. One Saturday afternoon, Amarjit and his little sister Rani went for a picnic to India Gate. There they saw ducks, water, and their friend Raj.

(ii) oh dear said the fir tree I like my old needle-like leaves best for goats don't eat them and no man can steal them

Ans. "Oh dear!," said the fir tree, "I like my old needle-like leaves best, for goats don't eat them and no man can steal them."

Let's Talk (NCERT Page 30)

Q.1 Look at the picture below. In the yellow box there are eight things. You can see six of them in the picture. You cannot see the other two. Write down the four things that you can see.

Ans. ducks, mat, boy, girl, tree, flowers (any 4)

Q.2 Look at the picture again. Describe the picture.

Ans. A boy and a girl have come to a park for a picnic. They are enjoying the natural scene by the side of a pond. Two ducks are swimming in the water. The girl has spread a mat on which she has put lunch box, bananas, a ball, etc. A bird is sitting near the mat. The boy is looking at the bird. He looks happy.

Fun Time (NCERT Page 31)

Q.1 Ajit loved flowers. He always wanted to have a garden for himself. Mohan, his friend gave him an idea. He said, "Why, we can have a garden in a dish!"

"Ha! Ha!" Ajit laughed. "A garden in a dish?"

"Yes, dish gardens are tiny gardens planted in a shallow dish. We must first put sand, manure and pebbles in a dish. Plant very tiny plants in it and place the dish on the window sill."

Ans. Do it yourself.

Q.2 Glass breaks easily when it is dropped. Do you think a mud flower pot, a glass spoon, a wooden table, a plastic cup, books or your plastic water bottle can break easily? Circle the things that can.

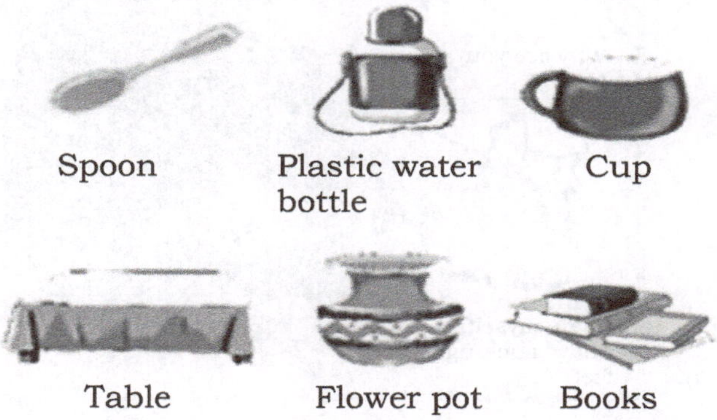

Ans. A mud flower pot and a glass spoon can break, but a plastic cup, wooden table, books and a plastic water bottle will not break.

Q.3 Which of the following actions would make others happy/unhappy?

- respecting elders
- caring for pets
- playing with friends
- watching television all day
- not saying thank you
- getting angry easily
- visiting a sick friend
- telling lies
- being polite
- being honest
- not sharing
- being greedy

Actions that make people happy	Actions that make people unhappy
respecting elders	watching television all day
caring for pets	not saying thank you
playing with friends	getting angry easily
visiting a sick friend	telling lies
being polite	not sharing
being honest	being greedy

Let's Listen, Read and Write (NCERT Page 33)

There was a thick jungle with beautiful green trees and birds. Koyal was singing happily. Suddenly she heard someone crying. It was her friend, the peacock. She flew to him and asked...

Some things make you feel happy. Some things make you feel sad. Write a poem on the picture.

Ans. Koyal was singing happily,
he heard the peacock cry.
the Koyal flew to him,
asked the peacock why?
The peacock replied,
"I have ugly feet.
I hate myself."
Let's make a word tree
The Koyal sang once again,
of the peacock's beautiful feet.

Let's Make a Word Tree (NCERT Page 34)

This is how you will do it.

- Take a long green sheet of paper or newspaper. Roll it like this.

- Hold the roll of paper firmly in one hand and cut four slits from the top to halfway down the roll.

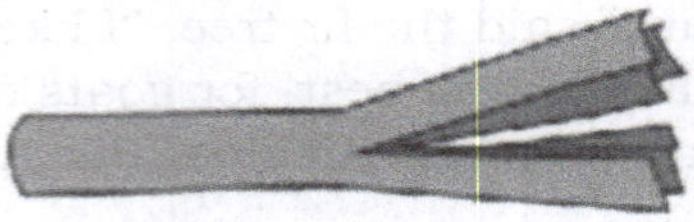

- Still holding the roll of paper firmly, bend back the four sections of the cut paper.

- Pull out the branches. Do this by pulling up the cut sections slowly and carefully from the centre of the roll.

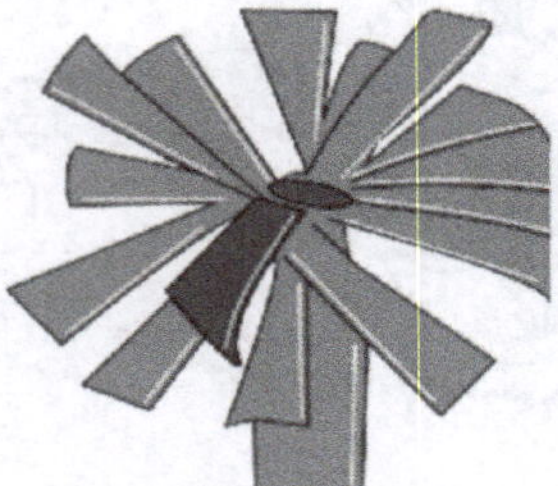

Write words related to leaves on the trees and make a Word Tree. Now make sentences with these words.

Ans.
- **Green** The leaves on the tree are bright green in the summer.
- **Fall** In autumn, the leaves fall to the ground.
- **Branch** The bird sat on a branch covered with leaves.
- **Soft** The soft leaves felt nice when I touched them.
- **Dry** The dry leaves crunched under my feet as I walked.
- **Shade** We sat under the tree to enjoy the cool shade from its leaves.
- **Fresh** The fresh leaves smelled good after the rain.

PRACTICE QUESTIONS

Multiple Choice Questions

1. What was the fir tree's first wish?
   (a) To grow taller
   (b) To have gold leaves
   (c) To have glass leaves
   (d) To have green leaves like its friends
2. What happened to the fir tree's gold leaves?
   (a) They were eaten by a goat
   (b) They were stolen by two men
   (c) They fell off during the night
   (d) They turned into glass leaves
3. What happened to the fir tree's glass leaves?
   (a) They turned into gold
   (b) They were eaten by a goat
   (c) They were stolen by men
   (d) The wind blew and broke them

Ans. 1. (d), 2. (b), 3. (d)

Fill in the Blanks

1. Shetty the magician granted the little fir tree _______ wishes.
2. The fir tree's glass leaves broke because of the strong _______.
3. The fir tree wished for gold leaves as _______ do not eat gold leaves.
4. The fir tree wished for _____ leaves after green and gold leaves were lost.
5. After getting back its old needle-like leaves, the little fir tree said, "Oh! I never was so _______."

Ans. 1. four, 2. wind, 3. goats, 4. needle-like 5. happy

True or False

1. Shetty saw an ugly fir tree.
2. Shetty wanted to enjoy the rain.
3. The golden leaves shone brightly in the Sun.
4. The fir tree got its needle shaped leaves back.
5. The tree didn't want the birds to make nests on it.

Ans. 1. False, 2. False, 3. True, 4. True, 5. False

Answer the Following Questions

1. How did the fir tree react when its gold leaves were stolen?

Ans. When its gold leaves were stolen, the fir tree was unhappy and wished to have glass leaves.

2. How did the fir tree feel about its needle-like leaves at the end?

Ans. The Fir tree learned that its needle-like trees were the best for it and that we should be happy with what we have.

3. What did the fir tree learn about its original leaves?

Ans. The Fir tree was very happy to have its needle-like tree back, as no goat would eat them and no men would steal them.

Writing Task

1. Write a paragraph on 'We should be happy with what we have'.

Ans. Satisfaction is a great virtue in life. Those who are contented with what life gives them, always remain in peace. And those, who are never satisfied with what life has given to them, never get anything worthwhile in life. People who are always dissatisfied always face problems. To fulfil their needs, they end up doing immoral or illegal acts that lands them in trouble. We have exploited resources and destroyed our environment. Hence, we should be happy with what we have.

CHAPTER 1 RUN!

Summary of the Poem In this poem, the poet asks the children to run away from the city and go to countryside to enjoy themselves.

Stanza-wise Explanation

Stanza 1

Away from the city Out to the country,
And into the sun, Run! Run! Run!

Word-Meaning *Country side - A rural area.*

Exp. The poet tells the children to leave the busy city and run towards the countryside, where they can enjoy the warmth and light of the sun.

Stanza 2

Run in the raindrops! Run little races
Run 'neath the trees! With each little breeze!

Word-Meaning *Breeze - A gentle, light wind.*

Exp. The poet is asking the children to run outside in the rain and under the trees. They can have fun racing with the wind as it blows gently.

Stanza 3

Run down the hillside, Run through the meadow,
Run up the lane; Then run back again!

Word-Meaning *Lane - A small road or pathl; Meadow - A field with grass and wildflowers.*

Exp. The poet tells the children to run down a hill, run up a street, run through a meadow and then run back to where they started. It's about enjoying running in different places and coming back to where you began.

Stanza 4

Run and be merry Run to the country,
All through the day! Away! Away!

Word-Meaning *Merry - Happy or cheerful.*

Exp. The poet suggests that the children should run and have fun all day long. He wants them to run to the countryside and enjoy being away from the city.

NCERT FOLDER

Reading is Fun (NCERT Page 40)

Q.1 What does the poem tell us to do?

Ans. The poem tells us to leave the city and enjoy running freely in the countryside.

Q.2 Write about the places where the poet wants us to run.

Ans. The poet wants us to run towards the countryside, through raindrops, under the trees, down the hillside, up the street and through the meadow.

Let's Talk (NCERT Page 40)

Q.1 Do you like to play and run about? Why?

Ans. Yes, I like to play and run about because it makes me feel happy and energetic.

Q.2 Running is very good exercise. Name any three games that you play, in which you have to run.

Ans. Three games in which we have to run are

- Race
- Cricket
- Football

Q.3 When you run fast, what do you feel is happening to your body?

Ans. When I run fast, I feel my heart beating faster, my breath getting heavier and my body becoming warmer.

Say Aloud (NCERT Page 40)

beneath	breeze
meet	fear
each	meadow

Ans. Do it yourself.

Let's Spell (NCERT Page 40)

Some letters are missing in each word.

Write **ee** or **ea** in each word.

(a) tr ___ ___ s (e) sl ___ ___ p

(b) pl ___ ___ se (f) b ___ ___ p

(c) t ___ ___ se (g) f ___ ___ t

(d) t ___ ___ ch (h) m ___ ___ t

Ans. (a) trees (b) please (c) tease
(d) teach (e) sleep (f) beep
(g) feet (h) meat

Now add more words with **ee** and **ea** and put them inside the bubbles

ee	ea
Green	Read
Deep	Team
Cheer	Seat
Need	Clean
Feel	Speak
Peel	Heal

Let's Listen (NCERT Page 41)

Q.1 Say the words aloud one by one. Follow the instructions and move your body accordingly.

Shoulders	Move them up and down.
Feet	Walk forward and backward.
Run	Fast and slow.
Hands	Move them left and right.

Ans. Do it yourself

Q.2 Now jump, hop, march and tiptoe.

Ans. Do it yourself

Let's Write (NCERT Page 42)

Q.1 Answer the questions by looking at the picture on the opposite page (given above)

Example : What is happening in picture 5?

The girl is diving into the water

(i) What is Mohan practising in picture 4?

He is ______________________

Ans. He is practising high jump.

(ii) What are Anil and his friends pulling in picture 3?

__________ are pulling __________

Ans. Anil and his friends are pulling a rope.

(iii) Where are the boats racing in picture 2?

__________ are __________

Ans. The boats are racing in the water.

(iv) What are the boys doing in picture 1?

__________ are __________

Ans. The boys are running a race.

(v) What are the girls doing in picture 6?

They are ______________________

Ans. They are swimming.

Q.2 Now make one more question for each picture. Write the question in the space below each picture. Use how many, what are, where are/is, how, why, to make questions.

(i) Picture 1: How many boys are running in the race?

(ii) Picture 2: How many boats are there in the picture?

(iii) Picture 3: Where are Anil and his friends pulling the rope?

(iv) Picture 4: What is the number on Mohan's shirt?

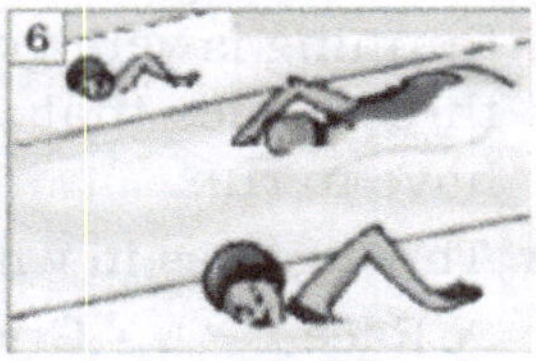

(v) Picture 5: Who is looking at the girl?

(vi) Picture 6: Where are the girls swimming?

PRACTICE QUESTIONS

Multiple Choice Questions

1. What does the poet want us to leave behind?
   (a) The city (b) The trees
   (c) The house (d) The mountains
2. According to the poem, where should we run under?
   (a) The sky (b) The river
   (c) The trees (d) The mountains
3. In the poem, where does the poet encourage us to run?
   (a) In the city
   (b) In the countryside
   (c) On the road
   (d) On the mountains
4. What feeling does the poet emphasise throughout the poem?
   (a) Freedom and joy (b) Fear
   (c) Sadness (d) Anxiety

Ans. 1. (a), 2. (c), 3. (b), 4. (a)

Fill in the Blanks

1. The poet encourages us to run away and be ________.
2. We are told to run back again after running through the ________.
3. The poem mentions running in the ________, enjoying the weather.
4. The poets wants us to race with the ________.

Ans. 1. merry, 2. meadow, 3. countryside, 4. breeze

True or False

1. The poem mentions running beside the river.
2. The poet asks us to run through the meadow.
3. The poet suggests that we run with the breeze.
4. The poem talks about running only on a sunny day.

Ans. 1. False, 2. True, 3. True, 4. False

Answer the Following Questions

1. What should you do in the raindrops?

Ans. We should run in the raindrops.

2. What are you advised to do all through the day?

Ans. We are advised to run and be happy throughout the day.

3. Describe the different places and activities the poem encourages you to run through.

Ans. The poet wants us to run from the city to the countryside. He wants us to run under the raindrops, under the trees, down the hillside, up the street, through the meadow and then, run back again.

Writing Task

1. Running is a form of exercise which keep us happy and fit. Realising this, write a story about a boy named Vihaan who learned the important of exercising daily.

Ans. Vihaan was not a lazy boy at all. However, he loved playing video games. He took a promise from his parents that if he scored well, he would be allowed to play video games during the summer vacations. He scored really well in the exams.

Summer vacations had started and Vihaan spent all his time in the room. He stopped going out to play with his friends. Soon, he started gaining a lot of weight. Soon, Vihaan was fat and unhealthy. When school started, everyone was shocked to see Vihaan. He looked so different. His teacher called him and asked him to come school half an hour early. Vihaan came to school early and exercised with his teacher. Gradually, he lost his weight and realised that he needed to exercise everyday to remain fit.

CHAPTER 2 NASRUDDIN'S AIM

Summary of the Chapter

Once Nasruddin boasted about his archery skills, claiming that his arrow always hit the target. His friends decided to test him and brought him a bow and some arrows. Nasruddin held the bow in his hands, strung it, aimed it at the target and shot an arrow. But the arrow did not hit the target. His friends began to laugh at him. He defended himself by saying that it was not his aim but Azad's aim. Then he picked up another arrow. Once again, he strung the bow, aimed at the target and shot the arrow, but failed to hit the target. At last, he got lucky and the arrow hit on the target. Nasruddin said triumphantly that it was his aim.

WORD-MEANING

Boast - Talk with pride; Skill - The ability to do something well; Archery - The art of shooting arrows; String - Provide the bow with a string; Target - Goal, aim; Bow - A weapon used for shooting arrows; Pointing - To focus on something; Defending - Protecting; Argued - Discussed; Stared - to look at something continuously; Agape - wide open.

NCERT FOLDER

Reading is Fun (NCERT Page 48)

Q.1 What did Nasruddin boast about?

Ans. Nasruddin boasted about his exceptional skill in archery.

Q.2 Why did Nasruddin take someone else's name each time he missed the target?

Ans. Nasruddin took someone else's name each time he missed the target as he did not want to show his poor skills in archery to his friends.

Q.3 Why did Nasruddin say, "It was my aim," the third time?

Ans. Nasruddin said, "It was my aim," the third time because he successfully hit the target and wanted to take credit for the success.

Q.4 Do you think Nasruddin was good at archery?

Ans. No, Nasruddin was not good at archery, as he missed the target multiple times before finally hitting it.

Read and Enjoy (NCERT Page 48)

Nasruddin Hodja

Be a Nasruddin Hodja Yourself

Q.1 What would you have done if your grandmother would have slipped?

Ans. I would help her to get up, comfort her and would pick up her glasses and stick.

I would hold her hand and lead her to her room to take rest and relax.

I would tell my parents about her fall so that they could call a doctor and could get her checked up.

Word Building (NCERT Page 50)

Q.1 Shoot the arrow and hit the target by matching the words with their correct meanings.

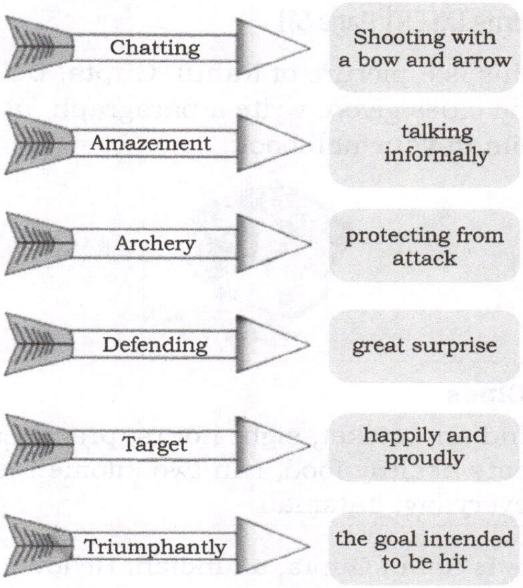

Ans. Chatting — talking informally
Amazement — great surprise
Archery — shooting with a bow and arrow
Defending — protecting from attack
Target — the goal intended to be hit
Triumphantly — happily and proudly

Q.2 Replace the bold word/words with a word from the quiver and re-write the sentence

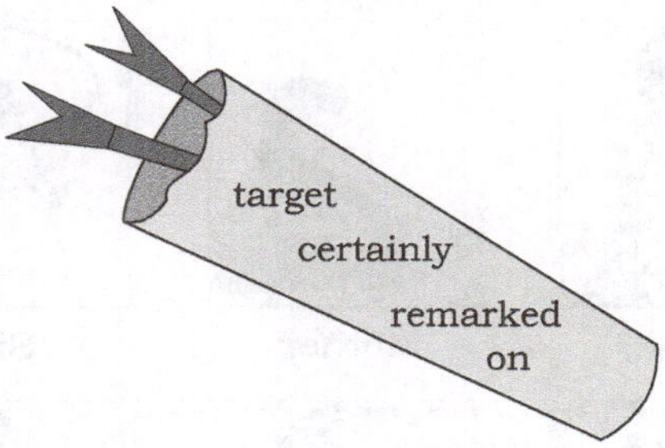

(a) In no time she hit the **object she aimed at.**

Ans. In no time she hit the target.

(b) Nasruddin was **surely** not a good archer

Ans. Nasruddin was certainly not a good archer.

(c) The teacher **said something about** his good handwriting. He felt very happy.

Ans. The teacher remarked about his good handwriting. He felt very happy.

Let's Write (NCERT Page 51)

Q.1 This is a picture of Rahul Gupta. Using the clues given, write a paragraph about him in your notebook.

Clues

Indian, cricket, eight hours, practises, eats healthy food, run two kilometres everyday, batsman

Ans. He is Rahul Gupta, an Indian. He loves to play cricket. He's trying hard to be a part of the Indian cricket team. To get selected to the Indian team, he practises cricket for over eight hours daily. To maintain good health, he run two kilometres everyday and does his exercises regularly. To stay fit and strong, he eats healthy food like vegetables, sprouts, eggs, meat, etc.

Q.2 This is Rajiv's family. They are a healthy family. See what each one does to remain healthy.

Father

Mother

Sita

Grandpa

Grandma

Rajiv

Ans.
- **Father** is lifting weights.
- **Mother** is doing yoga.
- **Sita** is skipping a rope.
- **Grandpa** is walking in the park.
- **Grandma** is drinking milk.
- **Rajiv** is jogging in the park.

Q.2 Use the words 'and' or 'but' and make as many sentences as you can about Rajivs family.

Example Grandpa and Grandma get up early in the morning.

Grandpa is walking but Rajiv is jogging.'

Ans. (i) Father and mother are exercising.

(ii) Grandpa and Rajiv's sister, Sita are walking.

(iii) Father is lifting weight but mother is doing yoga.

(iv) Grandpa is walking and Grandma is drinking milk.

(v) Rajiv is jogging but his sister, Sita is skipping a rope.

(vi) Rajiv and his family members wake up early in the morning.

Fun Time (NCERT Page 53)

Watch the arrow pierce the apple!

Would you like to see the arrow piercing the red apple?

Bring the page close to your face, touch the star with your nose, and then look at the picture!

Ans. Do it for yourself.

Let's Play (NCERT Page 54)

Q.1 Fill in the grid with words given below. You can use one word more than once.

stick bat/ball eleven table racket
ball football
stadium two to four ground

Ans.

Name of the game		What you play with	Where you play it	Number of players
(i)	Cricket	bat/ball	ground	eleven
(ii)	Hockey	stick/ball	stadium	eleven
(iii)	Table Tennis	racket	stadium	two to four
(iv)	Football	football	stadium	eleven

Q.2 Using the information in the grid, write a sentence about each game. One has been done for you.

(a) Cricket is an outdoor game. We play it with a bat and a ball. There are eleven players in this game.

Ans. (b) Hockey is an outdoor game. We play it with a stick and a ball. There are eleven players in this game.

(c) Table tennis is an indoor game. We play it on the table by using a racket and a ball. There are two to four players in this game.

(d) Football is an outdoor game. We play it with a football. There are eleven players in this game.

Q.3 The following words are used in various sports. List them under the sport that they are used in.

(a) googly (b) goal

(c) LBW (d) penalty

(e) free kick (f) penalty corner

Some words may be used in more than one game.

Ans.

Hockey	Cricket	Football
1. Penalty	1. Googly	1. Goal
2. Penalty corner	2. LBW	2. Free kick

Team Time (NCERT Page 56)

You can use an old tennis ball which has lost its bounce, to make the head of a puppet. She looks like a little girl in a skirt and is very quick and easy to make.

Look at the picture carefully and you will see how she works - your fingers are her arms!

You need - a tennis ball, needle, wool, coloured cloth.

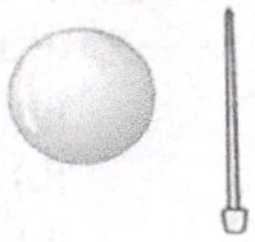

Method -

1. Start with the head. Make a small hole in the ball and push a long, thick knitting -needle (about size 3), into it.

2. The needle goes in on one side and right across inside the ball to touch the opposite side.
3. The hole needs to be very small, so that it is difficult to push the needle in. In this way it will fit tightly and remain firm when you play with your puppet.
4. Now cut the thick top off an old nylon sock and stretch it tightly round the ball, sewing it together down the back.

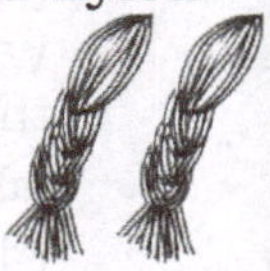

5. Take some coloured wool and stick on the ball. Make plaits. Paint the eyes and lips on the ball.

6. Cut two holes in the coloured cloth to put in your fingers.
7. Hold the needle in your hand to hold your puppet.

Write two sentences on your puppet.

Ans.
- The puppet dances very gracefully in the show.
- The puppet which I have is very beautifully dressed up.

PRACTICE QUESTIONS

Multiple Choice Questions

1. What was the result of Nasruddin's final shot?
   (a) It hit a tree (b) It hit the target
   (c) It missed the target (d) It hit a bird.
2. What did Nasruddin claim about his archery skills?
   (a) He was a beginner
   (b) He disliked archery
   (c) He could always hit the target
   (d) He didn't know anything about archery
3. How did Nasruddin's friends react after his first two shots?
   (a) They ignored him
   (b) They laughed at him
   (c) They clapped for him
   (d) They ignored him
4. What was Nasruddin's reaction when he missed the target first time?
   (a) He apologised
   (b) He blamed someone else
   (c) He became angry
   (d) He was very happy
5. Who did Nasruddin say was responsible for the second missed shot?
   (a) The king (b) His teacher
   (c) The Chief guard (d) Himself

Ans. 1. (b), 2. (c), 3. (b), 4. (c), 5. (c)

Fill in the Blanks

1. Nasruddin claimed that the first missed shot was ______ aim.
2. Nasruddin's third shot hit the target, and he said it was ______ aim.
3. Nasruddin's cleverness helped him avoid taking ______ for missed shots.
4. The friends couldn't believe it when Nasruddin's arrow ______ the target.
5. Nasruddin picked up the bow and arrow for the ______ time after missing twice.

Ans. 1. Azad's 2. his 3. blame
4. hit 5. third

True or False

1. Nasruddin hit the target on his first try.
2. Nasruddin took credit for his successful shot.
3. Nasruddin never managed to hit the target at all.
4. Nasruddin used excuses to explain why he missed the target.
5. Nasruddin's friends were impressed by his archery skills from the start.

Ans. 1. False, 2. True, 3. False, 4. True, 5. False

Answer the Following Questions

1. Why did Nasruddin's friends laugh at him?

Ans. Nasruddin's friends laughed at him because he failed to hit the arrows at the target in spite of boasting about his skills in archery.

2. What are the things that we require in archery?

Ans. We require a bow, an arrow, a string and a target in archery.

3. Why did Nasruddin take someone else's name each time he missed the target?

Ans. Nasruddin took someone else's name each time he missed to target because he did not want to take the blame for them.

Writing Task

1. Write a paragraph on 'My Aim in Life'.

Ans. My aim in life is to become a doctor. The idea of being able to help people and make a difference in their lives has always been a driving force for me. I believe that becoming a doctor is not just a career choice, but a desire to serve and care for others. I am eager to learn all that I can about the human body and the various medical treatments available. I am confident that I have the passion, dedication and compassion to become a successful and effective doctor.

CHAPTER 1 WHY?

Summary of the Poem In this poem, the poet talks about a little boy who is very curious. He always asks questions. The poet explains that some of the questions can be answered, while others remain unanswered.

Stanza-wise Explanation

Stanza 1

I know a curious little boy,
Who is always asking "Why?"
Why this, why that, why then, why now?
Why not, why by-the-by?

Word-Meaning *Curious - Wanting to learn more about something.*

Exp. The poet talks about a curious little boy who is always asking questions. He wants to know the reasons behind everything. He keeps asking 'why this?' and 'why that?' and 'why now?' or 'why not?'

Stanza 2

He wants to know why wood should swim,
Why lead and marble sink,
Why sun should shine and wind should blow
And why we eat and drink.

Word-Meaning *Lead - A heavy metal.*

Exp. The boy is curious about many things. He wonders why wood floats on water, while lead and marble sink. He also wants to know why the sun shines, why the wind blows, and why we need to eat and drink.

Stanza 3

He wants to know what makes the clouds
And why they cross the sky,
Why sinks the sun behind the hills
And why the flowers die.

Exp. He wonders what clouds are made of and why they move across the sky. He also wants to know why the sun sets behind the hills and why flowers die.

Stanza 4

Some of these why's are not too hard
To answer if you'll try;
Others no one ever yet
Has found the reason why.

Exp. The poet says that some of the boy's questions are easy to answer if someone tries. However, there are other questions that no one has been able to answer yet.

NCERT FOLDER

Reading is Fun (NCERT Page 62)

Q.1 Name a few things that sink.

Ans. Stone, keys, marble, cup, plate, spoon, rock, etc.

Q.2 List three questions that the little boy asks.

(a) ____________________

(b) ____________________

(c) ____________________

Ans. (a) Why do wood swim and marble sink?

(b) Why do the sun shine and the wind blow?

(c) Why do we eat and drink?

Q.3 What sort of a boy is described in the poem?

(a) sad

(b) curious

(c) brave

Ans. (b) curious

Let's Talk (NCERT Page 62)

Ram is a curious little boy. He is always asking questions. One day he came home and asked his grandfather questions like

(a) why can't we look at the sun during a solar eclipse?

(b) why can't we touch the sun?

(c) why can't we go out to play in the dark?

Discuss these questions with your teacher and class. Do you know the answers?

Ans. (a) We can't look at sun during a solar eclipse because the sun's rays can be harmful to our eyes.

(b) We can't touch the sun because it is too far to reach and touch. We cannot touch it as it is too hot.

(c) We can't go out to play in the dark because we cannot see in the dark. So, we may fall and hurt ourselves if we play in dark.

Word Building (NCERT Page 62)

Q.1 Fill in the blanks with words from the poem which rhyme with the coloured words in the sentences.

(a) **Why** is the __________ so high?

(b) Do you **know** the colour of __________?

(c) Have you **found** who made the __________?

(d) Put the glass in the **sink** after you finish your __________.

Ans. (a) sky (b) snow (c) cloud (d) drink

Q.2 The spellings of these words are jumbled. Put them right and make sentences of your own

(a) wokn

Ans. know - I don't know who made the painting.

(b) wism

Ans. Swim - I go for a swim every weekend.

(c) dael

Ans. Lead - Lead is a very heavy substance.

(d) blarme

Ans. Marble - Our house has marble flooring.

(e) llihs

Ans. Hills - Hills are very far away from the city

Let's Write (NCERT Page 62)

Q.1 Discuss and write

(a) Why do cats and dogs fight?

Ans. Cats and dogs are fight because they don't like each other. Dogs are not friendly with cats.

(b) Why do we walk across the road, not run?

Ans. In order to avoid accidents, we walk across the road and do not run.

(c) Why do people like ice-cream?

Ans. People like ice cream as it is a cold sweet thing which makes them happy.

Q.2 Write down at least two questions using 'why'?

(a) ______________________________

(b) ______________________________

Ans. (a) Why is father sleeping early?

(b) Why did you laugh so loudly?

Fun Time (NCERT Page 64)

Painting with ONION HALVES and BOTTLE TOPS

You need

two onion halves, two bottle tops, water colour, plate for mixing.

Method

Take an onion. Cut it into half. Mix some paint of any colour with a little water on a plate. Dip the cut side of the onion into the colour. Now press it on a paper to make designs.

Press the bottle top into the centre of the design.

You can use another colour for the other onion half and the other bottle top.

Ans. Do it yourself.

PRACTICE QUESTIONS

Multiple Choice Questions

1. How does the poet describe the boy's questions?
   (a) Simple and easy
   (b) Difficult and intriguing
   (c) Unnecessary and boring
   (d) Difficult and boring
2. What does the boy want to understand about the sun?
   (a) Why it shines
   (b) Why it sets early
   (c) Why it changes colour
   (d) Why it rises early
3. What is one thing the boy wonders about in relation to flowers?
   (a) Why they die
   (b) Why they smell good
   (c) Why they have different colours
   (d) Why they bloom

Ans. 1. (b), 2. (a), 3. (a)

Fill in the Blanks

1. He wonders why the ________ shines and why the ________ blows.
2. The little boy asks why ______ should swim,while ______ and ______ sink.
3. According to the poem, some questions about "why" have no ________ yet.

Ans. 1. sun, wind, 2. wood, lead, marble 3. answers

True or False

1. The poet knows a curious little boy ?
2. The boy wanted to know why we swim ?
3. The boy wanted to know why we eat and drink ?

Ans. 1. True 2. False 3. True

Answer the Following Questions

1. What the little boy always ask?

Ans. The boy always asks questions- why this, why that, why now and why not?

2. Name things that sink and float.

Ans. Wood floats while lead and marble sinks.

3. Were all the questions of the boy answered? Why?

Ans. No, not all of the boy's questions were answered. While of the questions asked by the boy were easy to answer, the others could not be answered by anyone.

4. Can you answer the little boy's question? 'why do we eat and drink'?

Ans. We eat and drink to grow and live a healthy life.

Writing Task

1. Look at the given image.

What does this image make you curious about? Write about 5 such things.

Ans.(1) I am curious about how the camera takes the picture and stores it.
(2) I am curious about how the boy hanging from the branch of the tree, came to that position.
(3) I am curious about why they are not sitting on the soft green grass.
(4) I am curious about what more things are kept in the basket.
(5) I am also curious to know if the sun is hidden behind the clouds.

CHAPTER 2 ALICE IN WONDERLAND

Summary of the Chapter

Alice was listening to a story from her sister when she saw a white rabbit. She was attracted towards it. The rabbit had pink eyes and was wearing a blue waistcoat. He took out a big watch from his waistcoat pocket. He hurried away saying that he would be late.

Being curious by nature, Alice followed the white rabbit. The rabbit suddenly jumped into a rabbit hole. Alice jumped into the hole too. They both kept falling down in the deep hole. She wondered if she would slip through the earth to the other side.

Suddenly, she landed on a pile of dry leaves and saw the white rabbit who disappeared saying that he was getting late. Alice stood up and saw a small door and then saw a glass table on which a golden key was kept. She took the key, opened the door and looked into the most beautiful garden. She could not get her head through the doorway and wished she could become smaller.

WORD-MEANING

Scamper by – To run or move quickly; Waistcoat – A sleeveless jacket Burning with – Excited with; Curiosity – A strong desire to know or learn something; Popped down – Moved suddenly, rushed; Thump – A loud, dull sound, when something heavy falls; Pile – A large quantity of things lying on top of one another; Disappeared – To go out of sight or become invisible; Whiskers – Long, stiff hairs growing on an animal's face; Delight – Great pleasure or happiness; Longed – To have a strong desire or wish for something; Exclaimed – To say something suddenly and loudly.

NCERT FOLDER

Reading is Fun (NCERT Page 68)

Q.1 While listening to the story, what did Alice see?

Ans. While listening to the story, Alice saw a white rabbit running.

Q.2 What was different about the rabbit that Alice saw?

Ans. The rabbit that Alice saw had pink eyes, wore a blue waistcoat and carried a watch. He could also talk like humans.

Q.3 Where did the rabbit go?

Ans. The rabbit went a deep rabbit hole.

Q.4 How did Alice reach Wonderland?

Ans. Alice followed the rabbit and jumped into the rabbit hole, which led her to the Wonderland.

Q.5 What strange things did Alice see?

Ans. At the bottom of the hole, she saw a very small door for her to go through. Then, she saw a glass table with a golden key on it. When she opened the door, she saw a lovely garden with beds of bright flowers and cool fountains.

Q.6 Describe in your own words the garden that Alice saw.

Ans. When Alice opened the door, she saw a beautiful garden. It was the most beautiful garden she had ever seen. There were flowers of different colours and they smelled wonderful. The garden also had fountains. Alice wished she could stay there forever.

Q.7 Draw the garden of your dreams.

Ans. You can draw

- a bed of flowers
- a lake
- trees
- children enjoying a picnic
- birds, flying as well as swimming

Tick (✓) the correct answer.

(i) The rabbit had

(a) white eyes (b) big eyes
(c) pink eyes

Ans. (c) pink eyes

(ii) Who was burning with curiosity?

(a) Alice (b) the rabbit
(c) children

Ans. (a) Alice

(iii) Who fell down and down and down?

(a) Alice (b) a mouse
(c) the rabbit

Ans. (a) Alice

(iv) Who said – "Oh, my ears and whiskers? How late it's getting!"

(a) the rabbit (b) Alice
(c) Alice's sister

Ans. (a) the rabbit

(v) The garden Alice saw was

(a) big (b) lovely
(c) small

Ans. (b) lovely

Let's Talk (NCERT Page 70)

Q.1 Describe some of the sounds you hear at night.

Ans. At night, I can hear the sounds of crickets, the wind blowing, dogs barking, and sometimes the noise of cars passing by.

Q.2 Imagine you are Alice and your partner is a rabbit. What would you do?

Ans. If I were Alice, I would first try to ask him how was he able to talk like us. I would tell him to take me to the wonderland. I would follow him wherever he will go and ask lots of questions.

Q.3 What do you think Alice saw in the garden?

Ans. I think Alice saw colourful flowers, green plants and beautiful fountains in the garden. It looked peaceful and magical.

Q.4 How could Alice have got into the garden?

Ans. Alice could have gotten into the garden if she became smaller, small enough to fit through the tiny door.

Let's Write (NCERT Page 70)

Q.1 Find one word from the story that means.

(a) To walk fast, h________.

(b) to think, w________.

(c) happy, d_______.

(d) to be seen nowhere, d_______.

(e) at once, q _____.

(f) move fast, s _____.

(g) to be inquisitive c_______.

Ans. (a) hurry (b) wonder

(c) delight (d) disappear

(e) quickly (f) scamper

(g) curious

Q.2 Give another word for the ones given below with similar meanings and make sentences. Now write the opposites of these describing words and make sentences with them –

	Opposite	Sentence
(a) lovely	________	________
(b) talking	________	________
(c) listening	________	________
(d) see	________	________
(e) centre	________	________

Ans. (a) Lovely

Similar : Beautiful - The lovely garden had many bright flowers.

Opposite : Ugly - The ugly painting on the wall was very plain and dull.

(b) Talking

Similar : Speaking - The talking parrot entertained everyone with its words.

Opposite : Silent - The Library was silent during the class.

(c) Listening

Similar : Hearing - I was listening to the birds chirping in the morning.

Opposite : Ignoring - He was ignoring the instructions given by the teacher.

(d) See

Similar : Look - I like to see the stars at night.

Opposite : Miss - I miss my best friend, Karan.

(e) Centre

Similar : Middle - The statue was placed in the centre of the town square.

Opposite : Edge - She stood at the edge of the sidewalk.

Q.3 Imagine you are going on a journey to the centre of the earth. What do you think you will see? What would you feel?

Ans. If I were going to the center of the Earth, I would see lots of rock and hot, melted lava. It would be very dark and very hot down there. I would feel scared and uncomfortable because it would be so different and hard to breathe. The journey would be both exciting and tough!

Q.4 Alice follows the strange rabbit because she wants to know a number of things. Re-arrange the words to make the questions that Alice has in her mind, and put a question mark (?).

(a) talk rabbit a how can

Ans. How can a rabbit talk?

(b) going he is where

Ans. Where is he going?

(c) read he can time the

Ans. Can he read the time?

(d) hurry is in a why he

Ans. Why is he in a hurry?

PRACTICE QUESTIONS

Multiple Choice Questions

1. What did Alice find at the small door?
   (a) A red key (b) A silver key
   (c) A golden key (d) A green key
2. What did Alice wish for when she saw the small door?
   (a) To fly
   (b) To become smaller
   (c) To become taller
   (d) To become famous
3. What did Alice land on when she fell down the rabbit hole?
   (a) A pile of dry leaves
   (b) A bed
   (c) A cushion
   (d) A pile of green leaves
4. How did Alice feel about the garden she saw?
   (a) She was scared
   (b) She wanted to stay there forever
   (c) She was indifferent
   (d) She was anxious.

Ans. 1. (c), 2. (b), 3. (a), 4. (b)

Fill in the Blanks

1. The rabbit's watch was used to tell ________.
2. Alice's fall seemed endless as she went down the ________ hole.
3. The garden had beds of bright ________ and cool ________.
4. Alice was with curious and wanted to know about the ________ rabbit.
5. The garden Alice saw was described as the ________ she had ever seen.

Ans. 1. time, 2. rabbit, 3. flowers, fountains, 4. white, 5. loveliest

True or False

1. The rabbit was pink coloured.
2. Alice wished she could be taller?
3. Alice and the rabbit sat on a cloud.
4. Rabbit took out a watch from his pocket.
5. The rabbit had pink eyes and wore a coat.

Ans. 1. True, 2. False, 3. False, 4. True, 5. True

Answer the Following Questions

1. What guesses did Alice make about her location?

Ans. Alice does not make any guesses about her location.

2. Where did the rabbit disappear? Why couldn't Alice follow him?

Ans. The rabbit disappeared after entering the small gate. Alice couldn't follow him because she was too big to enter the gate.

3. What did Alice see when she opened the door? How did she feel?

Ans. When Alice opened the door, she saw the loveliest garden she had ever seen. She felt very happy on seeing it but wished to be small to enter it.

4. What did Alice see on standing up from the pile of dry leaves?

Ans. When Alice stood up from the pile of dry leaves, she saw the white rabbit again.

Writing Task

1. Alice sees a lovely garden through the small door. Suppose you were in Alice's place, what would you have seen? Do not write a garden again.

Ans. If I were in Alice's place, I would come across a beautiful place with a huge palace near the lakeside. I would also like to find something that would allow me to enter the small gate. I want to scene to be filled with beautiful flowers, never seen creatures and crystal clear water. In the palace, I wish to see a big library with books so that I can read whatever I want. The palace would be beautiful and full of everything that I want.

CHAPTER 1 DON'T BE AFRAID OF THE DARK

Summary of the Poem In the poem, the poet tells the little children not to be afraid of the darkness of the night. The earth takes rest at night when the day is over. Therefore the poet wants children to be friends with the night.

Stanza-wise Explanation

Stanza 1

Don't be afraid of the dark, little one,
The earth must rest when the day is done.
The sun must be harsh, but moonlight - never!
And those stars will be shining forever and ever,

Word-Meaning *Afraid - Scared; Harsh - Too strong or rough.*

Exp. The poet tells the child not to be afraid of the dark because the earth needs to rest when the day is over. While the sun can be hot and bright, the moonlight is always gentle. The stars will continue to shine forever, so there's nothing to fear at night.

Stanza 2

Be friends with the Night, there is nothing to fear,
Just let your thoughts travel to friends far and near.
By day, it does seem that our troubles won't cease,
But at night, late at night, the world is at peace.

Word-Meaning *Troubles - Problems or difficulties that cause worry or stress; Cease - To stop or come to an end.*

Exp. The poet is telling us to not be scared of the night. We should become friends with night because there is nothing to fear. The poet suggests thinking about friends who are near and far away. During the day, we all face many problems but at night, the world becomes calm and peaceful.

NCERT FOLDER

Reading is Fun (NCERT Page 75)

Q.1 What is the poem about?

Ans. The poem is about children's fear of darkness of the night and the ways to overcome this fear.

Q.2 What happens when the day is over?

Ans. When the day is over, it gets dark, and the earth rests. The moon and stars come out, shining in the sky.

Q.3 What does the earth do when the day is over?

Ans. When the day is over, the night begins and the earth takes rest.

Q.4 What does the poet want us to do at night?

Ans. The poet wants us to not be afraid of the dark. The poet wants us to be friendly with night and think about our friends and relatives.

Q.5 Are these sentences True or False?

(a) The poet tells the child to be afraid when it is dark.

Ans. False

(b) The poet says that stars will always shine at night.

Ans. True

(c) The poet tells the child to think of friends after it is dark.

Ans. True

Word Building NCERT Page 75

(a) moon + light　(b) good + night
(c) water + fall　(d) break + fast
(e) day + break　(f) rain + bow

Ans. (a) moonlight　(b) goodnight
(c) waterfall　(d) breakfast
(e) daybreak　(f) rainbow

Q.1 Find a word in the poem which is the opposite of

(a) war ____________
(b) enemies ____________
(c) gentle ____________
(d) light ____________
(e) night ____________
(f) start ____________

Ans. (a) peace　(b) friends
(c) harsh　(d) dark
(e) day　(f) cease

Q.2 Look at these words in the poem

don't, won't

Here are their full forms

don't - do not　won't - will not

Now, write the full forms of the following words

(a) didn't　(b) shouldn't
(c) wouldn't　(d) couldn't
(e) mustn't

Ans. (a) did not　(b) should not
(c) would not　(d) could not
(e) must not

Let's Talk (NCERT Page 76)

Q.1 Are you afraid of the dark? Why?

Ans. No, I am not afraid of the dark because I sleep with my parents at night.

Q.2 What do you do when it is dark?

Ans. I busy myself with some fun activities like watching T.V., playing indoor games with my brother, etc.

Q.3 Have you ever been very frightened? Tell your partner about it.

Ans. Yes, I have been very frightened. One night when I was alone in my room, it started raining heavily outside. Then suddenly I heard a loud lightening sound outside. The loud noise scared me so much that I hid under the blanket for the rest of the night.

Say Aloud (NCERT Page 76)

Q.1 What is the word that starts with t, rhymes with 'cease', and means to playfully make fun of ?

Ans. Tease

Q.2 What is the word that starts with c, rhymes with 'near' and 'fear', and means easy to see, hear and understand?

Ans. Clear

Say t, t, t

Q.3 Where did the tip of the tongue touch?

Ans. Tip of the tongue touched the roof of the mouth.

Q.4 Listen and repeat Ca - t

Ans. Do it yourself.

Q.5 Did you hear what your tongue did?

Ans. Do it yourself.

Q.6 Say these words and feel what your tongue does when you say

toe, top, tie, ten

Ans. The tongue touches the roof of the mouth and then teeth.

Work in pairs

Make the 'cough' sound.

I came down
I coughed "K, k, k, k!"
And cough again "K, k, k, k!"

Did you hear the 'K' sound at the end of the word 'book'?

Repeat

book look neck duck chick
sack clock

All these words start with the same sound

kangaroo curtain king
key kind kitten

Team Time (NCERT Page 77)

Q.1 Divide the class into four groups.

Ans. Do in your classroom.

Q.2 Imagine life without the sun.

Ans. It's difficult to imagine life without the sun. We couldn't survive since plants would die without sunlight and there would be no oxygen/air and food on Earth.

Q.3 What are the things that may happen if there is no sunlight?

Ans. If there is no sunlight.

(i) It will always be dark, like night.
(ii) Days will become cold and gloomy.
(iii) We will need electricity constantly.
(iv) There will be no seasons or weather changes.
(v) Flowers will no longer bloom.
(vi) Plants will die, leaving us without food.

Q.4 Discuss with the group and write your ideas in your notebook.

Ans. Do it yourself.

Let's Write (NCERT Page 78)

Q.1 The red tea cups are filled with a particular word. Fill in the yellow tea cups with similar sounding words. Note the example given

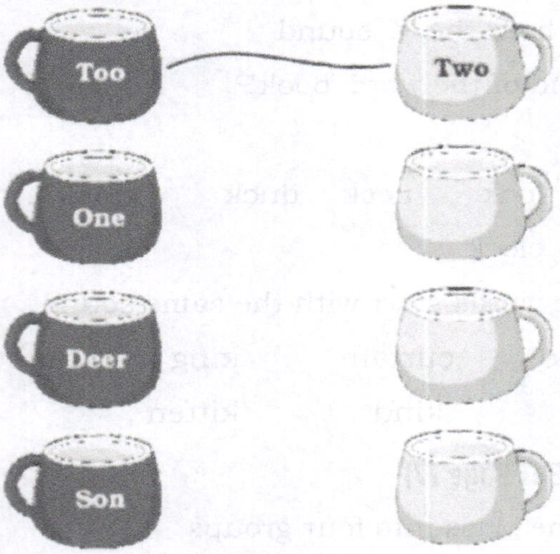

Ans. (a) Won (b) Dear (c) Sun

Q.2 Now complete the following sentences, choosing the right word

(a) The sum was __________ difficult for the class to solve. Only __________ students could do it. (two, too)

(b) There was only______ boy who______the prize. (one, won)

(c) The golden ________ was very ________ to him. (dear, deer)

(d) Ramu's ________ loved to play in the ________. (sun, son)

Ans. (a) too, two

(b) one, won

(c) deer, dear

(d) son, sun

Let's Listen (NCERT Page 79)

1. Relax your feet, legs and entire body. Be as quiet as you can.
2. Listen to the sounds around you.
3. Tell your partner softly what you heard and ask, "What did you hear?"
4. Let your partner talk about or copy those sounds.
5. Read out the following phrases aloud. Divide them into loud and softer sounds.

- clapping hands • a worm moving • stamping feet
- a bud blooming • a butterfly flying
- a feather dropping • an ant walking • a car moving
- the wind blowing • ssshhhh
- whisper • tiptoe • a leaf falling

Ans.

	Loud Sounds		Soft Sounds
1.	A car moving	1.	Tiptoe
2.	Stamping feet	2.	Whisper
3.	Clapping hands	3.	Ssshhhh
4.	The wind blowing	4.	A leaf falling
		5.	An ant walking
		6.	A worm moving
		7.	A bud blooming
		8.	A butterfly flying
		9.	A feather dropping

Let's Sing

Don't Give Up

If you keep on going, And never stop,
You can keep on going, You can make it to the top.
Life is full of mountains,
Some are big and some are small,
But if you don't give up, You can
overcome them all. So keep
on going, Try not to stop,
When you keep on going
You can make it to the top.

Look at the picture and describe it. Why do you think the boy is happy?

Ans. The boy seems happy because he has reached the top of the hill. He might feel proud and excited after the climb.
His raised arms show that he is celebrating his success or enjoying being on top of the hill.

PRACTICE QUESTIONS

Multiple Choice Questions

1. What must the earth do when the day is over?
(a) Rest (b) Work
(c) Shine (d) Play

2. How does the poet describe the moonlight?
(a) Bright (b) Harsh
(c) Gentle (d) Pleasant

3. What is the world like at night, as per the poet?
(a) Busy (b) Troubling
(c) At peace (d) Loud

4. What does the poet want us to become friends with?
(a) The day (b) The sun
(c) The night (d) The light

Ans. 1. (a), 2. (c), 3. (c), 4. (c)

Fill in the Blanks

1. The poet advises the child to _______ the night and not _______ it.
2. The _______ sky is filled with shining _______ that will remain forever.
3. Despite the _______ of the day, the _______ brings peace and stillness.
4. The night allows our thoughts to travel to friends both ______ and ______.
5. The poet says that while the _______ can be harsh, the _______ is always soft and calming.

Ans. 1. befriend, fear
2. night, stars
3. troubles, night
4. far, near
5. sun, moonlight

True or False

1. Troubles seem to remain during the day time.
2. If we befriend the night, we should fear everything.
3. The poet says that stars will always shine at night.
4. The poet tells little children to be afraid of the dark.
5. The poet tells the child to think of friends after it is dark.

Ans. 1. True 2. False
3. True 4. False
5. True

Answer the Following Questions

1. What does the poet want us to do?

Ans. The poet wants us stop fearing the night.

2. How is sunlight different from moonlight?

Ans. Sunlight is different from the moonlight because it is harsh while the moonlight is gentle.

3. What does the poet suggest us to do with the night?

Ans. The poet suggests us to become friends with the night.

CHAPTER 2

HELEN KELLER

Summary of the Chapter

Helen Keller was born a healthy and a normal child. However, one day she fell seriously ill. Although she recovered, she lost both her sight and hearing power. Helen was a bright girl but she often got angry. Her parents believed in her potential and decided to appoint a teacher for her.

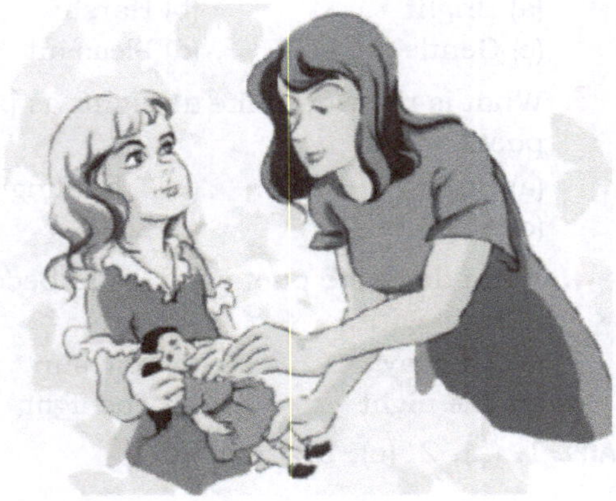

Miss Sullivan agreed to teach Helen how to understand the world. She started by giving Helen a doll and spelling "D-O-L-L" on her hand using special hand signs. Helen copied her and spelled the word too. One day, Miss Sullivan put Helen's hand in running water and spelt 'WATER'. As a result, Helen understood what water was. In this way, Miss Sullivan taught her many words, and slowly, Helen realized how important words were.

WORD-MEANING

Illness - Sickness; Felt sorry - Had sad feeling; Bright - Clever; Strict - Firm.

NCERT FOLDER

Reading is Fun (NCERT Page 84)

Q.1 "Something is wrong," said Helen's mother. What was wrong with Helen?

Ans. Helen could not hear or see after she became seriously ill.

Q.2 Although Helen could not hear or see, what kind of girl was she?

Ans. Although Helen could not hear or see, She was a smart and a bright little girl.

Q.3 Who agreed to help Helen?

Ans. Miss Sullivan, a young teacher, agreed to help Helen.

Q.4 How did Miss Sullivan help Helen?

Ans. Miss Sullivan taught Helen many words with the help of special hand signs. She made her understand the importance of words.

Q.5 What did Helen learn when the teacher put her hand into the running water?

Ans. Helen learnt the word WATER. She understood that water meant something wet.

Q.6 What was the most important thing that Helen finally understood?

Ans. The most important things that Helen finally understood was that words were the most important things in the world which would tell her everything she wanted to know.

Let's Talk (NCERT Page 84)

Q.1 Using sign language, make these letters with your hand.

'C', 'H', 'E', 'K'.

Ans. Do it yourself.

Q.2 Spell these words through hand signs.

(a) Helen (b) was

Ans. Do it yourself.

Q.3 How do people who cannot see, read?

Ans. The people who cannot see, read with the help of a special sign language.

Q.4 What is the script for children who cannot see called?

Ans. The script for children who cannot see is called 'Braille script'.

Q.5 How do you think you can help children who cannot see?

Ans. We can help children who cannot see by becoming their eyes. We can describe the things we see around and can read the books to them.

Let's Write (NCERT Page 87)

Q.1 Match the two parts of sentences given under column 'A' and 'B'. Add 'but' to join the two parts and write complete sentences.

	Column A		Column B
(i)	Helen lived after her illness	(a)	her mother thought she could learn.
(ii)	She could not see or hear	(b)	she did not understand what she was doing.
(iii)	People thought that she could not learn anything.	(c)	she could not hear or see.
(iv)	Helen copied the words	(d)	she was kind to Helen.
(v)	Miss Sullivan was strict	(e)	she was very intelligent.

Ans. (i) (c) Helen lived after her illness but she could not hear or see.

(ii) (e) She could not see or hear but she was very intelligent.

(iii) (a) People thought that she could not learn anything but her mother thought she could learn.

(iv) (b) Helen copied the words but she did not understand what she was doing.

(v) (d) Miss Sullivan was strict but she was kind to Helen.

Team Time (NCERT Page 88)

Q.1 Read the following sentences

(a) Her clothes were always dirty.

(b) She was often angry.

(c) Sometimes she lay on the floor.

(d) Her parents never scolded her

Ans. Do it yourself.

Q.2 Ask yourself the following questions. Put a tick (✓) under the right column.

Q.3 Now your friend will ask you the same questions.

	Questions	always	often	sometimes	never
	How often do you				
(a)	obey your parents?	✓			
(b)	visit your grandparents?			✓	
(c)	fight with your brother or sister?			✓	
(d)	help others?		✓		
(e)	throw waste in the dustbin?	✓			
(f)	switch off the lights,when you go out of the room?	✓			
(g)	leave the tap on while brushing your teeth?				✓
(h)	tear pages from your notebook?				✓

Let's Make Something (NCERT Page 89)

Q.1 From newspapers or old magazines collect stories/reports of courageous children

(a) Draw pictures of the story

(b) Talk about the stories.

Ans. Do it yourself.

PRACTICE QUESTIONS

Multiple Choice Questions

1. What happened to Helen Keller after she became ill?
   (a) She could not walk
   (b) She could not see or hear
   (c) She could not speak
   (d) She could not speak and hear
2. What did Helen's mother say after the illness?
   (a) Helen will be fine
   (b) She will get better soon
   (c) Something is very wrong
   (d) Helen is a strong girl
3. How did Helen behave as she grew older?
   (a) She became quiet
   (b) She became cheerful
   (c) She became wild and angry
   (d) She became an intelligent child
4. Who agreed to help Helen learn to see the world?
   (a) A doctor
   (b) Her mother
   (c) Miss Sullivan
   (d) Her father
5. How did Miss Sullivan spell words for Helen?
   (a) By showing pictures
   (b) By writing them on paper
   (c) By making hand signs in her palm
   (d) By speaking those words
6. If you were in the place of Miss Sullivan, Helen's teacher. How would you help Helen?
   (a) By beating her
   (b) By using sign language in which she understands life and be friends with her.

(c) By teasing her

(d) By making fun of her

Ans. 1. (b), 2. (c), 3. (c), 4. (b), 5. (c) 6. (b)

Fill in the Blanks

1. Helen's teacher's name was _______.
2. Helen Keller could not see or _______.
3. Helen was born in _______ in _______.
4. Helen would not let anyone _______ her hair.
5. Helen understood that _______ were the most important things in the world.

Ans. 1. Miss Sullivan 2. hear

3. Alabama, 1880 4. comb 5. words

True or False

1. Miss Sullivan was strict but kind.
2. Miss Sullivan gave Helen a toy car.
3. Helen Keller was a disciplined child.
4. Some people thought Helen could not learn anything.
5. Helen's parents found that she could see but could not hear.

Ans. 1. True, 2. False, 3. False, 4. True 5. False

Answer the Following Questions

1. Describe the character of Miss Sullivan.

Ans. Miss Sullivan was a kind but a strict teacher who managed a wild and angry Helen Keller with care.

2. Write a few qualities that Helen possessed.

Ans. Helen Keller was a child who could not see or hear. However, she was a smart, bright and an observant girl.

3. How did Miss Sullivan help Helen in learning?

Ans. Miss Sullivan taught Helen about many words and helped her in learning.

4. What was the reason behind Helen's extreme anger in her childhood? Diksha

Ans. I think Helen was not able to express her feelings to anyone because she did not know how to express herself till the time when her teacher Miss Sullivan was not with her. This may be the reason behind Helen's extreme anger in her childhood.

Writing Task

1. We came across many disabled people like Helen Keller but we often ignore them or treat them badly. People with disabilities should be dealt with love and care. Write a few ways in which you can make such people feel loved and cared for.

Ans. Respecting a person with a disability is not only crucial for ensuring their well-being, but also for encouraging a more inclusive society. Disabled persons face unique challenges in their daily lives.

When referring to a person's disability, it is important to use language that is respectful. Second, persons with disabilities may require more time to communicate, understand and respond.

We should be aware of any specific requirements or accommodations that may be needed, such as a wheelchair ramp or an interpreter.

Creating a positive environment where disabled persons feel supported and can thrive is essential for true inclusivity.

CHAPTER 1 HIAWATHA

Summary of the Poem Hiawatha was a young Red Indian boy. He lived in a hut with his old grandmother, Nokomia. He learnt the language of the birds and animals, their names and all their secrets. He also learnt the language of the beasts, their names and all their secrets. He talked with them and they to him.

Stanza-wise Explanation

Stanza 1

"Then the little Hiawatha
Learned of every bird its language,
Learned their names and all their secrets,
How they built their nests in Summer,
Where they hid themselves in Winter,
Talked with them whene'er he met them,
Called them 'Hiawatha's chickens.'

Word-Meaning *Learned - Get knowledge about something; Secrets - Hidden things or unknown facts; Hid - To keep something out of sight.*

Exp. Hiawatha, a young boy, learned to understand the birds. He learned their language, names and secrets. He knew how they built their nests in the summer and where they stayed in the winter. Whenever he met the birds, he would talk to them and called them "Hiawatha's chickens".

Stanza 2

Of all beasts he learned the language,
Learned their names and all their secrets,
How the beavers built their lodges,
Where the squirrels hid their acorns,
How the reindeer ran so swiftly,
Why the rabbit was so timid,
Talked with them whene'r he met them,
Called them 'Hiawatha's Brothers'."

Word-Meaning *Beasts - Animals, especially large or wild ones; Beavers - a small animal; Lodges - Homes or shelters, often used by animals like beavers, Acorns - Nuts from oak trees, which squirrels, eat, Reindeer - A kind of deer; Swiftly - Moving or happening very quickly; Timid - Shy or afraid; lacking courage.*

Exp. Hiawatha learnt how to understand the animals. He got to know their names and their habits. He learned how beavers built their homes and where squirrels stored their food.
He learnt how fast the reindeer could run and why rabbits were shy. Whenever he met them, he would talk and call - "Hiawatha's brothers".

NCERT FOLDER

Reading is Fun (NCERT Page 94)

Q.1 Who was Hiawatha?

Ans. Hiawatha was a young Red Indian boy.

Q.2 Who was Nokomis?

Ans. Nokomis was Hiawatha's old grandmother.

Q.3 What did he learn about the birds?

Ans. He learnt the language of the birds, including their names and secrets, how they build nests in summer, and where they hide themselves in winter.

Q.4 What secrets did he learn about beasts?

Ans. He learnt how to speak to all the beasts. He found out how beavers build their homes, where squirrels store their acorns, how quickly reindeer can run and why rabbits are so shy.

Let's Listen (NCERT Page 94)

Q.1 Whisper a secret in your partner's ear. The partner will in turn whisper his secret in your ear.

Now talk about the secret aloud.

Ans. Do it with your partner.

Chinese Whisper

Q.2 Form a circle and whisper a secret into the ear of the person on your right. He in turn whispers into the ear of the person on the right. Pass the secret on till it goes around the circle. The last person will tell the secret aloud.

Is the secret the same as what the first child had whispered?

Ans. Do it with your friends.

Let's Talk (NCERT Page 95)

Q.1 Do you think that

(a) Hiawatha liked learning new languages?

Ans. Yes, Hiawatha liked learning new languages.

(b) Hiawatha called the birds-'chickens' and the beasts 'brothers'. What do you think this shows?

Ans. This shows that Hiawatha was friendly with birds and animals.

(c) Do birds have secrets?

Ans. Yes, birds have their secrets.

(d) Do you know the secret language of any animal? Tell the class about it.

Ans. No, I don't know the secret language of any animal.

Say Aloud (NCERT Page 96)

squirrel	quarrel	queen	quick
quill	quilt	quiet	quality

Q.1 Use words beginning with 'h' sound like

hat, house, hen, hide, horse, heart, hand etc.

Make a pair of words, one a 'describing word' and one a 'naming word'.

Happy Hiawatha, hungry hippopotamus, high horse, heavy hand.

Ans. Hungry Hen, High House, Helpful Hand, Hot Horse, Happy Heart, Hasty Hare, Heavy Hammer, Healthy Hamster, Humble Hero, Hot Honey, High Hill, Hot Hamburger, etc.

Q.2 Have you seen

(a) a hippopotamus in a hat?

Ans. No

(b) a hen in a beehive?

Ans. No

(c) a helicopter with hair?

Ans. No

(d) a horse drink honey?

Ans. No

Let's Share (NCERT Page 96)

Make a story of the poem and share it with your friends. You can change Hiawatha's name and give the name of your classmate.

Start the story which other children can continue.

You could begin like this -

Once upon a time there was a boy called ...

Ans. Once upon a time, there was a boy called Arjun. He lived with his grandmother, who taught him about the wonderful world around them. Arjun learned to understand the language of the birds and animals. He found out how they built their nests in the summer and where they hid in the winter.

Let's Write (NCERT Page 97)

Q.1 This is a park where children talk to different animals and birds. Write four sentences about the picture. Use capital letters where required, complete sentences and punctuation.

Ans. (a) A girl is sitting happily in the park.

(b) The girl is sitting in the garden filled with lovely roses and flowers.

(c) Many birds and animals are around her talking to the girl.

(d) The girl, the birds and the animals are in a happy mood.

Now colour the picture.

Note : Colour the picture yourself with suitable colours.

Q.2 Where do the following live ?

(a) Birds live in ____________

Ans. Nests

(b) Rabbits live in ____________

Ans. Burrow

(c) Beavers live in ____________

Ans. Lodges

Q.3 Describe Hiawatha, his home and friends in ten lines.

Ans. Hiawatha was a young Native American boy. He lived with his old grandmother, Nokomis, in a wigwam. Nokomis taught Hiawatha about all the wonders around them. He learned to love the birds and animals. He talked to them whenever he met them. The birds and animals also loved him and talked back to him. All birds and animals were Hiawatha's friends.

He learned their languages, their names and all their secrets. Hiawatha called the birds 'Hiawatha's Chickens' and the animals 'Hiawatha's Brothers.'

Q.4 What did Hiawatha love?

Ans. Hiawatha loved learning the language of all the birds and animals as well as discovering the world around him, like the stars, trees, insects, and many other things.

Q.5 Match 'A' with 'B' and write the complete sentences below.

	A	B
(a)	Whenever	I go, I have friends
(b)	Whoever	I am hungry, I eat.
(c)	Wherever	comes first, wins.

Ans. (a) Whenever I am hungry, I eat.
(b) Whoever comes first, wins.
(c) Wherever I go, I have friends.

Q.6 Complete the following stories by using an appropriate word from the box given below

my, his, he, your

(A) Ram was a farmer. wanted to sell _____ goats and sheep. So he went to the market. There _____ sold all _____ animals to a rich man and got a lot of money. When he was going back to _____ village, three thieves stopped him. "Stop! Give us all _____ money."

Ram was very clever. He said, "I'll give _____ money to the strongest of you." On hearing this, the thieves started fighting amongst themselves. Ram slipped away quietly.

(B) Sitting on a tree, a crow was enjoying a piece of bread. A hungry fox wanted to have that bread. _____ said very sweetly, "Dear brother, I've heard that _____ voice is very sweet.

Please sing a song for me." The foolish crow opened _____ beak and the piece of bread fell down. The fox picked it up in _____ mouth and ran away.

Ans. (A) his, he, his, his, your, my.
(B) He, your, his, his

Q.7 Some words have similar sounds, but different meanings. Choose the correct word from the bracket and fill in the blanks.

(a) The bird sits on a _____. (bow, bough)
(b) The squirrel has a long _____. (tail, tale)
(c) I have to leave at _____. (too, two)
(d) This sum is _____. (right, write)
(e) I can _____ the bird's song. (hear, here)
(f) Do you _____ a secret? (no, know)
(g) The King sits on the _____. (thrown, throne)
(h) He is our school _____. (principal, principle)

Ans. (a) bough (b) tail (c) too
(d) right (e) hear (f) know
(g) throne (h) principal

PRACTICE QUESTIONS

Multiple Choice Questions

1. What did Hiawatha learn from the birds?
   (a) Their songs
   (b) Their colours
   (c) Their language
   (d) Their flying technique
2. What did Hiawatha call the birds?
   (a) His friends
   (b) Hiawatha's chickens
   (c) Little singers
   (d) His sisters
3. How did Hiawatha feel about the animals?
   (a) He considered them his brothers
   (b) He ignored them
   (c) He was afraid of them
   (d) He considered them his enemies
4. What did Hiawatha learn about beavers?
   (a) How they fly
   (b) How they swim
   (c) How they build their lodges
   (d) How they communicate
5. Why was the rabbit described as timid?
   (a) It is shy (b) It runs fast
   (c) It is very big (d) It is very lazy
6. What is common in Hiawatha and other creatures?
   (a) Hiawatha
   (b) Hiawatha's grandmother, Nokomis
   (c) Language
   (d) Wigwam

Ans. 1. (c), 2. (b), 3. (a), 4. (c), 5. (a), 6. (c)

Fill in the Blanks

1. Hiawatha was a young ________ boy.
2. He called the beasts "Hiawatha's ________."
3. He learnt where the squirrels hid their ________.
4. Hiawatha learned the language of all the ________.
5. He talked with the animals whenever he ________ them.

Ans. 1. Native American, 2. Brothers, 3. acorns, 4. birds, 5. met

True or False

1. Beavers build their homes called lodges.
2. Hiawatha did not care about the animals.
3. Hiawatha learned the names of all the beasts.
4. Hiawatha called the birds "Hiawatha's friends."
5. Hiawatha could talk to the birds and the animals.

Ans. 1. True, 2. False, 3. True, 4. False, 5. True

Answer the Following Questions

1. What qualities did the reindeer and the rabbit possess?

Ans. The reindeer ran fast while the rabbit was timid.

2. How did Hiawatha learn about the habits of the animals?

Ans. Hiawatha learnt the habits of the animals by learning their language and talking to them.

3. Why do you think Hiawatha called the birds 'Hiawatha's chickens' and the animals 'Hiawatha's Brothers'?

Ans. Hiawatha called the birds, Hiawatha chicken because of their small size. He called the other animals 'Hiawatha's brothers' to indicate their friendly relationship.

4. If you are among those people who speak foreign language and you don't understand even a bit of it, what would you do in that situation?

Ans. If I am among those people who speak foreign language and I don't understand even a bit of it, I would surely use my gestures to communicate with them.

Writing Task

1. You have just read Hiawatha's story. Write a letter to your friends telling him/her about the story.

Ans. XYZ Apartments

Patna, Bihar

23rd October, 20XX

Dear Kshitiz

How are you doing? I am doing great here and hope that you are hale and hearty. I just received your letter and I am so happy to learn that you are learning French. Your love for language reminded me of Hiawatha, a small boy from the poem I had read recently in my NCERT Book.

Hiawatha was a young Red Indian boy who lived with his grandmother. He loved to learn the language of birds and animals. As a results, he could talk to them and even know their secrets. He became their friend and enjoyed spending time with them. His love for learning the language reminded me of you. Juts like him, you also love learning languages.

Now I am reminding you of the monthly get together. I hope to meet you there and you can show me your new French skills.

Yours lovingly

Rishi

CHAPTER 2

THE SCHOLAR'S MOTHER TONGUE

Summary of the Chapter

One day, a learned Pundit visited Akbar's court. He could speak many languages fluently and challenged everyone to guess his mother tongue. No one succeeded. Finally, Birbal accepted the challenge. At night, he quietly went to the Pundit's room while he was sleeping. Birbal whispered into his ear and tickled him with a feather. The half-awake Pundit shouted in his mother tongue. The next day, Birbal declared in court that the Pundit's mother tongue was Telugu. He explained that when a person is in trouble, they naturally speak in their mother tongue, and shared how he discovered it.

WORD-MEANING

Learned - Having good knowledge; Court - The place where a king or royal officials meet; Courtier - Attendants at the court; Mastery - Full knowledge; Fluently - Speaking a language easily; Whispered - To speak very quietly; Tickled - To touch lightly.

NCERT FOLDER

Reading is Fun (NCERT Page 104)

Q.1 Who came to Akbar's court?

Ans. A learned Pundit came to Akbar's court.

Q.2 What did he claim to know?

Ans. He claimed to know many different languages. He could speak them fluently.

Q.3 How did he challenge everybody?

Ans. He challenged everybody to name his mother tongue.

Let's Talk (NCERT Page 104)

Q.1 What is your mother tongue?

Ans. Hindi

Q.2 Tell the class a joke in your mother tongue.

Ans. Do it yourself.

Q.3 Do you know any other language? Do you know a joke in English? Tell your friends.

Ans. Yes, I know English as well.

Note : Students can write about any other language that they know and tell a joke in that language.

Let's Listen (NCERT Page 104)

Q.1 Listen to your favourite advertisement on the radio or T.V. Repeat it with stress on the words. Act, draw and write the advertisement.

Ans. Easy Peasy cleaning! Tired of rubbing your burnt pan using different liquids. Now use XYZ, soak your pan for 5 minutes and Bam! Get your almost new looking pan back.

Say Aloud (NCERT Page 105)

ask bask mask task
scholar school scan skim

Ans. Do it yourself.

We say - I learnt my lesson. (action word)

But A learn - ed pundit came to the court. (describing word)

We pronounce it as learn-id to rhyme with- created, waited

Q.1 Tick (✓) the words which end with the sound **id**. Say each word aloud

accepted ☐	answered ☐	irritated ☐	failed ☐
completed ☐	challenged ☐	cried ☐	surprised ☐
find ☐	licked ☐	celebrated ☐	fried ☐

Word Building (NCERT Page 105)

Q.1 Make a class dictionary with words from the story. Try to find suitable words for them in your mother tongue. Say these words aloud. Then make sentences with those words in your class dictionary.

Ans.

Words in English	Sentences
Converse	I like to converse with my friends after school.
Tickle	My brother tried to tickle me and I started laughing.
Quietly	She walked quietly so she wouldn't wake the baby.
Whisper	He had to whisper during the meeting.
Surprise	The birthday party was a big surprise for her.
Difficult	This math problem is very difficult to solve.
Irritated	He felt irritated when the dog wouldn't stop barking.
Challenged	She challenged me to a game of chess.

Q.2 Write all the words that show you are happy

For example : Hurray, Ha! Ha!

Add more

_______ _______ _______

Ans. Yahoo!, Hip, Hip, Wow!, Oh! Wonderful!, etc.

Q.3 Tick (✓) the right answer.

(i) 'I visited the court of Akbar' means
(a) you always live there. ☐
(b) you came there for a short time. ☐
(c) you were born there. ☐

Ans. (b) you came there for a short time.

(ii) To imitate someone means to
(a) copy someone ☐
(b) tease someone ☐
(c) make someone angry ☐

Ans. (a) copy someone

Q.4 Look and fill in the columns. One has been done for you

quiet	quietly
(a) sad	_______
(b) fluent	_______
(c) fierce	_______

(d) angry __________

(e) gentle __________

Ans. (a) sadly (b) fluently

(c) fiercely (d) angrily (e) gently

Q.5 Match the words in Column A with words in Column B.

	Column A	Column B
(a)	king	children
(b)	teacher	patients
(c)	doctor	courtiers
(d)	bus driver	clients
(e)	lawyer	passengers
(f)	mother	students

Ans. (a) king - courtiers

(b) teacher - students

(c) doctor - patients

(d) bus driver - passengers

(e) lawyer - clients

(f) mother - children

Q.6 Play this game with a friend. Pick up what you want from any basket.

Add a or an before it.

Now say the sentences below, using these things-

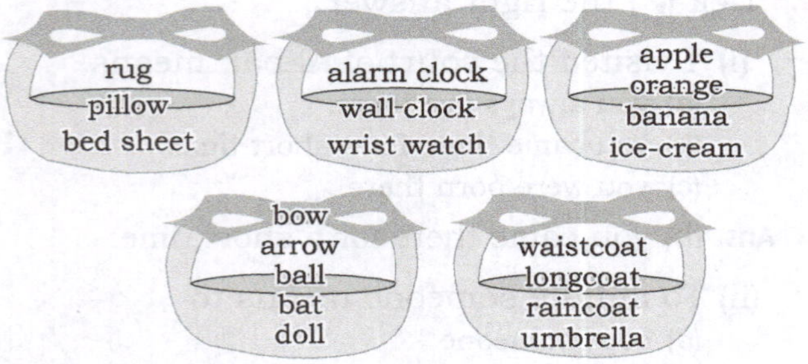

Ans.

a		an
rug	wristwatch	alarm clock
pillow	banana	apple
bedsheet	bow	orange
wall clock	ball	ice-cream
bat doll	raincoat	arrow
waistcoat	longcoat	umbrella

Neena : Can I have __________, please?

Rahul : Yes, here you are.

Jeevika : Can I have __________, too.

Nikhil : No, sorry. You can't have that.

Ans. an orange, a bow

Make more sentences using words from the baskets.

Rahul : Can I have a wristwatch please?

Neena : Yes, here you are.

Nikhil : Can I have an arrow too?

Jeevika : No, sorry. You can't have that.

Neena : Can I have an ice - cream, please?

Nikhil : No, sorry. You can't have that.

Jeevika : Can I have a banana too?

Rahul : Yes, here you are.

Nikhil : Can I have a raincoat please?

Neena : Yes, here you are.

Rahul : Can I have an umbrella too?

Jeevika : No, sorry. You can't have that.

Neena : Can I have an alarm clock, please?

Nikhil : No, sorry. You can't have that.

Let's Share (NCERT Page 108)

Q.1 How did Birbal find out about the Pundit's mother tongue?

Ans. Birbal entered quietly in the Pundit's room. He then whispered and tickled his ear. As a result, the Pundit shouted in his mother tongue. In this way, Birbal found out Pundit's mother tongue.

Q.2 Act this out with your friends and make it into a class play.

Ans. Do it yourself.

The Truth Balloon

Suppose you are going on a camping holiday. What are the four most important things you will carry with you?

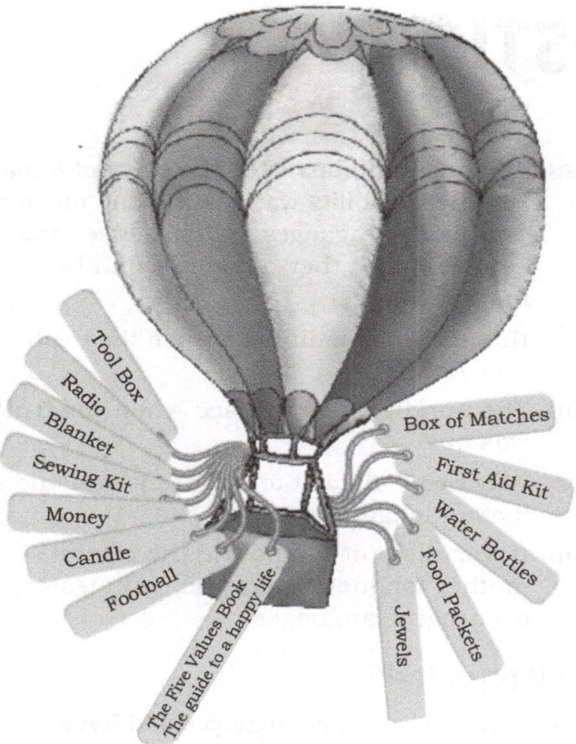

Choose from the tags attached to the hot air balloon.

Ans. (i) Food packets (ii) Water Bottles
(iii) Money (iv) First Aid Kit

Fun Time (NCERT Page 110)

Crossword fun

India is a country of many languages. Let's see if you know what the people of the states in this crossword puzzle speak. The clues are given below. The first letter of each answer has been filled in for you.

Across

(1) This language is spoken in Orissa

(2) It is spoken in karnataka

(4) The people of Assam speak this language

(7) This language is used in Andhra Pradesh

(8) You can hear this spoken in Maharashtra

Down

(3) The people of Kerala speak this language

(5) This language is spoken in most parts of North India

(6) The language of the Goan people

(7) This is spoken in Tamil Nadu

(9) It is widely spoken in Uttar Pradesh and elsewhere.

Ans.

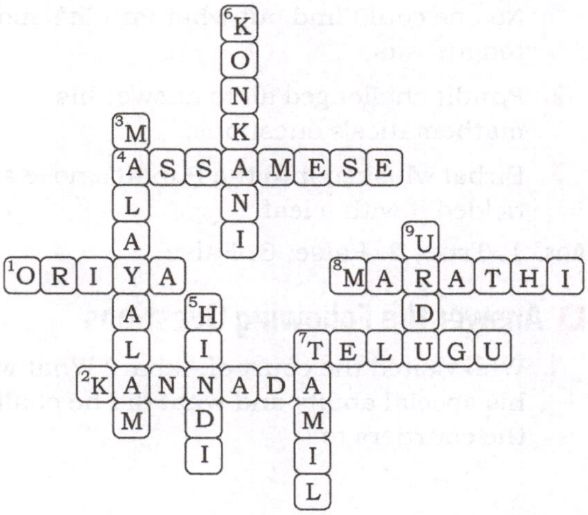

PRACTICE QUESTIONS

Multiple Choice Questions

1. What did the learned Pundit tell King Akbar and his courtiers?
   (a) He was a great warrior.
   (b) He wanted to leave the court.
   (c) He could only speak one language.
   (d) He had mastery over many different languages.
2. Who took up the challenge to find out the Pundit's mother tongue?
   (a) Akbar
   (b) Birbal
   (c) A courtier
   (d) The Pundit himself
3. What was the Pundit's mother tongue?
   (a) Hindi (b) Tamil
   (c) Telugu (d) Bengali

Ans. 1. (d), 2. (b), 3. (c)

Fill in the Blanks

1. Birbal tickled the Pundit's __________ .
2. The Pundit claimed to have mastered many __________.
3. Akbar asked Birbal how he discovered the Pundit's __________.

Ans. 1. ear, 2. languages, 3. mother tongue

True or False

1. No one could find out what Pundit's mother tongue was.
2. Pundit challenged all to answer his mathematics's questions.
3. Birbal whisked into the Pundit's nose and tickled it with a leaf.

Ans. 1. True, 2. False, 3. False

Answer the Following Questions

1. Who visited the court of Akbar? What was his special ability and what did he challenge the courtiers to?

Ans. A learned pundit visited the court of Akbar. His special ability was that he had mastery over many languages. He challenged the courtiers that they could not find his mother tongue.

2. How did the Pundit react when the truth was out?

Ans. The pundit was surprised when the truth was out.

3. Why was it difficult to find out what Pundit's mother tongue?

Ans. It was difficult to find out the pundit's mother tongue because he had mastery over many languages.

Writing Task

1. You love learning languages and have recently started learning a new language. Write a letter to your mother telling her about it.

Ans. ABC
New Delhi
22nd October, 20XX

Dear Mom

How are you? I am doing good here and hope that you are happy and healthy. I miss you all a lot. I know the decision to go to this school was difficult but I think it was good. I like the school because of its library and that I finally get to learn Japanese. Yes Mom, Can you believe it? They have Japanese teachers here so that all of us can learn Japanese properly.

I have started Japanese lessons and we are focusing on alphabets right now. Let me tell you. It is very interesting. In addition, the teachers are very kind and helpful.

I hope to see you soon and show off my new Japanese skills.

Yours lovingly
Son/Daughter.

Unit 7

CHAPTER 1 A WATERING RHYME

Summary of the Poem In the poem, the poet tells the right time to water the plants. He says that watering them early morning or evening is best. We should avoid watering plants at noon, as it can harm and kill them.

Stanza-wise Explanation

Stanza 1

Early in the morning,
Or the evening hour,
Are the times to water
Every kind of flower.

Watering at noonday,
When the sun is high,
Doesn't help the flowers,
Only makes them die.

Exp. The poet tells us that the best time to water plants is in the early morning or the evening. Watering them at noon, when the sun rays are very strong it is not good for the plants. Instead of helping, it can harm them.

Stanza 2

Also, when you water,
Water at the roots;
Flowers keep their mouths where
We should wear our boots.

Soak the earth around them,
Then through all the heat
The flowers will have water
For their thirsty 'feet'!

Word-Meaning *Boots - Big shoes which cover half legs; Soak - Absorb liquid, Feet - Roots.*

Exp. The poet says that we should water plants at their roots. The poet compares the roots to the plants' mouths. It's important to soak the soil around them so the plants can stay hydrated, especially on hot days. This helps keep the flowers healthy.

NCERT FOLDER

Reading is Fun (NCERT Page 116)

Q.1 What is the best time to water the plants?

Ans. The best time to water the plants is early morning or evening.

Q.2 When should we not water the plants?

Ans. We should not water the plants at noon when the sun is high.

Q.3 Which part of the plant should be watered?

Ans. The roots of the plant should be watered.

Word Building (NCERT Page 116)

Place letters in their right order to form the names of flowers.

(a) PAETWEES S _ _ _ _ _ _ A
(b) MRAIDOLG M _ _ _ _ _ _ D
(c) JMINEAS J _ _ _ _ _ E
(d) TLOUS L _ _ _ S
(e) ARGOM M _ _ _ A
(f) DHAAIL D _ _ _ _ A
(g) XOLHP P _ _ _ X
(h) ANSPY P _ _ _ Y
(i) BISIHCUS H _ _ _ _ _ _ S

Ans. (a) SWEETPEA (b) MARIGOLD
(c) JASMINE (d) LOTUS
(e) MOGRA (f) DAHLIA
(g) PHLOX (h) PANSY
(i) HIBISCUS

Fun Time (NCERT Page 117)

You have visited your school garden and seen different kinds of plants, shrubs and trees. This grid has the names of different parts of a tree. Look for these words - BUD, POD, LEAF STEM, ROOTS, THORNS, BRANCHES and FLOWERS as fast as you can - vertically, horizontally and diagonally.

B	P	R	S	T	Q	V	F	S	U	J	L
A	U	B	C	D	F	F	E	F	G	H	E
I	J	D	K	L	M	L	N	O	P	Q	A
R	S	T	U	V	W	X	O	Y	Z	A	F
B	C	T	D	E	P	O	D	W	F	G	H
I	J	H	E	K	L	M	M	O	E	P	Q
R	S	O	T	M	U	V	W	X	Y	R	Z
A	B	R	A	N	C	H	E	S	C	D	S
E	F	N	G	H	I	J	K	L	M	N	O
P	Q	S	R	S	T	U	R	O	O	T	S
V	W	X	Y	Z	A	B	C	D	E	F	G

Ans.

B	P	R	S	T	Q	V	F	S	U	J	L
A	U	B	C	D	F	F	E	F	G	H	E
I	J	D	K	L	M	L	N	O	P	Q	A
R	S	T	U	V	W	X	O	Y	Z	A	F
B	C	T	D	E	P	O	D	W	F	G	H
I	J	H	E	K	L	M	M	O	E	P	Q
R	S	O	T	M	U	V	W	X	Y	R	Z
A	B	R	A	N	C	H	E	S	C	D	S
E	F	N	G	H	I	J	K	L	M	N	O
P	Q	S	R	S	T	U	R	O	O	T	S
V	W	X	Y	Z	A	B	C	D	E	F	G

Let's Talk (NCERT Page 117)

Q.1 Do you have a garden?

Ans. Yes, I have a garden.

Q.2 Name some flowers which grow in your garden or near your house.

Ans. Rose, Marigold, Jasmine, etc.

Q.3 Give another word for 'thirsty feet'.

Ans. Dry roots

Q.4 What happens when we water plants in the morning?

Choose one answer.

(a) They will grow well.

(b) They will dry up.

Ans. (a) They will grow well.

Q.5 From where do flowers get water?

(a) From the bottom (roots)

(b) Form the top (leaves)

Ans. (a) From the bottom (roots).

Say Aloud (NCERT Page 118)

early curly surely	our hour are	flower flour shower	their there care	could hood should
where wear	seat sheet	shake sake	bread spread	high sigh

Ans. Do it yourself.

Pick out the silent letters from these words

hour	knit	wrong	doubt
often	know	night	could
write	knife	high	walk

Ans.

hour-h	knit-k	wrong-w	doubt-b
often-t	know-k	night-gh	could-l
write-w	knife-k	high-gh	walk-l

Let's Write (NCERT Page 118)

Q.1 Write rhyming words for the words given below. One has been done for you

(a) morning evening

(b) car

(c) high

(d) boots

(e) heat

(f) where

Ans. (b) bar (c) fly (d) roots

(e) beat (f) here

Q.2 Words like morning, evening, watering end in-ing. Write six more words to which -ing can be added at the end to form a new word.

Ans. (a) playing (b) swimming

(c) kicking (c) roaming

(e) hurrying (f) running

Q.3 Look for words in the poem which sound like the words given below.

(a) are (b) there (c) flour (d) where

(e) son (f) threw

Ans. (a) hour (b) thier (c) flower

(d) wear (e) sun (f) through

Q.4 In the sentences below the capital letters, commas, full stops and question marks are missing. Put these in the correct places.

(a) on monday I will go to school

Ans. On Monday, I will go to school.

(b) rahim ravi and raju are going to see the circus

Ans. Rahim, Ravi and Raju are going to see the circus.

(c) sita where are you looking

Ans. Sita, where are you going?

(d) the tailor went to the market mr singh.

Ans. The tailor went to the market, Mr. Singh.

(e) every sunday i go for a walk have breakfast read story books listen to music and watch television.

Ans. Every Sunday, I go for a walk, have breakfast, read story books, listen to music and watch television.

(f) Laxmi why are you crying

Ans. Laxmi, why are you crying?

(g) What is the colour of the sky

Ans. What is the colour of the sky?

(h) Oranges mangoes bananas and papayas are fruits

Ans. Oranges, mangoes, bananas and papayas are fruits.

Team Time (NCERT Page 120)

Write a Story

Write a story about a plant that is in danger. Write about how you might help to save it. Be sure the story has a beginning, a middle, and an end.

Ans. **The Little Plant in Danger**

Once, there was a small plant named Lily in a garden. She had green leaves and yellow flowers. One summer, the sun was too hot, and there was no rain. Lily started to dry up and was in danger.

A girl named Anya saw Lily struggling. She felt sad and decided to help. Anya watered Lily every morning and evening. She also made a small shade to protect Lily from the sun.

Soon, Lily became healthy again. Thanks to Anya's care, Lily was saved, and the garden was full of life again.

Prepare a Speech

Prepare a speech giving some reasons why it is important to protect flowers and plants. Include ways that you could help protect endangered plants in your school.

Ans. Good morning everyone,

Plants and flowers are essential to our environment and play a big role in keeping the Earth healthy. They give us oxygen, clean the air, and provide food for us and many animals. Without them, life would be very hard for all living things, including humans.

Protecting plants, especially endangered ones, is important because they help keep the balance in nature. They provide shelter for animals and insects, and they even help control the climate by making the air cooler. In our school, we can protect plants by growing more of them and taking care of the ones we already have. We can also remind each other not to harm the plants by being careful around them and making sure they have enough water.

Plants and flowers are a vital part of our lives, and it's up to us to protect them. Let's take this responsibility seriously and work together to protect the plants around us.

PRACTICE QUESTIONS

Multiple Choice Questions

1. When is the best time to water flowers according to the poem?
   (a) At noon
   (b) Late night
   (c) In the afternoon
   (d) Early morning or evening

2. What happens to flowers if they are watered at noonday?
   (a) They die
   (b) They grow faster
   (c) They bloom more
   (d) They stay the same

3. Where should you water the flowers?
   (a) At the roots
   (b) On the stems
   (c) On the leaves
   (d) On the flowers

4. What does the poet compare the flowers' mouths to?
   (a) Feet
   (b) Boots
   (c) Roots
   (d) Hands

5. What helps the flowers survive through the heat?
(a) Direct sunlight
(b) No water at all
(c) Watering only the leaves
(d) Water soaked in the earth

Ans. 1. (d), 2. (a), 3. (a), 4. (b), 5. (d)

Fill in the Blanks

1. The flowers keep their __________ where we wear our boots.
2. The __________ will help the flowers survive through the heat.
3. Watering in the __________ is harmful to the flowers when the sun is high.
4. The flowers will have water for their thirsty __________ if you water them correctly.
5. Flowers will remain hydrated if we water the soil around their __________.

Ans. 1. mouths, 2. water, 3. noon, 4. feet, 5. roots

True or False

1. At noon the sun is high.
2. We should water the plants at noon.
3. Plants need sunlight and water to live.
4. We should water the plants at their roots.
5. If we water the plants in the evening flowers will die.

Ans. 1. True, 2. False, 3. True, 4. True, 5. False

Answer the following Questions

1. How does watering the earth around the roots benefit the flowers?

Ans. Watering the earth around the roots benefit the flowers because roots are located there.

2. What happens to the flowers if they are watered when the sun is high?

Ans. When the flowers are watered when the sun is high, they die.

3. What will help the flowers survive through all the heat?

Ans. Watering the plants to its roots helps the flowers survive through the heat.

Writing Tasks

1. You have started your own garden. Your first plant is Jasmine and you have been taking caring of it for one month now. Recently your plant bore the first flower. You are very happy. What do you feel? Write your feelings about the entire process of growing the flower.

You can start with the following

I have recently started gardening ....

Ans. I have recently started gardening with my grandmother. My first plant that I took full responsibility was of the jasmine plant that my grandfather had got me. To plant my jasmine, I dug some soil put some fertiliser of the compost that my grandmother keeps and then, planted the tiny stem. I had to water it regularly and make sure that no animals came near it and destroy it. Soon, I saw the first bud on my plant. I was so excited to see my first flower. After a week, the bud bloomed into a . I fell in love with it.
I was going to pluck it when my grandmother told me that I should not do so. It is disrespectful to the plant. But she did tell me to click a picture which I took from my phone. It was a great experience.

CHAPTER 2

THE GIVING TREE

Summary of the Chapter

The story is about a tree that deeply loved a little boy. The boy enjoyed spending time with the tree, climbing its trunk, swinging on its branches, and eating its apples. Whenever he was tired, he would rest under the tree. As the boy grew older, he stopped visiting as often and started focusing on his own needs.

One day, when he needed money, the tree gave him apples to sell in the market. Later, when the boy became a young man, he asked the tree for a house. The tree happily told him to cut its branches to build a house.

Years later, the boy returned and wanted a boat to go on a business trip. The tree offered its trunk, and the boy sailed away. All that was left of the tree was a stump. Eventually, when the boy had become an old man, he returned to the tree looking for a quiet place to rest. The tree, now just a stump, offered it to him, and the old man sat down to rest.

WORD-MEANING

Company - The act of being with someone; Swing - To move back and forth; Trunk - The main wooden part of a tree; Pluck - Break off; Sail - To travel through water; Recognised - Knew or remembered someone or something; Sighing - Taking a deep breath, often showing sadness or relief; Stump - The bottom part of a tree that is left after it has been cut down.

NCERT FOLDER

Reading is Fun (NCERT Page 126)

Q.1 How did the boy enjoy the company of the tree?

Ans. The boy enjoyed the company of the tree by climbing its trunk and swinging from its branches. He played in its shade and ate its apples.

Q.2 How did the tree help the boy earn money?

Ans. The tree gave all its apples to the boy. The boy earned money by selling them in the market.

Q.3 What did the boy make with the branches of the tree?

Ans. The boy made a house for himself and his family with the branches of the tree.

Q.4 What did the boy make with the trunk of the tree?

Ans. The boy made a boat with the trunk of the tree.

Q.5 How was the stump of the tree useful?

Ans. The stump of the tree was useful because it provided the old man with a comfortable place to sit and rest.

Q.6 Why is the play called 'The Giving Tree'?

Ans. The play is named 'The Giving Tree' because it tells the story of a tree that selflessly gives parts of itself to a young boy without wanting anything back. The tree cares about what the boy needs and helps him by providing shade, fruit, branches and even its trunk.

Word Building (NCERT Page 126)

Q.1 Make new words and complete the sentences.

(a) The children love to sing ________.(loud)

(b) Read your lesson________. (silent)

(c) Throw the ball ________. (slow)

(d) The tree gave its fruit to the boy ________. (happy)

(e) Do your work ________. (neat)

Ans. (a) loudly (b) silently (c) slowly (d) happily (e) neatly

Q.2 Fill in the blanks with the correct word.

My mother went to the market and bought a kilogram of (a) ________ (apple/apples), a dozen (b) ________ (banana/bananas) and a dozen (c) ________ (orange/oranges). I love oranges. So I ate an (d) ________ (orange/oranges). My brother wanted a (e) ________ (banana/bananas) and my sister asked for an (f) ________ (apple /apples). A tree has one (g) ________ (trunk/trunks) but many (h) ________ (branch/branches). A (i) ________ (branch/branches) has a number of (j) ________ (leaf/leaves) and (k) ________ (flower/flowers).

Ans. (a) apples (b) bananas (c) oranges (d) orange (e) banana (f) apple (g) trunk (h) branches (i) branch (j) leaves (k) flowers

Let's Talk (NCERT Page 127)

Q.1 Why should we not cut trees?

Ans. We should not cut trees because

(a) they provide us with fruits, flowers, leaves, wood and shelter.

(b) they also help purify the air and enhance the beauty of our surroundings.

Q.2 At the end of the play, only the stump of the tree is left. Find out if it will grow into a tree again.

Ans. Once the trunk of the tree is cut off, it cannot grow back into a full tree. Leaves are essential for making food for the tree, and since a stump has no leaves, the tree will slowly die because it can no longer produce food for itself.

Q.3 Say the given sentences with different expressions.

(a) Come and play with me.

(b) I want to buy things and have fun.

(c) Come and climb up my trunk and swing from my branches.

(d) Cut down my trunk.

(e) I am too old to swing on branches.

(f) I am too tired to climb.

Ans. Do it yourself.

Let's Write (NCERT Page 127)

Q.1 Write these sentences in the correct order. Also, choose the right word from the box and add it before each sentence. Remember to put a comma after it, for example, Finally, ...

First	Then	After that	Finally

(a) It gave him its branches to make a house.

(b) It asked him to sit on the stump.

(c) It gave him its trunk to make a boat.

(d) The tree gave its apples to the boy.

Ans. (a) First, the tree gave its apples to the boy.

(b) Then, it gave him its branches to make a house.

(c) After that, it gave him its trunk to make a boat.

(d) Finally, it asked him to sit on the stump.

Q.2 Work in a group and decide the things that you can do to help your grandparents or any old person. Now, write five of these things that you will do.

Ans. (i) Go for walks with them.

(ii) Spend time talking to them.

(iii) Help with cleaning the house.

(iv) Show them how to use a phone.

(v) Remind them to take their medicine.

Let's Act (NCERT Page 128)

Q.1 You are reading and talking about trees. You are thinking about trees too. Can you make the shape of a tree with your body?

(a) Let's see your branches.

(b) Let's see a full tree with fruits and leaves.

(c) Enact a cut tree with only a trunk.

(d) Enact a tree with only a stump left.

(e) Communicate the idea in this play.

Ans. Do it yourself.

Q.2 Use your body to -

stretch	bend	jump	twist	hop	climb

Ans. Do it yourself.

Chintha Chettu

Chintha Chettu is a tamarind tree.

This famous tamarind tree is in Gwalior.

It grows over Tansen's tomb.

Tansen was a great singer.

People in Gwalior say:

"Eat the leaves of this tamarind tree

And you'll also sing like Tansen!"

Choose the right words.

Q.1 Chintha Chettu is a tamarind ________ (tree/ leaf).

Q.2 This famous tree is in ________ (Guntur/ Gwalior).

Q.3 Tansen was a famous ________ (singer/ dancer).

Q.4 The tamarind tree grows over Tansen's ________ (house/ tomb).

Q.5 "Eat the leaves of the tamarind tree, and you'll also sing like ________ (Tansen/ Akbar)."

Ans. 1. tree 2. Gwalior 3. singer 4. tomb 5. Tansen

PRACTICE QUESTIONS

Multiple Choice Questions

1. What does the tree give the boy when he asks for money?
   (a) A job
   (b) Coins
   (c) A wallet
   (d) Apples to sell
2. What does the tree offer when the boy asks for a boat?
   (a) Its trunk
   (b) Its roots
   (c) Its leaves
   (d) Its branches
3. What does the tree become at the end of the story?
   (a) A stump
   (b) A flower
   (c) A garden
   (d) A large tree

Ans. 1. (d), 2. (a), 3. (a)

True or False

1. The tree has a house to give to the boy.
2. The tree feels sad when the boy leaves.
3. The boy needs a boat when he is an old man.

Ans. 1. False, 2. True, 3. False

Fill in the Blanks

1. The boy enjoyed swinging from the tree's ______.
2. At the end of the story, the tree is just an old ______.
3. After cutting the trunk, the boy sailed away in a ______.

Ans. 1. branches, 2. stump, 3. boat

Answer the Following Questions

1. How did the boy have fun in 'The Giving Tree'?

Ans. The boy had fun in 'The Giving Tree' by enjoying time with the tree. He would climb its trunk, swing on its branches and eat its apples.

2. How did the tree help the boy to earn money?

Ans. The tree helped the boy in earning money by giving the boy its apples to sell.

3. What three things did the tree give to the little boy?

Ans. The tree gave its fruits- the apples, its branches and its trunk to help the boy.

Writing Task

1. The world today is seeing less parks, trees, and gardens but more buildings. This loss of greenery had impacted us negatively. Keeping this in mind, write a speech on 'The Importance of Forests'.

Ans. Forests are crucial for the well-being of living beings as they provide essential food and shelter for animals. Moreover, they play an important role in maintaining a clean environment by absorbing carbon dioxide and releasing oxygen. Additionally, forests help prevent soil erosion. It is important to protect forests to fight climate change, and protect environment.

Conserving forests is essential for sustaining life on Earth and ensuring a healthy environment for future generations.

CHAPTER 3 THE DONKEY

Summary of the Poem In this poem, a young boy imagines if he had a donkey, how he would treat it, if it refuses to obey. Instead of beating the donkey for not moving, he would choose kindness.

Stanza-wise Explanation

Stanza 1

If I had a donkey
And he wouldn't go,
Would I wallop him?
No, no, no.

Word-Meaning *Wallop - Beat roundly.*

Exp. The little boy wonders what he would do if he had a donkey that did not want to go when he asked it to. He quickly says that he would not hit or hurt the donkey, which shows he cares about it.

Stanza 2

I'd find a little hay
And give him some corn,
Then he'd be the best donkey
That ever was born.

Word-Meaning *Hay - Dry grass*

Exp. The boy thinks of a better way to handle the situation. He decides that instead of being harsh, he would find some hay and give the donkey corn to eat. He believes that by being kind and feeding the donkey, it would become the best donkey ever.

NCERT FOLDER

Fun Time (NCERT Page 131)

Q.1 Complete what is missing in these drawings. What work do these men or women do?

(a) A milkman

Ans. A milkman sells milk.

(b) A grocer

Ans. A grocer sells food items and household items.

(c) A policeman

Ans. A policeman ensures that law is enforced.

(d) An ice-cream man

Ans. An ice-cream man sells ice-cream.

(e) A wrestler

Ans. A wrestler builds his body and competes with other wrestlers.

Picture Story

Match pictures to the text and give an ending to the story by drawing the sixth picture. Give it a title.

1. He is heavy.
2. He is young.
3. I am sad.
4. I am happy now!
5. They are strong.
6. ________________ .

Ans. Title - Minu, The Donkey

PRACTICE QUESTIONS

Multiple Choice Questions

1. What does the boy think about hitting the donkey?
   (a) It is not the right thing to do.
   (b) It is fun.
   (c) It is necessary.
   (d) It will help him.
2. What does the boy plan to feed the donkey?
   (a) Bread (b) Apples
   (c) Carrots (d) Hay and corn
3. What does the boy want the donkey to do?
   (a) Sing (b) Jump
   (c) Go when asked (d) Dance
4. How does the boy feel about the donkey?
   (a) Angry
   (b) Loving and caring
   (c) Fearful
   (d) Indifferent
5. What would make the donkey the best donkey in the world, according to the boy?
   (a) Being hit
   (b) Running fast
   (c) Eating sweets
   (d) Receiving love and care

Ans. 1. (a), 2. (d), 3. (c), 4. (b), 5. (d)

Fill in the Blanks

1. He would give the donkey some ______ and corn.
2. The poem teaches us to be kind and ______ to animals.
3. The boy thinks he would not ______ the donkey for not moving.
4. He believed that with love and care, the donkey would be the best ______.
5. The boy imagines that if he took care of the donkey, it would _____ for him.

Ans. 1. hay, 2. gentle, 3. hit, 4. donkey, 5. go

True or False

1. The poem is about a girl and her donkey.
2. The boy thinks giving food to the donkey will help it.
3. The boy wants to punish the donkey for not obeying.
4. The donkey in the poem is described as a bad donkey.
5. The boy believes that kindness will make the donkey better.

Ans. 1. False, 2. True, 3. False, 4. False, 5. True

Answer the Following Questions

1. What would the poet do if the donkey wouldn't go?

Ans. The poet would not hurt or hit the donkey if he wouldn't go.

2. What would the poet give to the donkey to eat?

Ans. The poet would give hay and corn to the donkey to eat.

3. How would the donkey become the best donkey?

Ans. The donkey would become the best donkey with love and care.

4. What would the child find for the donkey?

Ans. The boy would find hay for the donkey.

Writing Task

1. Write a paragraph on 'Animals are our Friends'.

Ans. Throughout history, the bond between humans and animals has had a unique relationship marked. Pets, such as dogs and cats, have an innate ability to sense human emotions. They often act as a source of comfort during difficult times. For many, animals are more than just pets; they are family members that bring joy into everyday life. Caring for pets teaches us about the life values like kindness and care. They learn that animals, like humans, have needs and feelings that must be respected.

CHAPTER 1 THE BOOKS

Summary of the Poem In this poem, a child feels welcomed by the library door as he enters. He is amazed to see so many books inside. When the child opens one book and sits down to read, he discovers that the pictures inside tell their own stories. He thinks it's a wonderful book.

Stanza-wise Explanation

Stanza 1

"Come in, come in!"
Said the library door;
I opened it wide
And saw books galore!

Word-Meaning *Library* - *Place where books are kept;* *Wide* - *Broad;* *Galore* - *Plenty.*

Exp. The child imagines the library door inviting him inside. When he opens the door, he is excited to see a vast collection of books.

Stanza 2

Tall skinny books
Up high on the shelves;
Little fat books
That stood by themselves.

Word-Meaning *Skinny* - *Very thin;* *Shelves* - *Racks fixed in a cupboard.*

Exp. The child describes the different types of books he sees. Some books are tall and very thin. They are placed high on the shelves, while the thick books are kept separately.

Stanza 3

I opened one up
And sat down to look;
The pictures told stories!
What a wonderful book!

Exp. The child opens one of the books and sits down to read it. He finds that the pictures in the book tell their own stories. He finds the book to be amazing.

NCERT FOLDER

Readng is Fun (NCERT Page 136)

Q.1 What did the library door say?

Ans. The library door said, "Come in, come in."

Q.2 What did the books in the library look like?

Ans. Some of the books in the library were tall and skinny, while some were little and fat.

Q.3 Why did the child in the poem like looking at the pictures?

Ans. The child in the poem liked looking at the pictures because they told him stories.

Let's Listen (NCERT Page 136)

Q.1 Listen to the words

Come in, come in

Go out, go out

What word signs have you seen or heard

(a) at home ____________

(b) at the vegetable shop ____________

(c) at the library ____________

(d) at the doctor's place ____________

(e) at the bus stop ____________

(f) at the toy shop ____________

Ans. (a) Welcome Home (b) No bargain
(c) Keep silence (d) Emergency
(e) Ticket counter (f) Sale! Sale! Sale!

Let's Talk (NCERT Page 136-137)

Q.1 Do you like reading story books?

Ans. Yes, I like reading interesting story books with pictures in them.

Q.2 What kinds of stories do you like?

Ans. I like adventurous stories and fairy tales.

Q.3 The word galore means in great numbers. Do you also have a class library or a school library which keeps many books? Can you borrow books?

Ans. Yes, there is a huge library in my school and we can borrow books there.

Q.4 Tell the class about your favourite story book. Talk about the character you liked most in the book.

Ans. Do it yourself.

Fun Time (NCERT Page 137)

Let's play Book Chain

Form groups of five or six children in the class. Sit in circles. The first child will begin the book chain by saying the name of a story book. The next child extends the chain by saying the name of another book. In this way a book chain is formed. The more the rounds the children can go on for, the longer the book chain will be. See which group makes the longest book chain.

Ans. Do it yourself.

Let's Write (NCERT Page 138)

Make word families. The first word in each has been written for you.

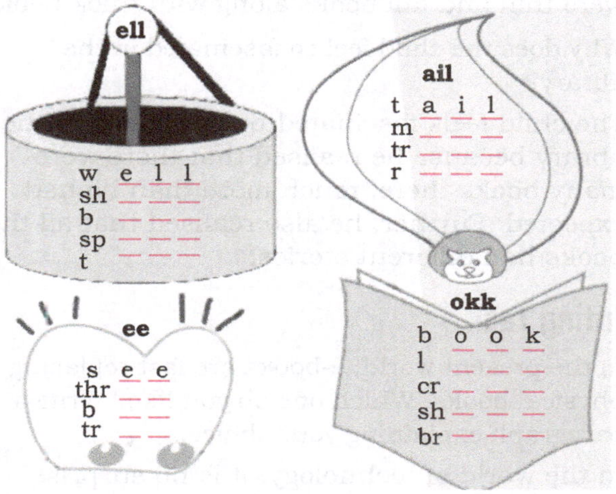

Ans.

ell	ail	ee	ook
shell	bell	spell	look
bell	trail	bee	crook
spell	rail	tree	shook
tell			brook

Look at this sentence

A library is a place where books are kept.

Now fill in the blanks after reading these sentences.

(a) An ______________ is a place where aeroplanes take off and land.

(b) A ______________ is a place where food is cooked.

(c) A ______________ is a place where sick people are taken care of.

(d) A ______________ is a place where you can buy things.

(e) A ______________ is a place where children study.

Ans. (a) airport
(b) kitchen
(c) hospital
(d) market
(e) school

PRACTICE QUESTIONS

Multiple Choice Questions

1. What does the child see inside the library?
(a) A few books
(b) Lots of books
(c) Only one book
(d) Pencils and paper

2. How are the tall books described in the poem?
(a) Wide and large (b) Skinny and tall
(c) Round and big (d) Short and fat

3. How are the small books described in the poem?
(a) Tall and slim
(b) Little and fat
(c) Heavy and old
(d) Large and thick

4. What makes the child love the book in the end?
(a) The cover
(b) The size of the book
(c) The colour of the pages
(d) The stories told by the pictures

5. What did the child do after opening the book?
(a) He sat down to look at it.
(b) He gave the book to a friend
(c) He closed the book immediately
(d) He put the book back on the shelf

Ans. 1. (b), 2. (b), 3. (d), 4. (d), 5. (a)

Fill in the Blanks

1. The child was welcomed by the ______ door.
2. The ______ told stories to the child in the book.
3. After opening a book, the child sat down to ______ it.
4. Some of the books on the shelves were tall and ______.
5. The child saw little ______ books standing by themselves.

Ans. 1. library, 2. pictures, 3. read, 4. skinny, 5. fat

True or False

1. The child thought the book was wonderful.
2. The library door told the child to stay outside.
3. The child found the pictures in the book boring.
4. The child sat down to look at a book after opening it.
5. The child saw both tall skinny books and little fat books.

Ans. 1. True, 2. False, 3. False, 4. True, 5. True

Answer the Following Questions

1. What kinds of books were there?

Ans. There were many kinds of books there. There were thin and tall books along with thick books.

2. Why does the child feel so fascinated in the library?

Ans. The child feels fascinated by the books in the library because he realised that there were many books there, much more than he had expected. Further, he also realised that all the books had different stories.

Writing Task

1. In the present world, e-books are fast replacing physical books. Which one do you like? Write a paragraph explaining your choice.

Ans. In the world of technology, it is no surprise that digital books or e-books, have become popular. However, despite these digital books, printed books still hold a special place in the hearts of readers and are often considered superior to e-books. I agree with it. One of the main reasons why printed books are better than their electronic formats is their nature. There is something magical about holding a physical book in your hands, feeling the weight, flipping through the pages and smelling the ink and paper. Printed books allow for a more personal reading experience.

CHAPTER 2

GOING TO BUY A BOOK

Summary of the Chapter

One day, a girl and her brother received money from their grandfather to buy books. Since they both loved reading, they decided to go to the bookshop immediately. They visited a small shop that had many books, and the shopkeeper was kind and helpful. He helped them in choosing books. After spending a lot of time reading, they finally decided which ones to buy. The girl chose a big book with many stories, while the boy chose a large book full of pictures. They went home, sat on their grandfather's bed, and started reading together.

NCERT FOLDER

Reading is Fun (NCERT Page 143)

Q.1 Why did grandfather give the children money?

Ans. Grandfather gave the money to the children to buy books.

Q.2 Where did they go to buy books?

Ans. They went to a small bookshop to buy books.

Q.3 Did the girl buy a picture book?

Ans. No, the girl bought a story book.

Let's Listen and Search (NCERT Page 143)

In small groups one child will give directions orally only once; the others will listen and hunt for the following:

1. a circle 
2. a square 
3. a triangle 
4. a piece of paper with three signatures 
5. a piece of paper with red colour 
6. a piece of paper with a number 

7. a piece of paper with the label of tea 
8. a twig in the shape of an alphabetic letter

10. a flower in the shape of a number

Ans. Do it yourself.

Let's Talk (NCERT Page 143)

Q.1 Is there a bookshop near your home? If there is, do you like to visit it?

Ans. Yes, there is a bookshop near my home. I like to visit it once a week.

Q.2 What are the different kinds of books in this bookshop or in any other bookshop you have seen? Tell the class.

Ans. There are many different types of books available in the bookshop like picture books, fairytales, non-fiction, poetry, novels, activity books, etc.

Let's Write (NCERT Page 144-145)

Q.1 Look at these sentences in the story -

(a) Should we go to the big market?

(b) Should we go to the small shop?

(c) Should I buy a thin book?

The coloured words above are describing words. Now fill in more describing words into the passage below -

It was a (a) ____________ night. A (b) ____________ girl sat up in bed listening to her mother tell a (c) ____________ story. Her (d) ____________ eyes opened wide and she gave a (e) ____________ smile. "Now go to sleep, Paro," her mother closed the book. "(f) ____________ dreams."

Ans. (a) cloudy (b) little (c) comic (d) black (e) big (f) Sweet

Q.2 Imagine that you will go to the bookshop tomorrow. What will you do there? Write five sentences beginning with

(a) I shall ____________

(b) I shall ____________

(c) I shall ____________

(d) I shall ____________

(e) I shall ____________

Ans. (a) I shall look for books with interesting stories.

(b) I shall ask the shopkeeper for suggestions.

(c) I shall choose a book with colourful pictures.

(d) I shall spend some time reading in the shop.

(e) I shall buy my favourite book to read at home.

Q.3 Tina goes to her school library to borrow a book. Complete her dialogue with the librarian by using and or or in the blanks.

Tina : Ma'am, I want to borrow a book

Librarian : Do you want a story book (a) ____________ a book of poems?

Tina : I want a story book.

Librarian : Do you like stories about animals (b) ____________ adventure stories?

Tina : I like both.

Librarian : Go to the second cupboard. On the first shelf, you will find animal stories (c) ____________ on the second, adventure stories.

Tina (after selecting two books) : Ma'am, I want Black Beauty (d) ____________ Panchantantra Stories.

Librarian : You can have either Black Beauty (e) ____________ Panchantantra Stories.

Ans. (a) or (b) or (c) and (d) and (e) or

Q.4 What is your favourite book? Write down the name of the book. Then write down the story.

Ans. **Charlie and the Chocolate Factory**
by Roald Dahl

The story is about a poor boy named Charlie Bucket who lives with his family. One day, Willy Wonka, the owner of the biggest chocolate factory in the world, announces that five lucky children who find golden tickets hidden in chocolate bars will get a special tour of his factory.

Charlie finds a golden ticket and visits the factory along with four other children. Inside, they experience magical things but due to their bad behaviour, the other children face funny consequences.

In the end, Willy Wonka chooses Charlie to inherit the factory because of his kind heart and humility. The story is full of adventure, imagination, and valuable life lessons.

Let's Make a Bookmark (NCERT Page 146)

Make your own bookmark

Remember to treat your books well. Never fold the corners of pages. This makes books look shabby and old.

A bookmark helps you to find the page you were on when you last read your book.

Here is a way to make your own beautiful Dove Bookmark.

You need

- An old greetings card/wedding card/scissors
- A black bindi for the eyes

Method

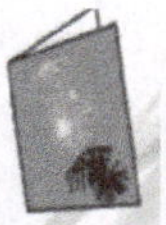

- Take the old card. You will need to use the inside of the card.

- Fold it into two as shown in the picture.

- Trace the outline of a dove on the card.
- Cut it along the lines.

- Make an outline with a black pen.
- Stick a bindi for the eye.
- Paste it on a strip of 2 inches x 4 inches.
- Your Dove Bookmark is now ready to be used.

Ans. Do it Yourself.

Let's Cover Our Book (NCERT Page 147)

1. Spread your notebook on a brown paper which is four inches bigger than your notebook, as shown in the picture.

2. Fold the paper into two halves with the book inside it in the middle.

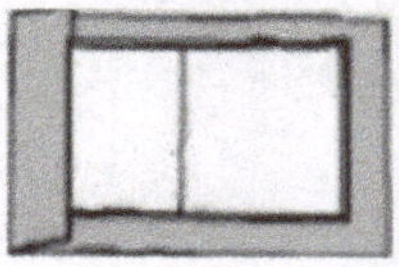

3. Fold the two open flaps of paper inside the first and the last page of the book and press to crease.

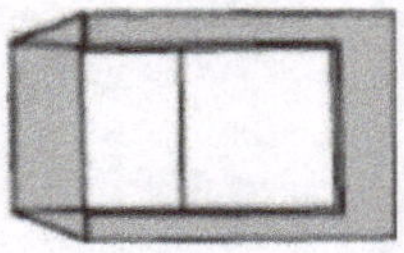

4. Fold the closed end of the two top and bottom flaps of the paper, forming a triangle. Crease the paper and cut it.

5. Fold the two front flaps inside the first page and crease it.

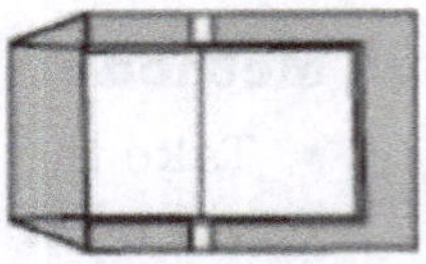

6. Fold the two back flaps under the last page and crease it.

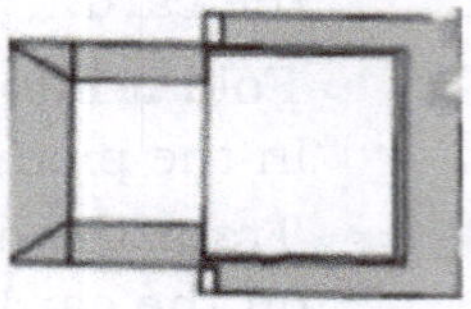

7. Now your book is neatly covered.
8. Write your name and class on the cover. Then write the subject you will use this notebook for.

Ans. Do it Yourself.

Do You Know? (NCERT Page 148)

The earliest books were written by hand. Two thousand years ago in India, birch bark (bhojapatra) and palm leaves (talapatra) were used for pages. A pen and black ink were used to write on birch bark. A sharp, iron spike was used for writing on palm leaves. Holes were drilled through the leaves and the book was held together by a string!

Enjoy and Read the Poem

Say in Chorus

Books are great! Books are fun!
Books let you do what you've never done!
Read a good mystery, solve a crime!
Read about history, go back in time!
Read about a lost dog, where can it be?
Read about a giant frog under the sea!
Read a very funny book, tears go away!
Read a bright, sunny book on a rainy day!

Chorus

Books are great! Books are fun!
Let's read books, everyone!

- Mash Goldfish (adapted)

PRACTICE QUESTIONS

Multiple Choice Questions

1. What did the grandfather give to the children?
   (a) Money (b) Toys (c) Food (d) Clothes
2. Where did the children decide to buy their books?
   (a) Mall (b) Big market
   (c) Small shop (d) Online store
3. How did the children feel while deciding which book to buy?
   (a) Angry (b) Confused (c) Bored (d) Excited
4. Which of the following is correct about the speaker and his brother?
   (a) They both love to read books.
   (b) They both fight with each other.
   (c) They do not know how to read.
   (d) They both love to play video games.

Ans. 1. (a), 2. (c), 3. (b), 4. (a)

Fill in the Blanks

1. The children decided to go to the ______ bookshop.
2. The children ran home to show their books to their ______.
3. The narrator sat on the ______ while reading in the bookshop.

Ans. 1. small, 2. grandfather, 3. relax

True or False

1. The narrator bought a thin book with pictures.
2. The children decided to go to the bookshop the next day.
3. The children spent two hours deciding which books to buy.

Ans. 1. False, 2. False, 3. True

Answer the Following Questions

1. Why did the children decide to go to the small shop?

Ans. The children decided to go to the small shop because it had many books and the man the shop was king and helpful.

2. How did the man in the small book shop help the children?

Ans. The man in the small bookshop helps the young children in selecting the books.

3. How did the grandfather treat the children?

Ans. The grandfather treats the children with love and care.

4. How did the children choose the books they wanted to buy?

Ans. The children read the books for two hours, after which they could select which books they wanted to buy.

Writing Task

1. Have you ever visited a library? Write a descriptive paragraph about your 'Visit to the Library'.

Ans. Yesterday, my friends and I decided to embark on a little adventure. We set out to explore our local library.

As we entered the library, we were greeted by the big collection of books kept neatly on the shelves. The room was filled with the smell of pages and the voices of other people. We were attracted to various types of books, each promising a new discovery.

We started selecting books that we wanted to read and sat down. Hours flew by and we all had to leave. We were sad but promised to come here every day for at least an hour.

CHAPTER 1 THE NAUGHTY BOY

Summary of the Poem In this poem, a naughty boy ran away to Scotland to see the people there. When he reached there, he was surprised to find that everything was the same as in England. He was confused and a little sad about why everything was so similar.

Stanza-wise Explanation

Stanza 1

There was a naughty boy,
And a naughty boy was he.
He ran away to Scotland,
The people there to see -
Then he found, That the ground
Was as hard, That a yard
Was as long, That a song
Was as merry,

Word-Meaning *Yard - Enclosed area adjoining a house; Merry - Sweet, happy, gay.*

Exp. A naughty boy decides to run away to Scotland to see the people there. When he arrives there, he realises that everything is similar to England. The ground is just as hard, the yard is of same length, and the songs were as happy.

Stanza 2

That a cherry
Was as red,
That lead
Was as weighty,
That fourscore
Was as eighty,
That a door was as wooden
As in England -
So he stood in his shoes
And he wondered,
He wondered,
He stood in his shoes,
And he wondered.

Word-Meaning *Fourscore - Eighty.*

Exp. The boy sees that things in Scotland are the same as in England. A cherry is red, lead is heavy, and fourscore means eighty. He notices that a door is wooden, just like in England. He stands there wondering why everything feels so similar.

NCERT FOLDER

Reading is Fun (NCERT Page 153)

Q.1 From where did the naughty boy come?

Ans. The naughty boy came from England.

Q.2 Where did the naughty boy go?

Ans. The naughty boy went to Scotland.

Q.3 Why did he go there?

Ans. He went to Scotland to see the people there and to see how different it was from England.

Q.4 What did the boy wonder about?

Ans. The boy wondered why all the things in Scotland like the ground, length of the yard, the song, the bright red cherries, heavy lead, the number fourscore and the door were same as of England.

Let's Listen (NCERT page 153)

Q.1 Listen to these instructions and follow them.

(a) naughty walk forward

(b) naughty walk backwards

(c) fall down

(d) do a funny trick

(e) walk on tiptoes

(f) drag your feet

(g) spin around

(h) jump like a horse

(i) walk with your shoes

(j) shuffle your feet

Ans. Do it yourself.

Let's Talk (NCERT Page 153)

Q.1 What do you think the naughty boy would see in India?

Ans. The naughty boy will see the natural landscapes, different languages, culture, traditions, classical dances and different types of food in India.

Q.2 Have you been to another place recently? What is it like? How is it different from your own place?

Ans. I went to a lovely hill station called Nainital recently. It was quite different from my busy city. Nainital had fresh, cool air and lots of green trees and colourful flowers all around. Unlike my city, which has many buildings and cars, this place was calm and quiet, filled with the sounds of nature.

The roads were narrow and winding, offering beautiful scenic views of the mountains. The food there was also tasty and special!

Q.3 All cultures have their own folk songs in which each line is repeated. This line is sung in a chorus. Sing a folk song in your own language.

Ans. Do it yourself.

Word Building (NCERT Page 154)

Q.1 Naughty is a describing word. Can you find more describing words in this maze?

A	C	J	V	W	X	B	X	T	I	L	P	O
F	W	B	E	A	U	T	I	F	U	L	Y	K
Q	T	C	N	O	N	O	J	S	G	R	E	O
W	P	G	O	C	A	L	M	E	L	Q	V	A
A	E	B	N	K	U	D	C	I	Y	D	O	L
N	C	E	L	I	G	O	O	D	A	I	R	P
B	M	S	I	E	H	E	A	L	T	H	Y	O
E	L	T	A	A	T	A	Y	R	U	D	E	A
B	N	R	P	D	Y	W	O	S	W	I	F	T
Y	L	O	R	O	K	E	A	L	P	A	I	P
Q	I	N	O	A	U	A	A	R	A	I	A	N
X	V	G	W	N	R	K	E	F	R	D	A	T

Ans.

A	C	J	V	W	X	B	X	T	I	L	P	O
F	W	B	E	A	U	T	I	F	U	L	Y	K
Q	T	C	N	O	N	O	J	S	G	R	E	O
W	P	G	O	C	A	L	M	E	L	Q	V	A
A	E	B	N	K	U	D	C	I	Y	D	O	L
N	C	E	L	I	G	O	O	D	A	I	R	P
B	M	S	I	E	H	E	A	L	T	H	Y	O
E	L	T	A	A	T	A	Y	R	U	D	E	A
B	N	R	P	D	Y	W	O	S	W	I	F	T
Y	L	O	R	O	K	E	A	L	P	A	I	P
Q	I	N	O	A	U	A	A	R	A	I	A	N
X	V	G	W	N	R	K	E	F	R	D	A	T

Q.2 Now write these words here.

(a) The peacock is a __________ bird.

(b) Pinocchio is a __________ puppet.

(c) I saw an __________ quarrel.

(d) Morning exercises make you ________ .

(e) A glass of milk makes your teeth ________ .

(f) Rita's ________ behaviour annoyed me.

(g) Rahul does not eat green vegetables, therefore his eyesight is ________.

Ans. (a) beautiful (b) naughty (c) ugly
(d) healthy (e) strong (f) rude
(g) weak

Let's Write (NCERT Page 155)

Q.1 Can you write six things that are made of wood?

Ans. Doors, benches, shelves, beds, cupboards, bats.

Q.2 Look at the words given below and put them under the things that they are made of

balloon chair table eraser shirt
pencil toys car trousers knife
scissors cap

Metal wood rubber cloth

Ans.

metal	wood	rubber	cloth
car	chair	balloon	shirt
knife	table	eraser	trousers
scissors	pencil	toys	cap

Q.3 Who do you think is the naughtiest child in your class? Describe her/him in five lines.

Ans. The naughtiest child in my class is Ravi. He is always full of energy and loves to play pranks on everyone. He talks a lot during lessons and makes funny faces to make us laugh.

Even though he gets into trouble, he is very friendly and always helps others. Despite his mischief, everyone likes him because he is fun to be around.

Say Aloud (NCERT Page 156)

hard yard | long song | red lead
weighty eighty | found ground

Fun Time (NCERT Page 156)

Let's make a mosaic hat for your clown

You need

- Mirrors/beads of different size and shapes
- Fevicol/glue/gum
- A piece of cardboard
- Sketch pens

Method

- Take a piece of old cardboard.
- Draw a colourful pattern on it.
- Take glue/gum and apply it on the surface and stick beads/mirrors/pulses on it.
- Fold it into a cone.
- Your lovely Mosaic Hat is now ready.
- Put it on your clown.

Q.1 Which country does your clown belong to?

Ans. Do it yourself.

Q.2 Now complete the table below

	Nation	Nationality
(a)	India	Indian
(b)	Scotland	
(c)	Australia	
(d)	France	
(e)	Japan	

Ans. (b) Scotish, (c) Australian, (d) French, (e) Japanese

PRACTICE QUESTIONS

1. What did the boy want to see in Scotland?
   (a) Rivers (b) People
   (c) Castles (d) Animals
2. How did the boy feel after discovering things were same in Scotland?
   (a) Angry (b) Bored
   (c) Excited (d) Surprised
3. What did the boy notice about the song in Scotland?
   (a) It was sad (b) It was loud
   (c) It was quiet (d) It was merry
4. How much is fourscore, as mentioned in the poem?
   (a) Forty (b) Sixty (c) Eighty (d) Twenty
5. In the end, what did the boy do after his discoveries?
   (a) Laughed
   (b) Sat down
   (c) Ran back to England
   (d) Stood and wondered

Ans. 1. (b), 2. (d), 3. (d), 4. (c), 5. (d)

Fill in the Blanks

1. He found that _______ was as heavy in Scotland as in England.
2. The number fourscore was the same as _______ in both places.
3. The naughty boy realised that a song was as _______ in Scotland as in England.
4. The boy discovered that a door was as _______ in Scotland as it was in England.
5. The boy stood in his shoes and _______ about the similarities between Scotland and England.

Ans. 1. lead, 2. eighty, 3. merry, 4. wooden, 5. wondered

True or False

1. The boy ran to Scotland to see if things were different.
2. The boy thought the ground in Scotland was softer than in England.
3. The boy realised that lead was as weighty in Scotland as in England.
4. The boy found that the yard in Scotland was shorter than in England.
5. The boy wondered about the similarities between Scotland and England.

Ans. 1. True, 2. False, 3. True, 4. False, 5. True

Answer the Following Questions

1. Why did the naughty boy run away to Scotland?

Ans. The naughty boy ran away to Scotland to see the people there and how they were different.

2. What did he learn about the similarities between Scotland and England?

Ans. The boy learnt that Scotland and England were similar. They had to same land, same yard, same wood, same lead, same cherry, etc.

3. What did the boy wonder about?

Ans. The boy wondered how similar Scotland and England were.

CHAPTER 2

PINOCCHIO

Summary of the Chapter

An old carpenter once found a strange piece of wood. As he worked on it, the wood suddenly spoke, which confused him. He decided to make a puppet out of it and named it Pinocchio. As soon as he finished making the eyes, they started moving. When he made the mouth, it began to laugh and its nose grew longer. After its hands were made, it caught the carpenter's wig and wore it.

When its legs and feet were done, they were too stiff, so the carpenter taught Pinocchio how to walk. The carpenter later sent Pinocchio to school, but Pinocchio often ran away from school. When asked why, he lied, and his nose grew even longer. In the end, Pinocchio promised to never lie again.

WORD-MEANING

Carpenter - A person who makes things from wood; Queer - Strange, old; Plane - A tool used by a carpenter; Tickling - A touch that causes laughter; Puzzled - Confused; Puppet - A kind of toy in the shape of a human; Amazed - Surprised; Snatched off - To take forcefully, grab, capture; Wig - False hair for the head; Stiff - A thing that bend easily; Rude - Harsh.

NCERT FOLDER

Reading is Fun (NCERT Page 160)

Q.1 What did the carpenter buy?

Ans. The carpenter bought a very odd piece of wood.

Q.2 What did he make out of it?

Ans. The carpenter made a boy puppet out of the odd piece of wood.

Q.3 What did he call his puppet?

Ans. He called his puppet Pinocchio.

Q.4 What did Pinocchio say in the end?

Ans. He said that he was glad to be a real boy. He would never lie again.

Let's Talk (NCERT Page 160)

Q.1 Have you ever seen a puppet?

Ans. Yes, I have seen a puppet.

Q.2 Tell the story of Pinocchio with actions.

Ans. Do it yourself.

Word Building (NCERT Page 160)

Word Fan

How many words can you make from PINOCCHIO? Fill them in the empty boxes.

PINOCCHIO	
PIN	HOP

Ans. (i) PIN (vi) ON
(ii) CHIN (vii) CHIP
(iii) HIP (viii) CHOP
(iv) NIP (ix) COP
(v) HOP (x) NO

Let's Write (NCERT Page 161)

Q.1 Make opposites with the words

dis in

(a) respect ______
(b) able ______
(c) efficient ______
(d) own ______
(e) capable ______
(f) secure ______

Ans. (a) disrespect (b) disable
(c) inefficient (d) disown
(d) incapable (f) insecure

Q.2 Make naming words by adding ness, ity, ty at the end of the words given below. One has been done for you.

	public	publicity		stupid	stupidity
(a)	forgive		(e)	blind	
(b)	kind		(f)	cruel	
(c)	polite		(g)	swift	
(d)	moral		(h)	solid	

Ans. (a) forgiveness (b) kindness
(c) politeness (d) morality
(d) blindnesss (f) cruelty
(g) swiftness (h) solidity

Q.3 Which of the following would you expect a carpenter to use at work?

bench, poker, plane, chisel, fork, spade, blotting paper, lawn-mower, telescope, pincers, jaw, scissors, hammer, map, nails, lathe, pencil, anvil.

Ans. Bench, plate, chisel, spade, hammer, nails, pencil, lathe.

Q.4 Now make sentences using some of the above words.

Ans. (a) **Fork** I used a fork to eat my salad at lunch.
(b) **Poker** He used a poker to stir the burning logs in the fireplace.
(c) **Map** We used a map to find the quickest route to the mountain.
(d) **Telescope** I saw many planets in the night sky using a telescope.
(e) **Anvil** The blacksmith placed the hot metal on the anvil to shape it.
(f) **Lawn-mower** He bought a lawn-mower to trim the grass of his garden.
(g) **Pincers** He grabbed the pincers to pull out the bent nail from the board.
(h) **Hammer** The carpenter used a hammer to drive the nails into the wood.

Q.5 Give another word from the story that means
(a) completed ______
(b) surprised ______
(c) strange ______
(d) make up your mind ______

Ans. (a) finished (b) amazed (c) queer
(d) decide

Q.6 Add '-er' or '-r' to the doing words below to make new words.
(a) stiff ______
(b) fight ______

(c) juggle ________
(d) speak ________
(e) write ________
(f) strange ________
(g) dance ________
(h) ride ________
(i) use ________
(j) joke ________

Ans. (a) stiffer (b) fighter (c) juggler
(d) speaker (d) writer (f) stranger
(g) dancer (h) rider (i) user
(j) joker

Comprehension Passage (NCERT Page 163)

Once a cunning jackal jumped into a big tub of blue dye.

"I am your king," he said. All the animals, big and small believed him and bowed before him. The clever jackal smiled. Now he was the most powerful animal in the forest. He was proud to be a king.

Once, the jackal woke up in the middle of the night. The jackals in the forest were howling at the full moon in the sky. The blue jackal forgot he was a king. He, too, began to howl.

"Hu...aah! Hu...aah!" he cried.

The animals ran out to see. "He is not a king. He is just a jackal!" they shouted. They rushed to attack him.

"Stop, stop! I am sorry I tricked you. Please do not punish me!" said the blue jackal.

The animals forgave him, but only after he vowed never to bother anyone again.

- A Panchtantra tale

Reading is Fun (NCERT Page 163)

Q.1 Why did the animals think that the jackal was a king?

Ans. The animals believed the jackal was a king because he had become blue, and nobody recognised him. Also, he declared himself to be a king.

Q.2 How did the jackal become blue?

Ans. The jackal become blue as he had jumped into a big tub of blue dye.

Q.3 What did the animals do when they saw the blue jackal?

Ans. As the animals believed the blue jackal to be the king, they bowed before him when they saw him.

Q.4 Why did the dogs feel scared when they saw the jackal?

Ans. The dogs felt scared when they saw the jackal because he was looking fearful in the blue colour.

Q.5 How did the animals know that the king was just a jackal?

Ans. One night, during the full moon, all the jackals started howling. The blue jackal forgot he was pretending to be a king and joined in. Because of this, the other animals realised that their "king" was actually just a jackal.

Say Aloud (NCERT Page 164)

laugh	fish	fan	few
cough	dish	van	view
rough	wish	ran	dew

Fun Time (NCERT Page 164)

Let's Make a Puppet

You need

A brown envelope, newspaper, stick, glue, paper, colours, sketch pen

Method

1. Make the face of a monkey on white paper and colour it.

2. Cut out the face and stick it on a brown envelope.

3. Crush the newspaper and fill it in the brown envelope

4. Put the stick inside the envelope.

5. Close the mouth of the envelope firmly with a tape or ribbon.

6. Your puppet is ready.

PRACTICE QUESTIONS

Multiple Choice Questions

1. What did the carpenter make out of the strange piece of wood?
   (a) A doll (b) A table
   (c) A chair (d) A puppet
2. What happened when Pinocchio lied?
   (a) His feet grew
   (b) His ears grew
   (c) His nose grew
   (d) He started crying
3. What did Pinocchio do at school?
   (a) He studied hard
   (b) He made new friends
   (c) He played with his friends
   (d) He looked for fun and ran away
4. What did Pinocchio do with the carpenter's wig?
   (a) He hid it (b) He wore it
   (c) He broke it (d) He threw it away
5. What did Pinocchio finally decide at the end of the story?
   (a) To run away again
   (b) To always tell the truth
   (c) To leave the carpenter
   (d) To buy a new wig for the carpenter

Ans. 1. (d), 2. (c), 3. (d), 4. (b), 5. (b)

Fill in the Blanks

1. Pinocchio often ran away from ______ to look for fun.
2. The carpenter made a puppet and named him ______.
3. When Pinocchio lied, his ______ grew longer and longer.
4. Pinocchio finally decided not to be ______ and not to lie again.
5. The carpenter showed Pinocchio how to use his ______ and feet.

Ans. 1. school, 2. Pinocchio, 3. nose, 4. rude, 5. legs

True or False

1. Pinocchio's feet were made stiff by the carpenter.
2. Pinocchio went to school but ran away to have fun.
3. Pinocchio's nose grew longer every time he told a lie.
4. In the end, Pinocchio decided to keep lying to everyone.
5. The carpenter was happy when Pinocchio snatched his wig.

Ans. 1. True, 2. True, 3. True, 4. False, 5. False

Answer the Following Questions

1. How did Pinocchio do in the school?

Ans. Pinocchio did very bad at school as it always wanted to have fun. So, he ran away from school.

2. What was so astonishing about his puppet?

Ans. The fact that the puppet could move was astonishing.

3. What did the carpenter do when he found that Pinocchio's legs were stiff?

Ans. The carpenter taught Pinocchio how to walk when he found that Pinocchio's legs were stiff.

4. Describe how the carpenter made Pinocchio's body parts one after other.

Ans. The carpenter made Pinocchio's body parts one after the other using a piece of wood and his tools.

Writing Task

1. Write a story teaching us how lies are dangerous.

Ans. Once upon a time in a small city, there lived two friends named Ayesha and Peehu. One day, Peehu borrowed Ayesha's favorite dress for a special occasion. While wearing the dress, Peehu accidentally spilled some food on it. Panicking, she decided to quickly clean the stain before Ayesha found out. Peehu could not tell Ayesha the truth. Instead, she told Ayesha that she had accidentally tore the dress while trying it on, and she would get it fixed. As the days passed, Ayesha started asking for the dress. Peehu had to lie to cover up her first lie. Ayesha asked Peehu's mother about it and when she got to know the truth, she got angry and sad.

As a result, Ayesha did not talk to Peehu for days. Peehu apologised to Ayesha and even bought a similar dress for her best friend as an apology. In the end, the best friends were able to repair their friendship, but the experience left a lasting impact on both of them.

रिमझिम

(हिंदी)

अध्याय 1

मन के भोले-भाले बादल

कविता का सार

प्रस्तुत कविता में कवि ने बादलों के अलग-अलग रूपों का वर्णन किया है। इन बादलों के बाल घुँघराले हैं और गाल गुब्बारे जैसे हैं। इन बादलों में से कुछ जोकर की तरह तोंद फुलाए तथा कुछ हाथी के जैसे सूँड उठाए हुए हैं। कुछ बादलों की पीठ पर ऊँटों की तरह कूबड़ दिखाई देता है, तो कुछ बादल परियों की तरह पंख लगाकर उड़ते हुए प्रतीत हो रहे हैं। कुछ बादल तूफ़ान लाते हैं, तो कुछ शैतानी करते हैं। कुछ बादल चुपके से आकर वर्षा कर जाते हैं। कभी-कभी ये बादल जिद्दी रूप धारण कर लेते हैं और नदी-नालों में बाढ़ ले आते हैं। इन सबके पश्चात् भी कवि को ये बादल अच्छे लगते हैं, क्योंकि ये मन के भोले-भाले होते हैं।

काव्यांशों की व्याख्या

काव्यांश 1

झब्बर-झब्बर बालों वाले
गुब्बारे से गालों वाले
लगे दौड़ने आसमान में
झूम-झूमकर काले बादल।
कुछ जोकर-से तोंद फुलाए
कुछ हाथी से सूँड उठाए
कुछ ऊँटों-से कूबड़ वाले
कुछ परियों-से पंख लगाए
आपस में टकराते रह-रह
शेरों से मतवाले बादल।

शब्दार्थ *झब्बर-घने बालों वाले, तोंद-पेट, कूबड़-किसी वस्तु का उभरा हुआ भाग, मतवाले-मस्ती में डूबे हुए।*

संदर्भ एवं प्रसंग प्रस्तुत पंक्तियाँ हमारी पाठ्यपुस्तक 'रिमझिम भाग-4' में संकलित कविता 'मन के भोले-भाले बादल' से ली गई हैं। इसके कवि 'कल्पनाथ सिंह जी' हैं। कविता के इस अंश में कवि बादलों को विभिन्न आकृतियों और जीवों के रूप में चित्रित कर रहा है।

व्याख्या प्रस्तुत पंक्तियों में कवि ने बादलों का खेलते हुए वर्णन किया है और उनकी तुलना इंसानों तथा जानवरों से की है। कवि कहता है कि बादलों के बाल घने और घुँघराले हैं। उनके गाल गुब्बारे की तरह फूले हुए हैं। काले बादल आसमान में झूम-झूमकर इधर-उधर दौड़ रहे हैं। इनमें से कुछ बादल जोकरों की तरह पेट फुलाए हुए

हैं, तो कुछ बादल हाथी की तरह सूँड उठाए हुए हैं। कुछ बादल ऊँट जैसे कूबड़ वाले दिखाई दे रहे हैं, तो कुछ परियों के जैसे पंख लगाकर उड़ रहे हैं। जब ये बादल आपस में टकराते हैं, तो ऐसा लगता है मानो मतवाले शेर मस्ती कर रहे हों।

काव्यांश 2

कुछ तो लगते हैं तूफ़ानी
कुछ रह-रहकर करते शैतानी
कुछ अपने थैलों से चुपके
झर-झर-झर बरसाते पानी
नहीं किसी की सुनते कुछ भी
ढोलक-ढोल बजाते बादल।

शब्दार्थ *तूफ़ानी-जो तूफ़ान लाने वाला हो, शैतानी-शरारतपूर्ण।*

प्रसंग प्रस्तुत पंक्तियों में कवि ने बादलों के तूफानी और शरारती रूपों का वर्णन किया है।

व्याख्या प्रस्तुत पंक्तियों में कवि कह रहा है कि कुछ बादल तूफान लाने वाले लग रहे हैं। कुछ बादल रह-रहकर अर्थात् रुक-रुककर शैतानी कर रहे हैं। कुछ बादल चुपके से आकर बारिश कर जाते हैं। ये बादल किसी की भी नहीं सुनते हैं। इनके आपस में टकराने से जो आवाज आती है, उससे ऐसा लगता है मानो बादल ढोल बजा रहे हों।

काव्यांश 3

रह-रहकर छत पर आ जाते
फिर चुपके ऊपर उड़ जाते
कभी-कभी जिद्दी बन करके
बाढ़ नदी-नालों में लाते
फिर भी लगते बहुत भले हैं
मन के भोले-भाले बादल।

शब्दार्थ *जिद्दी-जो अपनी बात पर अड़ा रहता हो।*

प्रसंग प्रस्तुत पंक्तियों में कवि ने बादलों के बदलते रूपों का वर्णन किया है।

व्याख्या प्रस्तुत पंक्तियों में कवि कहता है कि ये बादल रह-रहकर अर्थात् कभी भी छत पर जाते हैं और चुपके से फिर उड़ भी जाते हैं। ये बादल जब जिद्दी रूप धारण करते हैं, तो खूब बारिश करते हैं, जिससे नदी-नालों में बाढ़ आ जाती है। इतना कुछ करने के बाद भी बादल बहुत अच्छे लगते हैं, क्योंकि ये मन के भोले-भाले होते हैं।

NCERT फोल्डर

तुम्हारी समझ से

कभी कभी जिद्दी बन करके
बाढ़ नदी-नालों में लाते

(क) बादल नदी-नालों में बाढ़ कैसे लाते होंगे?

उत्तर बादल जब अधिक बारिश करते हैं, तो पानी तेजी से बहकर नदी-नालों में भर जाता है, जिससे नदी-नालों में पानी का स्तर बहुत बढ़ जाता है और बाढ़ आ जाती है।

नहीं किसी की सुनते कुछ भी
ढोलक-ढोल बजाते बादल

(ख) बादल ढोल कैसे बजाते होंगे?

उत्तर जब बादल आपस में टकराते हैं, तो वे जोर की गड़गड़ाहट करते हैं। कविता में बादलों की इस गड़गड़ाहट को ढोल बजाने की तरह बताया गया है।

कुछ तो लगते हैं तूफ़ानी
कुछ रह-रह करते शैतानी

(ग) बादल कैसी शैतानियाँ करते होंगे?

उत्तर बादल कई तरह की शैतानियाँ करते हैं। वे आसमान में तेजी से दौड़ लगाकर व जोर-जोर से गड़गड़ाहट करके, कभी हवा के साथ पानी बरसाकर और कभी दिन-रात वर्षा करके नदी-नालों में बाढ़ लाकर शैतानी करते होंगे।

कैसा-कौन

	कैसा	कौन
सूरज-सी	चमकीली	थाली
चंदा-सा		
हाथी-सा		
जोकर-सा		
परियों-सा		
गुब्बारे-सा		
ढोलक-सा		

उत्तर

	कैसा	कौन
सूरज-सी	चमकीली	थाली
चंदा-सा	गोल	चेहरा
हाथी-सा	बड़ा	शरीर
जोकर-सा	रंग-बिरंगा	चेहरा
परियों-सा	सुंदर	रूप
गुब्बारे-सा	फूला	मुँह
ढोलक-सा	गोल	पेट

कविता से आगे

(क) तूफ़ान क्या होता है? बादलों को तूफानी क्यों कहा गया है?

उत्तर तेज़ हवाओं, भारी बारिश और गरज-चमक को तूफ़ान कहा जाता है। बादलों को तूफानी इसलिए कहा गया है, क्योंकि ये कभी-कभी तेज हवा और गरज एवं चमक के साथ आँधी और मूसलाधार बारिश ले आते हैं।

(ख) साल के किन-किन महीनों में ज़्यादा बादल छाते हैं?

उत्तर साल के जुलाई और अगस्त के महीनों में ज़्यादा बादल छाते हैं।

(ग) कविता में 'काले बादलों' की बात की गई है। क्या बादल सचमुच काले होते हैं?

उत्तर बादलों के घने होने के कारण सूर्य की किरणें इनके आर-पार नहीं जा पाती हैं, जिसके कारण ये काले दिखाई देते हैं, लेकिन वास्तव में ये पूरी तरह काले नहीं होते हैं।

(घ) कक्षा में बातचीत करो और बताओ कि बादल किन-किन रंगों के होते हैं?

उत्तर बादल मुख्य रूप से सफेद, हल्के भूरे और काले रंग के होते हैं।

कैसे-कैसे बादल

(क) तरह-तरह के बादलों के चित्र बनाओ।

- काले-काले डरावने
- गुब्बारे-से गालों वाले
- हल्के-फुल्के सुहाने

उत्तर छात्र स्वयं करें।

(ख) कविता में बादलों को 'भोला' कहा गया है। इसके अतिरिक्त बादलों के लिए और कौन-कौन से शब्दों का प्रयोग किया गया है? नीचे लिखे अधूरे शब्दों को पूरा करो।

म …………… जि ……………

शै …………… तू ……………

उत्तर म - मतवाले जि - जिद्दी

शै - शैतान तू - तूफ़ानी

बारिश की आवाज़ें

कुछ अपने थैलों से चुपके
झर-झर-झर बरसाते पानी

पानी के बरसने की आवाज है झर-झर-झर! पानी बरसने की कुछ और आवाज़ें लिखो।

उत्तर टिप-टिप, छप-छप, रिमझिम, टप-टप, झमाझम आदि पानी के बरसने की आवाज़ें हैं।

कैसे-कैसे पेड़

बादलों की तरह पेड़ भी अलग-अलग आकार के होते हैं। कोई बरगद-सा फैला हुआ और कोई नारियल के पेड़ जैसा ऊँचा और सीधा।

अपने आसपास अलग-अलग तरह के पेड़ देखो। तुम्हें उनमें कौन-कौन से आकार दिखाई देते हैं? सब मिलकर पेड़ों पर एक कविता भी तैयार करो।

उत्तर मेरे आसपास अनेक प्रकार के पेड़ हैं। कुछ पेड़ बहुत छोटे तथा कुछ बहुत लंबे हैं। कुछ पेड़ों की पत्तियाँ बहुत घनी हैं और वे देखने में बिल्कुल किसी छाते की तरह लगते हैं।

कविता

पेड़ धरती की शान हैं,
जीवन की मुस्कान हैं।
पेड़-पौधों को पानी दो
जीवन को यही निशानी दो।
आओ पेड़ लगाएँ हम
पेड़ लगाकर जग महकाकर
जीवन सुखी बनाएँ हम।

अभ्यास प्रश्न

बहुविकल्पीय प्रश्न

1. कविता में बादलों के बालों की तुलना किससे की गई है?

(क) सींग से (ख) झब्बर-झब्बर बालों से
(ग) पंख से (घ) पतंग से

2. कविता में किसे 'गुब्बारे से गालों वाले' कहा गया है?

(क) जोकर को (ख) हाथी को
(ग) बादल को (घ) ऊँट को

3. कविता के अनुसार कुछ बादलों की तोंद कैसी होती है?

(क) पतली (ख) फूली हुई (ग) सीधी (घ) मुड़ी हुई

4. सूँड उठाए हुए बादलों की तुलना किससे की गई है?

(क) शेर से (ख) ऊँट से
(ग) हाथी से (घ) परियों से

5. बादलों के किस कार्य को कविता में 'ढोलक बजाने' के समान बताया गया है?

(क) बाढ़ लाना (ख) शैतानी करना
(ग) आपस में टकराना (घ) शोर मचाना

उत्तर

1. (ख) झब्बर-झब्बर बालों से 2. (ग) बादल को
3. (ख) फूली हुई 4. (ग) हाथी से
5. (घ) शोर मचाना

काव्यांश पर आधारित प्रश्न

निम्नलिखित काव्यांश को पढ़कर उस पर आधारित प्रश्नों के उत्तर दीजिए।

काव्यांश

कुछ तो लगते हैं तूफ़ानी
कुछ रह-रह करते शैतानी
कुछ अपने थैलों से चुपके
झर-झर-झर बरसाते पानी
नहीं किसी की सुनते कुछ भी
ढोलक-ढोल बजाते बादल
रह-रहकर छत पर आ जाते
फिर चुपके ऊपर उड़ जाते
कभी-कभी जिद्दी बन करके
बाढ़ नदी-नालों में लाते
फिर भी लगते बहुत भले हैं
मन के भोले-भाले बादल।

1. कुछ बादल किस प्रकार का व्यवहार करते हैं?

(क) सीधा-साधा (ख) तूफ़ानी और शैतानी
(ग) शांत और मधुर (घ) कठोर

2. बादल क्या बरसाते हैं?

(क) धूल (ख) धूप
(ग) पानी (घ) ओले

3. बादल किसकी तरह शोर मचाते हैं?

4. कभी-कभी बादल जिद्दी बनकर क्या लाते हैं?

उत्तर

1. (ख) तूफ़ानी और शैतानी
2. (ग) पानी
3. बादल ढोलक की तरह शोर मचाते हैं।
4. कभी-कभी बादल जिद्दी बनकर बाढ़ लाते हैं।

निम्नलिखित प्रश्नों के उत्तर दीजिए

1. कविता में बादलों की तोंद की तुलना किससे की गई है?

उत्तर कविता में बादलों की तोंद की तुलना जोकर से की गई है।

2. कविता में हाथी के किस अंग का उल्लेख किया गया है?

उत्तर कविता में हाथी की सूँड का उल्लेख किया गया है।

3. कविता में कौन-से बादल 'शेर' जैसे हैं?

उत्तर कविता में मतवाले बादल शेर जैसे हैं।

4. कविता में बादलों को 'भोले-भाले' क्यों कहा गया है?

उत्तर कविता में बादलों को भोले-भाले इसलिए कहा गया है, क्योंकि बादल हर बार अलग-अलग आकृतियों में दिखते हैं। इसके बावजूद भी ये बादल बहुत अच्छे हैं और मन के भोले-भाले हैं।

अध्याय 2

जैसा सवाल वैसा जवाब

पाठ का सार

बादशाह अकबर अपने बुद्धिमान मंत्री बीरबल को बहुत पसंद करते थे। इस कारण कुछ दरबारी, विशेषकर ख्वाजा सरा, उनसे जलते थे और बीरबल को किसी भी समस्या में फँसाने की सोचते रहते थे। इन्हीं में से एक खास दरबारी ख्वाजा सरा थे, जिन्हें अपनी विद्या और बुद्धि पर बहुत गर्व था। वे बीरबल को अपने सामने मूर्ख समझते थे। एक दिन ख्वाजा ने बीरबल को मूर्ख साबित करने के उद्देश्य से तीन मुश्किल प्रश्न तैयार किए। ख्वाजा सरा को उम्मीद थी कि बीरबल इन प्रश्नों का उत्तर नहीं दे पाएँगे। ख्वाजा ने अकबर के सामने जाकर बीरबल की बुद्धिमानी पर सवाल उठाया और अपने तीन प्रश्न पूछने की अनुमति माँगी। ख्वाजा ने उन प्रश्नों को लिखकर बादशाह अकबर को दे दिया। अकबर ने बीरबल को बुलाकर ख्वाजा के प्रश्नों का उत्तर देने को कहा। पहला प्रश्न था– "संसार का केंद्र कहाँ है?" बीरबल ने तुरंत अपनी छड़ी जमीन पर गाड़ते हुए उत्तर दिया कि "यही स्थान चारों ओर से दुनिया के बीचों-बीच पड़ता है।" उन्होंने ख्वाजा को चुनौती देते हुए कहा यदि उन्हें विश्वास न हो तो वे दुनिया नापकर साबित करें कि मेरी बात गलत है।

दूसरा प्रश्न था– "आकाश में कितने तारे हैं?" बीरबल ने एक भेड़ मँगवाई और कहा कि "जितने बाल इस भेड़ के शरीर पर हैं, उतने ही तारे आसमान में हैं।" उन्होंने कहा यदि ख्वाजा को संदेह हो, तो वे भेड़ के बालों को गिनकर तारों की संख्या से तुलना कर सकते हैं।

तीसरा प्रश्न था–"संसार की आबादी कितनी है?" बीरबल ने कहा कि "संसार की आबादी हर पल बदलती रहती है, क्योंकि हर समय लोग मरते और पैदा होते रहते हैं। उन्होंने कहा कि यदि सभी लोगों को एक जगह इकट्ठा किया जाए, तभी सही संख्या बताई जा सकती है।"

अकबर, बीरबल के उत्तरों से संतुष्ट हो गए, लेकिन ख्वाजा सरा नहीं। बीरबल ने कहा कि ऐसे सवालों के जवाब ऐसे ही होते हैं और ख्वाजा को अपने उत्तरों को गलत साबित करने की चुनौती दी, जिससे ख्वाजा चुप हो गए।

शब्दार्थ

दरबारी–राजा के दरबार में काम करने वाला व्यक्ति, मुसीबत–संकट, खास–महत्त्वपूर्ण, अभिमान–घमंड, नक्कारखाने–बड़े-बड़े ढोल रखे जाने वाली जगह, निरा–बिल्कुल, संतोषजनक–संतुष्ट करने वाला, ज्ञानी–बुद्धिमान, विश्वास–भरोसा, गोलमोल–स्पष्टता की कमी, इधर-उधर की बातें करना, कलई खुलना–राज का खुल जाना, चुनौती–कठिन कार्य के लिए आमंत्रण देना।

NCERT फोल्डर

तुम्हारी बात

(क) ख्वाजा सरा के तीनों सवालों का क्या कोई और जवाब हो सकता है? अपने मन से सोचकर लिखो।

उत्तर ख्वाजा सरा का पहला प्रश्न था कि "संसार का केंद्र कहाँ है?" इसका उत्तर यह हो सकता है कि "बादशाह का सिंहासन ही संसार का केंद्र है।" दूसरा प्रश्न था कि "आकाश में कितने तारे हैं?" इसका उत्तर यह हो सकता है कि "सिर पर जितने बाल हैं, आकाश में उतने ही तारे हैं।"

तीसरा प्रश्न था कि "संसार की आबादी कितनी है?" इसका उत्तर यह हो सकता है कि "पहले संसार के सभी लोगों को इकट्ठा करो फिर मैं गिनकर बता दूँगा।"

(ख) अगर तुम ख्वाजा सरा की जगह पर होते तो बीरबल को हराने के लिए कौन-से सवाल पूछते?

उत्तर अगर मैं ख्वाजा सरा की जगह पर होता तो बीरबल को हराने के लिए पूछता कि ऐसी कौन-सी चीज़ है, जिसे पहनकर उतारा नहीं जा सकता है?

(ग) ख्वाजा सरा का बस चलता तो वे बीरबल को हिंदुस्तान से निकाल देते। अगर तुम्हारा बस चले तो तुम कौन-कौन सी इच्छाएँ पूरी करना चाहोगे?

उत्तर अगर मेरा बस चले तो मैं समाज में जाति, धर्म और लिंग के भेदभाव एवं गरीबी ख़त्म करने का प्रयास करूँगा।

बस

नीचे लिखे वाक्य पढ़ो

- मैं **बस** में बैठकर स्कूल जाती हूँ।
- ख्वाजा सरा का **बस** चलता तो वे बीरबल को निकाल देते।
- **बस!** अब रुक जाओ।
- **बस** दो दिन की तो बात है। मैं आ जाऊँगी।

ऊपर लिखे वाक्यों में **बस** शब्द के अर्थ अलग-अलग हैं। अब इसी तरह **चल** शब्द से वाक्य बनाओ।

(संकेत चल, चल-चल, चला, चलें, चलना, चलती, चलो)

उत्तर
- **चल** आज मेरे साथ बाजार चल।
- **चल-चल** क्या चल-चल की रट लगाए हो।
- **चला** वह बाजार चला गया।
- **चलें** आओ घर चलें।
- **चलना** इस सँकरी गली में सँभलकर चलना।
- **चलती** वह गाड़ी समय पर चलती है।
- **चलो** तुम मेरे साथ चलो।

बढ़े कहानी

एक दिन अकबर ने बीरबल से पूछा, "बीरबल, दुनिया में सबसे अधिक शक्तिशाली कौन है?"

बीरबल ने क्या कहा होगा? कहानी आगे बढ़ाओ।

उत्तर एक दिन अकबर ने दरबार में बीरबल से पूछा, "बीरबल, दुनिया में सबसे अधिक शक्तिशाली कौन है?"

बीरबल ने मुस्कुराते हुए जवाब दिया, "जहाँपनाह! दुनिया में सबसे अधिक शक्तिशाली 'समय' है।"

अकबर ने आश्चर्य से कहा—"समय! वह कैसे?"

बीरबल ने समझाया—"जहाँपनाह! समय वह ताकत है, जो किसी भी राजा को रंक और रंक को राजा बना सकता है। कोई कितना भी ताकतवर क्यों न हो, समय के सामने सब हार जाते हैं। समय का सही उपयोग करना भी बहुत आवश्यक है। जो व्यक्ति समय का आदर करता है, वह बड़ी-से-बड़ी कठिनाइयों को मात दे देता है। जो व्यक्ति समय का सम्मान नहीं करता, उसे पछताना पड़ता है।"

बीरबल के इस उत्तर से प्रभावित होकर अकबर ने दरबार में बीरबल की बुद्धिमानी का सम्मान किया।

खोजो कहानियाँ

बीरबल की चतुराई के किस्से बहुत मशहूर हैं।

(क) तुम भी बीरबल का एक ऐसा ही किस्सा ढूँढो, जिसमें वह अपने जवाबों से सबका मुँह बंद कर देता है।

उत्तर एक बार की बात है, सर्दियों का मौसम था। अकबर बादशाह और बीरबल के बीच बातचीत हो रही थी। अकबर ने कहा कि "क्या कोई आदमी इतनी ठंडी रात में तालाब के ठंडे पानी में पूरी रात खड़ा रह सकता है?" यह काम किसी के लिए भी असंभव लग रहा था, लेकिन बीरबल ने एक गरीब आदमी को ढूँढ निकाला, जो इस चुनौती को स्वीकार करने के लिए तैयार था।

उस आदमी ने पूरी रात ठंडे पानी में बिताई। अगले दिन अकबर ने उसे इनाम देने का वादा किया, लेकिन कुछ दरबारियों ने बादशाह से कहा कि "उस आदमी ने तालाब के

किनारे एक जलते हुए दीपक को देखकर स्वयं को गर्म रखने की कोशिश की, इसलिए उसे इनाम नहीं दिया जाना चाहिए।'' अकबर ने दरबारियों की बात मान ली और गरीब आदमी को इनाम देने से मना कर दिया।

यह सुनकर बीरबल को बहुत गुस्सा आया। बीरबल ने अगले दिन दरबार में कोई काम नहीं किया। वे एक छोटे-से दीपक के ऊपर एक बर्तन लटकाकर खिचड़ी पकाने का नाटक करने लगे।

अकबर बादशाह ने यह देखकर हैरानी से पूछा, "बीरबल! तुम यह क्या कर रहे हो? इतने छोटे दीपक पर खिचड़ी कैसे पक सकती है?'' इस पर बीरबल ने हँसते हुए कहा, "जैसे दूर जलते हुए दीपक से आदमी स्वयं को गर्म रख सकता है, वैसे ही इस दीपक से खिचड़ी भी पक सकती है।''

अकबर बादशाह को बीरबल की बात समझ आ गई और उन्होंने उस गरीब आदमी को इनाम दे दिया।

इस तरह बीरबल ने अपनी चतुराई से अकबर का फैसला बदलवाकर गरीब आदमी को न्याय दिलाया।

(ख) **बीरबल की तरह बहुत-से अन्य व्यक्तियों की हाज़िरजवाबी के किस्से प्रसिद्ध हैं। उनके नाम पता करो।**

उत्तर बीरबल की तरह अन्य हाज़िरजवाब व्यक्तियों के नाम तेनालीराम, मुल्ला नसरुद्दीन, शेख चिल्ली और विक्रमादित्य हैं।

एक और शब्द

नीचे लिखे शब्दों की जगह और कौन-सा शब्द इस्तेमाल हो सकता है? खाली जगह में लिखो।

बुद्धिमान .... **मूर्ख** ....

अभिमान .... **विश्वास** ....

संसार .... **कोशिश** ....

उत्तर

बुद्धिमान	चतुर	**मूर्ख**	अज्ञानी
अभिमान	गर्व	**विश्वास**	आस्था
संसार	दुनिया	**कोशिश**	प्रयास

मुहावरे

नीचे लिखे मुहावरों का इस्तेमाल तुम कब-कब कर सकते हो? आपस में चर्चा करो। अब इनका वाक्यों में इस्तेमाल करो।

- **नाक-भौंह सिकोड़ना**
- **कलई खुलना**

उत्तर
- **नाक-भौंह सिकोड़ना** किसी चीज़ को नापसंद करना।
  वाक्य प्रयोग मम्मी ने जब कड़वी दवाई पीने के लिए कहा तो बच्चे ने नाक-भौंह सिकोड़ ली।
- **कलई खुलना** किसी की छिपी हुई बात सामने आना।
  वाक्य प्रयोग परीक्षा में नकल करते समय पकड़े जाने पर उसकी सारी कलई खुल गई।

अभ्यास प्रश्न

बहुविकल्पीय प्रश्न

1. ख्वाजा सरा ने बीरबल को कैसे चुनौती दी?
(क) शास्त्रार्थ के माध्यम से (ख) जादू करके
(ग) कठिन प्रश्न पूछकर (घ) शारीरिक शक्ति द्वारा

2. संसार का केंद्र किसने बताया?
(क) ख्वाजा सरा ने (ख) अकबर ने
(ग) बीरबल ने (घ) किसी और दरबारी ने

3. बीरबल ने आकाश में तारों की संख्या के प्रश्न का उत्तर कैसे दिया?
(क) गणना से
(ख) भेड़ के बालों की संख्या से तुलना करके
(ग) चंद्रमा की गणना से
(घ) अपनी कल्पना से

4. संसार की आबादी के प्रश्न पर बीरबल का क्या उत्तर था?
(क) 1 अरब (ख) पल-पल बदलती रहती है
(ग) 100 करोड़ (घ) स्थिर संख्या

5. बीरबल के उत्तरों ने उन्हें क्या साबित किया?
(क) ईमानदार (ख) साहसी
(ग) बुद्धिमान (घ) घमंडी

उत्तर

1. (ग) कठिन प्रश्न पूछकर 2. (ग) बीरबल ने
3. (ख) भेड़ के बालों की संख्या से तुलना करके
4. (ख) पल-पल बदलती रहती है
5. (ग) बुद्धिमान

रिक्त स्थान

नीचे दिए गए वाक्यों में रिक्त स्थान की पूर्ति उचित शब्द से कीजिए।

(भेड़, अभिमान, जलते)

1. बीरबल की बुद्धि के आगे बड़े-बड़ों की भी कुछ नहीं चल पाती थी, इसी कारण कुछ दरबारी बीरबल से .... थे।
2. अकबर के एक खास दरबारी ख्वाजा सरा को अपनी विद्या और बुद्धि पर बहुत .... था।
3. "आकाश में कितने तारे हैं?" इस प्रश्न का उत्तर देने के लिए बीरबल ने एक .... को मँगवाया।

उत्तर

1. जलते
2. अभिमान
3. भेड़

गद्यांश पर आधारित प्रश्न

निम्नलिखित गद्यांश को पढ़कर उस पर आधारित प्रश्नों के उत्तर दीजिए।

गद्यांश

बादशाह अकबर अपने मंत्री बीरबल को बहुत पसंद करते थे। बीरबल की बुद्धि के आगे बड़े-बड़ों की भी कुछ नहीं चल पाती थी। इसी कारण कुछ दरबारी बीरबल से जलते थे। वे बीरबल को मुसीबत में फँसाने के तरीके सोचते रहते थे।

अकबर के एक खास दरबारी ख्वाजा सरा को अपनी विद्या और बुद्धि पर बहुत अभिमान था। बीरबल को तो वे अपने सामने निरा बालक और मूर्ख समझते थे, लेकिन अपने ही मानने से तो कुछ होता नहीं! दरबार में बीरबल की ही तूती बोलती और ख्वाजा साहब की बात ऐसी लगती थी, जैसे नक्कारखाने में तूती की आवाज़। ख्वाजा साहब की चलती तो वे बीरबल को हिंदुस्तान से निकलवा देते, लेकिन निकलवाते कैसे!

1. अकबर अपने किस मंत्री को बहुत पसंद करता था?
   (क) तानसेन को (ख) बीरबल को
   (ग) मानसिंह को (घ) ख्वाजा सरा को
2. दरबारी बीरबल से क्यों जलते थे?
   (क) बीरबल बहुत अमीर था
   (ख) बीरबल की बुद्धिमत्ता के कारण
   (ग) बीरबल का उच्च पद था
   (घ) बीरबल राजा का रिश्तेदार था
3. ख्वाजा सरा बीरबल को किस प्रकार का व्यक्ति मानते थे?
4. ख्वाजा सरा बीरबल के साथ क्या करना चाहते थे?

उत्तर

1. (ख) बीरबल को
2. (ख) बीरबल की बुद्धिमत्ता के कारण
3. ख्वाजा सरा बीरबल को मूर्ख मानते थे।
4. ख्वाजा सरा बीरबल को हिंदुस्तान से बाहर निकलवाना चाहते थे।

निम्नलिखित प्रश्नों के उत्तर दीजिए

1. ख्वाजा सरा किस बात पर गर्व करते थे?

उत्तर ख्वाजा सरा अपनी विद्या और बुद्धि पर बहुत गर्व करते थे।

2. ख्वाजा सरा ने बीरबल को मूर्ख साबित करने के लिए क्या किया?

उत्तर ख्वाजा सरा ने बीरबल को मूर्ख साबित करने के लिए बहुत सोच-विचारकर कुछ मुश्किल प्रश्न तैयार किए।

3. ख्वाजा सरा ने बीरबल के उत्तरों के बारे में क्या कहा?

उत्तर ख्वाजा सरा ने बीरबल के उत्तरों के बारे में कहा कि "ऐसे गोलमोल जवाबों से काम नहीं चलेगा जनाब।"

4. बीरबल ने संसार के केंद्र के बारे में ख्वाजा सरा के प्रश्न का क्या उत्तर दिया?

उत्तर बीरबल ने संसार के केंद्र के बारे में ख्वाजा सरा को जमीन पर अपनी छड़ी गाड़कर उत्तर दिया कि "यही स्थान चारों ओर से दुनिया के बीचों-बीच पड़ता है।"

5. बीरबल ने आकाश में तारों की संख्या के प्रश्न का उत्तर कैसे दिया?

उत्तर बीरबल ने आकाश में तारों की संख्या के प्रश्न का उत्तर भेड़ के बालों को गिनवाकर दिया।

लेखन संबंधी प्रश्न

1. पुस्तकों पर एक अनुच्छेद लिखिए।

उत्तर पुस्तकें हमारी मित्र हैं। जिस व्यक्ति को पुस्तकों से लगाव होता है, वह कभी भी स्वयं को अकेला व कमजोर अनुभव नहीं कर सकता।

पुस्तकों से हमें अनेक लाभ हैं। पुस्तकें हमें ज्ञान देती हैं, हर प्रकार की जानकारी हमें पुस्तकों में मिलती है। पुस्तकों को पढ़कर ही ज्ञान-विज्ञान आज बहुत आगे है। पुस्तकें हमारे ज्ञानार्जन में सहायक हैं।

अध्याय 3

किरमिच की गेंद

पाठ का सार

गर्मियों की छुट्टियों में एक दिन दोपहर को दिनेश अपने घर में बैठकर एक कहानी पढ़ रहा था। तभी अचानक घर के पीछे बगीचे में किसी चीज के गिरने की आवाज़ आई। वह तुरंत बगीचे में गया और वहाँ लगे भिंडियों के पौधों और सीताफल की बेलों में उस वस्तु को ढूँढने लगा, परंतु उसे वहाँ कुछ नहीं मिला। वस्तु को ढूँढते-ढूँढते अचानक उसकी नजर घूँस द्वारा बनाए गए एक गड्ढे पर पड़ी, जहाँ एक नई चमचमाती हुई किरमिच की गेंद पड़ी थी। दिनेश ने अनुमान लगाया कि यह गेंद किसी ने ऊपर से फेंकी होगी। फिर उसने सोचा कि गेंद मोहल्ले के किसी बच्चे की हो सकती है।

गर्मियों की छुट्टियों में खेलने के लिए बच्चों ने एक क्लब बनाया हुआ था। शाम को क्लब में जब सभी बच्चे इकट्ठे हुए तो दिनेश ने गेंद के बारे में सबसे पूछा। अनिल, सुधीर और दीपक सहित कई बच्चों ने कहा कि गेंद उनकी है। दीपक ने गेंद को अपना साबित करने के लिए तरह-तरह के सबूत देने की कोशिश की। लेकिन अनिल और दिनेश ने उसकी बातों को मानने से मना कर दिया, क्योंकि उसके दावे और सच्चाई में फर्क था। दीपक ने कहा यदि गेंद मुझे नहीं मिली, तो मैं इसे सड़क पर फेंक दूँगा।

अंत में दिनेश ने फैसला किया कि झगड़ा छोड़कर पहले खेला जाए। कुछ देर खेलने के बाद गेंद उछलकर सड़क पर जाते हुए स्कूटर में बनी सामान रखने की जालीदार टोकरी में जाकर गिर गई। गेंद स्कूटर के साथ दूर चली गई। बच्चों ने कुछ दूर तक स्कूटर का पीछा किया, लेकिन उन्हें जल्दी ही समझ आ गया कि स्कूटर को पकड़ पाना मुश्किल है। अंत में सभी बच्चे एक-दूसरे की ओर देखकर जोर-जोर से हँसने लगे।

शब्दार्थ

किरमिच-चमड़े जैसी सतह वाली गेंद, लू-गर्म हवाएँ, क्यारी-पौधों को उगाने के लिए बनाई गई मिट्टी की जगह, मुँडेर-छत की बाउंड्री, तिमंजिली-तीन मंजिल वाली इमारत, चटाई-फर्श पर बिछाने वाली चादर, चिलचिलाना-तेज़ धूप का बहुत अधिक गर्म होना, क्लब-बच्चों द्वारा आपसी मनोरंजन और खेल के लिए बनाई गई संस्था, ठहाका-जोर से हँसने की आवाज, जालीदार-छेद वाली संरचना, टप्पा-गेंद का धरती पर उछलना, गुट-समूह, चिक-बाँस की तीलियों से बना बड़ा परदा, घूँस-बड़ा चूहा, जो धरती में गड्ढा करके रहता है।

NCERT फोल्डर

कहानी की बात

(क) दिनेश की माँ मशीन चलाते-चलाते बोलीं, “बेटा, कहाँ जा रहे हो?”

- **दिनेश की माँ कौन-सी मशीन चला रही होंगी?**
- **तुमने इस मशीन को कहाँ-कहाँ देखा है?**

उत्तर
- दिनेश की माँ संभवत: सिलाई मशीन चला रही होंगी।
- मैंने इस मशीन को घरेलू उपयोग में, कपड़ों की दुकान में, दर्ज़ी की दुकान में और आस-पड़ोस आदि जगहों पर देखा है।

(ख) दिनेश ने सारी सीताफल की बेल छान मारी।

- **दिनेश क्या खोज रहा था?**
- **दिनेश को कैसे पता चला होगा कि क्यारी में वही चीज़ गिरी है?**

उत्तर
- दिनेश एक नई किरमिच की गेंद खोज रहा था।
- दिनेश को गिरने की आवाज़ सुनकर पता चल गया था कि क्यारी में वही चीज (गेंद) गिरी है।

(ग) दिनेश अच्छी तरह जानता था कि गेंद दीपक की नहीं है।

- **दिनेश को यह बात कैसे पता चली कि गेंद दीपक की हो ही नहीं सकती?**
- **दीपक बार-बार गेंद को अपनी क्यों बता रहा होगा?**

उत्तर
- दिनेश को यह बात इस आधार पर पता चली कि दीपक की गेंद पाँच महीने पहले खो गई थी और यह गेंद बिल्कुल नई और चमकदार थी। ऐसा नहीं हो सकता कि कोई गेंद पाँच महीने मिट्टी में पड़ी रहे और उस पर कोई दाग न लगे।
- दीपक बार-बार गेंद को अपनी बताने का प्रयास इसलिए कर रहा था, क्योंकि उसकी गेंद खो गई थी और उसे एक गेंद चाहिए थी।

गेंद किसकी

(क) दीपक ने गेंद को अपना बताने के लिए उसके बारे में कौन-कौन सी बातें बताईं?

उत्तर दीपक ने गेंद को अपना बताने के लिए निम्नलिखित बातें बताईं
- उसकी गेंद पाँच महीने पहले खो गई थी।
- उसकी गेंद पर भी इसी गेंद की तरह लाल रंग का निशान था।
- उसकी गेंद के टप्पे की आवाज भी इसी गेंद की तरह आती थी।
- वह अपने पापा से कहलवा सकता है कि गेंद उसी की है।

(ख) अगर दीपक और दिनेश गेंद के बारे में फैसला करवाने तुम्हारे पास आते, तो तुम गेंद किसे देतीं? यह भी बताओ कि तुम यह फैसला किन बातों को ध्यान में रखकर करतीं?

उत्तर यदि दीपक और दिनेश गेंद के बारे में निर्णय लेने मेरे पास आते, तो मैं गेंद दिनेश को देती। मैं यह फैसला निम्न बातों को ध्यान में रखकर करती
- दीपक की गेंद पाँच महीने पुरानी थी, जबकि यह गेंद नई थी। दीपक का दावा उसके संकेतों पर आधारित था। उसका यह दावा संदिग्ध था।
- दीपक झूठ बोल रहा था।
- गेंद दिनेश के बगीचे में गिरी थी, परंतु वह ईमानदारी से सभी बच्चों से पूछ रहा था कि यह गेंद किसकी है।

गेंद की कहानी

**गेंद स्कूटर के साथ कहीं चली गई।
उसके बाद गेंद के साथ क्या-क्या हुआ होगा? सोचकर बताओ।**

उत्तर गेंद रास्ते में कहीं गिर गई होगी या स्कूटर वाले के साथ उसके घर चली गई होगी।

पहचान

मान लो तुम्हारा कोई खिलौना घर में ही कहीं खो गया है। तुमने अपने साथियों को घर पर बुलाया है, ताकि सब मिलकर उसे खोज लें। तुम अपने खिलौने की पहचान के लिए अपने साथियों को कौन-कौन सी बातें बताओगी? लिखो।

उत्तर यदि मेरा खिलौना घर में खो जाए तो मैं अपने साथियों को खिलौने के रंग, आकार और उसकी विशेषताओं के बारे में बताऊँगी। मैं यह भी बताऊँगी कि खिलौना किस जगह पर रखा जाता था। इसके अतिरिक्त मैं यह भी बताऊँगी कि वह खिलौना किस खेल में प्रयोग होता था।

कहाँ

सामने की क्यारी में भिंडियों के ऊँचे-ऊँचे पौधे थे। एक ओर सीताफल की घनी बेल फैली हुई थी।
सीताफल की बेल होती है और भिंडी का पौधा। बताओ और कौन-कौन सी सब्ज़ियाँ बेल और पौधे पर लगती हैं?

उत्तर

बेल	पौधा
कद्दू	हरी मिर्च
तरबूज	टमाटर
खीरा	बैंगन
लौकी	शिमला मिर्च

तरह-तरह की गेंदें

गेंदों के अनेक रंग-रूप होते हैं। अलग-अलग खेलों में अलग-अलग प्रकार की गेंदों का इस्तेमाल किया जाता है। नीचे दी गई जगह में खेलों के अनुसार गेंदों की सूची बनाओ।

उत्तर

क्रिकेट	किरमिच
फुटबॉल	रबड़
बास्केटबॉल	लेदर
टेबल टेनिस	प्लास्टिक
हॉकी	रबड़

खोजो आस-पास

दिनेश चिक सरकाकर बरामदे की ओर भागा।

(क) चिक पर्दे का काम करती है पर चिक और पर्दे में फर्क होता है। इन दोनों में क्या अंतर है? समूह में चर्चा करो। इसी तरह पता लगाओ कि इन शब्दों में क्या अंतर है?
- टहनी-तना
- पेड़-पौधा
- घूँस-चूहा
- मुँडेर-चारदीवारी

उत्तर चिक एक ठोस और मजबूत सामग्री की बनी होती है, जबकि पर्दा हल्के कपड़े से बना होता है।

- **टहनी-तना** टहनी शाखा से निकलती है, जो छोटी होती है, जबकि तना पेड़ का मुख्य और मजबूत भाग होता है।
- **पेड़-पौधा** पेड़ बड़ा और लंबा होता है। इसकी शाखाएँ अधिक होती हैं। पौधा छोटा और कम ऊँचाई वाला होता है।
- **घूँस-चूहा** घूँस चूहे से बड़ी होती है और जमीन में गड्ढा बनाकर रहती है। चूहा घूँस से आकार में छोटा होता है।
- **मुँडेर-चारदीवारी** मुँडेर घर की छत के चारों किनारों पर बनी दीवार होती है। इसकी ऊँचाई दीवार से कम होती है। चारदीवारी किसी स्थान को चारों ओर से घेरने के लिए बनाई जाती है। इसमें प्रवेश और निकास के लिए दरवाजे होते हैं।

(ख) चिक सरकंडे से भी बनती है और तीलियों से भी। सरकंडे से और क्या-क्या बनता है? अपने आस-पास पता करो और लिखो।

उत्तर सरकंडे से झाड़ू, चटाई और टोकरी आदि वस्तुएँ बनती हैं।

क्लब बनाएँ

मान लो तुम्हें अपने स्कूल में एक क्लब बनाना है, जो स्कूल में खेलकूद के कार्यक्रमों की तैयारी करेगा।

- इस क्लब में शामिल होने और इसको चलाने आदि के बारे में नियम सोचकर लिखो।
- तुम्हारे विचार से इस क्लब को अच्छी तरह चलाने के लिए नियमों की जरूरत है या नहीं? अपने जवाब का कारण भी बताओ।

उत्तर
- **क्लब के नियम** इसके नियम इस प्रकार होंगे
  - **सदस्यता** इसमें सभी छात्र प्रतिभाग कर सकते हैं। सदस्यता के लिए एक आवेदन की जरूरत होगा
  - **बैठक** क्लब की मासिक बैठक होगी, जिसमें सभी की उपस्थिति अनिवार्य होगी।
  - **कार्य** क्लब का उद्देश्य खेलकूद की योजना बनाना और आयोजन की तैयारी करना है।
  - **संचालन** क्लब में एक अध्यक्ष और एक सचिव होगा, जो क्लब के कार्यों का संचालन करेगा।
  - **सहयोग** सभी सदस्य सहयोग और सुझाव दे सकते हैं।
- क्लब को अच्छी तरह चलाने के लिए नियमों की जरूरत होती है, जिससे कि क्लब व्यवस्थित और प्रभावी ढंग से चलाया जा सके, क्योंकि नियम स्पष्टता, जिम्मेदारी और कार्यप्रणाली सुनिश्चित करते हैं। इससे गतिविधियाँ सुचारु रूप से संचालित होती हैं।

एक, दो, तीन

दिनेश ने तिमंजिली इमारत की ओर देखा।

जिस इमारत में तीन मंजिलें हों, उसे तिमंजिली इमारत कहते हैं। बताओ, इन्हें क्या कहेंगे?

- जिस मकान में दो मंज़िलें हों।
- जिस स्कूटर में दो पहिए हों।
- जिस झंडे में तीन रंग हों।
- जिस जगह पर चार राहें मिलती हों।
- जिस स्कूटर में तीन पहिए हों।

उत्तर • जिस मकान में दो मंज़िलें हों — दुमंजिला
• जिस स्कूटर में दो पहिए हों — दुपहिया
• जिस झंडे में तीन रंग हों — तिरंगा
• जिस जगह पर चार राहें मिलती हों — चौराहा
• जिस स्कूटर में तीन पहिए हों — तिपहिया

सब्जी एक नाम अनेक

एक ही सब्जी या फल के नाम अलग-अलग स्थान पर अलग-अलग होते हैं। नीचे ऐसे कुछ नाम दिए गए हैं।

सीताफल	काशीफल
कांदा	बैंगन
बटाटा	नेनुआ
अमरूद	तरबूज
तोरी	कुम्हड़ा
शरीफ़ा	घीया

• बताओ कि तुम्हारे घर, शहर या कस्बे में इनमें से कौन-कौन से शब्द इस्तेमाल किए जाते हैं?
• बाकी नामों का इस्तेमाल किन-किन स्थानों पर होता है? पता करो।

उत्तर • हमारे यहाँ इस्तेमाल होने वाले शब्द हैं — सीताफल, काशीफल, बैंगन, अमरूद, तरबूज, तोरी और कुम्हड़ा।
• उपर्युक्त बाकी शब्दों का इस्तेमाल निम्नलिखित जगहों पर
होता है

काशीफल—उत्तर भारत में।
कांदा—महाराष्ट्र में प्याज़ के लिए।
बटाटा—महाराष्ट्र और गोवा में आलू के लिए।
नेनुआ—उत्तर भारत और विशेषकर लखनऊ में तोरी के लिए।
कुम्हड़ा—पूरे भारत में कद्दू के लिए।
घीया—पूरे भारत में लौकी के लिए।

अभ्यास प्रश्न

बहुविकल्पीय प्रश्न

1. दिनेश ने बच्चों से गेंद के संबंध में क्या पूछा?
(क) किसी के पास नई गेंद है?
(ख) जिसकी गेंद खो गई हो, वह गेंद की पहचान बताकर मुझसे ले सकता है।
(ग) यह मेरी गेंद है, कोई इसे नहीं ले सकता।
(घ) इस गेंद से कौन खेलना चाहता है?

2. दीपक ने अपनी गेंद के खोने का समय क्या बताया था?
(क) चार महीने पहले (ख) पाँच महीने पहले
(ग) कल ही (घ) दो महीने पहले

3. खेलते समय दिनेश की गेंद कहाँ चली गई?
(क) घर के पीछे बगीचे में (ख) एक पेड़ के नीचे
(ग) स्कूटर की जालीदार टोकरी में (घ) बच्चों के क्लब के मैदान में

4. स्कूटर के पीछे भागने के बाद बच्चों ने क्या किया?
(क) खेलना शुरू कर दिया (ख) चुपचाप खड़े रहे
(ग) जोर से हँस पड़े (घ) झगड़ा करने लगे

5. दिनेश की माँ उसे बाहर जाने से क्यों मना कर रही थीं?
(क) बाहर बारिश हो रही थी (ख) बाहर लू चल रही थी
(ग) बाहर अँधेरा था (घ) बाहर बहुत ठंड थी

उत्तर

1. (ख) जिसकी गेंद खो गई हो, वह गेंद की पहचान बताकर मुझसे ले सकता है।
2. (ख) पाँच महीने पहले
3. (ग) स्कूटर की जालीदार टोकरी में
4. (ग) जोर से हँस पड़े
5. (ख) बाहर लू चल रही थी

रिक्त स्थान

नीचे दिए गए वाक्यों में रिक्त स्थान की पूर्ति उचित शब्द से कीजिए। (दीपक, भिंडियों, केले, गेंद, कहानी)

1. दोपहर के समय दिनेश घर में बैठा कोई .... पढ़ रहा था।
2. सामने की क्यारी में .... के ऊँचे-ऊँचे पौधे थे।
3. दिनेश ने हाथ बढ़ाकर .... उठा ली।
4. दिनेश अच्छी तरह जानता था कि यह गेंद ...... की नहीं है।
5. क्यारियों के चारों ओर हरे-हरे .... के वृक्ष लहरा रहे थे।

उत्तर

1. कहानी 2. भिंडियों 3. गेंद
4. दीपक 5. केले

गद्यांश पर आधारित प्रश्न

निम्नलिखित गद्यांश को पढ़कर उस पर आधारित प्रश्नों के उत्तर दीजिए।

गद्यांश

गर्मी की छुट्टियाँ थीं। दोपहर के समय दिनेश घर में बैठा कोई कहानी पढ़ रहा था। तभी पेड़ के पत्तों को हिलाती हुई कोई वस्तु धम से घर के पीछे वाले बगीचे में गिरी। दिनेश आवाज़ से पहचान गया कि वह वस्तु क्या हो सकती है? वह एकदम से उठकर बरामदे की चिक सरकाकर बगीचे की ओर भागा। "अरे अरे, बेटा कहाँ जा रहा है? बाहर लू चल रही है।" दिनेश की माँ मशीन चलाते-चलाते एकदम जोर से बोलीं, परंतु दिनेश रुका नहीं। उसने पैरों में चप्पल भी नहीं पहनी। जून का महीना था। धरती तवे की तरह तप रही थी पर दिनेश को पैरों के जलने की भी चिंता नहीं थी। वह जहाँ से आवाज़ आई थी, उसी ओर भाग चला।

1. **गद्यांश के अनुसार, जब बगीचे में कुछ गिरने की आवाज़ आई तब दिनेश क्या कर रहा था?**
   (क) खेल रहा था (ख) सो रहा था
   (ग) कहानी पढ़ रहा था (घ) खाना खा रहा था
2. **दिनेश की माँ ने उसे क्या चेतावनी दी?**
   (क) बाहर वर्षा हो रही है (ख) बाहर गर्मी है
   (ग) बाहर लू चल रही है (घ) बाहर ठंड है
3. **दिनेश को किसकी आवाज़ सुनाई दी?**
4. **दिनेश अचानक से कहाँ भागा?**

उत्तर

1. (ग) कहानी पढ़ रहा था
2. (ग) बाहर लू चल रही है
3. दिनेश को पेड़ के पत्तों को हिलाकर किसी वस्तु के गिरने की आवाज़ सुनाई दी।
4. दिनेश अचानक से बगीचे की ओर भागा।

निम्नलिखित प्रश्नों के उत्तर दीजिए

1. **जब गेंद के गिरने की आवाज आई, तब दिनेश क्या कर रहा था?**

उत्तर जब गेंद के गिरने की आवाज आई तो दिनेश घर में बैठकर कोई कहानी की किताब पढ़ रहा था।

2. **दिनेश की माँ क्या कर रही थीं?**

उत्तर दिनेश की माँ सिलाई मशीन चला रही थीं।

3. **स्कूटर में गेंद जाने के बाद बच्चों का क्या हाल हुआ?**

उत्तर स्कूटर में गेंद जाने के बाद बच्चे कुछ देर स्कूटर के पीछे आवाज देते हुए भागे, परंतु स्कूटर की गति इतनी तेज थी कि बच्चे समझ गए कि उसे पकड़ना मुश्किल है।

4. **गेंद स्कूटर में कैसे चली गई और बच्चों ने क्या किया?**

उत्तर गेंद जोर से उछली और सड़क पार करते हुए स्कूटर में सामान रखने वाली जालीदार टोकरी में जा गिरी। बच्चों ने स्कूटर का पीछा किया, परंतु गेंद न मिल सकी।

लेखन संबंधी प्रश्न

1. **इस पाठ में बच्चे क्रिकेट खेलना पसंद करते हैं। 'क्रिकेट' विषय पर एक अनुच्छेद लिखिए।**

उत्तर मुझे क्रिकेट खेलना बहुत अच्छा लगता है। क्रिकेट का खेल दो टीमों के मध्य खेला जाता है। यह खेल एक बड़े और खुले मैदान में बल्ले और गेंद के माध्यम से खेला जाता है। दोनों टीमों में से एक टीम बल्लेबाजी तथा एक टीम गेंदबाजी करती है।

गेंदबाज, बल्लेबाज की तरफ गेंद फेंकता है, जिसे बल्लेबाज मारने की कोशिश करता है। उसके बाद गेंदबाजी करने वाली टीम बल्लेबाजी करती है और पहली टीम द्वारा बनाए गए रनों से ज्यादा रन बनाने की कोशिश करती है।

अध्याय 4

पापा जब बच्चे थे

पाठ का सार

इस अध्याय में लेखक ने अपने पिताजी के बचपन की इच्छाओं और सपनों का वर्णन किया है। पापा जब छोटे थे, तो उनसे अकसर यह पूछा जाता था कि वे बड़े होकर क्या बनना चाहते हैं? पापा का जवाब हमेशा बदलता रहता था। वे सबसे पहले चौकीदार बनकर चौकीदारी करना चाहते थे, क्योंकि रात में जब सभी लोग सो रहे होंगे, तब वे शोर मचा सकेंगे। पापा ने जब आइसक्रीम वाले को देखा, तो सोचा कि वे आइसक्रीम बेचने वाला बनेंगे। उन्होंने सोचा कि इस काम में वे ठेला लेकर घूम सकते हैं और मनचाही आइसक्रीम खा सकते हैं। पापा के माता-पिता जब उनकी ऐसी बातें सुनते, तो खूब हँसते। एक बार उन्होंने रेलवे स्टेशन पर शंटिंग करने वाले को देखा, तो सोचा कि यह सबसे अच्छा काम है। वे भी शंटिंग करने वाला बनेंगे, तो किसी ने उनसे पूछ लिया कि फिर वे आइसक्रीम बेचने का काम कैसे करेंगे? पापा ने कहा कि वे दोनों काम एकसाथ करेंगे। सुबह आइसक्रीम बेचने के बाद वे स्टेशन जाकर शंटिंग का काम कर लेंगे, फिर शाम को आकर आइसक्रीम बेचेंगे। उनकी बात को सुनकर सभी लोग हँस पड़े, लेकिन लोगों के इस तरह हँसने से पापा नाराज हो गए।

पापा के सपनों का अंत यहीं नहीं हुआ और एक दिन उन्होंने वायुयान चालक बनने की सोची। इसके बाद उन्होंने अभिनेता, जहाजी और चरवाहा बनने के बारे में भी सोचा। एक दिन उन्होंने तय किया कि वे कुत्ता बनेंगे। यह उनकी सबसे अनोखी इच्छा थी। उस दिन पापा अजनबी लोगों पर कुत्ते की तरह भौंकते रहे। पापा ने भौंकना तो सीख लिया था, लेकिन कुत्ते की तरह पैर से कान के पीछे खुजाना नहीं सीख पाए। वे अपने पालतू कुत्ते के पास जाकर बैठ गए, क्योंकि वे उसे देखकर पैर से कान के पीछे खुजाना सीखना चाहते थे।

कुत्ता बनने की इस कोशिश में उन्होंने एक बूढ़ी महिला को काटने की भी कोशिश की। जब वे पैर से कान के पीछे खुजाना सीख रहे थे, तभी वहाँ से एक फौजी गुजरा। उसने पापा से पूछा कि ''तुम क्या कर रहे हो?'' पापा बोले कि ''मैं कुत्ता बनना सीख रहा हूँ। मैं काफी दिनों तक इंसान बनकर रह चुका हूँ।'' फौजी ने फिर पूछा – ''क्या तुम जानते हो कि इंसान किसे कहते हैं?'' पापा इसका जवाब नहीं दे सके और इसका उत्तर फौजी को ही बताने के लिए कहा। इस पर फौजी ने कहा कि ''इसके बारे में तुम स्वयं सोचो।'' इतना कहकर अफसर वहाँ से चला गया। काफी सोच-विचार करने के बाद पापा की समझ में बात आ गई। उन्होंने तय किया कि वे रोज-रोज अपना इरादा नहीं बदल सकते हैं। उन्होंने दृढ़ निश्चय किया कि वे एक अच्छा इंसान बनेंगे। अच्छा इंसान बनने का महत्त्व पापा की समझ में आ गया था।

शब्दार्थ

चटकदार-चमकदार, शंटिंग-रेलगाड़ियों के डिब्बों को यात्रा के बाद व्यवस्थित करने का काम, चरवाहा-पशुओं को चराने वाला, सहलाना-प्यार से हाथ फेरना।

NCERT फोल्डर

तुम्हारी बात

(क) पापा ने जितने काम सोचे, उनमें से तुम्हें सबसे दिलचस्प काम कौन-सा लगता है? क्यों?

उत्तर पापा ने जितने काम सोचे, उनमें से आइसक्रीम बेचने वाला काम सबसे दिलचस्प है। इस काम में बच्चों को मुफ्त में आइसक्रीम दे सकते हैं और स्वयं भी बहुत सारी आइसक्रीम खा सकते हैं।

(ख) क्या तुम्हें भी घर में बताया जाता है कि तुम्हें बड़े होकर क्या काम करना है? कौन-कौन कहता है? क्या कहता है?

उत्तर नहीं, मेरे घर में मुझे यह नहीं बताया जाता है कि बड़े होकर मुझे क्या काम करना है? घरवाले मुझसे कहते हैं कि अपनी रुचियों के अनुसार, उस काम को चुनो, जो तुम्हें संतुष्ट करे।

(ग) अपने मम्मी या पापा से पता करो कि वे जब बच्चे थे, तब बड़े होकर क्या-क्या करने की सोचते थे?

उत्तर मेरी मम्मी बताती हैं कि जब वे छोटी थीं, तो शिक्षिका बनना चाहती थीं, वहीं पापा का सपना था कि वे इंजीनियर बनें।

(घ) अपने घर के किसी भी एक सदस्य से उसके काम के बारे में जानकारी हासिल करो।

- **पता करो उनके काम को किस नाम से जाना जाता है?**
- **उस काम को अच्छी तरह करने के लिए कौन-कौन सी बातें मालूम होनी चाहिए?**
- **उन्हें अपने काम में किन बातों से परेशानी होती है?**

उत्तर मैंने अपने भैया से उनके काम के बारे में जानकारी ली है

- भैया के काम को इंजीनियरिंग के नाम से जाना जाता है।
- भैया जो काम करते हैं, उसको करने के लिए कंप्यूटर का अच्छा ज्ञान होना आवश्यक है।
- भैया को अपने काम में समय की कमी से परेशानी होती है। कभी-कभी नई तकनीक को सीखने में भी परेशानी होती है।

कहानी से आगे

शुरू-शुरू में पापा चौकीदार बनना चाहते थे।

(क) चौकीदार रात को भी काम करते हैं। इसके अलावा और कौन-कौन से कामों में रात को जागना पड़ता है?

उत्तर चौकीदारी के अतिरिक्त निम्नलिखित कामों में रात को जागना पड़ता है

- रेल व्यवस्था को सही ढंग से चलाने के लिए रेलवे कर्मचारियों को रात में जागना पड़ता है।
- शांति व्यवस्था बनाए रखने के लिए पुलिस कर्मचारियों को रात में जागना पड़ता है।
- सीमा की रक्षा करने के लिए सैनिक रात में जागते हैं।
- मरीजों का इलाज करने के लिए अस्पताल का स्टाफ रात में जागता है।
- खबरों को हम सभी तक पहुँचाने के लिए न्यूज़ एजेंसी के लोग भी रात में जागते हैं।
- कॉल सेंटर में काम करने वाले कर्मचारी रात में जागते हैं।

पापा कई तरह के काम करना चाहते थे।

(ख) क्या तुम किसी व्यक्ति को जानते हो, जो एक से ज्यादा तरह के काम करता है? उस व्यक्ति के बारे में बताओ।

उत्तर हाँ, मैं एक व्यक्ति को जानता हूँ, जो एक से ज्यादा तरह के काम करता है। मेरे दोस्त के पिता शिक्षक और लेखक दोनों हैं। वे दिन में स्कूल में पढ़ाते हैं और शाम को किताबें लिखते हैं। इसके साथ ही वे बच्चों को ट्यूशन भी पढ़ाते हैं, जिससे कि अतिरिक्त आय हो सके।

आओ खेलें-शेखचिल्ली कहता है

पापा अपने पैर से कान के पीछे नहीं खुजा पाते थे। आओ देखें, तुम कौन-कौन से काम कर सकती हो! एक खेल खेलते हैं। खेल का नाम है-शेखचिल्ली कहता है। तुममें से एक बनेगा शेखचिल्ली। जो शेखचिल्ली कहेगा, बाकी सबको वैसे ही करना है।

शेखचिल्ली इस तरह के आदेश दे सकता है

- **शेखचिल्ली कहता है-अपने दाएँ हाथ को सिर के पीछे से ले जाकर नाक को पकड़ो।**
- **अपने दाएँ हाथ को दाईं टाँग के नीचे से ले जाकर दायाँ कान पकड़ो।**
- **शेखचिल्ली कहता है-खड़े होकर झुको।**
- **अपने हाथों से पैरों को छुओ।**
- **सिर अपने घुटनों से लगाओ।**

ध्यान रहे, तुम्हें केवल वही आदेश मानना है, जिसके साथ जुड़ा हो–शेखचिल्ली कहता है। यदि तुमने कोई और आदेश मान लिया तो तुम खेल से बाहर हो जाओगे।

उत्तर इसे विद्यार्थी अपने समूह में खेलें।

सोच–विचार

अफसर के जाने के बाद पापा बहुत सोचते रहे। बताओ, वह क्या-क्या सोच रहे होंगे? सही (✓) का निशान लगाओ।

- यह अफ़सर आखिर है कौन?
- अब मैं रोज-रोज अपना इरादा नहीं बदल सकता।
- कुत्ता बनना बड़ा कठिन काम है।
- ये फौजी अफसर मुझ पर हँसा क्यों नहीं? बाकी सब तो हँसते हैं।
- इस अफसर को कुत्ता बनना नहीं आता, इसीलिए मुझे बहका रहा है।

उत्तर
- अब मैं रोज-रोज अपना इरादा नहीं बदल सकता। (✓)
- कुत्ता बनना बड़ा कठिन काम है। (✓)
- ये फौजी अफसर मुझ पर हँसा क्यों नहीं, बाकी सब तो हँसते हैं। (✓)

अगर.....

पापा ने कहा, "अपना ठेला मैं स्टेशन के पास ही खड़ा करूँगा।"

(क) अगर तुम पापा की जगह होती तो ठेला कहाँ लगाती? ऐसा तुमने क्यों तय किया?

उत्तर अगर मैं पापा की जगह होती तो ठेला किसी भीड़-भाड़ वाली जगह पर लगाती। वहाँ ज्यादा लोग आते हैं, जिससे बिक्री बढ़ती है।

(ख) अगर तुम रेल से सफर करोगी तो तुम्हें प्लेटफॉर्म और रेलगाड़ी में कौन-कौन लोग नज़र आएँगे?

उत्तर अगर मैं रेल में यात्रा करूँगी तो मुझे प्लेटफॉर्म पर कुली, यात्री, सफाई कर्मचारी और वेंडर आदि दिखेंगे। ट्रेन में टी.टी.ई., सहयात्री और सुरक्षा गार्ड नज़र आएँगे।

परिवार

पापा के पापा को दादा कहते हैं। इन्हें तुम अपने घर में क्या कहकर बुलाओगी?

- पापा के पापा
- माँ के पापा
- पापा की माँ
- माँ की माँ
- पापा के बड़े भाई
- माँ के भाई
- पापा की बहन
- माँ की बहन
- पापा के छोटे भाई
- बहन के पति

उत्तर

पापा के पापा	–	दादा
माँ के पापा	–	नाना
पापा की माँ	–	दादी
माँ की माँ	–	नानी
पापा के बड़े भाई	–	ताऊ
माँ के भाई	–	मामा
पापा की बहन	–	बुआ
माँ की बहन	–	मौसी
पापा के छोटे भाई	–	चाचा
बहन के पति	–	जीजा

एक शब्द के बदले दूसरा

पापा को वायुयान चालक बनने की सूझी। इसके बाद **उन्होंने** अभिनेता बनने की सोची। इसके अतिरिक्त **वह** जहाज़ी भी बनना चाहते थे।

ऊपर के वाक्यों में **उन्होंने** और **वह** का इस्तेमाल **पापा** की जगह पर हुआ है। हम अकसर एक ही शब्द को दोहराने के अतिरिक्त उसकी जगह किसी दूसरे शब्द का प्रयोग करते हैं। **मैं, तुम, इस** भी ऐसे ही शब्द हैं।

(क) पाठ में से ऐसे शब्दों के पाँच उदाहरण छाँटो।

(ख) इनकी मदद से वाक्य बनाओ।

उत्तर (क) उनसे, उन्हें, वह, मैं, उसे

(ख) **उनसे** पापा जब छोटे थे, तो उनसे अकसर पूछा जाता था कि वे बड़े होकर क्या बनेंगे?

उन्हें शुरू-शुरू में पापा चौकीदार बनना चाहते थे। उन्हें यह सोचना बहुत अच्छा लगता था कि जब सारा शहर सोता है, तब चौकीदार जागता है।

वह वह आइसक्रीम का ठेला लेकर दिन भर घूमता रहता है।

मैं मैं एक अच्छा नागरिक बनना चाहता हूँ।

उसे जब रेलगाड़ी अपनी यात्रा पूरी कर लेती है, तो उसे अगली यात्रा के लिए तैयार करना होता है।

कौन-किसमें तेज

सभी बच्चे और बड़े किसी-न-किसी काम में माहिर होते हैं। कोई साइकिल चलाने में होशियार होता है, तो कोई चित्र बनाने में तेज़ होता है। तुम्हारे दोस्तों और परिवार में कौन किस काम में माहिर है? उनके नाम लिखो।

- **जो बढ़िया कहानी गढ़ सकते हैं**
- **जो खूबसूरत कढ़ाई कर सकते हैं**
- **जो कलाबाजियाँ खा सकते हैं**
- **जो दूसरों की बढ़िया नकल उतार सकते हैं**
- **जो हाथ से बढ़िया स्वेटर बुन सकते हैं**
- **जो सबके सामने किसी चीज़ के बारे दो मिनट तक बता सकते हैं**
- **जो कठिन पहेलियाँ सुलझा सकते हैं**
- **जो खुलकर ज़ोर से हँस सकते हैं**
- **जो तरह-तरह की आवाज़ें बना सकते हैं**
- **जो अंदाजे से ही चीजों का सही माप या वज़न बता सकते हैं**
- **जो बढ़िया अभिनय कर सकते हैं**
- **जो बेकार पड़ी चीज़ों से सुंदर चीजें बना सकते हैं**
- **तुम किन-किन चीजों में माहिर हो, यह भी बताओ।**

उत्तर
- जो बढ़िया कहानी गढ़ सकते हैं —आयुष (दोस्त)
- जो खूबसूरत कढ़ाई कर सकते हैं—लता (मेरी मामी)
- जो कलाबाजियाँ खा सकते हैं—अमित (मेरा भाई)
- जो दूसरों की बढ़िया नकल उतार सकते हैं—विशाल (मेरा सहपाठी)
- जो हाथ से बढ़िया स्वेटर बुन सकते हैं—सुशीला (मेरी दादी)
- जो सबके सामने किसी चीज़ के बारे में दो मिनट तक बता सकते हैं—निखिल (मेरा दोस्त)
- जो कठिन पहेलियाँ सुलझा सकते हैं—सीमा (मेरी बहन)
- जो खुलकर जोर से हँस सकते हैं—कविता (मेरी दोस्त)
- जो तरह-तरह की आवाजें बना सकते हैं—राकेश (मेरा दोस्त)
- जो अंदाजे से ही चीजों का सही माप या वज़न बता सकते हैं—राहुल (मेरे पिता)
- जो बढ़िया अभिनय कर सकते हैं—साक्षी (मेरी दोस्त)
- जो बेकार पड़ी चीज़ों से सुंदर चीजें बना सकते हैं—सविता (मेरी माँ)

मैं कविता एवं कहानी लिख सकता हूँ और चित्रकारी भी कर सकता हूँ। मैं क्रिकेट भी अच्छा खेल लेता हूँ।

कैसे थे पापा

नीचे लिखी पंक्तियाँ पढ़ो। इन पंक्तियों के आधार पर बताओ कि तुम पापा के बारे में क्या सोचती हो?

(क) पापा के पास जवाब हमेशा तैयार होता था।
ऐसा लगता है कि ....

(ख) पापा का जवाब हमेशा अलग-अलग होता था।
ऐसा लगता है कि ....

(ग) मैं छोटे बच्चों को मुफ्त में आइसक्रीम दिया करूँगा।
ऐसा लगता है कि ....

(घ) रात में करने के लिए होता ही क्या है? रात में मैं चौकीदारी करूँगा।
ऐसा लगता है कि ....

उत्तर (क) ऐसा लगता है कि पापा बहुत चतुर थे।
(ख) ऐसा लगता है कि पापा बहुत रचनात्मक थे।
(ग) ऐसा लगता है कि पापा बच्चों को प्रेम करते थे।
(घ) ऐसा लगता है कि पापा समाज सेवा में विश्वास रखते थे।

अभ्यास प्रश्न

बहुविकल्पीय प्रश्न

1. पापा सबसे पहले क्या बनना चाहते थे?

(क) शंटिंग करने वाला (ख) चौकीदार
(ग) आइसक्रीम बेचने वाला (घ) अभिनेता

2. पापा ने आइसक्रीम बेचने वाला बनने के समय क्या सोचा था?

(क) वह आइसक्रीम बेचेंगे और स्वयं भी खाएँगे।
(ख) वह आइसक्रीम का व्यापार करेंगे।
(ग) वह आइसक्रीम की फैक्ट्री खोलेंगे।
(घ) वह केवल बच्चों को आइसक्रीम बेचेंगे।

3. शंटिंग करने वाले का क्या काम था?

(क) रेलगाड़ी को चलाना
(ख) रेलगाड़ी की सफाई करना और इंजन को तैयार करना
(ग) स्टेशन पर टिकट बेचने का काम करना
(घ) प्लेटफॉर्म की सफाई करना

4. अंततः पापा ने क्या बनने का निर्णय लिया?

(क) अभिनेता (ख) आइसक्रीम वाला
(ग) अच्छा इंसान (घ) शंटिंग करने वाला

उत्तर

1. (ख) चौकीदार
2. (क) वह आइसक्रीम बेचेंगे और स्वयं भी खाएँगे।
3. (ख) रेलगाड़ी की सफाई करना और इंजन को तैयार करना
4. (ग) अच्छा इंसान

गद्यांश पर आधारित प्रश्न

निम्नलिखित गद्यांश को पढ़कर उस पर आधारित प्रश्नों के उत्तर दीजिए।

गद्यांश

पापा जब छोटे थे, तो उनसे अकसर पूछा जाता था, ''बड़े होकर तुम क्या बनना चाहते हो?'' पापा के पास जवाब हमेशा तैयार होता, लेकिन उनका जवाब हर बार अलग-अलग होता था। शुरू-शुरू में पापा चौकीदार बनना चाहते थे। उन्हें यह सोचना बहुत अच्छा लगता था कि जब सारा शहर सोता है, तब चौकीदार जागता है। उन्हें यह सोचना भी अच्छा लगता था कि जब हर कोई सोया हुआ हो, वह खूब शोर मचा सकते हैं। उन्हें पक्का यकीन था कि बड़े होकर वह चौकीदार ही बनेंगे।

लेकिन एक दिन अपने चटकदार हरे ठेले को लिए आइसक्रीम वाला आ गया। भई वाह! पापा आइसक्रीम वाला बनेंगे। वह ठेले को लेकर घूम भी सकते हैं और जितना मन चाहे उतनी आइसक्रीम भी खा सकते हैं। पापा ने सोचा, ''मैं एक आइसक्रीम बेचूँगा तो एक खुद खाऊँगा। छोटे बच्चों को तो मैं मुफ़्त में आइसक्रीम दिया करूँगा।''

1. पापा को चौकीदार बनना क्यों पसंद था?

(क) जागने और शोर मचाने के लिए
(ख) सोने और आराम करने के लिए
(ग) ठेला लेकर घूमने के लिए
(घ) बच्चों को आइसक्रीम देने के लिए

2. पापा ने आइसक्रीम बेचने के लिए क्यों सोचा था?

(क) इसमें वे सो सकते थे
(ख) वह जितनी चाहें उतनी आइसक्रीम खा सकते थे
(ग) वह बच्चों के साथ घूम सकते थे
(घ) वह शहर में सफाई कर सकते थे

3. पापा ने आइसक्रीम बेचने का विचार कब किया?

4. पापा आइसक्रीम बेचते समय बच्चों के लिए क्या करना चाहते थे?

उत्तर

1. (क) जागने और शोर मचाने के लिए
2. (ख) वह जितनी चाहें उतनी आइसक्रीम खा सकते थे
3. एक दिन जब चटकदार हरे ठेले को लिए आइसक्रीम वाला आया तो उसे देखकर पापा ने तय किया कि वे आइसक्रीम बेचने वाला बनेंगे।
4. पापा आइसक्रीम बेचते समय बच्चों को आइसक्रीम मुफ्त में देना चाहते थे।

निम्नलिखित प्रश्नों के उत्तर दीजिए

1. पापा ने सबसे पहले क्या बनने के बारे में सोचा था?

उत्तर पापा सबसे पहले एक चौकीदार बनना चाहते थे।

2. पापा ने अंततः क्या बनने का निर्णय लिया?

उत्तर पापा ने अंततः एक अच्छा इंसान बनने का निर्णय लिया।

3. पापा ने कुत्ते के जैसा कौन-सा काम करने की कोशिश की?

उत्तर पापा ने कुत्ते के जैसा कान के पीछे खुजाने की कोशिश की, जो पापा नहीं कर सके।

4. पापा को चौकीदार बनना क्यों पसंद था?

उत्तर पापा चौकीदार इसलिए बनना चाहते थे कि जब सब सो रहे हों तब वे शोर मचा सकें।

अध्याय 5

दोस्त की पोशाक

पाठ का सार

कहानी में नसीरुद्दीन और उनके पुराने दोस्त जमाल साहब के बीच की मुलाकात को हास्यपूर्ण ढंग से प्रस्तुत किया गया है। नसीरुद्दीन बहुत दिनों के बाद अपने पुराने दोस्त जमाल साहब से मिले थे। काफी बातें करने के बाद नसीरुद्दीन ने अपने मित्र जमाल साहब को मोहल्ले में घूमने का प्रस्ताव दिया। जमाल साहब ने साधारण पोशाक पहन रखी थी, इसलिए उन्होंने बाहर जाने से मना कर दिया। नसीरुद्दीन ने उन्हें अपनी एक भड़कीली अचकन लाकर दी और कहा कि आप इसमें अच्छे दिखेंगे।

नसीरुद्दीन की दी हुई अचकन जमाल साहब ने पहन ली। नसीरुद्दीन जमाल साहब को अपने पड़ोसी के यहाँ ले गए और जमाल साहब का परिचय अपने पड़ोसी से करवाया। परिचय के इस क्रम में उन्होंने यह भी बता दिया कि जमाल साहब ने जो अचकन पहन रखी है, वह मेरी है। यह बात सुनकर जमाल साहब शर्मिंदा हो गए। उन्होंने नसीरुद्दीन को डाँटते हुए कहा कि यह बताने की क्या जरूरत थी कि अचकन तुम्हारी है। तब नसीरुद्दीन ने जमाल साहब से माफ़ी माँग ली। इसके बाद वे जमाल साहब को हुसैन साहब से मिलवाने ले गए। हुसैन साहब से जमाल साहब का परिचय करवाते हुए उन्होंने कहा कि जमाल साहब ने जो अचकन पहन रखी है, यह इनकी अपनी है। जमाल साहब यह सुनकर गुस्सा हो गए और कहा कि यह झूठ बोलने की क्या जरूरत थी? फिर नसीरुद्दीन ने वादा किया कि आगे से वे इस पोशाक के बारे में कुछ नहीं कहेंगे। हुसैन साहब से मिलने के बाद वे एक और पड़ोसी के यहाँ मिलने गए। नसीरुद्दीन ने अपने पड़ोसी से जमाल साहब का परिचय करवाया और बताया कि ये मेरे दोस्त हैं। आगे यह भी कहा कि ''इन्होंने जो अचकन पहन रखी है, उसके बारे में मैं चुप ही रहूँ तो अच्छा है।''

शब्दार्थ

गपशप–हल्की–फुल्की बातचीत, मामूली–साधारण, भड़कीली–चमकदार, अचकन–लंबा कोट, घड़ों पानी पड़ना–शर्मिंदा होना, सत्कार–आदरपूर्वक स्वागत।

NCERT फोल्डर

तुम्हारे सवाल

कहानी के बारे में कोई पाँच प्रश्न बनाकर नीचे दी गई जगह में लिखो। कॉपी में उनके उत्तर लिखो।

1. नसीरुद्दीन अपने किस दोस्त से मिले?

उत्तर नसीरुद्दीन अपने पुराने दोस्त जमाल साहब से मिले।

2. नसीरुद्दीन के दूसरे पड़ोसी का क्या नाम था?

उत्तर नसीरुद्दीन के दूसरे पड़ोसी का नाम हुसैन साहब था।

3. नसीरुद्दीन ने जमाल साहब को कौन-सी पोशाक पहनने के लिए दी?

उत्तर नसीरुद्दीन ने जमाल साहब को अपनी भड़कीली अचकन पहनने के लिए दी।

4. पहले पड़ोसी से मिलते समय नसीरुद्दीन ने अचकन के बारे में क्या कहा?

उत्तर पहले पड़ोसी से मिलते समय नसीरुद्दीन ने अचकन के बारे में कहा कि यह अचकन मेरी है।

5. नसीरुद्दीन ने तीसरे पड़ोसी से क्या कहा?

उत्तर नसीरुद्दीन ने तीसरे पड़ोसी से कहा कि "इन्होंने जो अचकन पहनी है, उसके बारे में मैं चुप ही रहूँ तो अच्छा है।"

तुम्हारी बात

नसीरुद्दीन और जमाल साहब बनठन कर घूमने के लिए निकले।

(क) तुम बनठन कर कहाँ-कहाँ जाते हो?

उत्तर मैं बनठन कर शादी, जन्मदिन की पार्टी और स्कूल के कार्यक्रम आदि में जाता हूँ। मैं कहीं बाहर घूमने जाते समय भी बनठन कर ही जाता हूँ।

(ख) तुम किस-किस तरह से बनते-ठनते हो?

उत्तर मैं विभिन्न अवसरों पर अलग तरह से बनता-ठनता हूँ। शादी या पार्टी में जाने के लिए शेरवानी, कुर्ता-पायजामा या सूट पहनता हूँ। स्कूल के कार्यक्रमों में यूनिफॉर्म या स्पेशल ड्रेस पहनता हूँ। त्योहारों पर पारंपरिक कपड़े पहनकर तैयार होता हूँ। इन सबके साथ मैं परफ्यूम जरूर लगाता हूँ।

तुम्हारी समझ से

(क) तीसरे मकान से बाहर निकलकर जमाल साहब ने नसीरुद्दीन से क्या कहा होगा?

उत्तर तीसरे मकान से बाहर निकलकर जमाल साहब ने नसीरुद्दीन से कहा होगा कि "मैंने कहा था कि पोशाक के बारे में कुछ नहीं कहना, लेकिन तुमने फिर से इसका उल्लेख कर दिया। अब कहीं और चलने से अच्छा है कि घर वापस चलो।"

(ख) जमाल साहब अपने मामूली से कपड़ों में घूमने क्यों नहीं जाना चाहते होंगे?

उत्तर जमाल साहब अपने मामूली से कपड़ों में घूमने इसलिए नहीं जाना चाहते होंगे, क्योंकि उन्हें डर था कि लोग उन्हें साधारण और कम महत्त्वपूर्ण व्यक्ति समझेंगे।

(ग) नसीरुद्दीन अपनी अचकन के बारे में हमेशा क्यों बताते होंगे?

उत्तर नसीरुद्दीन अपनी अचकन के बारे में हमेशा इसलिए बताते होंगे, क्योंकि उन्हें अचकन के बारे में बताने में मज़ा आता होगा। यह भी हो सकता है कि वे अपने मित्र को चिढ़ाने और लोगों का मनोरंजन करने के लिए ऐसा करते होंगे।

गपशप

जब जमाल साहब और नसीरुद्दीन हुसैन साहब के घर से बाहर निकले, तो उन्होंने अपनी बेगम को नसीरुद्दीन और जमाल साहब से मुलाकात का किस्सा सुनाया। उन दोनों के बीच में क्या बातचीत हुई होगी? लिखकर बताओ।

बेगम कौन आया था?

हुसैन साहब नसीरुद्दीन अपने दोस्त के साथ आया था।

उत्तर

बेगम कौन था उनका दोस्त?

हुसैन साहब उनका नाम जमाल साहब था। बहुत सीधे-साधे और अच्छे इंसान लगे।

बेगम पर, नसीरुद्दीन के साथ तो कुछ मज़ेदार बात ज़रूर हुई होगी!

हुसैन साहब अरे, वही तो! नसीरुद्दीन ने पहले तो कहा कि जमाल साहब ने मेरी अचकन पहनी है।

बेगम फिर क्या हुआ? क्या जमाल साहब नाराज हुए?

हुसैन साहब नाराज तो बाद में हुए होंगे, लेकिन जमाल साहब शर्मिंदा जरूर हो गए थे।

बेगम (हँसते हुए) नसीरुद्दीन का मजाक कभी खत्म नहीं होता। हर बार कुछ नया कर जाते हैं।

घूमना फिरना

नसीरुद्दीन ने कहा, 'चलो दोस्त, मोहल्ले में घूम आएँ।'

जब नसीरुद्दीन अपने दोस्त से मिले, वे उसे अपना मोहल्ला दिखाने ले गए। जब तुम अपने दोस्तों से मिलते हो, तब क्या-क्या करते हो?

उत्तर जब मैं अपने दोस्तों से मिलता हूँ, तो सबसे पहले क्रिकेट, फुटबॉल या लुका-छुपी खेलता हूँ। इसके बाद हम अपने-अपने घरों के बारे में बातें करते हैं और एक-दूसरे को नया खेल सिखाते हैं। कभी-कभी हम पार्क में भी घूमने जाते हैं या अपने मोहल्ले में साइकिल चलाते हैं।

करके दिखाओ

नीचे कुछ वाक्य लिखे हैं। तुम्हें इनका अभिनय करना है। तुम चाहो तो कहानी में देख सकते हो कि इन कामों का ज़िक्र कहाँ आया है।

- **बनठन कर घूमने के लिए निकलना।**
- **घड़ों पानी पड़ना।**
- **मुँह बनाकर शिकायत करना।**
- **गर्मजोशी से स्वागत करना।**
- **नाराज होना।**
- **देखते ही रह जाना।**

उत्तर छात्र स्वयं करें।

घड़ों पानी पड़ना

नसीरुद्दीन की बात सुनकर जमाल साहब पर तो मानो घड़ों पानी पड़ गया।

(क) घड़ों पानी पड़ना एक मुहावरा है। इसका क्या मतलब हो सकता है? पता लगाओ। तुम इसका मतलब पता करने के लिए अपने साथियों या बड़ों से बातचीत कर सकते हो या शब्दकोश देख सकते हो।

उत्तर 'घड़ों पानी पड़ना' मुहावरे का अर्थ है—बहुत अधिक शर्मिंदा होना।

(ख) इस मुहावरे को सुनकर मन में एक चित्र-सा बनता है। तुम भी किन्हीं दो मुहावरों के बारे में चित्र बनाओ। कुछ मुहावरे हम दे देते हैं। तुम चाहो तो इनमें से कोई पसंद कर सकते हो

- **सिर मुंडाते ही ओले पड़ना**
- **ऊँट के मुँह में जीरा**
- **दीया तले अँधेरा**

उत्तर छात्र स्वयं करें।

कौन है कैसा

नसीरुद्दीन एक भड़कीली अचकन निकालकर लाए। भड़कीली शब्द बता रहा है कि अचकन कैसी थी। कहानी में से ऐसे ही और शब्द छाँटो, जो किसी के बारे में कुछ बताते हों। उन्हें छाँटकर नीचे दी गई जगह में लिखो।

पुराना दोस्त ....

....

....

देखें, कौन सबसे ज्यादा ऐसे शब्द ढूँढ पाता है?

भड़कीली, पुराना जैसे शब्द किसी के बारे में कुछ खास या विशेष बात बता रहे हैं। इसलिए इन्हें विशेषण कहते हैं।

उत्तर **पुराना** दोस्त

मामूली-सी पोशाक

खास दोस्त

अन्य पड़ोसी

गर्मजोशी से उनका स्वागत सत्कार किया

अपनी अचकन

तुम्हारी अकल

कई सालों

इतनी-सी बात

पास-पड़ोस

पड़ोस के घर में जाकर नसीरुद्दीन पड़ोसी से मिले।

तुम अपने पड़ोसी बच्चों के साथ बहुत-से खेल खेलते हो। पर क्या तुम उनके परिवार के बारे में जानते हो?

चलो, दोस्तों के बारे में और जानकारी इकट्ठी करते हैं। यदि तुम चाहो तो उनसे ये बातें पूछ सकते हो

- **घर में कुल कितने लोग हैं?**
- **उनके नाम क्या हैं?**
- **उनकी आयु क्या है?**
- **वे क्या काम करते हैं?**

उत्तर
- माँ, पिताजी, एक बड़ा भाई और एक छोटी बहन।
- माँ का नाम स्मिता, पिताजी का नाम राहुल, बड़े भाई का नाम अमन और छोटी बहन का नाम रिया है।
- माँ की आयु 38 वर्ष है, पिताजी की आयु 40 वर्ष है, बड़े भाई की आयु 15 वर्ष है और छोटी बहन की आयु 8 वर्ष है।

- पिताजी अध्यापक हैं। माँ घर पर रहकर बच्चों की देखभाल करती हैं। बड़े भाई कॉलेज में पढ़ाई करते हैं और छोटी बहन स्कूल जाती है।

शब्दों का हेरफेर

झूठा–जूठा

इन शब्दों को बोलकर देखो। ये मिलती-जुलती आवाज वाले शब्द हैं। जरा-से अंतर से भी शब्द का अर्थ बदल जाता है।

नीचे इसी तरह के कुछ शब्दों के जोड़े दिए गए हैं। इन सबके अर्थ अलग-अलग हैं। इन शब्दों का वाक्यों में प्रयोग करो।

घड़ा-गढ़ा | घूम-झूम | राज-राज़

फ़न-फन | सजा-सज़ा | खोल-खौल

उत्तर
- घड़ा—वह पुराना **घड़ा** है।
  गढ़ा—कलाकार ने मूर्ति को बहुत सुंदर **गढ़ा** है।
- घूम—बच्चे पार्क में **घूम** रहे थे।
  झूम—संगीत सुनते ही सभी **झूम** उठे।
- राज—राजा ने बहुत दिन तक **राज** किया।
  राज़—अमित ने अपना **राज़** छिपा लिया।
- फ़न—सर्कस में जादूगर ने शानदार **फ़न** दिखाया।
  फन—साँप अपना **फन** उठाए हुए था।
- सजा—हमने दीपावली पर अपने घर को बहुत सुंदर तरीके से **सजा** लिया।
  सज़ा—यदि तुम नियम तोड़ोगे, तो तुम्हें **सज़ा** मिलेगी।
- खोल—कमरे की खिड़की **खोल** दो।
  खौल—रमेश की झूठी बात सुनकर अमित का खून **खौल** उठा।

अभ्यास प्रश्न

बहुविकल्पीय प्रश्न

1. नसीरुद्दीन ने जमाल साहब को भड़कीली अचकन पहनने के लिए क्यों दी?
(क) ताकि वे बेहतर दिख सकें
(ख) ताकि उनका मूड खराब हो
(ग) जिससे वे घर पर रह सकें
(घ) ताकि वे जल्दी घर लौट सकें

2. जमाल साहब ने क्यों कहा कि अचकन की बात नहीं करनी चाहिए?
(क) क्योंकि यह उनके लिए पुरानी थी
(ख) क्योंकि इससे उन्हें शर्मिंदगी हुई
(ग) क्योंकि यह अचकन बहुत महँगी थी
(घ) क्योंकि नसीरुद्दीन ने झूठ बोला

3. नसीरुद्दीन ने हुसैन साहब को जमाल साहब के बारे में क्या बताया?
(क) जमाल साहब ने अपनी अचकन पहन रखी है
(ख) जमाल साहब की अचकन मेरी है
(ग) जमाल साहब की अचकन बहुत पुरानी है
(घ) जमाल साहब ने अचकन बदल दी है

4. नसीरुद्दीन ने किससे माफ़ी माँगी थी?
(क) पहले पड़ोसी से (ख) हुसैन साहब से
(ग) जमाल साहब से (घ) हुसैन साहब की पत्नी से

5. जमाल साहब ने नसीरुद्दीन को क्या समझाया?
(क) अचकन के बारे में बात न करने को
(ख) झूठ बोलने को
(ग) घर से बाहर न जाने को
(घ) नसीरुद्दीन से नाराज़गी दिखाने को

उत्तर
1. (क) ताकि वे बेहतर दिख सकें
2. (ख) क्योंकि इससे उन्हें शर्मिंदगी हुई
3. (ख) जमाल साहब की अचकन मेरी है
4. (ग) जमाल साहब से
5. (क) अचकन के बारे में बात न करने को

सत्य–असत्य

नीचे दिए गए वाक्यों में से सत्य या असत्य कथन की पहचान कीजिए।

1. नसीरुद्दीन ने जमाल साहब को अपनी भड़कीली अचकन दी। (सत्य/असत्य)

2. नसीरुद्दीन ने माफ़ी माँगते हुए कहा, "गलती हो गई। अब ऐसा ही करूँगा।" (सत्य/असत्य)

3. नसीरुद्दीन ने हुसैन साहब से जमाल साहब का परिचय कराया। (सत्य/असत्य)

4. एक बार नसीरुद्दीन अपने बहुत पुराने दोस्त जमाल साहब से मिले। (सत्य/असत्य)

5. दोस्त को लेकर नसीरुद्दीन अपने घर गए। (सत्य/असत्य)

उत्तर

1. सत्य 2. असत्य 3. सत्य
4. असत्य 5. सत्य

रिक्त स्थान

नीचे दिए गए वाक्यों में रिक्त स्थान की पूर्ति उचित शब्द से कीजिए।

(पड़ोसी, भड़कीली, जमाल, नसीरुद्दीन, घड़ों)

1. एक बार नसीरुद्दीन अपने बहुत पुराने दोस्त .... साहब से मिले।
2. नसीरुद्दीन तुरंत उनके लिए अपनी एक .... अचकन निकालकर लाए।
3. दोस्त को लेकर नसीरुद्दीन .... के घर गए।
4. यह सुनकर जमाल साहब पर तो मानो .... पानी पड़ गया।
5. .... जमाल साहब को लेकर आगे बढ़े।

उत्तर

1. जमाल 2. भड़कीली
3. पड़ोसी 4. घड़ों
5. नसीरुद्दीन

गद्यांश पर आधारित प्रश्न

निम्नलिखित गद्यांश को पढ़कर उस पर आधारित प्रश्नों के उत्तर दीजिए।

गद्यांश

एक बार नसीरुद्दीन अपने बहुत पुराने दोस्त जमाल साहब से मिले। अपने पुराने दोस्त से मिलकर वे बड़े खुश हुए। कुछ देर गपशप करने के बाद उन्होंने कहा, "चलो दोस्त, मोहल्ले में घूम आएँ।" जमाल साहब ने जाने से मना कर दिया और कहा, "अपनी इस मामूली सी पोशाक में मैं लोगों से नहीं मिल सकता।" नसीरुद्दीन ने कहा, "बस इतनी सी बात!"

1. जमाल साहब ने घूमने से मना किया, क्योंकि
   (क) वे बीमार थे
   (ख) उनकी पोशाक मामूली थी
   (ग) उन्हें समय नहीं था
   (घ) वे घर से बाहर नहीं जाना चाहते थे
2. नसीरुद्दीन ने जमाल साहब की मामूली पोशाक को लेकर क्या कहा?
   (क) यह कोई समस्या नहीं है।
   (ख) यह बहुत सुंदर है।
   (ग) तुम्हें इसकी चिंता नहीं करनी चाहिए।
   (घ) तुम्हें इसे बदलना होगा।
3. नसीरुद्दीन और जमाल साहब ने मिलने पर क्या किया?
4. नसीरुद्दीन ने जमाल साहब के मनोबल को बढ़ाने के लिए क्या कहा?

उत्तर

1. (ख) उनकी पोशाक मामूली थी
2. (क) यह कोई समस्या नहीं है।
3. नसीरुद्दीन और जमाल साहब ने मिलने पर गपशप की।
4. नसीरुद्दीन ने जमाल साहब के मनोबल को बढ़ाने के लिए कहा कि "बस इतनी सी बात!"

निम्नलिखित प्रश्नों के उत्तर दीजिए

1. जमाल साहब ने मोहल्ले में घूमने से क्यों मना किया?

उत्तर जमाल साहब ने मोहल्ले में घूमने से इसलिए मना कर दिया, क्योंकि उन्होंने साधारण पोशाक पहन रखी थी।

2. नसीरुद्दीन ने जमाल साहब को कौन-सी पोशाक दी?

उत्तर नसीरुद्दीन ने जमाल साहब को अपनी एक भड़कीली अचकन लाकर दी।

3. जमाल साहब ने नसीरुद्दीन को क्या कहा?

उत्तर जमाल साहब ने नसीरुद्दीन को कहा कि यह बताने की क्या जरूरत है कि यह अचकन तुम्हारी है।

4. नसीरुद्दीन ने अपनी गलती मानते हुए क्या कहा?

उत्तर नसीरुद्दीन ने अपनी गलती मानते हुए कहा कि "वे आगे से ऐसा नहीं करेंगे।"

5. अचकन के बारे में जब नसीरुद्दीन ने अपने पड़ोसी से बताया कि यह मेरी है, तो जमाल साहब की क्या प्रतिक्रिया हुई?

उत्तर अचकन के बारे में जब नसीरुद्दीन ने अपने पड़ोसी को बताया कि यह मेरी है, तब यह बात सुनकर जमाल साहब शर्मिंदा हो गए।

अध्याय 6

नाव बनाओ नाव बनाओ

कविता का सार

इस कविता के कवि श्री हरिकृष्णदास गुप्त हैं। आसमान में घिरते बादल को देखकर एक बालक अनुमान लगाता है कि वर्षा होने वाली है। उसे लगता है कि खूब पानी बरसेगा, जिससे लंबी-चौड़ी गली में पानी भर जाएगा। इस पानी में वह कागज की नाव तैराना चाहता है। इस विचार से वह उत्साहित होकर अपने भाई से कहता है कि गुल्लक से पैसे निकालकर बाजार से चमकीला, रंग-बिरंगा कागज और कैंची ले आओ। बालक का बड़ा भाई कहता है कि यह उसके वश में नहीं है। बालक को पता है कि भैया आलस के कारण ऐसा कह रहे हैं। अत: वह अपने भाई से आलस छोड़कर जल्दी आने की प्रार्थना करता है।

काव्यांशों की व्याख्या

काव्यांश 1

नाव बनाओ, नाव बनाओ।
भैया मेरे, जल्दी आओ ।।
वह देखो, पानी आया है,
घिर-घिर कर बादल छाया है,
सात समुंदर भर लाया है,
तुम रस का सागर भर लाओ।

भैया मेरे, जल्दी आओ।।
पानी सचमुच खूब पड़ेगा,
लंबी-चौड़ी गली भरेगा,
लाकर घर में नदी धरेगा,
ऐसे में तुम भी लहराओ।
भैया मेरे, जल्दी आओ।।

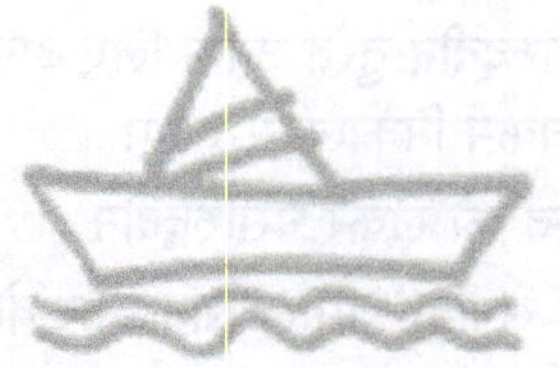

शब्दार्थ घिर-घिर-चारों ओर से घिरना, समुंदर-समुद्र, विशाल जलाशय, रस - आनंद, धरेगा-रखेगा।

संदर्भ एवं प्रसंग प्रस्तुत काव्य पंक्तियाँ हमारी पाठ्यपुस्तक 'रिमझिम भाग-4' में संकलित कविता 'नाव बनाओ, नाव बनाओ' से ली गई हैं। इसके कवि श्री ''हरिकृष्णदास गुप्त'' हैं। इस कविता में एक बच्चा कागज़ की नाव बनाने के लिए अपने भाई को बुला रहा है।

व्याख्या बालक अपने बड़े भाई से कागज़ की नाव बनाने के लिए कहता है। आसमान में घिरे बादलों को देखकर उसे लगता है कि बारिश होने वाली है। इन बादलों में सात समुंदर का पानी भरा हुआ है। अपने भाई से वह कहता है कि रस का सागर भरकर ले आओ। उसे लगता है कि खूब बारिश होगी और लंबी-चौड़ी गली में पानी भर जाएगा। इतना पानी भर जाएगा कि पानी घर में बहती हुई नदी के समान प्रतीत होगा। ऐसे सुंदर मौसम में वह अपने भाई से बार-बार नाव बनाने के लिए कहता है।

काव्यांश 2

गुल्लक भारी, अपनी खोलो,
हल्की मेरी, नहीं टटोलो,
पैसे नए-नए ही रोलो,
फिर बाजार लपक तुम लाओ।
भैया मेरे, जल्दी आओ।।
ले आओ कागज़ चमकीला,
लाल-हरा या नीला-पीला,
रंग-बिरंगा खूब रंगीला,
कैंची, चुटकी, हाथ चलाओ।
भैया मेरे, जल्दी आओ ।।

शब्दार्थ *गुल्लक-पैसे रखने का डिब्बा, टटोलो-छूकर ढूँढना, रोलो-लुढ़काओ, लपक-तेजी से जाना।*

प्रसंग प्रस्तुत पंक्तियों में कवि ने एक बच्चे की दृष्टि से बारिश की सुंदरता और बच्चे में छाए उत्साह का चित्रण किया है।

व्याख्या कविता के इस अंश में बच्चा अपने बड़े भाई से कह रहा है कि मेरी गुल्लक हल्की अर्थात् उसमें कम पैसे हैं। इसलिए तुम अपनी गुल्लक खोलकर पैसे निकालो, क्योंकि उसमें अधिक पैसे हैं।

इन पैसों से बाज़ार से चमकीला, रंग-बिरंगा कागज़ और कैंची लेकर आओ। उन रंग-बिरंगे कागज़ को कैंची से काटकर सुंदर नाव बनाओ। यह काम जल्दी करो।

काव्यांश 3

छप-छप कर कूड़े से अड़ती,
बूँदों-लहरों लड़ती-बढ़ती,
सब की आँखों चढ़ती-गढ़ती
नाव तैरा मुझको हर्षाओ।
भैया मेरे, जल्दी आओ।।
क्या कहते? मेरे क्या बस का?
क्यों? तब फिर यह किसके बस का?
खोट सभी है बस आलस का,
आलस छोड़ो सब कर पाओ।
भैया मेरे, जल्दी आओ।।

शब्दार्थ *अड़ती-बाधा डालना, हर्षाओ-खुश कर दो, खोट-कमी, आलस-सुस्ती।*

प्रसंग प्रस्तुत काव्य पंक्तियों में कवि ने बारिश के मौसम में बच्चों के उत्साह और मस्ती को दर्शाया है। कवि ने उनकी मासूम भावनाओं को प्रस्तुत किया है।

व्याख्या कविता के इस अंश में बच्चा अपने भाई से नाव बनाने के लिए कहता है। वह कहता है कि नाव कूड़े से अड़ते हुए छप-छपकर चलती है। जब वह बूँदों और लहरों से लड़ते हुए आगे बढ़ती है तो अच्छा लगता है। वह आगे कहता है कि भैया नाव तैराकर आप मुझे खुश कर दो। इस पर बड़े भैया कहते हैं कि यह काम मेरे वश का नहीं है। तभी बच्चा पूछता है कि फिर यह काम किसके वश का है? बच्चा जानता है कि बड़े भैया आलस के कारण ऐसा कह रहे हैं। वह कहता है कि आलस छोड़ दो, तो तुम सब कुछ कर सकते हो। वह भैया से जल्दी आकर नाव बनाने के लिए कहता है।

NCERT फोल्डर

कविता से

क्या कहते? मेरे क्या बस का?

(क) भैया ने क्या बहाना किया? क्यों?

उत्तर भैया ने यह बहाना किया कि नाव बनाना उनके वश की बात नहीं है। उन्होंने ऐसा इसलिए कहा, क्योंकि आलस के कारण वे बाजार जाकर कागज और कैंची नहीं लाना चाहते थे

बूँदों-लहरों लड़ती-बढ़ती

(ख) कौन बूँदों और लहरों से लड़ते हुए आगे बढ़ रही है?

उत्तर नाव बूँदों और लहरों से लड़ते हुए आगे बढ़ रही है। यह नाव कठिनाइयों का सामना करती हुई पानी में तैर रही है और अपने लक्ष्य की ओर बढ़ रही है।

गुल्लक भारी, अपनी खोलो।

(ग) किसकी गुल्लक भारी है? किसकी गुल्लक हल्की है?

उत्तर भैया की गुल्लक भारी है और बच्चे की गुल्लक हल्की है।

नाव की कहानी

एक बार फिर से कविता पढ़ो। इस कविता में एक नाव के बनने और पानी में सफर करने की कहानी छिपी है। मान लो तुम ही वह नाव हो। अब अपनी कहानी सबको सुनाओ।

शुरुआत हम कर देते हैं।

मैं एक नाव हूँ। मैं कागज़ से बनी हूँ। मुझे एक लड़के ने बनाया। उसका नाम तो मुझे नहीं पता पर.....

उत्तर मैं एक नाव हूँ। मुझे एक लड़के ने अपने नन्हें हाथों से बनाया। उसने बड़े ध्यान से कागज काटकर मुझे बनाया और फिर विभिन्न रंगों से सजाया। बाहर बारिश हो रही थी और सड़कों पर पानी जमा हो गया था। उसने मुझे उस पानी में धीरे से रखा और मैं धीरे-धीरे तैरने लगी। पानी की हल्की-हल्की लहरें मुझे आगे बढ़ा रही थीं। लड़का मुझे बड़े प्यार से देख रहा था।

कभी-कभी पानी की तेज लहरें मुझे घेरने की कोशिश करतीं, लेकिन मैं हिम्मत नहीं हारती। मुझे पता था कि मेरा सफर लंबा हो सकता है। हर बार जब मैं आगे बढ़ती, उसके चेहरे पर खुशी की लहर दौड़ जाती। मुझे तैरते हुए देखकर उसकी आँखों की चमक और भी बढ़ जाती।

अहा! बारिश!!

- **तुमने बरसात पर पहले भी कभी कोई कविता या लोकगीत सुना होगा। उसे नीचे दी गई जगह में लिखो।**

उत्तर जब-जब पानी आता है,
पत्ते, फूल खिलाता है।
बरखा रानी आती है,
रिमझिम पानी लाती है।।
पानी आता झर-झर,
बादल गरजते गर-गर-गर।
बिजली रानी चमकती है,
लगता अच्छा नभ मंडल।।
कभी आता ज्यादा पानी,
कभी आता पानी कम।
कभी कहीं पर बाढ़ बोलती,
कभी बोलता सूखापन।।

- **इस कविता को पढ़ते समय तुम्हारे मन में कई चित्र आए होंगे। उनके बारे में बताओ या उनका चित्र बनाओ।**

उत्तर इस कविता को पढ़ते समय मन में कई सुंदर चित्र उभरते हैं। इन प्रमुख चित्रों में जो भाव प्रकट होते हैं, वे इस प्रकार हैं

कविता की शुरुआत में बादलों के घिरने और पानी के आने का उल्लेख हुआ है। घने काले बादल आसमान में छाए हुए हैं। ऐसा लगता है मानो बादल समुंदर से पानी भरकर लाए हों।

छोटा बच्चा अपने भाई से कागज और कैंची लाकर नाव बनाने के लिए कहता है। बच्चा रंग-बिरंगा चमकीला कागज और कैंची लेकर खुशी-खुशी नाव बनाकर पानी में तैरा रहा है। नाव बूँदों और लहरों से टकराते हुए जब आगे बढ़ती है तो बच्चा खुश होता है।

सचमुच

पानी सचमुच खूब पड़ेगा।

सचमुच का इस्तेमाल करते हुए तुम भी दो वाक्य बनाओ।

उत्तर (i) आज **सचमुच** मौसम बहुत सुहाना है।
(ii) वह कहानी **सचमुच** दिलचस्प थी।

सात समुंदर

घिर-घिर कर बादल छाया है,
सात समुंदर भर लाया है।

(क) पता करो, सात समुद्र कौन-कौन से होंगे? जिनसे बादल पानी भरकर लाया है।

उत्तर सात समुंदरों के नाम निम्नलिखित हैं, जिनसे बादल पानी भरकर लाया है

1. उत्तर अटलांटिक महासागर
2. दक्षिण अटलांटिक महासागर
3. उत्तर प्रशांत महासागर
4. दक्षिण प्रशांत महासागर
5. हिंद महासागर
6. आर्कटिक महासागर
7. दक्षिणी महासागर (अंटार्कटिक महासागर)

(ख) क्या सचमुच बारिश के बादल समुद्र से पानी लाते हैं? वे इतना सारा पानी कैसे लाते होंगे? आपस में बातचीत करके पता करो। (तुम इस काम में बड़ों की या किताबों की मदद भी ले सकती हो।)

उत्तर हाँ, बारिश के बादल समुद्र से पानी लाते हैं। सूरज की गर्मी से समुद्र का पानी वाष्प बनकर हवा में उड़ता है, जिसे वाष्पीकरण कहते हैं। ऊँचाई पर पहुँचकर यह भाप ठंडी होकर बादल बन जाती है, जिसे संघनन कहते हैं। बादल भारी होने पर वर्षा के रूप में धरती पर गिरते हैं। यह प्रक्रिया जल चक्र का हिस्सा है।

तरह-तरह की नावें

तुम कागज़ से कितनी तरह की नाव बना सकते हो? बनाकर कक्षा में दिखाओ। उनमें से किसी एक के बारे में लिखकर बताओ कि तुमने वह कैसे बनाई?

उत्तर कागज से कई तरह की नाव बनाई जा सकती हैं; जैसे— साधारण कागज़ की नाव, त्रिकोणीय नाव और पतवार वाली

नाव। मैंने साधारण नाव बनाई है। इसके लिए मैंने कागज़ को बीच से मोड़ा, फिर दोनों कोनों को मोड़कर त्रिकोण बनाया। नीचे के किनारों को ऊपर की ओर मोड़ा और फिर इसे खोलकर नाव का आकार दिया।

आई बरसात

(क) बरसात के दिनों में अकसर घरों के दरवाजे और खिड़कियों से पानी की बौछार आ जाती है। कभी-कभी छत से पानी टपकता है, सीलन भी आ जाती है। ऐसी स्थितियों से निपटने के लिए तुम्हारे घर में क्या-क्या किया जाता है?

उत्तर बरसात के दिनों में घर में पानी की बौछार और सीलन से बचने के लिए कई सावधानियाँ बरती जाती हैं। दरवाजों और खिड़कियों पर प्लास्टिक के पर्दे लगाए जाते हैं, ताकि बारिश का पानी अंदर न आए। छत से पानी टपकने पर उसे तुरंत ठीक कराने की कोशिश की जाती है। सीलन से बचने के लिए दीवारों पर वाटरप्रूफ पेंट का इस्तेमाल किया जाता है।

(ख) बारिश के मौसम में गलियों और सड़कों पर भी पानी भर जाता है। तुम्हारे मोहल्ले और घर के आस-पास बारिश आने पर क्या-क्या होता है? बताओ।

उत्तर बारिश के मौसम में हमारे मोहल्ले की गलियों में पानी भर जाता है। इससे सड़कें पानी में डूब जाती हैं। नालियाँ जाम होने से कीचड़ और गंदगी फैल जाती है। लोगों को चलने में परेशानी होती है। मच्छरों का खतरा बढ़ जाता है। नालियों की सफाई करके समस्या को हल करने की कोशिश की जाती है।

काम वाले शब्द

(क) पिछले साल रिमझिम में तुमने पढ़ा था कि बनाना काम वाला शब्द होता है। काम वाले शब्दों को क्रिया कहते हैं। इस कविता में ढेर सारी क्रियाएँ या काम वाले शब्द आए हैं। उन्हें छाँटो और नीचे लिखो।

उत्तर इस कविता में कई क्रियाएँ आई हैं; जैसे— बनाओ, आओ, छाया, लाया, लहराओ, टटोलो, लाओ, चलाओ, तैरा, हर्षाओ, कहते, कर, छोड़ो और पाओ। ये सभी शब्द कविता में विभिन्न क्रियाओं को दर्शाते हैं; जैसे— नाव बनाना, बादलों का छाना, पानी लाना, लहरों में तैरना और आलस्य को छोड़कर काम करना।

(ख) तुमने जो क्रियाएँ छाँटी हैं, वर्णमाला के हिसाब से उनके आगे 1,2,3 आदि लिखकर उन्हें क्रम से लगाओ।

उत्तर

1. आओ	2. कर
3. कहते	4. चलाओ
5. छाया	6. छोड़ो
7. टटोलो	8. तैरा
9. पाओ	10. बनाओ
11. लाओ	12. लाया
13. लहराओ	14. हर्षाओ

अभ्यास प्रश्न

बहुविकल्पीय प्रश्न

1. कविता में बच्चा किस रंग के कागज़ की माँग करता है?

(क) सफेद (ख) लाल
(ग) काला (घ) भूरा

2. कविता में बच्चा किससे नाराज है?

(क) बारिश से (ख) बादल से
(ग) बड़े भाई के आलस से (घ) पानी से

3. बच्चा नाव के लिए कौन-कौन सी चीज़ें लाने के लिए कहता है?

(क) रंगीन कागज़ और कैंची (ख) कलम और स्केचबुक
(ग) चॉक और पेंसिल (घ) किताबें और नोट्स

4. कविता में पानी कहाँ से आया है?

(क) बादल से (ख) नदियों से
(ग) सात समुंदर से (घ) कुएँ से

5. कविता में बच्चा किस काम को त्यागने की सलाह देता है?

(क) मेहनत को (ख) आलस को
(ग) पढ़ाई को (घ) खेल को

उत्तर

1. (ख) लाल
2. (ग) बड़े भाई के आलस से
3. (क) रंगीन कागज़ और कैंची
4. (ग) सात समुंदर से
5. (ख) आलस को

सत्य-असत्य

नीचे दिए गए वाक्यों में से सत्य या असत्य कथन की पहचान कीजिए।

1. कविता में बच्चा अपने भाई से गाड़ी लाने के लिए कहता है। (सत्य/असत्य)
2. बच्चा अपने भाई से पैसे लाने की माँग करता है। (सत्य/असत्य)
3. कविता में बच्चा रंग-बिरंगे कागज़ की नाव बनाना चाहता है। (सत्य/असत्य)
4. कविता में आलस्य को त्यागने की सलाह दी गई है। (सत्य/असत्य)
5. कविता में बच्चे को कागज़ के अतिरिक्त और किसी चीज़ की ज़रूरत नहीं है। (सत्य/असत्य)

उत्तर

1. असत्य 2. सत्य 3. सत्य
4. सत्य 5. असत्य

रिक्त स्थान

नीचे दिए गए वाक्यों में रिक्त स्थान की पूर्ति उचित शब्द से कीजिए।

(आओ, लड़ती-बढ़ती, अड़ती, हर्षाओ, चढ़ती-गढ़ती)

1. छप-छप कर कूड़े से ……………….,
2. बूँदों-लहरों ……………….,
3. सब की आँखों ……………….
4. नाव तैरा मुझको ……………….।
5. भैया मेरे, जल्दी ……………….।।

उत्तर

1. अड़ती 2. लड़ती-बढ़ती
3. चढ़ती-गढ़ती 4. हर्षाओ
5. आओ

काव्यांश पर आधारित प्रश्न

निम्नलिखित काव्यांश को पढ़कर उस पर आधारित प्रश्नों के उत्तर दीजिए

काव्यांश

नाव बनाओ, नाव बनाओ।
भैया मेरे, जल्दी आओ।।
वह देखो, पानी आया है,
घिर-घिर कर बादल छाया है,
सात समुंदर भर लाया है,
तुम रस का सागर भर लाओ।
भैया मेरे, जल्दी आओ।।

1. बच्चा अपने भाई से क्या भरकर लाने की बात कहता है?
   (क) रस का सागर (ख) दूध का गिलास
   (ग) बादलों का जाल (घ) तालाब का पानी
2. किसके घिरने की बात कही गई है?
   (क) पहाड़ों के (ख) बादलों के
   (ग) जंगलों के (घ) समुंदर के
3. कविता में बच्चा किसको जल्दी आने के लिए कह रहा है?

उत्तर

1. (क) रस का सागर
2. (ख) बादलों के
3. कविता में बच्चा अपने बड़े भाई को जल्दी आने के लिए कह रहा है।

निम्नलिखित प्रश्नों के उत्तर दीजिए

1. कविता में बच्चे ने अपने भाई से क्या अनुरोध किया है?

उत्तर कविता में बच्चा अपने बड़े भाई से अनुरोध कर रहा है कि वह अपनी गुल्लक लाएँ, क्योंकि उसकी गुल्लक में ज्यादा पैसे हैं बच्चे की गुल्लक में कम।

2. बच्चा अपने भाई से कौन-सी सामग्री लाने के लिए कहता है?

उत्तर बच्चा अपने बड़े भाई से बाजार से रंग-बिरंगे कागज और कैंची लाने का अनुरोध कर रहा है।

3. कविता में बच्चा अपने भाई से किस तरह की नाव बनाने को कहता है?

उत्तर कविता में बच्चा अपने भाई से ऐसी नाव बनाने को कहता है, जो छप-छप करके कूड़े से टकराकर बारिश की बूँदों और पानी की लहरों से लड़ती हुई बिना रुके आगे बढ़ती जाए।

4. बच्चा नाव के बारे में क्या कहता है?

उत्तर बच्चा नाव के बारे में कहता है कि जब वह बूँदों और लहरों से लड़ती हुई आगे बढ़ती है, तो अच्छा लगता है।

5. कविता के आधार पर बताइए कि बारिश के मौसम में बच्चा किन गतिविधियों में शामिल होना चाहता है?

उत्तर बारिश के मौसम में बच्चा रंग-बिरंगे कागज की नाव बनाकर उसे बारिश के पानी में चलाना चाहता है।

अध्याय 7

दान का हिसाब

पाठ का सार

बहुत समय पहले की बात है। एक राजा था, वह अपने कपड़ों और सुख-सुविधाओं पर बहुत पैसा खर्च करता था, लेकिन दान या किसी अन्य सहायता के नाम पर वह एक रुपया भी नहीं देता था। प्रजा भी उससे बहुत दु:खी रहती थी। एक बार उस राजा के राज्य में अकाल पड़ गया। इस परेशानी के समय पूर्वी सीमा के लोग राजा के पास सहायता के लिए पहुँचे, लेकिन राजा ने उन लोगों की सहायता करने से मना कर दिया और उनसे कहा कि यह भगवान की मार है, इसमें मैं कुछ भी नहीं कर सकता हूँ। राजा की इन बातों से लोग निराश हो गए और खाली हाथ लौट गए। कुछ समय पश्चात् वे फिर राजा के पास गए और उन्होंने राजा से दस हजार रुपये की माँग की, लेकिन राजा यह छोटी-सी राशि भी देने के लिए तैयार नहीं था। लोग फिर से निराश होकर अपने घरों को लौट गए।

इस घटना के दो दिन बाद राजसभा में एक संन्यासी आया। उस संन्यासी ने राजा से अपनी एक इच्छा पूरी करने के लिए कहा। राजा के पूछने पर संन्यासी ने बताया कि मैं राजकोष से लगातार बीस दिनों तक मामूली भिक्षा लेना चाहता हूँ। भिक्षा लेने का नियम भी उसने बताया कि पहले दिन जितना लूँगा, दूसरे दिन उसका दोगुना, तीसरे दिन दूसरे दिन का दोगुना, चौथे दिन तीसरे दिन का दोगुना... इसी तरह प्रतिदिन राशि दोगुनी होती जाएगी। राजा के आदेशानुसार संन्यासी को राजकोष से भिक्षा दी जाने लगी। पहले दिन की भिक्षा के रूप में उसने एक रुपया माँगा। दो सप्ताह तक भिक्षा देने के बाद राज भंडारी ने हिसाब किया तो राजकोष से निकले हुए धन को देखकर वह हैरान और परेशान हो उठा। मंत्री भी राजकोष की स्थिति देखकर हैरान रह गया। उसने भंडारी को आदेश दिया कि बीस दिनों तक दी जाने वाली राशि का हिसाब करो। भंडारी ने हिसाब करके बताया कि यह राशि दस लाख अड़तालीस हजार पाँच सौ पचहत्तर रुपये होगी। इतनी बड़ी राशि सुनकर मंत्री घबरा गया और उसने बड़ी हिम्मत करके यह बात राजा को बताई।

संन्यासी जैसे ही दरबार में घुसा, तो राजा ने रोते हुए कहा कि आपके कहे अनुसार मैं भिक्षा देता रहा तो बीस दिन में मेरा पूरा राजकोष खाली हो जाएगा। राजा पर दया दिखाते हुए संन्यासी ने कहा कि अकाल पीड़ितों की सहायता के लिए मुझे केवल पचास हजार रुपये चाहिए। राजा व मंत्रियों ने संन्यासी से यह राशि कम करने के लिए कहा, लेकिन संन्यासी अपनी बात पर अड़ा रहा। अंतत: विवश होकर राजा ने संन्यासी को पचास हजार रुपये देने को कहा। राजा की इस दानवीरता से लोग बहुत खुश हुए और वह राजा की तुलना दानी कर्ण से करने लगे।

शब्दार्थ

लकदक-चमकदार वस्त्र, मुट्ठी बंद होना-कंजूस होना, सज्जन-भला व्यक्ति, अकाल-भुखमरी, दुहाई-गुहार लगाना, राजभंडार-राजा का खजाना, दिवालिया-आर्थिक रूप से बर्बाद, प्रकोप-भारी विपत्ति, उलझन-परेशानी, गिड़गिड़ाना-अनुरोध करना।

NCERT फोल्डर

कहानी से

(क) राजा किसी को भी दान क्यों नहीं देना चाहता था?

उत्तर राजा किसी को भी दान इसलिए नहीं देना चाहता था, क्योंकि वह कंजूस था। उसे लगता था कि यदि वह दान देता रहेगा तो एक दिन उसका खजाना खाली हो जाएगा।

(ख) राजदरबार के लोग मन-ही-मन राजा को बुरा कहते थे, लेकिन वे राजा का विरोध क्यों नहीं कर पाते थे?

उत्तर राजा के क्रोध के डर से लोग राजा का विरोध नहीं कर पाते थे। उन्हें डर लगता था कि क्रोधित होने पर राजा उन्हें दंडित करेगा।

(ग) राजसभा में सज्जन और विद्वान लोग क्यों नहीं जाते थे?

उत्तर राजसभा में सज्जन और विद्वान लोग इसलिए नहीं जाते थे, क्योंकि राजा केवल धनी और प्रतिष्ठित व्यक्तियों का ही स्वागत करता था। विद्वान और सज्जन लोगों का वहाँ कोई मान-सम्मान नहीं था।

(घ) संन्यासी ने सीधे-सीधे शब्दों में भिक्षा क्यों नहीं माँग ली?

उत्तर संन्यासी ने सीधे-सीधे भिक्षा इसलिए नहीं माँगी, क्योंकि वह राजा की कंजूसी को जानता था। वह यह भी जानता था कि उसे जितनी राशि चाहिए, राजा उतनी राशि उसे नहीं देगा।

(ङ) राजा को संन्यासी के आगे गिड़गिड़ाने की जरूरत क्यों पड़ी?

उत्तर राजा को संन्यासी के आगे गिड़गिड़ाने की जरूरत इसलिए पड़ी, क्योंकि संन्यासी के भिक्षा लेने के तरीके से उसे एहसास हुआ कि यदि भिक्षा का क्रम चलता रहा, तो राजकोष पूरी तरह से खाली हो जाएगा। अपनी संपत्ति और राज्य को बचाने के लिए राजा को संन्यासी के आगे गिड़गिड़ाना पड़ा।

अंदाज अपना-अपना

तुम नीचे दिए गए वाक्यों को किस तरह से कहोगे?

(क) दान के वक्त उनकी मुट्ठी बंद हो जाती थी।

उत्तर दान के नाम पर उससे एक पैसे नहीं निकलते।

(ख) हिसाब देखकर मंत्री का चेहरा फीका पड़ गया।

उत्तर हिसाब देखकर मंत्री के चेहरे की हवा उड़ गई।

(ग) संन्यासी की बात सुनकर सभी की जान में जान आई।

उत्तर संन्यासी की बात से सबको तसल्ली हुई।

(घ) लाखों रुपये राजकोष में मौजूद हैं। जैसे धन का सागर हो।

उत्तर राजकोष में बहुत पैसे हैं। राजकोष में पैसों की कमी नहीं है।

साथी हाथ बढ़ाना

कभी-कभी कुछ इलाकों में बारिश बिल्कुल भी नहीं होती। नदी-नाले, तालाब सब सूख जाते हैं। फसलों के लिए पानी नहीं मिलता। खेत सूख जाते हैं। पशु-पक्षी, जानवर एवं लोग भूखे मरने लगते हैं। ऐसे समय में वहाँ रहने वाले लोगों को मदद की ज़रूरत होती है। तुम भी लोगों की मदद ज़रूर कर सकते हो। सोचकर बताओ तुम अकाल में परेशान लोगों की मदद कैसे करोगे?

उत्तर मैं अकाल के समय धन, कपड़ा, भोजन, दवा आदि सामग्री को अकाल पीड़ितों तक पहुँचाकर उनकी मदद करूँगा।

जिम्मेदारी अपनी-अपनी

तुम्हारे विचार से राजदरबार में किसकी क्या-क्या जिम्मेदारियाँ होंगी?

(क) मंत्री (ख) भंडारी

उत्तर

(क) मंत्री का मुख्य कार्य राजा को राज्य के महत्त्वपूर्ण मामलों में सलाह देना होता है। वह नीतियों का निर्धारण करता है, प्रशासन की देखरेख करता है और राजकोष तथा राज्य के अन्य अधिकारियों के कार्यों की निगरानी करता है।

(ख) भंडारी का काम राजकोष की देखभाल करना होता है। वह खजाने का हिसाब-किताब रखता है, धन का संग्रहण और वितरण करता है। वह सुनिश्चित करता है कि राजकोष से धन का सही तरीके से उपयोग हो।

कर्ण जैसा दानी

सभी ने कहा, "हमारे महाराज कर्ण जैसे ही दानी हैं।" पता करो कि

(क) कर्ण कौन थे?

उत्तर कर्ण महाभारत के प्रसिद्ध योद्धा थे। वे अपनी उदारता और दानवीरता के लिए प्रसिद्ध थे। वे अपने शत्रुओं को भी बिना संकोच के दान देते थे। भले ही उसकी कीमत उनकी जान ही क्यों न हो।

(ख) 'कर्ण जैसे दानी' का क्या मतलब है?

उत्तर 'कर्ण जैसे दानी' का मतलब है कि सर्वस्व दान कर देने में भी कोई संकोच न हो। कर्ण की तरह दान देने वाला व्यक्ति अपनी संपत्ति या सामर्थ्य का बड़ा हिस्सा दूसरों की भलाई के लिए खुशी-खुशी समर्पित करता है।

(ग) दान क्या होता है?

उत्तर लोगों की सहायता के लिए दिया गया धन 'दान' कहलाता है।

(घ) **किन-किन कारणों से लोग दान करते हैं?**

उत्तर लोग धर्म, परोपकार, सामाजिक जिम्मेदारी, सहायता करने की भावना, पुण्य कमाने और आत्मिक शांति के लिए दान करते हैं।

कहानी और तुम

(क) **राजा राजकोष के धन का उपयोग किन-किन कामों में करता था?**

- **तुम्हारे घर में जो पैसा आता है वह कहाँ-कहाँ खर्च होता है? पता करके लिखो।**

उत्तर राजा राजकोष का धन अपने व्यक्तिगत ऐशो-आराम, सुगंधित वस्त्रों, मनोरंजन, महल की सजावट और पहरेदारों की खुराक आदि पर खर्च करता था।

मेरे घर में पैसा भोजन, कपड़े, शिक्षा, बिजली-पानी के बिल, घर की मरम्मत, दवाइयों और यात्रा आदि पर खर्च होता है। त्योहारों और विशेष अवसरों पर भी पैसा खर्च किया जाता है।

(ख) **अकाल के समय लोग राजा से कौन-कौन से काम करवाना चाहते थे?**

- **तुम अपने स्कूल या इलाके में क्या-क्या काम करवाना चाहते हो?**

उत्तर अकाल के समय लोग चाहते थे कि राजा दस हज़ार रुपये देकर उनकी जान बचाए और राहत प्रदान करे।

मैं अपने स्कूल में बेहतर खेल के मैदान और साफ-सफाई की सुविधा चाहता हूँ। अपने इलाके में सड़कों की मरम्मत, अधिक पौधारोपण और पानी की समुचित व्यवस्था चाहता हूँ, जिससे लोगों को साफ पानी मिल सके।

कैसा राजा!

(क) **राजा किसी को दान देना पसंद नहीं करता था। तुम्हारे विचार से राजा सही था या गलत? अपने उत्तर का कारण भी बताओ।**

उत्तर मेरे विचार से राजा गलत था, क्योकि एक राजा का कर्त्तव्य होता है कि वह अपनी प्रजा की सुरक्षा और कल्याण के लिए कार्य करे। अकाल के समय लोगों की मदद करना राजा की जिम्मेदारी थी। राजकोष में भंडार होते हुए भी वह जरूरतमंदों की सहायता नहीं कर रहा था। यह उसके स्वार्थ को दर्शाता है।

(ख) **राजा दान देने के अलावा और किन-किन तरीकों से लोगों की सहायता कर सकता था?**

उत्तर राजा दान देने के अलावा अकाल प्रभावित क्षेत्रों में पानी और अनाज की व्यवस्था कर सकता था। वह राहत शिविर स्थापित कर सकता था, जहाँ लोगों को भोजन, पानी और चिकित्सा सुविधाएँ मिलतीं।

पूर्व और पूर्व

पूर्वी सीमा के लोग भूखे प्यासे मरने लगे।

(क) 'पूर्व' शब्द के दो अर्थ हैं

पूर्व-एक दिशा

पूर्व-पहले।

नीचे ऐसे ही कुछ और शब्द दिए गए हैं, जिनके दो-दो अर्थ हैं। इनका प्रयोग करते हुए दो-दो वाक्य बनाओ।

- **जल** • **मन** • **मगर**

उत्तर
- **जल** (पानी)—सुबह उठकर ताजे **जल** का सेवन करना स्वास्थ्य के लिए अच्छा होता है।
  जल (जलना)—दूध **जल** गया है।
- **मन** (दिल)—उसके साथ समय बिताने से मेरा **मन** खुश हो जाता है।
  मन (भार मापने की इकाई)—बोरे में तीन **मन** गेहूँ है।
- **मगर** (मगरमच्छ)—नदी में एक बड़ा **मगर** रहता है।
  मगर (किंतु)—मैंने समय पर काम शुरू किया, **मगर** उसे पूरा नहीं कर सका।

(ख) नीचे चार दिशाओं के नाम लिखे हैं। तुम्हारे घर और स्कूल के आसपास इन दिशाओं में क्या-क्या है? तालिका भरो

दिशा	घर के पास	स्कूल के पास
पूर्व		
पश्चिम		
उत्तर		
दक्षिण		

उत्तर

दिशा	घर के पास	स्कूल के पास
पूर्व	पार्क और कुछ दुकानें हैं।	पुस्तकालय है।
पश्चिम	एक मंदिर है।	खेल का मैदान है।
उत्तर	कुछ आवासीय भवन हैं।	एक जिम है।
दक्षिण	नदी है।	एक अस्पताल है।

अभ्यास प्रश्न

बहुविकल्पीय प्रश्न

1. संन्यासी ने राजा से भिक्षा के रूप में कितनी राशि की माँग की थी?

(क) बीस हजार रुपये (ख) पचास हजार रुपये
(ग) एक लाख रुपये (घ) दस लाख रुपये

2. राजा ने संन्यासी को कितने दिन तक दान देने का आदेश दिया था?

(क) दस दिन तक (ख) बीस दिन तक
(ग) पचास दिन तक (घ) तीस दिन तक

3. इस कहानी के लेखक का नाम क्या है?

(क) सुकुमार राय (ख) ऋत्विक राय
(ग) प्रेमचंद (घ) सत्यजीत रे

4. प्रजा ने राजा की तुलना किस दानवीर से की?

(क) दुर्योधन से (ख) कर्ण से
(ग) कंस से (घ) युधिष्ठिर से

5. भंडारी का क्या काम था?

(क) प्रजा की रक्षा करना (ख) राजकोष की रक्षा करना
(ग) राजमहल की रक्षा करना (घ) राजा की रक्षा करना

उत्तर

1. (ख) पचास हजार रुपये 2. (ख) बीस दिन तक
3. (क) सुकुमार राय 4. (ख) कर्ण से
5. (ख) राजकोष की रक्षा करना

गद्यांश पर आधारित प्रश्न

निम्नलिखित गद्यांश को पढ़कर उस पर आधारित प्रश्नों के उत्तर दीजिए

गद्यांश

एक बार उस देश में अकाल पड़ गया। पूर्वी सीमा के लोग भूखे-प्यासे मरने लगे। राजा के पास खबर आई। वे बोले, "यह तो भगवान की मार है, इसमें मेरा कोई हाथ नहीं है।"

लोगों ने कहा, "महाराज, राजभंडार से हमारी सहायता करने की कृपा करें, जिससे हम लोग दूसरे देशों से अनाज खरीदकर अपनी जान बचा सकें।" राजा ने कहा, "आज तुम लोग अकाल से पीड़ित हो, कल पता चलेगा, कहीं भूकंप आया है। परसों सुनूँगा, कहीं के लोग बड़े गरीब हैं, दो वक्त की रोटी नहीं जुटती। इस तरह सभी की सहायता करते-करते जब राजभंडार खत्म हो जाएगा, तब खुद मैं ही दिवालिया हो जाऊँगा।" यह सुनकर सभी निराश होकर लौट गए।

1. राजा ने अकाल के समय गरीबों की सहायता करने से क्यों इंकार किया?

(क) राजकोष में पैसे कम थे।
(ख) उन्होंने कहा कि सभी की सहायता करते-करते राजभंडार खत्म हो जाएगा।
(ग) उन्हें गरीबों की समस्याओं से कोई फर्क नहीं पड़ता था।
(घ) उन्होंने महल की सजावट पर अधिक ध्यान दिया।

2. जब लोगों ने अकाल के समय सहायता माँगी तो राजा की राय क्या थी?

(क) उन्होंने तुरंत सहायता देने का वादा किया।
(ख) उन्होंने कहा कि उन्हें दान देने में कोई हिचक नहीं है।
(ग) उन्होंने सहायता देने से मना कर दिया।
(घ) उन्होंने कहा कि राजकोष का पूरा धन गरीबों पर खर्च करेंगे।

3. जब लोगों ने कहा कि राजकोष में लाखों रुपये हैं, तब राजा ने गरीबों को क्या प्रतिक्रिया दी?

4. राजा के अनुसार, यदि राजकोष खत्म हो जाता है, तो क्या होगा?

उत्तर

1. (ख) उन्होंने कहा कि सभी की सहायता करते-करते राज भंडार खत्म हो जाएगा।
2. (ग) उन्होंने सहायता देने से मना कर दिया।
3. राजा ने कहा कि राजकोष में अधिक धन है, लेकिन वह उसे दोनों हाथों से लुटा नहीं सकते।
4. राजा के अनुसार, यदि राजकोष खत्म हो जाएगा, तो वह खुद दिवालिया हो जाएँगे।

निम्नलिखित प्रश्नों के उत्तर दीजिए

1. संन्यासी ने पहले दिन कितने रुपये की भिक्षा माँगी?

उत्तर संन्यासी ने पहले दिन की भिक्षा के रूप में एक रुपया माँगा।

2. बीस दिन की कुल भिक्षा कितनी हुई थी?

उत्तर बीस दिन की कुल भिक्षा दस लाख अड़तालीस हजार पाँच सौ पचहत्तर हुई थी।

3. मंत्री ने राजा को किस प्रकार की सूचना दी?

उत्तर मंत्री ने राजा को सूचना दी कि इस तरह दान देने से तो संपूर्ण राजकोष खाली हो जाएगा।

4. अंततः संन्यासी ने कितने रुपये की माँग की?

उत्तर अंततः संन्यासी ने पचास हजार रुपये की माँग की।

अध्याय 4

कौन?

कविता का सार

प्रस्तुत कविता में कवि 'सोहनलाल द्विवेदी' जी ने एक शरारती चूहे की हरकतों का वर्णन किया है, जो घर के विभिन्न सामानों को कुतरता और नुकसान पहुँचाता रहता है। कवि बच्चों से पूछता है कि ऐसा कौन-सा जीव है, जो शरारत करता है। वह कौन जीव है, जो रातभर इधर-उधर दौड़कर आवाजें करता है और सोने नहीं देता है। कवि उस जीव का नाम नहीं बताता है, बच्चों से ही उसका नाम पूछता है।

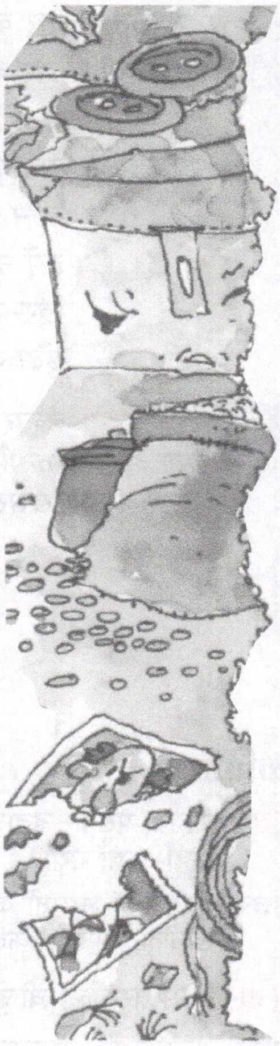

काव्यांशों की व्याख्या

काव्यांश 1

किसने बटन हमारे कुतरे?
किसने स्याही को बिखराया?
कौन चट कर गया दुबक कर
घर-भर में अनाज बिखराया?

दोना खाली रखा रह गया
कौन ले गया उठा मिठाई
दो टुकड़े तस्वीर हो गई
किसने रस्सी काट बहाई?

शब्दार्थ *कुतरे- काटकर छोटे-छोटे टुकड़े करना, स्याही - लिखने के लिए इस्तेमाल होने वाला रंग, चट कर गया-चोरी-छिपे खा जाना, दुबक कर-छिपकर, दोना-पत्तों से बना एक छोटा पात्र।*

संदर्भ एवं प्रसंग प्रस्तुत पंक्तियाँ हमारी पाठ्यपुस्तक 'रिमझिम भाग-4' में संकलित कविता 'कौन?' से ली गई हैं। इसके कवि सोहनलाल द्विवेदी हैं। काव्यांश में एक शरारती चूहे द्वारा घर के सामानों को नुकसान पहुँचाने की घटनाओं का वर्णन किया गया है।

व्याख्या कवि बच्चों से पूछता है कि वह कौन-सा जीव है, जिसने हमारे बटन को कुतर दिया है, स्याही को बिखरा दिया है? छिपकर अनाज खा जाता है और पूरे घर में अनाज को बिखेर देता है। वह कौन है, जिसने मिठाई खा ली है और दोना खाली छोड़ दिया है? किसने रस्सी को काट दिया है, जिससे तस्वीर के गिरकर दो टुकड़े हो गए।

काव्यांश 2

कभी कुतर जाता है चप्पल
कभी कुतर जूता है जाता,
कभी खलीता पर बन आती
अनजाने पैसा गिर जाता

किसने जिल्द काट डाली है?
बिखर गए पोथी के पन्ने।
रोज़ टाँगता धो-धोकर मैं
कौन उठा ले जाता छन्ने?

शब्दार्थ *खलीता*–छोटा बटुआ, *जिल्द*–*पुस्तक का कवर*, *पोथी*–पुस्तक।

प्रसंग पूर्ववत्।

व्याख्या कवि कहता है कि वह कभी जूते-चप्पल को कुतर देता है, तो कभी पैसों की थैली को कुतर देता है, जिससे पैसे गिर जाते हैं। वह कौन है, जिसने किताबों की जिल्द काट दी है, जिससे उसके पन्ने बिखर गए हैं। कौन छन्ने उठाकर ले जाता है, जिसे मैं रोज धोकर टाँगता हूँ।

काव्यांश 3

कुतर-कुतर कर कागज़ सारे
रद्दी से घर को भर जाता।
कौन कबाड़ी है जो कूड़ा
दुनिया भर का घर भर जाता?
कौन रात भर गड़बड़ करता?
हमें नहीं देता है सोने,
खुर-खुर करता इधर-उधर है
ढूँढा करता छिप-छिप कोने?

शब्दार्थ *रद्दी*–बेकार कागज़, *कबाड़ी*–वह व्यक्ति, जो कबाड़ खरीदता और बेचता है, *गड़बड़*–अव्यवस्था, *खुर-खुर*–चूहे द्वारा होने वाली हल्की खसखस की आवाज़, *छिप-छिप*–चुपके से।

प्रसंग पूर्ववत्।

व्याख्या कवि कहता है कि वह जीव कागज को कुतरकर रद्दी से सारे घर को भर देता है। वह कौन कबाड़ी है, जो पूरी दुनिया का कबाड़ मेरे घर में भर जाता है? पूरी रात कौन गड़बड़ी करता है और हमें सोने नहीं देता है? कौन पूरी रात खुर-खुर करके खाने की चीजें ढूँढता रहता है और फिर कोने में छिप जाता है।

काव्यांश 4

रोज़ रात-भर जगता रहता
खुर-खुर इधर-उधर है धाता
बच्चों उसका नाम बताओ
कौन शरारत यह कर जाता?

शब्दार्थ *जगता*–जागना, *धाता*–दौड़ना, *शरारत*–शैतानी।

प्रसंग पूर्ववत्।

व्याख्या कवि कहता है कि वह शरारती जीव रातभर जागता है और खुर-खुर की आवाज़ करके इधर-उधर दौड़ता है। कवि बच्चों से पूछता है कि उस जीव का नाम बताओ जो यह शरारत करता है?

NCERT फोल्डर

कविता से

(क) कविता पढ़कर बताओ कि यह शरारती जीव घर में कहाँ-कहाँ गया?

उत्तर कविता में शरारती जीव घर में चप्पल-जूते रखने के स्थान, खलीता, मिठाई, किताबें, कागज़ और छन्नी आदि पर गया है।

(ख) किस तरह की चीज़ों का सबसे ज्यादा नुकसान हुआ?

उत्तर सबसे ज्यादा नुकसान जूते-चप्पल, किताब-कागज़ और घरेलू सामान का हुआ है।

(ग) कविता में बहुत-से नुकसान गिनाए गए हैं। तुम्हारे हिसाब से इनमें से कौन-सा नुकसान सबसे बड़ा है? क्यों?

उत्तर सबसे बड़ा नुकसान किताबों का है, क्योंकि इनके नुकसान से शिक्षा और जानकारी की उपलब्धता प्रभावित होती है।

(घ) इस कविता में किसकी शैतानियों की बात कही गई है? तुमने कैसे अनुमान लगाया?

उत्तर कविता में चूहे की शैतानियों की बात की गई है। इसका अनुमान उसकी शरारतों और रातभर की जाने वाली इधर-उधर की भागदौड़ से लगाया जा सकता है।

कभी कुतर जाता है चप्पल

शरारती जीव ने बहुत सारी चीजों को कुतरा, बिखराया और काटा। अब तुम बताओ कि किन-किन चीज़ों को

कुतरा जा सकता है	बिखराया जा सकता है	काटा जा सकता है

उत्तर

कुतरा जा सकता है	बिखराया जा सकता है	काटा जा सकता है
रोटी	कागज	फल
बिस्किट	रेत	कपड़ा
पेंसिल	खिलौने	सब्जी
ब्रेड	चावल	पेड़

कबाड़ का हिसाब

(क) कबाड़ी क्या-क्या सामान खरीदते हैं?

उत्तर कबाड़ी पुराने कागज़, बर्तन, लकड़ी, प्लास्टिक और अन्य बेकार सामान खरीदते हैं।

(ख) तुम्हारे घर से सामान ले जाकर कबाड़ी उसका क्या करते हैं?

उत्तर कबाड़ी घर से सामान ले जाकर उसे फिर से बेचते हैं और फिर वह सामान फैक्ट्रियों में जाता है, जहाँ इन्हें गलाकर नई वस्तुएँ बनाई जाती हैं।

(ग) पता करो कि पुराना अखबार या रद्दी किस भाव से बिकते हैं?

उत्तर पुराना अखबार या रद्दी आमतौर पर किलोग्राम के हिसाब से बिकते हैं। मूल्य स्थानीय बाजार और सामग्री की स्थिति पर निर्भर करता है।

(घ) अगर कबाड़ी तुम्हारे घर का कबाड़ न खरीदे तो क्या होगा?

उत्तर अगर कबाड़ी हमारे घर का कबाड़ न खरीदे, तो बेकार सामान जमा होता रहेगा और घर में गंदगी फैल जाएगी।

घुसपैठ

(क) तुम्हारे घर में भी यदि यह शरारती जीव है या उसकी फौज घुस गई है, तो पता करो कि उससे कैसे निपटा जाता है?

उत्तर अगर घर में शरारती जीव चूहे हैं, तो उन्हें पकड़ने के लिए चूहे पकड़ने वाले पिंजरे या जाली का उपयोग किया जाता है।

(ख) इस शरारती जीव के अलावा और कौन-कौन से जीव तुम्हारे घर में घुस जाते हैं?

उत्तर इस शरारती जीव के अलावा घर में सामान्यतः मक्खियाँ, कीट, बिल्ली और चींटियाँ आदि घुस जाती हैं।

बूझो

नीचे लिखी कविता की पंक्तियाँ पढ़ो। जिन शब्दों के नीचे रेखा खिंची है, उनका अर्थ आपस में चर्चा करके बताओ।

(क) कभी <u>खलीता</u> पर बन आती अनजाने पैसा गिर जाता।

उत्तर छोटा बटुआ

(ख) रोज टाँगता धो-धोकर मैं कौन उठा ले जाता <u>छन्ने</u>।

उत्तर छानने का उपकरण

(ग) रोज रात-भर जगता रहता खुर-खुर इधर-उधर है <u>धाता</u>।

उत्तर दौड़ता

अभ्यास प्रश्न

बहुविकल्पीय प्रश्न

1. बटन किसने कुतर दिए?

(क) चूहे ने (ख) बिल्ली ने
(ग) कुत्ते ने (घ) तोते ने

2. खलीता का अर्थ है

(क) कबूतर (ख) थैली (ग) बंदर (घ) किताब

3. खुर-खुर करने से किसको नींद नहीं आती है?

(क) साँप को (ख) कवि को
(ग) बच्चों को (घ) पक्षी को

4. किसके पन्ने बिखर गए थे?

(क) पुस्तक के (ख) अखबार के
(ग) स्कूल के (घ) शिक्षक के

5. शरारती जीव का नाम कौन पूछ रहा है?

(क) शिक्षक (ख) कवि (ग) नेता (घ) प्राचार्य

उत्तर

1. (क) चूहे ने 2. (ख) थैली
3. (ख) कवि को 4. (क) पुस्तक के
5. (ख) कवि

सत्य–असत्य

नीचे दिए गए वाक्यों में से सत्य या असत्य कथन की पहचान कीजिए।

1. चूहा अनाज बिखराता है। (सत्य/असत्य)
2. कविता में चूहे ने मिठाई नहीं उठाई। (सत्य/असत्य)
3. चूहा रोज़ रात भर शरारत करता है। (सत्य/असत्य)
4. कविता में चूहे ने पोथी के पन्ने बिखराए। (सत्य/असत्य)

उत्तर 1. सत्य 2. असत्य 3. सत्य 4. सत्य

रिक्त स्थान

नीचे दिए गए वाक्यों में रिक्त स्थान की पूर्ति उचित शब्द से कीजिए।

(अनाज, दुबक, बटन, स्याही, दोना)

1. किसने ········ हमारे कुतरे?
2. किसने ······ को बिखराया?
3. कौन चट कर गया ······· कर?
4. घर-भर में ········ बिखराया?

उत्तर 1. बटन 2. स्याही 3. दुबक 4. अनाज

काव्यांश पर आधारित प्रश्न

निम्नलिखित काव्यांश को पढ़कर उस पर आधारित प्रश्नों के उत्तर दीजिए।

काव्यांश

किसने बटन हमारे कुतरे?
किसने स्याही को बिखराया?
कौन चट कर गया दुबक कर
घर-भर में अनाज बिखराया?

दोना खाली रखा रह गया
कौन ले गया उठा मिठाई
दो टुकड़े तस्वीर हो गई
किसने रस्सी काट बहाई?

1. शरारती जीव का नाम कौन पूछ रहा है?
   (क) कवि (ख) रहीम (ग) बच्चे (घ) शिक्षक
2. चूहे ने क्या काट दिया था?
   (क) कपड़ा (ख) रस्सी (ग) पेड़ (घ) टेबल
3. चूहे ने क्या बिखेर दी थी?
4. मिठाई ले जाने के बाद क्या खाली रह गया था?

उत्तर

1. (क) कवि 2. (ख) रस्सी
3. चूहे ने स्याही बिखेर दी थी।
4. मिठाई ले जाने के बाद दोना खाली रह गया था।

निम्नलिखित प्रश्नों के उत्तर दीजिए

1. प्रस्तुत कविता के कवि का क्या नाम है?

उत्तर प्रस्तुत कविता के कवि का नाम सोहनलाल द्विवेदी है।

2. जूते को कौन कुतर देता है?

उत्तर जूते को चूहा कुतर देता है।

3. तस्वीर के कितने टुकड़े हो गए थे?

उत्तर तस्वीर के दो टुकड़े हो गए थे।

4. खलीते में क्या रखा जाता है?

उत्तर खलीते में पैसे रखे जाते हैं।

व्याकरण संबंधी प्रश्न

1. दिए गए मुहावरों का अर्थ बताइए
   - डूबे हुए चूहे जैसे दिखना
   - पेट में चूहे कूदना
   - नौ सौ चूहे खाकर बिल्ली चली हज को।
   - चूहे के चाम से नगाड़े नहीं मढ़े जाते।

उत्तर

1. • पूरी तरह भीग जाना।
   • जोर की भूख लगना।
   • खुद गलत काम करना दूसरों को अच्छी सलाह देना।
   • सीमित साधनों से बड़े काम नहीं होते।

लेखन संबंधी प्रश्न

1. दिए गए चित्र का अपने शब्दों में वर्णन कीजिए।

उत्तर
- यह होली का चित्र है।
- इस चित्र में तीन लड़के और दो लड़कियाँ दिखाई दे रही हैं।
- कुछ बच्चों के पास रंग-बिरंगी पिचकारियाँ हैं।
- एक लड़का एक लड़की पर पिचकारी से रंग डाल रहा है।
- एक लड़के ने अपने गले में ढोलक डाल रखी है।

अध्याय 9 स्वतंत्रता की ओर

पाठ का सार

धनी नौ वर्ष का एक लड़का था, जो महात्मा गाँधी के साबरमती आश्रम में अपने माता-पिता के साथ रहता था। इस आश्रम में पूरे भारत से लोग रहने और काम करने के लिए आते थे। आश्रम में सभी को काम करना पड़ता था; जैसे—कपड़े धोना, बर्तन धोना, खाना पकाना आदि। धनी आश्रम में अपनी बकरी की देखभाल करता था, जिसका नाम बिन्नी था। एक दिन धनी को लगा कि आश्रम में कोई बड़ी योजना बन रही है। धनी को लोग बच्चा समझते थे, इसलिए बहुत सारी बातें उससे साझा नहीं करते थे। अधिक जानकारी के लिए वह अपनी माँ से इसके बारे में पूछने चला गया। तो उसकी माँ ने बताया कि वे समुद्र के पास कहीं एक यात्रा पर जा रहे हैं। इसके बाद धनी ने यही बात बिंदा चाचा से पूछी। उन्होंने बताया कि गाँधीजी और उनके साथी गुजरात में दांडी नाम की जगह पर जा रहे हैं।

वहाँ वे समुद्र के किनारे नमक बनाएँगे। धनी ने कहा कि नमक तो किसी दुकान से खरीदा जा सकता है, इसका जवाब देते हुए बिंदा चाचा ने बताया कि ब्रिटिश सरकार ने नमक पर कर लगा रखा है। सभी अमीर-गरीब व्यक्ति को भी कर चुकाना पड़ता है। इसी कर का विरोध करने और भारतीयों को भी नमक बनाने का अधिकार दिलाने के लिए गाँधीजी यह यात्रा कर रहे हैं।

उसने अपने पिता से पूछा कि क्या आप और माँ दांडी यात्रा पर जा रहे हैं, तब उन्होंने कहा कि हाँ, परंतु तुम्हें यहीं रहना पड़ेगा। जब धनी इस यात्रा में जाने की जिद करने लगा तो उसके पिता ने बताया कि गाँधीजी ने जिन लोगों को इस यात्रा के लिए चुना है, वही जाएँगे। बरामदे में चरखे के पास बैठे गाँधीजी ने धनी को पुकारा। वह गाँधीजी के पास गया और पूछा कि क्या वह भी आपके साथ दांडी यात्रा पर चल सकता है? गाँधीजी ने उसे समझाया कि वह अभी बहुत छोटा है तथा यात्रा बहुत लंबी और कठिन है। इस यात्रा पर केवल बड़े लोग ही जा रहे हैं। धनी बोला, आप तो नौजवान नहीं हैं, आप भी तो थक जाएँगे। उसकी जिद को देखकर गाँधीजी ने कहा, यदि तुम चले गए, तो तुम्हारी बकरी 'बिन्नी' की देखभाल कौन करेगा? धनी की समझ में यह बात आ गई और उसने गाँधीजी से वादा किया कि वह आश्रम में रहकर बिन्नी की देखभाल करेगा और गाँधीजी के लौटने का इंतजार करेगा।

शब्दार्थ

बड़बड़ाना–अपने आपसे बोलना, चरखा–सूत कातने वाली मशीन, सत्याग्रह–अन्याय के खिलाफ अहिंसक तरीके से विरोध करना, हठ–ज़िद करना, गौशाला–गायों के रहने की जगह, धीरज–सब्र।

NCERT फोल्डर

प्यारे बापू

इस कहानी को पढ़कर तुम्हें बापू के बारे में कई बातें पता चली होंगी। उनमें से कोई तीन बातें यहाँ लिखो।

उत्तर • गाँधीजी प्रतिदिन सुबह उठकर आश्रम की देखभाल करने के बाद चरखे पर सूत कातते थे।
- गाँधीजी ने ब्रिटिश सरकार के नमक कर का विरोध करने के लिए दांडी यात्रा का निर्णय किया।
- गाँधीजी छोटे बच्चों से भी स्नेहपूर्वक मिलते थे और उन्हें अच्छी सीख देते थे।

चूल्हा

धनी की माँ चूल्हा फूँक रही थीं।

धनी की माँ खाना पकाने के लिए चूल्हे का इस्तेमाल करती थीं। नीचे कुछ चित्र बने हैं। इनके नाम पता करो और लिखो।

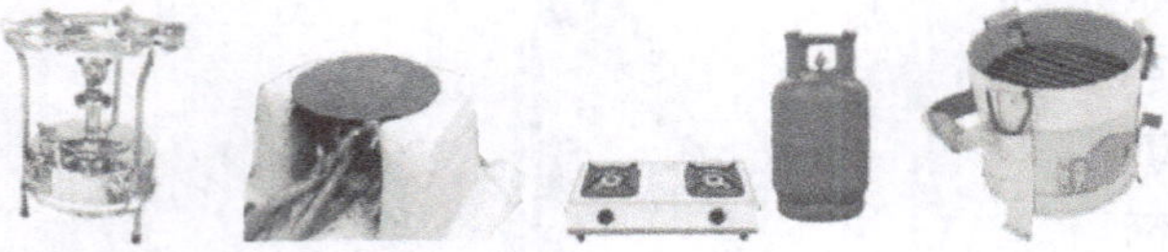

इनमें कौन-कौन से ईंधन का इस्तेमाल किया जाता है?

तुम्हारे घर में खाना पकाने के लिए इनमें से किसका इस्तेमाल किया जाता है?

उत्तर • **स्टोव** इसमें मिट्टी के तेल का प्रयोग होता है।
- **मिट्टी का चूल्हा** इसमें लकड़ी और गोबर के उपले का प्रयोग होता है।
- **गैस स्टोव** इसमें एल.पी.जी. गैस का उपयोग होता है।
- **भट्ठी** इसमें कोयले का प्रयोग होता है।
- मेरे घर में खाना पकाने के लिए मिट्टी के चूल्हे और गैस दोनों का प्रयोग किया जाता है।

कहानी से आगे

नीचे कहानी में आए कुछ शब्द लिखे हैं। कक्षा में चार-चार के समूह में एक-एक चीज़ के बारे में पता करो।

- स्वतंत्रता
- सत्याग्रह
- खादी
- चरखा

तुम इस काम में अपने दोस्तों से, बड़ों से, शब्दकोश या पुस्तकालय से सहायता ले सकते हो। जानकारी इकट्ठा करने के बाद कक्षा में इसके बारे में बताओ।

उत्तर **स्वतंत्रता** अपनी इच्छा और अधिकारों के अनुसार बिना किसी बाहरी दबाव के जीवन जीने की स्थिति को स्वतंत्रता कहते हैं।

सत्याग्रह सत्य और अहिंसा के सिद्धांतों पर आधारित अन्याय के खिलाफ़ अहिंसक प्रतिरोध को सत्याग्रह कहते हैं।

खादी यह हाथ से काता और बुना गया प्राकृतिक कपड़ा है, जिसे भारतीय स्वतंत्रता संग्राम के दौरान स्वदेशी आंदोलन का प्रतीक माना गया था।

चरखा एक पारंपरिक यंत्र, जिससे सूत काता जाता है। यह भारतीय स्वावलंबन और स्वतंत्रता संग्राम का महत्त्वपूर्ण प्रतीक है।

आगे की कहानी

गाँधीजी ने धनी से कहा, "क्या तुम आश्रम में ही रहकर मेरे लिए बिन्नी की देखभाल करोगे?"

धनी ने गाँधीजी की बात मान ली।

जब गाँधीजी दांडी यात्रा से लौटे होंगे, तब आश्रम में क्या-क्या हुआ होगा? आगे की कहानी सोचकर लिखो।

उत्तर जब गाँधीजी दांडी यात्रा से लौटे होंगे, तब सभी ने आश्रम में उनका गर्मजोशी से स्वागत किया होगा। आश्रम में गाँधीजी की सफलता पर उत्सव मनाया गया होगा और सभी लोग स्वतंत्रता आंदोलन के प्रति और अधिक प्रेरित हुए होंगे। धनी ने गर्व से बिन्नी की देखभाल का जिक्र किया होगा और गाँधीजी ने उसे सराहा होगा।

कहानी से

(क) धनी ने गाँधीजी से सुबह के समय बात करना क्यों ठीक समझा होगा?

उत्तर धनी ने गाँधीजी से सुबह के समय बात करना इसलिए ठीक समझा होगा, क्योंकि सुबह के समय गाँधीजी का समय अपेक्षाकृत खाली होता था। सुबह वे आश्रम में टहलते हुए लोगों से मुलाकात भी करते थे।

(ख) धनी बिन्नी की देखभाल कैसे करता था?

उत्तर धनी बिन्नी को हरी घास खिलाता और उसके पानी के बर्तन को भरता था। वह बिन्नी को आश्रम में घुमाता था और उससे बातें भी करता था।

(ग) धनी को यह कैसे महसूस हुआ होगा कि आश्रम में कोई योजना बनाई जा रही है?

उत्तर धनी ने महसूस किया कि आश्रम में कोई योजना बनाई जा रही है, क्योंकि गाँधीजी और बाकी लोग कमरे में बैठकर बातचीत करते थे।

कहानी और तुम

(क) धनी यात्रा पर जाने के लिए उत्सुक क्यों था?
अगर तुम धनी की जगह होते तो क्या तुम यात्रा पर जाने की जिद करते? क्यों?

उत्तर धनी यात्रा पर जाने के लिए इसलिए उत्सुक था, क्योंकि वह गाँधीजी के साथ दांडी यात्रा का हिस्सा बनना चाहता था और स्वतंत्रता संग्राम में अपना योगदान देना चाहता था।

अगर मैं धनी की जगह होता, तो शायद मैं भी यात्रा पर जाने की जिद करता, क्योंकि यह एक ऐतिहासिक और महत्त्वपूर्ण घटना थी।

(ख) गाँधीजी ने धनी को न जाने के लिए कैसे मनाया?
क्या तुम गाँधीजी के तर्क से सहमत हो? क्यों?

उत्तर गाँधीजी ने धनी को बिन्नी की देखभाल करने की जिम्मेदारी देकर और यह कहकर मनाया कि उसकी गैर-मौजूदगी में बिन्नी ठीक से खा-पी नहीं सकेगी। हाँ, मैं गाँधीजी के तर्क से सहमत हूँ, क्योंकि यह जिम्मेदारी का पाठ सिखाने के साथ-साथ धनी के लिए उचित था।

ताकत के लिए

गाँधीजी ने कहा, "जब मैं वापस आऊँगा तो मुझे खूब सारा दूध पीना पड़ेगा, जिससे कि मेरी ताकत लौट आए।"

बताओ, खूब सारी ताकत और अच्छी सेहत के लिए तुम क्या-क्या खाओगे-पिओगे?

- चटपटी अंकुरित दाल
- गर्म समोसे
- करारे गोलगप्पे
- कुरकुरी मक्का की रोटी
- खुशबूदार दाल
- मसालेदार अचार
- मीठा दूध
- रसीला आम
- गर्मागर्म साग
- ठंडी आइसक्रीम
- रंग-बिरंगी टॉफी
- ठंडा शरबत

उत्तर
- चटपटी अंकुरित दाल
- मीठा दूध
- रसीला आम
- गर्मागर्म साग
- कुरकुरी मक्का की रोटी
- खुशबूदार दाल
- ठंडा शरबत

विशेषता के शब्द

अभी तुमने जिन खाने-पीने की चीज़ों के नाम पढ़े, उनकी विशेषता बता रहे हैं ये शब्द
चटपटी, मीठा, गर्म, ठंडा, कुरकुरी आदि

नीचे लिखी चीज़ों की विशेषता बताने वाले शब्द सोचकर लिखो

- हलवा
- नमक
- पत्थर
- चश्मा
- पेड़
- चींटी
- कुरता
- झंडा

उत्तर
- गर्मागर्म हलवा
- लंबा पेड़
- थोड़ा नमक
- लाल चींटी
- रंगीन पत्थर
- पुराना कुरता
- काला चश्मा
- तिरंगा झंडा

चाँद की बिंदी

नीचे लिखे शब्दों में सही जगह पर ँ या ं लगाओ।

- धुआ
- फूक
- स्वतत्र
- मा
- बदगोभी
- पसद
- कुआ
- कहा
- बाध
- गाव
- इतज़ार

उत्तर
- धुआ – धुआँ
- कुआ – कुआँ
- फूक – फूँक
- कहा – कहाँ
- स्वतत्र – स्वतंत्र
- बाध – बाँध
- मा – माँ
- गाव – गाँव
- बदगोभी – बंदगोभी
- इतज़ार – इंतज़ार
- पसद – पसंद

किसकी जिम्मेदारी?

धनी को बिन्नी की देखभाल करने की जिम्मेदारी दी गई थी। इनकी क्या-क्या ज़िम्मेदारियाँ थीं?

- माँ
- पिता
- बिंदा

उत्तर
- **माँ** आश्रम में आने वाले लोगों के लिए खाना बनाना।
- **पिता** चरखा कातकर धागा बनाना।
- **बिंदा** आश्रम में सब्जियाँ उगाना।

अभ्यास प्रश्न

बहुविकल्पीय प्रश्न

1. धनी साबरमती आश्रम में किसकी देखभाल करता था?

(क) गाय की (ख) बकरी की
(ग) कुत्ते की (घ) घोड़े की

2. गाँधीजी दांडी यात्रा पर क्यों जा रहे थे?

(क) नमक कर के विरोध में
(ख) नई योजना बनाने के लिए
(ग) अंग्रेजों से समझौता करने के लिए
(घ) खादी प्रचार के लिए

3. धनी के पिता गाँधीजी के साथ दांडी यात्रा पर क्यों जा रहे थे?

(क) चरखा कातने (ख) गाँधीजी के साथ सत्याग्रह करने
(ग) नमक बनाने (घ) गाँवों का दौरा करने

4. धनी ने बिंदा चाचा से जब सवाल किया तब वे किस काम में व्यस्त थे?

(क) सब्ज़ी उगाने में (ख) चरखा कातने में
(ग) बर्तन धोने में (घ) खादी बनाने में

5. गाँधीजी ने धनी से कहा कि वह आश्रम में रहकर किसकी देखभाल करेगा?

(क) अपने माता-पिता की (ख) बिन्नी की
(ग) आश्रम की गायों की (घ) सब्ज़ियों की

उत्तर

1. (ख) बकरी की 2. (क) नमक कर के विरोध में
3. (ग) नमक बनाने 4. (क) सब्ज़ी उगाने में
5. (ख) बिन्नी की

गद्यांश पर आधारित प्रश्न

निम्नलिखित गद्यांश को पढ़कर उस पर आधारित प्रश्नों के उत्तर दीजिए।

गद्यांश

धनी को पता था कि आश्रम में कोई बड़ी योजना बन रही है, पर उसे कोई कुछ न बताता। "वे सब समझते हैं कि मैं नौ साल का हूँ इसलिए मैं बुद्धू हूँ। पर मैं बुद्धू नहीं हूँ!" धनी मन ही मन बड़बड़ाया। धनी और उसके माता-पिता, बड़ी खास जगह में रहते थे अहमदाबाद के पास, महात्मा गाँधी के साबरमती आश्रम में। जहाँ पूरे भारत से लोग रहने आते थे। गाँधीजी की तरह वे सब भी भारत की स्वतंत्रता के लिए लड़ रहे थे। जब वे आश्रम में ठहरते तो चरखों पर खादी का सूत कातते, भजन गाते और गाँधीजी की बातें सुनते।

1. धनी कहाँ रहता था?

(क) मुंबई में
(ख) दिल्ली में
(ग) अहमदाबाद के पास साबरमती आश्रम में
(घ) बनारस में

2. लोग साबरमती आश्रम में किसलिए आते थे?

(क) स्वतंत्रता संग्राम के लिए (ख) व्यापार के लिए
(ग) पढ़ाई के लिए (घ) तीर्थ यात्रा के लिए

3. धनी लोगों के बारे में क्या सोचता था?

4. आश्रम में लोग कौन-सा कार्य करते थे?

उत्तर

1. (ग) अहमदाबाद के पास साबरमती आश्रम में
2. (क) स्वतंत्रता संग्राम के लिए
3. धनी सोचता था कि लोग उसे नौ साल का बच्चा जानकर समझदार नहीं मानते हैं।
4. आश्रम में लोग खादी का सूत कातते थे, भजन गाते थे और गाँधीजी की बातें सुनते थे।

निम्नलिखित प्रश्नों के उत्तर दीजिए

1. धनी किसके साथ साबरमती आश्रम में रहता था?

उत्तर धनी अपने माता-पिता के साथ महात्मा गाँधी के साबरमती आश्रम में रहता था।

2. धनी का आश्रम में क्या काम था?

उत्तर धनी का आश्रम में बकरियों की देखभाल का काम था।

3. गाँधीजी और उनके साथी दांडी यात्रा पर क्यों जा रहे थे?

उत्तर गाँधीजी और उनके साथी दांडी यात्रा पर समुद्र के किनारे नमक बनाने जा रहे थे।

4. धनी को आश्रम की सभी बकरियों में कौन-सी बकरी पसंद थी?

उत्तर धनी को आश्रम की सभी बकरियों में 'बिन्नी' नाम की बकरी पसंद थी, जिसे वह बहुत प्यार करता था।

5. धनी ने गाँधीजी से किस बारे में पूछा?

उत्तर धनी ने गाँधीजी से पूछा कि क्या वह भी दांडी मार्च की यात्रा पर चल सकता है।

अध्याय 10

थप्प रोटी थप्प दाल

पाठ का सार

पर्दा उठता है और बच्चे नाटक खेलते हुए दिखाई देते हैं। इसी बीच मुन्नी दौड़ती हुई आती है और नीना को बुलाती है। वह नीना को बताती है कि उसने घर से आटा, घी, दाल, दही, साग, चीनी, मक्खन सारी चीजें ले ली हैं और अब रोटी का खेल खेलेंगे। नीना ताली बजाकर चुन्नू और बाकी बच्चों को बुलाती है और रोटी का खेल खेलने के लिए कहती है। मुन्नी, चुन्नू और टिंकू को बाज़ार से साग-सब्ज़ी लाने का काम सौंपती है, लेकिन नीना उनसे दाल पकवाने का काम करने के लिए कहती है।

सरला कहती है कि वह दही का मट्ठा चलाएगी, जबकि तरला कहती है कि वह मुन्नी के साथ रोटी बनाएगी। नीना मजाक में कहती है कि मैं बिल्ली बनकर सबकी चीजें खा जाऊँगी। सरला और तरला मट्ठा चलाने का अभिनय करती हैं। चुन्नू और टिंकू कंधे पर बोझ रखे साग-सब्ज़ी लाने का अभिनय करते हैं। मुन्नी उन्हें दाल पकाने के लिए कहती है। चुन्नू और टिंकू आग जलाने और दाल पकाने का प्रयास करते हैं।

इस बीच लड़कियाँ रोटी पकाने का अभिनय करती हैं और गाती हैं ''थप्प रोटी थप्प दाल, खाने वाले हो तैयार।'' लड़के आकर खाने की माँग करते हैं और गाते हैं ''लाओ रोटी लाओ दाल, लाओ खूब उड़ाएँ माल।'' लड़के पहले चिढ़ाते हैं कि खाना खट्टा है, फिर बताते हैं कि खाना मीठा है। बिल्ली मक्खन और रोटी खाने का अभिनय करती है। बिल्ली के जाने के बाद, सरला उठकर मक्खन के बर्तन को खाली देखकर चुन्नू और टिंकू को पुकारती है।

सभी बच्चे बिल्ली को ढूँढते हैं। बिल्ली भागने की कोशिश करती है, लेकिन बच्चे उसे घेर लेते हैं। नाटक का अंत बच्चों के 'पकड़ो-पकड़ो' के शोर और बिल्ली के भागने के साथ होता है।

शब्दार्थ

तरकारी-सब्जी, करारी भूख-बहुत जोर से भूख, भात-पका हुआ चावल, अभिनय-नाटक करना, मटकाते-हिलाना, कलछी-बड़ा चमचा, छींके-लटकने की जाली, झट से-तुरंत, सरपट-तेजी से।

NCERT फोल्डर

कोई और शीर्षक

नाटक का नाम 'थप्प रोटी थप्प दाल' क्यों है? तुम इसे क्या शीर्षक देना चाहोगे?

उत्तर नाटक का नाम 'थप्प रोटी थप्प दाल' इसलिए है, क्योंकि इसमें रोटी-दाल पकाने का अभिनय किया गया है। मैं इसे 'रोटी और बिल्ली' शीर्षक देना चाहूँगा।

आवाज वाले शब्द

थप्प रोटी थप्प दाल

'थप्प' शब्द से लगता है किसी तरह की आवाज़ है। आवाज़ का मज़ा देने वाले और भी बहुत-से शब्द हैं; जैसे- टप, खट। ऐसे ही कुछ शब्द तुम भी लिखो।

उत्तर धप, ठनठन, पट, छन-छन, फट, गटगट।

कौन-कौन से खेल

इस नाटक में बच्चे रोटी बनाने का खेल खेलते हैं। तुम अपने साथियों के साथ कौन-कौन से खेल खेलती हो? उनके नाम लिखो।

उत्तर लुका-छिपी, चोर-सिपाही, गिल्ली-डंडा और कबड्डी।

सोचकर बताओ

(क) नीना, चुन्नू और टिंकू से ही दाल क्यों बनवाना चाहती होगी?

उत्तर नीना, चुन्नू और टिंकू से इसलिए दाल बनवाना चाहती होगी, क्योंकि उसे पता था कि ये लड़के हैं। इन्हें दाल बनाना तो छोड़िए आग जलाना भी नहीं आता होगा। इनके द्वारा गलती करने पर खेल में और मनोरंजन आएगा।

(ख) बच्चों ने खाने-पीने की चीजें छींके में क्यों रखीं?

उत्तर बच्चों ने खाने-पीने की चीजें छींके में इसलिए रखीं, जिससे कोई बिल्ली या अन्य जानवर इन्हें चुरा न ले।

(ग) चुन्नू ने दाल को पहले खट्टा फिर मीठा क्यों बताया?

उत्तर लड़कियों को चिढ़ाने के लिए चुन्नू ने पहले दाल को खट्टा और फिर मीठा बताया।

तुम्हारी बात

तुम्हारे घर में खाना कौन बनाता है? तुम खाना बनाने में क्या-क्या मदद करते हो? नीचे दी गई तालिका में लिखो।

उत्तर

खाना कौन बनाता है?	मैं क्या मदद कर सकता हूँ?	मैं क्या मदद करता हूँ?
माँ	सब्जी काट सकता हूँ।	सब्जी धोता और काटता हूँ।
दादी	बर्तन धो सकता हूँ।	दाल फ्राई करता हूँ।
बहन	चूल्हा जला सकता हूँ।	खाना परोसता हूँ।

तुम क्या बनाती

इन बच्चों की जगह तुम होती तो खाने के लिए कौन-से तीन पकवान बनाती? उन्हें बनाने के लिए किन चीजों की जरूरत पड़ती? पता करो और सूची बनाओ।

उत्तर

पकवान का नाम	किन चीजों की जरूरत होगी?
पूरी	आटा, पानी, तेल
चावल	चावल, पानी
दाल	दाल, पानी, हल्दी, नमक, टमाटर, जीरा, मिर्च, प्याज आदि।
सब्जी	आलू, प्याज, मिर्च, धनिया, हल्दी, मसाला आदि।

मट्ठा बनाएँ

(क) सरला ने कहा-मैं दही का मट्ठा चला दूँगी। दही का मट्ठा चलाने का मतलब है

दही बिलोना

दही से लस्सी या छाछ बनाना

सरला को इस काम के लिए किन-किन चीजों की जरूरत होगी? उनके नाम लिखो।

उत्तर उपर्युक्त काम के लिए सरला को दही, हांडी, मथनी, पानी आदि की जरूरत होगी।

(ख) बिलोना, घोलना, फेंटना इन तीनों कामों में क्या फ़र्क है? बातचीत करो और पता लगाओ।

उत्तर • मक्खन निकालने के लिए मट्ठा को लकड़ी या मशीन से घुमाने की प्रक्रिया को 'बिलोना' कहते हैं।

- किसी ठोस चीज़ को पानी में मिलाकर पतला करने को 'घोलना' कहते हैं।
- चीजों को हल्का और फूला हुआ बनाने के लिए तेजी से मिलाने को 'फेंटना' कहते हैं; जैसे— बेसन फेंटना।

(ग) किन्हीं दो-दो चीज़ों के नाम बताओ, जिन्हें बिलोते, घोलते और फेंटते हैं।

- **बिलोते हैं** • **घोलते हैं** • **फेंटते हैं**

उत्तर • बिलोते हैं—मट्ठा, लस्सी
- घोलते हैं—दूध-चीनी, नमक-पानी-नींबू
- फेंटते हैं—अंडे को मैदा के साथ, पानी और बेसन

(घ) सरला ने रई से मट्ठा बिलोया। रई को मथनी भी कहते हैं। रसोई के दूसरे बर्तनों को तुम्हारे घर की भाषा में क्या कहते हैं? कक्षा में इस पर बातचीत करो और एक सूची बनाओ।

उत्तर पतीला, कढ़ाई, थाली, कटोरी, चम्मच, गगरी, तवा, कलछी आदि।

आओ तुकबंदी करें

नाटक में बच्चों ने अपनी बात को कई बार कविता की तरह कहा है; जैसे-

टिंकू ने पकाई बड़ियाँ,
चुन्नू ने पकाई दाल
टिंकू की बड़ियाँ जल गईं,
चुन्नू का बुरा हाल

अब तुम भी नीचे लिखी पंक्तियों में कुछ जोड़ो

घंटी बोली टन-टन-टन
कहाँ चले भई कहाँ चले
रेल चली भई रेल चली
कल की छुट्टी परसों इतवार
रोटी दाल पकाएँगे

उत्तर घंटी बोली टन-टन-टन
घर की ओर चले हम
कहाँ चले भई कहाँ चले
पैदा होकर जहाँ पले
रेल चली भई रेल चली
स्टेशन पर मची खलबली
कल की छुट्टी परसों इतवार
नहीं उठाना होगा बस्ते का भार
रोटी दाल पकाएँगे
बैठ के टोली में खाएँगे।

अभ्यास प्रश्न

बहुविकल्पीय प्रश्न

1. मुन्नी ने नीना को क्यों बुलाया?
(क) गाने के लिए (ख) रोटी का खेल खेलने के लिए
(ग) स्कूल जाने के लिए (घ) बाजार जाने के लिए

2. बिल्ली ने क्या चुराकर खाया?
(क) चावल और दाल (ख) मक्खन और रोटी
(ग) सब्जी और दही (घ) साग और चीनी

3. बिल्ली के आने पर बच्चों ने क्या किया?
(क) सो गए (ख) खेलना बंद कर दिया
(ग) बिल्ली को पकड़ने की कोशिश की
(घ) दाल और रोटी बनाने लगे

4. सरला और तरला ने कौन-सा अभिनय किया?
(क) रोटी बनाने का (ख) रई से मट्ठा चलाने का
(ग) मक्खन बनाने का (घ) साग पकाने का

उत्तर
1. (ख) रोटी का खेल खेलने के लिए
2. (ख) मक्खन और रोटी
3. (ग) बिल्ली को पकड़ने की कोशिश की
4. (ख) राई से मट्ठा चलाने का

रिक्त स्थान

नीचे दिए गए वाक्यों में रिक्त स्थान की पूर्ति उचित शब्द से कीजिए।

(माल, रोटी, गरम-गरम, थप्प, आँसू)

1. मुन्नी और तरला की सहेलियों ने रोटी पकाने का अभिनय करते हुए गीत गाया, 'थप्प रोटी, ... दाल।'

2. चुन्नू और टिंकू ने दाल पकाते समय धुएँ की वजह से .... पोंछने का अभिनय किया।

3. बिल्ली ने रोटी चुराने से पहले कहा, "रोटी कैसी ………… है, घी से चुपड़ी नरम-नरम है।"

4. बिल्ली ने मक्खन, रोटी, चावल और दाल खाकर कहा, 'जी भर खाया कित्ता …………।'

5. बच्चों ने बिल्ली को पकड़ने के बाद कहा, 'अब खाएगी मेरी …………? अब खाएगी मेरी दाल?'

उत्तर

1. थप्प 2. आँसू 3. गरम-गरम
4. माल 5. रोटी

गद्यांश पर आधारित प्रश्न

निम्नलिखित गद्यांश को पढ़कर उस पर आधारित प्रश्नों के उत्तर दीजिए।

गद्यांश

पर्दा खुलने पर बच्चे खेलते हुए दिखाई पड़ते हैं। सब बच्चे हल्ला मचाते, हँसते हुए बड़े उत्साह के साथ खेल रहे हैं। अचानक मुन्नी अपने घर से भागी-भागी वहाँ आती है और नीना को पुकारती है। नीना खेल छोड़कर सामने एक किनारे पर आ जाती है। पीछे बच्चों का खेल चलता रहता है।

- **मुन्नी** (पुकारकर) ओ नीना, नीना सुन!
- **नीना** (पास आते हुए) क्यों, क्या बात है, मुन्नी?
- **मुन्नी** देख नीना, आज मैंने अम्मा से आटा, घी, दाल, दही, साग, चीनी, मक्खन सब चीजें ले ली हैं। चल, रोटी का खेल खेलेंगे।
- **नीना** हाँ, खूब मजा आएगा। चलो, उन लोगों को भी बुला लें। (ताली बजाकर)
- अरे चुन्नू, सुनो! अब इस खेल को खेलते तो बहुत देर हो गई। चलो, अब रोटी का खेल खेलें।
- **सब** हाँ, हाँ! यह ठीक है।
- **मुन्नी** अच्छा-अच्छा चलो। देख चुन्नू, तू और टिंकू, बाज़ार से साग-सब्ज़ी लाने का काम करना।

1. **मुन्नी ने नीना को किस खेल के लिए बुलाया?**
(क) खेलना (ख) रोटी का खेल
(ग) दही बनाना (घ) सब्जी लाना

2. **मुन्नी ने चुन्नू और टिंकू के लिए क्या करने का प्रस्ताव रखा?**
(क) दाल बनाना (ख) मट्ठा चलाना
(ग) रोटी बनाना (घ) सब्जी लाना

3. **मुन्नी ने घर से क्या-क्या सामान लिया?**

4. **नीना ने क्या कहा जब मुन्नी ने उसे बुलाया?**

उत्तर

1. (ख) रोटी का खेल 2. (घ) सब्जी लाना
3. मुन्नी ने घर से आटा, घी, दाल, दही, साग, चीनी और मक्खन लिया।
4. जब मुन्नी ने नीना को बुलाया तो उसने पूछा, 'क्यों, क्या बात है, मुन्नी?'

निम्नलिखित प्रश्नों के उत्तर दीजिए

1. **मुन्नी ने अपने घर से कौन-कौन सी चीजें ली थीं?**

उत्तर मुन्नी ने अपने घर से आटा, घी, दाल, दही, मक्खन ये सभी चीजें ली थीं।

2. **नीना ने किस चीज़ का अभिनय करने के लिए सोचा?**

उत्तर नीना ने बिल्ली बनने का अभिनय करने के लिए सोचा।

3. **चुन्नू और टिंकू किस काम के लिए बाजार गए थे?**

उत्तर चुन्नू और टिंकू साग-सब्जी लाने के लिए बाजार गए थे।

4. **बच्चों ने रोटी और दाल पकाने के लिए क्या किया?**

उत्तर बच्चों ने रोटी और दाल पकाने के लिए तरह-तरह के अभिनय किए।

5. **बिल्ली ने रोटी और मक्खन को देखकर क्या कहा?**

उत्तर बिल्ली ने रोटी और मक्खन को देखकर कहा "यदि तुम लोग सोते रहे तो मैं फिर से खा जाऊँगी।"

लेखन संबंधी प्रश्न

1. **'सच्चा मित्र' पर अनुच्छेद लिखिए।**

उत्तर सच्चा मित्र वही है, जो हमारे सुख-दुःख में पूरा-पूरा साथ दे। हमें सोच-समझकर ही मित्र बनाना चाहिए। मित्र उसी को बनाना चाहिए, जिसके विचार हमसे मिलते हों। हमें रहन-सहन, स्वभाव, परिवार, आदतें, रुचियाँ आदि की जानकारी प्राप्त करने के बाद ही मित्र बनाना चाहिए। मित्र का प्रभाव व्यक्ति के जीवन पर अत्यधिक पड़ता है। यदि हम गलती कर रहे हों तो मित्र का कर्त्तव्य है कि वह हमें गलत काम करने से रोके और सही मार्ग दिखाए।

अध्याय 11

पढ़क्कू की सूझ

कविता का सार

'पढ़क्कू की सूझ' कविता में कवि रामधारी सिंह 'दिनकर' ने एक पढ़क्कू व्यक्ति का वर्णन किया है। वह पढ़क्कू व्यक्ति तर्कशास्त्र पढ़ता था। एक दिन वह यह सोचकर असमंजस (चिंता) में पड़ गया कि बिना चलाए ही बैल कोल्हू में कैसे घूमते हैं? इसके मालिक को जरूर कोई तरीका आता होगा।

काव्यांशों की व्याख्या

काव्यांश 1

एक पढ़क्कू बड़े तेज़ थे, तर्कशास्त्र पढ़ते थे,
जहाँ न कोई बात, वहाँ भी नई बात गढ़ते थे।
एक रोज़ वे पड़े फिक्र में समझ नहीं कुछ पाए,
'बैल घूमता है कोल्हू में कैसे बिना चलाए?'
कई दिनों तक रहे सोचते, मालिक बड़ा गज़ब है?
सिखा बैल को रक्खा इसने, निश्चय कोई ढब है।

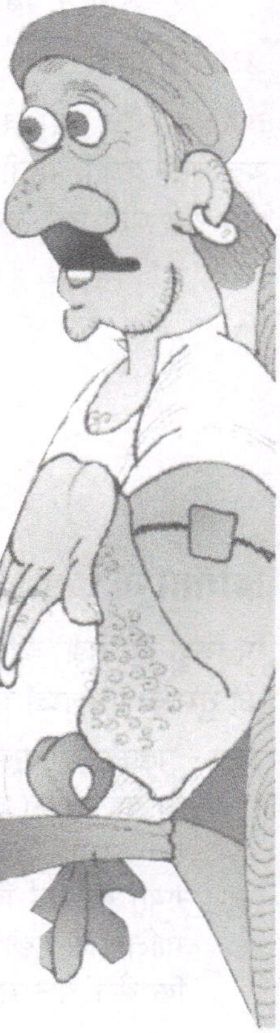

शब्दार्थ *पढ़क्कू–बहुत पढ़ने वाला, गढ़ते–बनाते, गजब–अनोखा, फ़िक्र–चिंता, ढब–तरीका।*

संदर्भ एवं प्रसंग प्रस्तुत पंक्तियाँ हमारी पाठ्यपुस्तक 'रिमझिम भाग–4' में संकलित कविता 'पढ़क्कू की सूझ' से ली गई हैं। इसके कवि रामधारी सिंह 'दिनकर' हैं। इस कविता में एक पढ़क्कू के माध्यम से बताया गया है कि अत्यधिक तर्कशास्त्र में उलझने वाला व्यक्ति व्यावहारिक जीवन की सरल सच्चाइयों को नहीं समझ पाता है।

व्याख्या काव्यांश में एक ऐसे व्यक्ति की बात की जा रही है, जो बहुत पढ़क्कू और तेज है। तर्कशास्त्र पढ़ने के कारण वे जहाँ कोई भी बात नहीं होती थी, वहाँ भी नई-नई बातें बना लेते थे। एक दिन कोल्हू में बैल को चलते हुए देखकर वे चिंता में पड़ गए कि बिना चलाए ही बैल कोल्हू में कैसे घूम रहा है? वे इस बारे में कई दिनों तक सोचते रहे। उन्हें लगा कि जरूर मालिक ने बैल को कोई तरीका सिखा रखा होगा।

काव्यांश 2

आखिर, एक रोज़ मालिक से पूछा उसने ऐसे,
'अजी, बिना देखे, लेते तुम जान भेद यह कैसे?
कोल्हू का यह बैल तुम्हारा चलता या अड़ता है?
रहता है घूमता, खड़ा हो या पागुर करता है?'
मालिक ने यह कहा, 'अजी, इसमें क्या बात बड़ी है?
नहीं देखते क्या, गर्दन में घंटी एक पड़ी है?'

शब्दार्थ *भेद–राज या रहस्य, अड़ता–रुकता, पागुर–जुगाली।*

प्रसंग पूर्ववत्।

व्याख्या पढ़क्कू व्यक्ति को यह समझ में नहीं आया कि बैल बिना चलाए कैसे चलता रहता है? एक दिन उन्होंने मालिक से जाकर पूछ ही लिया कि तुम्हें कैसे पता चलता है कि बैल चल रहा है कि नहीं?

यह कैसे जान लेते हो कि बैल घूम रहा है, खड़ा है या जुगाली कर रहा है? मालिक ने कहा कि इसमें कोई विशेष बात नहीं है। उसने बैल की गर्दन में पड़ी घंटी की ओर इशारा करते हुए बताया कि सब इसी की मदद से होता है।

काव्यांश 3

'जब तक यह बजती रहती है, मैं न फ़िक्र करता हूँ,
हाँ, जब बजती नहीं, दौड़कर तनिक पूँछ धरता हूँ।'
कहा पढ़क्कू ने सुनकर, 'तुम रहे सदा के कोरे!
बेवकूफ! मंतिख की बातें समझ सकोगे थोड़े!
अगर किसी दिन बैल तुम्हारा सोच-समझ अड़ जाए,
चले नहीं, बस, खड़ा-खड़ा गर्दन को खूब हिलाए।'

शब्दार्थ *तनिक-थोड़ा, पूँछ धरता-बैल की पूँछ ऐंठना, कोरे-अनुभवहीन, बेवकूफ, मूर्ख, मंतिख-तर्कशास्त्र, अड़ जाए -आगे न बढ़े।*

प्रसंग पूर्ववत्।

व्याख्या बैल और कोल्हू के मालिक ने बताया कि जब तक यह घंटी बजती रहती है, तब तक मैं कोई चिंता नहीं करता हूँ। जब यह घंटी नहीं बजती है, तो समझ जाता हूँ कि वे खड़े हैं। मैं तुरंत ही दौड़कर उनकी पूँछ ऐंठ देता हूँ। पढ़क्कू ने यह सुनकर मालिक से कहा कि तुम बिल्कुल मूर्ख हो। तुम्हें तर्कशास्त्र की बात समझ में नहीं आएगी। यदि किसी दिन तुम्हारा बैल जानबूझकर खड़े होकर गर्दन हिलाता रहा, तब क्या होगा?

काव्यांश 4

घंटी टुन-टुन खूब बजेगी, तुम न पास आओगे,
मगर बूँद भर तेल साँझ तक भी क्या तुम पाओगे?
मालिक थोड़ा हँसा और बोला कि पढ़क्कू जाओ,
सीखा है यह ज्ञान जहाँ पर, वहीं इसे फैलाओ।
यहाँ सभी कुछ ठीक-ठाक है, यह केवल माया है,
बैल हमारा नहीं अभी तक मंतिख पढ़ पाया है।

शब्दार्थ *टुन-टुन-घंटी बजने की आवाज, साँझ-शाम, माया-भ्रम।*

प्रसंग पूर्ववत्

व्याख्या पढ़क्कू ने मालिक से कहा बैल खड़ा होकर गर्दन हिलाता रहेगा तो घंटी भी बजती रहेगी। तुम बैल को चलता हुआ समझकर उसके पास नहीं जाओगे, लेकिन शाम को जब देखोगे तो तुम्हें एक भी बूँद तेल नहीं मिलेगा। मालिक ने हँसते हुए पढ़क्कू से कहा कि यह ज्ञान जहाँ से सीखा है, वहीं पर जाकर इसे फैलाओ। यहाँ सब कुछ ठीक-ठाक है। तुम्हारी बात भ्रम फैलाने वाली है। मेरा बैल अभी तक तर्कशास्त्र नहीं पढ़ पाया है। वह बिल्कुल सीधा-साधा है।

NCERT फोल्डर

कविता में कहानी

'पढ़क्कू की सूझ' कविता में एक कहानी कही गई है। इस कहानी को तुम अपने शब्दों में लिखो।

उत्तर 'पढ़क्कू की सूझ' कविता में एक पढ़क्कू व्यक्ति की कहानी है। वह व्यक्ति तर्कशास्त्र का ज्ञाता था। वह एक दिन कोल्हू के बैल को बिना किसी के चलाए घूमते देखकर हैरान हो गया। वह कई दिनों तक इस पर सोचता रहा। उसने बैल के मालिक से पूछा कि बिना देखे ही उसे कैसे पता चल जाता है कि बैल चल रहा है। मालिक ने बताया कि बैल की गर्दन में बँधी घंटी चलने पर बजती रहती है। पढ़क्कू व्यक्ति ने तर्क दिया कि बैल खड़ा होकर भी तो गर्दन हिलाकर घंटी बजा सकता है। इस पर मालिक ने हँसते हुए कहा कि उसके बैल ने अभी तक तर्कशास्त्र नहीं पढ़ा है।

कवि की कविताएँ

तीसरी कक्षा में तुमने रामधारी सिंह 'दिनकर' की कविता 'मिर्च का मजा' पढ़ी थी। अब तुमने उन्हीं की कविता 'पढ़क्कू की सूझ' पढ़ी।

(क) दोनों में से कौन-सी कविता पढ़कर तुम्हें ज्यादा मज़ा आया? (चाहो तो तीसरी की किताब फिर से देख सकते हो।)

उत्तर दोनों ही कविताओं को पढ़कर मजा आया। इस कविता में पढ़क्कू तर्कशास्त्री का बैल के मालिक से पूछा गया सवाल मूर्खतापूर्ण था। यह सवाल इस कविता को और अधिक रोचक बना देता है।

(ख) तुम्हें काबुली वाला ज्यादा अच्छा लगा या पढ़क्कू? या कोई भी अच्छा नहीं लगा?

उत्तर मुझे दोनों ही अच्छे लगे।

(ग) अपने साथियों के साथ मिलकर एक-एक कविता ढूँढो। कविताएँ इकट्ठा करके कविता की एक किताब बनाओ।

उत्तर छात्र स्वयं करें।

मेहनत के मुहावरे

कोल्हू का बैल ऐसे व्यक्ति को कहते हैं, जो कड़ी मेहनत करता है या जिससे कड़ी मेहनत करवाई जाती है।

मेहनत और कोशिश से जुड़े कुछ और मुहावरे नीचे लिखे हैं। इनका वाक्यों में इस्तेमाल करो।

- दिन रात एक करना
- पसीना बहाना
- एड़ी-चोटी का जोर लगाना

उत्तर
- **दिन रात एक करना** महेश को अपना लक्ष्य पाने के लिए दिन-रात एक करना पड़ा।
- **पसीना बहाना** अच्छा परिणाम पाने के लिए विद्यार्थियों को परीक्षा की तैयारी में पसीना बहाना पड़ता है।
- **एड़ी-चोटी का जोर लगाना** खेल में सफल होने के लिए राजू ने एड़ी-चोटी का ज़ोर लगा दिया।

पढ़क्कू

(क) पढ़क्कू का नाम पढ़क्कू क्यों पड़ा होगा?

उत्तर दिन-रात पढ़ते रहने की आदत के कारण पढ़क्कू का नाम पढ़क्कू पड़ा होगा।

(ख) तुम कौन-सा काम खूब मन से करना चाहते हो? उसके आधार पर अपने लिए भी पढ़क्कू जैसा कोई शब्द सोचो।

उत्तर मैं लोगों को खूब सलाह देना चाहता हूँ। इसके आधार पर मैं 'रायचंद' के नाम से जाना जा सकता हूँ।

अपना तरीका

हाँ जब बजती नहीं, दौड़कर तनिक पूँछ धरता हूँ

पूँछ धरता हूँ का मतलब है पूँछ पकड़ लेता हूँ।

नीचे लिखे वाक्यों को अपने शब्दों में लिखो।

(क) मगर बूँद भर तेल साँझ तक भी क्या तुम पाओगे?

उत्तर शाम तक तुम तेल की एक बूँद भी नहीं पाओगे।

(ख) बैल हमारा नहीं अभी तक मंतिख पढ़ पाया है।

उत्तर हमारा बैल अभी तर्कशास्त्र नहीं पढ़ा है।

(ग) सिखा बैल को रखा इसने निश्चय कोई ढब है।

उत्तर इसने बैल को जरूर कोई हुनर सिखा रखा है।

(घ) जहाँ न कोई बात, वहाँ भी नई बात गढ़ते थे।

उत्तर जहाँ कोई बात नहीं होती थी, वहाँ भी वे बातें गढ़ लेते थे।

गढ़ना

पढ़क्कू नई-नई बातें गढ़ते थे। बताओ, ये लोग क्या गढ़ते हैं?

- सुनार
- कवि
- लुहार
- कुम्हार
- ठठेरा
- लेखक

उत्तर

- सुनार – जेवर
- कवि – कविता
- लुहार – लोहे का सामान
- कुम्हार – घड़ा
- ठठेरा – बर्तन
- लेखक – कहानियाँ

अर्थ खोजो

नीचे दिए गए शब्दों के अर्थ अक्षरजाल में खोजो

ढब, भेद, गजब, मंतिख, छल

त	र्क	शा	स्त्र	म्र
रा	ज	त	क	ब
जू	स	री	मा	धो
रा	ज़	का	ल	खा
धो	क	म	ल	ड़

उत्तर
- ढब – तरीका
- भेद – राज़
- गजब – कमाल
- मंतिख – तर्कशास्त्र
- छल – धोखा

अभ्यास प्रश्न

बहुविकल्पीय प्रश्न

1. पढ़क्कू कौन-सा विषय पढ़ते थे?

(क) विज्ञान (ख) गणित
(ग) तर्कशास्त्र (घ) भूगोल

2. पढ़क्कू ने मालिक से किस चीज़ के बारे में पूछा?

(क) बैल के खाने के बारे में
(ख) कोल्हू में बैल के घूमने के बारे में
(ग) बैल की घंटी के बारे में
(घ) तेल निकालने के बारे में

3. मालिक को कैसे पता चलता है कि बैल चल रहा है?

(क) वह बैल को देखता है (ख) बैल की घंटी की आवाज़ से
(ग) वह बैल को छूता है (घ) वह तेल की मात्रा से समझता है

4. पढ़क्कू के अनुसार बैल कोल्हू में क्यों रुक सकता है?

(क) थकान के कारण
(ख) मालिक की नज़र से बचने के लिए
(ग) तेल खत्म होने पर
(घ) घंटी बजाने के लिए

5. पढ़क्कू की किस विशेषता का उल्लेख कविता में हुआ है?

(क) समझदारी (ख) बेवकूफी
(ग) धैर्य (घ) साहस

उत्तर

1. (ग) तर्कशास्त्र
2. (ख) कोल्हू में बैल के घूमने के बारे में
3. (ख) बैल की घंटी की आवाज़ से
4. (घ) घंटी बजाने के लिए
5. (ख) बेवकूफी

काव्यांश पर आधारित प्रश्न

निम्नलिखित काव्यांश को पढ़कर उस पर आधारित प्रश्नों के उत्तर दीजिए।

काव्यांश

एक पढ़क्कू बड़े तेज़ थे, तर्कशास्त्र पढ़ते थे,
जहाँ न कोई बात, वहाँ भी नई बात गढ़ते थे।
एक रोज़ वे पड़े फ़िक्र में समझ नहीं कुछ पाए,
'बैल घूमता है कोल्हू में कैसे बिना चलाए?'
कई दिनों तक रहे सोचते, मालिक बड़ा गज़ब है?
सिखा बैल को रक्खा इसने, निश्चय कोई ढब है।

1. पढ़क्कू कौन-सा विषय पढ़ते थे?

(क) गणित (ख) तर्कशास्त्र
(ग) साहित्य (घ) इतिहास

2. पढ़क्कू को किस बात पर हैरानी थी?

(क) बैल की चाल पर
(ख) बैल के कोल्हू में घूमने पर
(ग) बैल के खाने पर
(घ) मालिक की समझदारी पर

3. पढ़क्कू किस बात को लेकर फ़िक्र में थे?

4. मालिक के बारे में पढ़क्कू ने क्या सोचा?

उत्तर

1. (ख) तर्कशास्त्र
2. (ख) बैल के कोल्हू में घूमने पर
3. पढ़क्कू इस बात को लेकर फ़िक्र में थे कि बैल बिना किसी के चलाए कोल्हू में कैसे घूमता है।
4. पढ़क्कू ने सोचा कि मालिक ने बैल को किसी विशेष ढंग से सिखाया है, जो बड़ा गज़ब है।

निम्नलिखित प्रश्नों के उत्तर दीजिए

1. बैल कहाँ घूमता था?

उत्तर बैल कोल्हू में घूमता था।

2. मालिक बैल की गतिविधियों का ध्यान कैसे रखता था?

उत्तर मालिक ने बताया कि जब तक यह घंटी बजती रहती है, तब तक मैं कोई चिंता नहीं करता हूँ, लेकिन जब यह घंटी नहीं बजती तो मैं समझ जाता हूँ कि बैल खड़े हैं।

3. पढ़क्कू ने मालिक को क्या कहा?

उत्तर पढ़क्कू ने मालिक से कहा कि तुम्हें कैसे पता कि बैल चल रहा है या नहीं?

4. बैल की गर्दन में क्या बँधा था?

उत्तर बैल की गर्दन में घंटी बँधी थी।

अध्याय 12

सुनीता की पहिया कुर्सी

पाठ का सार

सुनीता सुबह सात बजे उठी तो उसको याद आया कि उसे आज बाजार जाना है। आज अकेले बाजार जाने की ख़ुशी से उसकी आँखों में चमक आ गई। पलंग का सहारा लेते हुए वह पहिये वाली कुर्सी तक गई। सुनीता चलने-फिरने के लिए पहिये वाली कुर्सी का सहारा लेती थी। घर के सभी काम निपटाकर वह नहा धोकर तैयार हो गई। उसकी माँ ने मेज पर नाश्ता लगाकर अलमारी से अचार ले लेने के लिए कहा। नाश्ता करते हुए उसने माँ से पूछा कि आज बाजार से क्या-क्या लाना है? माँ ने कहा कि एक किलो चीनी लानी है। माँ ने उसे झोला और पैसे पकड़ा दिए।

अपनी पहिये वाली कुर्सी पर बैठकर वह बाजार की ओर चल पड़ी। आज वह अकेले ही बाजार जा रही थी, इसलिए उसे सभी चीजें आकर्षित कर रही थीं। छुट्टी का दिन होने के कारण सभी बच्चे खेलते हुए दिखाई दे रहे थे। सुनीता उन्हें रुककर देखती रही। वह इन लोगों को देखकर उदास हो गई, क्योंकि वह भी खेलना चाहती थी। उसने देखा कि एक बच्चे को अन्य सभी बच्चे छोटू-छोटू कहकर चिढ़ा रहे थे। सुनीता को यह अच्छा नहीं लगा। रास्ते में जब लोग उसे देखकर मुस्कुराते थे तो उसे यह अच्छा लगता था। एक लड़की ने सुनीता से पूछा कि तुम्हारे पास यह क्या है? सुनीता जवाब देती उससे पहले ही उस लड़की की माँ ने सुनीता से उसे दूर हटा दिया। उस लड़की की माँ ने समझाया कि फरीदा इस तरह का प्रश्न नहीं पूछा जाता है। तभी वह लड़का आया, जिसे अन्य बच्चे छोटू-छोटू कहकर चिढ़ा रहे थे।

उसने अपना नाम अमित बताया और मदद करने का प्रस्ताव दिया। सुनीता ने भी अपना परिचय दिया और पीछे के पैडल को पैर से दबाने के लिए कहा। उस लड़के ने मदद की और सुनीता ने उसे धन्यवाद दिया। उसने दुकान में जाकर चीनी ली, लेकिन दुकानदार का व्यवहार उसे अच्छा नहीं लगा। सुनीता ने सोचा कि लोग मेरे साथ ऐसा व्यवहार क्यों करते हैं जैसे कि मैं कोई अजीब लड़की हूँ। अमित ने कहा कि पहिया कुर्सी पर चलने के कारण शायद लोग तुम्हारे साथ ऐसा व्यवहार करते हैं। अमित ने बताया कि वह उन सभी कामों को कर सकता है, जो दूसरे बच्चे करते हैं। फिर भी मैं उन लोगों से अलग हूँ। अमित और सुनीता दोनों साथ-साथ चलने लगे। बाहर लोग उन्हें घूर रहे थे, लेकिन सुनीता ने इसकी कोई परवाह नहीं की।

शब्दार्थ

स्वयं-खुद, तरीका-उपाय, सहारा-मदद, सहायता, फुर्ती-तेजी, जिंदगी-जीवन, व्यवहार-बर्ताव, रोजाना-प्रतिदिन, अजीबोगरीब-अनोखी, विचित्र, परवाह-ख्याल, ध्यान।

NCERT फोल्डर

कहानी से

1. सुनीता को सब लोग गौर से क्यों देख रहे थे?

उत्तर सुनीता पहिया कुर्सी पर बैठकर चल रही थी, इसलिए लोग उसे गौर से देख रहे थे।

2. सुनीता को दुकानदार का व्यवहार क्यों बुरा लगा?

उत्तर सुनीता को दुकानदार का व्यवहार इसलिए बुरा लगा, क्योंकि दुकानदार ने उसे इस लायक भी नहीं समझा कि वह स्वयं चीनी ले सकती है। दुकानदार ने उसकी गोद में चीनी का थैला रख दिया था।

मजेदार

सुनीता को सड़क की जिंदगी देखने में मजा आता है।

(क) तुम्हारे विचार से सुनीता को सड़क देखना अच्छा क्यों लगता होगा?

उत्तर सुनीता अपने पैरों पर चलने में असमर्थ थी। उसे बाहर निकलने और घूमने का अवसर बहुत कम मिल पाता था। इसीलिए वह जब भी बाहर निकलती थी, तो सड़क की चहल-पहल देखकर उसे अच्छा लगता था।

(ख) अपने घर के आसपास की सड़क को ध्यान से देखो और बताओ

- **तुम्हें क्या-क्या चीजें नज़र आती हैं?**
- **लोग क्या-क्या करते हुए नज़र आते हैं?**

उत्तर
- मुझे सड़क पर लोगों की भीड़, सब्जी, बिकने वाली अन्य सामग्री, साइकिल, ठेला और गाड़ियाँ आदि चीजें नजर आती हैं।
- सड़क पर मुझे लोग बात करते हुए, आते-जाते हुए और गाड़ियाँ चलाते हुए नज़र आते हैं।

मनाही

फ़रीदा की माँ ने कहा, "इस तरह के सवाल नहीं पूछने चाहिए।"

फ़रीदा पहिया कुर्सी के बारे में जानना चाहती थी पर उसकी माँ ने उसे रोक दिया।

- **माँ ने फ़रीदा को क्यों रोक दिया होगा?**

उत्तर माँ ने फरीदा को इसलिए रोक दिया होगा, क्योंकि शारीरिक रूप से अक्षम व्यक्ति से ऐसे प्रश्न पूछना उसे अपमानित करने वाले लग सकते हैं।

- **क्या फ़रीदा को पहिया कुर्सी के बारे में नहीं पूछना चाहिए था? तुम्हें क्या लगता है?**

उत्तर इसका कोई सीधा उत्तर नहीं हो सकता है, क्योंकि फ़रीदा छोटी थी। उसे इस बात की जानकारी नहीं थी कि किससे किस तरह के प्रश्न पूछने चाहिए?

- **क्या तुम्हें भी कोई काम करने या कोई बात कहने से मना किया जाता है? कौन मना करता है? कब मना करता है?**

उत्तर छात्र स्वयं करें।

मैं भी कुछ कर सकती हूँ

(क) यदि सुनीता तुम्हारी पाठशाला में आए तो उसे किन-किन कामों में परेशानी आएगी?

उत्तर यदि सुनीता मेरे स्कूल में आए तो उसे सीढ़ी चढ़ने, बच्चों के साथ खेलने और प्रार्थना के समय खड़े रहने आदि कार्यों में परेशानी आएगी।

(ख) उसे यह परेशानी न हो इसके लिए अपनी पाठशाला में क्या तुम कुछ बदलाव सुझा सकती हो?

उत्तर उसे परेशानी न हो या कम-से-कम हो, इसके लिए रैंप बनवाए जा सकते हैं। सुनीता जैसे बच्चों के लिए सहायक भी नियुक्त किया जा सकता है।

प्यारी सुनीता

सुनीता के बारे में पढ़कर तुम्हारे मन में कई सवाल और बातें आ रही होंगी। वे बातें सुनीता को चिट्ठी लिखकर बताओ।

उत्तर

परीक्षा भवन

दिल्ली।

दिनांक 10 सितंबर, 20XX

प्रिय सुनीता,

तुम्हारी कहानी पढ़कर मुझे बहुत प्रेरणा मिली। तुमने अपनी पहिया कुर्सी को अपनी ताकत बनाया है। यह दिखाता है कि तुम कितनी

साहसी और आत्मनिर्भर हो। बाज़ार अकेले जाने का तुम्हारा फैसला और कठिनाइयों का सामना करने का तुम्हारा हौसला प्रशंसनीय है। अमित के साथ तुम्हारी बातचीत ने मुझे सिखाया कि हम सब अपनी-अपनी तरह से खास होते हैं, चाहे हमारी चुनौतियाँ कुछ भी हों। तुमने मुझे यह समझाया कि मुश्किलों के बावजूद हमें आत्मविश्वास नहीं खोना चाहिए। मुझे तुमसे बहुत प्रेरणा मिली है।

तुम्हारी सहेली

क.ख.ग.

कहानी से आगे

सुनीता ने कहा, "मैं पैरों से चल ही नहीं सकती।"

(क) सुनीता अपने पैरों से चल-फिर नहीं सकती। तुमने पिछले साल पर्यावरण अध्ययन की किताब आस-पास में रवि भैया के बारे में पढ़ा होगा। रवि भैया देख नहीं सकते फिर भी वे किताबें पढ़ लेते हैं।

- **वे किस तरह की किताबें पढ़ सकते हैं?**
- **उस तरह की किताबों के बारे में सबसे पहले किसने सोचा?**

उत्तर • रवि भैया ब्रेल लिपि में लिखी पुस्तकें पढ़ सकते हैं।

- उस तरह की किताबों के बारे में सबसे पहले लुई ब्रेल ने सोचा था।

(ख) आस-पास में कुछ ऐसे लोगों के बारे में भी बात की गई है, जो सुन-बोल नहीं सकते हैं।

- **क्या तुम ऐसे किसी बच्चे को जानते हो, जो सुन-बोल नहीं सकता?**
- **तुम उसे किस तरह से अपनी बात समझाते हो?**

उत्तर • हाँ, मैं एक ऐसे लड़के को जानता हूँ। मैं पहले जिस स्कूल में पढ़ता था, उसी में वह भी पढ़ता था। उसका नाम महेश है।

- मैं उसे इशारे के माध्यम से अपनी बात समझाता हूँ।

मेरा आविष्कार

सुनीता जैसे कई बच्चे हैं। इनमें से कुछ देख नहीं सकते तो कुछ बोल या सुन नहीं सकते। कुछ बच्चों के हाथों में परेशानी है, तो कुछ चल नहीं सकते।

तुम ऐसे ही किसी एक बच्चे के बारे में सोचो। यदि तुम्हें कोई शारीरिक परेशानी है, तो अपनी चुनौतियों के बारे में भी सोचो। उस चुनौती का सामना करने के लिए तुम क्या आविष्कार करना चाहोगे? उसके बारे में सोचकर बताओ कि

- **तुम वह कैसे बनाओगे?**

उत्तर मैं उसे लैब में विभिन्न यंत्रों की मदद से बनाऊँगा।

- **उसे बनाने के लिए किन चीजों की जरूरत होगी?**

उत्तर उसे बनाने के लिए चिकित्सा विज्ञान में उपयोग किए जाने वाले यंत्रों की जरूरत पड़ेगी।

- **वह चीज़ क्या-क्या काम कर सकेगी?**

उत्तर वह चीज बोलने और सुनने में मदद करेगी।

- **उस चीज का चित्र भी बनाओ।**

उत्तर छात्र स्वयं करें।

अभ्यास प्रश्न

बहुविकल्पीय प्रश्न

1. सुनीता पहली बार अकेले कहाँ जा रही थी?

(क) स्कूल (ख) बाज़ार (ग) पार्क (घ) दोस्त के घर

2. सुनीता की बाज़ार में किसने मदद की?

(क) दुकानदार ने (ख) फ़रीदा ने
(ग) अमित ने (घ) उसकी माँ ने

3. सुनीता ने बाज़ार से क्या खरीदा?

(क) आटा (ख) चावल
(ग) चीनी (घ) दूध

4. सुनीता को देखकर लोग क्यों मुस्कुराते थे?

(क) क्योंकि वह पहिया कुर्सी पर थी
(ख) क्योंकि वह बहुत हँसमुख थी
(ग) क्योंकि वह अच्छे कपड़े पहनकर आई थी
(घ) क्योंकि वह बहुत तेज़ चल रही थी

उत्तर

1. (ख) बाज़ार
2. (ग) अमित ने
3. (ग) चीनी
4. (क) क्योंकि वह पहिया कुर्सी पर थी

रिक्त स्थान

नीचे दिए गए वाक्यों में रिक्त स्थान की पूर्ति उचित शब्द से कीजिए।

(अलमारी, छोटे, एक, सीढ़ियाँ, पहिया कुर्सी)

1. सुनीता को चलने-फिरने के लिए ………… की मदद लेनी पड़ती है।
2. बाज़ार जाते समय सुनीता ने ….. बच्चों को खेलते हुए देखा।
3. सुनीता ने बाज़ार से ………… किलो चीनी खरीदी।
4. सुनीता की माँ ने उसे …… से अचार लेने को कहा।
5. सुनीता के लिए दुकान में घुसना मुश्किल था, क्योंकि वहाँ ………….. थीं।

उत्तर

1. पहिया कुर्सी 2. छोटे 3. एक
4. अलमारी 5. सीढ़ियाँ

गद्यांश पर आधारित प्रश्न

निम्नलिखित गद्यांश को पढ़कर उस पर आधारित प्रश्नों के उत्तर दीजिए

गद्यांश

सुनीता सुबह सात बजे सोकर उठी। कुछ देर तो वह अपने बिस्तर पर ही बैठी रही। वह सोच रही थी कि आज उसे क्या-क्या काम करने हैं? उसे याद आया कि आज तो बाज़ार जाना है। सोचते ही उसकी आँखों में चमक आ गई। सुनीता आज पहली बार अकेले बाज़ार जाने वाली थी। उसने अपनी टाँग को हाथ से पकड़कर खींचा और उन्हें पलंग से नीचे की ओर लटकाया। फिर पलंग का सहारा लेती हुई अपनी पहिया कुर्सी तक बढ़ी। सुनीता चलने-फिरने के लिए पहिया कुर्सी की मदद लेती है। आज वह सभी काम फुर्ती से निपटाना चाहती थी। हालाँकि कपड़े बदलना, जूते पहनना आदि उसके लिए कठिन काम हैं। पर अपने रोज़ाना के काम करने के लिए उसने स्वयं ही कई तरीके ढूँढ निकाले हैं।

1. सुनीता आज किस काम के लिए तैयार हो रही थी?
   (क) स्कूल जाने के लिए (ख) बाज़ार जाने के लिए
   (ग) पार्क जाने के लिए (घ) खेलने के लिए
2. सुनीता चलने-फिरने के लिए किसकी मदद लेती है?
   (क) अपने भाई की
   (ख) पहिया कुर्सी की
   (ग) माँ की
   (घ) अपने दोस्तों की
3. सुनीता सुबह कितने बजे सोकर उठी?
4. सुनीता को कपड़े बदलना और जूते पहनना क्यों कठिन लगता है?

उत्तर

1. (ख) बाज़ार जाने के लिए 2. (ख) पहिया कुर्सी की
3. सुनीता सुबह सात बजे सोकर उठी।
4. सुनीता को कपड़े बदलना और जूते पहनना इसलिए कठिन लगता है, क्योंकि वह पहिया कुर्सी पर बैठी होती है।

निम्नलिखित प्रश्नों के उत्तर दीजिए

1. सुनीता किस समय सोकर उठी?

उत्तर सुनीता सुबह सात बजे सोकर उठी।

2. सुनीता को बाज़ार से क्या लानी थी?

उत्तर सुनीता को बाजार से एक किलो चीनी लानी थी।

3. सुनीता की मदद करने वाला लड़का कौन था?

उत्तर सुनीता की मदद करने वाला लड़का अमित था, जिसे अन्य बच्चे 'छोटू-छोटू' कहकर बुलाते थे।

4. सुनीता को दुकानदार का व्यवहार क्यों बुरा लगा?

उत्तर सुनीता को दुकानदार का व्यवहार इसलिए बुरा लगा कि दुकानदार ने चीनी की थैली उसके हाथ में न पकड़ाकर उसकी गोद में रख दी थी।

लेखन संबंधी प्रश्न

1. दिए गए चित्र का अपने शब्दों में वर्णन कीजिए।

उत्तर यह चित्र एक पिकनिक का है। इस चित्र में एक परिवार पिकनिक मनाने आया है, जिसमें माता-पिता और उनके तीन बच्चे हैं। इनके पास कुछ खाने-पीने का भी सामान रखा हुआ है। इस चित्र में चारों तरफ हरियाली छाई है। चित्र में तीन कुत्ते भी दिखाई दे रहे हैं। एक बच्चा बोतल से दूध पी रहा है। एक लड़की अपने पिता के कंधे पर बैठी है।

अध्याय 13

हुदहुद

पाठ का सार

बादशाह सुलेमान अपने उड़नखटोले से उड़ते हुए कहीं जा रहे थे। गर्मी के दिन थे, इसलिए वे धूप से परेशान होने लगे। धूप से बचने के लिए उन्होंने गिद्धों से मदद माँगी और कहा कि तुम लोग अपने पंखों से मेरे ऊपर छाया करे दो। गिद्धों ने बहाना बनाया कि हम तो बहुत छोटे हैं, इसलिए आपके ऊपर छाया नहीं कर पाएँगे। बादशाह सुलेमान आगे बढ़ गए। आगे जाने पर बादशाह की मुलाकात हुदहुदों के मुखिया से हुई। बादशाह ने उनसे भी मदद माँगी। हुदहुदों के मुखिया ने सभी हुदहुदों को इकट्ठा किया और बादशाह के ऊपर छाया कर दी। बादशाह हुदहुदों से काफी खुश हुए। उन्होंने उनसे कोई वरदान माँगने के लिए कहा। हुदहुदों के मुखिया ने कहा कि ऐसा वरदान दीजिए कि हमारे सर पर सोने की कलगी निकल आए। बादशाह ने पुनः विचार करने के लिए कहा। इस पर हुदहुदों के मुखिया ने कहा कि हमने इस पर सोच-विचार कर लिया है। बादशाह सुलेमान ने मुखिया की प्रार्थना स्वीकार कर ली और सभी हुदहुदों के सिर पर सोने की कलगी निकल आई। लोग हुदहुदों को मारकर सोना इकट्ठा करने लगे। इससे हुदहुदों के वंश पर संकट छा गया। हुदहुदों का मुखिया पुनः बादशाह सुलेमान के पास पहुँचा और उसने अपनी समस्या बताई। सुलेमान ने उनकी समस्या का हल निकालते हुए कहा कि आज से सोने की जगह सुंदर परों की कलगी होगी। इस घटना के बाद से ही हुदहुदों के सिर पर सुंदर कलगी शोभायमान है। इसके बाद कहानी में हुदहुदों के बारे में जानकारी दी गई है।

हुदहुद एक सुंदर पक्षी है। इसका शरीर सुंदर है। इसकी कलगी विशेष रूप से सुंदर है। इसका पूरा शरीर रंग-बिरंगा होता है। इसके पंख काले होते हैं, जिन पर मोटी सफेद धारियाँ बनी होती हैं। गर्दन का अगला हिस्सा बादामी रंग का होता है। चोटी भी बादामी रंग की होती है, लेकिन उसके सिरे काले और सफेद होते हैं। दुम का भीतरी हिस्सा सफेद और बाहरी हिस्सा काले रंग का होता है। चोंच पतली, लंबी तथा तीखी होती है। इसे कई नामों से जाना जाता है। इन नामों में नहरनी, हजामिन, अंग्रेजी में हुप ऊ, हिंदी में हुदहुद, पदुबया और शाह सुलेमान आदि प्रमुख हैं। मादा हुदहुद तीन से दस अंडे तक देती है और उन अंडों से जब तक बच्चे नहीं निकल आते हैं, तब तक वह उन अंडों की देखरेख करती है। इस समय भोजन की व्यवस्था नर हुदहुद करता है। हुदहुद की बोली में मिठास नहीं होती और न ही इसे पालतू बनाया जा सकता है।

शब्दार्थ

कलगी–पक्षियों के सिर पर पंखों का गुच्छा, परामर्श–सलाह, चटकीला–बहुत चमकदार, नहरनी–नाखून काटने का औजार, दूब–लंबी व नर्म घास।

NCERT फोल्डर

तुम्हारी समझ

(क) हुदहुद को कहीं 'हजामिन' चिड़िया और कहीं 'पदुबया' के नाम से पुकारते हैं। क्यों?

उत्तर हुदहुद की चोंच नाखून काटने की नहरनी से मिलती है, इसलिए इसे 'हजामिन' कहा जाता है। यह दूब में कीड़ा खोजकर खाती है, इसलिए इसे 'पदुबया' के नाम से पुकारते हैं।

(ख) हुदहुद की चोंच पतली, लंबी और तीखी होती है। इस बात को ध्यान में रखकर बताओ

- **वे कैसा भोजन खाते होंगे?**
- **चोंच से वे क्या-क्या काम ले सकते होंगे?**

उत्तर
- हुदहुद कीड़े-मकोड़े और छोटे जीव खाते होंगे।
- हुदहुद चोंच से भोजन निकालने और घोंसला बनाने का काम कर सकते होंगे।

मैंने जाना

पाठ में से ऐसे शब्दों की सूची बनाओ जो पक्षियों के लिए इस्तेमाल होते हैं।

जानती थी	पढ़कर मालूम हुआ	जानना चाहती हूँ	कैसे कहाँ से पता लगाऊँगी?

उत्तर

जानती थी	पढ़कर मालूम हुआ	जानना चाहती हूँ	कैसे कहाँ से पता लगाऊँगी?
चोंच	कलगी	हुदहुद की उम्र	किताब से
चिड़िया	हजामिन चिड़िया	हुदहुद का जीवन चक्र	इंटरनेट से
पंख	पदुबया	हुदहुद के दुश्मन	पक्षी विशेषज्ञ से
घोंसला	शाह सुलेमान	हुदहुद का प्रवासी व्यवहार	डॉक्यूमेंट्री से
अंडे	हुप-हुप-हुप की आवाज	हुदहुद नर-मादा में अंतर	अभयारण्य से

पाठ पढ़ने के बाद अपनी कॉपी में एक तालिका तैयार करो और उस तालिका में मालूम की गई जानकारी लिखो।

उत्तर छात्र स्वयं करें।

पहचानें कैसे?

(क) अगर तुम्हें हुदहुद को पहचानने में किसी की मदद करनी है तो तुम उसे कौन-सी बातें बताओगे? चार-पाँच वाक्यों में लिखो।

उत्तर हुदहुद एक रंग-बिरंगा और सुंदर पक्षी होता है। इसकी चोंच लंबी, पतली और तीखी होती है, जिससे यह ज़मीन के भीतर छिपे कीड़े-मकोड़ों को ढूँढता है। इसके सिर पर एक सुंदर कलगी होती है, जो आमतौर पर समेटी रहती है, लेकिन आवाज़ सुनकर यह उसे फैला लेता है। इसके पंख काले होते हैं, जिन पर सफेद धारियाँ होती हैं। इसके बोलने की आवाज़ 'हुप-हुप-हुप' जैसी होती है।

(ख) अब कौवे या कबूतर को पहचानने के लिए चार-पाँच बिंदु लिखो। यह लिखने के लिए तुम्हें इन पक्षियों को कुछ समय तक बहुत गौर से देखना होगा।

उत्तर कौवे का रंग काला होता है और उसकी चोंच भी काली और मजबूत होती है। उसकी आँखें भी काली होती हैं। उसकी आवाज़ 'काँव-काँव' होती है। वह बहुत चतुर और सामाजिक होता है। इसे आमतौर पर कूड़े में खाना ढूँढते हुए देखा जाता है।

कबूतर का शरीर सफेद, भूरे या नीले रंग का हो सकता है। उसकी चोंच छोटी और नुकीली होती है। कबूतर बहुत शांत पक्षी होता है और अकसर घरों की छतों पर बैठे हुए देखा जा सकता है। इनकी आवाज़ 'गुटर-गू' होती है।

तरह-तरह के नाम

तुम्हारे आसपास कौन-कौन से पक्षी पाए जाते हैं, उनके नामों की सूची बनाओ। तुम्हारे और तुम्हारे दोस्तों के घर की भाषा में इन्हें क्या कहते हैं? जिन पक्षियों के नाम तुम्हें पता नहीं हैं, उनके नाम तुम्हें पता करने होंगे।

उत्तर हमारे घर के आसपास कौआ, कबूतर, गौरैया, तोता, मोर, बगुला और तीतर आदि पक्षी पाए जाते हैं।

बातचीत

तुमने हुदहुद से जुड़ी एक कहानी पढ़ी है। उस कहानी को बातचीत के रूप में लिखो। नीचे हमने इस बातचीत को तुम्हारे लिए शुरू कर दिया है

शाह सुलेमान अरे भाई गिद्ध! जरा मेरी बात तो सुनो।

गिद्ध (उड़ते-उड़ते) कहिए, मगर जरा जल्दी से।

शाह सुलेमान ....

गिद्ध ....

तुम अपने दोस्तों के साथ बातचीत को कक्षा में नाटक के रूप में प्रस्तुत कर सकते हो।

उत्तर

शाह सुलेमान मैं बहुत गर्मी में हूँ। क्या तुम अपने पंखों से मुझे थोड़ी छाया दे सकते हो?

गिद्ध (हँसते हुए) अरे महाराज, हम तो छोटे-छोटे हैं। हमारी गर्दन पर तो पंख भी नहीं हैं, हम आपको छाया कैसे देंगे?

शाह सुलेमान ओ हुदहुद के मुखिया, क्या तुम मेरी मदद करोगे? मुझे छाया की ज़रूरत है।

हुदहुद के मुखिया (चतुराई से) जी महाराज, हम तुरंत अपने दल को इकट्ठा कर देते हैं।

शाह सुलेमान (हँसते हुए) इसका फल क्या होगा, यह तुमने सोचा?

मुखिया जी हाँ, मैंने परामर्श कर लिया है।

शाह सुलेमान ठीक है, तुम्हारी प्रार्थना स्वीकार है।

मुखिया (कुछ समय बाद चिंतित होकर) महाराज, यह कलगी तो हमारे वंश का विनाश कर रही है!

शाह सुलेमान मैंने तुम्हें चेतावनी दी थी। अब से तुम्हारे सिर पर सुंदर परों का ताज होगा।

मुखिया (खुश होकर) धन्यवाद, महाराज!
(हुदहुद अपनी नई कलगी के साथ उड़ने लगते हैं।)

रंगा-रंग

(क) हुदहुद का सारा शरीर रंग-बिरंगा और चटकीला होता है।
हुदहुद का रंग चटकीला बताया गया है। रंग कैसे हैं- यह बताने के लिए कुछ शब्दों का इस्तेमाल किया जा सकता है; जैसे- फीके रंग, चटकीले रंग आदि।
बताओ कि ऐसे रंग किन-किन चीज़ों के होते हैं?

उत्तर

रंग का नाम	इस रंग की चीजों के नाम
गहरा काला	कोयला, काली बिल्ली, गहरी रात
फीका हरा	पत्ता, घास, कपड़ा
भड़कीला लाल	शादी का जोड़ा, ट्रैफिक सिग्नल की बत्ती, लाल गुब्बारा
सुनहरा पीला	सूरजमुखी, सोने का सिक्का

(ख) यूनी ने आसमानी रंग की कमीज पहनी है।
'आसमानी' रंग का नाम कैसे बना होगा? सोचो।

ऐसे ही कुछ और रंगों के नाम लिखो, जो किसी चीज़ के नाम पर पड़े हैं।
(संकेत- फल, सब्ज़ी, पत्तों आदि के नामों पर)

उत्तर
- गुलाबी गुलाब के नाम पर
- बैंगनी बैंगन के नाम पर
- चॉकलेटी चॉकलेट के नाम पर
- केसरी केसर के नाम पर
- मटमैला मिट्टी के नाम पर
- जामुनी जामुन के नाम पर
- नारंगी संतरे के नाम पर

शब्द एक-अर्थ अनेक

- शाह की भेंट हुदहुदों के मुखिया से हुई।
- मुझे मेरी बहन ने एक बहुत सुंदर भेंट दी।

ऊपर वाले वाक्य में भेंट का मतलब **मुलाकात** से है, नीचे वाले वाक्य में **उपहार** से। तुम भी कोई ऐसे चार शब्द सोचो जिनके दो मतलब निकलते हों। उनका वाक्यों में प्रयोग करो।

उत्तर

(i) **कलम**
- उसकी **कलम** बहुत सुंदर है। (पेन)
- बगीचे में आम की एक नई **कलम** लगाई गई है। (पेड़ की शाखा या पौधा)

(ii) **नाव**

- मछुआरे ने अपनी **नाव** को किनारे खड़ा कर दिया। (पानी में चलने वाला वाहन)
- रमेश मुश्किल से घर-गृहस्थी की **नाव** खे रहा है। (चलाना)

(iii) **बाँध**

- इस नदी पर एक बड़ा **बाँध** बनाया गया है। (पानी इकट्ठा करने के लिए अवरोध)
- उसने अपने बालों को रिबन से **बाँध** लिया। (कसकर पकड़ना)

(iv) **दूरी**

- मेरे घर और स्कूल के बीच काफी **दूरी** है। (भौतिक फासला)
- इस विषय पर हमारे विचारों में **दूरी** है। (मतभेद)

नाम

हुदहुद एक बहुत ही सुंदर **पक्षी** है। हुदहुद और पक्षी, दोनों को ही हम संज्ञा कहते हैं। अब नीचे दी गई तालिका को आगे बढ़ाओ।

हुदहुद	पक्षी
भारत	देश
अनार	फल
हाथी	जानवर
गंगा	नदी
दिल्ली	शहर

अभ्यास प्रश्न

बहुविकल्पीय प्रश्न

1. हुदहुद को कलगी क्यों मिली?

(क) उसने बादशाह सुलेमान की मदद की थी
(ख) वह सबसे सुंदर पक्षी था
(ग) वह सबसे चतुर पक्षी था
(घ) उसने गिद्धों की मदद की थी

2. गिद्धों ने सुलेमान की मदद क्यों नहीं की?

(क) वे छोटे थे और पंखों से छाया नहीं कर सकते थे
(ख) वे सुलेमान को पसंद नहीं करते थे
(ग) वे सोने की कलगी चाहते थे
(घ) वे उड़ान भर रहे थे

3. हुदहुद की चोंच कैसी होती है?

(क) छोटी और मोटी
(ख) लंबी और पतली
(ग) मुड़ी हुई
(घ) चौड़ी

4. बादशाह सुलेमान ने हुदहुदों को क्या वरदान दिया?

(क) पंखों का ताज
(ख) सोने की कलगी
(ग) उड़ने की शक्ति
(घ) सुंदर घोंसला

5. हुदहुद किसकी वजह से 'शाह सुलेमान' के नाम से भी जाना जाता है?

(क) सुंदरता की वजह से (ख) चोंच की वजह से
(ग) कलगी की वजह से (घ) आवाज़ की वजह से

उत्तर

1. (क) उसने बादशाह सुलेमान की मदद की थी
2. (क) वे छोटे थे और पंखों से छाया नहीं कर सकते थे
3. (ख) लंबी और पतली
4. (ख) सोने की कलगी
5. (ग) कलगी की वजह से

रिक्त स्थान

नीचे दिए गए वाक्यों में रिक्त स्थान की पूर्ति उचित शब्द से कीजिए।

(सोने, सफेद, तीखी, तीन, छाया)

1. हुदहुद की चोंच पतली, लंबी और ·········· होती है।
2. सुलेमान बादशाह ने गिद्धों से ······ करने के लिए कहा।
3. हुदहुदों के सिर पर पहले ········· की कलगी थी।
4. हुदहुद के पंखों पर मोटी ··········· धारियाँ होती हैं।
5. मादा हुदहुद ··········· से दस तक अंडे देती है।

उत्तर

1. तीखी
2. छाया
3. सोने
4. सफेद
5. तीन

गद्यांश पर आधारित प्रश्न

निम्नलिखित गद्यांश को पढ़कर उस पर आधारित प्रश्नों के उत्तर दीजिए।

गद्यांश

एक बार सुलेमान नामक बादशाह आकाश में उड़ने वाले अपने उड़नखटोले पर बैठे कहीं जा रहे थे। बड़ी गर्मी थी। वह धूप से परेशान हो रहे थे। आकाश में उड़ने वाले गिद्धों से उन्होंने कहा कि अपने पंखों से तुम लोग मेरे सिर पर छाया कर दो। पर गिद्धों ने ऐसा करने से मना कर दिया। उन्होंने बहाना बनाते हुए कहा, "हम तो इतने छोटे-छोटे हैं। हमारी गर्दन पर पंख भी नहीं हैं। हम छाया कैसे कर सकते हैं!"

सुलेमान आगे बढ़ गए। कुछ दूर जाने पर उनकी भेंट हुदहुदों के मुखिया से हुई। सुलेमान ने उससे भी मदद माँगी। वह चतुर था। उसने फ़ौरन अपने दल के सभी हुदहुदों को इकट्ठा करके बादशाह सुलेमान के ऊपर छाया कर दी। सुलेमान बोले, "मैंने गिद्धों से भी मदद माँगी थी। वे मेरी मदद कर सकते थे, पर उन्होंने मेरी मदद नहीं की। तुम गिद्धों से छोटे तो हो पर चतुर अधिक हो। तुम सबने मिलकर मेरी सहायता की है। मैं तुमसे बहुत प्रसन्न हूँ। मैं तुम्हारी कोई इच्छा पूरी करूँगा। बताओ, तुम्हारी क्या इच्छा है?"

1. **बादशाह सुलेमान ने सबसे पहले किससे मदद माँगी थी?**
   (क) हुदहुद से (ख) गिद्धों से
   (ग) बाज से (घ) तोते से
2. **सुलेमान ने दूसरी बार किससे मदद माँगी?**
   (क) गिद्धों से (ख) हुदहुदों से
   (ग) मैना से (घ) सैनिकों से
3. **सुलेमान किस पर बैठे हुए थे?**
4. **हुदहुदों ने सुलेमान की मदद कैसे की?**

उत्तर

1. (ख) गिद्धों से
2. (ख) हुदहुदों से
3. सुलेमान उड़नखटोले पर बैठे हुए थे।
4. हुदहुदों ने अपने पंखों से सुलेमान के ऊपर छाया कर दी।

निम्नलिखित प्रश्नों के उत्तर दीजिए

1. **बादशाह सुलेमान ने सबसे पहले किस पक्षी से मदद माँगी?**

उत्तर बादशाह सुलेमान ने सबसे पहले गिद्धों से मदद माँगी।

2. **हुदहुद को किसकी वजह से 'हजामिन चिड़िया' कहा जाता है?**

उत्तर हुदहुद की चोंच पतली, तीखी तथा लंबी होती है, जिस कारण इसे 'हजामिन चिड़िया' भी कहते हैं।

3. **हुदहुद को अंग्रेजी में क्या कहा जाता है?**

उत्तर हुदहुद को अंग्रेजी में हूपो (Hoopoe) कहते हैं।

4. **हुदहुद का शरीर कैसा होता है?**

उत्तर हुदहुद एक सुंदर पक्षी है। इसकी कलगी विशेष रूप से सुंदर है। इसका पूरा शरीर रंग-बिरंगा होता है। इनके पंख काले होते हैं। गर्दन का हिस्सा बादामी रंग का होता है।

लेखन संबंधी प्रश्न

1. **अपने मित्र को उसके जन्मदिन पर बधाई पत्र लिखिए।**

उत्तर परीक्षा भवन,

दिल्ली

दिनांक 10 अक्टूबर, 20XX

प्रिय मित्र,

नमस्ते, मैं और मेरे माता-पिता सकुशल हैं। आशा है कि तुम भी कुशलपूर्वक होगे। तुम्हारे जन्मदिन का निमंत्रण पत्र मिला। मेरे व मेरे परिवार की तरफ से तुम्हें जन्मदिन की हार्दिक शुभकामनाएँ। ईश्वर तुम्हें लंबी उम्र दें। मैं तुम्हें एक छोटा-सा उपहार भेज रहा हूँ, जो तुम्हें अवश्य पसंद आएगा। एक बार पुन: जन्मदिन की बधाई।

तुम्हारा मित्र

हर्षित

अध्याय 14

मुफ्त ही मुफ्त

पाठ का सार

एक दिन भीखूभाई का मन नारियल खाने को किया। उन्होंने अपनी यह इच्छा लाभुबेन को बताई, तो उसने कहा कि नारियल बाजार में जाकर लाना पड़ेगा। बाजार में उन्होंने नारियल वाले से पूछा कि नारियल का दाम कितना है, तो नारियल वाले ने दो रुपये बताए। भीखूभाई ने नारियल एक रुपये में देने को कहा, तो नारियल वाले ने कहा कि एक रुपये में नारियल चाहते हो तो मंडी में जाकर ले लो। मंडी में जाकर देखा तो वहाँ एक रुपये में नारियल मिल रहे थे। भीखूभाई ने नारियल पचास पैसे में लेना चाहा। नारियल वाले ने मना कर दिया और कहा कि पचास पैसे में चाहते हो तो बंदरगाह पर जाओ, वहाँ मिल जाएगा। भीखूभाई बंदरगाह की ओर चल पड़े। वहाँ सागर किनारे एक नाववाला था, जिसके सामने कुछ नारियल रखे हुए थे।

भीखूभाई ने नारियल का दाम पूछा, तो उसने पचास पैसे बताए। भीखूभाई ने इससे भी कम दाम पर नारियल लेना चाहा। नाववाले ने कहा इससे भी कम दाम पर लेना है, तो नारियल के बगीचे में चले जाओ। बगीचे वाले ने नारियल का दाम पच्चीस पैसे बताए। भीखूभाई ने सोचा कि इतनी दूर आकर भी पैसे देने पड़ रहे हैं। बगीचे वाले ने कहा कि ये पैसे नारियल तोड़ने में लगने वाली मेहनत के हैं। यदि मुफ़्त में चाहते हो, तो पेड़ पर चढ़कर तोड़ लो।

वे पेड़ पर चढ़ गए तथा उन्होंने जैसे ही एक नारियल को पकड़कर तोड़ना चाहा, उनका पैर फिसल गया और वे एक नारियल पकड़कर लटक गए। बगीचे वाले ने भी उनकी मदद नहीं की। तभी उधर से एक ऊँट वाला गुजरा, तो भीखूभाई ने उससे मदद करने को कहा। उसने ऊँट की पीठ पर खड़े होकर जैसे ही भीखूभाई के पैर को पेड़ पर टिकाने की कोशिश की, तो ऊँट हरे-हरे पत्ते देखकर आगे बढ़ गया। अपनी जान बचाने के लिए ऊँट वाला भीखूभाई के पैर पकड़कर लटक गया। थोड़ी देर बाद एक घुड़सवार उधर से गुजरा तो दोनों ने उससे मदद करने को कहा। वह मदद करने के लिए जैसे ही घोड़े पर खड़ा हुआ, तो हरी-हरी घास देखकर घोड़ा भी आगे बढ़ गया। अब तीनों एक के नीचे एक लटके हुए थे। घुड़सवार ने भीखूभाई से कहा कि काका कसकर पकड़े रहना छोड़ना नहीं, मैं तुम्हें सौ रुपये दूँगा, तभी ऊँट वाले ने दो सौ रुपये देने को कहा। भीखूभाई बहुत खुश हो गए और उन्होंने अपनी दोनों बाहें फैला दीं। बाँह फैलाते ही नारियल छूट गया और तीनों नीचे गिर गए। गिरने के बाद तभी एक बड़ा नारियल भीखूभाई के सिर पर गिरकर फूट गया। यह नारियल भीखूभाई के लिए बिल्कुल मुफ़्त था।

शब्दार्थ

चटकारा-स्वाद लेना, कंजूस-पैसे न खर्च करने वाला, कोलाहल-शोर, हक्के-बक्के-आश्चर्यचकित, दुहाई-विनती, धड़ाम-गिरने की आवाज़।

NCERT फोल्डर

तुम्हारी समझ

(क) हर बार भीखूभाई कम दाम देना चाहते थे। क्यों?

उत्तर भीखूभाई हर बार इसलिए कम दाम देना चाहते थे, क्योंकि वे कंजूस थे।

(ख) हर जगह नारियल के दाम में फ़र्क क्यों था?

उत्तर नारियल के दाम में फ़र्क आने का कारण मजदूरी और परिवहन व्यय है। जहाँ पर इसकी खेती होती है, वहाँ परिवहन व्यय शून्य होता है, इसलिए यह वहाँ सस्ता मिलेगा। जबकि बाजार तक आते-आते परिवहन और मजदूरी के कारण दाम अधिक हो जाता है।

(ग) क्या भीखूभाई को नारियल सच में मुफ़्त में ही मिला? क्यों?

उत्तर भीखूभाई को नारियल मुफ़्त में नहीं मिला था, क्योंकि उस एक नारियल के बदले उन्होंने पैदल चलकर लंबी दूरी तय की थी और पसीने से लथपथ हो गए थे। वहीं बिना पैसे दिए नारियल पाने के लिए उन्हें पेड़ पर भी चढ़ना पड़ा और कई समस्याओं का सामना भी करना पड़ा।

(घ) वे खेत में बूढ़े बरगद के नीचे बैठ गए। तुम्हारे विचार से कहानी में बरगद को बूढ़ा क्यों कहा गया होगा?

उत्तर बरगद को बूढ़ा इसलिए कहा गया होगा, क्योंकि वह बहुत पुराना रहा होगा।

भीखूभाई ऐसे थे

कहानी को पढ़कर तुम भीखूभाई के बारे में कुछ बातें बताओ।

(क) उन्हें खाने-पीने का शौक था।

(ख) ....

(ग) ....

(घ) ....

(ङ) ....

उत्तर

(क) उन्हें खाने-पीने का शौक था।

(ख) वे बहुत कंजूस थे।

(ग) सस्ता पाने के चक्कर में वे कहीं भी जा सकते थे।

(घ) पैसा बचाने के लिए वे बहुत मेहनत करते थे।

(ङ) वे नारियल के शौकीन थे।

क्या बढ़ा, क्या घटा

कहानी जैसे-जैसे आगे बढ़ती है, कुछ चीजें बढ़ती हैं और कुछ घटती हैं। बताओ इनका क्या हुआ, ये घटे या बढ़े?

नारियल का दाम	....
भीखूभाई का लालच	....
रास्ते की लंबाई	....
भीखूभाई की थकान	....

उत्तर

नारियल का दाम	घटा
भीखूभाई का लालच	बढ़ा
रास्ते की लंबाई	बढ़ी
भीखूभाई की थकान	बढ़ी

कहो कहानी

यदि इस कहानी में भीखूभाई को नारियल नहीं बल्कि आम खाने की इच्छा होती तो कहानी आगे कैसे बढ़ती? बताओ।

उत्तर छात्र स्वयं करें।

बात की बात

कहानी में नारियल वाले और भीखूभाई की बातचीत फिर से पढ़ो। अब इसे अपने घर की बोली में लिखो।

उत्तर 1. ऐ भाई, नारियल कइसे दे रहा हो?

2. काका, बस दो रुपये में ले लो।

3. अरे, दो रुपये बहुत हैं, एक रुपये में दे दे।

4. ना काका, एक में ना होगा, दो रुपये ही लगेंगे।

5. अच्छा तो बताओ, एक रुपये में कहाँ मिलेगा?

6. मंडी में मिल सकता है, उधर जाकर देख लो।

शब्दों की बात

नाना-नानी पतीली-पतीला

ऊपर दिए गए उदाहरणों की मदद से नीचे दी गई जगह में सही शब्द लिखो।

उत्तर

काका	काकी
दर्जी	दर्जिन
मालिन	माली
टोकरी	टोकरा
मटका	मटकी
गद्दा	गद्दी

मंडी

"मंडी में कोलाहल फैला हुआ था। व्यापारियों की ऊँची-ऊँची आवाज़ें गूँज रही थीं।"

(क) मंडी में क्या-क्या बिक रहा होगा?

उत्तर मंडी में आलू, टमाटर, मिर्च, गाजर, मूली, कद्दू, लौकी, प्याज, लहसुन आदि बिक रहा होगा।

(ख) मंडी में तरह-तरह की आवाजें सुनाई देती हैं। जैसे– ताज़ा टमाटर! बीस रुपया! बीस रुपया! बीस रुपया! मंडी में और कैसी आवाजें सुनाई देती हैं?

उत्तर आलू ले लो, सस्ता आलू! दस रुपये किलो!
प्याज़-प्याज़! ताज़ा प्याज़, बीस रुपये किलो!
हरी मिर्ची! मसालेदार मिर्ची! दस रुपये की ढेरी!
धनिया-पत्ता! एकदम ताज़ा हरा धनिया! पाँच रुपये का गुच्छा!
गोभी-गोभी! बंदगोभी सिर्फ पंद्रह रुपये!
संतरे-संतरे! मीठे संतरे, बीस रुपये किलो!

(ग) क्या तुम अपने आसपास की ऐसी जगह सोच सकते हो, जहाँ बहुत शोर होता है। उस जगह के बारे में लिखो।

उत्तर हमारे शहर का मुख्य बाजार बहुत शोरगुल वाला होता है। वहाँ दुकानदारों की आवाज़ें, गाड़ियों के हॉर्न और भीड़-भाड़ से हमेशा हलचल मची रहती है।

गुजरात की झलक

(क) 'मुफ्त ही मुफ्त' गुजरात की लोककथा है। इस लोककथा के चित्रों में ऐसी कौन-सी बातें हैं, जिनसे तुम यह अंदाज़ा लगा सकते हो?

उत्तर इस लोककथा में कुछ चीजें ऐसी आई हैं, जिससे अनुमान लगाया जा सकता है कि यह गुजरात की लोककथा है भीखूभाई और लाभुबेन के नाम से

- पाठ में दिए गए चित्र से जिसमें भीखूभाई गुजराती परिधान पहने हैं
- बंदरगाह के वर्णन से
- पात्रों के द्वारा उपयोग की गई भाषा से

(ख) गुजरात में किसी का आदर करने के लिए नाम के साथ भाई, बेन (बहन) जैसे शब्दों का प्रयोग होता है। तेलुगू में नाम के आगे 'गारू' और हिंदी में 'जी' जोड़ा जाता है। तुम्हारी कक्षा में भी अलग-अलग भाषा बोलने वाले बच्चे होंगे! पता करो और लिखो कि वे अपनी भाषा में किसी को आदर देने के लिए किन-किन शब्दों का इस्तेमाल करते हैं?

उत्तर छात्र स्वयं करें।

अभ्यास प्रश्न

बहुविकल्पीय प्रश्न

1. भीखूभाई को क्या खाने का मन हुआ था?
(क) आम (ख) नारियल (ग) गाजर (घ) बटाटा

2. नारियल वाला भीखूभाई से कितने पैसे माँग रहा था?
(क) एक रुपया (ख) दो रुपये
(ग) पचास पैसे (घ) पच्चीस पैसे

3. भीखूभाई ने नाववाले से कितने पैसे में नारियल लेना चाहा?
(क) एक रुपये में (ख) पचास पैसे में
(ग) पच्चीस पैसे में (घ) मुफ्त में

4. भीखूभाई ने सबसे पहले किससे मदद माँगी?
(क) नारियल वाले से (ख) ऊँटवाले से
(ग) घुड़सवार से (घ) नाववाले से

5. आखिर में भीखूभाई के सिर पर क्या गिरा?
(क) नारियल (ख) घास
(ग) पत्थर (घ) लकड़ी

उत्तर
1. (ख) नारियल 2. (ख) दो रुपये
3. (ग) पच्चीस पैसे में 4. (ख) ऊँटवाले से
5. (क) नारियल

रिक्त स्थान

नीचे दिए गए वाक्यों में रिक्त स्थान की पूर्ति उचित शब्द से कीजिए।

(हरी घास, बाजार, पेड़ पर, नारियल, मुफ्त में)

1. भीखूभाई नारियल खरीदने के लिए पहले ······ गए थे।
2. माली ने भीखूभाई से कहा कि नारियल तोड़ने के लिए उन्हें ········ चढ़ना पड़ेगा।
3. जब भीखूभाई का पैर फिसला, तो उन्होंने ········ को पकड़ लिया।
4. घोड़े ने ·········· देखते ही अपनी जगह छोड़ दी।
5. भीखूभाई को नारियल ········· मिला।

उत्तर

1. बाजार 2. पेड़ पर 3. नारियल
4. हरी घास 5. मुफ़्त में

गद्यांश पर आधारित प्रश्न

निम्नलिखित गद्यांश को पढ़कर उस पर आधारित प्रश्नों के उत्तर दीजिए।

गद्यांश

एक दिन भीखूभाई का मन नारियल खाने का हुआ। ताज़ा-मुलायम, कसा हुआ, शक्कर के साथ। म्म्म्म ! उसके बारे में सोचते ही भीखूभाई ने अपने होंठों को चटकारा, "वाह क्या मीठा-मीठा सा स्वाद होगा!" लेकिन एक छोटी-सी समस्या थी। घर में तो एक भी नारियल नहीं था। 'ओहो! अब मुझे बाज़ार जाना पड़ेगा,' उन्होंने अपनी पत्नी लाभुबेन से कहा।

लाभुबेन अपने कंधे उचकाकर बोलीं, 'खाना है तो जाना है।' एक समस्या और थी।

भीखूभाई ने कहा, "पैसे खर्च करने पड़ेंगे,"

लाभुबेन बोली, "हाँ। पैसे तो खर्च करने पड़ेंगे।।"

अब तक तो तुम्हें पता लग गया होगा कि भीखूभाई ज़रा कंजूस थे। वे सीधे खेत में बूढ़े बरगद के नीचे जाकर बैठ गए और सोचने लगे, 'क्या करूँ? मैं क्या करूँ?'

1. भीखूभाई के घर में क्या नहीं था?
   (क) सेब (ख) नारियल
   (ग) आम (घ) अंगूर
2. लाभुबेन ने भीखूभाई से क्या कहा?
   (क) घर पर नारियल है (ख) तुम्हें बाजार जाना पड़ेगा
   (ग) नारियल मत खाओ (घ) बाज़ार मत जाओ
3. भीखूभाई किस पेड़ के नीचे जाकर बैठे?
4. जब भीखूभाई ने बाज़ार जाने की बात की तो लाभुबेन ने क्या कहा?

उत्तर 1. (ख) नारियल
2. (ख) तुम्हें बाजार जाना पड़ेगा
3. भीखूभाई बूढ़े बरगद के नीचे जाकर बैठे।
4. खाना है तो जाना है।

निम्नलिखित प्रश्नों के उत्तर दीजिए

1. भीखूभाई की पत्नी का नाम क्या था?

उत्तर भीखूभाई की पत्नी का नाम लाभुबेन था।

2. माली ने भीखूभाई से नारियल के कितने पैसे माँगे?

उत्तर माली ने भीखूभाई से नारियल के पच्चीस पैसे माँगे।

3. भीखूभाई को किसने मुफ्त में नारियल तोड़ने का सुझाव दिया?

उत्तर भीखूभाई को बगीचे वाले ने मुफ्त में नारियल तोड़ने का सुझाव दिया।

4. भीखूभाई ने नारियल तोड़ने के लिए किस पेड़ पर चढ़ने की कोशिश की?

उत्तर भीखूभाई ने नारियल तोड़ने के लिए नारियल के पेड़ पर चढ़ने की कोशिश की।

5. भीखूभाई को नारियल अंत में किस कीमत पर मिला?

उत्तर भीखूभाई को नारियल अंत में बिल्कुल मुफ्त में मिला, क्योंकि वह नारियल उनके सिर पर आ गिरा था।

लेखन संबंधी प्रश्न

1. अमन और फलवाले के बीच होने वाला संवाद लिखिए।

उत्तर **अमन** भैया लीची कितने रुपये किलो दीं?
फलवाला साठ रुपये किलो।
अमन ये तो बहुत महँगी हैं।
फलवाला दूसरी टोकरी में चालीस रुपये किलो हैं।
अमन नहीं भैया, ये तो अच्छी नही हैं। सेब कैसे दिए?
फलवाला सेब अस्सी रुपये किलो हैं।
अमन आधा किलो सेब दे दीजिए।
फलवाला ये लीजिए, आधा किलो सेब।
अमन लीजिए भैया पैसे।
फलवाला धन्यवाद।

Looking Around (EVS)

CHAPTER 1

GOING TO SCHOOL

About the Chapter

In this chapter, we will learn how children in different parts of India go to school. In some places, children walk through thick jungles or in the snow to reach school. In places with heavy rain, they cross rivers on bamboo and rope bridges. They balance carefully as they walk.

In Ladakh, children use a wooden trolley to cross wide and deep rivers. The trolley is tied to strong ropes and 4 to 5 children sit in it. A pulley moves the trolley safely across the river. In Kerala, children travel in small wooden boats called *vallams*.

In deserts like Rajasthan, children ride camel carts to school. In some villages, they use bullock carts. In cities and towns, children cross strong bridges made of cement, bricks, or iron rods. In many places, children ride bicycles to school.

GLOSSARY

Pulley A machine that helps to lift or move things using a wheel and rope.

Vallam A small wooden boat used to cross rivers, especially in Kerala.

Jungle Path A jungle path is a way through a thick forest, where you can see birds and animals.

Snowy Path A path covered in snow. It is found in high-altitude regions.

Rocky Path A rocky path is a rough road covered with stones, usually found in the mountains.

NCERT FOLDER

Try these (Page 1)

Q.1 Collect some bricks. Lay them on the ground in a line as shown in the picture. Try walking on them. Was it easy?

Ans. Walking on the bricks was a little hard at first. But after trying a few times, it became easier.

Q.2 Make a small bridge by tying 4 or 5 bamboo poles together. Ask your teacher to help you. Now walk on your bridge. How did you feel? Did you fall down? If you walk like this a few times, you will start finding it easy.

Ans. At first, I was scared that I would fall. I felt a little unsteady. But after trying a few times, I found it easier to walk on the bamboo bridge.

Q.3 Do you think it would be easier to walk on this bridge barefoot or with shoes or slippers? Why?

Ans. It might be easier to walk with shoes because shoes can give a better grip.

Let us Do (Page 2)

Q.1 Observe pictures 1 and 2. In the pictures, children are pulling the buckets from the well. Can you tell the difference in both the pictures? Which would be easier-using the pulley or not using it to lift things?

Ans. In picture 1, the child is not using a pulley, so it looks harder to lift the bucket.
In picture 2, the child is using a pulley, which makes lifting the bucket much easier.

Q.2 Look around you–where all do you see the use of pulleys? List them.

Ans. I see pulleys being used in many things. For example, pulleys are used wells to pull up water. They are used in elevators to move up and down and sometimes in construction sites to lift heavy materials.

Page 3

Q.1 How is this bridge different from a bamboo bridge?

Ans. The bridge is stronger and more durable. It is made of materials like bricks, cement, and iron. A bamboo bridge is made using bamboo. It is lighter and not as strong as a cement bridge.

Q.2 How many people do you think can cross the bridge at one time?

Ans. Around 20-30 people can cross the cement bridge at one time because it is strong and wide.

Q.3 If you had a chance, which bridge would you like to use? Why?

Ans. I would like to use a cement bridge because it feels safer and more solid.

Q.4 Do you have to cross any bridge on the way to your school? If yes, what is the bridge like? Draw its picture.

Ans. Yes, I have to cross a bridge on the way to my school. It is a bridge made up of cement.

Q.5 Find out from your grandparents, what kinds of bridge were there when they were young?

Ans. My grandparents said that there were wooden and bamboo bridges when they were young. They were not as strong as the bridges we have now.

Page 4

Q.1 Is there any bridge near your house? Find out more about the bridge.

Ans. Yes, there is a bridge near my house.

Q.2 Where is the bridge – over water, over a road, between two mountains or somewhere else?

Ans. The bridge is over a small river that flows in my neighbourhood.

Q.3 Who all use the bridge? Is it used by people on foot and also by vehicles and animals?

Ans. The bridge is used by people on foot, bicycles, and vehicles like cars and buses. Sometimes, animals like cows and dogs also use the bridge.

Q.4 Does the bridge seem to be old or is it new?

Ans. The bridge looks a bit old, but it is still strong and safe to use.

Q.5 Find out what materials are used in making this bridge. List some of them.

Ans. The bridge is made of cement, iron rods, and bricks. There are also some metal railings for safety.

Q.6 Draw a picture of the bridge in your notebook. Do not forget to draw the train, vehicles, animals or people who cross the bridge.

Ans.

Q.7 Imagine what difficulties there would be, if the bridge was not there?

Ans. If the bridge was not there, it would be difficult for people to cross the river. They would have to go a long way around, or they might need a boat to cross. It would take much longer to reach places on the other side of the river.

Page 5

Q.1 Have you seen any other kind of boats?

Ans. Yes, I have seen boats like motorboats and rowboats.

Q.2 Can you think of other ways by which we can travel on water?

Ans. We can travel on water using ships, ferries, and even rafts.

Q.3 Have you ever sat in a camel-cart or horse carriage (tonga)? Where? Did you climb on it yourself, or did someone help you?

Ans. Yes, I sat in a horse carriage once during my trip to Mussorie. My father helped me climb onto it because it was high.

Q.4 How did you feel riding in the cart? Also, share your experience in the class.

Ans. It was fun to ride in the cart. The horse moved slowly, and it was a bit bumpy. I was scared but also excited for the ride.

Page 6

Q.1 Do you have bullock-carts where you live?

Ans. No, we don't have bullock-carts where I live. But I have seen them in villages.

Q.2 Does it have a roof?

Ans. Some bullock-carts have roofs, and some don't.

Q.3 What kind of wheels do they have?

Ans. They have wooden wheels.

Q.4 Make a drawing of the cart in your notebook.

Ans.

Q.5 Can you ride a bicycle? If yes, who taught you to ride?

Ans. Yes, I can ride a bicycle. My parents taught me.

Q.6 How many children come on bicycles to your school?

Ans. About 30 children come to my school on bicycles.

Page 7

Q.1 Have you ever been in a thick jungle or any such place? Write your experiences in the notebook.

Ans. Yes, I went to a thick jungle once. The jungle was full of thick green trees. There were different types of plants, animals and birds around the jungle. It was a thrilling experience.

Q.2 Can you recognise some birds by their sounds? Can you imitate the sounds of some birds? Do it.

Ans. Yes, I can recognise the sounds of sparrows and crows. I can try to imitate them too.

Page 8

Q.1 Have you ever seen so much snow? Where? In films or somewhere else?

Ans. I have seen snow in pictures and movies, but I have never seen it in real life.

Q.2 Do you think that such places have snow all the time? Why?

Ans. No, I don't think such places have snow all the time. Snow usually falls in winter, when it is very cold. In summer, the snow melts, and the weather becomes warmer in those places.

Page 9

Q.1 Do you face difficulties on the way to your school?

Ans. No, my way to school is easy, and there are no big difficulties.

Q.2 Which is the best month, in which you like to go to school? Why?

Ans. I like going to school in December because the weather is cool and pleasant.

See Me Walk! (Page 9)

Go to a ground or an open space with your friends. Act the way you will walk in these situations:

- The ground is made of soft and smooth rose petals.
- The ground is covered with thorns and there is tall grass on the sides.
- The ground is covered with snow.

Was there a difference in the way you walked each time? Discuss.

Ans. Yes, there was a big difference. On the smooth rose petals, I had to walk gently. On the thorns, I was very careful and slow. On the snow, I had to balance myself to avoid slipping. Different surfaces make us walk differently!

Talk and Share about it (Page 10)

Q.1 Do you also have punishment in your school? What kind?

Ans. Yes, in my school, we sometimes get punishments like standing outside the classroom or not being allowed to play during recess. The punishments are not very harsh.

Q.2 Do you think that punishment should not be there in schools?

Ans. I think there should be no punishment in schools. Instead, teachers should help us understand what we did wrong and guide us to do better.

Q.3 If you come across any such incident, whom will you inform?

Ans. If I come across any such incident, I will inform my teacher or the school principal.

Q.4 How will you make a complaint?

Ans. I will tell the teacher or principal about the issue. I can also write my complaint on a piece of paper and give it to them.

Q.5 Is punishment the only solution to misdeeds? Make some rules for school to prevent misdeeds.

Ans. No, punishment is not the only solution to misdeeds. Students should be guided not to do any misdeeds.

There should be rewards for good behaviour. Teachers should select student of the month on the basis of good behaviour.

Q.6 Draw a picture of your 'dream school' in your notebook and write about it and share in the class.

Ans. My dream school will have big classrooms with colorful walls.

It will have a large playground with swings and slides. There will be no punishments. We will have lots of game periods.

CHAPTER 2 EAR TO EAR

About the Chapter

In this chapter, we will learn about different animals, their ears and skin patterns. Different animals have different types of ears. In some animals, we can see the ears while in other animals, we cannot see them. Birds usually have tiny holes covered with feathers on the sides of their heads. Different animals also have different skin patterns. The different patterns on animals are due to the hair on their skin. Animals give birth in different ways. Some animals lay eggs while others give birth to babies. Some animals like dinosaurs used to live on Earth many years ago. Animals like crocodiles and lizards look like them.

GLOSSARY

Patterns The designs or marks on an animal's skin, usually caused by hair or fur.

NCERT FOLDER

Page 11

Q.1

Are these animals looking funny? The artist has drawn the wrong ears on the heads of the animals. Give correct ears to the animals in the space given below.

Animal	Ear
Elephant	Mouse
Rabbit	
Mouse	
Giraffe	
Dog	
Buffalo	
Deer	

Ans. Yes, the animals in the picture do look funny.

Animal	Ear
Elephant	Mouse
Rabbit	Giraffe
Mouse	Dog
Giraffe	Elephant
Dog	Rabbit
Buffalo	Deer
Deer	Buffalo

Page 12

Q.2 Different animals have different kinds of ears. Among the animals given below, which one have ears that you can see? In which animal can you not see the ears? Write in the table below.

Deer, Frog, Tiger, Sparrow, Pig, Duck, Fish, Buffalo, Giraffe, Ant, Crow, Snake, Lizard, Elephant, Cat

Animals whose ears we can see	Animals whose ears we cannot see

Ans.

Animals whose ears we can see	Animals whose ears we cannot see
Deer	Frog
Tiger	Sparrow
Pig	Duck
Buffalo	Fish
Giraffe	Ant
Elephant	Crow
Cat	Snake
	Lizard

Q.3 Do you think that the animals whose ears we cannot see, really do not have ears?

Ans. No, animals whose ears we cannot see, still have ears. They have different types of ears. For example, birds, frogs and snakes have tiny ear holes, which help them to hear.

Let us Observe this Picture

Q.4 Name the animals in the pictures.

Ans. Here are the names of the animals in the picture

- Chicken (or Hen)
- Sparrow
- Duck
- Crow
- Parrot
- Frog

Q.5 Can you see their ears?

Ans. No, we cannot see the ears of the animals in the picture.

Page 13

Q.1 Find out some other animals which have ears that we cannot see. Write their names.

Ans. Here are some animals whose ears we cannot see

- Snake
- Dolphin
- Turtle
- Crocodile
- Frog
- Fish
- Whale
- Lizard

Read and Write (Page 13)

Q.1 An animal with ears like fans.

Ans. Elephant

Q.2 An animal with ears like leaves.

Ans. Deer

Q.3 An animal with ears on the top of its head.

Ans. Rabbit

Q.4 An animal with ears on both sides of its head.

Ans. Buffalo

Page 14

Q.1 Match the animals shown here with the pictures of their skin. Make the correct pattern of the skin on the picture of each animal.

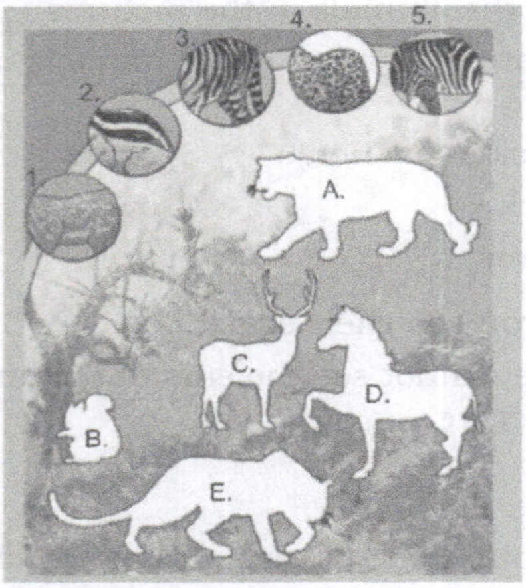

Ans. A-3, B-2, C-1, D-5, E-4

Page 15

Q.1 You might have seen some of the animals given below.

Fox	Elephant	Sparrow	Pigeon
Frog	Crow	Peacock	Pig
Mouse	Cat	Buffalo	Duck
Hen	Camel	Lizard	Cow

Put the names of the animals in the table below.

Ears can be seen	Has hair on skin	Ears cannot be seen	Has feathers on skin

Ans.

Ears can be seen	Has hair on skin	Ears cannot be seen	Has feathers on skin
Elephant	Cow	Sparrow	Duck
Fox	Buffalo	Frog	Hen
Cat	Cat	Duck	Crow
Pig	Pig	Crow	Pigeon
Mouse	Mouse	Hen	Sparrow
Cow	Camel	Pigeon	Peacock
Camel	Fox	Lizard	
Buffalo		Peacock	

Q.2 In which list did you put the cow and the buffalo?

Ans. I put cow and buffalo in the list of animals whose ears can be seen and have hair on skin.

Q.3 From a distance, can you see the hair on their skin?

Ans. No, I cannot see hair on their skin from a distance.

Q.4 Try to go near one of them. Could you see the hair?

Ans. Yes, I could see the hair now.

Q.5 If you were to meet an elephant, would you dare to touch it?

Ans. If I were to meet an elephant, I would not dare to touch it.

Page 16

Q.1 Can you tell which of the animals mentioned in the list lay eggs? Find out and write the names of these animals in the box. Which of the animals in the list give birth to babies? Write their names in the box.

Animals who give birth to babies	

Animals who lay eggs	

Ans.

Animals who give birth to babies	
Deer	Elephant
Cow	Buffalo
Cat	Pig
Giraffe	

Animals who lay eggs	
Fish	Lizard
Frog	Snake
Crow	Ant
Duck	Sparrow

Page 17

Q.1 Have you seen animals around your house or school that have small babies? Write their names in your notebook.

Ans. Yes, I have seen animals around my house or school that have small babies. The names of those animals are Cat, Dog, Cow, Buffalo, Bird, Rabbit, Pig.

Q.2 Have you ever kept a pet? Does anyone you know keep a pet?

Ans. Yes, I have kept a pet. My uncle also has a pet.

Q.3 Which animal is it?

Ans. It's a dog.

Q.4 Does it have a name? What is it?

Ans. Yes, its name is Max.

Q.5 Who gave it this name?

Ans. My mother chose the name Max.

Q.6 What does it like to eat?

Ans. Max likes to eat dog food, chicken and his treats.

Q.7 How many times a day is it given food?

Ans. Max gets his dog food twice a day, once in the morning and once in the evening.

Q.8 When does it sleep? For how long does it sleep?

Ans. Max usually sleeps a lot during the day and night. He might sleep for about 12-14 hours in total.

Q.9 Is there any special way to look after this animal? How?

Ans. Yes, Max needs regular walks, fresh water, and its fur needs to be brushed. Also, we take him to the vet for check-ups.

Q.10 Does it get angry? When? How do you know it is angry?

Ans. Yes, it can get angry if someone takes its toys or food or if another dog comes near it. It growls and barks loudly when it is angry.

Page 18

Q.1 Does it have hair or feathers on its skin?

Ans. It has hair on its skin.

Q.2 Can you see its ears?

Ans. Yes, I can see its ears. It has floppy ears.

Q.3 Is it a baby or a young animal or a full-grown animal?

Ans. Max is a young dog, not a baby. He is not full grown yet.

Q.4 Will this pet animal lay eggs or give birth to babies?

Ans. No, Max will not lay eggs. Dogs give birth to puppies.

Q.5 Does it have young ones?

Ans. Max does not have young ones right now.

Q.6 Draw a picture of this animal and colour it. Give it a name of your own choice.

Ans.

Page 19

Q.1 Look at this picture. Colour the parts which have even numbers (2, 4, 6, 8...). What do you see? Find out the name of the animal.

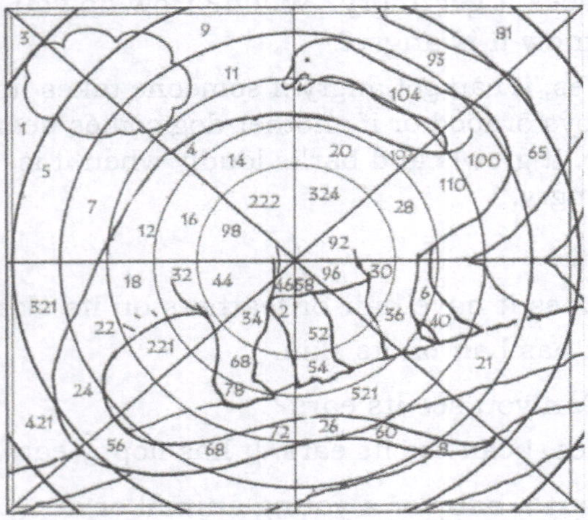

Ans. It is a dinosaur.

Q.2 Have you seen any animal that looks a little like a dinosaur? Do you know its name?

Ans. Yes, some animals look a bit like dinosaurs. One example is the lizard.

Q.3 Look at this animal. Write its name. Do you know that this is our National Animal?

Ans. It's a tiger. Yes, I know this is our national animal.

Q.4 Where does it live?

Ans. It lives in the forest.

Q.5 The number of this animal are going down in India. Discuss why this could be happening?

Ans. The number of tigers is going down in India. It is happening because of the following reasons

- Tigers lose their homes when people cut down trees or build on their land.
- People sometimes hunt tigers, which can make their numbers go down.
- Changes in weather can make it hard for tigers to find food and stay safe.

CHAPTER 3 A DAY WITH NANDU

About the Chapter

This chapter is about Nandu, a baby elephant living in a herd in the jungle. It describes how elephants live, eat and play together. Nandu's herd, led by his grandmother, moves through the jungle, eating twigs and leaves and enjoying the river.

Baby elephants like Nandu play in the water. After sunset, they return to the jungle. Adult elephants can eat over 100 kilograms of leaves and twigs daily. Elephants have large ears that help them stay cool. They live in herds, which usually consist of females and babies, while male elephants leave the herd at 14 or 15 years of age.

GLOSSARY

Trunk The long nose of an elephant, used for eating, drinking, playing and communicating.
Blink Quickly opening and closing your eyes.
Trumpeting A loud sound made by elephants.
Twig A small, thin branch from a tree or bush.
Riverbank The land along the side of a river.
Mud bath Rolling in mud to keep cool.
Herd A group of elephants or other animals that live together and move around together.

NCERT FOLDER

Find out (Page 22-23)

Q1. Nandu is only three months old, but he weighs 200 kilograms. What is your weight?

Ans. My weight is 20 kilograms.

Q.2 Can you find out - the weight of how many children like you will add up to Nandu's weight?

Ans. The weight of 10 children like me will add up to Nandu's weight.

Page 24

Q.1 If you were Nandu and you lived in a herd, what kind of things would you do?

Ans. If I were Nandu, I would play in the water with my cousins. I would roam around all day playing, eating, dancing and chatting. At night, I would sleep with my mother.

Q.2 In the elephant herd, the oldest female elephant decides everything. Who takes decisions in your family?

Ans. In my family, decisions are usually made by my grandparents.

Page 25

Q.1 Nandu did things that he liked to do. If you could spend a whole day with your friends, what all would you do?

Ans. If I could spend a whole day with my friends, we would play games, ride bicycles and have fun in the park. We would also have snacks and tell stories to each other.

Q.2 Find out and write, which other animals live in herds.

Ans. Some other animals that live in herds are deer, zebras, sheep, cows and buffaloes.

Q.3 Do you also live in a group? Do you like to live together like that? Why would you like or not like to live in a group?

Ans. Yes, I live with my family. I like to live together with my family.

The reason why I would like to live in a group because we could help each other. We can share things and have fun together.

The reason why I would not like to live together in a group is because sometimes it's noisy. I don't always get my own space and sometimes we argue on silly things.

Q.4 How do elephants feel when they are kept in chains? Discuss and share your feelings.

Ans. Elephants feel sad when they are kept in chains. They cannot move freely and they miss their family and the jungle. It is not good to keep them in chains because they should be free to live in the wild.

Page 26

Q.1 Have you ever taken a ride on an elephant? How did it feel?

Ans. Yes, I have taken a ride on an elephant. It felt very high up and a little bumpy, but it was exciting and fun.

Q.2 Which animals have you sat on? Write their names.

Ans. I have sat on a horse and a camel. Both were fun rides.

Q.3 You must have seen many animals around you - in books, in movies. Some may be alone, some in groups. Find out more about any one of these animals and write about it.

Ans. Lions are big, strong animals. They live in groups called prides. In a pride of lions, there are male lions, female lions and cubs. The females usually hunt for food and the males protect the pride.

Think and Write (Page 27)

Q.1 Why do you think the egret is sitting on the buffalo?

Ans. The egret sits on the buffalo to eat small insects from its skin. It helps the buffalo stay clean.

Q.2 Have you seen any animal riding on another animal? Write its name.

Ans. Yes, I have seen a monkey riding on an elephant.

Q.3 Which animals do we use for riding?

Ans. Animals we use for riding are horses, camels, elephants.

Q.4 Which animals do we use for carrying loads?

Ans. Animals we use for carrying loads are donkeys, mules, camels.

What Do They Say? (Page 29-30)

Look at these pictures and read what these animals are sharing with their friends. Discuss these narratives sensitively in the class.

Discuss

Q.1 You have read what these animals say. Why do you think that some of them are sad?

Ans. Some animals are sad because they are forced to do things they don't want to do, like dancing or carrying heavy loads. They are not free to live in their natural homes, like the jungle.

Q.2 How do you think they are different - the monkeys that dance to entertain people and the monkeys that are free?

Ans. Monkeys that dance to entertain people are forced to do it and don't get to live freely. Free monkeys can live in the jungle, climb trees, and play whenever they want.

Page 30

Q.1 How many legs does this elephant have?

Ans. This elephant has four legs.

CHAPTER 4 THE STORY OF AMRITA

About the Chapter

In this chapter, we will learn about the importance of trees and how people of Khejadli village saved the trees. Amrita, who lived in the village near Jodhpur, loved the Khejadi trees. These trees didn't need much water and their bark was used to make medicine. One day, some men came to cut down the trees. To protect them, Amrita hugged a tree, but the men followed the king's orders and cut it.

Many villagers, including Amrita, hugged the trees to save them and some of them died. When the king saw how much the villagers cared the trees, he decided to protect them. The people of the village are called Bishnois and they still protect the trees and animals today.

GLOSSARY

Bishnoi Community The Bishnoi people are a community in Rajasthan known for their strong belief in protecting nature.
Axe A tool with a sharp blade used for cutting wood.
Roam To move or wander around freely without a specific direction.

NCERT FOLDER

Page 32

Q.1 Is there a place near your house, school, or along the roadside, where trees have been planted?

Ans. Yes, there are trees planted along the roadsides and in the parks in my neighbourhood.

Q.2 Why were they planted there?

Ans. Trees are planted to provide shade and clean air. They make the area look beautiful.

Page 33

Q.1 Have you seen anyone taking care of the trees? Who does this?

Ans. Yes, gardeners take care of the trees by watering them and cutting their branches.

Q.2 Have you seen fruits on any of the trees? Who eats these fruits?

Ans. Yes, I have seen mangoes and guavas growing on trees.
Birds, squirrels and people eat these fruits.

Q.3 Lalita feels that grass and small plants growing near her school wall have not been planted by anyone. Do you know of any place where grass, small plants, or trees are growing on their own without being planted by anyone?

Ans. Yes, in some fields and open spaces, grass and plants grow naturally without being planted.

Q.4 Why do you feel they are growing on their own?

Ans. These plants grow on their own because no one has planted them.

Page 34

Q.1 Do you remember what the elders of this village used to say?

Ans. Yes, the elders used to say, "*Agar perh hain to hum hain*". It means plants and animals can survive without us, but we cannot survive without them.

Q.2 Do you think we could survive if there were no trees and no animals?

Ans. No, we cannot survive without trees because they give us oxygen to breathe, provide clean air and food to eat. Animals are also important for the balance of nature.

Page 35

Q.1 Do you remember that in Class III, you had made a tree your friend? How is your friend now?

Ans. Yes, I made a mango tree my friend in Class III. It has grown taller and has more branches now.

Q.2 Why don't you make a new friend this year? Have you seen how your friends - the trees, change in some ways, in different months of a year?

Ans. Yes, I will make a new friend this year, maybe a neem tree. Trees change a lot during the year. In summer, they have lots of green leaves, and in winter, many trees lose their leaves.

Q.3 Write about any one tree.

Ans. I have a mango tree near my house. It is very big and provides a lot of shade. In summer, it grows delicious mangoes.

Q.4 Does the tree have flowers?

Ans. Yes, the mango tree has small white flowers in spring.

Q.5 Do the flowers remain on the tree throughout the year?

Ans. No, the flowers bloom in spring and fall off after some time.

Q.6 In which month do their leaves fall?

Ans. The leaves of mango trees fall mostly in autumn, around October or November.

Page 36

Q.1 Do fruits grow on the tree?

Ans. Yes, mangoes grow on this tree.

Q.2 In which months do they grow?

Ans. The mangoes usually grow between May and July.

Q.3 Have you eaten these fruits?

Ans. Yes, I have eaten the ripe mangoes from this tree and they are very sweet.

Discuss

Q.1 Why do people hunt?

Ans. Some people hunt for food, while others hunt for sport or to sell animal products like skin and fur.

Q.2 There are rules against hunting some animals. Why do you think there is punishment for hunting?

Ans. There are rules to protect animals. Hunting can reduce their numbers, and punishments help to stop this.

Talk to your grandparents and find out.

Q.3 Which birds did your grandparents see when they were young?

Ans. My grandparents saw many sparrows, mynahs and crows when they were young.

Q.4 Have the number of some of these birds become less?

Ans. Yes, the number of sparrows and other small birds has become less due to changes in the environment.

Q.5 Are there some birds or animals which they cannot see anymore?

Ans. Yes, some birds and animals like vultures and eagles are rarely seen now.

Page 37

Q.1 Shanti's grandfather told her that when he was a small child he saw more birds like sparrows and mynah than he sees today. Can you make two guesses why their numbers have become less?

Ans. There are fewer birds today because of hunting and cutting down of trees and pollution.

Q.2 The Khejadi tree was the most common tree that grew in Amrita's village. Which kind of trees can you see a lot of, in your area? Name two such trees.

Ans. In my area, there are many neem and banyan trees.

Q.3 Find out more about these trees from your elders.

Ans. **Neem tree** My elders told me that the neem tree is very useful. Its leaves are used for medicine, and its shade keeps the area cool. It also helps clean the air.

Banyan tree The banyan tree grows very large and gives shade to many people. Its roots grow down from the branches, and it is considered sacred in our culture.

CHAPTER 5

ANITA AND THE HONEYBEES

About the Chapter

This chapter shows how learning new things, like beekeeping, can help people earn money and improve their lives. It also teaches us the importance of going to school and working hard. Anita is a girl who lives in a village in Bihar. Her family was poor and her parents didn't want to send her to school because they thought girls shouldn't go to school. But Anita was determined to learn, so she worked hard, taught students and earned money from it.

In India, every child has the right to go to school under the RTE Act 2009. One day, Anita learned about keeping bees and collecting honey. She found it exciting and saved money from her teaching to start a honey business. By selling honey, she earn money and helped her family. Every beehive has a Queen Bee that lays eggs. Most bees are worker bees that make honey, and there are only a few male bees.

GLOSSARY

Bee-Keeping The practice of raising and maintaining bee colonies, primarily to collect honey and beeswax.

Hives Hives are the home of bees, where they make honey, store food and take care of baby bees.

Nectar A sweet liquid found in flowers, which worker bees collect and turn into honey.

Wholesaler A person or business that buys goods in large quantities and sells them to small shopkeepers.

NCERT FOLDER

Q.1 Find out how much money do you spend in one year for various school-related things.

	Things	Money Spent
1.	Travel to school and back	
2.	Notebooks	
3.	Pens-Pencils/Stationery	
4.	Uniforms	
5.	School bag	
6.	Lunch box	
7.	Shoes	
8.	Other things (i)	
	(ii)	
	Total	

Ans.

	Things	Money Spent
1.	Travel to school and back	24000
2.	Notebooks	5000
3.	Pens-Pencils/Stationery	2000
4.	Uniforms	10000
5.	School bag	1000
6.	Lunch box	500
7.	Shoes	1500
8.	Other things (i) Fees	36000
	(ii) Books	20000
	Total	100000

Page 40

Q.1 How much money did you spend on your books this year?

Ans. This year, I spent ₹ 20000 on books.

Q.2 What kind of school uniform would you like to wear?

Ans. I would like to wear a comfortable and neat uniform with my favourite colours.

Q.3 Make two groups in the class. Debate the topic-'We should have uniforms in school.'

Ans. You can the following points for debate :

For

- Uniforms help reduce differences between students and make everyone feel equal.
- They create a sense of discipline.
- It reduces bullying

Against

- Uniforms can be uncomfortable for some students.
- They are expensive and cannot be afforded by everyone.

Q.4 Do you know someone who wanted to study, but could not do so?

Ans. Yes, children of our househelp wanted to study but couldn't go to school because their families needed them to help at home.

Page 41

Q.1 Every child has a right to free education up to Class VIII. Do you think all children are able to study up to Class VIII?

Ans. No, not all children are able to study up to Class VIII because of financial problems or family issues.

Q.2 Have you seen any insects near flowers? Find out their names.

Ans. Yes, I have seen bees, butterflies and ants near flowers.

Q.3 Draw and colour their pictures in the notebook.

Ans.

Page 42

Q.1 Why do you think they come to the flowers?

Ans. They come to the flowers to collect nectar and food.

Q.2 When honeybees fly, there is a kind of sound. Can you try to copy this sound?

Ans. Students should try themselves to copy the sound of honeybee.

Find Out (Page 43)

Q.1 What do people in your area put on the part of the body where the bee has stung?

Ans. In my area, people usually apply ice or a paste of baking soda and water to the sting to reduce pain and swelling.

Q.2 Draw a picture of a honeybee in your notebook. Colour it and give it a name.

Ans.

Q.3 What will be the total cost of Anita's 20 boxes?

Ans. Each box costs ₹ 2000, so 20 boxes would cost ₹ 2000 × 20 = ₹ 40,000.

Find Out (Page 44)

Q.1 Anita and others in her village get ₹ 35 for one kilogram of honey. How much does one kilogram of honey cost in your town?

Ans. One kilogram of honey costs ₹ 800 in my town.

Q.2 What are the different colors of honey that you have seen?

Ans. I have seen honey of golden and dark brown colour.

Q.3 Is honey used in your house? What is it used for?

Ans. Yes, honey is used in my house for sweetening green tea, spreading on bread, or as medicine for cold and cough.

Page 45

Q.1 Which are some other insects that live together in a group, like honeybees?

Ans. Ants, termites and wasps live together in groups like honeybees.

Q.2 Have you seen where ants live?

Ans. Yes, I have seen ants build nests in the ground or on the walls.

Q.3 What kind of eatables attract ants? List them.

Ans. Ants are attracted to sweet foods like sugar, candy and fruits.

Q.4 Look at a line of ants. What is its colour?

Ans. They are of black, red and brown.

Page 46

Q.1 Have you been bitten by an ant? What was the ant like - black or red, big or small?

Ans. Yes, I was bitten by a small red ant once.

Q.2 Do ants ever come near you? When?

Ans. Yes, ants come near me when I drop food or snacks on the ground.

Q.3 Look carefully at some big and small ants. How many legs does an ant have?

- Big ant
- Small ant

Ans. Both big and small ants have six legs.

Q.4 Draw an ant in your notebook and colour it.

Ans.

Q.5 While eating peanuts you probably throw away the shells. Why don't you try to make some insects by using the shells? Do not forget to colour them.

Ans. Students should try themselves to make the model of insects with peanuts shells.

CHAPTER 6

OMANA'S JOURNEY

About the Chapter

This chapter is about Omana's exciting train journey and her experience of the train. Omana and Radha had planned to travel together but Radha got injured. Omana keeps a diary to tell Radha about the journey. We learn about the trip from her diary. Omana and her family started their trip on 16th May from Gandhidham station in Gujarat.

Omana and her brother sat on the middle seat and their parents sat on the lower seat. Her mother brought lots of food and snacks for the trip. Omana enjoyed looking out of the train window. The train stopped at Valsad station for two minutes, where they bought some fruits. Omana made two new friends, Sunil and Ann who gave her storybooks to read. When she went to brush her teeth, there was no water in the bathroom.

GLOSSARY

Reservation Chart A list displayed at the train station showing the names of passengers and their assigned seats for the journey.

Luggage Baggage used for carrying a person's clothes and things on a journey.

Berth A place for sleeping or sitting on a train.

Coach A separate section of the train that carries passengers.

NCERT FOLDER

Page 49

Q.1 Why was it so crowded at the door of the coach?

Ans. It was crowded because some people were getting off the train and others were trying to get on the train, all through one door.

Q.2 Have you ever travelled in a train? When?

Ans. Yes, I have travelled by train many times. Last month, I travelled in a train when I went to visit my grandparents.

Q.3 What food would you like to take with you when you travel? Why?

Ans. I would take sandwiches, fruits, and snacks because they are easy to carry and eat while travelling.

Q.4 What does the ticket-checker do?

Ans. The ticket-checker checks the tickets of passengers to make sure they are sitting in the right seats.

Q.5 How will you recognise the ticket- checker?

Ans. The ticket-checker usually wears black uniform with a tie and carries a list of passenger names and ticket details.

Page 51

Q.1 What did Omana see from the window?

Ans. Omana saw dry, brown fields, small villages, and a beautiful orange sunset in the evening from the window.

Q.2 What are some of the things that are sold at railway stations?

Ans. Vendors at railway stations sell items like hot tea, *batata vada*, *puri-shaak*, cold milk, and fruits like bananas and *chikoos*.

Page 52

Q.1 Why do you think there was no water in the bathroom of the train? Discuss.

Ans. There was no water because the train had not yet reached a big station where the water tanks could be refilled.

Q.2 Imagine that you are going on a long train journey. What are the things that you will take with you to help pass the time?

Ans. I would take some books, snacks, games like ludo, and a notebook to write about the journey.

Q.3 Can you recognise who are these people shown in the picture? What work do they do? Discuss.

Ans.
1. Porter He helps people to carry their luggage.
2. Railway Guard He signals trains to start or stop.
3. Railway Driver He drives and control the train.
4. Ticket Checker He checks the tickets of the passengers.
5. Railway Police He provides security to the passengers.
6. Sweeper He cleans the platform and the trains.
7. Ticket Seller She sells the ticket.

CHAPTER 7 FROM THE WINDOW

About the Chapter

In this chapter, we learn more about Omana's train journey. On 17th May, the train stopped at Madgaon station in Goa early in the morning. Omana saw a beautiful view with red soil, green crops and hills full of trees. The air was cooler. She also noticed many vehicles waiting at a level crossing. Later, the train crossed a big river and also went through a tunnel.

As they travelled South, Omana saw many coconut trees and noticed that the houses and clothes looked different from those in Ahmedabad. Passengers got off at different stations and Sunil's family left at Kozhikode in the evening. That night, Omana's family was going to get off at Kottayam, where they would take a bus to Valiyamma's house the next day.

GLOSSARY

Level Crossing A point where a railway track crosses a road, often with gates to stop vehicles when a train is passing.

Tunnel A man-made passage dug through mountains or hills to allow trains or vehicles to pass through.

Rattling It means making a series of short, sharp noises, often like something shaking.

NCERT FOLDER

Page 54-55

Q.1 What was the difference in the scene that Omana saw from the train on the first day and the second day?

Ans. On the first day, Omana saw dry landscapes, but on the second day, the scene was filled with green fields, hills, ponds, and water bodies. The air was cooler and there was more greenery.

Q.2 Omana saw many kinds of vehicles at the level-crossing. Which of them run on diesel or petrol?

Ans. The vehicles that run on diesel or petrol are buses, cars, trucks, auto-rickshaws, motorbikes and scooters.

Q.3 Why was there so much smoke and noise from the vehicles at the level crossing?

Ans. There was smoke and noise because some people do not switch off the engines of their vehicle even while waiting at the level crossing.

Q.4 What can we do to reduce noise of the vehicle and save petrol and diesel? Discuss.

Ans. To reduce noise and save fuel, people should turn off their vehicles while waiting at a level crossing. This will reduce both noise and air pollution.

Discuss (Page 55-59)

Q.1 Sometimes people cross the tracks even when the crossing is closed. What do you feel about this?

Ans. People should not cross the tracks when the crossing is closed as it is very dangerous.

Q.2 Have you seen any bridges? Where?

Ans. Yes, I have seen many bridges in my city.

Q.3 Have you ever crossed a bridge? Where?

Ans. Yes, I have crossed many bridges in Varanasi over river Ganga.

Q.4 What was the bridge built over?

Ans. The bridge was built over a large river.

Q.5 What did you see below the bridge?

Ans. Below the bridge, I saw water and boats.

Q.6 Find out why bridges are made.

Ans. Bridges are made to help people and vehicles cross things like rivers, valleys or roads.

Q.7 Have you ever been through a tunnel? How did you feel?

Ans. Yes, I have been through a tunnel. I felt very scared.

Q.8 The route from Goa to Kerala has a total of 2000 bridges and 92 tunnels. Why do you think there are so many bridges and tunnels ?

Ans. There are many rivers and mountains between Goa and Kerala, so bridges and tunnels are necessary to allow the train to cross these paths.

Q.9 Imagine and draw in your notebook what Omana saw under the bridge when her train crossed it?

Ans. Omana must have seen a river with many fishes. She could have also seen some people taking boat rides or doing rafting.

Q.10 Imagine, if on the way there had been no tunnels and bridges, how would Omana's train have crossed the mountains and rivers?

Ans. If there were no tunnels and bridges, Omana's train would not have crossed the mountains and rivers.

Q.11 Which languages do you speak at home?

Ans. I speak Hindi at home.

Q.12 On the way from Gujarat to Kerala, Omana's train went through several states of our country. Find out and list which states it crossed.

Ans. Omana's train passed through Gujarat, Maharashtra, Goa and Kerala.

Q.13 Did you ever have coconut water? How did you find it? Discuss.

Ans. Yes, I had coconut water many times. It was sold by a local vendor outside my house.

Q.14 Draw a coconut tree and discuss in the class about it.

Ans.

Q.15 Find out in which states these languages are spoken

Language	**Where it is spoken** (State)
Malayalam	
Konkani	
Marathi	
Gujarati	
Kannada	

Ans.

Language	**Where it is spoken** (State)
Malayalam	Kerala
Konkani	Goa
Marathi	Maharashtra
Gujarati	Gujarat
Kannada	Karnataka

Q.16 What do you call them?

Mother's sister:

Mother's mother:

Father's sister:

Father's mother:

Ans.
- Mother's sister: Mausi
- Mother's mother: Nani
- Father's sister: Bua
- Father's mother: Dadi

CHAPTER 8

REACHING GRANDMOTHER'S HOUSE

About the Chapter

In this chapter, we learn how Omana's journey ends. After a long train ride, Omana's family reached Kottayam at night and took two auto-rickshaws to Valiyamma's house. Omana was so tired that she went to sleep after taking a bath, without eating anything. They woke up again after some time and went to the bus stand to travel to Ammumma's house. They bought the tickets and got on the bus. It was crowded and some passengers had to share seats.

After the bus ride, they had to cross a river on a ferry. On the ferry, Omana saw people fishing, washing clothes and bathing by the water. Before the sunset, Omana and her family finally reached Ammumma's house after their long, exciting journey.

GLOSSARY

Ferry A boat used to transport people and goods from one side to another side of a river.

NCERT FOLDER

Page 62-65

Q.1 Omana travelled by different kinds of transport after she got down from the train. Can you remember what these were?

Ans. Omana travelled by auto-rickshaw, bus, and ferry after getting off the train.

Q.2 On which vehicles have you travelled?

Ans. I have travelled on all vehicles like auto-rickshaw, bus, car, metro and ferry.

Q.3 Which ride did you enjoy the most? Why?

Ans. I enjoyed the ferry most because there was no traffic on the water.

Q.4 Omana left Ahmedabad on 16 May. How many hours did it take for her to reach *Ammumma's* place?

Ans. It took Omana almost 36 hours to reach *Ammumma's* house after leaving Ahmedabad.

Q.5 Have you ever been on a long journey? Where did you go?

Ans. Yes, I have been on a long journey from Patna to Bangalore.

Q.6 Name the different kinds of transport that you used during the journey.

Ans. I used a train and an auto-rickshaw during the journey.

Q.7 How long did your journey take?

Ans. My journey took 45 hours.

Q.8 Omana's *Appa* bought tickets for the train and the bus. Can you think of other means of transport for which we need to buy tickets?

Ans. We need to buy tickets for means of transport like planes.

Q.9 Sometimes we need to buy tickets to enter a place. Can you think of such places?

Ans. We need to buy tickets to enter places like zoos, museums, cinemas and theme parks.

Q.10 Look at this picture of a railway ticket. Find the following information on the ticket and circle them with different colours and discuss.

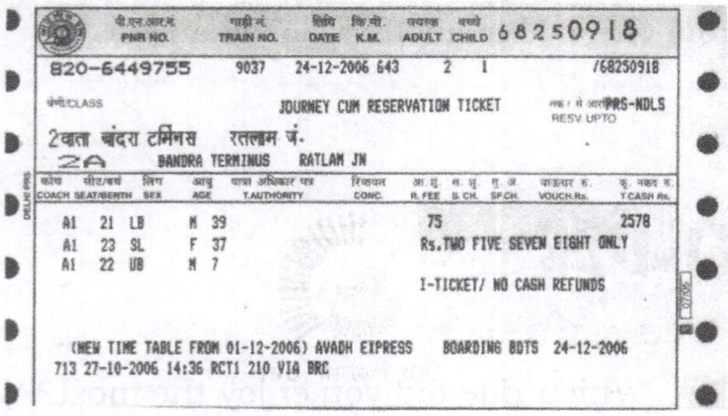

PNR NO. TRAIN NO. DATE K.M. ADULT CHILD 68250918
820-6449755 9037 24-12-2006 643 2 1 /68250918
CLASS JOURNEY CUM RESERVATION TICKET PRS-NDLS RESV UPTO
2वाता बांद्रा टर्मिनस रतलाम जं.
2A BANDRA TERMINUS RATLAM JN
COACH SEAT/BERTH SEX AGE T.AUTHORITY CONC. R.FEE S.CH. SF.CH. VOUCH.Rs. T.CASH Rs.
A1 21 LB M 39 75 2578
A1 23 SL F 37 Rs.TWO FIVE SEVEN EIGHT ONLY
A1 22 UB M 7
I-TICKET/ NO CASH REFUNDS
(NEW TIME TABLE FROM 01-12-2006) AVADH EXPRESS BOARDING BDTS 24-12-2006
713 27-10-2006 14:36 RCT1 210 VIA BRC

1. The train number ________
2. The date of the start of the journey ___
3. The berth and the coach numbers ___
4. The fare (the cost of the ticket) ______
5. The distance (in km) _______

Ans. 1. The train number - 9037
2. The date of the start of the journey- 24.12.2006
3. The berth and the coach numbers- A1- 21, 22 and 23
4. The fare (the cost of the ticket)- ₹ 2,578
5. The distance (in km)- 643 km

Q.11 Write what other information you can find out from the ticket.

Ans.
- Name of the train: Avadh Express
- Boarding station: Bandra Terminus
- Destination station: Ratlam Junction
- PNR No: 820-6449755
- No. of adults: 2 (1 male, 1 female)
- No. of children: 1

Some portions of the time-table for the route of the train on which Omana travelled are given. Look carefully at it and answer the following questions.

16635 GANDHIDHAM NAGERCOIL EXPRESS

S. No.	Station Name	Arrival time	Departure Time	Distance (km)	Day
1	Gandhidham	–	05:15	0	1
2	Ahmedabad	11:30	11:50	301	1
3.	Vadodara	14:03	14:10	401	1
4.	Surat	16:15	16:20	530	1
5.	Valsad	17:23	17:25	598	1
6.	Bhiwandi Road	21:10	21:12	772	1
7.	Madgaon	07:35	07:45	1509	2
8.	Udupi	12:06	12:18	1858	2
9.	Kozhikode	17:45	17:50	2165	2
10.	Trichur	21:05	21:10	2280	2
11.	Ernakulam Town	22:35	22:40	2356	2
12	Kottayam	23:50	23:55	2418	2
13.	Trivandrum CNTL	03:05	03:10	2578	3
14.	Nagarcoil	04:45	00:00	2649	3

Q.12 Circle the names of all the stations in the table that are mentioned in Omana's diary.

Ans. Circle these station: Gandhidham, Ahmedabad, Valsad, Madgaon, Udupi, Kozhikode, Kottayam.

Q.13 From which station did the train start?

Ans. The train started from Gandhidham.

Q.14 How many minutes did the train stop at Ahmedabad station?

Ans. The train stopped for 20 minutes at Ahmedabad station.

Q.15 On which day of the journey did the train reach Madgaon?

Ans. The train reached Madgaon on the second day of the journey.

Q.16 Sunil and Ann got off at Kozhikode station. Omana got off at Kottayam station. How many hours does the train take to reach Kottayam from Kozhikode?

Ans. It takes around 6 hours for the train to reach Kottayam from Kozhikode.

Q.17 What is the distance that the train travelled over the whole route?

Ans. The train travelled 2,649 kilometers from Gandhidham to Nagercoil.

Q.18 How many kilometers did Omana travel by train?

Ans. Omana traveled 2,418 kilometers by train from Gandhidham to Kottayam.

Q.19 Would you like to keep a diary? Take a notebook or a diary. Everyday for a week, write about what you did. Also write your thoughts and feelings. Share your diary with your friends.

Ans. During late night hour, we boarded the train from Shivaji Terminal for Goa. We were going on a trip with our family members to celebrate my parents' anniversary. My mother packed a lot of food items for the journey. I took the middle berth. The scenes outside the window were very beautiful.

I could see the yellow lighting in the fields making it look like fire flies. It was almost time to sleep. I went and brushed my teeth. Then, we all played cards and went to sleep after some time.

Students can record their entries for a week.

CHAPTER 9 CHANGING FAMILIES

About the Chapter

In this chapter, we will learn how families change over time. We will also learn about the importance of education. All families change in some way or other because of various reasons like birth of a baby, promotion or transfer at work and marriage of a family member. Nimmi, Tsering and Nazil's family changed due to these reasons. Many girls have to leave school and get married before they are eighteen years old. There are some girls like Susheela from Ranga Reddy district who are going back to school with the help of the Panchayat. Her village Panchayat believed that young children should play and study instead of getting married.

GLOSSARY

Promotion When someone is given a higher position or rank at their job.
Panchayat A local village council in India that helps people with important issues like education, work, and family matters.

NCERT FOLDER

Page 67

Look at the pictures and write

Q.1 Who were the members of Nimmi's family before the arrival of her baby sister?

Ans. Nimmi, her parents, grandmother and uncle were the members of Nimmi's family before the arrival of her baby sister.

Q.2 How many members are there in Nimmi's family now?

Ans. There are six members in Nimmi's family now. Nimmi, her mother, father, grandmother, uncle and the new baby sister.

Let us Talk (Page 67-70)

Q.1 How do you think the lives of Nimmi's family members have changed after the arrival of the new baby?
For example

(a) How will Nimmi spend her day now?

Ans. Nimmi will have new responsibilities, such as helping take care of the baby.

(b) What new work will her mother do now?

Ans. Her mother will be busy, especially with feeding and looking after the baby.

(c) There will be a change in the daily work of Nimmi's father, grandmother and uncle with the arrival of the new baby. Can you tell how?

Ans. Nimmi's father, grandmother and uncle will also help with tasks like caring for the baby or helping around the house.

Q.2 Has a small brother or sister been born in your home or in any house in your neighbourhood?

Ans. Yes, a baby boy was born in my neighbourhood.

(a) How does it feel to have a new baby at home?

Ans. There is excitement all around and everyone plays with the baby all the time. All family members help in taking care of the baby.

(b) How have things changed at home with the new baby?

Ans. Everyone is busy with the new baby. They are taking care of the baby and spending their days playing with him.

Q.3 Find out all about the youngest child in your home or in the home of a relative. Then write -

(a) When was the baby born?

Ans. The baby was born last month.

(b) Is the baby a boy or a girl?

Ans. The baby is a boy.

(c) How are you related to him or her?

Ans. I am his neighbour.

(d) Where was the baby born?

Ans. The baby was born in the hospital.

(e) Who does the baby look like?

Ans. The baby looks like his father.

(f) What is the colour of his or her hair?

Ans. The colour of his hair is brown.

(g) What is the colour of his or her eyes?

Ans. The colour of his eyes in black.

(h) Does the baby have any teeth?

Ans. No, the baby does not have any teeth.

(i) What do we feed the baby with?

Ans. We feed the baby with milk.

(j) What is the baby's length?

Ans. Baby's length is about two feet.

(k) How many hours a day does the baby sleep?

Ans. Baby sleeps for 14-15 hours.

(l) What different sounds does the baby make?

Ans. Baby cries when he is hungry.

(m) Who does the baby stay with most of the time?

Ans. The baby stays with his mother most of the time.

(n) Stick a photograph of the baby or draw a picture in your Notebook.

Ans. Do it yourself.

Q.4 When Tsering's father showed the letter to his family, how do you think the different members would have felt?

Ans. All the family members were happy when Tsering's father got a promotion. Tsering was excited because he would be moving to a new town. However, Tsering's father, mother, and grandparents felt a little worried since they had to organise everything for moving to the new place.

Q.5 What will change in Tsering's family after his father's transfer?

For example

(a) Who from Tsering's family will live with his father at the new place? Which school will Tsering go to now? Will he have new friends?

Ans. Tsering, his sister and his mother will live with his father at the new place.

He will go to a new school now.
Yes, he will have new friends.

(b) Has anybody in your family moved to a new place because of work?

Ans. Yes, my uncle moved to Delhi because of work.

(c) What do you feel about this change?

Ans. I feel good as it gives the opportunity to visit a new place.

Q.6 Is there anyone in your class or school who has come to your school from another place? If so, talk to him or her.

Ans. Yes, a girl came from another city.

(a) Where has she or he come from?

Ans. She has come from Hyderabad.

(b) What was his or her old school like?

Ans. Her old school was not very big. But, she had many friends there.

(c) What does he or she find different here?

Ans. She finds everything new here. The teachers and her classmates are very friendly here.

(d) Does he or she like the change?

Ans. Yes, she likes the change.

Let us Talk (Page 71-74)

Q.1 Do you think there will be any change in Nazli's family after this wedding? What will change?

Ans. Yes, there will be change in Nazli's family after this wedding. A new member will live with Nazli's family.

(a) Do you think there will be changes in the home from where the new bride has come? What kind of changes?

Ans. The bride's own family will also experience change as she leaves her parents' home to live with her husband.

(b) Talk to your mother and aunts in the family. Ask them about where they lived before they got married.

Ans. They lived with their parents before marriage.

(c) Who were the members in their families then?

Ans. Before my mother's marriage, there was her father, her mother and her sister in my mother's family.

(d) Has anybody in your family been married recently? Who?

Ans. Yes, my mother's sister (my aunt) has been married recently.

Q.2 Talk to your classmates and write all about what happens during weddings in their families.

(a) What kind of special food is cooked?

Ans. Do it yourself.

(b) What special clothes do the bride and bridegroom wear?

Ans. The bridegroom wears dhoti and kurta. The bride wears saree or lehenga.

Q.3 What did you see at the wedding that you attended? Draw some pictures in your notebook. Then look at the pictures drawn by your classmates.

Ans. Do it yourself.

Q.4 We saw changes taking place in the families of Nimmi, Tsering and Nazli because of different reasons. Write down the reasons for these changes:

(a) In Nimmi's family -

Ans. A new baby was born, which brings new responsibilities and changes in daily life.

(b) In Tsering's family

Ans. The father's promotion means the family will move to a new city, bringing changes to their home and school life.

(c) In Nazli's family

Ans. A wedding adds a new member to the family.

Q.5 There can be many reasons for changes in families. Can you think of some more reasons?

Ans. Families can change for many reasons. Some examples include

- A family member getting a new job or a promotion.
- Moving to a new house or city.
- A new baby is being born.
- Someone getting married.
- Children growing up and going to a new school.
- A family member passing away.
- Adopting a pet.
- Changes in health or responsibilities of family members.

Q.6 Talk to three old people - one from your family, one from your friend's family and one from a family in your neighbourhood. Ask them these questions and fill in the table.

Ans.

Questions	Your Family	Friend's Family	Neighbour's Family
Since how many years has your family been staying here?	15 years	10 years	5 years
Where did your family live before coming here?	Almore, Uttarakhand	Patna, Bihar	Raipur, Chhattisgarh
How many members are there in your family today?	7	4	4
How many members were there in your family 10 years ago?	6	5	7
What were the reasons for the changes in your family in the last 10 years?	Birth of my sister.	Death of grandfatherand transfer of his uncle	Transfer due to job Earlier living with his grandparents and uncle
How do you feel about all these changes?	I am very happy	He is sad because of his grandfather's death.	They are happy as they are visiting new places
What problems do you face with changes in technology?	Learning new devices or software	Keeping up with updates	Keeping up with updates

Page 74

Q.7 All families change in some way or the other because of different reasons. Has your family changed too?

Ans. Yes, my family has changed due to the birth of my sister.

Q.8 When your grandmother and grandfather were children like you, was your family just like it is today?

Ans. No, it was different from today. There were more family-members who lived together.

Q.9 Do you remember the picture of Sitamma's family tree which we saw in Class III?

Ans. Yes.

(a) You had also drawn a family tree of your own family. Let us again draw the family tree of last year in your notebook.

Ans.

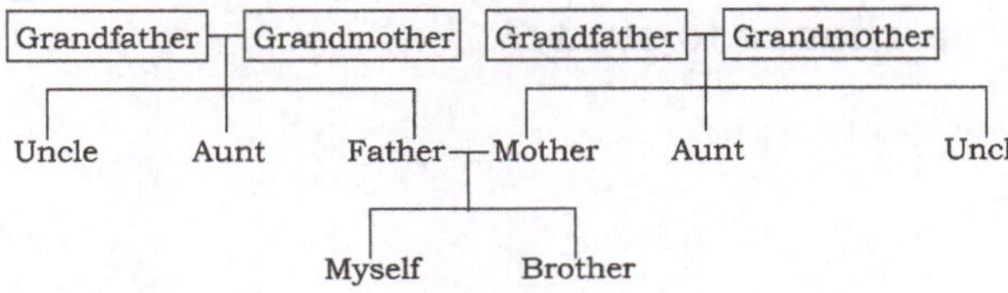

(b) Ask your grandmother or grandfather, how many members were there in their family when they were your age? Then draw a family tree in your notebook of their family when they were young.

Ans. Do it yourself.

(c) Can you see yourself, your brother or your sister, your mother or your father, anywhere in this family tree?

Ans. No, I cannot see myself but I can see my father.

(d) Now draw a family tree of your present family in your notebook.

Ans. Do it yourself.

Q.10 Can you see yourself anywhere in this family tree? Who are the members of your family today? Where are your grandparents?

Ans. Do it yourself.

Let us Talk (Page 75)

Q.1 Can you tell in what ways the family tree of your grandmother or grandfather in their childhood is different from your family tree today?

Ans. In my grandparents' time, their families were larger. They had 12 members. Today, in my family there were only four members.

Q.2 Upto which class do you want to study?

Ans. I want to study up to college, or even beyond.

Q.3. Upto which class have your parents studied?

Ans. They have studied till college.

Q.4 Till which class did your grandmother get a chance to study?

Ans. She has studied till class 8.

Q.5 At what age did your grandmother get married?

Ans. Do it yourself.

Q.6 Have you heard of a law about the minimum age for marriage?

Ans. Yes, the law states that girls must be 18 years old and boys should be 21 years old to get married.

Page 76

Find Out and Write

Q.1. Are there any such children in your neighbourhood who had to drop out of school? Do they want to go back to school?

Ans. There are no children in my neighbourhood who had to drop out of school.

Q.2 What are they doing these days?

Ans. They all are studying.

Q.3 Has anybody in your family got married recently? Who?

Ans. Yes, my uncle.

Q.4. What was the age of the bride and groom?

Ans. The bride was 23 years old and groom's age was 28 years.

Q.5 What kind of dresses they wore?

- Bride
- Groom

Ans. **Bride** She wore a saree.

Groom He wore a sherwani.

Q.6 What kind of dishes were served at the wedding? Name them.

Ans. Dishes like biryani, paneer tikka, chicken curry, puri sabzi, sweets like gulab jamun or jalebi and drinks like juice or soda were served at the wedding.

CHAPTER 10 HU TU TU, HU TU TU

About the Chapter

This chapter introduces Kabaddi and its challenges. Shyamala plays Kabaddi with six other girls and wins. Kabaddi is known by various names like Chegguguddu and Ha-du-du. It involves pushing, pulling and touching opponents while holding one's breath and saying "Kabaddi-Kabaddi." The game requires teamwork and strategy.

Jwala, Leela and Heera are three sisters from Mumbai who faced opposition for playing Kabaddi but overcame it. They formed a Kabaddi Club, which still exists today. The chapter also tells us about Karnam Malleshwari, a weightlifter from Andhra Pradesh, who began lifting at 12 years of age and has won 29 international medals.

GLOSSARY

Coach A person who trains players in a game or sport, teaching them skills and helping them improve.

Central Line The line in the middle of the Kabaddi court that players must cross to tag the other team and return safely.

Insist To say strongly that you must have or do something

Drag To pull somebody with difficulty

NCERT FOLDER

Page 79

Q.1 When you play Kabaddi, how many players do you have in a team?

Ans. A Kabaddi team has 8 players.

Q.2 How many players got out when Shyamala touched the line?

Ans. 8 players from the other team got out when Shyamala touched the line.

Q.3 Do you have ways to resolve disputes in games?

Ans. Yes, we can discuss the rules and agree on a fair decision.

Page 80

Q.1 Try to hold your breath and keep saying Kabaddi- Kabaddi. How many times could you say it?

Ans. I could easily say it 20-25 times.

Q.2 How many times can you say it, while you are playing Kabaddi? Is there any difference?

Ans. I can say it about 15-18 times. Yes, there is a difference of 5- 10 counts.

Q.3 Make a picture in your notebook to show how Shyamala managed to get the entire opposing team 'out' in one go.

Ans. Do it yourself.

Q.4 What does it mean to be out in games? When does one gets 'out' in Kabaddi?

Ans. To be out in the game means that the player who is out will not be allowed to play the game.

A player is "out" if they get caught by the opposing team or if they take a breath before reaching their side.

Q.5 In some games it is very important to touch the player. For example, in the game of Kho-Kho, you get 'out' when someone touches you. You also get your turn by someone's touch. Name some games in which it is very important to touch the players?

Ans. Some games are hide and seek, lock and key and ice and water.

Q.6 In Kabaddi, the entire team was 'out', because Shyamala had touched the line. What are some other games in which the central line is very important?

Ans. Some games in which central line is important are football, tug of war and hockey.

Q.7 What are the games in which , besides the players, you have to touch some things or colours?

Ans. Touching a thing: Kho-kho

Touching a colour: Colour race

Page 81

Q.1 Do you play Kabaddi? Is there a girls Kabaddi team in your school? Do you think that your grandmother played Kabaddi when they were your age? Ask them.

Ans. Yes, I play Kabaddi.

Yes, there is a girls Kabaddi team in my school. No, my grandmother has not played Kabaddi.

Page 83

Q.1 Have you learnt any game from a coach? Which one?

Ans. Yes, I have learnt badminton from a coach.

Q.2 Do you know of anyone who has learnt any game from a coach?

Ans. Yes, my brother has learnt cricket from a coach.

Discuss

Q.1 How does a coach teach? How does a coach make a player practice? How hard do you think the players have to work?

Ans. A coach teaches by showing the players how to play the game and explaining the rules. The coach also helps the players to practice.

Q.2 Have you ever thought of making a club for your favourite game?

Ans. Yes, I have thought about making a club for my favourite game, which is football. I would invite my friends to join and we could practice every weekend.

Q.3 Imagine that there are 15 childrens to play Kho-Kho. They must form two teams with equal numbers (7 each). Then one player will be left. What will you do if this happens? Have you ever become the 'extra person' in the middle? Write about this.

Ans. If we have 15 players, I would ask the extra person to be the referee for that round. They can help keep score or watch to make sure the game is fair.

Yes, I have been the extra person in the middle before. At first, I felt a little left out, but then I got to help the coach and cheer for my team. It was still fun because I knew I would get a turn in the next game.

Q.4 Every game has some rules. The game is played according to those rules. Let us see what happens if the rules are changed. For example, in cricket, a batsman gets 'out', if the bails fall off the stumps. Imagine if there is a rule that the entire team will be 'out', if all the three stumps fall. Would it be fun!

Ans. Changing the rules would make the game very different. If all three stumps fall, it means the whole team is out. The game would be faster and more exciting. Teams will also get more careful while playing the game.

Q.5 Try and play the game with this rule. Similarly, make some rules for other games and play.

Ans. Do it yourself.

CHAPTER 11 THE VALLEY OF FLOWERS

About the Chapter

In this chapter, we will learn about the Valley of Flowers and different uses of Flowers. In Uttarakhand, there is a beautiful place called Valley of Flowers. The valley is full of flowers of different colours like red, white, yellow and blue. They bloom only for a few weeks in the year.

Flowers have many uses in daily life. They are cooked and eaten as vegetables, used to make medicines, used to make natural colours, used for making perfumes, and they are an important part of festivals. Madhubani painting is an ancient form of folk art from Madhubani district in Bihar. It involves floral patterns created using a paste of powdered rice mixed with natural colours.

GLOSSARY

Valley A valley is a long, low-lying area of land that is usually found between mountains or hills.
Bloom It means to produce flowers.
Madhubani Art A traditional form of painting from Bihar that features floral designs made from natural colours derived from flowers and plants.
Folk Art It is art that reflects the life, history, geography, stories and culture of a group of people.
Dyeing To change the colour of something by adding a chemical to it.
Itr A perfume made from flowers.

NCERT FOLDER

Page 84

Q.1 Now close your eyes and imagine that you have reached such a place. How does it feel? Which songs do you feel like singing?

Ans. It feels very beautiful. I like to sing the Daffodil song.

Q.2 Have you ever seen so many flowers grow together anywhere? Where?

Ans. Yes, I have seen many flowers growing together in Mughal garden in Delhi.

Q.3 How many differently coloured flowers have you seen?

Ans. I have seen 6 differently coloured flowers.

Q.4 Write their colours.

Ans. White, red, pink, blue, orange and yellow.

Page 85

Q.1 Now you were just left counting, weren't you?

Ans. Yes, but it is difficult to count the flowers in a garden.

Q.2 Are there any things in your house which have designs of flowers made on them like clothes, sheets, vases, etc.?

Ans. Yes, in my house teacups and bedsheets have designs of flowers made on them.

Q.3 Draw your own design in your notebook and colour it as well.

Ans.

Q.4 Look at the designs made by your friends as well.

Ans.

Page 86-87 The World of Flowers

Q.1 Here are some pictures of flowers. Mark a (✓)on the flowers which you recognise. Write their names too if you know.

Ans. 1. Hibiscus, 2. Rose, 3. Sunflower, 4. Marigold, 5. Champa, 6. Jasmine, 7. Tulsi, 8. Crown flower, 9. Dahlia flower

Q.2 From the pictures given above and other flowers that you know, give names of two which

a. grow on trees __________ __________

b. grow on bushes __________ __________

c. grow on creepers __________ __________

d. grow on water plants __________ __________

e. bloom only at night __________ __________

f. bloom in the day and close at night __________ __________

Ans. a. grow on trees- Gulmohar, Kadam

b. grow on bushes- Lavender, Hibiscus

c. grow on creepers- Champa, Coral vine

d. grow on water plants- Water lilly, Lotus

e. bloom only at night- Moon flower, Queen of Night

f. bloom in the day and close at night- Sunflower, Poppy

Page 87

Q.1 Which flowers can you recognise by their scent, even with your eyes closed?

Ans. I can recognise rose and jasmine by their scent, even with my eyes closed.

Q.2 Which flowers bloom all the year round? Which flowers bloom only in certain months?

Ans. Rose and jasmine bloom all the year round. Flowers such as Tulips usually bloom in the spring season.

Q.3 Are there any trees or plants which never have any flowers? Find out and write.

Ans. Yes, money plants and snakeplant never have any flowers.

Why this?

Q.1 Have you ever seen a board like this put up anywhere?

Ans. Yes, I have seen such a board put up in parks and gardens.

Q.2 Do people pluck flowers even when this board is there?

Ans. Yes, people do usually pluck flowers even when they see this board placed.

Q.3 Why do you think they do this?

Ans. They do this as they do not respect the rules.

Q.4 Should they do this?

Ans. No, it's against the rule, and people should not pluck flowers.

Q.5 What would happen if everybody plucked flowers?

Ans. If everybody plucked flowers, then there wouldn't be any flowers left in the parks and gardens. Also, it will destroy the beauty of the place.

Let us look closely (Page 88)

Make groups of three or four children and look at one flower carefully

Q.1 What is the colour of the flower?

Ans. It's red in colour.

Q.2 What kind of a scent does it have?

Ans. It has a very lovely scent.

Q.3 What does it look like - a bell, a bowl, a brush or anything else?

Ans. It looks bowl-shaped.

Q.4 Do these flowers grow in bunches?

Ans. No, they do not grow in bunches usually.

Q.5 How many petals does it have?

Ans. It has about 40 to 80 petals.

Q.6 Are all the petals joined together or separate?

Ans. The petals of the flower are separate.

Q.7 Outside the petals, can you see any green leafy structure? How many are there?

Ans. Yes, I can see four such structures.

Q.8 Inside the petals, in the middle of the flower, can you see some thin structures? Write its colour.

Ans. Yes, the colour of this structure is pink-red.

Page 89

Q.9 When you touch these, do you find a powdery thing on your hands?

Ans. Yes, I found a powdery thing on my hands when touching it.

Blooming Buds

Q.1 What differences do you find between a flower and a bud?

Ans. A bud is smaller than a flower. It's the bud that develops into a flower.

Q.2 Can you tell how many days will a bud take to bloom into a flower? Let us try and find out.

(a) Choose a bud that is growing on a plant and look at it every day. Write the name of the plant.

Ans. It takes about 4 to 5 days for a bud to bloom into a flower. It is a rose plant.

(b) When you first saw this bud, the date was ________. Now when the bud has bloomed into a flower, the date is _______. How many days did the bud take to become a flower?

Ans. When I first saw this bud, the date was 12th March. Now when the bud has bloomed into a flower, the date is 19th March. It took 7 days for the bud to become a flower.

(c) Ask your friends the names of the different flowers that they have seen. How much time did it take their buds to become flowers?

Ans. The bud of a hibiscus takes about seven days and a sunflower's bud takes about seven to eight days.

(d) Also observe how many days the same flower took to dry.

Ans. Hibiscus takes about 30 days to become dry and sunflower takes about 30 to 40 days to become dry.

Page 90

Q.1 Are flowers cooked in your home as a dry vegetable, a gravy dish or as a chutney? Find out which flowers are used for these.

Ans. Yes, flowers of some plants are cooked as a dry vegetable, gravy dish or as chutney. Flowers of banana, sahjan, kachnar, etc are used as vegetables and gravy. Flowers of shefalika are used for making chutney.

Q.2 Find out names of any two flowers which are used for making medicines.

Ans. Cedar and rose are used for making medicines.

Q.3 How is rose water used in your house? Is it used as medicine, sweets, lassi or something else? Find out and tell others.

Ans. Rose water is used as a medicine for the eyes and skin and is also used to mix with sweets and lassi.

Page 91

Q.1 Find out and write the names of some more flowers that are used for making colours.

Ans. Rose, saffron and hibiscus are some of the flowers that are used for making colours and dyes.

Q.2 Can you think of a colour of which there is no flower?

Ans. I think there are no golden and silver colour flowers.

Q.3 Write the names of such flowers which are used to make scents.

Ans. Lavender, jasmine, rose and many other flowers are used to make scents.

Page 92

Q.1 Have you ever read or heard any songs about flowers?

Ans. Yes, I have read or heard songs about flowers.

Talk about it

Q.1 Do you know when such songs are sung?

Ans. Yes, such songs are sung on the occasion of marriages.

Q.2 Do you or anybody else at home know other such songs? Collect songs, poems, etc., on flowers.

Ans. My mother and aunty know several such songs.

Q.3 Are any special flowers used on certain occasions/festivals by your elders? Make a list of different occasions and the flowers used at each.

Ans.

Occasions/Festivals	Name of Flower
Marriage	Rose, Marigold
Pooja	Marigold
Birthday	Rose, tulips

Let us Know some more (Page 93)

Have you ever seen anyone selling flowers anywhere? If there are any flower-sellers nearby ask them these questions and write.

Q.1 What are the different flowers that they sell? Ask them the names of three flowers.

Ans. Rose, jasmine, marigold and orchids are different flowers sold.

Q.2 Where do they bring these flowers from?

Ans. They bring these flowers from horticulture farms and gardens.

Q.3 Why do people buy flowers?

Ans. People buy flowers for various purposes like decoration, pooja and for gifting them to others.

Q.4 In what forms do flower sellers sell their flowers? Look at these pictures. Tick against those forms that you have seen.

(i)

(ii)

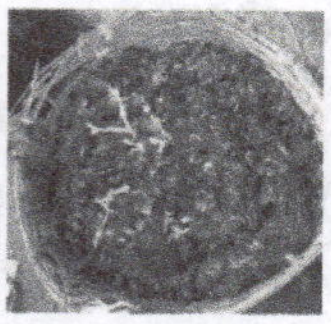

(iii)

(iv)

(v)

(vi)

Ans. (ii), (iii), (iv), (vi)

Page 94

Q.1 Any other form that you have seen.

Ans. No, I have not seen.

Q.2 Have you seen flowers offered at many religious places?

Ans. Yes, I have seen different types and colours of flowers offered at many religious places.

Q.3 What do we do when they dry up?

Ans. We dispose the dry flowers as waste.

Q.4 How will you use them?

Ans. I will use them to make greeting card.

Q.5 Some flowers are used in different forms - like rose and marigold are used in garlands and as loose petals too.

(a) Find out the prices of these different forms.

(i) One flower ________

(ii) One garland ________

(iii) One bouquet ________

Ans. (i) One flower - ₹ 15

(ii) One garland - ₹ 70

(iii) One bouquet - ₹ 300

(b) Has the flower-seller learnt to make bouquets or a net of flowers from anybody? From whom?

Ans. Yes, the flower-seller learnt to make bouquets or net flowers from his father.

(c) Would they like the other members of their family to do this work? Why?

Ans. Yes, they'd like to include other family members to do this work as it helps the flower-seller earn some extra money.

CHAPTER 12

CHANGING TIMES

About the Chapter

This chapter is about Chetandas, an elderly man who shares the changes he has seen throughout his life. As a child, he lived in Dera Gazikhan, now part of Pakistan, but his family moved to Delhi during the partition of the country into India and Pakistan. They later settled in Sohna village, where they built a simple house using mud, cow dung and wood. Over time, as Chetandas and his family grew, they made improvements to the house, by adding rooms like a new kitchen and a separate toilet. They used materials like cement and unbaked bricks.

Later, when his son was getting married, they made changes to the house by using baked bricks, lintel roof, marble chips and gas stove in the kitchen. Chetandas moved to Delhi with his son, where they saw modern buildings and renovated their home further. In his 70 years, Chetandas saw many changes in his home and surroundings.

GLOSSARY

Chulha A traditional clay stove used for cooking, often found in older homes.

Unbaked Bricks Bricks that are not baked in a kiln but are used to build houses and require regular maintenance.

Lintel A lintel is a strong, straight piece of wood or stone placed above a door or window to support the wall above it.

Renovate It means to fix up or make something old look new again, like painting or repairing the house.

Coated It means something is covered with a layer of another material.

Sand Sand is tiny, soft grains of rock that you often find at the beach or in a sandbox.

NCERT FOLDER

Find Out and Write (Page 98)

Q.1 Talk to any one of your grandparents or any other elderly person. Find out when she or he was eight-nine years old -

(a) Where did she or he live? Name that place.

Ans. She lived in a village named Cheyyar.

(b) From what material was her or his house made?

Ans. Her house was made of materials like wood, thatched bamboo, mud and straw.

(c) Did they have a toilet in their house? If no, where was it?

Ans. Yes, they had a toilet in their house.

(d) In which part of the house was food cooked?

Ans. Food was cooked in the verandah, which was separated by a wall.

(e) A lot of mud was used when Chetandas' house was made. Why?

Ans. A lot of mud was used when Chetandas' house was made to protect the house from heat and cold.

Page 99

Q.1 Chetandas tells that people from the basti used to come to clean the toilets and take away the waste. They were not allowed to enter the house.

(a) The people who used the toilets did not clean them. Discuss.

Ans. The people who used the toilets did not clean them, as they thought that it was a dirty job. Therefore, people from basti cleaned the toilets and took away the waste.

(b) Is there a toilet in your house? Who cleans it?

Ans. Yes, there are toilets in my house. My entire family cleans them on a weekly basis.

Page 101

Q.1 What materials have been used in making your house?

Ans. The materials used in making my house are cement, bricks, concrete, sand, iron rod and wood.

Q.2 Find out the material from which your friend's house is made? Is there any difference? Write about it.

Ans. My friend's house is made up of materials like sand, cement, iron rods and bricks. No, there is no difference.

Q.3 What kind of house do you think Chetandas' grandchildren will live in?

Ans. Chetandas' grandchildren will live in skyscrapers made up of cement and iron.

Page 102

Q.4 Where would you like to live when you grow up? What kind of house would you like?

Ans. I would like to live in a metropolitan city in a bungalow when I grow up.

Q.5 You had written about the things that your grandparent's house was made of. Have some of those materials been used in your house? Name them.

Ans. No, those kinds of materials are not used in my house, except for doors and windows, which are made of wood.

Q.6 People are given names according to the work they do. For example, a person who works with wood is called a carpenter.

(a) In your place, what do you call a person who works with wood?

Ans. In my place, a person who works with wood is called a Badhai.

Q.7 Now, look at the picture and fill in the table.

What kind of work is being done by different people here? What tools are they shown using in the picture? Write them in the given table.

Work	Tool	What is the person called
1.		
2.		
3.		
4.		

Ans.

Work	Tool	What is the person called
1. Mixing of sand and cement	Trowel, hammer	Mason
2. Fixing taps and pipes	Pipe cutter, wrench	Plumber
3. Fixing electrical wires	Wires, screw drivers	Electrician
4. Carrying bricks	Iron pans	Labourer

Page 103

Q.1 Do you know people who do this type of work? Talk to them and find out about their work. Discuss it with your friends.

Ans. Yes, I know people who work as electricians, masons and plumbers.

Find these people and ask them questions about what they do. Then, discuss with you friends.

Q.2 With your teacher or someone from home, go to a place where a building is being constructed. Talk to the people working there and find out the answers to these questions.

(a) What is being built there?

Ans. A big mall is being built there.

(b) How many people are working there?

Ans. Approximately 400 people are working there.

(c) What kind of work are they doing?

Ans. Masons were putting cement on lintels and roofs, engineers were supervising the work, and labourers were carrying materials. Other people were operating cranes and other machines.

(d) How many men and women are there?

Ans. About 300 men and 100 women are there.

Page 104

(e) Are any children working there? What are they doing?

Ans. No, children are not working there.

(f) How much money do these people get paid daily? Ask any three different people.

Ans. Mason - ₹ 2,500/-
Carpenter - ₹ 2,500/-
Helper - ₹ 1,800/-

(g) Where do these people live?

Ans. These people live in tents located near construction places, while others come from their houses.

(h) What are the materials being used to make the building?

Ans. The materials being used to make the building are cement, wood, iron rods, sand, stone chips, bricks, etc.

(i) Try and guess how many trucks of bricks and bags of cement will be used to make the building.

Ans. 8,000 trucks of bricks and 2,00,000 bags of cement will be used to make the building.

Q.3 How do the materials reach the building site? (By truck, handcart, or any other vehicle.) List them.

Ans. The materials reach the building site by trucks.

Q.4 Find out the price of

(a) One bag of cement ______

(b) One brick ______

(c) One truck of sand ______

Ans. (a) One bag of cement - ₹ 260/-

(b) One brick - ₹ 5/-

(c) One truck of sand - ₹ 7,000/-

Page 105

Q.1 Ask a few other questions and write their answers.

(a) How much sand is mixed with cement?

Ans. 6 bags of sand are mixed with 1 bag of cement.

(b) Who makes the map of buildings?

Ans. The map of buildings is made by architects.

(c) Why are cranes used at construction sites?

Ans. Cranes are used at construction sites to lift heavy objects.

Q.2. Over the sixty years, different materials were used at different times in Chetandas' house. List these in the correct order.

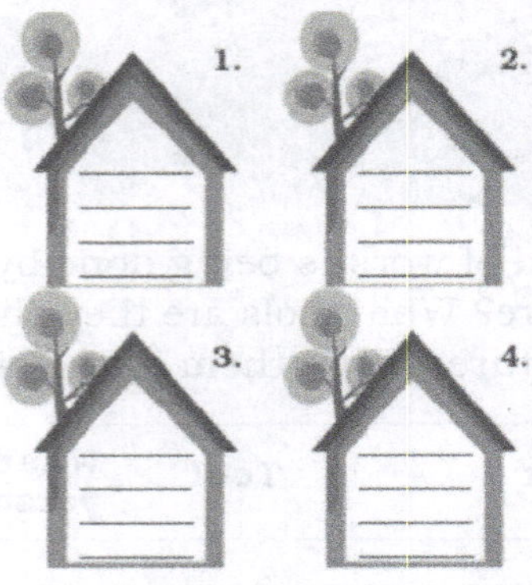

Ans. 1. (a) Bamboo (b) Muds (c) Straw (d) Ropes

2. (a) Nut and bolt (b) Wood (c) Bamboo (d) Iron rods

3. (a) Iron rod (b) Sand (c) Cement (d) Wood

4. (a) Cement (b) Sand (c) Plastic (d) Marble

Let us make houses

Q.3 Divide the children in the class into 3-4 groups. Let each group make a model of a different house. For this you can use mud, wood, paper, pieces of cloth, shoe-boxes, match boxes and colours.

Ans. Do it yourself.

Q.4 Place all the houses so as to construct a neighbourhood colony.

Ans. Do it yourself.

CHAPTER 13 A RIVER'S TALE

About the Chapter

In this chapter, we will learn about the journey of the river and how it changes on its way. The river flows through villages, towns and cities. The water changes when the river flows. People use the river for washing clothes, bathing animals and cleaning utensils.

These activities make the water dirty. Many things dissolve easily in water, making it dirty and harmful for our health. It is important to clean water before drinking it. Boiling is one of the best ways to clean water.

GLOSSARY

Dissolve When a substance mixes completely with water and disappears, like sugar or salt. Some things like oil do not dissolve in water.

Utensils Containers used in the kitchen for cooking and serving food. Examples include pots, pans, spoons and forks.

NCERT FOLDER

Page 106

Q.1 Look carefully at the picture of the river. Read the words given below.

Boat, flowing water, blue, fish, water-plants, river, foul smell, big ship, oil, river banks, factories, washing clothes, animals, other work, change, city.

Use these words to make a story. Give a title to your story also.

Ans. River Pollution

Once upon a time, there was a river with clear blue water and many fishes. There were also some plants in the river. A factory was made near the river and a city grew near it. Goods required for the factory were supplied through the river with the help of big ships. Oil waste from the factory was drained in the river. People from the nearby cities also bathed their animals and washed clothes in the river. This made the river dirty. It was no longer a river with clear water.

Page 107

Look at the pictures and answer the following questions.

Q.1 What is the colour of the river where it begins?

Ans. The colour of the river is blue where it begins.

Q.2 At some places, there are many fish in the river, at others, there are only a few and at some places, there are dead fish. What could be the reason for this? Discuss.

Ans. Fish need fresh and clean water. There are more fishes when water is clean. When the water gets dirty or polluted, the fishes die. This is why, some places have few or dead fish.

Q.3 What can be seen in the river before it reaches the village?

Ans. A large number of fishes can be seen in the river before it reaches the village.

Q.4 At which places did the colour of the water in the river change? Why did this happen? Discuss.

Ans. The colour of the water in the river changed near towns and villages.

It happened because of pollution caused by the people who throw waste in the river.

Q.5 Which of the places shown in the picture would you like to live in? Why?

Ans. I would like to live in the place where the river started. The water is clean and pure, and there are so many trees.

Q.6 Would you like to change any of the things that you see in the picture? Why and how?

Ans. I would like to remove all the waste from the water and also clean river bank. Due to these wastes, the water gets polluted.

Q.7 Have you seen people throwing different things into rivers or water bodies?

Ans. Yes, I have seen people throwing harmful chemicals, coins, domestic waste, etc., into rivers and other water bodies.

Q.8 What could be done to keep rivers clean? Discuss.

Ans. Following are the things that could be done to keep the rivers clean

- People living near the river banks should not bathe their animals and wash their clothes in the river.
- The industrial waste should not be thrown into the river.
- Treatment plants should be set up to remove chemicals and other wastes before letting it into the river.

Page 108

Q.1 If you wanted to drink some water, from which part of the river would you like to drink? Why?

Ans. I would like to drink some water at the place from which the river starts.

The water at the beginning of the river is clean and safe for drinking.

Q.2 In the last part of the picture, the river flows into the sea. Have you ever seen the sea? Where? In a movie, or somewhere else?

Ans. Yes, I have seen the sea. I once saw the sea when I went to Mumbai.

Q.3 Have you ever been near a river or sea? When?

Ans. Yes, there is a river in my city. I go there sometimes.

Q.4 Show with your hands, how the waves in the sea move.

Ans. Do it yourself.

Q.5 Is the water from the sea drinkable? Why?

Ans. The water from the sea is not drinkable, as it is salty.

Q.6 Do you think that there would be changes taking place in a river, pond or stream at different times of the year? What kind of changes would these be? Discuss.

Ans. Yes, there would be changes taking place in a river, pond or stream at different times of the year. The water level would be high during the rainy season and it would be lesser in the summer months.

Page 109

Q.7 Will there be the same amount of water in the ponds or rivers during the rainy season and in summer?

Ans. No, there will not be the same amount of water in the ponds or rivers during the rainy season and in summer. Water level will be more in the rainy season and it will be lesser in summer.

Q.8 Is there a pond, river or lake near your town or city?

Ans. Yes, there is a river near my city.

Find out (Page 109)

Q.1 Are there any changes in the water during summers, the rainy season and in winters?

Ans. Yes, in summers, the level of water is less. During the rainy season, the water level is more and in winters, the water level is medium.

Q.2 What are the different kinds of water animals found there?

Ans. The different kinds of animals found in water are fishes, frogs and crabs.

Q.3 What kind of trees and plants grow around it?

Ans. Thick trees, grasses and bushy plants grow around it.

Q.4 What are the kinds of birds that come there?

Ans. Swan, crow, eagle, etc., are the kinds of birds that come there.

Q.5 Have you ever seen or read about floods? Where?

Ans. Yes, I have read about floods which occurred in Bihar.

Q.6 What happens when there is a flood?

Ans. Railway tracks, roads, houses, etc., get drowned during a flood.

Q.7 Have you seen dirty water in a river or pond? Where?

Ans. Yes, I have seen dirty water in a river and in ponds in my village.

Q.8 How would you know if the water is dirty? If the water looks clean, can you be sure that it is alright to drink that water? Discuss.

Ans. If the water is dirty, it looks muddy and gives a bad smell. If the water looks clean, it may still not be safe to drink, as it may contain some bacteria and other germs.

Page 110

Q.1 Where do you get your drinking water? A river or a lake?

Ans. I get drinking water from a river.

Q.2 Do you think that like the river in the picture, your river or lake can also be affected?

Ans. Yes, the river located in my town is affected by pollution.

Page 110-111

Q.3 Fill about half of each bottle or glass with water. Make sure that all have the same amount of water. Now, one by one, put each of the things in the water. For example, haldi in the first glass oil in the second glass and soda in the third glass until you have one thing in each glass. Mix each thing in the water and see what happens. Write your observations in the table. What did you observe? Put (✓) mark in the right places.

Things	Dissolved (mixed in water)	Did not dissolve in water	Colour of water changes	Colour of water does not change
Sugar				
Salt				
Lemon juice				
Haldi				
Soap water				
Flour				
Dal				
Sherbet				
Cooking soda				
Oil (Mustard, Til or any other)				

Ans. **Dissolved** (mixed in water) Sugar, salt, lemon juice, haldi, soap water, sherbet, cooking soda

Did not dissolve in water Flour, dal, oil

Colour of water changes Haldi, soap water, flour, sherbet, oil

Colour of water does not change Sugar, salt, lemon juice, cooking soda

Page - 111

Now, on the basis of your observations, tell

Q.4 Do all things dissolve in water?

Ans. No, all things do not dissolve in water.

Q.5 Does the colour of the water always change?

Ans. No, the colour of the water does not always change.

Q.6 Did oil dissolve in water? How can you say whether it has dissolved or not?

Ans. No, oil does not dissolve in water. Things which are insoluble in water either come up or settle down. For example, oil floats on water.

Q.7 Colour of the water may not change even after some things are dissolved in it. Would you say that these are absent in water?

Ans. No, these things are not absent in water. They are present and have mixed up with water.

Q.8 Imagine how it would be if things like sugar, salt, lemon juice, sherbet, etc., could not dissolve in water.

Ans. If things like sugar, salt, lemon juice, sherbet, etc., could not dissolve in water, cooking food and preparing things like cold drinks, coffee, tea, etc., will not be possible.

Q.9. Imagine how it would be if things like stones, chalk, plastic and garbage would dissolve in water.

Ans. If things like stones, chalk, plastic and garbage would dissolve in water, they would make the water dirty.

Q.10 How is drinking water cleaned in your house?

Ans. The drinking water in our house is cleaned using a water filter.

Q.11 Find out the many different ways of cleaning water at home.

Ans. Different ways of cleaning water at home are

- By adding chlorine tablet to the clean water.
- By boiling water.

Q.12 Draw pictures showing any two ways of cleaning the water.

Ans. (i) Boiling water

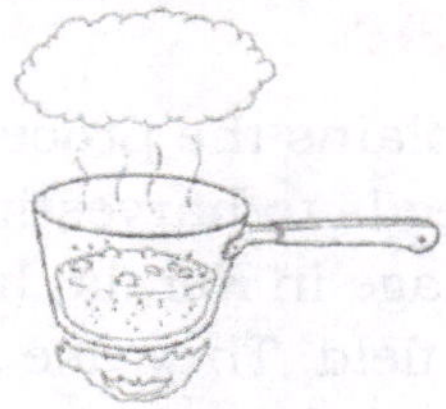

(ii) Water purification by filter

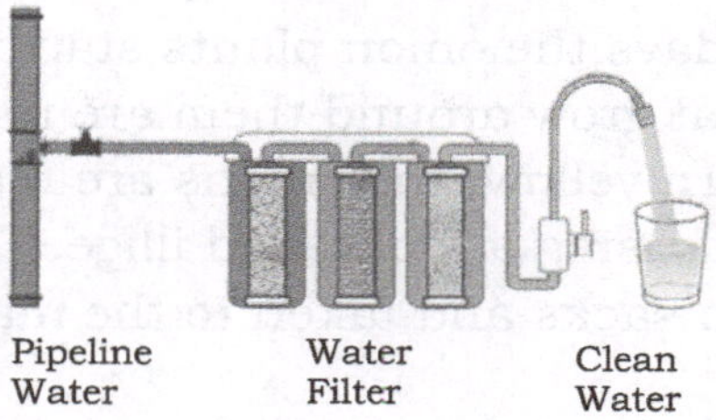

CHAPTER 14

BASVA'S FARM

About the Chapter

This chapter explains the process of farming, from planting seeds to harvesting crops. Basva, a boy from a village in Kerala, helps his father, a farmer, in the field. They use a Khunti to loosen the soil and they plant seeds with a Kurige which is pulled by bullocks.

After 20 days,the onion plants start to sprout and weeds that grow around them are removed. When the leaves turn yellow, the onions are ready to be harvested using a tool called illige. The onions are then packed in sacks and taken to the market to be sold.

GLOSSARY

Khunti An iron rod used to dig and loosen soil in preparation for planting.

Sowing The act of planting seeds in the ground to grow plants.

Kurige A ploughing tool pulled by bullocks to prepare the field for sowing seeds.

Weeds Unwanted plants that grow in fields and gardens, taking up space and nutrients needed by crops.

Harvesting It means gathering or collecting crops, fruits, or vegetables from the fields when they are fully grown and ready to be eaten or used.

Sprinkling It means to throw drops of water or any liquid on a surface.

NCERT FOLDER

Find out (Page 113)

Q.1 In Basva's area, an implement called Khunti is used to loosen the soil. What is the kind of implement called in your area? Draw it and discuss.

Ans. The implement used to loosen the soil in my area is called *Khunti* only.

Q.2 Find out from a farmer or some elders in your family, what kinds of crops are grown in your area?

Ans. Vegetables, mustard, rice, gram, maize, wheat, etc., are the crops grown in my area.

Page 114

Q.3 What other ways could be used to plough the fields instead of animals? Discuss.

Ans. Tractors can be used to plough the fields instead of animals.

Page 115

Q.4 Draw any crop which you have seen in the field.

Ans.

Q.5 Basva helps his father in the field. Do you help the elders in your family in their work? What do you help with?

Ans. Yes, I help elders in my family with their work. I help my father in buying groceries for our house and my mother in cooking food.

Page 116

Q.6 Do you enjoy doing that work?

Ans. Yes, I enjoy doing that work.

Page 116

Write answers in your notebook

Q.1 Why should Basva help Appa in the field only after school hours and on holidays?

Ans. Basva should help Appa in the field only after school hours and on holidays because he needs to focus on his studies during school time.

Q.2 Are there any fields near your house? What is grown there?

Ans. Yes, there is a field near my house. Rice and wheat are grown in that field.

Q.3 Basva's Appa takes the onions to the market in a truck. Think, how would fruits and vegetables be taken to another place, if there were no proper roads.

Ans. It is very difficult to carry fruits and vegetables, if there are no proper roads. In the olden days, people carried fruits, vegetables and crops to the market in bullock carts, boats, donkeys, etc.

Q.4 What kind of vehicles are used to carry fruits and vegetables? Draw a picture of one of these vehicles in your notebook.

Ans. Thela, rikshaw, tempo, trucks and tractors, etc., are used to carry fruits and vegetables.

Truck

Page 117

Find out and write

Q.1 Given here are pictures of some implements used by Basva's family. Write the names of the implements. Also write what these are called in your area? What work are they used for?

(i) Name (in this chapter) ______

Name in your area ______

Work ______

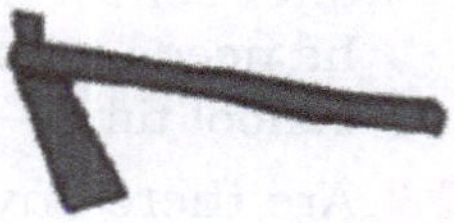

(ii) Name (in this chapter) ______

Name in your area ______

Work ______

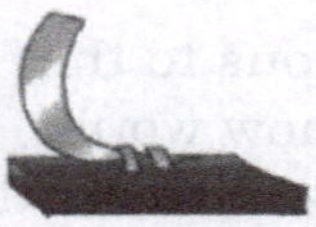

(iii) Name (in this chapter) ______

Name in your area ______

Work ______

Ans. (i) Kurige, Kudal, Ploughing

(ii) Khunti, Khunti, Digging

(iii) Illige, Sickle, Digging

Page 118

Q.2 Many steps are needed to grow crops. Look at the pictures and mark them in the correct order.

Ans. 5, 3, 2, 1, 4, 6

Q.3 Find out about a crop that is grown in your area. Also, find out the steps that are part of this work. Draw them in your notebook.

Ans. Rice, wheat, mustard, vegetables, etc., are grown in my area.

Draw them yourself.

CHAPTER 15 FROM MARKET TO HOME

About the Chapter

This chapter is about Vaishali, a young girl whose family sells vegetables. Her whole family, including Amma, Babuji, Bhaiya and Chotu, wake up at 3 am to start their day. First, they remove the old vegetables to make space for the new ones. Babuji, Bhaiya and her uncle buy fresh vegetables like brinjals, potatoes, tomatoes, okra and more from the mandi.

Babuji goes to the market at 7 a.m. after arranging vegetables on the handcart. After that, Vaishali attends school. Chotu helps at the cart in the morning because he goes to school in the afternoon. Babuji and Bhaiya sell vegetables all day, making sure to sell the old ones first. They keep the vegetables fresh by sprinkling water on them. They return home by 10 p.m., go to bed at 11:30 p.m., and wake up after four hours to start their day.

GLOSSARY

Gunny Bags Large, sturdy sacks made from jute or other materials.

Handcart A two-wheeled cart pushed or pulled by hand, used by vegetable sellers to carry and display their vegetables in the *bazaar*.

Sorting The process of separating things of one type from others.

NCERT FOLDER

Page 119

Q.1 Does anyone in your house have to get up very early? What time do they get up? Why do they need to get up so early?

Ans. Yes, my elder brother gets up early. He gets up by 5:30 a.m. to visit the gym to stay fit.

Let us talk (Page 122)

Q.1 Babuji sells the previous day's vegetables first. Why do you think he does this?

Ans. He sells the previous day's vegetables first as they might get spoilt.

Q.2 Have you seen dried or spoilt vegetables? Where?

Ans. Yes, I have seen dried and spoilt vegetables. I have seen them at home.

Q.3 How did you know that the vegetables were spoilt?

Ans. When vegetables are spoilt, wrinkles appear, moulds grow and they give a bad smell.

Q.4 Chhotu is helping his family. What do you think Chhotu has learnt from it?

Ans. Chhotu has learnt to help others.

Q.5 How do you help the elders in your family?

Ans. I help the elders in my family by picking up things which are heavy or distant to them by handing these things to them.

Q.6 Look at the clocks given below. Write what you do, and what Vaishali does, at the time which the clocks are showing.

Ans.

Morning Morning Night

Ans.

Name/Time	3 o'clock morning	6 o'clock morning	10 o' clock night
Vaishali	Takes out vegetables	Putting vegetables in the bag	Sleeping
Me	Sleeping	Getting ready for school	Sleeping

Q.7 From where do you get vegetables for your home? Who brings the vegetables?

Ans. We get vegetables from the nearby market. My mother and father bring them home.

Some Fun with Vegetables (Page 123)

Q.1 The next time when you get okra (*Bhindi*) at home, look at them carefully. Are all of them the same size?

Ans. No, all of them are not of the same size.

(a) Find the longest and the shortest one. Measure them.

Ans. The longest lady finger was 4 inches and the shortest one was 2.5 inches.

(b) Do all the okra (*Bhindi*) have the same thickness and colour? Cut two okra (*Bhindi*) lengthwise. Do both of them have the same number of seeds? Draw them in your notebook.

Ans. All of them have different thicknesses but are of the same colour. No, they do not have the same number of seeds.

(c) Seema's mother has brought some fruits and vegetables from the market. Can you find them in this picture? Colour them and write their names alongside.

Ans. I can find tomato, carrot, potato, spinach, brinjal, pumpkin and lady finger.

Find Out (Page 124)

Q.1 Given here is a list of vegetables and fruits. Which of these will spoil earlier, and which will stay for some days?

Write the names in the correct column. You can add more names to the list.

Spinach, Potato, Banana, Tomato, Pear Chikoo, Pineapple, Gourd, Onion, Cabbage Cucumber, Grapes, Ginger

Fruits and vegetables that spoil quickly	Fruits and vegetables that can stay for some days

Ans.

Fruits and vegetables that spoil quickly	Fruits and vegetables that can stay for some days
Pineapple	Potato
Banana	Cucumber
Spinach	Onion
Tomato	Chikoo
Pear	Cabbage
Grapes	Gourd
	Ginger

Q.2 Some of these fruits and vegetables are smooth to touch, while some are rough. From the list above, put the names in the correct column.

Smooth	Rough

Ans.

Smooth	Rough
Tomato	Onion
Brinjal	Cabbage
Potato	Pineapple
Apple	Gourd

Q.3 Which vegetable do you find the heaviest to carry? Write its name and draw its picture in your notebook.

Ans. Pumpkin is the heaviest.

Q.4 Which is the lightest fruit or vegetable that you have eaten? Write its name and draw the picture in your notebook.

Ans. Grapes is the lightest fruit.

Q.5 Write the names of three vegetables which do not have seeds.

Ans. Cabbage, potato and cauliflower are vegetables which do not have seeds.

Q.6 Fill in the table given below. You can add three more names and fill in the table.

	Colour	Length	Weight	Price
Apple			(½ kilo)	
Banana			(1dozen)	
Potato			(½ kilo)	

Ans.

	Colour	Length	Weight	Price
Apple	Red	5 cm	(½ kilo)	₹100
Banana	Yellow	12 cm	(1 dozen)	₹40
Potato	Yellow	4 cm	(½ kilo)	₹50
Tomato	Red	4 cm	(½ kilo)	₹45
Lady's finger	Green	6 cm	(1 kg)	₹30
Cabbage	Green	10 cm	(1 kg)	₹40

Q.7 Talk with a vegetable seller in your area. Ask the following questions and make a brief report in the notebook.

(a) What is his name?

Ans. His name is Bhola Prasad.

(b) How many people are there in his house? How many children are there at home?

Ans. There are 6 people in his house. There are 4 children at home.

(c) What are the names of the children? How old are they?

Ans. The names and ages of the children are as follows

Raju - 15 years old

Ashok - 13 years old

Priyanka - 5 years old

Geeta- 2 years old

(d) Who all help in the work of selling vegetables?

Ans. His wife and his elder son Raju helps in the work of selling vegetables.

(e) Who all stay with the vegetable cart or in the shop?

Ans. His wife and his daughters stay at the shop.

(f) What vegetables do they sell?

Ans. They sell all kinds of vegetables.

(g) What time do they start work?

Ans. They start their work in the early morning at 4:30 a.m.

(h) For how many hours in a day do they work?

Ans. They work for nearly 14 to 15 hours a day.

(i) Ask them about any three vegetables that they sell.

Ans.

	Vegetable 1	**Vegetable 2**	**Vegetable 3**
Name of the vegetable	Potato	Onion	Tomato
The price of the vegetable	60	70	75
Where does it come from?	Patna Mandi	Patna Mandi	Patna Mandi
How much of the vegetabale do they buy at one time?	2 kg	5 kg	1 kg
In which months	All	All	All
Does this vegetable usually come?			

CHAPTER 16 A BUSY MONTH

About the Chapter

This chapter is a letter written by Gijubhai Bhdeka on 13th April, 1936, about birds during the nesting season. Birds like sparrows, sunbirds and doves build nests for their eggs. Different birds build nests in different places. Crows build nests high in trees, while doves build theirs nests in mehendi hedges. Birds like the koel, barbet, tailor bird and sunbird make their nests in different ways. Sometimes animals like cows, cats and rats try to steal eggs or break the nests.

Birds use nests to lay eggs and raise their chicks. Once the chicks grow, they leave the nest and live in different atmospheres. Birds also have different kinds of feet and beaks and animals have different types of teeth. Cows have short teeth, while cats have sharp teeth. The front teeth of squirrel's keep growing.

GLOSSARY

Nesting The process by which birds build a nest to lay their eggs and raise their chicks.
Binoculars A tool used to view distant objects clearly, often used to watch birds.

NCERT FOLDER

Page 130-132

Q.1 How many years ago did Gijubhai write this letter?

Ans. Gijubhai wrote this letter 88 years ago.

Q.2 Find out how old your grandfather and grandmother were at that time.

Ans. My grandfather was five years old and my grandmother was one year old.

Q.3 This letter talks about many different birds. How many of these birds have you seen?

Ans. I have seen different kinds of birds, like robins, cuckoos, crows, pigeons, etc.

Q.4 How many other birds have you seen? Which ones?

Ans. I have seen several other birds, like parrots, eagles, sparrows, vultures, etc.

Q.5 Have you seen a bird's nest? Where did you see it?

Ans. Yes, I have seen a bird's nest. I saw it on a tree in our garden.

Q.6 Which is your favourite bird? Can you show your friends in the class how it flies and what sound it makes?

Ans. My favourite bird is pigeon.

Q.7 Guess what this bird is

'A crown on the head and coins on the tail, So many shades of blue from top to tall.'
Clue : It is our national bird.

Ans. This bird is a peacock.

Q.8 Do you know of any other bird that makes its nest in a tree trunk as the barbet does?

Ans. Yes, the woodpecker makes its nest in a tree trunk as the barbet does.

Q.9 If there is a nest inside or around your house, look carefully at it. Remember, do not go too near the nest and do not touch it. If you do, then the bird will not come to the nest again.

Observe the nest for some days and note down the following things:

(a) Where is the nest made?

Ans. The nest is made on my roof.

(b) What is the nest made of?

Ans. The nest is made of dried leaves and straw.

(c) Is the nest ready or are the birds still making it?

Ans. Yes, the nest is ready.

(d) Can you recognise which bird has made the nest?

Ans. Yes, the crow has made the nest.

(e) What things does the bird bring to the nest?

Ans. The bird brings worms, straws, twigs, etc., to the nest.

(f) Is there any bird sitting in the nest?

Ans. Yes, one crow is sitting in the nest.

(g) Do you think there are any eggs in the nest?

Ans. There are two eggs in the nest.

(h) Can you hear any sound like 'chee chee' from the nest?

Ans. Yes, I can hear a sound like 'chee chee' from the nest.

(i) If there are chicks in the nest, what do the parent birds bring for them to eat?

Ans. Parent birds bring grains and insects for them to eat.

(j) How many times in one hour do the birds come to the nest?

Ans. The birds come to the nest two to three times in one hour.

(k) After how many days did the chicks leave the nest?

Ans. The chicks left the nest after three months.

(l) Make a picture of the nest in your notebook.

Ans.

Q.10 You have seen how birds use many different things to make their nests. Use some of these things and make a nest. Make a small paper bird to put in your nest.

Ans. Do it yourself.

Let Us Have Some Fun (Page 132)

Q.1 Make three groups in the class. Each child must draw a picture of an animal and colour it. They should then cut each picture out.

Ans. Do it yourself.

Q.2 Children in one group will take cut-outs of the pictures of animals that live on land. They should then draw soil, grass and some trees on chart paper. Stick the pictures of the land animals at the correct places on the chart.

Ans. Do it yourself.

Q.3 The second group will take cut-outs of the pictures of animals that live in the water. They should then colour a chart paper blue to show water. They should also draw water plants, stones, etc. They should then stick the pictures of the animals that live in the water on the chart.

Ans. Do it yourself.

Q.4 The third group will take cut-outs of pictures of animals that live on trees. One child in the group will draw a big three on a chart paper and colour it. Then, all the children in the group must stick their cut-outs of the pictures on the chart paper of their group.

Ans. Do it yourself.

Q.5 Put up all three charts in your class and discuss about them.

Ans. Do it yourself.

Find Out About Your Own Teeth and Write (Page 135)

Q.1 Your age.

Ans. My age is 10 years.

Q.2 How many teeth do you have?

Ans. I have 16 teeth.

Q.3 Have any of your teeth fallen or broken? How many?

Ans. Yes, 6 of my teeth have fallen.

Q.4 How many new teeth do you have?

Ans. I have 4 new teeth.

Q.5 How many of your milk teeth have fallen, but no new teeth have come in their place?

Ans. 6 of my milk teeth have fallen, but no new teeth have come in their place.

Find Out More About Teeth (Page 135)

Q.1 Look at your friend's teeth. Are there different kinds of teeth?

Ans. Yes, there are different kinds of teeth in my friend's mouth.

Q.2 Draw one front tooth and one back tooth in your notebook.

Ans.

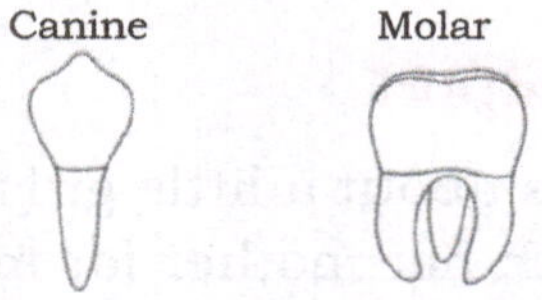

Q.3 Can you see any difference between these teeth?

Ans. Yes, there are differences between these teeth. The back tooth is broad and thick, whereas the front tooth is sharp and flat.

Imagine and Share (Page 136)

Q.1 If you did not have front teeth (both top and bottom), how would you eat a guava? Act and show how.

Ans. If I did not have front teeth (both top and bottom), I would eat a guava like an old man.

Q.2 You have your front teeth but no teeth at the back. Someone gives you a roti. Show how would you eat it.

Ans. Do it yourself.

Q.3 You do not have any teeth in your mouth. What kind of things would you be able to eat?

Ans. If I do not have any teeth in my mouth, I will be able to eat only soft things like bananas, ice-cream, etc.

Q.4 Draw a picture in your notebook – How would you look if you had no teeth?

Ans. Do it yourself.

Q.5 Find out from old people who do not have teeth – what are the kinds of things that they can not eat?

Ans. Old people who do not have teeth cannot eat hard things like fried grams, paratha, chapati, chips, etc.

CHAPTER 17 NANDITA IN MUMBAI

About the Chapter

This chapter is about a little girl named Nandita, who moves from her village to the big city of Mumbai with her mother for medical treatment. They stayed at her uncle's (Mama's) house, which was a small room where everyone lived and did everything like sleeping and cooking. Nandita takes the bus to visit her mother in the hospital. They have to use a dirty public toilet at the end of the street and wake up early to collect water from a public tap.

In her village, Nandita also didn't have a tap and collected water from a pond. In Mumbai, Nandita goes with her Mami where she works and sees tall buildings, big houses. She learns that they have lifts, many rooms, and proper water, which is different from her village and Mama's house. One day, Nandita's uncle gets a notice to move because a new hotel is being built. They are given a new place to live that is far away and has no water or electricity.

GLOSSARY

Crowded A place full of people, where it is difficult to move freely.

Courtyard An open area or space around a house, often used for activities like playing or cooking.

NCERT FOLDER

Page 39

Q.1 Why did Nandita have to bring her mother from the village to Mumbai?

Ans. Nandita had to bring her mother from the village to Mumbai for treatment.

Q.2 Nandita used to feel like vomiting when at first she had to use the toilet where Mama lived. Why?

Ans. Nandita used to feel like vomiting when at first she had to use the toilet where Mama lived because the toilet was used by everyone in the street. It was always dirty and smelled very bad.

Page 40

Q.3 In what ways did Nandita find her Mama's house to be different from her house in the village?

Ans. Nandita found her Mama's house to be different from her house in the village because Nandita's house in the village had a separate cooking area. But in Mama's house, there was only one room and everything including cooking was done there only.

Q.4 What differences did Nandita find between getting water from the public tap and in the village?

Ans. There is no tap in Nandita's Mama's house for water. They have to stand in a line for water from a public tap, where there is a lot of rush. Nandita's village house also doesn't have taps but they don't have to stand in a queue for water. They get water from a pond in their village and even if the water dries up there, they can walk to a river and get water from there.

Q.5 Was there electricity at the place where Nandita's Mama lived? Guess.

Ans. Yes, there was electricity at the place where Nandita's Mama lived.

Let us Talk (Page 141)

Q.1 Do you know anyone who was admitted to a hospital?

Ans. Yes, my grandfather was admitted to a hospital.

(i) For how many days was he or she in the hospital?

Ans. He was admitted for 5 days in the hospital.

(ii) Did you visit the person in the hospital?

Ans. Yes, I visited him in the hospital.

(iii) Who was looking after the patient at the hospital?

Ans. The nurses and my father were looking after her at the hospital.

Q.2 Have you ever seen a tall building? Where?

Ans. Yes, I have seen a very tall building in Delhi.

Q.3 How many floors did the building have?

Ans. The building had 25 floors.

Q.4 How many floors did you climb?

Ans. I climbed to the 5 floors.

Page 142

Q.1 When Nandita first came to Mumbai, what were the things that she was afraid to do?

Ans. When Nandita first came to Mumbai, she was afraid of

- getting into crowded buses
- getting into the lift
- looking down from higher floors

Page 143

Q.2 What were the differences between the houses where Mama lived and the houses in the high-rise buildings?

Houses in the area where Mama lived	Houses in a high-rise building

Ans.

Houses in the area where Mama lived	Houses in a high-rise building
Public toilets	Personal toilets for each family
No separate kitchen	Separate kitchens
No water taps in the house	Water taps in every house
No glass windows	Glass windows

Q.3 Discuss why there were differences.

Ans. There were differences because Mama didn't have money to live in a house in the high-rise buildings. These houses in high-rise buildings are very costly and have all kinds of amenities.

Tell about yourself

Q.1 Draw a circle around the kind of house you live in. Is it like the house of –

Nandita, Mama, Babloo, Any other kind

Ans. Babloo

Q.2 Where does the water come from in your house?

Ans. The water comes from taps in my house.

Q.3 Is there an electricity connection in your house? How many hours in a day do you get electricity?

Ans. Yes, there is an electricity connection in my house. We get electricity all the time.

Q.4 Which is the nearest hospital in the area where you live?

Ans. The nearest hospital in the area where I live is a big private hospital.

Q.5 How far are these from your house?

	Minutes to Walk	In Kilometers
Bus Stop		
School		
Market		
Post Office		
Hospital		

Ans.

	Minutes to Walk	In Kilometers
Bus Stop	10	1/2
School	40	3
Market	15	1
Post Office	15	1
Hospital	10	1/2

Q.6 Draw a picture in your notebook of the different kinds of houses in your area.

Ans. Do it yourself.

Write in your notebook (Page 145)

Q.1 Why does Mama have to change his house?

Ans. Mama had to change his house because he was given the notice to move out of his place. A big hotel will be built where Mama lived.

Q.2 Have you ever moved from your house? If yes, why did you have to move?

Ans. No, I have never moved from my house.

Q.3 Do people in your family have to go far for their work? Where do they go? How far do they have to go?

Ans. No, people in my family do not have to go far for their work. My father goes to the nearby bank and my mother goes to a school. My father travels 3 km for work and my mother goes 2 km for work.

Discuss

Q.1 Is it right that Mama and others have to move because a hotel is going to be built there?

Ans. No, it is not right that Mama and others have to move because a hotel is going to be built there.

Q.2 Who will benefit from this?

Ans. The owner of the hotel will benefit from this.

Q.3 Who will face difficulties?

Ans. People currently living in that area will face difficulties.

Q.4 Do you know of any people who have faced problems similar to Nandita's Mama? Talk about it in class.

Ans. Yes, I know of some people who have faced problems similar to Nandita's Mama. There were around 40 such families who were forced to move out of those houses because a road was constructed there.

Q.5 Draw a picture of house of your choice and colour it.

Ans. Do it yourself.

CHAPTER 18 TOO MUCH WATER, TOO LITTLE WATER

About the Chapter

This chapter is about the uneven distribution of water in different parts of the country and how it affects people. We see many examples of water shortages. Suguna lives with her family in Nallama village, Andhra Pradesh, where they don't have clean drinking water. That is why they have to serve cold drinks to guests instead. In Bazaar Gaon, Rohan and Reena visit a water park and notice that while people are facing water shortages in the area, kids are wasting water at the park.

In Mumbai, Deepak goes to Razia Madam's house with his mother on a holiday. There, they see that dirty gutter water has mixed with drinking water. Razia tells them to boil water for drinking and to take some boiled water with them. Deepak feels happy because he doesn't have to wait in line to get water.

GLOSSARY

Water hose A flexible tube, usually made of rubber or plastic, that is used to transport water.
Clinging To hold on tightly to somebody/something.
Diarrhoea A common health condition in which a person passes loose motions frequently.

NCERT FOLDER

Discuss (Pg 147)

Q.1 How can unclean or dirty water harm our body?

Ans. Dirty water can cause serious illnesses and make us sick.

Q.2 Have you ever got dirty or unclean water in your area? What was the reason for this?

Ans. Yes, sometimes our tap water is dirty due to the leakage in the pipeline.

Q.3 Do you know anyone who has fallen sick because of such water? Talk about this.

Ans. Yes, I know some people who fell sick because of drinking dirty water. Some people in our colony do not use RO or filters for drinking water, so they get sick whenever there is an issue with the quality of water supply.

Q.4 When the guest came to Suguna's house, they offered him a cold drink, because they thought he should not drink such water. What do you think Suguna's family must be doing for their own drinking water?

Ans. Suguna's family must be boiling the water and filtering it.

Q.5 The guest said he did not take cold drinks. Why do you think he said this?

Ans. Cold drinks are not good for our health. That is why I think the guest must have refused to take it.

Read and Write (Pg 148)

Q.1 Have you ever faced a shortage of water in your house? When?

Ans. Yes, sometimes there is an issue with the pipeline and we do not get water in our area for hours.

Q.2 What did you do then?

Ans. We called a water tanker and used some of the stored drinking water from the refrigerator.

Q.3 Have you ever played in water? Where and when?

Ans. Yes, I have played in the water in the local swimming pool, during summer vacations.

Q.4 Are there times when you are not allowed to play in water?

Ans. Yes, during winters and rainy season, I am not allowed to play in water as the weather gets cold during that time. Also, when the water is dirty or looks unsafe, my parents don't allow me to play in it.

Q.5 What are the reasons for this?

Ans. The reason for this is my own safety and health. Our parents tell us not to play with water when it is too deep, dirty or too cold as they care for our health and safety.

Q.6 Have you seen wastage of water in your area? Discuss.

Ans. Yes, I have seen wastage of water in my area. There are some people who waste a lot of water to clean their cars everyday. This can be easily avoided if they use a bucket of water instead of pipes and clean their car only once a week.

Q.7 The water park had a lot of water to play in but the nearby village people did not have water even to drink. Think about it and discuss.

Ans. Water parks are owned and run by private authorities. They provide profits to the authorities, hence, their water supply is regular and carefully managed. However, the water in the village is supplied by the government. Due to uneven distribution and poor management by the government, the village people were not getting regular water supply.

Q.8 If you go to a water park, find out from where the water comes to the park.

Ans. Water in the water park comes through pipelines connected to nearby water bodies.

Write in your Notebook (Pg 150)

Q.1 Why was Raziya worried when she read the newspaper?

Ans. Raziya was worried as there was news in the newspaper about clean water getting mixed with dirty water from the gutter.

Q.2 Raziya asked that all the water that was filled the previous day should be thrown. Could this water have been used for something else? What kind of things?

Ans. Yes, it could have been used for cleaning or watering the plants after boiling and cooling it.

Q.3 In what way did she plan to clean the water?

Ans. She planned to do so by boiling the water to kill the germs.

Q.4 Do you know of different ways to clean the water? Describe them.

Ans. Yes, some ways to clean water are boiling, filtering, adding chlorine and using alum.

Q.5 Suppose, Raziya had not read the news and everyone had drunk the water without boiling it, what could have happened?

Ans. Raziya and her family could have fallen sick if she had not read the news. They could have got a serious stomach infection.

Do and Discuss (Pg 151)

Q.1 Look through the newspapers of the last one month. Look for all news-items related to water. Cut them out. Stick all the cuttings together on a big paper to make a big collage.Talk about what you have collected. Discuss in the class.

Ans. Do it yourself.

Water Survey in School (Pg 151-153)

Make three groups of students in your class.

(a) One group will find out about the arrangements of drinking water in the school.

(b) The second group will find out about the arrangement of toilet in the school.

(c) The third group will find out about illness affecting children in the class.

The questions given below will help the groups to collect information.

Group 1

Observe and Note

Put a (✓) in right box or boxes

Q.1 Where does the water in your school come from?

(i) Tap ☐ (ii) Tank ☐

(iii) Handpump ☐ (iv) Any other ☐

Ans. (i) Tap

In your school, from where do you take water to drink?

(i) Tap ☐ (ii) Tank ☐

(iii) Handpump ☐ (iv) Any other ☐

Ans. (i) Tap

Q.3 If there is no tap, *matka* or handpump, then how do you get drinking water?

Ans. We get packaged drinking water from the water suppliers near our school.

Q.4 Is there water in all the taps or handpumps?

Ans. Yes, there is water in all the taps and handpumps.

Q.5 Is there any tap which is leaking or dripping?

Ans. Yes, there are some taps that are constantly dripping.

Q.6 Are all the *matkas* filled with water and are they covered?

Ans. Yes, all the matkas are filled with water and they are covered.

Q.7 Are the *matkas* and other water containers cleaned regularly?

Ans. Yes, they are cleaned regularly.

Q.8 How is water made safe for drinking?

Ans. The drinking water in our school comes from the tank which has a filter attached to it. So, the water is made safe for drinking by filtering it.

Q.9 Is there a long-handled ladle to take water from the *matka* or container? How many ladles are there per container?

Ans. Yes, each *matka* has one ladle to take water from it.

Q.10 Is the place around the drinking water, taps or *matkas* cleaned regularly?

Ans. Yes, the place around the *matkas* is cleaned regularly.

Think and Discuss (Pg 153)

Q.1 Why do the drinking water places get dirty?

Ans. The drinking water places get dirty as some people spill the water while taking it and some use it to wash hands.

Q.2 What can we do to keep these places clean?

Ans. We can keep these places clean by avoiding washing our hands with the drinking water and by cleaning the area regularly.

Find Out and Write in your Notebook (Pg 153)

Q.1 How often (once a day, once in two days, etc.) are the containers or *matkas* and ladles cleaned? Who cleans them?

Ans. The ladles and *matkas* are cleaned everyday by the cleaning staff of our school.

Q.2 How many children are there in your school? How many taps, *matkas* or handpumps are there? Are these sufficient for children?

Ans. There are 500 students in my school and there are 5 drinking water taps and 10 *matkas* which are sufficient for everyone.

Q.3 Who cleans the places near the water?

Ans. The cleaning staff cleans the places near the water.

Q.4 Where does the water that is spilt go?

Ans. The water that is spilt goes in a small bucket kept under the matkas which is emptied during the lunch break.

Pg 153-154

Group 2

Observe and Note

Put a (✓) in right box or boxes

Q.1 Where are the toilet arrangements in your school?

(i) Built toilet ☐ (ii) Open area ☐

Ans. (i) Built toilet

Q.2 How many toilets are there?

Ans. There are 10 toilets.

Q.3 Are there separate toilets for girls and boys?

Yes ☐ No ☐

Ans. Yes

Q.4 Is there water in the toilets?

Yes ☐ No ☐

Ans. Yes

Q.5 What does the water come from?

(i) The tap Yes ☐ No ☐

(ii) Filled containers Yes ☐ No ☐

(iii) Has to be brought from home Yes ☐ No ☐

Ans. (i) The tap - Yes

Q.6 Is there water for washing hands near the toilet?

Yes ☐ No ☐

Ans. Yes

Q.7 Do you wash your hands after using the toilet?

Yes ☐ No ☐

Ans. Yes

Q.8 Is there any tap that is leaking or dripping?

Yes ☐ No ☐

Ans. Yes

Q.9 Are the toilets kept clean?

Yes ☐ No ☐

Ans. Yes

Find Out and Write (Page 154)

Q.1 How many boys and girls are there in your school?

Girls ☐ Boys ☐

Ans. 331 girls and 330 boys.

Q.2 How many toilets are there for girls, and how many for boys?

Girls ☐ Boys ☐

Ans. Girls - 5, Boys - 5

Q.3 If there are no taps, who brings the water for the toilet? From where does the water have to be brought?

Ans. The water tanker is called in case there is no water in the overhead water tank.

Q.4 Who keeps the place clean?

Ans. School's cleaning staff keeps it clean.

Talk About It (Pg 155)

Q.1 What can be done to keep the toilets clean?

Ans. Regular cleaning is important to keep the toilets clean.

Q.2 What can each of us do for this?

Ans. Each of us should also maintain cleanliness and not leave the place dirty.

Q.3 Have you seen toilets at bus stands or railway stations? How are they different from the toilets at home?

Ans. Yes, I have seen the toilets at the bus stands and railway stations. They are not very clean as they are used by many people and are not cleaned regularly.

Page 155

Group 3

Talk with the children in your class and fill in the table given below. In the last few months, how many children in the class have suffered from any of these?

Diarrhoea, loose motions	Vomiting	Loose motion and vomiting	Yellow urine, yellow (pale) skin and eyes, mild fever	Stomach ache

Discuss with your teacher what you have found out from your survey. Now make a report with your findings and suggestions. Read your report in the assembly. Put it up on the notice bhoard.

Ans. Do it yourself.

CHAPTER 19 ABDUL IN THE GARDEN

About the Chapter

This chapter is about the different parts of plants and trees and how they grow. Abdul is a young boy who helps his father in the garden on a holiday. They pull out dried leaves and grass and Abdul learns that the grass has strong roots that need to be dug out. They also pull out some radishes, which are root vegetables.

A branch of the neem tree breaks due to rain and strong winds in Abdul's garden but the tree stays strong because it has deep roots. Some trees, like the banyan and oak, have special roots. In India, there is a law that protects trees, which means people cannot cut or harm them without permission. If someone wants to cut branches from a tree, they need to get written permission from the government.

GLOSSARY

Knocked Down It means to destroy or damage something.

Roots The part of plants that grows under the ground and helps in absorbing food and water from the soil.

Climber A plant that attaches itself to something, such as a wall or stick for support while growing.

Courtyard An area that is partly or completely surrounded by the walls of a building and does not have a roof over it.

NCERT FOLDER

Abdul in the garden (Page 158-160)

Q.1 The stick which was stuck in the ground fell very easily. It was difficult to pull out a small grass. Why ?

Ans. Roots of the grass hold the soil, therefore it was difficult to pull it out. The stick has no roots, so it fell very easily.

Q.2 Do all plants have roots ?

Ans. Yes, all plants have roots.

Q.3 Look at some plants and trees around you. Imagine how deep and spread out the roots of these are.

Ans. Small plants have very small roots, which are spread only a few inches around the plant.

The big trees have larger roots which are spread deeper in the ground.

Q.4 After three days, Abdul saw that one broken part of the pea plant had dried. Guess which part would have dried up? Why?

Ans. The leaves and stem of the broken pea plant must have dried up as the water from the soil could not reach them.

Q.5 Why do you think the neem tree did not fall despite the strong wind ?

Ans. Neem trees have big, deep and strong roots in the soil. They hold the tree firmly in its place. Therefore, the neem tree does not fall despite the strong winds.

Q.6 On putting water in the soil where the plants are growing, the drooping leaves become fresh again. How ?

Ans. Roots help the plant get all the minerals and water from the soil. Due to this, the drooping leaves become fresh again when water is put in the soil where the plants are growing.

Q.7 What do you feel, do all plants need water?

Ans. Yes, all the plants need water.

Q.8 Which of the plants around you need regular watering ?

Ans. Plants that have flowers growing on them need regular watering.

Q.9 What will happen, if nobody gives water to these plants ?

Ans. These plants will get all dried up and die if nobody waters them.

Q.10 Abdul realised that he never watered the huge neem tree. "Where did it get its water from?", he thought. Which of the plants around you do not need watering. Where do they get water from? Make two guesses.

Ans. The big trees like neem tree and mango tree do not need watering. Such trees have roots that go deep into the soil in search of water. They get water when it rains. They also get water from the ground.

Q.11 Abdul wondered whether radish was a root. Why did he think so?

Ans. Radish is a root vegetable. Abdul thought that radish was a root because it grows under the ground.

Q.12 Look at the pictures below and find out which of these vegetables are roots.

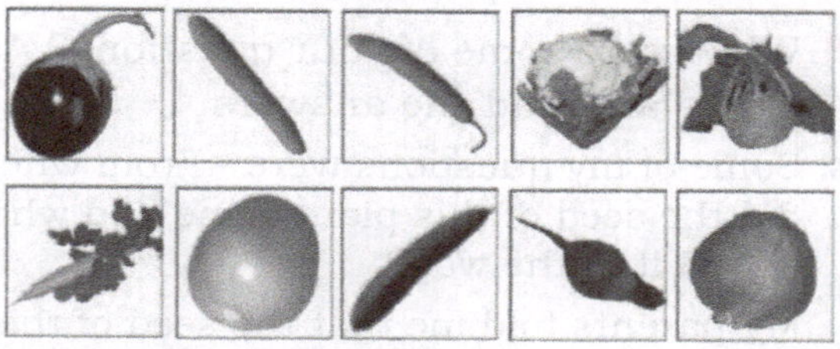

Ans. The following vegetables are roots - Radish, carrot, beetroot and cabbage.

Abdul Has More Questions (Page 160-161)

Abdul saw a plant growing out of a wall in school. He wondered.

Q.1 How deep must the roots of this plant be going?

Ans. The roots of this plant must be going up to at least 10-15 inches deep.

Q.2 How do the roots get water?

Ans. The roots get water from the moisture in the wall.

Q.3 How big will this plant grow?

Ans. If it keeps getting enough water, this plant can grow very big.

Q.4 What will happen to the wall?

Ans. If the plant grows big, the wall will have cracks and break after some time.

Q.5 Can you give the name of the plant in the picture?

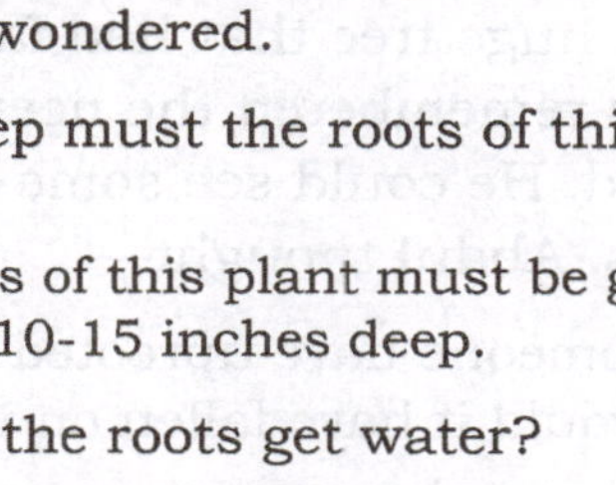

Ans. Sacred fig (*Peepal* tree)

Q.6 Have you ever seen a plant growing from a crack in a wall? Where was it?

Ans. Yes, I have seen a plant growing from a crack in the boundary wall of our school.

Q.7 Did you have any questions when you saw it?

Ans. Yes, I had many questions when I saw it.

Q.8 What were some of your questions? Ask elders and find the answers.

Ans. Some of my questions were - From where did the seed of this plant come and who sowed it in the wall?

My parents told me that the seed of the plant could have been dropped by a bird.

Q.9 Find out the name of the plant you saw.

Ans. The plant that I saw was peepal.

Page 161

Abdul saw a huge tree that had fallen on the roadside. He remembered the neem tree in his courtyard. He could see some of its broken roots. Abdul thought—

Q.1 Would someone have uprooted such a big tree or would it have fallen on its own?

Ans. The strong winds must have uprooted the tree.

Q.2 How old would this tree be?

Ans. This must have been more than 50 years old.

Q.3 Abdul on seeing a tree surrounded by cemented ground, thought that how will it get rain water?

Ans. This tree will get water from its deep roots in the soil.

Let Us talk

Q.1 Which are the oldest trees in your area? Find out from your elders how old the trees are?

Ans. The oldest tree in my area is the banyan tree. According to my grandparents, it is more than 60 years old.

Q.2 Name animals who live on this tree.

Ans. Different kinds of birds, squirrels, lizards and monkeys live on this tree.

Q.3 Have you ever seen any big tree that had fallen down? What did you think when you saw it?

Ans. Yes, during a storm a big tree near my house got uprooted by the strong winds. I saw it on my way to school.

Unusual Roots

Q.1 Have you swung from a banyan tree?

Ans. Yes, I swung from a banyan tree when I was smaller.

Q.2 What did you hold to swing?

Ans. I held on to the rope like parts of the branches.

Let Us Do This (Page 162-164)

Get together with 3-4 of your friends. From the list of things given, decide who will bring which thing. A transparent glass tumbler or bottle with a wide mouth, rubber band or thread, some seeds of moong, wheat, bajra, mustard, *channa* (chick peas) or *rajma* (red beans) and a wad of cotton wool. Each group will work with only one kind of seed. Soak a few seeds (5-6) overnight in a bowl full of water.

Take the wad of cotton wool and wet it. Put it on the mouth of the tumbler. Tie it tight to the mouth with rubber band or thread. Remove soaked seeds from water and place them on the cotton wool. You will have to take care that the cotton wool does not dry. Observe the changes that take place for the next 10 to 12 days. Did you observe the seedlings come out of the seeds?

Draw the picture of the seedling as it looks on the fourth and the eighth day.

Ans. The seedlings came out after 4 days.

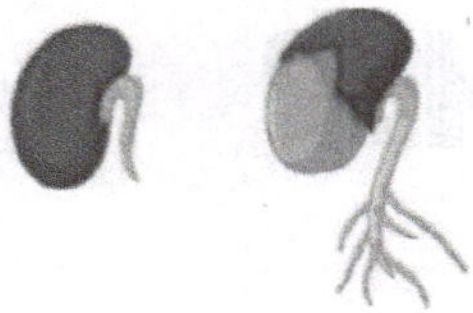

Write in Your Notebook

Q.1 What difference did you observe in the seeds after soaking? Compare with dry seeds and write.

Ans. After soaking the seeds, they became softer and bigger in size.

Q.2 What do you think would happen if the cotton wool had been left dry?

Ans. There will be no change in the seeds present in it.

Q.3 In which direction did the roots grow? And the stem?

Ans. The roots grew downwards and the stem grew upwards.

Q.4 How big did the plant grow in the cotton wool?

Ans. It grew about 5 cm.

Q.5 Did small plants come out from all the seeds?

Ans. Yes

Q.6 What is the colour of the roots?

Ans. The roots were white in colour.

Q.7 Did you see any hair on the roots?

Ans. Yes, there were small hair on the roots after 10 days.

Q.8 Try and pull out one little plant from the cotton wool. Were you able to pull it out? Why?

Ans. Yes, I was able to pull it out but it was not easy. This happened because the roots were holding the cotton wool strongly.

Q.9 Did you see how the roots grip the cotton wool? Do you think that the roots hold the soil in the same way? Also look at the plants grown by your friends.

Ans. Yes, I saw the roots gripping the cotton wool and I think they hold the soil the same way. The plants grown by my friends also looked the same.

What Grows? Page 164

Q.1 What do you think? Which of these things listed by Arif and Roopali grow?

Ans. All the things listed in Arif and Roopali's list grow.

Q.2 Why don't you make your own list of things that grow? Your list can include the names of things that are in Arif's and Roopali's list.

Ans. Some things that grow are animals like cats, monkeys, dogs, plants, trees, hair and nails.

Q.3 Think about yourself—in what ways have you changed over a period of time ? Have you grown in any way? For example—Has your height increased?

Ans. Yes, my height has increased and my hair is also longer.

Q.4 How much taller have you grown in the last one year?

Ans. I have grown 1.5 inches taller in the last one year.

Q.5 Imagine that you had never cut your nails! Draw a picture of your fingers in the notebook to show how they would have looked.

Ans. Do it yourself.

Q.6 What other part of your body (some people cut it regularly) keeps growing?

Ans. Hair keeps growing even if we cut it regularly.

CHAPTER 20

EATING TOGETHER

About the Chapter

This chapter is about the importance of eating together and celebrating festivals like Bihu. We will also learn about the mid-day meal scheme. In this chapter, children are excited to get back to school after holidays. They decide to have a party together with delicious food, games, singing and dancing. Food also plays an important part in festivals like Bihu.

During the Bihu festival, people make a *Bhela ghar* using grass and bamboo, and collect money to buy fish and vegetables. They make *pitha* and prepare cheva rice in a large vessel called tao. Everyone in the village wears traditional clothes and enjoys the food together at the feast. In our country, mid-day meals are provided in government schools. It is a fresh, healthy and properly cooked meal for all children studying in schools.

GLOSSARY

Harvest Act of cutting and gathering a crop.
Vessel A container for holding or storing something.
Pat and Muga Mekhala-chador A traditional attire worn by women from Assam.
Mezi A traditional bonfire made from wood, bamboo and hay that is lit during the Bihu festival.

NCERT FOLDER

Write in Your Notebook (Page 167)

Q.1 Do you like to eat with others?

Ans. Yes, I like to eat with my friends and my family.

Q.2 On what occasions do you eat together with your friends?

Ans. I eat with my friends everyday during the lunch break. During festivals or special occasions too, I like to eat with my friends.

Q.3 Have you ever had a party in your class? When? What all did you do to arrange a party?

Ans. Yes, we had a party in our class on Children's day. We all brought balloons and decorative items to decorate our class. We also brought different snacks and collected money to buy cupcakes from the school's canteen.

Q.4 What did you and your classmates bring to the party?

Ans. I brought big balloons for decoration and samosas for everyone in the class. My friend brought some glitter tape and chocolates for everyone.

Q.5 What all did you eat?

Ans. I ate cupcake, samosa, chocolate and pasta.

Q.6 Who were the people you invited for your party?

Ans. We invited our teachers and parents to our party.

Q.7 Were there some people who work in your school, whom you could not invite? Who were these people?

Ans. Yes, we could not invite our school's principal as he was on leave that week.

Q.8 Did you wear any special dress for the party?

Ans. Yes, all of us were well-dressed for the party.

Q.9 What are the things that you can do to make the party greater fun for everyone? Discuss.

Ans. To make the party more fun for everyone, we could play games, sing songs and dance together.

Let us Talk (Page 169)

Q.1 Where is the festival of Bihu celebrated?

Ans. Bihu is celebrated in Assam.

Q.2 Which are the festivals you celebrate together with other families?

Ans. We celebrate Holi, Lohri, Navratri, Eid and Christmas together with other families.

Q.3 Does everyone cook and eat together on such festivals? What are some of the special dishes that are cooked? How are they cooked?

Ans. No, people do not cook together, but they share sweets and celebrate these festivals together. Some special dishes that are cooked on these festivals are gujiya, halwa, seviyan and plum cake. Gujiya, halwa, seviyan are cooked in a kadhai and plum cake is baked in an oven.

Q.4 Are some special vessels used for cooking these items? What are they?

Ans. Yes, a big kadahi is used to fry gujiya and to make seviyan and halwa. For making the plum cake, a baking dish is used.

Q.5 Which is the biggest vessel that is used? Can you draw a picture of it? Can you guess how many people can eat the food that is cooked in it at one time?

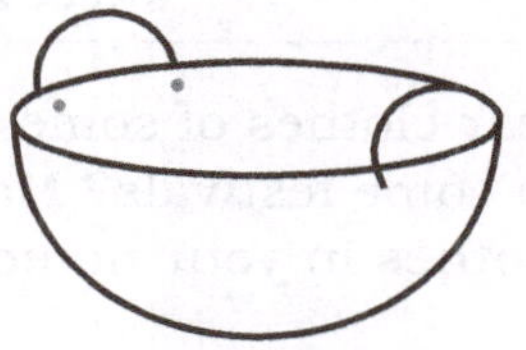

Ans. I think 20-30 people can eat the food that is cooked in this kadahi at one time.

Find Out and Do (Page 170)

Q.1 Can you guess how many people must have eaten together in the village feast?

Ans. I guess more than 500 people must have eaten together in the village feast.

Q.2 Have you ever seen the Bihu dance? Did you like it?

Ans. Yes, I have seen the Bihu dance. It was performed in our school's annual day programme. I really liked it.

Q.3 Find out from the students in your class, the festivals that they celebrate and the special food that they eat on these days. Who cooks the special food for festivals?

Ans.

Festival	Special Dish	Prepared by
Diwali	Sweets like Gulab Jamun, Kaju Katli, and Laddoos	Gulab Jamun and Kaju katli are bought from the sweet shop and Laddoos are made by the mothers/ grandmothers at home.
Holi	Gujiya and Thandai	Everyone prepares it at home.
Ganesh Chaturthi	Modak	Some buy Modaks from the sweet shop and some make it at home.
Durga Puja	Sandesh	Bought from the sweet shop.

Q.4 Do you wear clothes of some special colours on some festivals? Make a picture of these clothes in your notebook.

Ans.

Q.5 Are there special songs that are sung at different festivals in your place? Learn some of these songs and sing them in the class.

Ans. Do it yourself.

Q.6 Learn some special festival dances. Perform these with your friends in your school assembly.

Ans. Do it yourself.

Q.7 When you meet friends, of your own age do you do anything special—like play a game, chat or watch a movie? What else do you do?

Ans. When I meet my friends, we always play and have fun together. We also like to share and eat our chocolates and snacks.

Find Out and Write in Your Notebook (Page 172)

Q.1 Write about the food given in your school. If you do not get food in school, ask a friend or someone else who gets food in school.

Ans. I asked my friend about the food given in his school and he answered the following questions.

Q.2 What time is the meal served?

Ans. The meal is served at 12:30 p.m.

Q.3 What do you get in the meal at school?

Ans. He gets dal, rice, sabzi, upma and roti. Sometimes he also gets boiled eggs, cooked vegetables and bread. Everyday the menu is different.

Q.4 Do you like the mid-day meal that you get?

Ans. He says he likes the meal he gets.

Q.5 Is the food that you get enough for you?

Ans. Yes, it is enough.

Q.6 Do you bring your own plate, or do you get it in school?

Ans. No, the plates are provided by the school.

Q.7 Who serves the food?

Ans. The catering staff serves the food.

Q.8 Do your teachers eat with you?

Ans. Yes, the teachers eat with the students.

Q.9 Is the week's menu put up on the school board?

Ans. Yes, it is put up on the school's notice board.

Q.10 What will you get on Wednesday and Friday?

Ans. The students get vegetable curry and rice on Wednesday and chhole, sabzi and roti on Friday.

Q.11 If you got a chance to change the menu for the meal in your school, what would you like to change? What would you like to eat? Make your own menu.

Day	Food items
Monday	
Wednesday	
Friday	

Ans. Monday - Aloo paratha with curd and papad
Wednesday - Rajma with rice and curd
Friday - Vegetable pasta with banana milkshake

Q.12 If you do not get food in the school, find out why?

Ans. Most of the students preferred to bring their own lunch from home. This is why the food is not offered in our school.

Q.13 Where will you lodge your complaint about the mid-day meal?

Ans. A complaint about the mid-day meal can be registered to local authorities or at the online portal of government.

Q.14 Find out the toll free phone number, the website or e-mail address to make a complaint.

Ans. **Toll free no** : 1800-345-6208
Email : Ikomdm@gmail.com

CHAPTER 21 FOOD AND FUN

About the Chapter

This chapter describes how food is an important part of celebration, gatherings and social events. It highlights the role of food in bringing people together. Four friends Manpreet, Gurnoor, Divya and Swastik go to the Gurudwara. They enter the kitchen after covering their heads and see the large vessels used to cook food for langar. Gurnoor' s father was preparing *kadhah prasad* in a big kadhai.

Everyone was contributing in preparing the food by arranging material and working together to cook the food. It brings a sense of community. After the *ardaas, kadhah prasad* was served and people in the Gurudwara sat down to eat langar. During langar, everyone helped to serve the food and clean the utensils.

GLOSSARY

Kadhah Prasad Halwa prepared as an offering to God and then, to people in a Gurudwara.
Ardaas A prayer
Langar A communal kitchen and dining hall in a Gurudwara.

NCERT FOLDER

Page 175

Do you study in a boarding school? If you do not, try to talk with someone who goes to a boarding school and find out .

Q.1 In what ways is boarding school different from other schools?

Ans. Boarding schools are different from other schools because children live there instead of going home every day. They have their own rooms, eat all their meals at the school, and do their homework there.

Q.2 What kind of food do they get there?

Ans. They get a variety of food, like rice, vegetables, dal, and sometimes even pizza, dosa, noodles or burgers.

Q.3 Where do the children sit and eat in the boarding school?

Ans. Children in boarding schools usually eat in a big dining hall. They sit at long tables and eat together.

Q.4 Who cooks food for the children in the boarding school? Who serves the food?

Ans. The food is cooked by the cooks who work at the school. Sometimes, older students or teachers help serve the food.

Q.5 Who washes the vessels?

Ans. There are people whose job it is to wash the dishes and keep the kitchen clean.

Q.6 Do the children miss home-made food sometimes?

Ans. Yes, sometimes children miss the food their parents make at home. But they also learn to appreciate the food they get at boarding school.

Q.7 Would you like to go to a boarding school? Why?

Ans. I'm not sure if I would like to go to a boarding school. It would be fun to live with my friends and have so many activities to do, but I would miss my family a lot.

Talk about it (Page 177)

Q.1 The 'cooking and eating together' in a Gurudwara is called langar. Have you ever eaten in a langar ? Where and when?

Ans. Yes, I have eaten in a langar once. It was at the Gurudwara near my house during Diwali.

Q.2 How many people were cooking and how many were serving the food there?

Ans. There were many people cooking and serving food. Some were volunteers from the Gurudwara community and others were people who had come to celebrate Diwali.

Q.3 Are there other occasions when you have eaten with many people? Where and when? Who cooked and served the food there?

Ans. Yes, I have eaten with many people at my school during lunch. Sometimes, my parents also cook food for a lot of people on special occasions like birthdays or festivals. We usually cook and serve the food ourselves.

CHAPTER 22 THE WORLD IN MY HOME

About the Chapter

This chapter discusses about social issues and how children learn behaviour from their families. Different families have different traditions and ways of doing things. In Marietta's family, they had a disagreement about what to watch on TV, but in the end, they all watched the football match because Daddy wanted to watch the football match. This teaches us to respect our elders' decisions.

Pratibha wasn't allowed to play outside late in the evening, but her brothers were allowed. It shows that sometimes boys and girls are treated differently.

Pilloo aunty teaches kindness by paying the right amount to the kulfi seller when he makes a mistake in counting. Akshay's grandmother didn't want him to eat at Anil's house because their family was different, showing how families have different values.

Dhondu had a good business idea, but his uncle didn't agree with him. Finally, Ritu's story teaches us to be aware of good and bad touch. She didn't like how Meena's uncle touched her hand.

GLOSSARY

Quarreling To have a verbal argument or fight about something.
Giant Wheel A giant wheel is a big, circular ride that spins around.
Pleaded It means to request somebody to do something.

NCERT FOLDER

Let us talk (Tug of War) (Page 180)

Q.1 In your home too, do people quarrel over fans, TV, newspapers, chairs or anything else?

Ans. Yes, me and my brother always quarrel over the TV.

Q.2 In your home, who settles such quarrels?

Ans. My mother settles such quarrels by telling us to take turns while watching TV.

Q.3 Talk about an interesting incident at home when there was a quarrel over such things.

Ans. One day I wanted to eat aloo paratha but my brother wanted to eat rajma and rice.

So, we both started quarrelling about it. To settle this, our mother prepared a vegetable omelette which we both liked.

Q.4 Have you ever seen people quarrelling over something elsewhere? What?

Ans. Yes, I have seen people quarrelling at the restaurants with the staff about getting their order ready early. I have also seen people quarrelling over parking space in our colony.

Let us talk (Why the difference ? (Page 180 and 181)

Q.1 Does this kind of thing happen in your house or in any of your friend's house? What do you think about this?

Ans. No, this does not happen in my house or my friend's house. I think it is not fair to have different rules for boys and girls.

Q.2 Do you think that there should be different rules for girls and boys, women and men?

Ans. No, I don't think that there should be different rules for girls and boys, women and men.

Q.3 Think-what would happen if girls had to follow rules made for boys and boys had to follow rules made for girls.

Ans. I think it will create a lot of confusion and it would still be unfair.

Pilloo Aunty (Page 181 & 182)

Q.1 If you were to write a different ending for this story, how will you end it?

Ans. If I could change the ending of this story, I would write - The *kulfi* seller was amazed by Pilloo Aunty's honesty so he asked her to take one *kulfi* as a gift, but she did not take it. So, he bought some balloons and offered them to all the children.

Q.2 Is there anyone in your family who is like Pilloo Aunty? Who?

Ans. Yes, both my parents are like Pilloo Aunty.

Q.3 What would the children have thought if Pilloo Aunty had paid less money to the *kulfi* seller? What do you think about this?

Ans. I think that all the children would have learned that it was fine to be dishonest if Pilloo Aunty had paid less money to the *kulfi* seller.

Talk about it (What should I do?) (Page 183)

Q.4 What do you think Akshay will do?

Ans. I think Akshay will drink the water.

Q.5 Why was Akshay confused?

Ans. Akshay was confused because Anil was his friend and he did not see any problem with the water that he had offered him. He could not understand why his grandmother did not want him to eat or drink from his house.

Q.6 Why do you think Akshay's grandmother warned him not to drink even water in Anil's house?

Ans. Akshay's grandmother told him that Anil's family was different from their family and therefore, he must not eat or drink at their house.

Q.7 Do you know of anybody who thinks like Akshay's grandmother?

Ans. No, I do not know anybody who thinks like Akshay's grandmother.

Q.8 Do you agree with Akshay's grandmother?

Ans. No, I don't agree with Akshay's grandmother.

Q.9 What do you think Akshay should do?

Ans. I think Akshay should drink the water.

Page 184 Talk about it (Who will decide?)

Q.1 If you were in Dhondu's place what would you do?

Ans. If I were in Dhondu's place, I would try to convince my uncle.

Q.2 Has it ever happened with you that you wanted to do something but the elders in the family did not allow you?

Ans. Yes, sometimes my elders stop me from doing something but they also make me understand why it is not right.

Q.3 Who takes important decisions in your family? What do you feel about this?

Ans. My parents take important decisions in our family. I think it is right as they are older and experienced.

Q.4 How would you like if only one person made all the decisions for your family?

Ans. I will not like it.

Page 185 Talk about it (I don't like it!)

Q.1 Have you ever disliked anybody's touch? Whose touch did you dislike?

Ans. Yes, I do not like when someone touches me without my permission.

Q.2 If you were in Ritu's place, what would you do?

Ans. I would tell my parents about Meena's uncle.

Q.3 What else can be done when such things happen? Discuss.

Ans. When such things happen, we should immediately share it with our parents.

Q.4 Everybody's touch is not the same. Ritu did not like it when Meena's uncle held her hand, but she liked to hold Meena's hand. Why do you think there was this difference?

Ans. Any touch that makes us feel uncomfortable, scared, or confused can be considered as a bad touch. This is why Ritu did not like Meena's uncle's touch as he was a stranger to her and she felt uncomfortable when he held her hand.

CHAPTER 23

POCHAMPALLI

About the Chapter

This chapter is about the weavers of Pochampalli and their art of weaving. It shows us how important traditional arts and crafts are and why we need to protect them.

Vani and Prasad's family live in Mukhtapur, a village in Pochampalli town, Telangana, where most families are weavers. They have been making Pochampalli cloth for a long time.

Weaving requires hard work and involves many steps. First, the threads are washed, dyed and rolled into bundles. Then, these bundles are woven on a loom with different threads to create beautiful sarees in bright colours.

It takes many days of hard work to make these sarees. However, many people are leaving this craft because silk is becoming expensive and the weavers are not getting good prices for their sarees. It is important to preserve the Pochampalli weaving tradition.

GLOSSARY

Weavers They are the people who create fabric by interlacing threads or yarn by using looms.
Weaving It is the art of creating fabric using yarn or threads, making different patterns using special looms.
Looms They are special type of machines used to create different weaving patterns.
Craft It refers to the skill of making things by hand, often using traditional techniques.
Bundle It means to collect and tie a number of things together.
Fabric A type of cloth or soft material used for making clothes.

NCERT FOLDER

Discuss (Page 189)

Q.1 Vani and Prasad learnt this beautiful craft from their family members. When they grow up, do you think they will be able to teach their children the skills of this craft?

Ans. Yes, when they grow up, they will be able to teach their children the skills of this craft.

Write in Your Notebook (Page 189)

Q.1 Have you ever seen anybody weave something on a loom? What were they weaving and where?

Ans. Yes, I have seen it on TV as well as in my grandparent's village. They were weaving a shawl.

Q.2 The threads of a saree are dyed. Do you know of any other thing that is dyed?

Ans. Woollen threads, cotton cloth and polyester are also dyed.

Q.3 If you visit Vani's village it seems as if the entire village is weaving sarees. Do you know of any other work which many people living in one place do?

Ans. Yes, I have seen many people living in one place doing pottery.

Q.4 Do they make some article?

Ans. Yes, they make some clay pots and earthen utensils.

Q.5 Find out the process of making the article? What are the different steps?

Ans. The process of pottery is as follows

- Clay is collected and dried. It is then ground into powder and sieved to remove any unwanted particles.
- Fine clay is mixed with water and a dough is kneaded out of it.
- Clay dough is placed on a potter's wheel. It is shaped using hands in different sizes and shapes.
- Pots are dried in the Sun and then baked in a special oven called a kiln. They are painted and different patterns are drawn on them.

Q.6 Do men and women do different kinds of work to make this article?

Ans. No, men and women do the same kind of work to make this article.

Q.7 Do children also contribute in making this article?

Ans. Yes, children also help in making this article.

Find Out and Write (Page 189-190)

Q.1 Talk to an ironsmith, a carpenter and a potter about the nature of their work.

Ans. An ironsmith makes things using iron.

A carpenter makes wooden objects like tables, chairs, etc. A potter makes earthen pots using clay.

Q.2 Where did they learn to do their work?

Ans. They learned the work from their parents.

Q.3 What else did they need to learn to be able to do this work?

Ans. They needed the skill of creativity and imagination to do this work.

Q.4 Have they taught this work to anybody in their family, or to anyone else?

Ans. Yes, they have taught this work to their children and other family members. They also teach this to anyone who wants to learn it.

Q.5 The table below has a list of different kinds of work that people do. Do you know people who do such work? Write their names in the first column. In the next column write from whom have they learnt their work?

Ans.

Kind of work	Name of the people you know who do this work	Where did they learn this work from?
Cloth weaving	Prasad and Vani's parents	From their elders
Cooking	Shivesh Jain	In the Hotel Management Institute
Cycle Repair	Raj Kumar Chottu	From his father
Flying aeroplanes	Captain Vivek Oberoi	In the flying school
Sewing and embroidery	Pooja Arora	In fashion school
Singing	Kamal Ghuman	From his music teacher
Making shoes	Suresh Kumar	From his father
Flying kites	Mudit	From his elder brother
Farming	Hasmukh	From their elders
Cutting hair	Javed	From his father

CHAPTER 24 HOME AND ABROAD

About the Chapter

In this chapter, we learn about the differences between India and countries like the United Arab Emirates (UAE). Maalu's uncle and his family return from Abu Dhabi to Kerala on a flight and talk about these differences. Abu Dhabi is the capital of the UAE. Maalu learns that flights are faster than trains for travelling.

Many parts of Abu Dhabi are deserts with sand dunes of different colour soil. (There is not much greenery and water is a precious thing there because it is not easily available.)

The UAE has a lot of oil underground. India has plenty of greenery and many fruit trees but in Dubai, there are mostly date palm trees. The money used in the UAE is called Dirham, which is different from Indian currency. The weather in Dubai is very hot, so people wear loose cotton clothes to stay cool.

GLOSSARY

Greenery Green plants or trees together in one place.
Storeys Floors or levels of a tall building.

NCERT FOLDER

Discussion and Write (Page 195)

Q.1 You can also make a small report comparing Abu Dhabi with the place where you live. You can use some of these points mentioned below while writing the report. You can also draw pictures or put photographs.

- The climate and weather
- What people wear
- The trees and plants
- The kind of buildings
- The traffic on the roads (kinds of vehicles)
- The common food items
- The language

Ans.

Points of Comparison	Abu Dhabi	New Delhi
The climate and weather	Very dry	Hot and humid in summers
What people wear	Men wear kandura and agal; women wear burqa and hijab	Men usually wear kurta pyjamas, jeans and shirts; women wear suit, saree.
The trees and plants	Dates	Banyan, Neem
Buildings	Skyscrapers (tall multi-floor buildings)	Flats and houses
Common food items	Meat, Dates, Biryani	Chole Bhature, Poori Aloo, Dal Makhni, Chicken
The language	Arabic	English, Hindi

Q.2 Why do you think many trees cannot grow in desert areas?

Ans. Many trees cannot grow in desert areas because there is no water and the climate is very dry. In a desert, there is mostly sand.

Q.3 Do you have any relatives who live in another country?

Ans. Yes, one of my aunts lives in the USA.

Q.4 How long have they lived there? Did they go there for studies or for work? Was there any other reason?

Ans. My aunt and her family have been living there for ten years. She went there for studies but now she is doing a job.

Q.5 Look at these currency notes. Write the value of each note in the box near its picture.

(i)

(ii)

(iii)

(iv)

(v)

Ans. (i) Ten rupees (ii) Twenty rupees (iii) Hundred rupees (iv) Two hundred rupees (v) Five hundred rupees

Page 197

Q.1 To which country does this currency belong? How did you know?

Ans. This currency belongs to India. We know because 'Reserve Bank of India' is written on Indian currency.

Q.2 Whose picture can you see on the notes?

Ans. I can see Mahatma Gandhi's picture on the notes.

Q.3 Can you find any number on the notes (other than the value)?

Ans. Yes, I can see numbers other than the value on the notes. It is the serial number of the note.

Q.4 Do you think that two notes can have the same number?

Ans. No, two notes cannot have the same number.

Q.5 Take a ten rupee note and observe it carefully. How many languages can you see on the note?

Ans. I can see fifteen languages on the note.

Q.6 Write the name of the bank given on the note.

Ans. Reserve Bank of India.

Match the coins (Page 197-198)

Q.1 How many of these coins do you recognise?

Ans. I can recognise all the coins.

Q.2 What is written on each coin other than the value?

Ans. Other than the value, 'India' is written on each coin.

Q.3 Look at these notes. Do they all belong to India? Put a circle around notes that are not Indian. Find out which country do they belong to.

(i)

(ii)

(iii)

(iv)

(v)

(vi)

(vii)

(viii)

(ix)

Ans. (i), (iii), (iv), (vi), (viii) and (ix) does not belong to India.

They belong to

(i) Egypt,

(iii) Europe,

(iv) United Arab Emirates,

(vi) United States of America,

(viii) Oman,

(ix) China

CHAPTER 25

SPICY RIDDLES

About the Chapter

In this chapter, we will learn about different spices and their uses. Some spices can be grinded into fine powder like red chilli, turmeric, etc. but other spices can be ground into large particles like black pepper, fennel, etc. Spices like red chilli are very hot and spicy. Turmeric can be used to give yellow colour to our food and it is also used to heal wounds.

Black pepper gives a sharp and spicy taste. Jeera is very small and skinny and has a strong fragrance. Fennel (*saunf*) is green in colour and it is very good for our stomach. Clove looks like a nail and it also has a very strong smell. It is used to cure toothaches. This is how different spices are used in different ways.

GLOSSARY

Gasp It means to breathe-in suddenly and sharply, often because of surprise, shock, or pain.
Coarse It means ground into large pieces or particles.
Fragrance It is a type of good smell.
Heal To make something well or healthy again using some medication or herbs.
Grind To break or reduce something to small particles or powder.

NCERT FOLDER

Page 199

Q.1 I can be powdered fine
To make food hot and spicy,
If too much of me is added
I make you gasp-shheee ..... shheee ....
Your eyes and nose begin to water
And you cry!
Think and tell me who am I?
Tell me quickly, who am I?

Ans. Red Chilli

Q.2 Grind me and powder me
To make your food look yellow,
I am mixed in oil by granny
And applied to wounds quickly,
I heal all wounds–big and small,
That is why I am loved by all!
Think and tell me who am I?
Tell me quickly, who am I?

Ans. Turmeric

Q.3 Small and round like a pearl,
I am black when I am whole.
I can be powdered coarse or fine
A sharp and spicy taste is mine,
Whether it is salty or sweet
I am added as a special treat,
Think and tell me who am I?
Tell me quickly, who am I?

Ans. Black Pepper

Q.4 I am a small and skinny chap
Sometimes I am brown and sometime black,
Added to hot oil and ghee
I spread my fragrance all around me,
When I am roasted.
Curd and jaljeera are favourite to me.
Think and tell me who am I?
Tell me quickly, who am I?

Ans. Cumin

Q.5 I look like jeera though green am I,
To make your stomach healthy
I always try,
Eat me always after your meal
I refresh your mouth, you surely feel,
Think and tell me who am I?
Tell me quickly, who am I?

Ans. Fennel

Q.6 I look like a nail but a bud am I,
Chocolate brown colour and a strong smell
have I.
When your toothache makes you shout,
I soothe the pain in your mouth.
and tell me who am I?
Tell me quickly, who am I?

Ans. Clove

Page 201

Q.1 Now try and make your own riddles about two other spices. Ask those riddles in your class. Draw pictures of the two spices in your notebook and write their names.

Ans. I look like a bark,
a spice, a flavour bold.
Often used in desserts,
a story untold.
What am I?
I am like sand,
I give out my oil,
I am used in Poha and Dhokla
and many things you name.
What am I?

Q.2 Find out which spices are used in your house for cooking. Make a list and look at your friends' lists too.

Ans. Turmeric, red chilli, ginger, coriander powder, amchur, saunf, clove, pepper, saffron, etc. are some spices used in my house. Spices used in my friends house; black pepper, turmeric, cinnamon, cumin, etc.

Q.3 When your grandparents were young, which spices were used most in their kitchens? Find out from them and write here.

Ans. Red chilli, turmeric, black pepper, salt, cumin were used most when our grandparents were young.

Q.4 Name one spice which is put into both sweet and salty things.

Ans. Cardamom (elaichi) or cinnamon is put into both sweet and salty things.

Q.5 Find out what is put into food to make it taste sour.

Ans. Lemon, amchur, anardana and imli are put into food to make it sour.

Page 202

I am Kuttan. I live in Kerala. There is a garden of spices in the backyard of my house. There, I see plants of tejpatta, small and big cardamoms and black pepper grow.

Q.1 Find out whether any spices are grown in your area. Write their names here.

Ans. Yes, in my area, chilli, turmeric, ginger and garlic are grown.

Q.2 Bring some whole spices to class. Write their names in the table. Close your eyes and try to recognise each spice by smelling and touching each one in turn. Put a (✓) mark in front of the ones you recognise. If you do not recognise any, put a (×) mark.

No.	Smell	Touch	Name of the spice
1.			
2.			
3.			
4.			
5.			

Ans.

No.	Smell	Touch	Name of the spice
1.	✓	✓	Chilli
2.	✓	✓	Jeera
3.	✓	×	Haldi
4.	✓	✓	Ginger
5.	✓	×	Coriander

Let Us Try making a Spicy Potato Chaat

For this you need

- Boiled potatoes, enough for everybody in the class.
- Salt, red chilly powder, mango powder (amchur) or lemon, according to taste.
- Roasted cumin seeds (jeera), black salt and garam masala, if it is possible.
- Fresh coriander leaves.

Peel the boiled potatoes and cut them into small pieces. Now add salt, red chilly powder, mango powder or lemon juice according to taste. To make your chaat more delicious, add a little roasted cumin seeds, black salt and coriander powder. A pinch of garam masala can also be added at the end. Mix the potatoes well. Sprinkle chopped coriander leaves on top and hurrah! Your spicy chaat is ready to eat!

Q.3 Did you enjoy the potato chaat?

Ans. Yes, I enjoyed the potato chaat.

Q.4 Just imagine, if there were no spices to make the potato chaat, how would it taste?

Ans. It would taste very bad without spices.

Q.5 Try to learn and make a different kind of chaat and enjoy it with all your friends in class.

Ans. Do it yourself.

Q.6 How do spice-less and very spicy things feel on your tongue?

Ans. Spicy things give a sensation on my tongue. I start crying when I eat very spicy things. Less spicy things do not give any sensation.

CHAPTER 26 DEFENCE OFFICER : WAHIDA

About the Chapter

This chapter is about Wahida Prism, a Lieutenant Commander in the Indian Navy. It talks about her childhood, education, and job. Wahida comes from a small village called Thannamandi in the Rajouri district of Jammu and Kashmir. She finished her schooling at a government school and studied M.B.B.S at Jammu Medical College.

Wahida always dreamed of joining the army. She loves travelling and enjoys working at sea. As a doctor in the Indian Navy, her responsibilities include taking care of everyone on the ship, keeping the ship clean and helping people in emergencies. Wahida was chosen as the first woman to lead a parade, and she practised hard for it. Her father gave her the name "Prism", which means a glass that reflects all seven colours of nature.

GLOSSARY

Armed forces Groups of people who are trained to fight for their country like soldiers, sailors and airmen.
Naval It refers to anything related to ships, the navy or the sea.
Submarine It is a type of closed ship that can travel underwater.
Sailors They are people who work on ships and help to move the ship, operate the sails and keep the ship safe.
First Aid It is the immediate medical care given to a person who has been injured or suddenly becomes ill.
Platoons A small group of soldiers, typically made up of 30-50 soldiers, led by an officer.
Command It is an order or instruction given to someone, telling them what to do.
Spectators People who watch an event or performance.

NCERT FOLDER

Page 208

Q.1 Do you know anyone who is in defence services? Is the person in the Navy, Army or Air Force?

Ans. Yes, my mother is in defence services. She is in the Air Force.

Q.2 What work do they do in the force?

Ans. She is a pilot. She flies fighter planes.

Q.3 Would you like to join the defence services?

Ans. Yes, I would like to join the defence services.

Q.4 Which of the three would you like to join- the Army, the Navy or the Air Force?

Ans. I would like to join the Navy.

Page 209

Q.1 In which other jobs do people wear uniforms as in defence services?

Ans. People wear uniforms in jobs like police forces, doctors, nurses, lawyers and in paramilitary forces.

Q.2 Wahida works as a doctor in the Indian Navy. Can you name five other occupations in the Navy?

Ans. Captain, sailors, cooks, cleaner and medical assistants.

Q.3 Have you ever seen a parade? Hold a parade in your own school and try giving thirty-six-commands– for example, "Parade, Eyes Right", "Don't move", "Close in", "Open file". Can you add some more commands to this list?

Ans. Yes, I have seen a parade. Some other commands are "Attention!", "Stand at ease!", "Salute", "Left-right-left".

Q.4 Talk to a doctor and find out about her/his work.

Ans. A doctor carefully examines the patients, asks them questions and diagnoses the disease. He/She gives proper medicines to the patients. He also helps them with any other medical assistance.

Q.5 Do you know any woman who has done something unusual?

Ans. Yes, I know about Kiran Bedi. She was the first Indian IPS officer. It was a great achievement because women were not even allowed to study at that time.

Q.6 Talk to her in the same way as we talked to Lt. Cdr. Wahida Prism. Think of the questions that you will ask. Find out why she has chosen that work. What were the difficulties she faced in her life?

Ans. Interview Questions

Question — How did you feel when you were selected for the Indian Police Service.

Kiran Bedi — I felt as if 'all my dreams have come true'. I was feeling on top of the world.

Question — Why did you want to join the police forces? Did somebody inspire you?

Kiran Bedi — I wanted to prove that women can do anything that men can. I wanted to show that we also have physical and mental strength.

My father supported me in my dream.

Question — What problem did you face?

Kiran Bedi — Many people tried to discourage me. Some of my male colleagues tried to bully me. I also faced a lot of criticism.

CHAPTER 27 CHUSKIT GOES TO SCHOOL

About the Chapter

In this chapter, we learn about a girl named Chuskit who lives in a remote village in Ladakh. Chuskit is excited to go to school, but she faces challenges because she cannot walk. With the help of her family and friends, she overcomes these challenges. They all work together to make sure she can reach school by making a levelled road, and a wooden bridge so that she could take her wheelchair to the school easily. It shows that support and determination are important. Chuskit finally goes to school, loves learning and enjoys being with her friends at school.

GLOSSARY

Eager It means full of interest in something.
Level It means to make the surface of the road flat or even.

NCERT FOLDER

Page 212

Q.1 How do you go to school?

Ans. I go to school by school bus.

Q.2 Find out where Ladakh is. What kind of a place is it?

Ans. Ladakh is one of the Union Territories of India. It is in the extreme North side. It is the highest plateau of the country, situated at the great height of 3000 m. It is a hilly and cold place.

Page 213

Q.1 What are the things that you enjoy doing in school?

Ans. In school, I enjoy learning and playing with my friends.

Q.2 Do you like going to school?

Ans. Yes, I like going to school very much.

Q.3 Would you like it if you never could go to school?

Ans. No, I cannot even think about not going to school.

Talk about it (Page 215)

Q.1 Who all helped Chuskit to reach school?

Ans. Abdul, the Headmaster, teachers and the children of the school helped Chuskit to reach school.

Q.2 If you were Abdul what would you have done?

Ans. If I was Abdul, I would have done the same thing and made a plan to help Chuskit in reaching the school.

Q.3 At last, Chuskit could reach school. Do you think that she may face some difficulties in school? What kind of difficulties? If you were Chuskit's friend, how would you help her?

Ans. She would face difficulties like moving from one place to another, climbing the stairs, sitting on her chair, going to the playground, etc.

If I was Chuskit's friend, I would help her in moving from place to place and helping her reach wherever she wants to go.

Q.4 Do you have ramps in your school on which a wheelchair can move?

Ans. Yes, our school has proper ramps where a wheelchair can move.

Q.5 Do you know any child near your house who cannot go to school because of some difficulty? Would you like to help such a child? How will you help?

Ans. Yes, one of the children in my neighbourhood cannot go to school because he is blind. Yes, I would like to help such a child. I would teach him at home and read stories for him.

Q.6 Look at the buildings around your house. Can a wheelchair go inside the building?

Ans. Yes, a wheelchair can easily go inside the building.

Let us do (Page 215)

Q.1 Draw pictures of a ramp and a wheelchair in your notebook.

Ans.

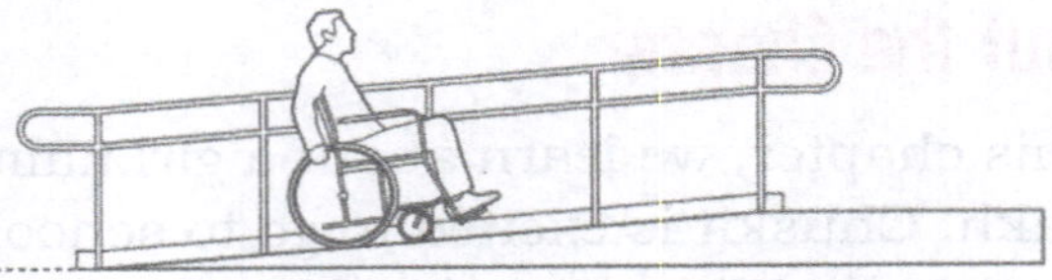

Q.2 Why not make your own bridge? For this, use material that you can find around you . Ice cream sticks, plastic spoons, small sticks, rope, string etc. Your friends can also make bridge.

Ans.

Q.3 In a group of friends make a model showing fields, rivers, mountains, roads, and railway tracks, etc. You can use clay, sand, pebbles, twigs, leaves. Place your bridges at different positions on this model.

Ans. Do it yourself.